INTERMEI
COLLEGE MECHANICS

A Vectorial Treatment

Dan Edwin Christie
Associate Professor of Physics
and Mathematics, Bowdoin College

1952
McGRAW-HILL BOOK COMPANY, INC.
New York Toronto London

INTERMEDIATE COLLEGE MECHANICS

Library of Congress Catalog Card Number: 51-12593

II

PREFACE

In the education of a scientist or engineer the study of mechanics plays several significant overlapping roles. It is a foundation on which further studies in quantitative science can be based. It is an excellent example of a well-developed physical theory. It provides an opportunity to apply standard mathematics at an elementary level, and it may be used as a means of introducing useful varieties of special mathematics such as vector analysis. It helps to develop skill in setting up solutions of practical problems. It may include forays into the mechanical theories of other branches of physics. The present textbook is an attempt to present mechanics at an intermediate level in such a way that all of these important roles may be at least partially fulfilled.

This book in mimeographed form has been used in classes composed mainly of students who were taking simultaneously a second year of college mathematics and who were planning to major in physics or mathematics. Many of them were looking ahead to graduate work in science or to a "combined plan course" at a school of engineering. For students of this sort an early use of calculus and vectors is desirable. Yet the relative lack of experience with advanced mathematics makes it advisable to introduce certain new ideas from the intuitive point of view, leaving more rigorous study to later courses in mathematics. Thus in this book no advanced knowledge of mathematical concepts is presupposed, yet experience in the use of mathematics is continually afforded.

The techniques of vector analysis are especially suited to mechanics. This method is particularly desirable because it is so concise and natural, but it cannot seem natural to a student who meets it in too much of a hurry along with other distracting difficulties. For this reason the language and algebra of vectors are here introduced rather thoroughly before more than simple geometrical applications are encountered. If the student can be persuaded to think in terms of vectors before he starts really to use them in physics, the path ahead will be much simpler.

A student can, however, hardly think in terms of vectors without using them and also knowing when he is using them. The use of boldface type signalizes vectors admirably in print, but the handwritten symbols on paper or blackboard are often ambiguous or irritatingly laden with special arrows, underlines, or overlines. Even the use of separate colors for vectors and scalars is irksome. The solution used in this book is not altogether desirable, for any departure from precedent in nomenclature is rightly open to suspicion. The departure here, however, is not great, and the pedagogical benefits seem to justify it. The symbolism used is close enough to those in common use so that no difficulty of readjustment is encountered in later courses where heavier demands upon alphabets preclude this expedient.

Vectors are printed boldface as usual, but only capitals are used. Scalars are printed in italics but only lower-case symbols are used. Thus a student with his pencil or the teacher with his chalk does not have to distinguish between **v** and *v* or between **V** and *V*. For example the magnitude of **V** is *v*. The unit vectors parallel to the coordinate axes are **I, J,** and **K.** A vector equation such as

$$\mathbf{V} = v_x\mathbf{I} + v_y\mathbf{J} + v_z\mathbf{K}$$

is easily mimicked on the blackboard by something like

$$\mathrm{V} = \mathrm{v_xI} + \mathrm{v_yJ} + \mathrm{v_zK}.$$

The student comes to think in terms of vectors, and embarrassing ambiguities are avoided.

The first two chapters are devoted to vector algebra. Unit vectors, components, and position vectors are stressed. The fundamental proofs concerning products are done gradually so that the vector properties used can be well understood. Once the vector language is available, it is used freely. Theory is generally developed in vector form. Both analytical and graphical methods for solving problems are included.

The basic material of an elementary mechanics course is developed in Chaps. 3 to 11. Major physical concepts determine the outline for this part of the course. The key concepts are force, torque, velocity, mass and acceleration, energy, momentum. Numerous worked examples assist the student in acquiring technique for the solution of problems. The concept of isolation is stressed, as it must be in any successful mechanics course. Additional vector tools are given, as intuitively as possible, when they are needed. Many problems are included in the belief that much practice is essential. Exercises are, in fact, provided for most of the numerous sections, so assignments are easily made. Answers are appended for most of the odd-numbered exercises. Many of the exercises have theoretical content and thus extend or supplement the theory presented in the text.

For students of limited experience, the first eleven chapters form the core of the course. The instructor will observe that this core material is easily shortened by skipping the last section or two in several of these chapters. In these basic chapters perhaps more attention than usual is given to couples, to relative motion, to moments of inertia, and to methods involving energy.

The remaining six chapters are of quite a different character. They help the student to make a natural transition from drill work in basic mechanics to the appreciation and use of mechanical principles in reading about other fields. These chapters may be regarded partly as "reading assignments" to follow the preliminary emphasis on "language" and "grammar." They consist of selected topics in mechanical physics, together with additional vector tools. In each case, naturally, the material presented is selected arbitrarily with many attractive topics omitted. Except for the sections on vector analysis these topics are generally independent of each other; so courses of different length are readily arranged.

Chapter 12 concerns free, damped, and forced oscillations presented from the point of view of electrical analogues. Chapter 13 introduces the point of view of fields, giving an intuitive approach to directional derivatives and gradients. Applications are made to simple gravitational and electrical cases. Chapter 14 applies the previous work on displacements and equilibrium to an elementary analysis of strain and stress. Vector methods are used. Applications are given to special cases. Chapter 15, by developing the fundamental equations of hydrodynamics, provides as much of an introduction to the concepts of curl and divergence as most physics undergraduates require for such courses as electromagnetism. Chapter 16 is a one-dimensional treatment of wave motion, due attention being given to energy propagation. Chapter 17 gives a taste of the classical mechanical theory of thermal phenomena.

These last six chapters, by their nature and purpose, are less burdened with exercises and numerical examples, although such aids are given in sections where they are appropriate. For students already versed in fundamentals, such topics may form the major part of the course. The transition from course work to normal use may, of course, be carried further. It has been the author's practice to ask each student to write a Chapter 18 of his own, on some suitable mechanical topic of his own choice. It must be admitted that Chapter 18 has proved the most educational chapter of the course for many of these men. Favorite topics have been "Engineering Structures," "Relativity," "Aerodynamics," "Surface Phenomena," "Lagrange's Equations," "Friction," etc. A number of suitable books for outside reading are included among the references at the end of this volume.

The list of Suggested References is made up largely of books which I have found especially useful as aids or as texts in teaching mechanics. They are therefore books to which I am greatly indebted, and it is a pleasure to acknowledge this debt. During the years that this book has been used in temporary form I have benefited from the cooperative criticism of numerous discerning students and assistants. For this assistance I am very grateful. I am particularly indebted to my colleagues Profs.

Noel C. Little and Myron A. Jeppesen for their encouragement and counsel, to Dr. Harold O. Curtis for reading the manuscript and offering very helpful suggestions, to T. P. Sylvan for working all the exercises, and to Eleanor W. Christie for continual assistance and especially for typing the entire manuscript.

DAN E. CHRISTIE

BRUNSWICK, ME.
January, 1952

CONTENTS

CHAPTER 5

Motion of a Particle

CHAPTER 6

Motion of a Rigid Body

CHAPTER 7

Particle Dynamics

CHAPTER 8

Rigid-body Dynamics

CHAPTER 9

Work and Kinetic Energy

CHAPTER 10

Potential Energy and Virtual Work

CHAPTER 11

Impulse and Momentum

CHAPTER 12

Mechanical Vibrations in One Dimension

CHAPTER 13

Motion in a Conservative Force Field

CHAPTER 14

Deformable Bodies in Equilibrium

CHAPTER 15

Mechanics of an Ideal Fluid

CHAPTER 16

Wave Motion in One Dimension

CHAPTER 17

Kinetic Theory

INTRODUCTION

In the science of mechanics a study is made of the *motions of physical objects*. The revolutions of wheels and planets, the trajectories of baseballs and rockets, the starting and stopping of automobiles, the oscillations of pendulums and pistons, the falling of raindrops and the rising of balloons, and even the nonmotion of bridges and towers lie in its domain. There are two main aspects of the subject of mechanics. One may study motion *experimentally* by making careful observations and precise measurements of positions, times, and forces; or one may approach the problem from the *theoretical* point of view by setting up a mathematical model or "theory" whose properties are analogous to observed phenomena.

A mathematical science such as mechanics tends to advance in alternating strides, theory and experiment progressing in turn. Conclusions deduced from the theory suggest experimental tests, while experimental results often necessitate modifications of the theory. In this course we shall explore a relatively simple theory which has been found to be in remarkably close accord with experiment. It was at one time thought to be the key to all the secrets of the universe, and the mechanistic point of view became dominant in many fields of thought. It is now known that the model has distinct limitations: it does not, for instance, represent adequately the phenomena of atomic physics or of motion at speeds close to that of light. New and much less simple theories have been created within the last half century to handle many such problems. For ordinary objects at ordinary speeds (as in ballistics, mechanical engineering, aerodynamics, etc.), the simpler classical theory is entirely satisfactory.

The steps in the setting up of our theory will be spread out through the course. At this stage, however, a preview may be given. In terms of idealized space and time we shall study the motion of such unnatural objects as material points and absolutely rigid bodies. The starting point, aside from customary geometrical assumptions, will be certain dynamical *laws*, roughly as stated by Sir Isaac Newton. These basic postulates for the mathematical theory are both suggested and checked by experimental observations. From these assumed principles one may deduce mathematically conclusions which may be applied with reasonable confidence to physical situations. These conclusions enable us to predict as well as to describe motion. Results about particles may be applied to problems involving projectiles or planets. And properties discovered for ideal rigid bodies have significance when applied to the design of practical machinery.

The study of mechanics, even in elementary form, presents most students with an array of difficulties. It is sometimes hard for a beginner to appreciate theoretical developments, especially when they are carried out in the unfamiliar shorthand of vector analysis. Theory which is understood only partially may seem unrelated to practical problems. The student and the teacher must unite efforts to overcome these difficulties.

It must, in the first place, be recognized that vector notation is introduced as a natural and economical means of describing physical situations. The student should resolve to master this technique. He should not be satisfied until he can carry out vector operations with ease and can see the physical meaning of each vector expression involving forces, velocities, etc. The number of basic principles used in this treatment is extremely small. They should be studied and thought over until they are thoroughly comprehended. It will then be found that the vector equations are merely a precise crystallization of fundamental ideas.

The solution of many, many problems is indispensable to the achievement of a reasonable mastery of mechanics. Formal manipulations and physical doctrines are appreciated fully only when they have been approached and utilized in many different ways. It should be unnecessary to insist that exercises be done thoughtfully. While technique is of extreme importance, the aim of a problem assignment is not merely a list of correct numerical answers; it is also a fuller understanding of the theory and of the relationships between theoretical principles and specific physical situations. The student should strive to develop power and confidence in analyzing problems. When the fundamentals have been mastered in this way, a reliable basis will exist for future studies in applied mathematics, theoretical physics, and engineering analysis.

CHAPTER 1

DISTANCE, POSITION, AND VECTORS

Is geometry a subdivision of mechanics? It is probably too early in the course for us to deal satisfactorily with such a technical though unimportant question. We can assert, however, that the study of some geometry is essential in a mechanics course, for the student of mechanics needs geometrical tools. It will also appear that many mathematical devices suitable for geometry have wide application in various parts of mechanics. The subject matter of this first chapter is thus doubly important, for it emphasizes the language of vectors in geometrical situations. This chapter also has a special tactical significance for the beginning student; in later chapters this same vector language will be used in unfamiliar situations. So here, against the familiar background of everyday geometry, is the place for acquiring a thorough understanding of vectors.

1.1. Distance. In order to describe quantitatively the motion of a body or even of a point, some standard of distance or length is necessary. The metric unit of length, the meter, is defined in terms of marks on a standard meter bar under stated conditions or in terms of the wavelength of a characteristic cadmium or mercury isotope radiation. The English unit of length, the foot, may be taken as approximately 0.305 meter. In this course we shall not attempt a full analysis of the philosophical or practical difficulties associated with the problem of measurement. We merely state that from the experimental point of view length is the result of measuring a distance with a suitable instrument: meter stick, micrometer, cathetometer, comparator, etc. From the point of view of our mathematical theory, on the other hand, length is a primitive concept to which numerical values may be assigned and in terms of which other concepts (such as volume and speed) might be defined.

1.2. Reference Frames. One aim of this chapter is to provide a language for answering a question such as "Where is the point?" This question is fully meaningful only if a specific reference body is understood. The selection of a suitable reference body is in itself an interesting enterprise. We feel intuitively, perhaps, that it should be absolutely at rest; but this requirement is meaningless as reflection will show. In most of our mechanics problems the earth or a somewhat rigid extension of the earth such as a room will be an adequate reference body. When the effects of the earth's motion are to be taken into account, one may imagine a reference frame which is fixed in our solar system and which does not rotate with respect to the stars fixed in our galaxy.

It is customary and convenient to select in the reference body fixed straight lines known as *axes.* In Fig. 1.1 the dotted lines represent the body. A point O fixed in the body is chosen as *origin;* a set of three mutually perpendicular lines through O are chosen as axes. O divides each line into halves, one of which is arbitrarily called positive, the other negative. When the positive x and positive y directions have been chosen, the positive z direction is usually taken so that the 90° rotation carrying the positive x axis into the positive y axis will appear counterclockwise to an observer looking back toward O from the positive z axis. This is a right-handed set of axes; the opposite choice of the positive z axis would yield a left-handed set. Why is this frame called "right-handed?" If the thumb, forefinger, and middle finger of the right hand are held at right angles representing the x, y, and z axes, the answer is apparent. Another approach is that the rotation described would cause a z axis which was threaded like an ordinary screw to advance in its positive direction.

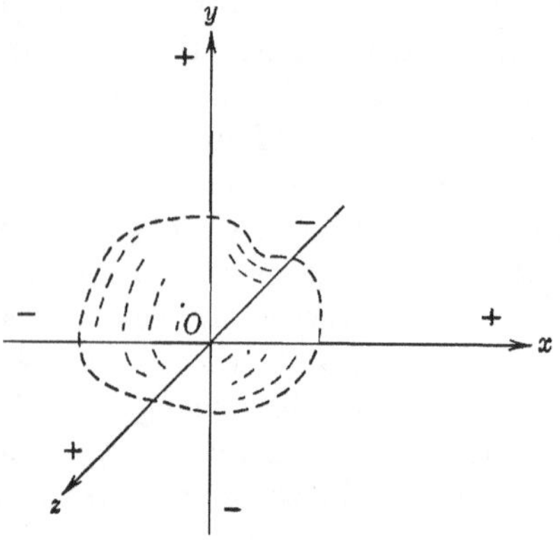

FIG 1.1.

1.3. Rectangular Coordinates. Once a standard of length, a reference body, and a set of axes have been established, it is very easy to specify the position of a point. It is assumed that the student is familiar with rectangular coordinates as used in plane analytic geometry; therefore the discussion here will be brief. The x coordinate of a point is defined as its distance from the yz plane, that is, the plane determined by the y and z axes; it is positive if the point is on the same side of the plane as the positive x axis. Similarly the y and z coordinates of the point are the distances from the xz and xy planes, respectively. These three coordinates listed in order are a unique name for the point. For example, (0,0,0) is the name of the origin, $(-3,0,0)$ is the name of a point three units distant from the origin on the negative x axis, $(2,0,-4)$ is a point in the xz plane. (x,y,z) might denote any point, it being understood that x, y, and z are suitable numbers. The coordinates of the point P in Fig. 1.2 are all positive.

In dealing with many aspects of vector analysis and mechanics it is exceedingly helpful to be able to visualize geometrical relationships in three dimensions. Good practice is afforded by sketching the position of points of various coordinates, using box diagrams as in Fig. 1.2. For example, the point $P(4,-4,6)$ might be sketched as in Fig. 1.3.

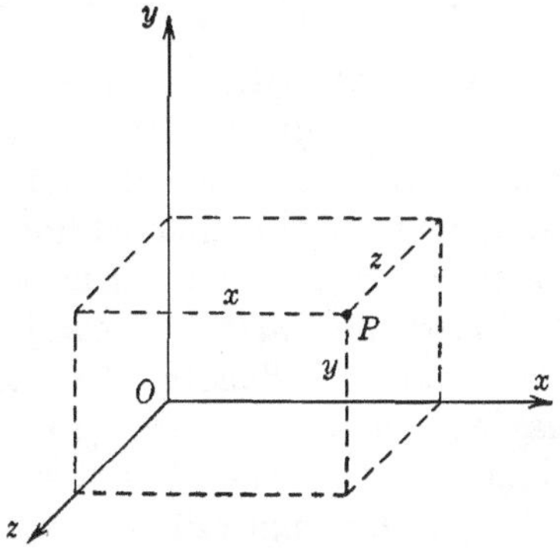

FIG. 1.2.

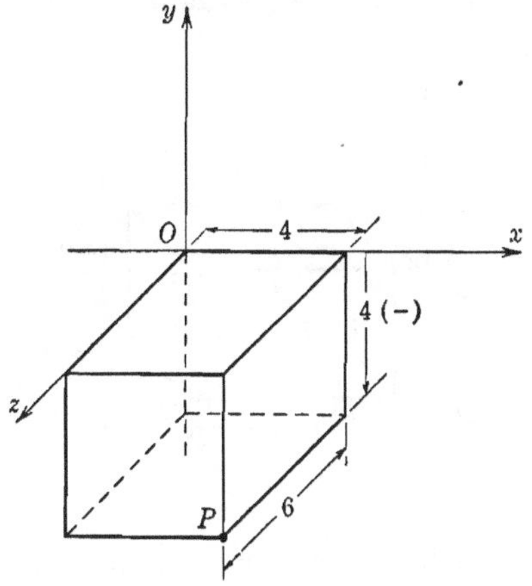

FIG. 1.3.

EXERCISES

1. Use box diagrams to plot the points (5,3,4), (−3,5,4), (−3,0,0).

2. Figure 1.4 represents a rectangular room 24 ft by 18 ft by 8 ft. K is the center of the wall $ABCD$. M and N are centers of edges AE and BF. If G is taken as origin, GF as the positive x axis, GC as the positive y axis, and GH as the negative z axis, find the coordinates of A, B, C, D, E, F, H, K, M, N.

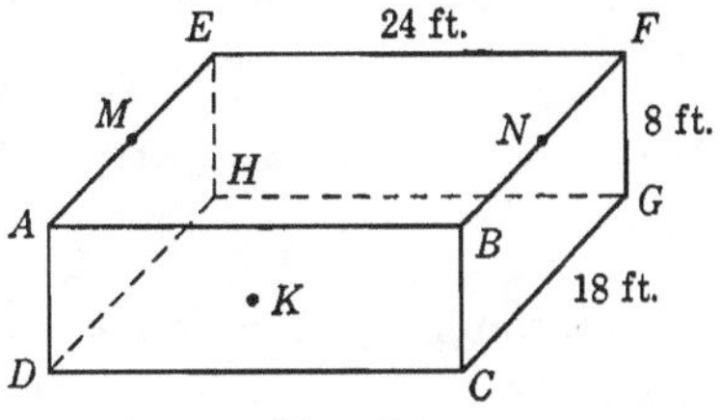

FIG. 1.4.

1.4. The Geometry of the Line Segment. The study of motion obviously entails the idea of displacement or change of position. If a particle is initially at point P and later at point P', the net displacement is determined by the *directed segment* PP'. A directed segment such as PP', or, more fully, a *directed line segment*, is two things at once. It is the portion of a straight line between the points P and P', and at the same time it is a statement that P is the *initial point* and P' the *final point.* For the directed segment $P'P$ the roles of these points are reversed. $P'P$ is directed *opposite* to PP'. In mechanics both the magnitude and the direction of such a segment are of prime interest. Both aspects of the geometry of a line segment can be studied readily with the aid of box diagrams such as were used in the preceding section in describing the position of a single point with respect to the origin. Let $P(x,y,z)$ and $P'(x',y',z')$ be any two points. Through each of these points imagine to be constructed planes parallel to the three planes determined by the axes. The six planes thus constructed enclose a boxlike region as shown in Fig. 1.5. (In special cases the box is "degenerate," *i.e.*, one or more sides may have length zero.) The lengths of the sides of this box (except possibly for sign) are

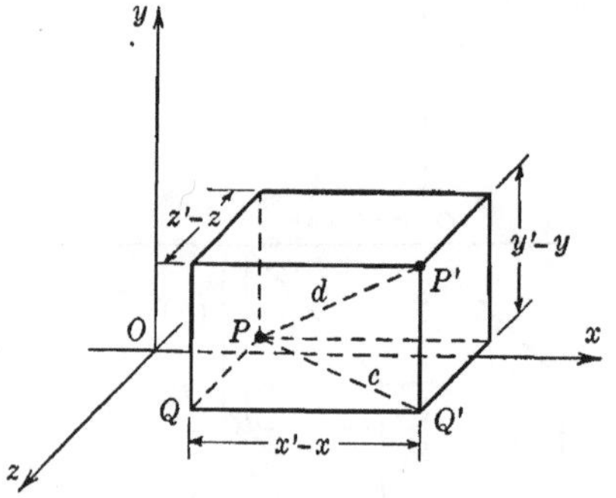

FIG. 1.5.

$$x' - x, \qquad y' - y, \qquad z' - z.$$

These three numbers are often called, respectively, the x component, the y component, and the z component of the directed line segment PP'. We first derive a formula for the *length* of the segment PP'. Let Q' denote the corner having coordinates (x',y,z'). We shall use the letter d as a symbol for the length of the segment PP' and c for the length of the segment PQ'. Two applications of the famous theorem of Pythagoras will lead to an expression for d in terms of the coordinates of P and P'. First note that PQQ' is a right triangle. Consequently

$$c^2 = (x' - x)^2 + (z' - z)^2.$$

Note furthermore that $PQ'P'$ is a right triangle. It follows that

$$d^2 = c^2 + (y' - y)^2.$$

If the value for c^2 is substituted in this equation, d is expressed thus:

$$d = \sqrt{(x' - x)^2 + (y' - y)^2 + (z' - z)^2}. \tag{1.1}$$

This formula by itself is one of the most effective tools of solid analytic geometry. In this course especially it should be used in concert with a mental picture of a rectangular box and its diagonals. That the lengths of the edges of the box are merely differences in coordinates is an immediate consequence of its orientation with respect to the axes. The displacement from P to P' may then be thought of (see Fig. 1.6) as an x displacement of length $\Delta x = x' - x$ followed by a y displacement of length $\Delta y = y' - y$ followed by a z displacement of length $\Delta z = z' - z$. Then the net displacement has magnitude d given by

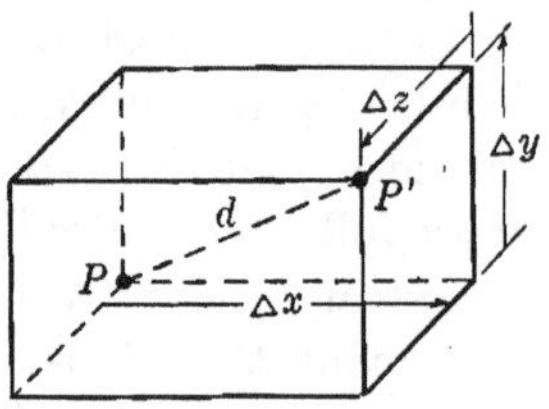

FIG. 1.6.

$$d = \sqrt{(\Delta x)^2 + (\Delta y)^2 + (\Delta z)^2}. \tag{1.2}$$

The *direction* of the segment can be specified by stating the angles between PP' and the positive axes (that is, by the angles between PP'

and lines through P parallel to these axes). These angles are labeled α, β, and γ in Fig. 1.7. In actual practice it is usually more convenient to state the cosines of these angles.

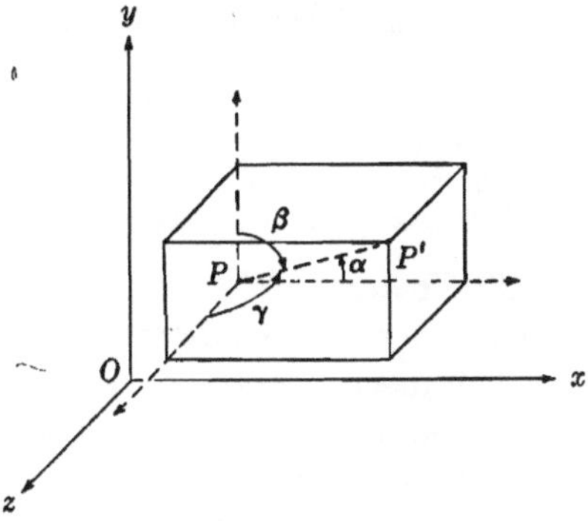

FIG. 1.7.

$$(1.3) \qquad l = \cos\alpha = \frac{\Delta x}{d}, \quad m = \cos\beta = \frac{\Delta y}{d}, \quad n = \cos\gamma = \frac{\Delta z}{d}.$$

The quantities l, m, n are called *direction cosines.*

If both sides of Eq. (1.2) be divided by d, an interesting identity is discovered:

$$\frac{d}{d} = \sqrt{\left(\frac{\Delta x}{d}\right)^2 + \left(\frac{\Delta y}{d}\right)^2 + \left(\frac{\Delta z}{d}\right)^2},$$

or

$$(1.4) \qquad l^2 + m^2 + n^2 = 1.$$

Example 1. What is the distance from $P(-1,-4,5)$ to $P'(3,-2,2)$?

SOLUTION. The displacement from P to P' is equal to the result of an x displacement, $\Delta x = 4$; a y displacement, $\Delta y = 2$; and a z displacement, $\Delta z = -3$. The distance then is

$$d = \sqrt{(4)^2 + (2)^2 + (-3)^2} = \sqrt{29} = 5.4.$$

Example 2. What are the direction cosines of the directed line segment PP' described in the preceding example?

SOLUTION

$$l = \frac{4}{5.4} = 0.74, \qquad m = \frac{2}{5.4} = 0.37, \qquad n = \frac{-3}{5.4} = -0.56.$$

(The angles between PP' and the positive axes are then 42°, 68°, 124°.)

EXERCISES

1. A helicopter flies 500 ft vertically upward, then 700 ft horizontally south, and then 300 ft horizontally east. How far is it from the starting point?

2. P and Q are points with coordinates $(3,-2,1)$, $(-1,1,1)$. (*a*) What is the distance from P to Q? (*b*) What are the direction cosines of the directed line segment PQ?

3. The positive x axis is horizontal and east, the positive y axis vertical upward, and the positive z axis horizontal and south. An observer sits on the ground at the origin. The peak of a spire has an angle of elevation above the horizontal of 30° in a direction 50° east of south. What are the direction cosines of the line from the observer to the spire?

4. The point P having coordinates $(2,5,d)$ is at a distance 5 from the point $(-1,1,4)$. Find d.

5. O is the origin, P a second point. The segment OP makes an angle of 60° with the positive x axis, 45° with the positive y axis. What can be said about its angle with the positive z axis?

6. What angle does OP make with the positive axes if P is the point $(3,3,3)$?

1.5. Vectors. We have already seen how a change in position, *i.e.*, a displacement, can be described by a directed line segment. In mechanics we shall meet many other concepts which similarly have both magnitude and direction. These are called *vector concepts.* Examples are force, velocity, acceleration, momentum, angular velocity, and torque. These concepts have so many significant properties in common that a separate study of this common ground is richly worth while. This subject is known as vector analysis. Only the elementary aspects are considered in this course. We shall begin with some definitions.

Vector. A vector is a directed line segment or arrow having definite length and definite direction. This reference to direction implies that a reference frame has already been selected. The definite direction might be expressed by giving a unique set of direction cosines. In a given discussion only one frame will ordinarily be used. Figure 1.8 is a portrait of a vector. The length of the arrow is the *magnitude* of the vector. It is imagined that the arrow in the figure is drawn in the direction of the vector. A vector quantity (*i.e.*, a specific example of a vector concept) may be represented by a vector in an obvious way. The vector in the figure might represent a 100-lb force in the direction shown. A 50-lb force would be represented by an arrow just half as long. The figure might equally well represent a velocity in the indicated direction of 75 miles per hour (mph). In that case an arrow twice as long would represent a velocity of 150 mph. In general, then, the figures are drawn to scale so that lengths are proportional to the magnitudes represented.

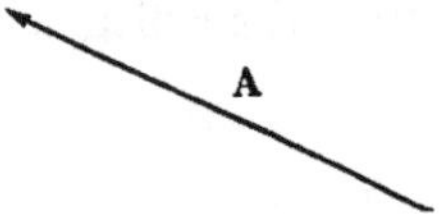

FIG. 1.8.

Scalar. In this context the word scalar is used to denote ordinary real numbers. Thus a *scalar concept,* in contrast with a vector concept, is one which can be specified by a numerical or scale value (positive, negative, or zero) without requiring any statement about direction. Examples are temperature, time, energy, and mass. We shall use *boldface capital letters* for vector quantities and *italic small letters* for scalar quantities. Thus in Fig. 1.8 the *vector* is labeled **A**. Its *magnitude,* a nonnegative scalar, would be written a or, when more convenient, $|\mathbf{A}|$.

Equality of Vectors. Two vectors will be called equal if both their directions and their magnitudes are identical. In Fig. 1.9, **A** and **B** are equal. **A** and **C** are not equal, for their directions are opposite. Likewise **A** and **D** are not equal, for their magnitudes differ. Symbolically,

$$\mathbf{A} = \mathbf{B}, \qquad \mathbf{A} \neq \mathbf{C}, \qquad \mathbf{A} \neq \mathbf{D}.$$

Using small letters to denote magnitudes, as suggested above, we may write

$$a = b = c, \qquad a \neq d.$$

It should be noticed that equal vectors may represent vector quantities which are not equivalent. For instance, two forces represented by **A** and **B** in Fig. 1.9 are not equivalent for their lines of action do not agree. This should not, however, disturb us. The scalars 3 and 3 are equal; but this does not mean that three degrees centigrade and three degrees Kelvin are equivalent temperatures. A similar amount of discernment in particular applications will enable us to use the idea of vector equality successfully.

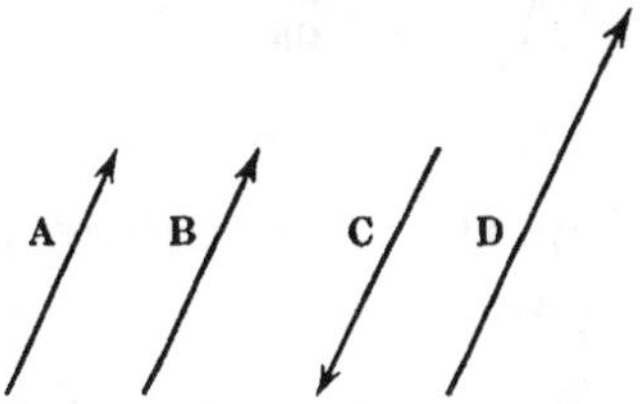

FIG. 1.9.

Minus a Vector. If two vectors, **A** and **C**, have the same magnitudes but opposite directions (as in Fig. 1.9), we shall write

$$(1.5) \qquad \mathbf{A} = -\mathbf{C} \quad \text{or} \quad -\mathbf{A} = \mathbf{C}.$$

We say that **A** is the *opposite* of **C** and that **C** is the *opposite* of **A**.

EXERCISES

1. A parallelogram is made up of four line segments. If its diagonals are drawn, four more segments (the semidiagonals) are added. Change these eight segments into vectors by indicating directions (*a*) so that no two vectors are equal; (*b*) so that there are four pairs of equal vectors.

2. Four successive straight displacements all of equal magnitude bring a moving point back to the starting point. Show that this may be done in such a way that the vectors representing the displacements satisfy the following statements: (*a*) the vectors form two distinct *opposite* pairs, that is, **A**, −**A**, **B**, −**B**, where $\mathbf{B} \neq \mathbf{A} \neq -\mathbf{B}$ (the order need not be as given in this list); (*b*) the vectors form two *equal* pairs; (*c*) no two of the vectors are either *equal* or *opposite*.

1.6. Vector Addition. An *operation* on vectors is a rule for combining vectors with vectors or vectors with scalars in such a way as to yield new vectors or scalars.

Some of these operations may seem at first to be arbitrary and artificial. Their utility for dealing with spatial situations will, however, appear in the exercises. In later parts of the course the elementary relationships of mechanics will be expressed in terms of them. The operation called *vector addition* will be no surprise to a student who has had some experience with statics in an elementary physics course. The introduction of two kinds of *products* will seem less natural, perhaps, but in this connection it should be recalled from elementary physics that two quite different concepts, work and torque, are measured in foot-pounds.

In this section we define an operation which, for convenience, is called *addition.* This operation is an exceedingly natural way of combining vectors. It is most easily described in terms of displacements. If one walks from a point P to a point Q and then from Q to a third point R, the net result is the same as a single displacement from P to R. As is shown in Fig. 1.10, if we denote the first displacement as **PQ** and the second as **QR,** then the resultant displacement **PR** may be thought of as the result of combining **PQ** with **QR.** The relationship is expressed concisely in the equation

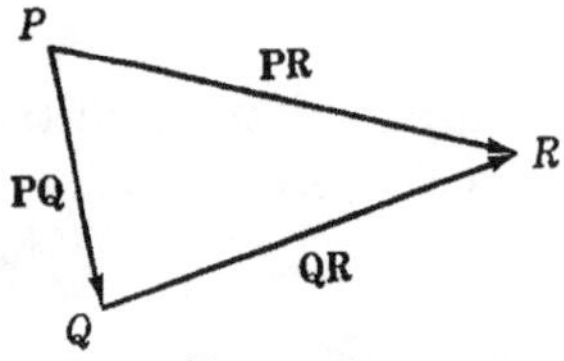

FIG. 1.10.

$$\mathbf{PQ} + \mathbf{QR} = \mathbf{PR}. \tag{1.6}$$

This is a typical case of *vector addition.* In general, given two vectors **A** and **B,** their sum **A** + **B** is defined to be equal to the third vector obtained by combining **A** and **B** (or vectors equal to them) as if they were successive displacements. This is illustrated in Fig. 1.11. The two given vectors are **A** and **B.** To find a vector equal to the sum **A** + **B,** a copy of **B** is drawn adjacent to **A.** Then the vector from the "initial point" of **A** to the "final point" of **B** is drawn. This vector is the desired sum. The roles of **B** and **A** may be interchanged; then the sum **B** + **A** is obtained. These two operations may be combined in a single diagram, as shown in Fig. 1.12. The fact that the diagonal of the parallelogram is the same whether viewed from above or below constitutes an extremely important proposition in vector algebra: *the commutative law for vector addition.* It is restated symbolically in the following equation:

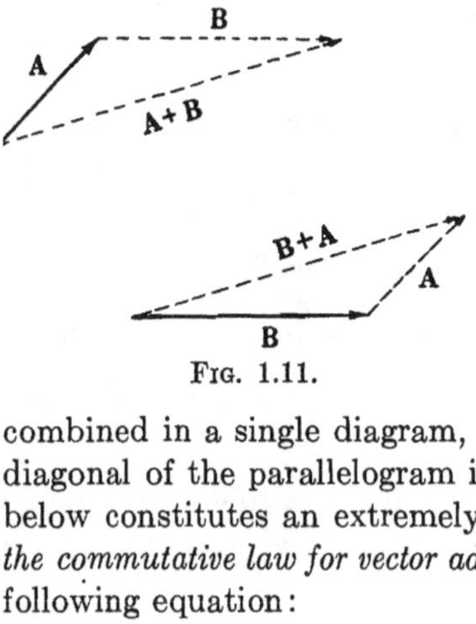

FIG. 1.11.

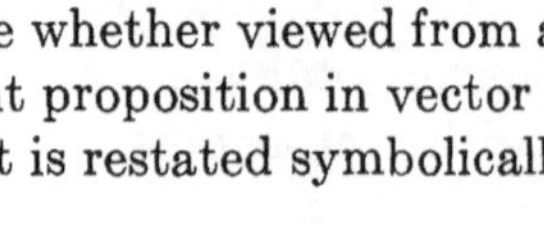

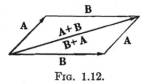

FIG. 1.12.

$$\mathbf{A} + \mathbf{B} = \mathbf{B} + \mathbf{A}. \tag{1.7}$$

Figure 1.12 illustrates the familiar "parallelogram rule" for vector addition.

The Null Vector. It is highly desirable that an operation *always* be defined. In particular, given *any* two vectors, a unique vector equal to their sum should exist. The sum of a vector and its opposite poses a problem. A displacement **A** followed by the displacement −**A** results in a net effect of no displacement at all. Clearly a *null* displacement does not satisfy our criterion for a vector quantity: it has no unique direction. Just as a matter of convenience then we decide to create a null vector **O** to express the result of all additions such as

$$\mathbf{A} + (-\mathbf{A}) = \mathbf{O}. \tag{1.8}$$

Successive Additions. Thus far we have considered sums for pairs of vectors. Figure 1.13 shows how the definition may be extended. To the sum **A** + **B** the vector **C** is added, giving the vector (**A** + **B**) + **C**. This vector can be described as extending from the initial point of **A** to the final point of **C**. It appears, moreover, from Fig. 1.13 that the sum **A** + (**B** + **C**) is precisely the same vector. This fact constitutes a second important proposition of vector algebra: *the associative law of vector addition*

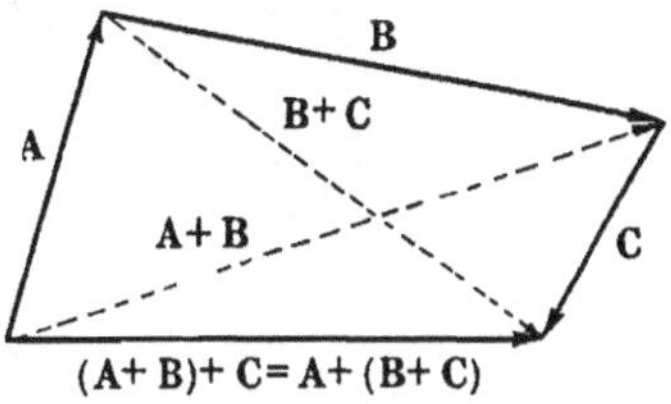

FIG. 1.13.

$$(\mathbf{A} + \mathbf{B}) + \mathbf{C} = \mathbf{A} + (\mathbf{B} + \mathbf{C}). \tag{1.9}$$

This together with the commutative law ensures that successive additions of several vectors will have a unique result independent of the order in which vectors are combined. As an illustration of the essential simplicity

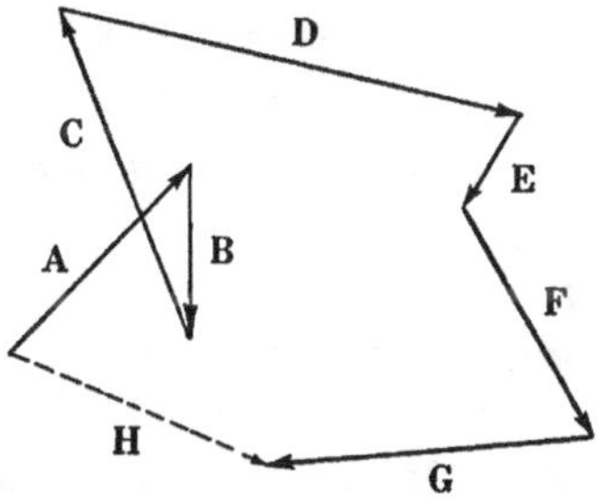

FIG. 1.14.

of successive vector additions, a number of vectors are added in Fig. 1.14. It represents the equation

$$\mathbf{A} + \mathbf{B} + \mathbf{C} + \mathbf{D} + \mathbf{E} + \mathbf{F} + \mathbf{G} = \mathbf{H}.$$

Vector Subtraction. The difference of two vectors is defined in terms of addition and minus a vector by the following equation:

$$\mathbf{A} - \mathbf{B} = \mathbf{A} + (-\mathbf{B}). \tag{1.10}$$

In Fig. 1.15 this is shown. From the geometry of the parallelograms in this figure it is clear that

$$\mathbf{A} - \mathbf{B} = -(\mathbf{B} - \mathbf{A}).$$

The construction used in Fig. 1.15 involved two steps: the construction of the opposite of one of the vectors and then addition. The result, however, suggests a shorter construction:

(1.11) *If the vectors are drawn with the same initial point* (as in Fig. 1.15), *then the vector between their final points is the difference.* This is

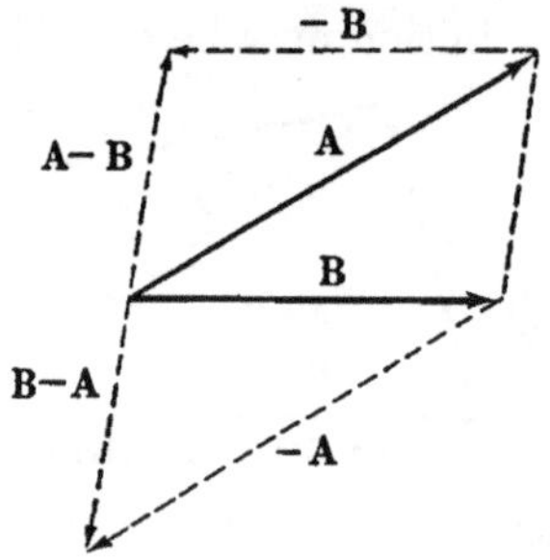

FIG. 1.15.

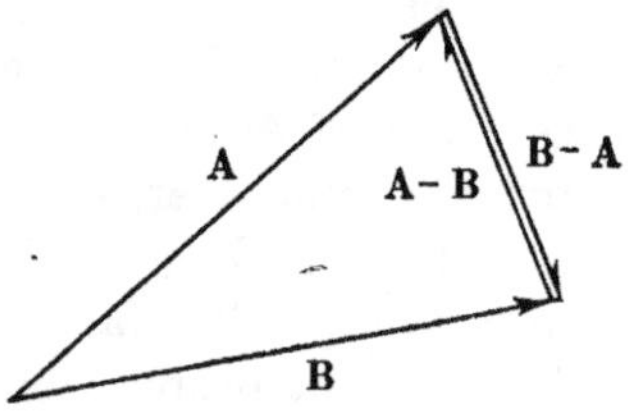

FIG. 1.16.

illustrated in Fig. 1.16. The student should convince himself that the difference **B** − **A** is the unique solution of the equation

$$\mathbf{A} + \mathbf{X} = \mathbf{B}.$$

EXERCISES

1. Draw four vectors **A, B, C, D,** of random length and direction. Using graphic methods (*e.g.* constructions with ruler, compass, or protractor), find a fifth vector **E** such that

$$\mathbf{A} + \mathbf{B} + \mathbf{C} + \mathbf{D} + \mathbf{E} = \mathbf{O}.$$

2. M is the mid-point of a segment AB. Construct graphically and compare the two vector sums $OA + OB$ and $OM + OM$.

3. ABC is a triangle. G is the point of intersection of its medians, and M is the mid-point of the side BC. Construct the vector sums

$$OG + OG + OG, \qquad OM + OM + OA, \qquad OA + OB + OC.$$

4. $ABCD$ is a square, M is its center, and O is any other point in its plane. Construct and compare

$$OA + OB + OC + OD, \qquad OM + OM + OM + OM, \qquad MA + MB + MC + MD.$$

5. Use the definition given for the null vector to show that for any vector **A**,

$$\mathbf{A} + \mathbf{O} = \mathbf{A}.$$

6. For two nonparallel vectors **A** and **B** draw a figure to show that

$$\mathbf{A} + \mathbf{B} - \mathbf{A} - \mathbf{B} = \mathbf{O}.$$

7. Prove that the equation **A** + **C** = **B** + **C** always implies **A** = **B**.

1.7. Polar Notation for Plane Vectors. In many mechanics problems we shall find that coordinate axes may be chosen in such a way that most if not all of the vectors under discussion are in or parallel to the xy plane. Such a vector is described uniquely if its magnitude and its angle with the positive x axis are specified. This angle is usually called positive if it is measured counterclockwise from the positive x axis. Thus in Fig. 1.17 the vector shown may be written

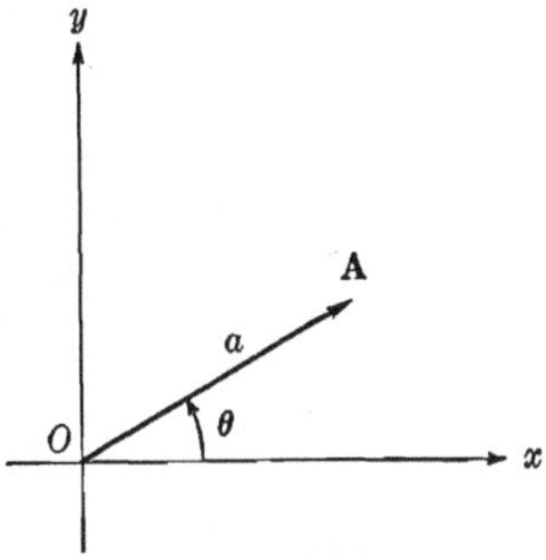

FIG. 1.17.

(1.12) $$\mathbf{A} = a\underline{/\theta}.$$

Some numerical examples are given in Fig. 1.18. Since no analytical methods have been developed thus far in the course, it is assumed that most of the following exercises will be done graphically (measuring angles with a protractor); therefore extreme accuracy is not expected.

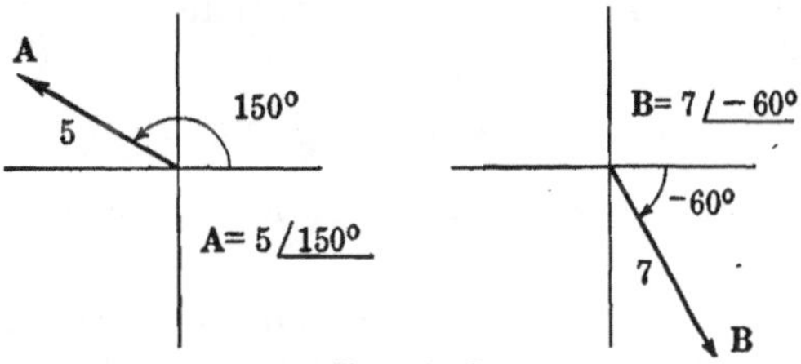

FIG. 1.18.

EXERCISES

1. Plot to scale the vectors $3\underline{/0°}$, $4\underline{/45°}$, $5\underline{/90°}$, $4.5\underline{/150°}$, $3.8\underline{/-90°}$.

2. Show that, reasonably interpreted, the following are true:

(*a*) $a\underline{/\theta°} = a\underline{/\theta° + n360°}$, for any integer n.

(*b*) $-a\underline{/\theta°} = a\underline{/\theta° \pm 180°}$.

(*c*) $a\underline{/\theta°} + b\underline{/\theta°} = (a + b)\underline{/\theta°}$.

3. Compute the following graphically:

(*a*) $4\underline{/90°} + 3\underline{/0°}$.

(*b*) $5\underline{/30°} + 5\underline{/120°}$.

(*c*) $10\underline{/60°} - 8.7\underline{/30°}$.

(*d*) $10\underline{/180°} - 10\underline{/90°}$.

4. Express in polar form displacements of length 5 whose direction cosines are (*a*) $-0.707, +0.707, 0$; (*b*) $0.866, -0.500, 0$.

1.8. Products of Vectors by Scalars. In the problems on Sec. 1.6, such sums as $OM + OM$, $OM + OM + OM$ occurred. It is a natural and convenient abbreviation to write instead $2OM$, $3OM$. This notation suggests the following definition: for any positive scalar c and any non-null vector $\mathbf{A}$ the product $c\mathbf{A}$ is a vector parallel to $\mathbf{A}$ and having magnitude c times the magnitude of $\mathbf{A}$; that is,

(1.13) $$|c\mathbf{A}| = c|\mathbf{A}|.$$

This definition is extended to the cases where the scalar multiple is zero or negative as follows:

$$(-c)\mathbf{A} = -c\mathbf{A} \tag{1.14}$$

$$0\mathbf{A} = \mathbf{O}. \tag{1.15}$$

In this last equation it should be realized that the "0" in the left member is the scalar "zero" but that the "**O**" in the right member denotes the "null vector." The three cases may be summarized in a single statement: the product of a scalar c by a vector **A** is a vector whose magnitude is equal to the magnitude of **A** multiplied by the absolute value of the scalar c; it is parallel to **A** if c is positive, opposite to **A** if c is negative. For a converse of this statement, see Exercise 5 below. Illustrations are given in Fig. 1.19. That this operation is associative, distributive with respect to scalar addition, and distributive with respect to vector addition is easily shown. The demonstrations are left as exercises (see Exercises 1*a*,*b*,*c* below).

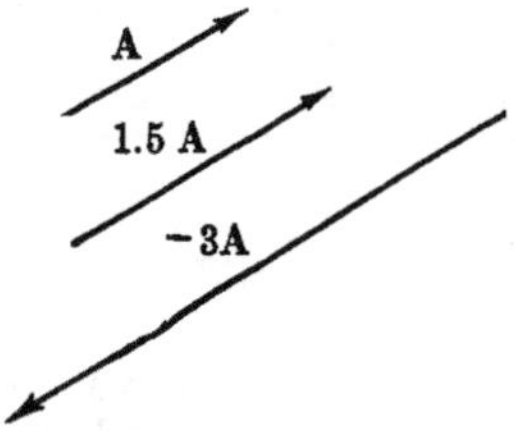

FIG. 1.19.

EXERCISES

1. Using the definitions above, prove each of the following for any scalars c, c' and any vectors **A**, **A**′:

(*a*) $c(c'\mathbf{A}) = (cc')\mathbf{A}$.
(*b*) $(c + c')\mathbf{A} = c\mathbf{A} + c'\mathbf{A}$.
(*c*) $c(\mathbf{A} + \mathbf{A}') = c\mathbf{A} + c\mathbf{A}'$.
(*d*) $1\mathbf{A} = \mathbf{A}$.
(*e*) $(-c)(-\mathbf{A}) = c\mathbf{A}$.

2. Given the two vectors $\mathbf{A} = 10\underline{/0°}$ and $\mathbf{B} = 10\underline{/60°}$, construct graphically each of the following:

$$\mathbf{A} + 2\mathbf{B}, \quad -\mathbf{A} + 2\mathbf{B}, \quad -\mathbf{A} - 2\mathbf{B}, \quad \mathbf{A} - 2\mathbf{B}.$$

3. AB is a line segment and O is a point not on the line. Show that the mid-point M of AB is determined by

$$OM = 0.5\,OA + 0.5\,OB.$$

4. Show that any vector $\mathbf{A} = a\underline{/\theta°}$ in the xy plane can be expressed as the sum of multiples of $1\underline{/0°}$ and $1\underline{/90°}$, *i.e.*, that this equation will hold for the correct choice of scalars c and d:

$$a\underline{/\theta°} = c(1\underline{/0°}) + d(1\underline{/90°}).$$

Express c and d in terms of a and θ.

5. If **A** is parallel to **B** (or to its opposite vector), show that for some scalar c this equation holds:

$$\mathbf{A} = c\mathbf{B}.$$

6. If **A** and **B** are nonparallel vectors and **C** is parallel to the plane they determine, prove that for some scalars c and d, $\mathbf{C} = c\mathbf{A} + d\mathbf{B}$. Illustrate with several diagrams showing possible arrangements. SUGGESTION: Show that if **C** is parallel to neither

A nor **B** it is possible to draw a triangle with sides parallel to **A, B,** and **C**; so that for suitable scalars a', b', c' one can write

$$a'\mathbf{A} + b'\mathbf{B} + c'\mathbf{C} = \mathbf{O}.$$

1.9. Unit Vectors. In order that our algebra of vectors be a flexible tool, it is important that we have a convenient way of denoting both the direction and the magnitude of any vector which we may encounter. The polar notation of Sec. 1.7 provides such a means in the plane case. Now that the operation of multiplication by scalars has been introduced, a second approach is immediately suggested. Any direction can be described in terms of any vector in that direction, but for simplicity's sake we shall specify such directions by means of a vector of length one, *i.e.*, by a *unit vector*. In the first place, given any vector **A**, a parallel unit vector **E** may be determined just by multiplying **A** by the scalar $1/a$:

$$\mathbf{E} = \frac{1}{a}\mathbf{A} = \frac{1}{|\mathbf{A}|}\mathbf{A}. \tag{1.16}$$

FIG. 1.20.

This means that any vector **A** can be expressed as the product of its length by a unit vector having the same direction

$$\mathbf{A} = a\mathbf{E} \quad \text{or} \quad \mathbf{A} = |\mathbf{A}|\mathbf{E}, \tag{1.17}$$

as is shown in Fig. 1.20. The letter **E** will be used as a generic symbol for unit vectors in any context. In theoretical discussions then, **E** may be used simply as a symbol for direction. In particular problems it is usual to consider the directions of the axes as preferred directions. Unit vectors parallel to the positive x, y, and z axes will be denoted, respectively, by **I, J,** and **K.** In problems confined to the xy plane the symbol **I** is interchangeable with the symbol $1\underline{/0°}$ and the symbol **J** is interchangeable with $1\underline{/90°}$. Figure 1.21 shows these unit vectors in the customary setting. In later sections the letters **L, M, T, N,** etc., will be introduced as unit vectors having particular connotations.

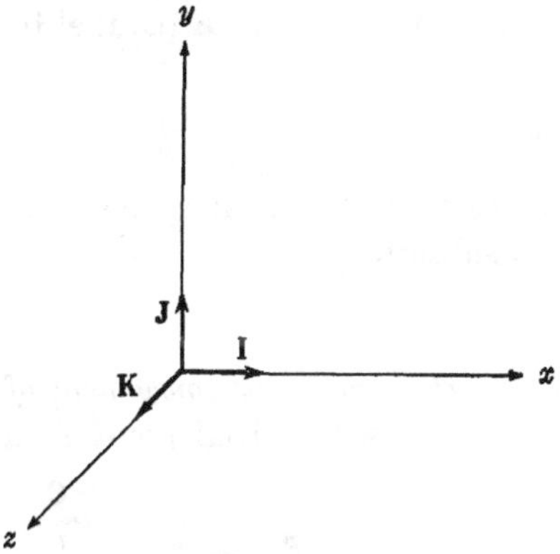

FIG. 1.21.

EXERCISES

1. Express in the form $a\underline{/\theta°}$ a unit vector in the direction of (*a*) $\mathbf{I} + \mathbf{J}$; (*b*) $2\mathbf{I} - \mathbf{J}$; (*c*) $5.00\underline{/45°} + 8.66\underline{/135°}$. (Either graphic methods or simple trigonometry may be used.)

2. Solve the equation $a\mathbf{E} = a_x\mathbf{I} + a_y\mathbf{J}$ for a and $\mathbf{E}$ (in polar form) when
(*a*) $a_x = 5$, $a_y = 12$. (*b*) $a_x = 20$, $a_y = -21$.

3. Solve the equation $\mathbf{A} = a_x\mathbf{I} + a_y\mathbf{J}$ for a_x and a_y when $\mathbf{A}$ is the vector $10\underline{/\theta}$ and θ is (*a*) 30°; (*b*) 90°; (*c*) 180°; (*d*) 300°.

4. Show that if $\mathbf{E}$ is a unit vector parallel to $\mathbf{A} = a\underline{/\theta°}$, then

$$\mathbf{E} = \cos\theta\,\mathbf{I} + \sin\theta\,\mathbf{J}.$$

1.10. Components of a Vector. In Sec. 1.4 we studied a displacement from P to P' in terms of an x displacement Δx, and a y displacement Δy, and a z displacement Δz. The quantities Δx, Δy, and Δz are often called the components parallel to the axes of the displacement. We shall generalize this idea by defining what shall be meant by the component of a vector in any direction whatever. Since we are now getting accustomed to stating directions in terms of a unit vector, we shall define the *scalar component of a vector* **A** *in the direction of a unit vector* **E** as the product of the magnitude of **A** by the cosine of the angle ϕ between the two vectors. Just what is meant by the angle between any two vectors is apparent if the vectors are drawn as in Fig. 1.22 with a common initial point, and by our definition of equality of two vectors it is clear that we may draw them that way if convenient. The symbol for the scalar component of **A** parallel to **E** will be a_E; thus

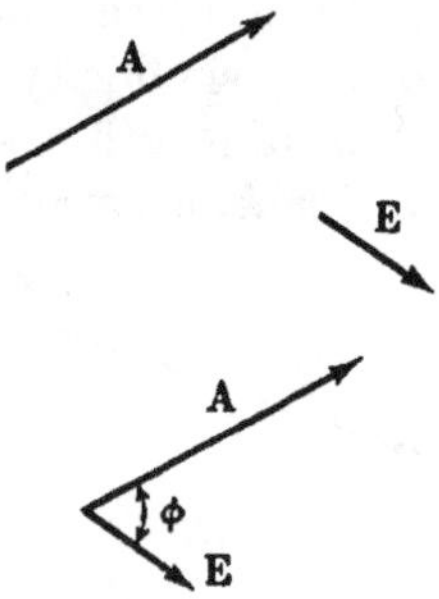

FIG. 1.22

$$a_E = a\cos\phi. \tag{1.18}$$

In cases where the unit vector determines a coordinate axis, the symbol for that coordinate may be used as the subscript:

$$a_I = a_x, \qquad a_J = a_y, \qquad a_K = a_z.$$

A closely related notion is that of *projection or vector component of a vector* in a given direction. Let **A** be a vector with initial point P and terminal point Q and let l be a line or axis whose direction is given by a unit vector **E**, as in Fig. 1.23. Let P' and Q' be the feet of the perpendiculars dropped from P and Q to l. Then the vector $P'Q'$ is the *projection of* **A** *on* l or the *vector component of* **A** *parallel to* **E**. It should be clear that this vector is given by

$$P'Q' = (a_E)\mathbf{E}. \tag{1.19}$$

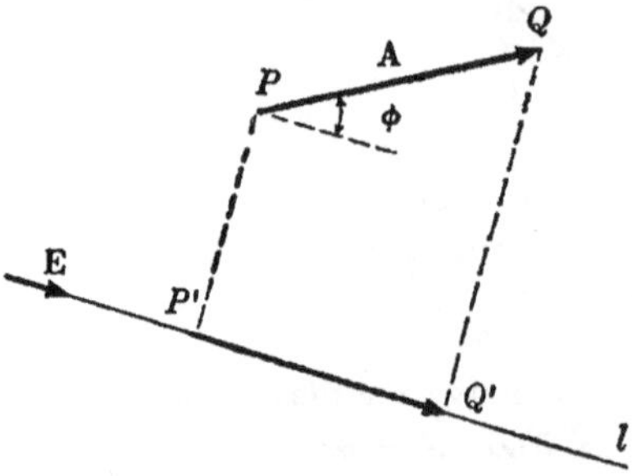

FIG. 1.23.

It should be noted that a_E is a positive scalar when ϕ is an acute angle, that it is zero when ϕ is 90°, and that it is negative when ϕ is obtuse. Of the two angles determined by two vectors we shall always choose the smaller; therefore ϕ will not exceed 180°. In Fig. 1.24, scalar components are represented as signed lengths of projections upon a line having the direction of a unit vector **E**.

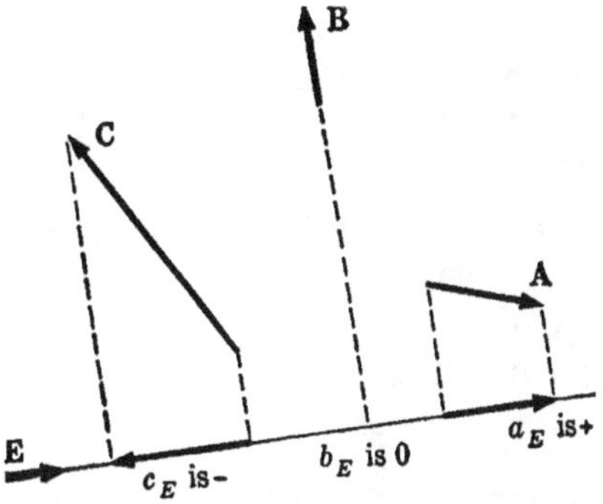

FIG. 1.24.

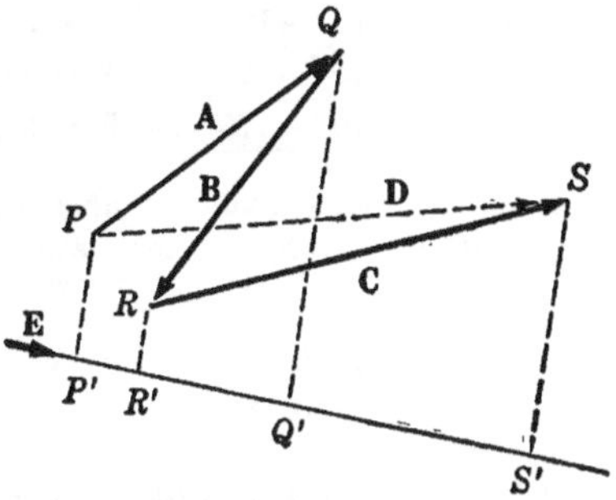

FIG. 1.25.

An important proposition concerning projections is that *the projection of the sum of two (or more) vectors is equal to the sum of their projections.* This is illustrated in Fig. 1.25 where it is apparent that the sum of the projections $P'Q' + Q'R' + R'S'$ is precisely the vector $P'S'$. But $P'S'$ is the projection of PS which is equal to the sum $PQ + QR + RS$. In terms of the notations which have been described, this equality appears as

(1.20) $$(a_E)\mathbf{E} + (b_E)\mathbf{E} + (c_E)\mathbf{E} = (d_E)\mathbf{E};$$

or, using one of the distributive laws for multiplication of vectors by scalars,

(1.21) $$(a_E + b_E + c_E)\mathbf{E} = (d_E)\mathbf{E}.$$

By the definition of equality of vectors, however, two vectors can be equal only if their magnitudes are equal; hence

(1.22) $$a_E + b_E + c_E = d_E.$$

(Of course the left member may be negative, but only if the right one is also.) We conclude that

(1.23) *Parallel to any unit vector* **E** *the sum of the components of a number of vectors is equal to the component of their sum.*

This has been verified for both scalar and vector components.

Example. In discussing a displacement from $P(x,y,z)$ to $P'(x',y',z')$, it was remarked that the whole could be regarded as the result of three displacements parallel to the axes. In terms of the symbols here used this might be stated:

$$PP' = \Delta x\,\mathbf{I} + \Delta y\,\mathbf{J} + \Delta z\,\mathbf{K}.$$

EXERCISES

1. Compute the scalar component of **A** in the direction of **E** and illustrate with a diagram for each of the following cases:

(a) $\mathbf{A} = 10\underline{/-120^\circ}$ and $\mathbf{E} = \mathbf{I}$. (b) $\mathbf{A} = 10\underline{/-120^\circ}$ and $\mathbf{E} = \mathbf{J}$.
(c) $\mathbf{A} = 10\underline{/-120^\circ}$ and $\mathbf{E} = 1\underline{/30^\circ}$. (d) $\mathbf{A} = 10\underline{/-120^\circ}$ and $\mathbf{E} = 1\underline{/-150^\circ}$.
(e) $\mathbf{A} = 10\underline{/-120^\circ}$ and $\mathbf{E} = 1\underline{/150^\circ}$. (f) $\mathbf{A} = 10\underline{/-120^\circ}$ and $\mathbf{E} = 1\underline{/50^\circ}$.

2. Compute the scalar component of $\mathbf{A} = 5\mathbf{I} + 6\mathbf{J}$ parallel to **E** in each of the following cases. (NOTE: Results on components of sums may be used.)

(a) $\mathbf{E} = \mathbf{I}$. (b) $\mathbf{E} = \mathbf{J}$.
(c) $\mathbf{E} = 1\underline{/30^\circ}$. (d) $\mathbf{E} = 1\underline{/135^\circ}$.
(e) $\mathbf{E} = 1\underline{/300^\circ}$. (f) $\mathbf{E} = 1\underline{/-130^\circ}$.

1.11. x, y, and z Components of a Vector. The situation described in the example in the preceding section is typical. Given *any vector* **A,** we shall often wish to make use of the fact that **A** can be represented as the vector sum of its vector components in the directions of the three axes; we shall usually express it as follows:

(1.24) $$\mathbf{A} = a_x\mathbf{I} + a_y\mathbf{J} + a_z\mathbf{K}.$$

This is illustrated in Fig. 1.26.

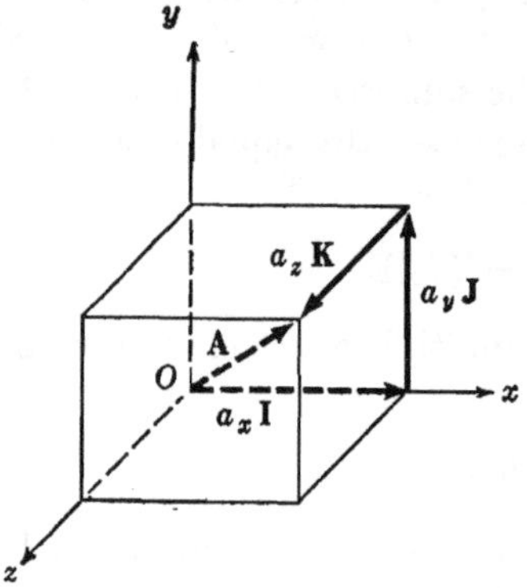

FIG. 1.26.

It follows from Eq. (1.2) that the magnitude of **A** is given by

(1.25) $$|\mathbf{A}| = a = \sqrt{a_x^2 + a_y^2 + a_z^2}.$$

If **A** is given as above and **B** by the equation

$$\mathbf{B} = b_x\mathbf{I} + b_y\mathbf{J} + b_z\mathbf{K},$$

then, using the associative and commutative laws for addition and the distributive laws for products by scalars, we may write

(1.26) $$\mathbf{A} + \mathbf{B} = (a_x + b_x)\mathbf{I} + (a_y + b_y)\mathbf{J} + (a_z + b_z)\mathbf{K}.$$

Since this is an assertion that *the x component of* **A** + **B** *is the x component of* **A** *plus the x component of* **B,** etc., it may be regarded as corroborating the statements made earlier in the preceding section about sums of projections and sums of components. From the equations

(1.27) $$c\mathbf{A} = c(a_x\mathbf{I} + a_y\mathbf{J} + a_z\mathbf{K}) = ca_x\mathbf{I} + ca_y\mathbf{J} + ca_z\mathbf{K}$$

we may similarly conclude that *the x component of the product of a vector by a scalar is equal to the product of the x component of the vector by the scalar;* and similarly for components in other directions.

If it is given that two vectors are equal,

$$\mathbf{A} = \mathbf{B}$$

it follows that

$$\mathbf{A} - \mathbf{B} = \mathbf{O} = (a_x - b_x)\mathbf{I} + (a_y - b_y)\mathbf{J} + (a_z - b_z)\mathbf{K}.$$

Since the component in any direction of a null vector is zero, we have as a consequence

$$a_x = b_x, \qquad a_y = b_y, \qquad a_z = b_z. \tag{1.28}$$

Thus *two vectors are equal if and only if their x, y, and z components are, respectively, equal.*

In Sec. 1.4 the direction cosines l, m, and n of a segment were derived by multiplying the x, y, and z components of the displacement by the reciprocal of the length of the displacement. It follows that the vector having l, m, and n as components parallel to the axes is a unit vector parallel to the displacement:

$$\mathbf{E} = l\mathbf{I} + m\mathbf{J} + n\mathbf{K} = \cos\alpha\,\mathbf{I} + \cos\beta\,\mathbf{J} + \cos\gamma\,\mathbf{K}. \tag{1.29}$$

This fact ties together two of our devices for describing direction: *the x, y, and z components of any unit vector are its direction cosines.*

EXERCISES

1. Express in the form $e_x\mathbf{I} + e_y\mathbf{J} + e_z\mathbf{K}$ a unit vector in each of the following directions:

(*a*) Parallel to $\mathbf{I} + \mathbf{J}$.
(*b*) Parallel to $10\underline{/150°}$.
(*c*) Parallel to $4\mathbf{I} - 3\mathbf{J}$.
(*d*) Parallel to $6\mathbf{J} + 8\mathbf{K}$.
(*e*) Parallel to $6\mathbf{I} - 3\mathbf{J} - 6\mathbf{K}$.
(*f*) Parallel to a displacement from the point with coordinates (5,0,3) to the point with coordinates (−7,0,8).
(*g*) Parallel to a displacement from the point with coordinates (5,0,3) to the point with coordinates (3,4,−1).

2. Express in the form $a_x\mathbf{I} + a_y\mathbf{J} + a_z\mathbf{K}$ each of the following vectors:

(*a*) $15\underline{/140°}$.
(*b*) $5\underline{/-90°}$.
(*c*) The magnitude is 100, and the direction is parallel to the unit vector $0.8\mathbf{J} - 0.6\mathbf{K}$.
(*d*) The magnitude is 70, and the direction is parallel to the vector $2\mathbf{I} + 3\mathbf{J} - 6\mathbf{K}$.
(*e*) The magnitude is 50, and the angles with the positive x, y, and z axes are 60°, 45°, 120°.

3. Find the magnitude and direction cosines of each of the following vectors:

(*a*) $-33\mathbf{I} + 56\mathbf{K}$. (*b*) $-14\mathbf{I} + 7\mathbf{J} + 14\mathbf{K}$.
(*c*) $-30\mathbf{K}$. (*d*) $8\mathbf{I} - 7\mathbf{J} - 6\mathbf{K}$.

4. Find the magnitude of each of the following sums and express in the form $e_x\mathbf{I} + e_y\mathbf{J} + e_z\mathbf{K}$ a unit vector parallel to the sum:

(*a*) $\mathbf{I} + \mathbf{J} + \mathbf{K}$. (*b*) $(\mathbf{I} + \mathbf{J}) + (-\mathbf{J} + \mathbf{K})$.
(*c*) $(2\mathbf{I} - 3\mathbf{K}) + (\mathbf{I} + 6\mathbf{J} - 3\mathbf{K})$. (*d*) $10\underline{/120°} + 10\underline{/45°}$.
(*e*) $7\underline{/30°} + 7\underline{/150°}$.

5. Any vector **A** in the xy plane can be expressed as a linear combination of two independent vectors such as $(\mathbf{I} + \mathbf{J})$ and $(2\mathbf{I} - \mathbf{J})$, that is, $\mathbf{A} = m(\mathbf{I} + \mathbf{J}) + n(2\mathbf{I} - \mathbf{J})$ for suitable scalars m and n. Find the correct values of m and n for the following cases:

(*a*) $\mathbf{A} = \mathbf{I}$. (*b*) $\mathbf{A} = \mathbf{J}$.
(*c*) $\mathbf{A} = \mathbf{O}$. (*d*) $\mathbf{A} = \mathbf{I} + 2\mathbf{J}$.

6. Starting at the point with coordinates (1,2,3) a displacement of length 6 is made in a direction whose direction cosines are -0.81, 0.32, -0.49. What are the coordinates of the stopping point?

1.12. Position Vectors. It has already been remarked that in our study of mechanics we shall require concise and lucid means of describing motion. The answer to the question "Where is the point?" can be given by stating the coordinates of the point with respect to an established frame of reference. This point of view, developed in Sec. 1.3, is very efficient when specific numerical information is needed, but it is unnecessarily clumsy and obscure in theoretical or qualitative discussions. Vector notation affords a means of stating position which is equivalent to coordinate notation in numerical work but which is simpler and more intuitive for general discourse. Given a point (x,y,z), we call the vector drawn from the origin to that point its *position vector*. The most frequently used symbol will be **R**. It is presumably obvious that the components of **R** (see Fig. 1.27) parallel to the axes are precisely the coordinates x, y, and z. Thus we may write

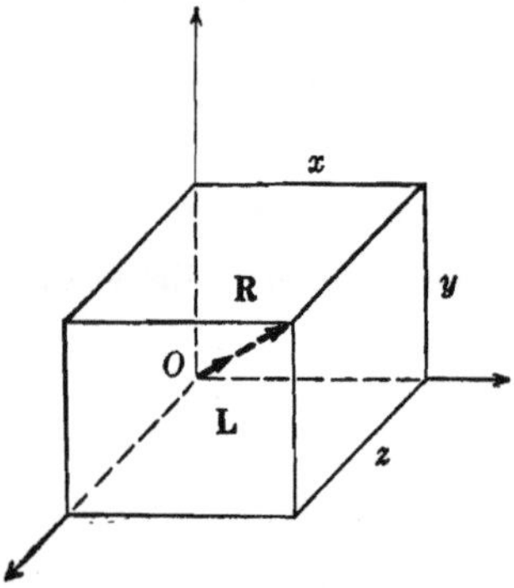

FIG. 1.27.

$$\mathbf{R} = x\mathbf{I} + y\mathbf{J} + z\mathbf{K}. \tag{1.30}$$

The magnitude of **R** will usually be denoted by r and the unit vector parallel to it by **L**; thus we write the equation

$$\mathbf{R} = r\mathbf{L}. \tag{1.31}$$

The position vector **R** and the unit radial vector **L** are easily visualized as means of describing position. Imagine that you are studying the motion of an airplane by following its course with a monocular. Regard your eye as the origin and the airplane as a moving point. Then the line of sight from your eye to the airplane serves as the position vector of the point. The length of this position vector is continually varying, but the monocular represents a parallel vector of fixed length always pointing at the airplane. Regard the monocular, then, as a model of the unit vector **L** which designates the direction to the moving point but ignores the distance. Some such intuitive feeling for vector notation must be deliberately cultivated by the student if he is to reap the full benefit of its use.

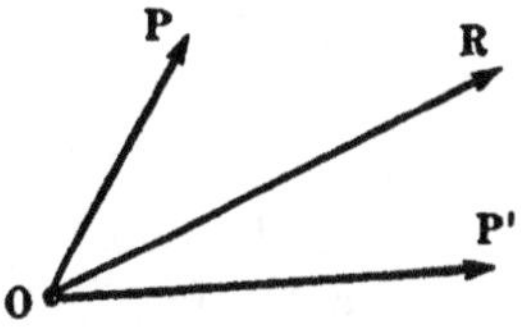

FIG. 1.28.

Since every point has a unique position vector and every vector starting at the origin determines a specific point, it will be convenient and economical to use the same symbol for both point and vector, as in Fig. 1.28. Thus **R** will be called the position vector of the point **R**. Similarly if **P** is a point, **P** will be the name of its position vector. The letter **O** now has two meanings: name of the origin and null vector. Since the position vector of the origin with respect to itself is assuredly a null vector, no serious ambiguity results.

Motion means change of position; therefore it is exceedingly gratifying to discover that displacements are easily described in terms of position vectors. Consider the displacement **PP′** from the point **P** (and hence with position vector **P**) to the point **P′**. Since position vectors have by definition the same initial points, it follows that a displacement is equal to a difference of position vectors (see rule for subtraction in Sec. 1.6). Thus a displacement is, as it should be, a change in position.

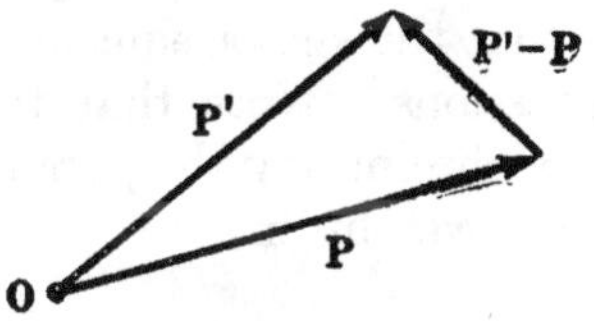

FIG. 1.29.

$$\mathbf{PP'} = \mathbf{P'} - \mathbf{P} = \Delta\mathbf{P}. \tag{1.32}$$

This is illustrated in Fig. 1.29. This symbolism may be compared with corresponding expressions for change of coordinate in a displacement:

$$\Delta x = x' - x, \qquad \Delta y = y' - y, \qquad \Delta z = z' - z.$$

Example. Find the magnitude and direction cosines of the displacement from $(-1,4,2)$ to $(3,2,-2)$.

SOLUTION. In terms of position vectors the displacement is from $\mathbf{P} = -\mathbf{I} + 4\mathbf{J} + 2\mathbf{K}$ to $\mathbf{P'} = 3\mathbf{I} + 2\mathbf{J} - 2\mathbf{K}$. The displacement $\Delta\mathbf{P}$ is thus given by $\Delta\mathbf{P} = \mathbf{P'} - \mathbf{P} = 4\mathbf{I} - 2\mathbf{J} - 4\mathbf{K}$. The magnitude is $\sqrt{4^2 + (-2)^2 + (-4)^2} = 6$. A unit vector parallel to the displacement is obtained by dividing $\Delta\mathbf{P}$ by 6. Its components, 0.667, −0.333, −0.667, are the direction cosines.

Vector Equation of a Straight Line. As an application of the language of this section let us write a vector equation for a line through $\mathbf{P}'$ and parallel to the unit vector $\mathbf{E}$. As usual in a locus problem, we first pick a variable point, $\mathbf{P}$, on the line. Treating this line as an axis with $\mathbf{P}'$ as origin, denote by s the scalar coordinate of $\mathbf{P}$. Then (see Fig. 1.30)

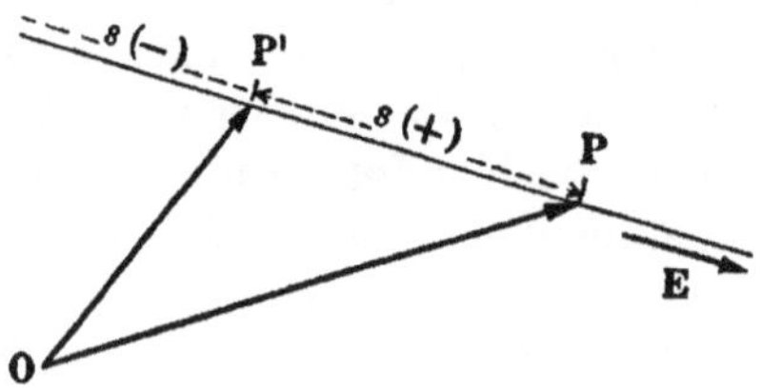

FIG. 1.30.

$$\mathbf{P'P} = s\mathbf{E}$$

so that

$$\mathbf{P} = \mathbf{P}' + s\mathbf{E}. \tag{1.33}$$

This is an equation, in parametric form, of the line. Assuming that $\mathbf{P}$ has coordinates (x,y,z), that $\mathbf{P}'$ has coordinates (x',y',z'), and that the components of $\mathbf{E}$ are the direction cosines l, m, n, this simple equation can be expanded thus

$$(x\mathbf{I} + y\mathbf{J} + z\mathbf{K}) = (x'\mathbf{I} + y'\mathbf{J} + z'\mathbf{K}) + s(l\mathbf{I} + m\mathbf{J} + n\mathbf{K}),$$

which yields, using previous results on equality of vectors and multiplication by scalars, three scalar equations of the same form:

$$x = x' + sl, \qquad y = y' + sm, \qquad z = z' + sn. \tag{1.34}$$

This *transition from one vector equation to three scalar equations* is representative of what may be done at any stage of a development in vector mechanics. It illustrates the remarkable conciseness and simplicity of vector notations and at the same time it shows that the vector equations are equivalent to suitable sets of scalar expressions. Note that the scalar parametric equations can be combined by eliminating the parameter. Solving each for s and equating the results, we obtain

$$\frac{x - x'}{l} = \frac{y - y'}{m} = \frac{z - z'}{n}. \tag{1.35}$$

This symmetric form is a standard result of solid analytic geometry.

EXERCISES

1. Evaluate the components parallel to the axes of the unit radial vector $\mathbf{L}$ associated with each of the following points:

(*a*) (1,0,1). (*b*) (1,−1,1). (*c*) (−10,12,−8).

2. Find the magnitude and direction cosines of the displacement from $\mathbf{P}$ to $\mathbf{P}'$ when (*a*) $\mathbf{P} = (-5,0,5)$ and $\mathbf{P}' = (0,0,0)$; (*b*) $\mathbf{P} = (-5,0,5)$ and $\mathbf{P}' = (2,8,14)$.

3. Find the position vectors of the two points 5 units from $\mathbf{P}$ on a line through $\mathbf{P}$ having direction cosines (0.500, −0.707, 0.500). $\mathbf{P}$ is the point (1,1,1).

4. Assuming that $(\bar{x},\bar{y},\bar{z})$ are the coordinates of $\bar{\mathbf{R}}$, (x_1,y_1,z_1) of $\mathbf{R}_1$, etc., write three scalar equations equivalent to the vector equation

$$10\bar{\mathbf{R}} = 2\mathbf{R}_1 + 5\mathbf{R}_2 + 3\mathbf{R}_3.$$

5. Show that the point $\mathbf{P}$ dividing the segment $\mathbf{P}'\mathbf{P}''$ in the ratio $r:(1 - r)$ is given by $\mathbf{P} = (1 - r)\mathbf{P}' + r\mathbf{P}''$.

6. Write three scalar equations equivalent to the ratio formula derived in Exercise 5.

7. State and derive a formula for the mid-point $\mathbf{P}$ of a segment $\mathbf{P}'\mathbf{P}''$.

8. Show that the result of Exercise 7 implies that the diagonals of a parallelogram bisect each other.

CHAPTER 2

PRODUCTS OF VECTORS

The first chapter introduced vectors from the geometrical point of view: geometrical tools such as coordinates, distances, and components were used in describing vectors. After getting accustomed to this new concept, we were able to reverse roles: vectors appeared as a natural tool for use in describing geometric relationships. The present chapter will add greatly to our ability to use vectors. This time the emphasis will be on algebraic operations, but many applications will be of geometric character.

2.1. Scalar Products of Two Vectors. Two operations have already been discussed for vectors: addition, in which two vectors are combined to give a third vector, and multiplication by scalars, in which a vector and a scalar are combined to give a new vector. In this section an operation is defined by which two vectors are combined to give a scalar. This scalar is the *scalar product* or the *inner product* of the two vectors. Let **A** and **B** denote any two vectors and θ the angle between them as in Fig. 2.1. Then the scalar product of **A** and **B**, denoted by $\mathbf{A} \cdot \mathbf{B}$ (and hence often called a "dot product"), is defined as the product of the magnitudes of the two vectors by the cosine of the angle:

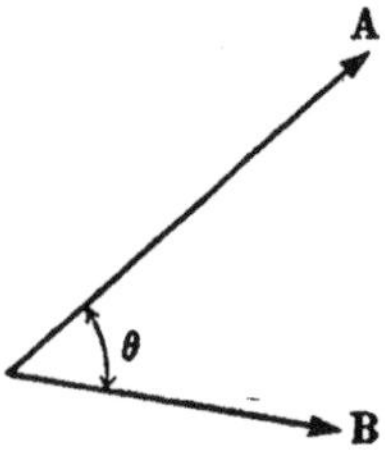

FIG. 2.1.

$$\mathbf{A} \cdot \mathbf{B} = ab \cos \theta. \tag{2.1}$$

Example 1. Consider $\mathbf{A} \cdot \mathbf{B}$, where $\mathbf{A} = 5\underline{/40^\circ}$ and $\mathbf{B} = 2\underline{/-20^\circ}$. Then

$$\theta = 40^\circ - (-20^\circ) = 60^\circ.$$
$$\mathbf{A} \cdot \mathbf{B} = (5)(2) \cos 60^\circ = 5.$$

Example 2. Consider $\mathbf{A} \cdot \mathbf{B}$ where $\mathbf{A} = 5\underline{/40^\circ}$ and $\mathbf{B} = 2\underline{/160^\circ}$. Then

$$\theta = 160^\circ - 40^\circ = 120^\circ.$$
$$\mathbf{A} \cdot \mathbf{B} = (5)(2) \cos 120^\circ = -5.$$

SPECIAL CONCLUSIONS. 1. Note that for any vector **A**

$$\mathbf{A} \cdot \mathbf{A} = |\mathbf{A}|^2 = a^2 \tag{2.2}$$

since in this case $\theta = 0^\circ$. $\mathbf{A} \cdot \mathbf{A}$ is often written as $\mathbf{A}^2$.

2. Consider the cases in which $\mathbf{A} \cdot \mathbf{B} = 0$. From the definition it is apparent that this is true whenever one of the vectors is a null vector. *Aside from this special case, it is apparent that*

$$\mathbf{A} \cdot \mathbf{B} = 0$$

means **A** *and* **B** *are perpendicular.*

3. Note that

$$\begin{aligned} \mathbf{I} \cdot \mathbf{I} = \mathbf{J} \cdot \mathbf{J} = \mathbf{K} \cdot \mathbf{K} = 1 \\ \mathbf{I} \cdot \mathbf{J} = \mathbf{J} \cdot \mathbf{I} = \mathbf{J} \cdot \mathbf{K} = \mathbf{K} \cdot \mathbf{J} = \mathbf{K} \cdot \mathbf{I} = \mathbf{I} \cdot \mathbf{K} = 0. \end{aligned} \tag{2.3}$$

4. Note that for any two unit vectors **E** and **F**, having between them an angle θ

$$\mathbf{E} \cdot \mathbf{F} = \cos \theta. \tag{2.4}$$

Similarly the angle between any two vectors **A** and **B** has a cosine given by

$$\cos \theta = \frac{\mathbf{A}}{a} \cdot \frac{\mathbf{B}}{b} = \frac{\mathbf{A} \cdot \mathbf{B}}{ab}. \tag{2.5}$$

5. The scalar product of a vector **A** by a unit vector **E** has special significance:

$$\mathbf{A} \cdot \mathbf{E} = (a)(1) \cos \theta = a \cos \theta = a_E. \tag{2.6}$$

That is, the scalar product of a vector by a unit vector is equal to the scalar component of the vector in the direction of the unit vector. For instance,

$$a_x = \mathbf{A} \cdot \mathbf{I}, \qquad a_y = \mathbf{A} \cdot \mathbf{J}, \qquad \ldots .$$

This property will be used frequently; therefore the student should take care to fix firmly in his mind the equivalence just described. It may be noted further that the *vector component* of **A** parallel to **E** is simply $(\mathbf{A} \cdot \mathbf{E})\mathbf{E}$.

Algebraic Properties. From the symmetry of the definition and the fact that

$$ab = ba$$

it follows that *scalar multiplication of vectors is commutative:*

$$\mathbf{A} \cdot \mathbf{B} = \mathbf{B} \cdot \mathbf{A}. \tag{2.7}$$

It is easy to show that scalar factors may be factored out of a scalar product:

$$(c\mathbf{A}) \cdot (d\mathbf{B}) = cd(\mathbf{A} \cdot \mathbf{B}). \tag{2.8}$$

The proof is listed as an exercise.

We have seen how this new operation may be combined with multiplication by scalars. We now consider its use in conjunction with the operation of addition. Consider the product $(\mathbf{A} + \mathbf{B}) \cdot \mathbf{C}$. Let us write $\mathbf{C}$ as $c\mathbf{E}$, where as usual $\mathbf{E}$ represents a unit vector in the desired direction. Factoring out the scalar multiple c, we are left with c times $(\mathbf{A} + \mathbf{B}) \cdot \mathbf{E}$ which we have just seen to be equal to the scalar component of $(\mathbf{A} + \mathbf{B})$ parallel to $\mathbf{E}$. But in Sec. 1.10 it was shown that such a component of a sum is equal to the sum of the components in the same direction of the vectors being added, that is,

$$(\mathbf{A} + \mathbf{B}) \cdot \mathbf{E} = \mathbf{A} \cdot \mathbf{E} + \mathbf{B} \cdot \mathbf{E}.$$

If both sides of this equation be multiplied by c, we have

$$(\mathbf{A} + \mathbf{B}) \cdot \mathbf{C} = c(\mathbf{A} + \mathbf{B}) \cdot \mathbf{E} = c(\mathbf{A} \cdot \mathbf{E}) + c(\mathbf{B} \cdot \mathbf{E})$$

or, using the rule for scalar factors,

$$(2.9) \quad (\mathbf{A} + \mathbf{B}) \cdot \mathbf{C} = (\mathbf{A} \cdot c\mathbf{E}) + (\mathbf{B} \cdot c\mathbf{E}) = (\mathbf{A} \cdot \mathbf{C}) + (\mathbf{B} \cdot \mathbf{C}).$$

This shows that *scalar multiplication of vectors is distributive with respect to vector addition.* Using this result together with the commutative law, one may derive a second form of the distributive law:

$$(2.10) \qquad \mathbf{A} \cdot (\mathbf{B} + \mathbf{C}) = \mathbf{A} \cdot \mathbf{B} + \mathbf{A} \cdot \mathbf{C}.$$

By successive application of the commutative and distributive laws it is possible to justify free manipulation of the operations thus far defined according to the rules of elementary algebra. Of course, one must keep in mind that a scalar is not a vector, so that, for instance, it is meaningless to write $(\mathbf{A} \cdot \mathbf{B}) \cdot \mathbf{C}$ unless one understands that this must mean the same as $(\mathbf{A} \cdot \mathbf{B})\mathbf{C}$.

As an example of such manipulations, we shall compute a working formula for scalar products in terms of components. Let us evaluate

$$\mathbf{A} \cdot \mathbf{B} = (a_x\mathbf{I} + a_y\mathbf{J} + a_z\mathbf{K}) \cdot (b_x\mathbf{I} + b_y\mathbf{J} + b_z\mathbf{K}).$$

Expanding the right member, using the distributive property, we get nine terms such as

$$(a_x\mathbf{I} \cdot b_x\mathbf{I}), \qquad (a_y\mathbf{J} \cdot b_z\mathbf{K}), \ . \ . \ . \ .$$

By the rule for factoring out scalar factors, they may be rewritten as

$$a_xb_x(\mathbf{I} \cdot \mathbf{I}), \qquad a_yb_z(\mathbf{J} \cdot \mathbf{K}), \ . \ . \ . \ .$$

It is now apparent that six of the nine terms are equal to zero.

$$(\mathbf{J} \cdot \mathbf{K} = 0, \ . \ . \ .);$$

hence, if we replace $(\mathbf{I}\cdot\mathbf{I})$ by its value one (and similarly for $\mathbf{J}\cdot\mathbf{J}$ and $\mathbf{K}\cdot\mathbf{K}$), we shall have as an end result:

$$\mathbf{A}\cdot\mathbf{B} = a_xb_x + a_yb_y + a_zb_z. \tag{2.11}$$

This is a formula of great utility.

Example 3. Find the scalar component of $\mathbf{A} = 9\mathbf{I} - 3\mathbf{J} + 6\mathbf{K}$ parallel to the unit vector $\mathbf{E} = (\frac{2}{3})\mathbf{I} - (\frac{1}{3})\mathbf{J} + (\frac{2}{3})\mathbf{K}$.

SOLUTION

$$a_E = \mathbf{A}\cdot\mathbf{E} = (9)(\tfrac{2}{3}) + (-3)(-\tfrac{1}{3}) + (6)(\tfrac{2}{3}) = 11.$$

Example 4. Find the angle subtended at the origin by the points with coordinates (3,4,0) and (0,−8,6).

SOLUTION. The vectors from the origin to these points are

$$\mathbf{A} = 3\mathbf{I} + 4\mathbf{J} \qquad \text{and} \qquad \mathbf{B} = -8\mathbf{J} + 6\mathbf{K},$$

then

$$\cos\theta = \frac{\mathbf{A}\cdot\mathbf{B}}{ab} = \frac{-32}{5\times 10} = -0.64,$$

whence

$$\theta = 129.8°.$$

EXERCISES

1. Find the scalar product of each of the following pairs of vectors:

(*a*) $25/\underline{0°}$ and $10/\underline{110°}$.
(*b*) $5/\underline{-50°}$ and $6/\underline{40°}$.
(*c*) $1/\underline{70°}$ and $1/\underline{130°}$.
(*d*) $1/\underline{30°}$ and $1/\underline{210°}$.
(*e*) $15/\underline{155°}$ and $\mathbf{J}$.
(*f*) $2\mathbf{I} + \mathbf{J}$ and $2\mathbf{I} - \mathbf{J}$.
(*g*) $\mathbf{I} - 2\mathbf{J} + 3\mathbf{K}$ and $\mathbf{J} - \mathbf{K}$.
(*h*) $2\mathbf{I} - \mathbf{J} - 3\mathbf{K}$ and $4\mathbf{I} + 5\mathbf{J} + \mathbf{K}$.

2. Find the angle between (*a*) the vectors $2\mathbf{I} - 2\mathbf{J} + \mathbf{K}$ and $4\mathbf{I} - 3\mathbf{K}$; (*b*) the position vectors of the points with coordinates (2,0,5) and (3,−6,−6); (*c*) the lines *AB* and *AC* where *A*, *B*, and *C* are points with coordinates (3,−2,6), (5,−2,7), and (1,−1,6), respectively; (*d*) the directions having direction cosines $(\frac{2}{3})$, $(\frac{1}{3})$, $(-\frac{2}{3})$ and $(\frac{1}{3})$, $(\frac{2}{3})$, $(\frac{2}{3})$.

3. The vector $a\mathbf{I} - 2\mathbf{J} + \mathbf{K}$ is perpendicular to the vector $\mathbf{I} - 2\mathbf{J} - 3\mathbf{K}$. Find a.

4. $\mathbf{E}$ and $\mathbf{F}$ are unit vectors. Under what conditions can the sum $\mathbf{E} + \mathbf{F}$ be a unit vector? (HINT: Expand the scalar product of $\mathbf{E} + \mathbf{F}$ with itself.)

5. The vectors $\mathbf{A} + \mathbf{B}$ and $\mathbf{A} - \mathbf{B}$ are perpendicular. Use the scalar product as a means of arriving at a conclusion concerning the magnitudes of $\mathbf{A}$ and of $\mathbf{B}$.

6. Find the scalar component of the vector $2\mathbf{I} - 3\mathbf{J} + 6\mathbf{K}$ parallel to (*a*) the unit vector $0.33\mathbf{I} - 0.67\mathbf{J} + 0.67\mathbf{K}$; (*b*) the *z* axis; (*c*) the vector $3\mathbf{I} - 9\mathbf{J} - 2\mathbf{K}$; (*d*) the vector $3\mathbf{I} + 2\mathbf{J}$.

7. Find the vector component of $6\mathbf{I} - 6\mathbf{J} - 7\mathbf{K}$ (*a*) parallel to the *y* axis; (*b*) parallel to $3\mathbf{I} - 4\mathbf{K}$.

8. A unit vector $\mathbf{E}$ makes angles of 45°, 60°, and 120°, respectively, with the coordinate axes. Find the component parallel to $\mathbf{E}$ of the vector $\mathbf{I} - \mathbf{J} - \mathbf{K}$.

9. A vector **V** has magnitude 10 and direction cosines 0.5, 0.707, and −0.5. Find the component of **V** parallel to the z axis; parallel to the vector $4\mathbf{I} - 3\mathbf{K}$.

10. Given two nonperpendicular vectors **A** and **B**. For some scalar k, the vector $k\mathbf{B}$ has a component in the direction of **A** which is exactly equal to **A**. Prove that

$$k = \frac{\mathbf{A} \cdot \mathbf{A}}{\mathbf{A} \cdot \mathbf{B}}.$$

11. **E** and **F** are unit vectors. $\mathbf{E} - \mathbf{F}$ is also a unit vector. Use scalar products to draw a further conclusion about **E** and **F**.

12. **E** and **F** are unit vectors. $\mathbf{E} - 2\mathbf{F}$ has magnitude 2. Use scalar products to draw a further conclusion about **E** and **F**.

13. If $\mathbf{A} = (\mathbf{A} \cdot \mathbf{B})\mathbf{B}$, prove that **B** is a unit vector.

14. For vectors **A**, **B** and scalars c, d prove that the following identity is valid:

$$(c\mathbf{A}) \cdot (d\mathbf{B}) = cd(\mathbf{A} \cdot \mathbf{B}).$$

15. Under what conditions is cancellation of the common factor **C** valid in an equation such as $\mathbf{A} \cdot \mathbf{C} = \mathbf{B} \cdot \mathbf{C}$? Prove your answer carefully.

16. Use scalar products to prove that any vector which is perpendicular to both **A** and **B**,

$$\mathbf{A} = a_x\mathbf{I} + a_y\mathbf{J} + a_z\mathbf{K}, \qquad \mathbf{B} = b_x\mathbf{I} + b_y\mathbf{J} + b_z\mathbf{K},$$

is a scalar multiple of the vector

$$\mathbf{C} = (a_yb_z - a_zb_y)\mathbf{I} + (a_zb_x - a_xb_z)\mathbf{J} + (a_xb_y - a_yb_x)\mathbf{K}.$$

2.2. Applications of the Scalar Product. In this section a few geometric applications of scalar products will be given. The geometry itself is interesting, but here the primary aim is to develop familiarity with this new operation. These applications are listed just as illustrative examples in the use of scalar products. Further situations are presented in the exercises.

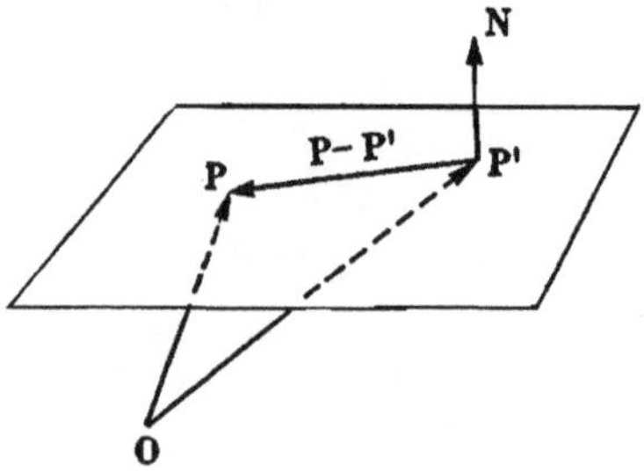

FIG. 2.2.

Example 1. Write an equation for a plane through **P**′ and perpendicular to a unit vector **N**.

SOLUTION. Pick a variable point **P** on the plane (see Fig. 2.2). Then the vector from **P**′, $\mathbf{P} - \mathbf{P}'$, is perpendicular to **N**. Hence

$$(\mathbf{P} - \mathbf{P}') \cdot \mathbf{N} = 0. \tag{2.12}$$

This is the desired equation. It is a scalar equation in terms of vectors. If **N** has direction cosines l, m, and n, **P** has coordinates (x,y,z), and **P**′ (x',y',z'), then the above equation is equivalent to

$$l(x - x') + m(y - y') + n(z - z') = 0. \tag{2.13}$$

Example 2. Determine the vector obtained by projecting a vector **A** onto a plane which is normal to a unit vector **N**.

SOLUTION. Denote this vector by $\mathbf{A}'$. Since lines drawn from the ends of $\mathbf{A}'$ to the corresponding ends of $\mathbf{A}$ are parallel to $\mathbf{N}$, it is apparent (see Fig. 2.3) that $\mathbf{A}$ is equal to the vector sum of $\mathbf{A}'$ and the vector component of $\mathbf{A}$ parallel to $\mathbf{N}$; thus

$$\mathbf{A} = \mathbf{A}' + (\mathbf{A} \cdot \mathbf{N})\mathbf{N}.$$

Thus $\mathbf{A}'$ is expressible by the equation

$$\mathbf{A}' = \mathbf{A} - (\mathbf{A} \cdot \mathbf{N})\mathbf{N}. \tag{2.14}$$

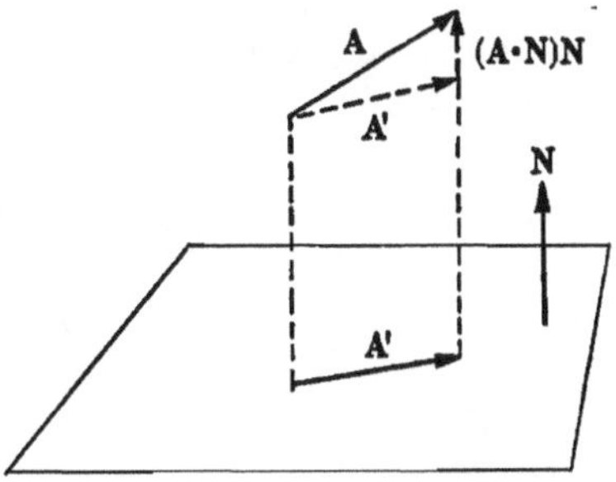

FIG. 2.3.

In terms of this expression it is easy to prove a theorem about projections onto a plane which is analogous to the one proved in Sec. 1.10 about projections onto a line. The statement is the same as before: *The projection of the sum of two (or more) vectors is equal to the sum of their projections.* The proof is as follows. Let $\mathbf{A}'$ and $\mathbf{B}'$ denote the projections onto the plane of the vectors $\mathbf{A}$ and $\mathbf{B}$. If $\mathbf{N}$ is a

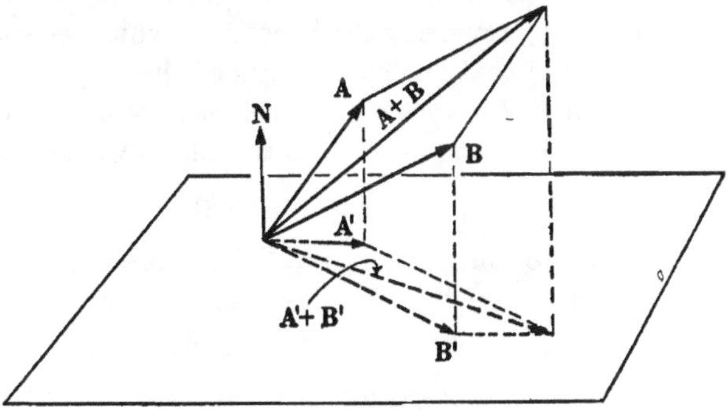

FIG. 2.4.

unit normal to the plane, then, as just stated above (see Fig. 2.4),

$$\mathbf{A}' = \mathbf{A} - (\mathbf{A} \cdot \mathbf{N})\mathbf{N} \qquad \text{and} \qquad \mathbf{B}' = \mathbf{B} - (\mathbf{B} \cdot \mathbf{N})\mathbf{N}.$$

Using the associative and commutative laws for vector addition, the sum $\mathbf{A}' + \mathbf{B}'$ may be written

$$\mathbf{A}' + \mathbf{B}' = \mathbf{A} + \mathbf{B} - (\mathbf{A} \cdot \mathbf{N})\mathbf{N} - (\mathbf{B} \cdot \mathbf{N})\mathbf{N}.$$

But by the distributive law for multiplication by a scalar we may factor out the $\mathbf{N}$ from the last two terms.

$$\mathbf{A}' + \mathbf{B}' = \mathbf{A} + \mathbf{B} - [(\mathbf{A} \cdot \mathbf{N}) + (\mathbf{B} \cdot \mathbf{N})]\mathbf{N}.$$

Then finally the distributive law for scalar products yields

$$\mathbf{A}' + \mathbf{B}' = \mathbf{A} + \mathbf{B} - [(\mathbf{A} + \mathbf{B}) \cdot \mathbf{N}]\mathbf{N}.$$

But the right member of this equation is immediately recognizable as the projection onto the plane of the vector $\mathbf{A} + \mathbf{B}$; therefore we have

$$\mathbf{A}' + \mathbf{B}' = (\mathbf{A} + \mathbf{B})', \tag{2.15}$$

as was to be proved.

Example 3. Find the distance from a point **P** to a plane through the point **P′** and perpendicular to the unit vector **N** (see Fig. 2.5).

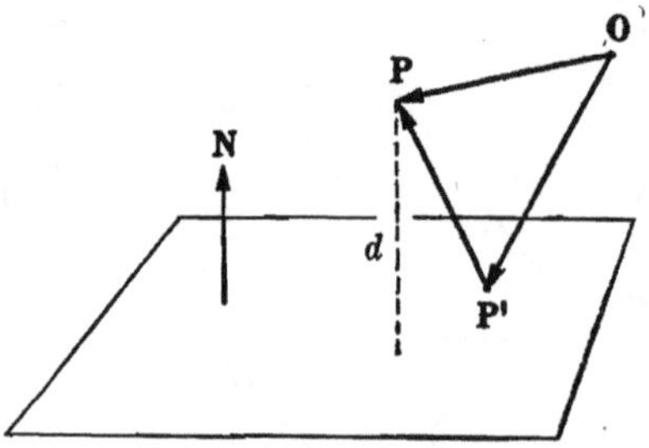

FIG. 2.5.

SOLUTION. What is desired is clearly the magnitude of the scalar component of the vector from **P′** to **P** parallel to **N**. Thus

$$d = |(\mathbf{P} - \mathbf{P}') \cdot \mathbf{N}|. \tag{2.16}$$

NOTE: In each of the examples involving planes, the plane has been described in terms of a unit normal vector **N** and a point **P′**. In numerical problems these are easy to find. If the equation of the plane is given, one can show directly (by reversing the procedure which we used in finding an equation for a plane) that the coefficients of the x, y, and z terms are x, y, and z components of a vector (not necessarily unit) normal to the plane. Thus $a\mathbf{I} + b\mathbf{J} + c\mathbf{K}$ is normal to the plane whose equation is

$$ax + by + cz + d = 0.$$

From this a unit vector may be found. The problem of finding the coordinates of a point **P′** on the plane is even simpler. For instance if $a \neq 0$, then $(-d/a,0,0)$ is such a point.

EXERCISES

1. Show how the law of cosines of trigonometry can be derived from an expansion of the scalar product

$$(\mathbf{A} + \mathbf{B}) \cdot (\mathbf{A} + \mathbf{B}).$$

2. The vector components of **A** parallel and perpendicular to a unit vector **E** have been shown to be, respectively, equal to $(\mathbf{A} \cdot \mathbf{E})\mathbf{E}$ and $\mathbf{A} - (\mathbf{A} \cdot \mathbf{E})\mathbf{E}$. Use the rules for scalar multiplication to show that these two components are perpendicular to each other.

3. Find the scalar component of the vector $2\mathbf{I} - 3\mathbf{J} + 6\mathbf{K}$ parallel to the xy plane.

4. Find the vector component of $6\mathbf{I} - 6\mathbf{J} - 7\mathbf{K}$ (*a*) parallel to the plane $x - 2y - 2z = 0$; (*b*) perpendicular to the vector $\mathbf{I} + \mathbf{J}$ (that is, parallel to a plane normal to this vector); (*c*) perpendicular to the vector $3\mathbf{I} + \mathbf{K}$.

5. Write an equation for the plane through the origin and perpendicular to the vector $\mathbf{I} - 2\mathbf{J} - 3\mathbf{K}$.

6. Write an equation for the plane whose normal has direction cosines 0.500, 0.707, −0.500 and which passes through the point (−2, 0,1).

7. Use the scalar product as a tool for finding the distance from the point (1,1,1) to the plane through (4,6,2) normal to the unit vector $0.6\mathbf{I} - 0.8\mathbf{J}$.

8. Find the distance from the plane $6x - 2y + 3z = 10$ to the point (10,4,0).

9. Use the scalar product as a tool for finding the distance from the point (0,0,0) to the line through the points $(5,-7,2)$ and $(-1,1,2)$. (HINT: The altitude of a triangle is equal to the scalar component perpendicular to the base of one of the other sides.)

10. Find the shortest distance from the point $(-1,0,2)$ to the line through the points $(3,-1,3)$ and (2,2,0).

2.3. Vector Products of Two Vectors. The remaining operation to be introduced at this stage is in many ways the most interesting of all. When applied to two vectors, the operation yields a new vector. The procedure resembles multiplication enough to deserve the name *vector product;* yet many of the usual properties of a product are missing. Since the result of this operation is a vector, both a direction and a magnitude must be specified. For two nonparallel vectors **A** and **B,** the direction is that of a unit vector **N** perpendicular to the plane determined by the two vectors **A** and **B.** Two such unit vectors are possible (**N** and $-$**N** in Fig. 2.6), but we choose **N** so that the rotation of **A** into **B** as seen from the

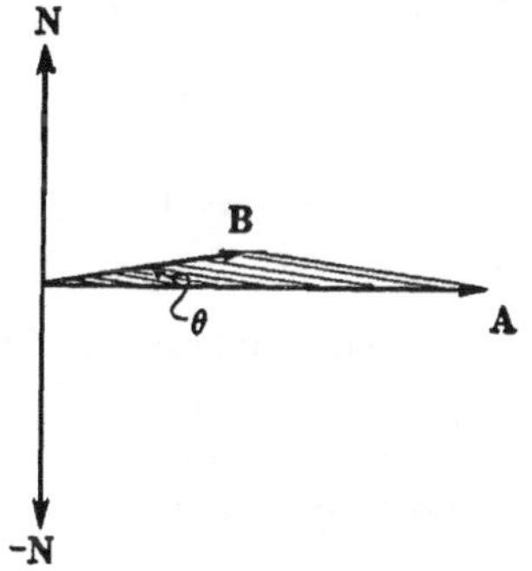

FIG. 2.6.

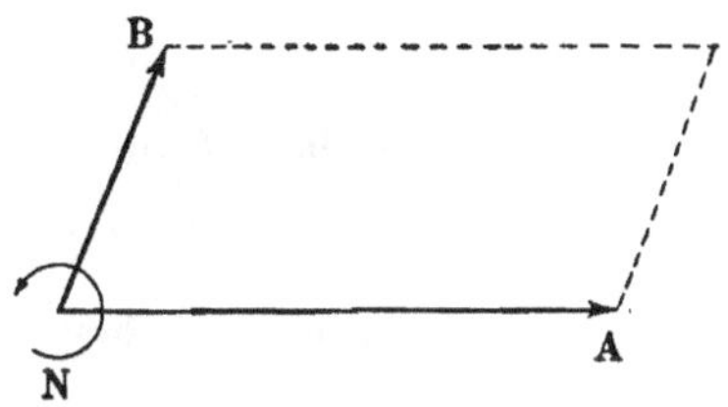

FIG. 2.7.

tip of **N,** looking back at the plane, is counterclockwise. The same kind of choice was made in Sec. 1.2 in selecting a positive z axis. In Fig. 2.7, **N** is directed out of the page toward the reader. The magnitude of this vector product is defined to be the product of the magnitudes of the two vectors times the sine of the angle between. A defining equation for the vector product of **A** times **B** (denoted by **A** $\times$ **B,** and hence often called the "cross product") is

$$\mathbf{A} \times \mathbf{B} = ab \sin \theta \, \mathbf{N}. \tag{2.17}$$

It is interesting to note that the magnitude of **A** $\times$ **B** is equal to the area of the parallelogram determined (as in Fig. 2.7) by the vectors **A** and **B.** Thus

$$\mathbf{A} \times \mathbf{B} = (\text{area})\mathbf{N}. \tag{2.18}$$

From the definition of **N** it should be at once obvious that this kind of multiplication is not commutative:

$$\mathbf{A} \times \mathbf{B} = -\mathbf{B} \times \mathbf{A}. \tag{2.19}$$

In describing the direction of **N**, we considered **A** and **B** as being non-parallel. For parallel vectors, however, $\sin\theta$ is zero; thus our defining equation may be used for all cases.

This suggests the following useful criterion for parallelism (or anti-parallelism) of two non-null vectors **A** and **B**, namely,

$$\mathbf{A} \times \mathbf{B} = \mathbf{O}.$$

Example 1. Consider $\mathbf{A} \times \mathbf{B}$, where $\mathbf{A} = 5\underline{/40^\circ}$ and $\mathbf{B} = 2\underline{/-110^\circ}$. Then

$$\mathbf{A} \times \mathbf{B} = (5)(2)(\sin 150^\circ)(-\mathbf{K}) = -5\mathbf{K}.$$

Similarly,

$$\mathbf{B} \times \mathbf{A} = (5)(2)(\sin 150^\circ)(\mathbf{K}) = 5\mathbf{K}.$$

SPECIAL CONCLUSIONS. 1. $\mathbf{A} \times \mathbf{A} = \mathbf{O}$. This is, of course, a special case of the criterion just stated.

2. Note that

$$\begin{array}{lll} \mathbf{I} \times \mathbf{J} = \mathbf{K}, & \mathbf{J} \times \mathbf{K} = \mathbf{I}, & \mathbf{K} \times \mathbf{I} = \mathbf{J}, \\ \mathbf{J} \times \mathbf{I} = -\mathbf{K}, & \mathbf{K} \times \mathbf{J} = -\mathbf{I}, & \mathbf{I} \times \mathbf{K} = -\mathbf{J}. \end{array} \tag{2.20}$$

3. For two unit vectors **E** and **F** having between them an angle θ,

$$\mathbf{E} \times \mathbf{F} = \sin\theta\, \mathbf{N}. \tag{2.21}$$

Hence the sine of the angle is given by the magnitude of the vector product:

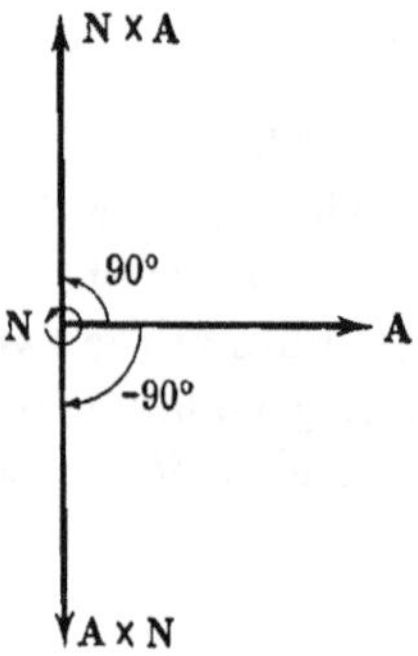

FIG. 2.8.

$$\sin\theta = |\mathbf{E} \times \mathbf{F}|. \tag{2.22}$$

More generally for any two vectors **A** and **B**

$$\sin\theta = \left|\frac{\mathbf{A} \times \mathbf{B}}{ab}\right|. \tag{2.23}$$

4. Suppose that **N** is a *unit vector perpendicular to* **A**. Then $\mathbf{N} \times \mathbf{A}$ is a vector equal to **A** but at right angles to **A** (as in Fig. 2.8).

(2.24) *The operation* $\mathbf{N} \times$ *may be thought of as merely rotating* **A** *through* 90°. (*Similarly the operation* $\times \mathbf{N}$ *may be thought of as merely rotating* **A** *through* −90°.)

Note that $\mathbf{N} \times (\mathbf{N} \times \mathbf{A}) = -\mathbf{A}$. This suggests an analogy between the operation $\mathbf{N} \times$ and multiplication by $i = \sqrt{-1}$ in the algebra of complex numbers.

5. Just as all parallelograms with the same base and altitude have the same area, it is interesting and profitable to observe that

$$\mathbf{A} \times \mathbf{B} = \mathbf{A} \times \mathbf{B}', \tag{2.25}$$

where $\mathbf{B}'$ is the component of $\mathbf{B}$ perpendicular to $\mathbf{A}$. Moreover (referring to Fig. 2.9), $\mathbf{A} \times \mathbf{B} = \mathbf{A} \times \mathbf{B}''$ if $\mathbf{B}$ and $\mathbf{B}''$ have equal components perpendicular to $\mathbf{A}$. The student should use the definition of vector product to verify these relations and also the following similar ones:

$$\mathbf{A}' \times \mathbf{B} = \mathbf{A} \times \mathbf{B} = \mathbf{A}'' \times \mathbf{B}. \tag{2.26}$$

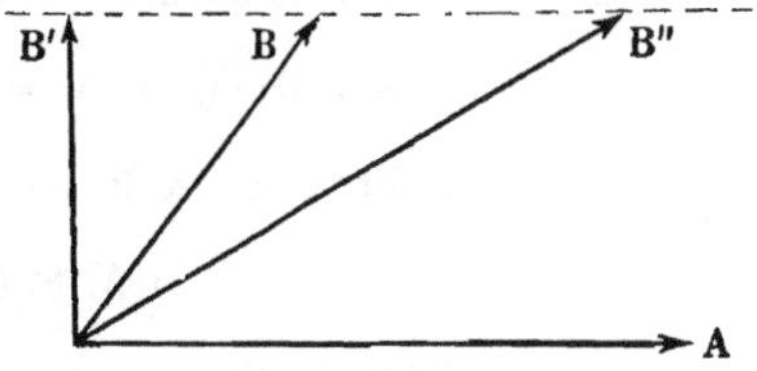

FIG. 2.9.

Algebraic Properties. It is easy to show that scalar factors may be factored out of a vector product:

$$(c\mathbf{A}) \times (d\mathbf{B}) = cd(\mathbf{A} \times \mathbf{B}). \tag{2.27}$$

The proof is listed as an exercise.

We have seen already that vector multiplication is not commutative:

$$\mathbf{A} \times \mathbf{B} \neq \mathbf{B} \times \mathbf{A}.$$

Later it will be shown that this kind of multiplication is not associative:

$$\mathbf{A} \times (\mathbf{B} \times \mathbf{C}) \neq (\mathbf{A} \times \mathbf{B}) \times \mathbf{C}.$$

We shall next seek to prove that vector multiplication is distributive with respect to vector addition, *i.e.*, that the following equation is in general valid.

$$\mathbf{A} \times (\mathbf{B} + \mathbf{C}) = \mathbf{A} \times \mathbf{B} + \mathbf{A} \times \mathbf{C}.$$

The proof is given in Sec. 2.4.

EXERCISES

1. Use the defining equations for vector products to compute in **IJK** form the vector product of each of the following pairs of vectors:

(*a*) $\mathbf{A} = 4\underline{/20^\circ}$, $\mathbf{B} = 7\underline{/-25^\circ}$. (*b*) $\mathbf{A} = 5\underline{/-55^\circ}$, $\mathbf{B} = 10\underline{/125^\circ}$.
(*c*) $\mathbf{A} = 5\underline{/55^\circ}$, $\mathbf{B} = 10\underline{/35^\circ}$. (*d*) $\mathbf{A} = 5\underline{/40^\circ}$, $\mathbf{B} = 5\underline{/40^\circ}$.
(*e*) $\mathbf{A} = \mathbf{I} + \mathbf{J}$, $\mathbf{B} = \mathbf{J} + \mathbf{K}$.

2. Compute in polar form the following vector products:

(*a*) $\mathbf{K} \times \mathbf{I}$. (*b*) $\mathbf{K} \times 10\underline{/30^\circ}$.
(*c*) $\mathbf{K} \times \mathbf{J}$. (*d*) $\mathbf{K} \times (2\mathbf{I} + 2\mathbf{J})$.
(*e*) $10\underline{/30^\circ} \times \mathbf{K}$. (*f*) $\mathbf{K} \times \{\mathbf{K} \times [\mathbf{K} \times (\mathbf{K} \times 2\underline{/36^\circ})]\}$.

3. $\mathbf{R}$ is a vector in the xy plane. $\mathbf{I}$ as usual is a unit vector parallel to the x axis. It is given that

$$\mathbf{I} \times \mathbf{R} = \mathbf{K},$$

where **K** is the unit vector parallel to the z axis. How much can be concluded about **R**? Describe the locus of points in the xy plane for which **R** may be position vector.

4. Use the definition of scalar and vector products to prove the following: if

$$\mathbf{A} \times \mathbf{B} = \mathbf{C} \quad \text{and} \quad \mathbf{B} \times \mathbf{C} = \mathbf{A},$$

then

$$\mathbf{B} \cdot \mathbf{A} = 0, \quad \mathbf{C} \cdot \mathbf{A} = 0, \quad \mathbf{B} \cdot \mathbf{C} = 0, \quad \mathbf{A} \cdot \mathbf{A} = \mathbf{C} \cdot \mathbf{C}, \quad \mathbf{B} \cdot \mathbf{B} = 1.$$

5. Use the definitions of scalar and vector products to prove

$$(\mathbf{A} \times \mathbf{B}) \cdot (\mathbf{A} \times \mathbf{B}) = (\mathbf{A} \cdot \mathbf{A})(\mathbf{B} \cdot \mathbf{B}) - (\mathbf{A} \cdot \mathbf{B})(\mathbf{A} \cdot \mathbf{B}).$$

6. Prove that for vectors **A**, **B** and scalars c, d the following identity is valid:

$$(c\mathbf{A}) \times (d\mathbf{B}) = cd(\mathbf{A} \times \mathbf{B}).$$

2.4. The Distributive Law for Vector Products. It is so natural to accept equations like

$$2 \times 3 = 3 \times 2, \qquad 3 \times (1 + 2) = 3 \times 1 + 3 \times 2$$

as inevitable truisms that proofs of corresponding vector relationships might first impress the student as unnecessary. Any such complacency should be dispelled by the discovery in the preceding section that the operation called *vector product* is not commutative. The distributive law to which this section is devoted is of unusual interest because of its very close connection with certain problems in statics. Fairly detailed attention to the law and its applications will help greatly in getting accustomed to this rather strange new operation.

Let us now proceed with a proof of

$$\mathbf{A} \times (\mathbf{B} + \mathbf{C}) = \mathbf{A} \times \mathbf{B} + \mathbf{A} \times \mathbf{C}. \tag{2.28}$$

Let $(\mathbf{B} + \mathbf{C})'$ denote the component of $(\mathbf{B} + \mathbf{C})$ perpendicular to **A**. As was pointed out in Special Conclusion 5, Sec. 2.3,

$$\mathbf{A} \times (\mathbf{B} + \mathbf{C}) = \mathbf{A} \times (\mathbf{B} + \mathbf{C})'.$$

But $(\mathbf{B} + \mathbf{C})'$ is merely the projection of the sum $\mathbf{B} + \mathbf{C}$ onto a plane normal to **A**. It was shown in Sec. 2.2 that

$$(\mathbf{B} + \mathbf{C})' = \mathbf{B}' + \mathbf{C}',$$

where $\mathbf{B}'$ and $\mathbf{C}'$ are the projections of **B** and **C** onto a plane perpendicular to **A**. Substituting this expression for $(\mathbf{B} + \mathbf{C})'$ and writing $a\mathbf{E}$ for **A** (that is, we denote the unit vector $\mathbf{A}/a$ by **E**), we have

$$\mathbf{A} \times (\mathbf{B} + \mathbf{C}) = a\mathbf{E} \times (\mathbf{B}' + \mathbf{C}'),$$

where **E** is a unit vector perpendicular to both $\mathbf{B}'$ and $\mathbf{C}'$. In Special Conclusion 4, Sec. 2.3, it was observed that the operation $\mathbf{E} \times$ merely rotates vectors normal to **E** through 90°, as in Fig. 2.10. If the parallelogram representing the addition of **B**′ and **C**′ is rotated in its own plane by 90°, each of the three vectors **B**′, **C**′, and **B**′ + **C**′ is also rotated through 90°. In symbols, then

$$\mathbf{E} \times (\mathbf{B}' + \mathbf{C}') = \mathbf{E} \times \mathbf{B}' + \mathbf{E} \times \mathbf{C}'.$$

(This equation is, of course, a statement of the distributive law for a very special case.) Substituting this in the previous equation, we get

$$\mathbf{A} \times (\mathbf{B} + \mathbf{C}) = a(\mathbf{E} \times \mathbf{B}' + \mathbf{E} \times \mathbf{C}').$$

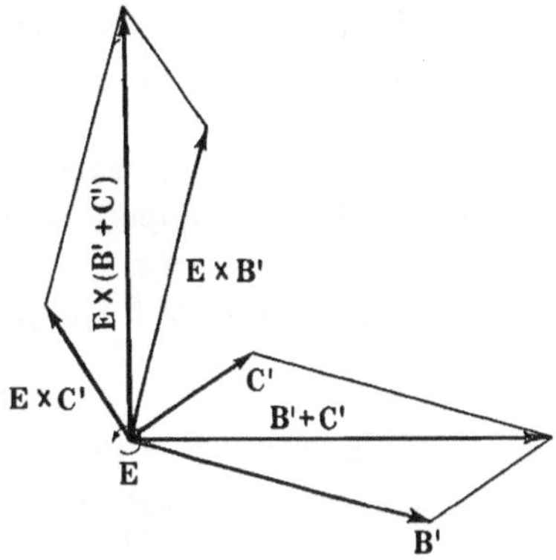

FIG. 2.10.

Using the distributive property of the operation of multiplication of vectors by scalars (see exercises of Sec. 1.8), using again the result on projections, etc., we have

$$\begin{aligned}\mathbf{A} \times (\mathbf{B} + \mathbf{C}) &= a(\mathbf{E} \times \mathbf{B}') + a(\mathbf{E} \times \mathbf{C}') \\ &= a\mathbf{E} \times \mathbf{B}' + a\mathbf{E} \times \mathbf{C}' \\ &= \mathbf{A} \times \mathbf{B}' + \mathbf{A} \times \mathbf{C}' \\ &= \mathbf{A} \times \mathbf{B} + \mathbf{A} \times \mathbf{C}.\end{aligned}$$

It is left as an exercise to show that the reverse form of the distributive law also holds, *i.e.*, that

$$(\mathbf{A} + \mathbf{B}) \times \mathbf{C} = \mathbf{A} \times \mathbf{C} + \mathbf{B} \times \mathbf{C}, \tag{2.29}$$

and that the laws hold in more extensive form,

$$\mathbf{A} \times (\mathbf{B} + \mathbf{C} + \mathbf{D}) = \mathbf{A} \times \mathbf{B} + \mathbf{A} \times \mathbf{C} + \mathbf{A} \times \mathbf{D}. \tag{2.30}$$

Having established the distributive law for vector multiplication, we are now able to derive a formula for such a product in terms of x, y, and z components. By a direct substitution we have

$$(\mathbf{A} \times \mathbf{B}) = (a_x\mathbf{I} + a_y\mathbf{J} + a_z\mathbf{K}) \times (b_x\mathbf{I} + b_y\mathbf{J} + b_z\mathbf{K}).$$

Now using the distributive laws, the law for factoring out scalars, the commutative and associative laws for vector addition, etc., we get

$$\mathbf{A} \times \mathbf{B} = (a_yb_z - a_zb_y)\mathbf{I} + (a_zb_x - a_xb_z)\mathbf{J} + (a_xb_y - a_yb_x)\mathbf{K}. \tag{2.31}$$

Note that one can get one component from the preceding by a cyclic substitution of subscripts: y for x, z for y, x for z. A compact way of writing this result is in terms of a determinant:

$$\mathbf{A} \times \mathbf{B} = \begin{vmatrix} a_x & a_y & a_z \\ b_x & b_y & b_z \\ \mathbf{I} & \mathbf{J} & \mathbf{K} \end{vmatrix} = \begin{vmatrix} a_y & a_z \\ b_y & b_z \end{vmatrix}\mathbf{I} + \begin{vmatrix} a_z & a_x \\ b_z & b_x \end{vmatrix}\mathbf{J} + \begin{vmatrix} a_x & a_y \\ b_x & b_y \end{vmatrix}\mathbf{K}. \tag{2.32}$$

The student who has had no previous work with determinants should not be dismayed by the introduction of this notation. All that is desired is a systematic way of computing components of the vector product. The x component of the product is obtained from the y and z components of the factors by subtracting the "diagonal products" of the square array shown before the **I** above, and similarly for other components, cyclic order being observed in each case: x from y and z, y from z and x, z from x and y. It just happens that the determinant machinery handles the same kind of problem.

If we denote the vector **A** × **B** by the letter **C**, so that

$$\mathbf{C} = \mathbf{A} \times \mathbf{B},$$

then it should be clear that the components c_x, c_y, and c_z are contained in the columns indicated in the diagram below.

$$\begin{matrix} & \overbrace{\begin{matrix} a_y & a_z \\ b_y & b_z \end{matrix}}^{c_x} & \\ \end{matrix}$$

$$\underbrace{\begin{matrix} a_x & a_y \\ b_x & b_y \end{matrix}}_{c_z} \quad \underbrace{\begin{matrix} a_z & a_x \\ b_z & b_x. \end{matrix}}_{c_y}$$

Taking the difference of diagonal products in each case, one obtains

$$c_x = a_yb_z - a_zb_y, \qquad c_y = a_zb_x - a_xb_z, \qquad c_z = a_xb_y - a_yb_x.$$

Example 1. Compute the components of the vector product **A** × **B**, where **A** = 3**I** − 7**J** and **B** = **I** + **J** − 2**K**.

SOLUTION. Writing down the array of components of **A** and **B** in cyclic order,

$$\begin{matrix} 3 & -7 & 0 & 3 \\ 1 & 1 & -2 & 1 \end{matrix}$$

the components of the product may be read off as

$$\begin{aligned} c_x &= (-7)(-2) - (0)(1) = 14, \\ c_y &= (0)(1) - (3)(-2) = 6, \\ c_z &= (3)(1) - (-7)(1) = 10. \end{aligned}$$

Collecting these results, we have

$$\mathbf{A} \times \mathbf{B} = 14\mathbf{I} + 6\mathbf{J} + 10\mathbf{K}.$$

EXERCISES

1. Compute in **IJK** form the vector product of each of the following pairs of vectors:

(*a*) **A** = 2**J**, **B** = **I** + **J** + **K**.

(*b*) **A** = **I** + 2**J** + 3**K**, **B** = 3**I** + 2**J** + **K**.

(*c*) **A** = 2**I** − 4**K**, **B** = −0.5**I** + **K**.

2. The vectors 2**I** − 3**J** + 4**K** and **I** + b**J** + c**K** are parallel. Use a vector product to find b and c.

3. If the vectors **R, R′**, and **F**, and **N** have, respectively, the components x, y, z; x', y', z'; f_x, f_y, f_z; and n_x, n_y, n_z, write three scalar equations equivalent to the vector equation

$$\mathbf{N} = (\mathbf{R} - \mathbf{R}') \times \mathbf{F}.$$

4. Using the distributive law as originally established in this section, devise careful proofs for each of the following:

(*a*) $(\mathbf{A} + \mathbf{B}) \times \mathbf{C} = \mathbf{A} \times \mathbf{C} + \mathbf{B} \times \mathbf{C}$.

(*b*) $\mathbf{A} \times (\mathbf{B} + \mathbf{C} + \mathbf{D}) = \mathbf{A} \times \mathbf{B} + \mathbf{A} \times \mathbf{C} + \mathbf{A} \times \mathbf{D}$.

5. Under what conditions is cancellation possible in an equation such as

$$\mathbf{A} \times \mathbf{C} = \mathbf{B} \times \mathbf{C}?$$

Prove your answer.

2.5. Applications of the Vector Product. For practice in visualizing vector products, a number of geometric examples are presented in this section. The student should try to get a clear mental picture of the geometric situations and also to sharpen his algebraic techniques.

Example 1. Find direction cosines for a line normal to any plane which is parallel to both the vectors $\mathbf{I} - 2\mathbf{J}$ and $\mathbf{I} + 2\mathbf{K}$.

SOLUTION. The vector product $(\mathbf{I} - 2\mathbf{J}) \times (\mathbf{I} + 2\mathbf{K})$ is normal to the plane since it is perpendicular to both of the given vectors. A unit vector parallel to this product will have components equal to suitable direction cosines (as shown in Sec. 1.11). Carrying out the computations, we get

$$(\mathbf{I} - 2\mathbf{J}) \times (\mathbf{I} + 2\mathbf{K}) = -4\mathbf{I} - 2\mathbf{J} + 2\mathbf{K}.$$

This is a vector of magnitude

$$\sqrt{(-4)^2 + (-2)^2 + (2)^2} = 4.9.$$

A parallel vector of magnitude one is

$$\frac{-4}{4.9}\mathbf{I} + \frac{-2}{4.9}\mathbf{J} + \frac{2}{4.9}\mathbf{K} = -0.82\mathbf{I} - 0.41\mathbf{J} + 0.41\mathbf{K}.$$

The two possible sets of direction cosines are then either $(-0.82, -0.41, +0.41)$ or $(+0.82, +0.41, -0.41)$.

Example 2. An interesting geometrical example of the vector product is found in the computation of the distance between two skew lines in space. Such a distance is measured along a common normal. If the two lines in Fig. 2.11 are **AB** and **A′B′**, respectively (where the letters denote the position vectors of the points so named), the vector product

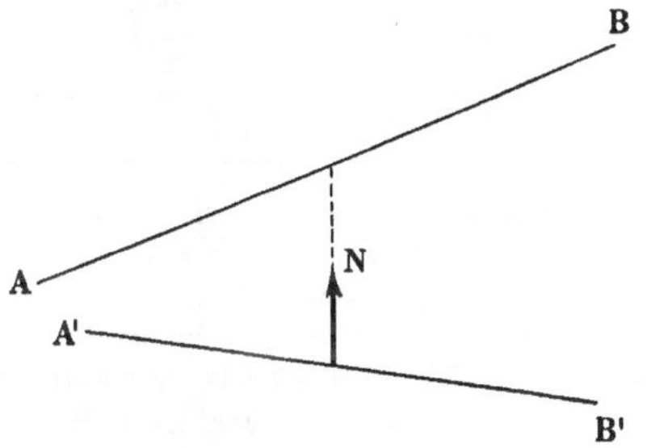

FIG. 2.11.

$$(\mathbf{B} - \mathbf{A}) \times (\mathbf{B}' - \mathbf{A}')$$

gives the direction of such a normal. Let **N** be a unit vector in this direction. Then the distance between the lines is equal to the scalar component in the direction of **N** of some vector (such as **AB′**, or **BB′**) originating on one line and ending on the other.

Example 3. In Sec. 1.12 a parametric approach to equations of a line in space was given. Now in terms of the vector product a simple vector formulation is possible. As before consider a line as in Fig. 2.12 through **P′** parallel to **E**. If **P** is a variable point on the line, then, regardless of the origin used, **P** − **P′** is parallel to **E**. Hence we may write

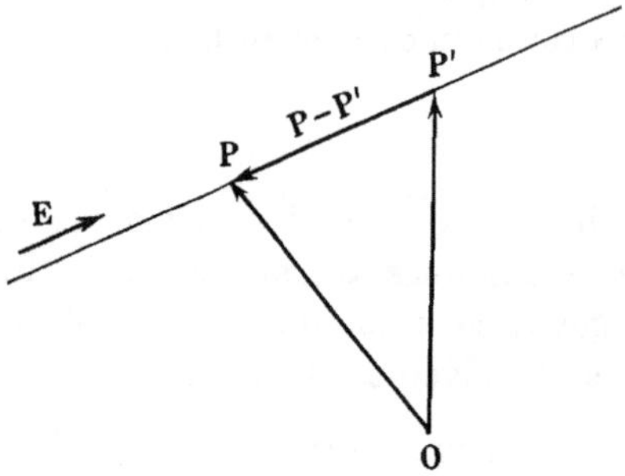

FIG. 2.12.

$$\mathbf{E} \times (\mathbf{P} - \mathbf{P}') = \mathbf{O} \tag{2.33}$$

as a vector equation for the line. If **P** and **P′** have coordinates (x,y,z) and (x',y',z'), respectively, and if the components of **E** are the direction cosines l, m, and n, then we may get coordinate equations for the line as follows

$$\mathbf{E} \times (\mathbf{P} - \mathbf{P}') = \begin{vmatrix} l & m & n \\ x - x' & y - y' & z - z' \\ \mathbf{I} & \mathbf{J} & \mathbf{K} \end{vmatrix} = \mathbf{O}.$$

Equating the coefficients of **I**, **J**, and **K** separately to zero, we have

$$\begin{aligned} m(z - z') - n(y - y') &= 0, \\ n(x - x') - l(z - z') &= 0, \\ l(y - y') - m(x - x') &= 0, \end{aligned}$$

which are equations for three planes through the line. As before they may be rewritten in the symmetric form

$$\frac{x - x'}{l} = \frac{y - y'}{m} = \frac{z - z'}{n}.$$

EXERCISES

1. Find a unit vector perpendicular to the plane parallel to both of the following vectors: **I** + 2**K** and **I** + **J**.

2. Find direction cosines for a line normal to the plane through the three points (0,0,0), (1,0,2), and (1,1,0).

3. Find the direction cosines for a vector normal to the plane through the three points (4,2,2), (10,−7,10), and (1,0,−2).

4. Given the three vectors **A**, **B**, **C** as below, compute the x, y, and z components of **A** × (**B** × **C**) and (**A** × **B**) × **C**. (Perform the multiplication within the parentheses first.)

$$\mathbf{A} = \mathbf{I} + \mathbf{J}, \qquad \mathbf{B} = \mathbf{J} + \mathbf{K}, \qquad \mathbf{C} = \mathbf{K} + \mathbf{I}.$$

5. For the vectors **A, B,** and **C** listed in Exercise 4, compute

$$(\mathbf{A} \times \mathbf{B}) \cdot \mathbf{C} \quad \text{and} \quad \mathbf{A} \cdot (\mathbf{B} \times \mathbf{C}).$$

6. Compute the distance between the line through the points (1,2,3) and (3,4,3) and the line through the points (4,6,8) and (4,5,6).

7. Given the line through (1,1,0) parallel to the vector $\mathbf{I} + \mathbf{J} + \mathbf{K}$. How close does this line come to the x axis?

8. For two perpendicular vectors **A** and **B** prove that the locus of points having position vector **P** such that

$$\mathbf{A} \times \mathbf{P} = \mathbf{B}$$

is a straight line.

9. Use the vector product as a device for obtaining scalar equations for a line perpendicular to the plane

$$x - 8y + 4z + 6 = 0$$

and through the point (1,2,3).

10. Find scalar equations for the line through the origin and perpendicular to both of the following vectors: $3\mathbf{I} - 2\mathbf{K}$, $3\mathbf{I} + 3\mathbf{J}$.

2.6. The Scalar Triple Product. We have seen how for any two vectors **A** and **B** two products $\mathbf{A} \cdot \mathbf{B}$ and $\mathbf{A} \times \mathbf{B}$ are defined. If either **A** or **B** happens to have entered the discussion as the result of vector multiplication, we are confronted by triple products such as

$$\mathbf{A} \cdot (\mathbf{C} \times \mathbf{D}), \qquad (\mathbf{C} \times \mathbf{D}) \cdot \mathbf{B}, \qquad \mathbf{A} \times (\mathbf{C} \times \mathbf{D}), \qquad (\mathbf{C} \times \mathbf{D}) \times \mathbf{B}.$$

Such combined products have a number of interesting and useful properties.

Consider for three vectors **A, B,** and **C** the product $\mathbf{A} \cdot (\mathbf{B} \times \mathbf{C})$. This is called a *scalar triple product.* Note first that the parentheses may be omitted since $(\mathbf{A} \cdot \mathbf{B}) \times \mathbf{C}$ is meaningless, or, giving it an obvious meaning, we should use the notation $(\mathbf{A} \cdot \mathbf{B})\mathbf{C}$. The product $\mathbf{B} \times \mathbf{C}$ has magnitude equal to the area of the parallelogram determined by **B** and **C**; therefore let us write

$$\mathbf{B} \times \mathbf{C} = (\text{area})\mathbf{N}$$

and

$$\mathbf{A} \cdot \mathbf{B} \times \mathbf{C} = (\text{area})(\mathbf{A} \cdot \mathbf{N}).$$

Since $\mathbf{A} \cdot \mathbf{N}$ is the component of **A** normal to the plane of the parallelogram it is evident that this expression is equal to a volume if the angle θ between **A** and **N** is acute or to minus a volume if θ is obtuse. The volume clearly is that of the parallelepiped having edges **A, B,** and **C** (see Fig. 2.13).

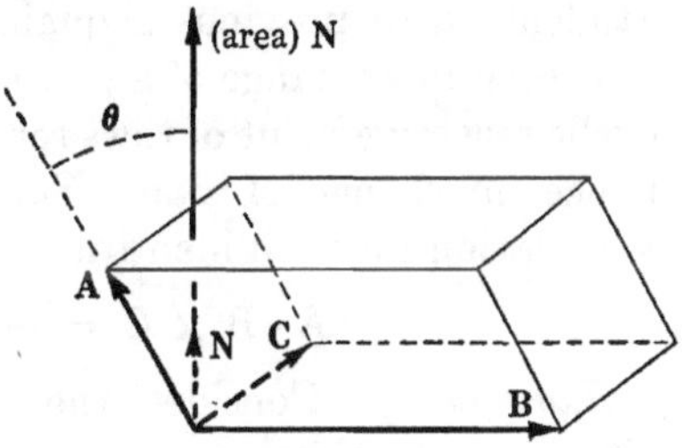

FIG. 2.13.

$$(2.34) \qquad \mathbf{A} \cdot \mathbf{B} \times \mathbf{C} = \pm \text{volume}.$$

The volume of the solid does not depend on the point of view of the observer. The three vectors have similar roles in determining the parallelepiped. This fact leads, as an examination of a number of figures would show, to the following identities:

$$\mathbf{A} \cdot \mathbf{B} \times \mathbf{C} = \mathbf{B} \cdot \mathbf{C} \times \mathbf{A} = \mathbf{C} \cdot \mathbf{A} \times \mathbf{B}. \tag{2.35}$$

Further verification will be found later when expressions for these products in terms of components are examined. Since scalar products commute, we may write

$$\mathbf{A} \cdot \mathbf{B} \times \mathbf{C} = \mathbf{B} \times \mathbf{C} \cdot \mathbf{A}$$

and similarly for the other products. In the light of the other identities we conclude that the $\times$ and the $\cdot$ may be interchanged; thus

$$\mathbf{A} \cdot \mathbf{B} \times \mathbf{C} = \mathbf{A} \times \mathbf{B} \cdot \mathbf{C} \tag{2.36}$$

and similarly for the other products. If $\mathbf{B} \times \mathbf{C}$ is replaced by $\mathbf{C} \times \mathbf{B}$, the sign is reversed, since θ is replaced by its supplement. Thus

$$\mathbf{A} \cdot \mathbf{C} \times \mathbf{B} = \mp \text{volume}.$$

In summary, it is apparent that scalar triple products of three vectors **A, B,** and **C** fall into two groups: those with cyclic order of **ABC** and those having the opposite cyclic order **ACB.** One order yields equal positive results; the other yields the same magnitude but the opposite sign.

$$\begin{aligned} \pm\text{Volume} &= \mathbf{A} \cdot \mathbf{B} \times \mathbf{C} = \mathbf{B} \cdot \mathbf{C} \times \mathbf{A} = \mathbf{C} \cdot \mathbf{A} \times \mathbf{B} \\ &= \mathbf{A} \times \mathbf{B} \cdot \mathbf{C} = \mathbf{B} \times \mathbf{C} \cdot \mathbf{A} = \mathbf{C} \times \mathbf{A} \cdot \mathbf{B}. \\ \mp\text{Volume} &= \mathbf{A} \cdot \mathbf{C} \times \mathbf{B} = \mathbf{C} \cdot \mathbf{B} \times \mathbf{A} = \mathbf{B} \cdot \mathbf{A} \times \mathbf{C} \\ &= \mathbf{A} \times \mathbf{C} \cdot \mathbf{B} = \mathbf{C} \times \mathbf{B} \cdot \mathbf{A} = \mathbf{B} \times \mathbf{A} \cdot \mathbf{C}. \end{aligned} \tag{2.37}$$

The relationships just derived may be regarded also as immediate algebraic consequences of the following expression for the scalar triple product in terms of the usual components of the vectors.

$$\mathbf{A} \cdot \mathbf{B} \times \mathbf{C} = \begin{vmatrix} a_x & a_y & a_z \\ b_x & b_y & b_z \\ c_x & c_y & c_z \end{vmatrix} = \mathbf{A} \times \mathbf{B} \cdot \mathbf{C}. \tag{2.38}$$

Students with previous acquaintance with determinants will remember that each interchange of a pair of rows results in a change of sign, while a cyclic rearrangement of rows requires an even number of interchanges and hence no change of sign. Such considerations provide an alternative verification for such identities as

$$\mathbf{A} \cdot \mathbf{B} \times \mathbf{C} = -\mathbf{A} \cdot \mathbf{C} \times \mathbf{B} = \mathbf{C} \cdot \mathbf{A} \times \mathbf{B}.$$

Example 1. Consider the product $\mathbf{A} \times \mathbf{B} \cdot \mathbf{A}$. By the identities already given this is equal to $\mathbf{A} \times \mathbf{A} \cdot \mathbf{B}$. But $\mathbf{A} \times \mathbf{A} = \mathbf{O}$. Therefore the product vanishes. Conversely it is interesting to point out that whenever the triple scalar product of nonzero vectors is equal to zero it must follow that the vectors are parallel to a single plane (for their parallelepiped has zero volume).

Example 2. Evaluate $\mathbf{A} \times \mathbf{B} \cdot \mathbf{C}$ where $\mathbf{A} = \mathbf{I} + \mathbf{J} - \mathbf{K}$, $\mathbf{B} = \mathbf{I} - \mathbf{J} + \mathbf{K}$, and $\mathbf{C} = -\mathbf{I} + \mathbf{J} + \mathbf{K}$. One way of proceeding is to compute first the vector product $\mathbf{A} \times \mathbf{B} = -2\mathbf{J} - 2\mathbf{K}$ and then to compute the scalar product with $\mathbf{C}$:

$$\mathbf{A} \times \mathbf{B} \cdot \mathbf{C} = (0)(-1) + (-2)(1) + (-2)(1) = -4.$$

Alternatively one may set up the determinant and evaluate it using any of the methods which one has at his command.

$$\begin{vmatrix} 1 & 1 & -1 \\ 1 & -1 & 1 \\ -1 & 1 & 1 \end{vmatrix} = -4.$$

Example 3. Geometric situations related to some of those investigated in other sections occasionally involve this type of combined product. For instance, find an equation for the plane through the three fixed points $\mathbf{P}'$, $\mathbf{Q}'$, $\mathbf{R}'$ (see Fig. 2.14). The vector $(\mathbf{P} - \mathbf{P}')$ for any variable point $\mathbf{P}$ in the plane must lie in the plane and hence be perpendicular to the normal

$$(\mathbf{Q}' - \mathbf{P}') \times (\mathbf{R}' - \mathbf{P}').$$

We have then

$$(\mathbf{P} - \mathbf{P}') \cdot (\mathbf{Q}' - \mathbf{P}') \times (\mathbf{R}' - \mathbf{P}') = 0$$

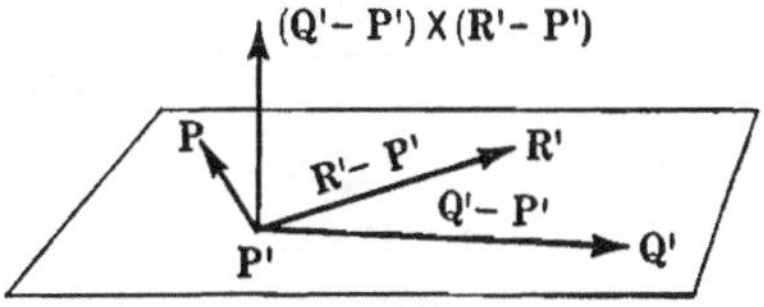

FIG. 2.14.

which is a suitable equation for the plane.

Example 4. It has been pointed out that $\mathbf{A} \cdot \mathbf{E}$ is the scalar component of $\mathbf{A}$ parallel to the unit vector $\mathbf{E}$. It is obvious then that the scalar component of the vector product $\mathbf{B} \times \mathbf{C}$ parallel to $\mathbf{E}$ is given by the scalar triple product $\mathbf{B} \times \mathbf{C} \cdot \mathbf{E}$. This use of a combined product will occur frequently.

EXERCISES

1. Given the four points $\mathbf{A}(3,0,1)$, $\mathbf{B}(1,-5,1)$, $\mathbf{C}(6,0,2)$, and $\mathbf{D}(4,-3,2)$. Evaluate $(\mathbf{B} - \mathbf{A}) \times (\mathbf{C} - \mathbf{A}) \cdot (\mathbf{D} - \mathbf{A})$.

2. $\mathbf{A}(-5,0,1)$ is a vertex of a parallelepiped. Edges run from $\mathbf{A}$ to $\mathbf{B}(2,-2,5)$, to $\mathbf{C}(-1,5,7)$, and to $\mathbf{D}(-2,4,6)$. What is the volume of the parallelepiped?

3. The vector $x\mathbf{I} - 3\mathbf{J} + 4\mathbf{K}$ is parallel to the plane determined by $\mathbf{I} - \mathbf{J} + 2\mathbf{K}$ and $2\mathbf{I} - \mathbf{K}$. Find x.

4. Find an expression in terms of x, y, and z components for $(\mathbf{R} - \mathbf{R}') \times \mathbf{F} \cdot \mathbf{E}$, where the vectors listed have components, respectively, as follows:

$$x,\ y,\ z;\ x',\ y',\ z';\ f_x,\ f_y,\ f_z;\ l,\ m,\ n.$$

5. Use the scalar triple product to prove that a non-null vector **C** which can be written $\mathbf{C} = l\mathbf{A} + m\mathbf{B}$ for scalars l and m is parallel to the plane determined by vectors **A** and **B**.

6. Write a vector equation for the plane through the origin and parallel to both the vectors **U** and **V**.

7. Given the vectors $\mathbf{A} = \mathbf{I} - 3\mathbf{J} + 2\mathbf{K}$ and $\mathbf{B} = 2\mathbf{I} + \mathbf{J} - \mathbf{K}$. Find the component of $\mathbf{A} \times \mathbf{B}$ parallel to $5\mathbf{I} - \mathbf{K}$.

2.7. The Vector Triple Product. Next we shall devote some attention to a combined product of the form $\mathbf{A} \times (\mathbf{B} \times \mathbf{C})$. This is often called the *vector triple product.* Since $\mathbf{B} \times \mathbf{C}$ is normal to the plane of **B** and **C** (see Fig. 2.15) and $\mathbf{A} \times (\mathbf{B} \times \mathbf{C})$ is perpendicular to this normal, it follows that $\mathbf{A} \times (\mathbf{B} \times \mathbf{C})$ is parallel to the plane of **B** and **C**. Similarly

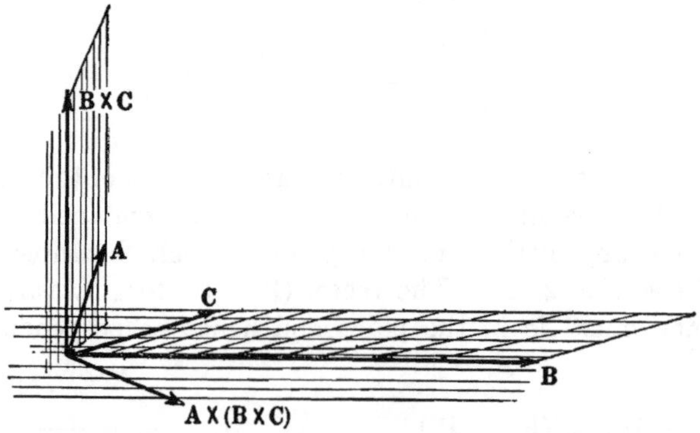

FIG. 2.15.

one may conclude that $(\mathbf{A} \times \mathbf{B}) \times \mathbf{C}$ is parallel to the plane of **A** and **B**. In general then the two expressions are not equal. This is a denial of the associative law for this type of multiplication:

$$\mathbf{A} \times (\mathbf{B} \times \mathbf{C}) \neq (\mathbf{A} \times \mathbf{B}) \times \mathbf{C}. \tag{2.39}$$

Example 1. In Sec. 2.1 it was demonstrated that the vector component of **A** parallel to a unit vector **E** is given by $(\mathbf{A} \cdot \mathbf{E})\mathbf{E}$. It is easy to show that the vector component of **A** perpendicular to **E** may be written as $\mathbf{E} \times (\mathbf{A} \times \mathbf{E})$. The proof is left as an exercise.

Suppose that **N** is a unit vector perpendicular to a given plane. Then the projection of a vector **A** onto the plane is given by $\mathbf{A}' = \mathbf{N} \times (\mathbf{A} \times \mathbf{N})$, for the term "projection of **A** onto a plane of normal **N**" is just another way of saying "component of **A** perpendicular to **N**." In terms of this expression it is easy to re-prove the proposition of Sec. 2.2 on projections of sums of vectors. All that is needed is two applications of the distributive law for vector multiplication. Using the notation of Sec. 2.2,

$$\begin{aligned}(\mathbf{A} + \mathbf{B})' &= \mathbf{N} \times [(\mathbf{A} + \mathbf{B}) \times \mathbf{N}] = \mathbf{N} \times [(\mathbf{A} \times \mathbf{N}) + (\mathbf{B} \times \mathbf{N})] \\ &= \mathbf{N} \times (\mathbf{A} \times \mathbf{N}) + \mathbf{N} \times (\mathbf{B} \times \mathbf{N}) = \mathbf{A}' + \mathbf{B}'.\end{aligned}$$

Example 2. Find an equation for a line through a fixed point $\mathbf{P}'$ and parallel to each of two planes whose normals are parallel, respectively, to $\mathbf{N}$ and $\mathbf{N}'$. For a variable point $\mathbf{P}$ on the line, the vector $(\mathbf{P} - \mathbf{P}')$ (see Fig. 2.16) is perpendicular to both $\mathbf{N}$ and $\mathbf{N}'$, and hence it is parallel to their vector product. Thus we may write

$$(\mathbf{P} - \mathbf{P}') \times (\mathbf{N} \times \mathbf{N}') = \mathbf{O},$$

which is a suitable equation for the line.

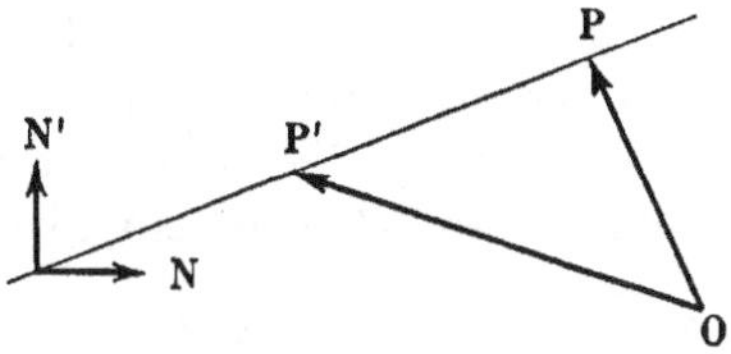

FIG. 2.16.

A Crucial Vector Identity. If $\mathbf{A} \times (\mathbf{B} \times \mathbf{C})$ is parallel to the plane of $\mathbf{B}$ and $\mathbf{C}$ it must be possible to express it as the sum of a vector in the $\mathbf{B}$ direction plus a vector in the $\mathbf{C}$ direction (compare Exercise 6, Sec. 1.8). A precise statement of this very important relationship is given in the following remarkable identity:

$$\mathbf{A} \times (\mathbf{B} \times \mathbf{C}) = (\mathbf{A} \cdot \mathbf{C})\mathbf{B} - (\mathbf{A} \cdot \mathbf{B})\mathbf{C}. \tag{2.40}$$

It is possible to prove this in various ways. One very direct approach, using x, y, and z components, is left as an exercise. In this section we shall approach the problem through a sequence of special cases which will perhaps clarify the significance of the identity while establishing it and will at the same time afford some practice in using techniques developed in earlier sections.

FIRST SPECIAL CASE. We first consider a triple product in which the first factor is repeated. If $\mathbf{N}$ denotes the unit vector in the direction of $\mathbf{A} \times \mathbf{B}$, we may write, using the definition of vector product

$$\mathbf{A} \times (\mathbf{A} \times \mathbf{B}) = \mathbf{A} \times (ab \sin \theta)\mathbf{N} = (ab \sin \theta)\mathbf{A}',$$

where the vector $\mathbf{A} \times \mathbf{N}$ is denoted by $\mathbf{A}'$. Since $\mathbf{N}$ is perpendicular to $\mathbf{A}$, we know from Special Conclusion 4, Sec. 2.3, that $\mathbf{A}'$ is $\mathbf{A}$ rotated through $-90°$. Since $\mathbf{A}$ and $\mathbf{A}'$ are perpendicular, one can easily resolve $\mathbf{B}$ into components in their directions (see Fig. 2.17):

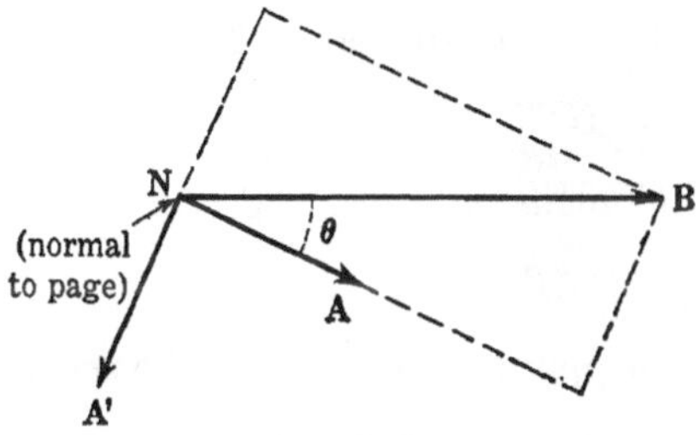

FIG. 2.17.

$$\mathbf{B} = (b \cos \theta)\,\frac{\mathbf{A}}{a} - (b \sin \theta)\,\frac{\mathbf{A}'}{a}.$$

Solving for $\mathbf{A}'$,

$$\mathbf{A}' = \left(\frac{\cos \theta}{\sin \theta}\right)\mathbf{A} - \left(\frac{a}{b \sin \theta}\right)\mathbf{B}.$$

We may conclude then

$$\mathbf{A} \times (\mathbf{A} \times \mathbf{B}) = (ab \sin \theta)\mathbf{A}' = (ab \cos \theta)\mathbf{A} - (a^2)\mathbf{B}$$
$$= (\mathbf{A} \cdot \mathbf{B})\mathbf{A} - (\mathbf{A} \cdot \mathbf{A})\mathbf{B}.$$

Thus our identity is verified for the first special case.

A variant of this special case, readily proved from it, is next recorded: the reasons for the steps in the proof are omitted, since only basic and obvious properties are employed.

$$\mathbf{A} \times (\mathbf{B} \times \mathbf{A}) = -\mathbf{A} \times (\mathbf{A} \times \mathbf{B}) = -(\mathbf{A} \cdot \mathbf{B})\mathbf{A} + (\mathbf{A} \cdot \mathbf{A})\mathbf{B}$$
$$= (\mathbf{A} \cdot \mathbf{A})\mathbf{B} - (\mathbf{A} \cdot \mathbf{B})\mathbf{A}.$$

SECOND SPECIAL CASE. We now prove the identity for the special case where **A** is parallel to the plane of **B** and **C**. In such a case we can write **A** as a "linear combination" of **B** and **C**:

$$\mathbf{A} = m\mathbf{B} + n\mathbf{C},$$

for suitable scalars m and n. We have then, substituting this expression and using the distributive property of vector products,

$$\mathbf{A} \times (\mathbf{B} \times \mathbf{C}) = (m\mathbf{B} + n\mathbf{C}) \times (\mathbf{B} \times \mathbf{C}) = m[\mathbf{B} \times (\mathbf{B} \times \mathbf{C})]$$
$$+ n[\mathbf{C} \times (\mathbf{B} \times \mathbf{C})].$$

If we now use the identity for the first special case, this becomes

$$\mathbf{A} \times (\mathbf{B} \times \mathbf{C}) = m(\mathbf{B} \cdot \mathbf{C})\mathbf{B} - m(\mathbf{B} \cdot \mathbf{B})\mathbf{C} + n(\mathbf{C} \cdot \mathbf{C})\mathbf{B} - n(\mathbf{C} \cdot \mathbf{B})\mathbf{C}.$$

Using the distributive properties of the scalar product, the associative law for vector addition, and various properties of multiplication by scalars, we regroup the terms to get

$$\mathbf{A} \times (\mathbf{B} \times \mathbf{C}) = [(m\mathbf{B} + n\mathbf{C}) \cdot \mathbf{C}]\mathbf{B} - [(m\mathbf{B} + n\mathbf{C}) \cdot \mathbf{B}]\mathbf{C}.$$

Resubstituting **A** for $m\mathbf{B} + n\mathbf{C}$, we have, as desired,

$$\mathbf{A} \times (\mathbf{B} \times \mathbf{C}) = (\mathbf{A} \cdot \mathbf{C})\mathbf{B} - (\mathbf{A} \cdot \mathbf{B})\mathbf{C}.$$

THE GENERAL CASE. Now let **N** be the unit vector in the direction of $\mathbf{B} \times \mathbf{C}$, and let $\mathbf{A}'$ be the component of **A** perpendicular to **N**:

$$\mathbf{A}' = \mathbf{A} - (\mathbf{A} \cdot \mathbf{N})\mathbf{N}$$

(as in Fig. 2.3). Then, using Special Conclusion 5, Sec. 2.3,

$$\mathbf{A} \times (\mathbf{B} \times \mathbf{C}) = \mathbf{A}' \times (\mathbf{B} \times \mathbf{C}),$$

where $\mathbf{A}'$ lies in the plane of **B** and **C**. Applying the result of the second special case,

$$\mathbf{A} \times (\mathbf{B} \times \mathbf{C}) = (\mathbf{A}' \cdot \mathbf{C})\mathbf{B} - (\mathbf{A}' \cdot \mathbf{B})\mathbf{C}.$$

We now evaluate the coefficients of **B** and **C**, using the expressions for **A**′ above.

$$(\mathbf{A}' \cdot \mathbf{C}) = (\mathbf{A} \cdot \mathbf{C}) - (\mathbf{A} \cdot \mathbf{N})(\mathbf{N} \cdot \mathbf{C}).$$

But

$$\mathbf{N} \cdot \mathbf{C} = 0.$$

Hence

$$(\mathbf{A}' \cdot \mathbf{C}) = (\mathbf{A} \cdot \mathbf{C}).$$

Likewise

$$(\mathbf{A}' \cdot \mathbf{B}) = (\mathbf{A} \cdot \mathbf{B}).$$

For the general case then we can conclude, as before,

$$\mathbf{A} \times (\mathbf{B} \times \mathbf{C}) = (\mathbf{A} \cdot \mathbf{C})\mathbf{B} - (\mathbf{A} \cdot \mathbf{B})\mathbf{C}. \tag{2.40}$$

EXERCISES

1. Verify the identity $\mathbf{A} \times (\mathbf{B} \times \mathbf{C}) = (\mathbf{A} \cdot \mathbf{C})\mathbf{B} - (\mathbf{A} \cdot \mathbf{B})\mathbf{C}$ by computing the x component of each member in terms of the components $a_x, a_y, a_z, b_x, b_y, b_z, c_x, c_y, c_z$.

2. The scalar product of a vector by itself $\mathbf{A} \cdot \mathbf{A}$ is often written as the vector squared $\mathbf{A}^2$. Use the results of this chapter to verify the identity

$$(\mathbf{A} \times \mathbf{B})^2 + (\mathbf{A} \cdot \mathbf{B})^2 = \mathbf{A}^2\mathbf{B}^2.$$

What familiar trigonometric identity is closely related to this?

3. If $\mathbf{E} \times \mathbf{B} = \mathbf{C}$ and $\mathbf{B} \times \mathbf{C} = \mathbf{E}$, where **E** is a unit vector, use direct substitutions and the methods of this chapter to prove that $\mathbf{C} \times \mathbf{E} = \mathbf{B}$.

4. Prove that the component of **A** perpendicular to the unit vector **E** is $\mathbf{E} \times (\mathbf{A} \times \mathbf{E})$.

5. Prove that the projection of $\mathbf{A} \times \mathbf{B}$ onto a plane of unit normal **N** is given by

$$(\mathbf{A} \times \mathbf{B})' = (\mathbf{B} \cdot \mathbf{N})(\mathbf{A} \times \mathbf{N}) - (\mathbf{A} \cdot \mathbf{N})(\mathbf{B} \times \mathbf{N}).$$

6. Prove that the projection onto a plane of the cross product of two vectors plus the cross product of their projections is equal to their cross product; *i.e.*,

$$\mathbf{A} \times \mathbf{B} = (\mathbf{A} \times \mathbf{B})' + \mathbf{A}' \times \mathbf{B}'.$$

7. The point (x', y', z') lies on the intersection of the two planes

$$ax + by + cz + d = 0 \quad \text{and} \quad a'x + b'y + c'z + d' = 0.$$

Show that a set of equations for the line of intersection is the following:

$$\frac{x - x'}{bc' - cb'} = \frac{y - y'}{ca' - ac'} = \frac{z - z'}{ab' - ba'}.$$

8. Prove that the following identity is valid:

$$\mathbf{A} \times (\mathbf{B} \times \mathbf{C}) + \mathbf{B} \times (\mathbf{C} \times \mathbf{A}) + \mathbf{C} \times (\mathbf{A} \times \mathbf{B}) = 0.$$

9. Prove that the following identity is valid:

$$(\mathbf{A} \times \mathbf{B}) \times \mathbf{C} + (\mathbf{A} \cdot \mathbf{B})\mathbf{C} = (\mathbf{A} \times \mathbf{C}) \times \mathbf{B} + (\mathbf{A} \cdot \mathbf{C})\mathbf{B}.$$

CHAPTER 3

FORCES

In our approach to the science of mechanics, *force*, along with distance and time, will be a basic ingredient. The concept of distance is the only such ingredient to be treated so far, for the geometry of position uses distances as coordinates. The vector language of the first two chapters will be as useful in the study of forces as it was in the study of position.

3.1. The Nature of a Force. We shall first review some of its intuitive aspects by considering examples. (*a*) When an object falls freely, we say that a gravitational force called the weight is pulling it down. (*b*) If a drawer sticks, we apply a force to close it. (*c*) If an object hangs in equilibrium at the end of a string, we say that it is prevented from falling by a force called the tension exerted by the string. (*d*) When an automobile skids to a stop, we say that a frictional force caused it to stop. In each of the examples cited, the force had a *direction*. The gravitational force was down, the tension in the string was up, the push on the drawer was deliberately directed as the need required, the frictional force was in a direction opposed to the motion.

Forces also have *magnitudes*. We continually distinguish between large and small forces, and we are accustomed to assigning numerical values to forces. The magnitude of a force may be measured directly by counterbalancing it with a calibrated spring, by removing it and then producing identical effects with such a spring, or it may be measured indirectly by observing its effects when it is left unbalanced. The study of effects of unbalanced forces is deferred until Chap. 7. The metric unit of force, the newton, may be defined in terms of a reference object, the "standard kilogram," prototypes of which are preserved in bureaus of standards. Such a definition could be based on the character of the motion of the standard object when subjected to an unbalanced force. A more convenient approach for us at this juncture is contained in the statement: The gravitational force or weight in a standard locality on a standard kilogram is 9.80665 newtons. A precise statement of just what constitutes a "standard locality" would drive us back to the indirect approach; but let it be said that any locality on the surface of the earth is nearly a standard locality, the deviation seldom being as much as one-quarter of 1 per cent. For the exercises in this treatment we shall round off the value to 9.81 newtons per kilogram and shall regard all surface situations as standard unless otherwise specified. The English unit of force, the pound, is equal to 4.4482 newtons. Here it may be assumed that the conversion factor is 4.45. Other units of force will be mentioned later.

Since forces have direction and magnitude, it is natural that they should be represented by *vectors*. In Fig. 3.1, the vectors **W, F, T, F′** and **F″**

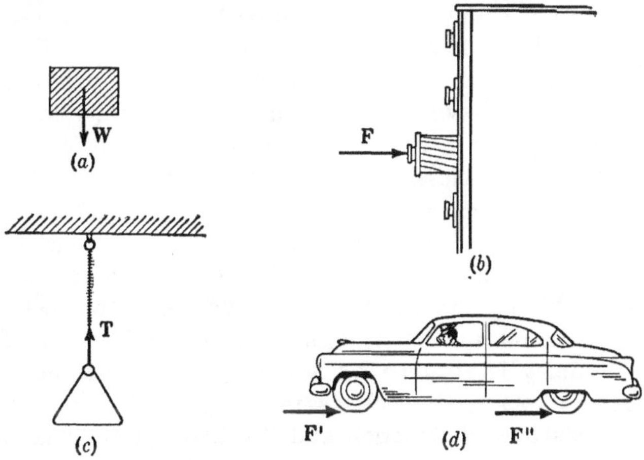

FIG. 3.1.

represent the weight, push, tension, and frictional forces which were described in the examples listed above.

Actually it is not enough to say that forces can be represented as vectors. More will be said about this in Sec. 3.4. For the present let it merely be stated that a force is completely specified if we know its magnitude, its direction, *and* the point at which it is applied. In these first simple analyses we shall assume outright that when two bodies touch, the contact forces act at the point or points of contact. We shall also assume that the weight of a body may be thought of as acting at its center if it is symmetrical and homogeneous; otherwise it may act at some other intermediate point.

3.2. Particles and Rigid Bodies. Even in the early part of this course we shall envisage forces as acting on objects in great variety. Yet we cannot investigate separately the behavior of automobiles, balls, doors, drawers, bridges, and people. Our theory must be general enough to apply to many such things. This theory in its simplest form will deal with forces as applied to particles. *Particle* is a technical term denoting any physical object whose extent is negligible. For instance, a falling stone may act as if all forces influencing it were directed through its center. In such a circumstance it is treated as a particle. A boy on a sled may be considered as a particle as he slides smoothly downhill. The moon may be treated as a particle for some investigations. Whenever we apply our theory of particles to a practical problem involving a physical object, we must remember that we implicitly assume that the object acts like a particle and hence that our results involve an approximation of a basic sort.

Any investigator will of course discover that even in simple situations an object may not behave like a single particle. In that case we often shall try to regard it as a set of interacting particles. This approach extends the coverage of our theory tremendously. It is apparent that an object like a tree blowing in the wind could be studied in this manner. One would rightly guess, however, that complexity of structure would make the problem hopeless. Much of our work will, in the interest of simplicity, be limited to collections of particles whose relative positions are fixed. Such a collection is called a *rigid body*. Wheels, automobiles, and ladders are examples of objects which it is advantageous to treat as rigid bodies. While we expect in the laboratory to meet no perfect portrayals of the roles of particle and rigid body, it will be found that adequate accuracy is attained by assuming that many objects behave like a member of one of these elemental categories.

3.3. Newton's Law of Reaction and the Concept of Isolation. Much of the theory presented in this course is based on the remarkably clear and fruitful *laws of motion* enunciated by Sir Isaac Newton. His third law stated in effect that every action causes an equal and opposite reaction. This has been abundantly verified experimentally. We shall *assume it* as a postulate, restating it as follows:

(3.1) *Forces always act in pairs, equal in magnitude, along the same line, but opposite in direction.*

To see the significance of this postulate, let us reexamine the examples of Sec. 3.1. In (*a*) we accepted the idea of a gravitational force acting on a body and causing it to fall. The reaction postulate reminds us that an equal force was simultaneously pulling up on the earth. Because of the disparity of the objects involved only the effect of one of the two objects is observable; but it is a fact that Newton's theory of gravitation is perfectly symmetrical. If the sun attracts the earth, so does the earth attract the sun. In (*b*) the push exerted on the drawer gives rise to a force of opposition acting on the pusher. In (*c*) the suspended object pulls down on the cord just as hard as the cord pulls up on it. In (*d*) the tires push ahead on the road surface with exactly the same intensity that the road surface pushes back on the tires. If the road were not anchored firmly, this force might displace it just as an unanchored rug slips when a running person suddenly stops on it.

Since forces occur in pairs, it is important to decide for each pair which of the two will be of interest in a given problem. If an object under consideration has n distinct interactions with other objects, then $2n$ forces are involved. But of these $2n$ forces we shall invariably interest ourselves in the n forces acting *on* the object. The process of focusing one's attention on a single object and of sifting out all the forces acting on it from the outside is called *isolating* the object. The isolation process is aided by diagrams. First draw an outline of the isolated object. Then at each point of interaction draw vectors to represent the forces acting on the body from without. Such a diagram is often called a *free-body diagram.*

Examples. A number of illustrations are listed. Note that gravitational forces are drawn as acting at the center of uniform bodies. Justification will be given later. Note also that forces acting at a smooth surface are normal to the plane of contact. This also will be given more attention later.

1. Ball on string (as in Fig. 3.2). **T** is the tension of the string; **W** is weight of the ball.

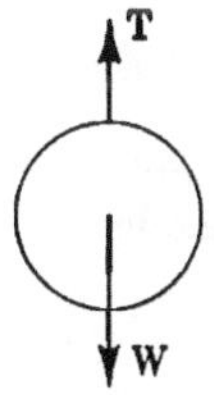

FIG. 3.2.

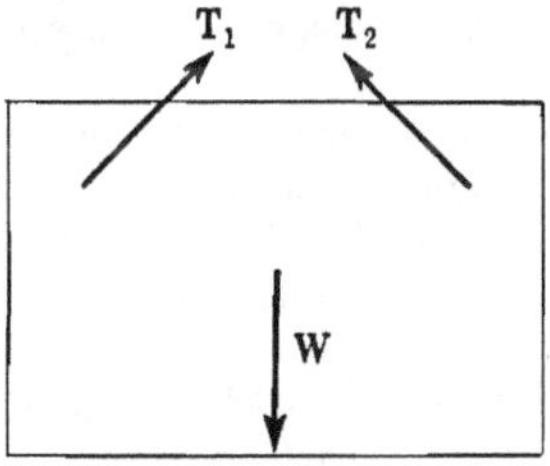

FIG. 3.3.

2. Picture hung by wire (as in Fig. 3.3). $\mathbf{T}_1$ and $\mathbf{T}_2$ are the forces exerted by the wire; **W** is the weight of the picture.

3. Sled on a smooth hill (as in Fig. 3.4). **W** is the weight of the sled; **N** is the normal reaction force of the hill on the sled.

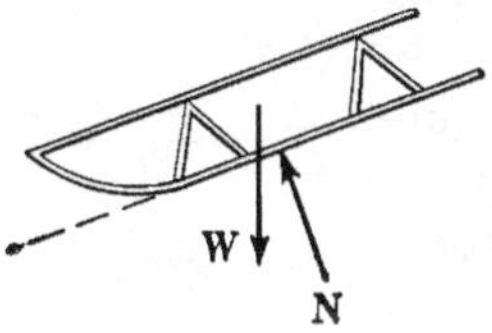

FIG. 3.4.

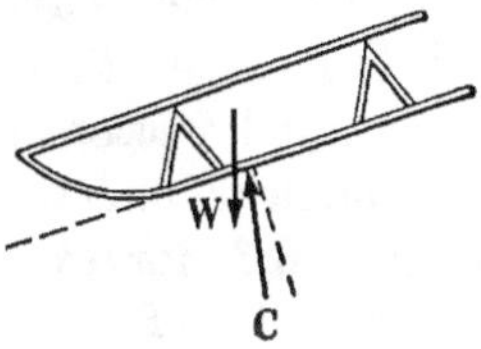

FIG. 3.5.

4. Sled on slightly rough hill (as in Fig. 3.5). **W** is the weight of the sled; **C** is the contact reaction of the hill on the sled (no longer normal).

5. Uniform ladder on rough ground against smooth wall (as in Fig. 3.6). **W** is the weight of the ladder; **C** is the reaction of the ground on the ladder (not normal); **N** is the reaction of smooth wall on the ladder (normal).

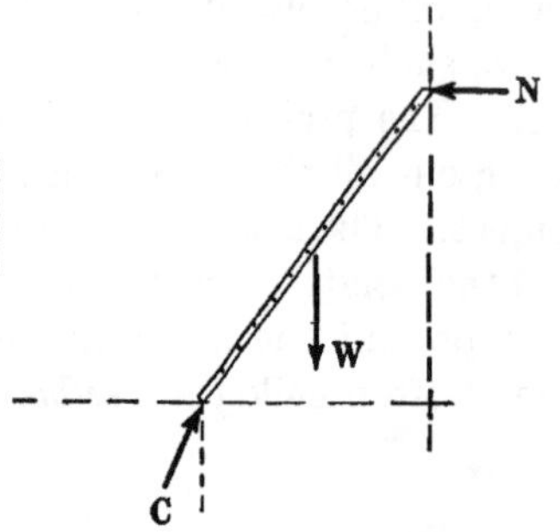

FIG. 3.6.

The following exercises require for perfect execution knowledge of mechanics as yet not introduced. The student should try to concentrate on two aspects: representation of known forces by suitable vectors, and qualitatively correct isolation of bodies. Of course, common sense and any previous contact with physics or forces will aid the student in getting reasonable results.

EXERCISES

1. Using a scale of 100 lb/in., draw a free-body diagram of yourself sitting in a chair, feet on floor, with 75 per cent of your weight resting on the chair, the rest through feet on floor.

2. Draw a free-body diagram of an automobile ascending a grade inclined at 20° with the horizontal.

3. An athlete's hammer is swung in a vertical circle. Draw a free-body diagram for it in three of its positions: top, side, bottom.

4. A man stands on the ladder which was used in Example 5 above. (*a*) Isolate the man and draw a free-body diagram. (*b*) Isolate the ladder and draw a free-body diagram.

5. A boy pulls a loaded cart by a rope inclined at 15°. Isolate the cart and draw a diagram.

6. Two boys, weighing 70 lb and 100 lb, balance on a seesaw. Draw three diagrams, isolating each of the boys and the seesaw separately.

3.4. Equivalence of Forces. We have seen that it is natural and convenient to represent forces by vectors. We must, however, use caution in applying the results of vector algebra developed in Chap. 1. For instance, two vectors are equal if they have the same magnitude and the same direction. But two forces having equal vectors may have quite different mechanical effects on a physical object. In Fig. 3.7, for example, the forces represented by vectors **F** and **F′** produce quite dissimilar effects: **F** causes rotation of the propellor, but **F′** merely causes a reaction at the bearing. Yet **F** and **F′** are equal vectors.

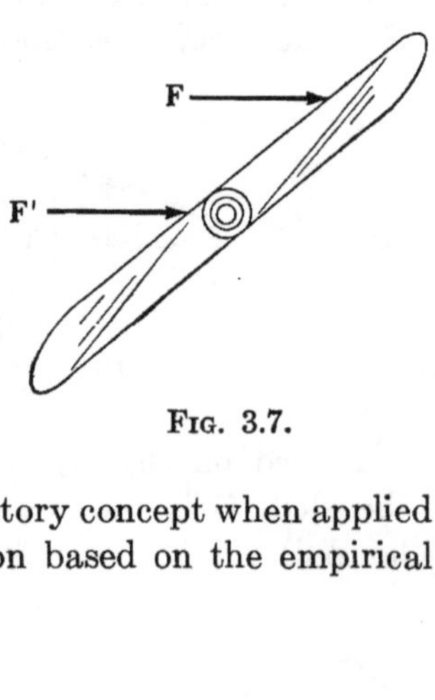

FIG. 3.7.

Since vector equality is by itself an unsatisfactory concept when applied to forces, we shall introduce a narrower notion based on the empirical effects of forces. Two sets of forces will be called *equivalent* if their instantaneous effects on a particle or a rigid body would necessarily be the same. As in Sec. 3.3, significant experimental results will serve as working postulates for the further development of the theory. The first conclusion is this: The effects on an essentially rigid body of two equal and parallel forces having the same line of action are indistinguishable. Consequently, a force may be displaced along its line of action without changing its effect. In Fig. 3.8, equivalent forces are shown acting on

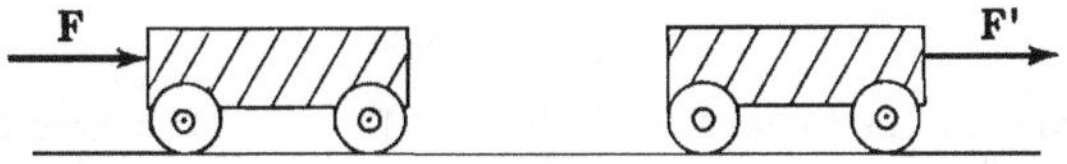

FIG. 3.8.

identical carts. Equivalent forces need not be equally easy to apply or to maintain; but as far as effect on a rigid body or particle is concerned, a push is as good as a pull. This property is often called the *principle of transmissibility of forces.* For future reference, we state our postulate thus:

(3.2) *Two forces are equivalent if (a) they are represented by equal vectors and (b) their lines of action coincide.*

A third noteworthy experimental fact about forces is that concurrent forces may be combined according to the rules of vector addition. This too will be stated as a postulate in terms of the notion of equivalence:

(3.3) *If* $\mathbf{F}$ *and* $\mathbf{F}'$ *are vectors representing two forces whose lines of action have a common point, then the vector* $\mathbf{F} + \mathbf{F}'$ *represents an equivalent single force whose line of action passes through the same point.*

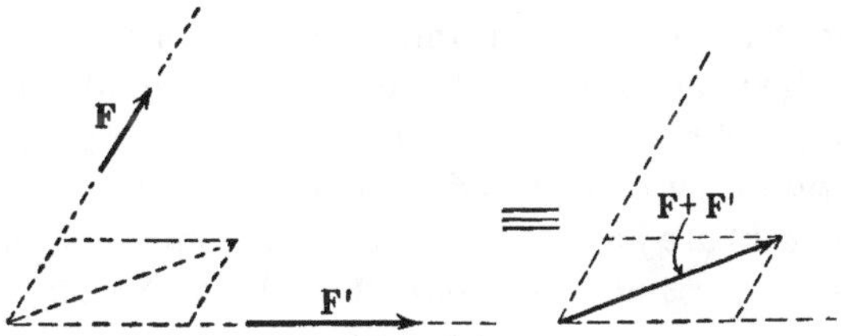

FIG. 3.9.

This is illustrated in Fig. 3.9. (In what follows the same symbol will be used for a force and for the vector representing it.) Postulate (3.3) is often called the *parallelogram law of composition.* It is an extremely useful tool. It justifies replacing a number of concurrent forces by one force. This one force is unique, of course, for the order in which vectors are added is immaterial. It also justifies replacing any one force by a convenient selection of equivalent forces.

Example 1. Any force **F** may be replaced by the three concurrent forces whose vectors are $f_x\mathbf{I}$, $f_y\mathbf{J}$, and $f_z\mathbf{K}$.

Example 2. Two equal and opposite forces having the same line of action are equivalent to a null force. Hence any family of forces may be augmented by two such forces without changing the effect of the family.

Example 3. If the forces $a_x\mathbf{I} + a_y\mathbf{J} + a_z\mathbf{K}$ and $b_x\mathbf{I} + b_y\mathbf{J} + b_z\mathbf{K}$ are concurrent, they are equivalent to the single force

$$(a_x + b_x)\mathbf{I} + (a_y + b_y)\mathbf{J} + (a_z + b_z)\mathbf{K}.$$

EXERCISES

1. (*a*) Plot to scale the forces $\mathbf{F} = 4\underline{/65°}$ and $\mathbf{F}' = 6\underline{/20°}$, where **F** acts at the point (5, −2) and **F**′ at (0,0).

(*b*) Use Postulates (3.2) and (3.3) to construct graphically a single force equivalent to **F** and **F**′ in combination.

(*c*) Measure from the result of part (*b*) the magnitude and the angle of this force.

(*d*) Using analytical methods compute from the data the angle and magnitude of $\mathbf{F} + \mathbf{F}'$.

2. Given two forces **A** and **B** acting at the origin $5\underline{/-20°}$ and $3\underline{/50°}$. (*a*) Plot the vectors to scale. (*b*) Construct graphically the projections a_x, b_x, $a_x + b_x$, a_y, b_y, and $a_y + b_y$. (*c*) From the results of (*b*) construct $\mathbf{A} + \mathbf{B}$. (*d*) Check your results analytically.

3. The following forces act at one point:

A: 10 lb, parallel to the vector $\mathbf{I} + \mathbf{J}$
B: 15 lb, with direction cosines 0.0, −0.8, 0.6
C: $3\mathbf{I} + 15\mathbf{J} + \mathbf{K}$ lb
D: 5 lb, parallel to the negative x axis
E: 5 lb, making angles of 90°, 135°, and 135° with the positive coordinate axes

Find the magnitude and direction cosines of a single vector equivalent to the family of five forces.

3.5. Resultants. If a set of forces is equivalent to a single force $\bar{\mathbf{F}}$, then $\bar{\mathbf{F}}$ is called the *resultant* of the set. A generalization of this term will appear in Sec. 4.6. In terms of this concept the principal fact of the preceding section may be restated as follows:

(3.4) *If* **F** *and* **F**′ *are forces whose lines of action meet in a common point, then they have as a resultant the force* $\mathbf{F} + \mathbf{F}'$ *acting through the point of intersection.*

This statement may obviously be extended to cover any number of *concurrent forces, i.e.*, forces whose lines of action have a common point.

(3.5) *The resultant of a collection of concurrent forces* $\mathbf{F}_1, \mathbf{F}_2, \ldots, \mathbf{F}_n$ *is a single force* $\mathbf{F}_1 + \mathbf{F}_2 + \cdots + \mathbf{F}_n$ *through the point of concurrence.*

Such a vector summation we shall usually abbreviate as $\Sigma\mathbf{F}$, the Σ indicating that the vectors in question are to be added. Sometimes a more specific use of the symbol may be required; for instance, $\Sigma_2^5\mathbf{F}_i$ indicates the sum of $\mathbf{F}_2$, $\mathbf{F}_3$, $\mathbf{F}_4$, $\mathbf{F}_5$ only.

Example 1. A small particle is subject to forces expressed by the following vectors: $\mathbf{F}_1 = 3\mathbf{I} - 7\mathbf{K}$, $\mathbf{F}_2 = -12\mathbf{J}$, $\mathbf{F}_3 = \mathbf{I} + 4\mathbf{J}$. Compute the resultant.

SOLUTION. Since the forces all act on a small particle, we may consider them as concurrent. Hence the resultant is a single force acting on the particle:

$$\bar{\mathbf{F}} = \mathbf{F}_1 + \mathbf{F}_2 + \mathbf{F}_3 = 4\mathbf{I} - 8\mathbf{J} - 7\mathbf{K}.$$

Example 2. Find graphically the resultant of the three forces shown in Fig. 3.10.

SOLUTION. In Fig. 3.10 the solution is effected by first forming $\mathbf{F}_1 + \mathbf{F}_2$ and then $(\mathbf{F}_1 + \mathbf{F}_2) + \mathbf{F}_3$.

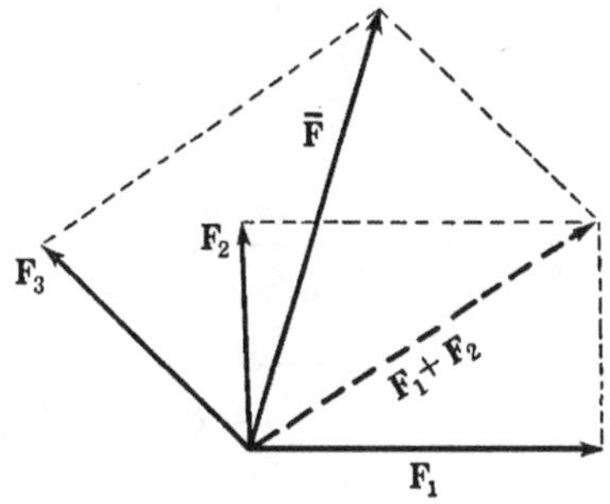

FIG. 3.10.

Example 3. Construct graphically the resultant of the two forces $\mathbf{F}$ and $\mathbf{F}'$ shown in Fig. 3.11.

FIG. 3.11.

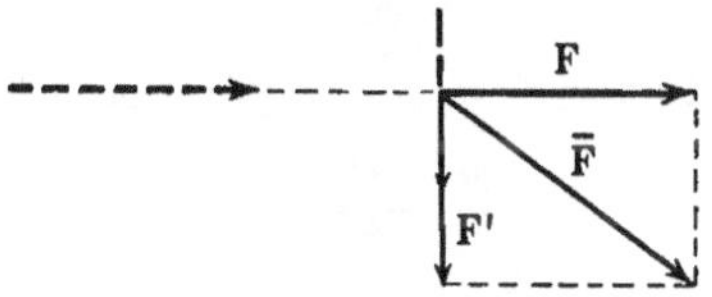

FIG. 3.12.

SOLUTION. Here we use both of the techniques of Sec. 3.4. First slide the forces along their lines of action until they both act on the point of concurrence. Then use the parallelogram law for combining them. The result appears in Fig. 3.12.

Resultants of Parallel Forces. Although *parallel forces* have lines of action which do not intersect, their resultants also may often be determined by repeated use of Postulate (3.4). Consider two forces **A** and **B** such that for some scalar k

$$\mathbf{A} = k\mathbf{B}.$$

Introduce at right angles (a graphical convenience, but skew angles will do) in the plane of **A** and **B** a pair of equal and opposite forces **C** and $-\mathbf{C}$ having a common line of action. As has been pointed out before, this enlarged set is equivalent to the original one. By Postulate (3.4) **A** and **C** have a resultant $\mathbf{A} + \mathbf{C}$ while **B** and $-\mathbf{C}$ have a resultant $\mathbf{B} - \mathbf{C}$. But these two forces will usually be concurrent; thus they will have a resultant $\bar{\mathbf{F}}$ passing through the point of concurrence. The vector $\bar{\mathbf{F}}$ is given by

$$\bar{\mathbf{F}} = (\mathbf{A} + \mathbf{C}) + (\mathbf{B} - \mathbf{C}) = \mathbf{A} + \mathbf{B}.$$

In Fig. 3.13 the construction is shown for the case where **A** and **B** point in the same direction. The success of this construction hinges on the nonparallelism of **A** + **C** and **B** − **C**. In Fig. 3.13 it seems quite obvious that they are not parallel. It may be much less obvious in the antiparallel case diagramed in Fig. 3.14, even though the steps of the construction are identical. Let us examine this point more critically. If the two vectors happen to be parallel, then for some scalar h we may write

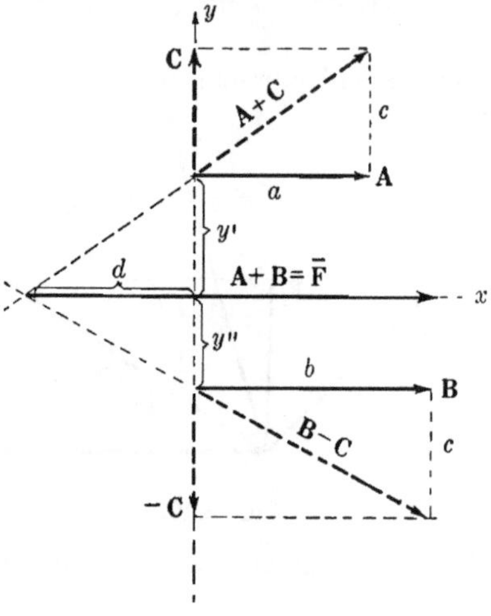

FIG. 3.13.

$$\mathbf{A} + \mathbf{C} = h(\mathbf{B} - \mathbf{C}),$$

or, since $\mathbf{A} = k\mathbf{B}$,

$$(h - k)\mathbf{B} = (h + 1)\mathbf{C}.$$

Since **B** and **C** are not parallel, it follows that the scalar coefficients

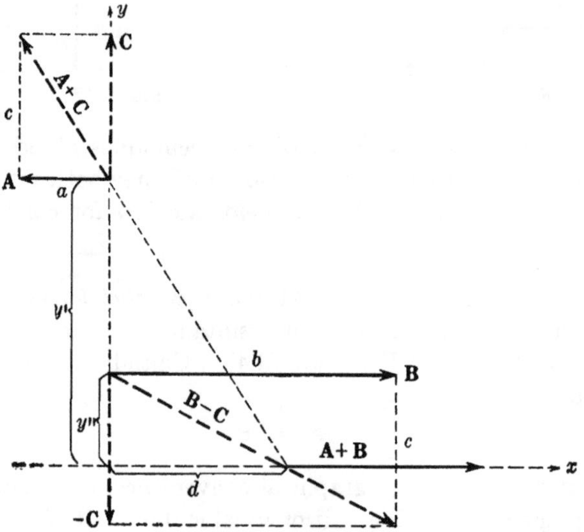

FIG. 3.14.

vanish and that

$$k = h = -1,$$

or that

$$\mathbf{A} = -\mathbf{B}.$$

Thus the reduction of two parallel forces to a single resultant force is valid except for the case where the given forces are equal in magnitude, opposite in direction, and with different lines of action. Such a pair of forces constitutes a *couple*. Figure 3.15 is a portrait of a couple. Special properties of couples will be investigated later.

In each of the cases considered (parallel and antiparallel) the resultant force is given by the vector **A** + **B**. The line of action of this force was found to lie between the two given forces (and nearer to the larger) in the parallel case. In the antiparallel case it was outside but nearer to the larger force, as one would expect. From the geometry of Figs. 3.13 and 3.14 one can quickly arrive at quantitative conclusions concerning this line of action. Let y' and y'' be the positive distances from the line of the resultant to **A** and **B**, respectively. Then from similar triangles one may write

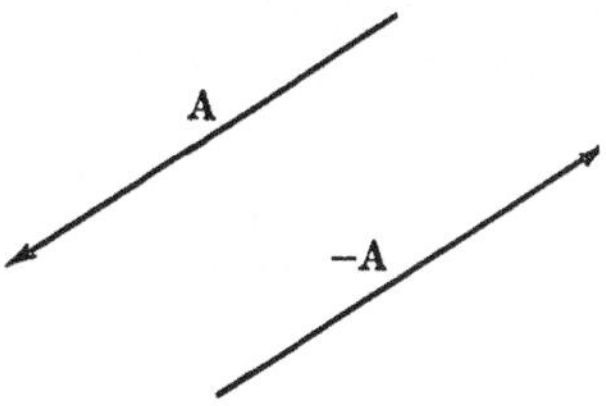

FIG. 3.15.

$$(3.6) \qquad \frac{c}{a} = \frac{y'}{d} \quad \text{and} \quad \frac{c}{b} = \frac{y''}{d}, \quad \text{whence } \frac{y'}{y''} = \frac{b}{a}.$$

Thus the resultant is separated from the two given parallel forces by distances inversely proportional to the magnitudes of the forces.

Example 4. The resultant of a set of forces will often be zero. In each of the diagrams in Fig. 3.16 that is the case. When the resultant

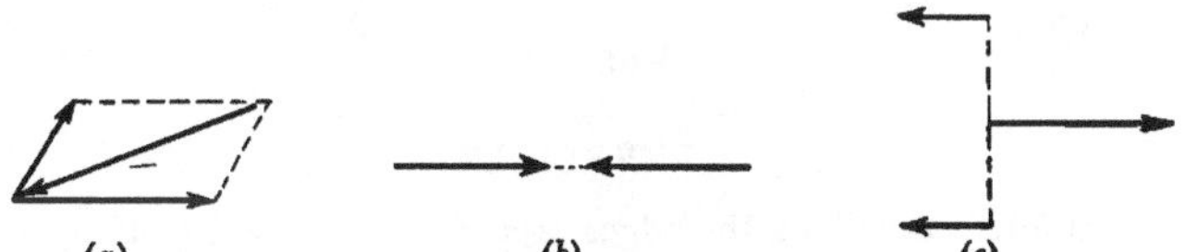

FIG. 3.16.

of a family of forces is zero, each force in the family is equal but opposite to the resultant of the remaining forces in the family. The student should convince himself of the truth of this assertion.

Example 5. Four equal forces act along the sides of a square as shown in Fig. 3.17*a*. Construct their resultant.

SOLUTION. However we may proceed to combine the forces, we know in advance that the resultant, as a vector, is equal to the vector sum of the four given vectors. Let a denote the magnitude of each of the forces. Then the resultant has magnitude $2.828a$; for **A** + **D** = **B** + **C**, and each of these sums is equal in magnitude to $1.414a$.

The direction of the resultant and its line of action may be arrived at in various ways. Let us carry out the construction in different orders. First combine **A** and **B**; then **C** and **D**. Since **A** + **B** = **C** + **D**, this resultant lies halfway between and is twice as large (Fig. 3.17*b*). As an alternative construction, first form **A** + **D**, then **B** + **C**. Since these two vectors have the same line of action, their resultant also has this same line of action (Fig. 3.17*c*). Finally, as a third approach, let us combine **A** and **C** to get a vector twice as large halfway between; then treat **B** and **D** similarly (Fig. 3.17*d*).

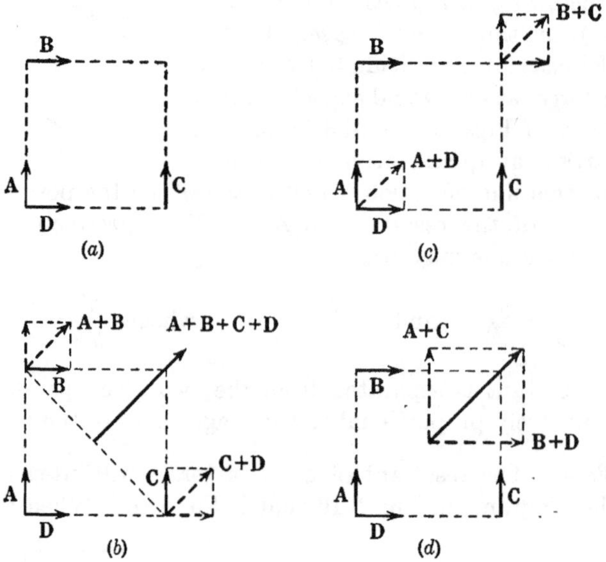

FIG. 3.17.

EXERCISES

1. Four equal forces act along the edges of a square in the directions shown in Fig. 3.18. Use careful graphical constructions to find their resultant. Measure the length of your resultant vector to be sure that it is twice as long as the given vectors.

FIG. 3.18.

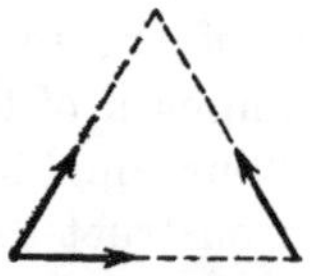

FIG. 3.19.

2. Three equal forces act along the edges of an equilateral triangle in the senses shown in Fig. 3.19. Construct their resultant in three distinct ways (*i.e.*, vary the order in which you combine the forces).

3. Given two nonparallel forces in a diagram such that their point of intersection lies off the paper. Devise and execute a graphical procedure such that the line of action of the resultant can be found all on the given sheet. In Fig. 3.20 the dotted lines indicate the boundaries of the paper.

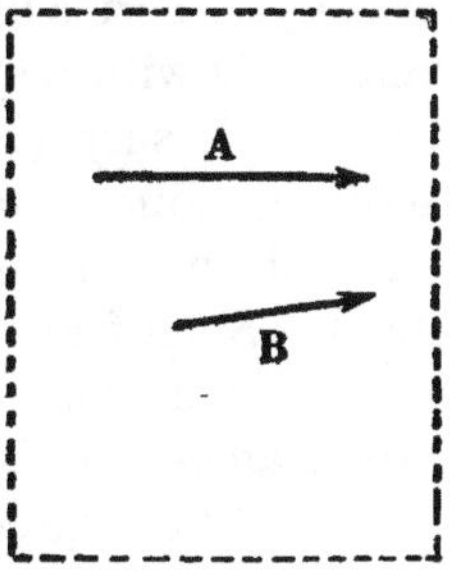

FIG. 3.20.

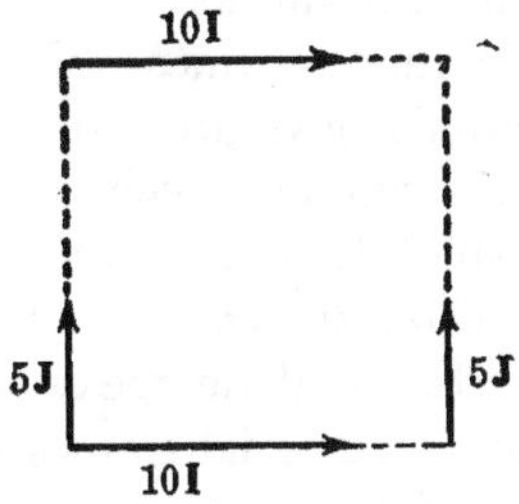

FIG. 3.21.

4. Find the resultant of the forces shown in Fig. 3.21.

5. Forces F, 2F, and 3F are equally spaced as is shown in Fig. 3.22. Find their resultant.

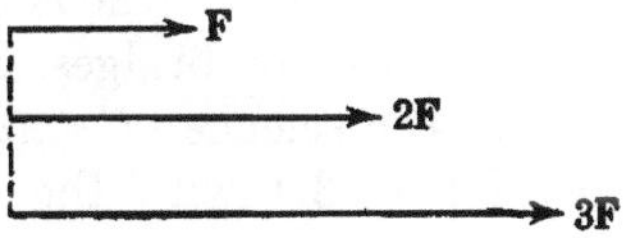

FIG. 3.22.

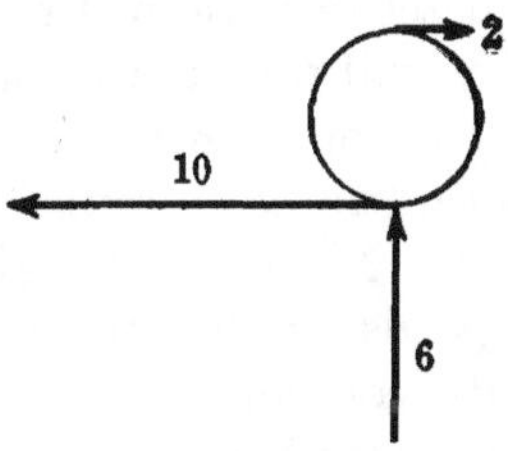

FIG. 3.23.

6. Find by graphical construction the magnitude and line of action of a single force which together with the forces shown in Fig. 3.23 will have a zero resultant.

3.6. Newton's Laws of Inertia and Static Equilibrium. Forces are interesting mainly as they act on *things*. We have so far discussed forces in the abstract with only incidental reference to objects and structures. Forces are brought to bear on all objects large and small. Gravitational pulls are universal. Whenever bodies touch, contact forces result. What are the effects of such forces? The first two laws of Newton are a good starting point for such a discussion. Their substance, amply verified experimentally, is as follows:

(3.7) *First Law. A body subject to no forces must remain at rest or in continued uniform motion.*

(3.8) *Second Law. A body subject to unbalanced forces experiences a rate of change of momentum proportional to the vector sum of these forces.*

As yet we have given no definition of *momentum;* therefore the second law will not be studied at all fully until a later section. From the definition of equivalence we may, however, at once conclude:

(3.9) *If two sets of forces are equivalent, then their vector sums are equal.*

The first law may already be interpreted without too much difficulty. Later it will become apparent that the first may be considered as a corollary of the second.

One aspect of these laws requires some scrutiny. Terms like "at rest" and "in uniform motion" can have significance only with respect to well-defined reference frames. Consequently, it is not surprising to learn that Newton's laws are valid in some reference frames and invalid in others. Elementary mechanics usually deals only with frames of reference for which these laws are assumed to hold. Such frames are sometimes called *inertial frames.* Reference frames such as were described in Sec. 1.2 are to a high degree of accuracy inertial frames. Frames rotating with respect to inertial frames lose this character to a degree dependent on the rate of rotation. Accelerated frames likewise are not inertial.

A body is "at rest" when its position within the reference frame is constant. It is in "uniform motion" when the character of its motion does not vary with time in either direction or magnitude. Thus if a pitched baseball could be freed from the effects of gravity and of frictional forces it would travel at a constant rate in a straight line with a uniform rate of spin about an axis of fixed orientation. Bodies behaving in this way are said to be *in equilibrium.* The case of actual rest is especially important. Much structural engineering—design of bridges, buildings, etc.—depends on the science of *statics, i.e.,* the science of *static equilibrium.* By combining the terminology of Sec. 3.4 with the empirical evidence crystallized in Newton's laws we may assume as a fourth postulate for forces:

(3.10) *A family of forces acting on a particle or rigid body will produce equilibrium if and only if it is equivalent to no forces (i.e., a vacuous set of forces).*

A useful corollary in terms of the ideas of Sec. 3.5 is

(3.11) *If the resultant of the forces acting on a particle or rigid body is zero (i.e., no forces), then the body is in equilibrium, and vice versa.*

Another corollary [from Proposition (3.9)] is

(3.12) *For a particle or rigid body to be in equilibrium, it is necessary that the vector sum of the forces acting on it be zero (i.e., a null vector).*

The state of affairs described in this corollary is not enough to *ensure* equilibrium for a rigid body. A couple, for example, is a set of forces satisfying this condition; but a body subject to an unbalanced couple is not in equilibrium. This is intuitively obvious and will later be deduced from the second law. For the present it is assumed:

(3.13) *A couple is not equivalent to zero.*

3.7. Statics of a Particle. Let us apply the conclusions of the preceding sections to the problem of equilibrium of a particle. Using Propositions (3.5) and (3.11), we may state at once:

(3.14) *A particle is in equilibrium if and only if the vector sum of the forces acting on it is zero (i.e., a null vector).*

We are now in a position to solve problems concerning statics of a particle. First we isolate the particle. Then we make whatever use seems convenient of the condition

$$\Sigma \mathbf{F} = \mathbf{F}_1 + \mathbf{F}_2 + \cdots + \mathbf{F}_n = \mathbf{O}. \tag{3.15}$$

This is equivalent to a set of three scalar equations:

$$\begin{aligned} \Sigma f_x &= f_{x_1} + f_{x_2} + \cdots + f_{x_n} = 0, \\ \Sigma f_y &= f_{y_1} + f_{y_2} + \cdots + f_{y_n} = 0, \\ \Sigma f_z &= f_{z_1} + f_{z_2} + \cdots + f_{z_n} = 0. \end{aligned} \tag{3.16}$$

The graphical interpretation of Proposition (3.14) is also often useful, especially when the forces are all parallel to a plane; for it says that if the vectors representing the forces are arranged in tandem, head to tail as in Fig. 3.24, then the figure must be a *closed polygon*. In this figure,

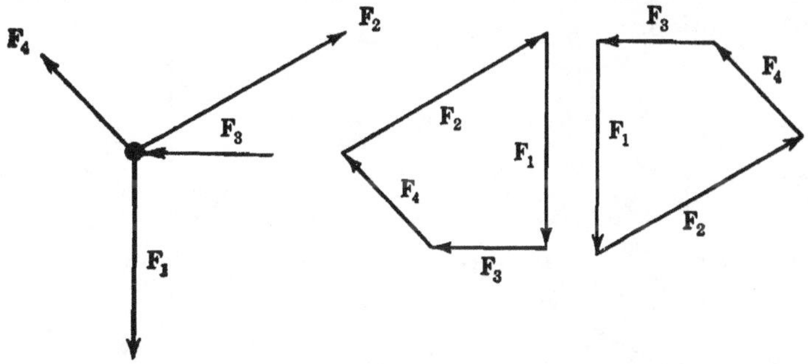

FIG. 3.24.

four forces act on a particle. If the particle is in equilibrium, the four vectors arranged head to tail in any order must form a closed quadrilateral. Two possible force polygons are shown. Others are, of course, possible, depending on the order in which the forces happen to be portrayed.

Example 1. Suppose a particle is subjected to two forces **F** and **F′**. The condition for the particle to be in equilibrium is then

$$\mathbf{F} + \mathbf{F}' = \mathbf{O}.$$

Using the rules of vector algebra, this tells us

$$\mathbf{F} = -\mathbf{F}'.$$

In other terms, a particle is in equilibrium under two forces only if the forces are equal but opposite. These forces cannot constitute a couple since they are concurrent.

Example 2. Suppose a particle is subjected to three forces **F**, **F′**, and **F″**. The force polygon, if there is equilibrium in this case, is a triangle. Hence, if the particle is in equilibrium under three forces, the forces all lie in the same plane and their vectors form a closed triangle. We shall now consider a numerical illustration.

Example 3. A 1-ton load is supported by two cables, making angles with the horizontal, respectively, equal to 60° and 30°. Find the tensions in the two cables.

In any solution of such a problem a useful first step is to draw a figure showing the essential data of the problem (Fig. 3.25). The first real step is to *isolate something,* as described in Sec. 3.3. In this case let us isolate the load, assuming that the forces are concurrent. Let **T** and **T′** denote the unknown tensions; t and t' will denote their magnitudes. The result of the isolation appears in Fig. 3.26. From now on different procedures are possible. Let us consider both an analytical and a graphical solution.

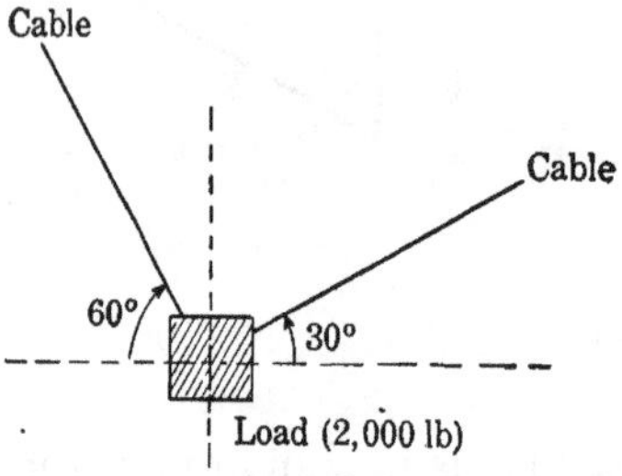

FIG. 3.25.

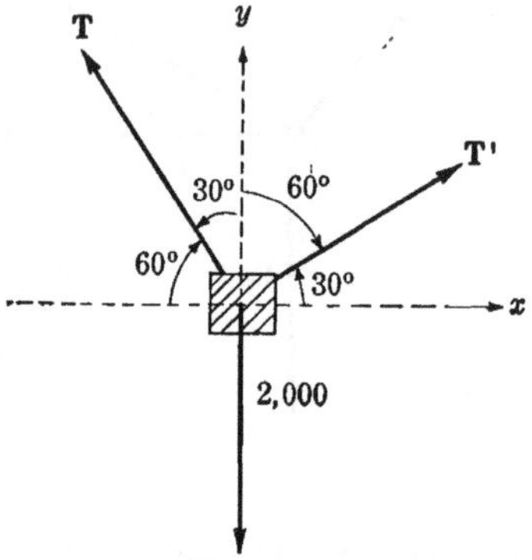

FIG. 3.26.

ANALYTICAL SOLUTION. In applying Eqs. (3.16), we are free to choose axes as we please. Let us take them as horizontal and vertical, as shown in the figure. Now following the first equation of (3.16) we put the sum of the scalar x components of the isolating forces equal to zero:

$$-t \cos 60° + t' \cos 30° = 0.$$

Treating the y components similarly we have

$$t \cos 30° + t' \cos 60° - 2{,}000 = 0.$$

It is a simple algebraic problem to solve these equations simultaneously and to arrive at the solutions:

$$t = 1{,}732 \text{ lb}, \qquad t' = 1{,}000 \text{ lb}.$$

GRAPHICAL SOLUTION. Let us plot the vector polygon to scale, using all the given data (see Fig. 3.27). The unknowns may be measured from the diagram; or they may be computed with the aid of the figure. Here we have given the direction and magnitude of the weight, the direction of **T**, and the direction of **T′**.

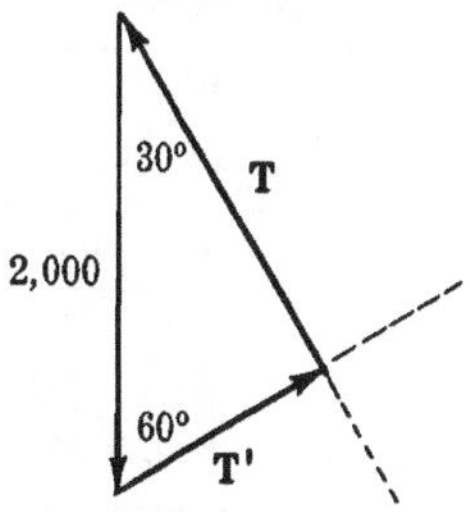

FIG. 3.27.

This is a simple problem, but the methods of attack are typical. In using the analytical approach, one merely chooses axes as cannily as possible; then one writes down the conditions of equilibrium and pushes through an algebraic solution. The equations are simpler if the axes are chosen so that as many forces as possible are parallel to them: then scalar components tend either to be zero or to be equal to the magnitude of the force. In using the graphical approach, one should use graph paper, choose a suitable scale for as large a figure as practical, draw with a fine line the vectors which are completely specified, and then construct the loci corresponding to the vectors specified only partly. Thus if the magnitude of a vector is known, the locus is a circle; if the direction is known, the locus is a line (as in the example just worked). When the diagram is complete, magnitudes may be read with a ruler; angles may be read roughly with a protractor, or more accurately by use of linear measurements and trigonometric tables. The details in special cases are left to the student's ingenuity and to class discussions.

EXERCISES

1. A particle is subject to forces whose vectors (in pounds) are given by $\mathbf{F}_1 = 8\mathbf{I} + 6\mathbf{J}$, $\mathbf{F}_2 = 10\underline{/100°}$, and $\mathbf{F}_3 = 10\underline{/-45°}$. Use graph paper to plot to scale a polygon of forces. From this figure, find the force $\mathbf{F} = f\underline{/\theta°}$ which must be added to ensure equilibrium for the particle. Check your result analytically.

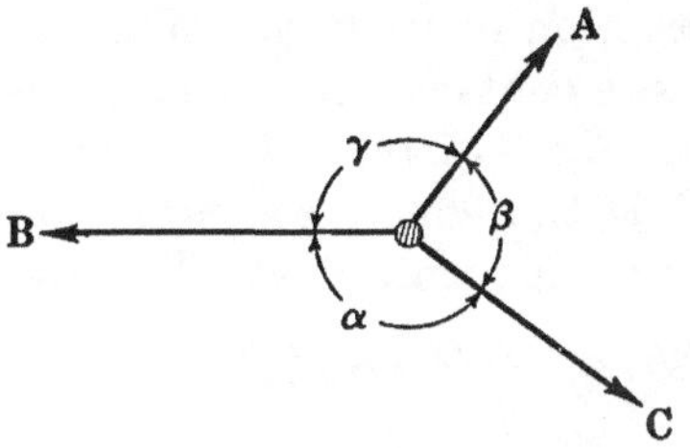

FIG. 3.28.

2. A particle is subject to three forces **A**, **B**, and **C** making angles of α, β, and γ with each other as shown in Fig. 3.28. If the particle is in equilibrium, show that (*Lamy's theorem*)

$$\frac{a}{\sin \alpha} = \frac{b}{\sin \beta} = \frac{c}{\sin \gamma}.$$

Does this condition, conversely, ensure equilibrium?

3. The ends of a rope 77 ft long are attached to hooks 63 ft apart on a horizontal girder. A 200-lb load is attached to the rope 25 ft from one end so that the load and the hooks form a triangle of sides 25, 52, and 63 ft. Find the tensions in the rope on either side of the load.

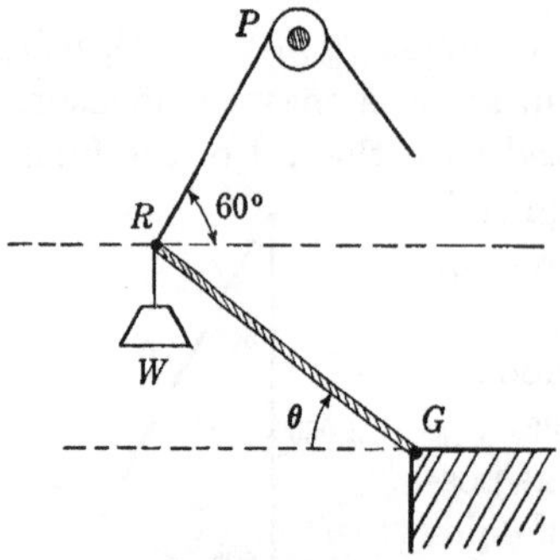

FIG. 3.29.

4. A 500-lb load W (see Fig. 3.29) is suspended by a cable WRP which passes over a pulley P. The cable is to be displaced to one side by a strut GR which is to sustain a compression along its length of 300 lb, so that RP makes an angle of 60° with the horizontal. (*a*) Find two possible angles θ which the strut GR may make with the horizontal. (*b*) Compute the corresponding tensions in the cable RP.

5. Show how a 2-lb force and a 4-lb force together can be used to hold a 3-lb force in equilibrium.

6. A 100-lb chandelier is supported by three chains symmetrically arranged and each making an angle of 30° with the vertical. Find the tension sustained by each of the chains.

7. A steel ball bearing weighing 1 lb rests in a V-shaped trough one side of which is vertical and the other side of which makes an angle of 30° with the vertical. Both sides are smooth; therefore reaction forces may be considered as perpendicular to the sides. How great are these forces?

8. A boulder is lifted by three ropes all in one vertical plane. One rope inclined at 150° with the horizontal has a tension of 300 lb; the second at 135° has a tension of 200 lb; the third is inclined at 30°. Find the weight of the boulder and the tension in the third rope.

9. A 100-kg cylinder rests between two smooth planes whose inclinations are, respectively, 30° and 60°. The planes meet in a horizontal line. Find in newtons the reaction forces between the cylinder and each of the planes.

10. A particle is in equilibrium when subjected to forces as shown in Fig. 3.30. Find the magnitude of the weight **W** and of the force **F**.

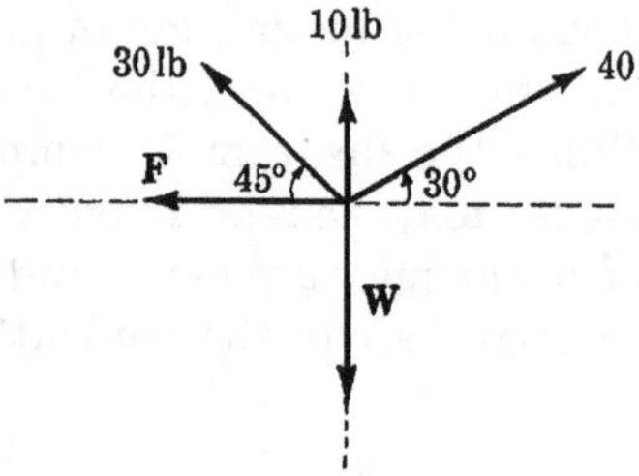

FIG. 3.30.

3.8. Problems Involving Interactions. In this section we shall consider special types of statics problems.

Friction. The first type involves the reaction forces when two bodies are in contact and centers around a discussion of friction. When two objects touch, the pair of equal and opposite contact forces may or may not be normal to the plane of contact. In Fig. 3.31 body a is in contact with body b at **Q**. Isolate a. Then **C** is the effective contact force exerted on a by b. Let us resolve **C** into components **F** and **N**, respec-

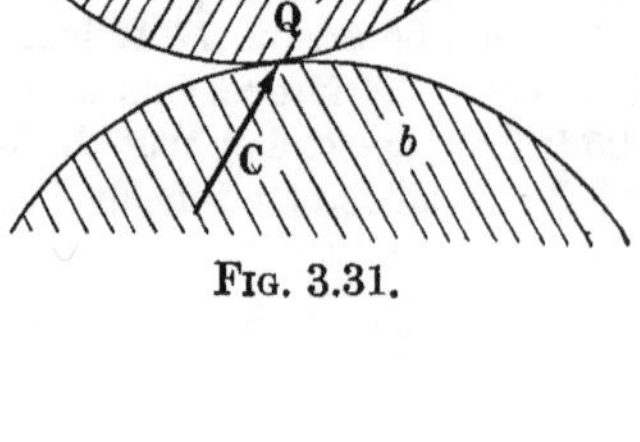

FIG. 3.31.

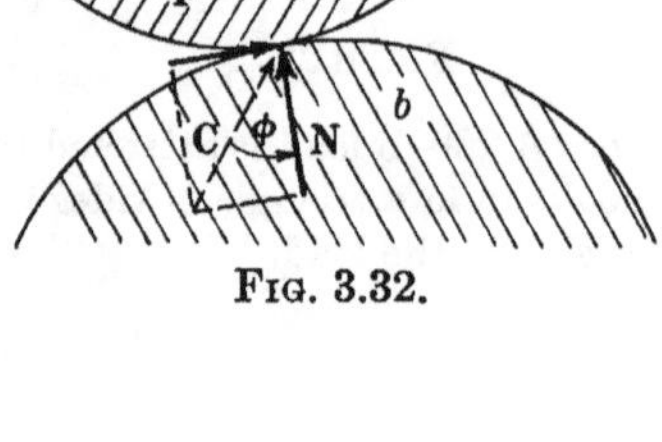

FIG. 3.32.

tively, tangential and normal to the contact surface, as in Fig. 3.32. **F** is called the *frictional force*, **N** the *normal reaction force*. As an example consider a sled resting on bare horizontal ground. If no effort is made to move the sled, **F** is zero. If one tries to slide the sled, an opposing force **F** is generated. If the effort is gradually increased, **F** also will gradually increase up to a maximum at which actual sliding takes place. During sliding, **F** remains nearly constant at a magnitude nearly as large as the maximum. The ratio of this maximum magnitude for **F** to the corresponding magnitude for **N** is called the coefficient of friction, denoted by μ.

$$\mu = \frac{f_{max}}{n}. \tag{3.17}$$

The coefficient of sliding friction is actually less than the coefficient of starting friction; but so little precision seems to be possible that we shall not pursue the matter far. It will merely be assumed that the coefficient is a constant, depending on the nature but not the size of the surfaces in contact. From the context the student will judge which kind of coefficient is intended. The angle ϕ between the resultant reaction **C** and the normal is often called the *angle of friction:*

$$\tan \phi = \mu. \tag{3.18}$$

Example 1. A 100-lb box resting on a horizontal floor barely starts to slide when pulled by a 25-lb tug directed 30° above the horizontal. What is the coefficient of friction?

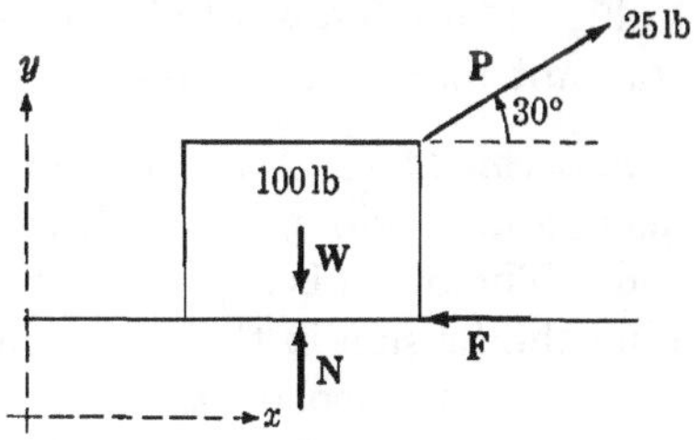

FIG. 3.33.

ANALYTICAL SOLUTION. Choose axes horizontal and vertical. The isolating forces are shown in Fig. 3.33. Use the conditions of equilibrium:

$$\Sigma f_x = 0 = 25 \cos 30° - f, \qquad \text{or} \qquad f = 21.7 \text{ lb}.$$
$$\Sigma f_y = 0 = n - 100 + 25 \sin 30°, \qquad \text{or} \qquad n = 87.5 \text{ lb}.$$

Consequently

$$\mu = \frac{f}{n} = \frac{21.7}{87.5} = 0.247.$$

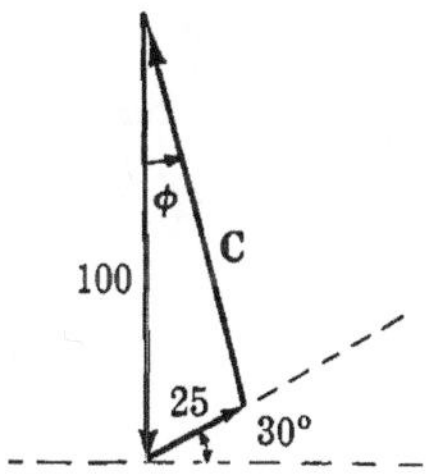

FIG. 3.34.

GRAPHICAL SOLUTION. Draw a force triangle as in Fig. 3.34. The angle between **C** and **W** is the angle of friction. One may use trigonometric techniques or direct measurement to determine this angle. Then its tangent may be looked up to evaluate the coefficient of friction.

Thrusts and Tensions. In many problems involving structures, beams are assumed to have negligible weight. This assumption is often justified in view of the loads sustained by the beams. Such an assumption makes for a simple solution of an important class of problems. Consider such a light strut with forces applied only at the ends, as in Fig. 3.35. This may be attained by fastening the strut to other members of the structure by frictionless pins, one at each end of the beam. The condition for

FIG. 3.35.

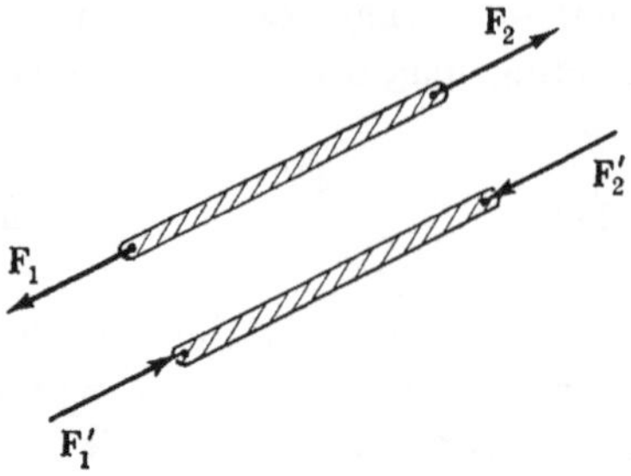

FIG. 3.36.

equilibrium, in view of Propositions (3.11) and (3.13), is that the forces at the two ends are equal but opposite and directed along the beam, as in Fig. 3.36. Thus a light beam with forces acting only at its ends can transmit forces only in its own direction.

Example 2. A 1,000-lb load is attached to the end of a light beam making an angle of 60° with the vertical and hinged freely at the lower end. The beam is supported by a cable making an angle of 45° with it. Find the tension in the cable and the thrust provided by the beam.

SOLUTION. Isolate the tip of the beam to which cable and load are attached (Fig. 3.37). Since we know that the thrust of the beam is

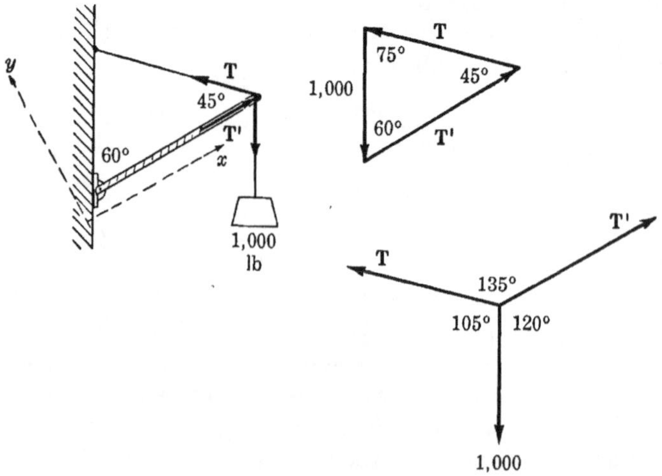

FIG. 3.37.

directed along the beam, we can easily draw a force triangle or apply Lamy's theorem (Exercise 2, Sec. 3.7) using the third diagram in Fig. 3.37. Let us also consider a routine analytical solution. Take axes parallel and perpendicular to the beam:

$$\Sigma f_x = 0 = t' - t \cos 45° - 1{,}000 \cos 60°,$$
$$\Sigma f_y = 0 = t \cos 45° - 1{,}000 \cos 30°.$$

From these equations we easily compute $t' = 1{,}366$ lb, $t = 1{,}225$ lb.

Complex Structures. In each of the problems studied thus far a single thing has been isolated. In problems involving several parts, we can make direct use of our first assumption (3.1) about forces. By isolating parts in succession and using the fact that interaction forces occur in equal but opposite pairs, we can write successive sets of equilibrium equations using the same unknowns. Similarly the force polygons for adjacent members of a structure will have equal but opposite sides; therefore they may be drawn in juxtaposition.

Example 3. Two blocks weighing, respectively, 10 and 5 newtons rest side by side on a plane inclined at 30°, as in Fig. 3.38. The coefficients of friction are, respectively, 0.2 and 0.1. What horizontal force is necessary to prevent slipping? The contact between the two blocks is smooth.

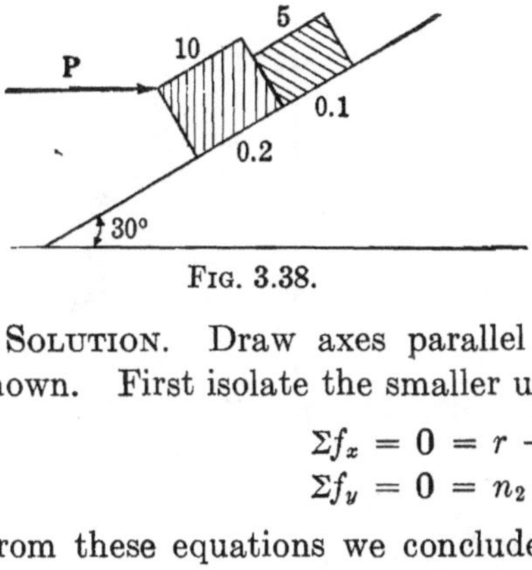

FIG. 3.38.

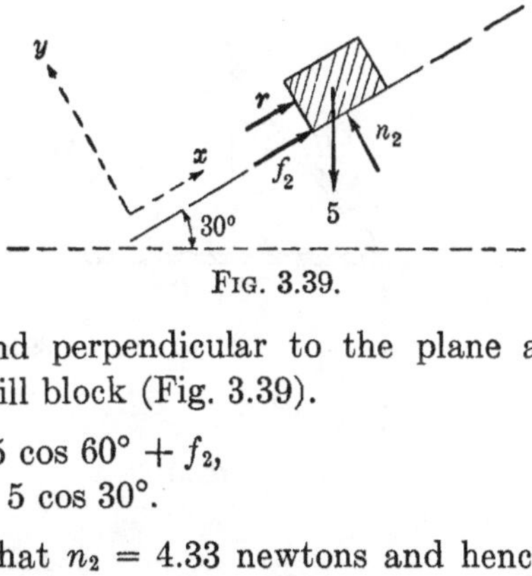

FIG. 3.39.

SOLUTION. Draw axes parallel and perpendicular to the plane as shown. First isolate the smaller uphill block (Fig. 3.39).

$$\Sigma f_x = 0 = r - 5 \cos 60° + f_2,$$
$$\Sigma f_y = 0 = n_2 - 5 \cos 30°.$$

From these equations we conclude that $n_2 = 4.33$ newtons and hence, since slipping is imminent, that $f_2 = 0.433$ newtons. Then we can compute r as $2.5 - 0.43$, or 2.07 newtons. Now isolate the other block (Fig. 3.40).

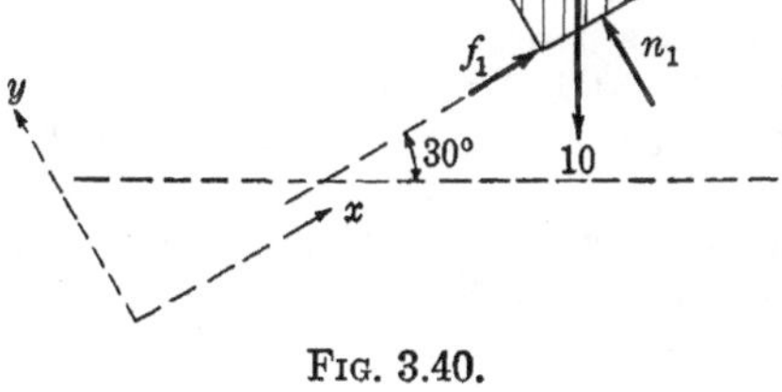

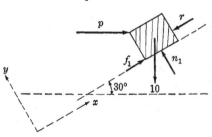

FIG. 3.40.

$$\Sigma f_x = 0 = p \cos 30° + f_1 - 2.07 - 10 \cos 60°,$$
$$\Sigma f_y = 0 = -p \cos 60° + n_1 - 10 \cos 30°.$$

Using the fact that $f_1 = 0.2n_1$, we may solve this pair of equations for p, getting $p = 5.32$ newtons.

A graphical solution is quite possible. Figure 3.41 shows such a solution. Starting with the small block, draw the vector triangle for the forces: weight $\mathbf{W}_2$ known in direction and magnitude; reaction $\mathbf{R}$ with other block, known in direction; and contact reaction $\mathbf{C}_2$ with plane, known in direction, at angle ϕ_2 whose tangent is 0.1, by Eq. (3.18). Now reverse $\mathbf{R}$ and draw for the first block the weight $\mathbf{W}_1$ known in direction and magnitude and the contact reaction force at an angle ϕ_1 with the normal. The force $\mathbf{P}$ is known in direction; thus with its line of action the figure may be completed. The length of the arrow $\mathbf{P}$ may be measured directly from the figure, or trigonometric computations may be used.

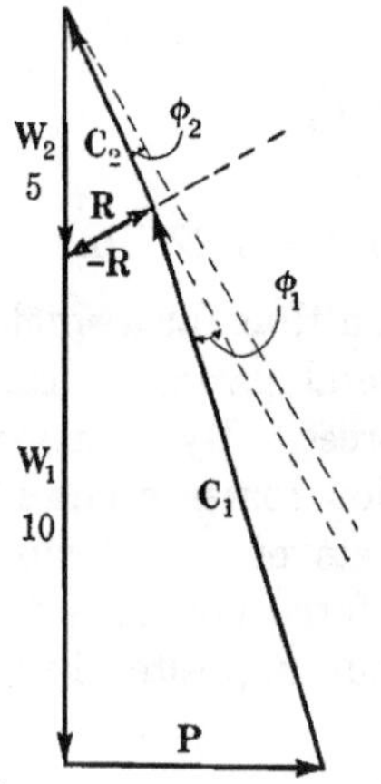

FIG. 3.41.

Example 4. The method of this section is particularly applicable to problems concerning simple trusses, *i.e.*, frames whose members are light beams freely pinned at the ends. In Fig. 3.42, such a structure is shown. In Fig. 3.43, the vector triangles generated by isolating each of the three vertex pins are shown.

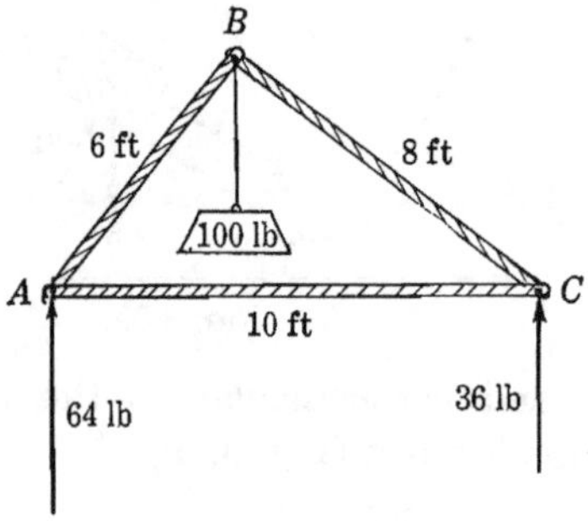

FIG. 3.42

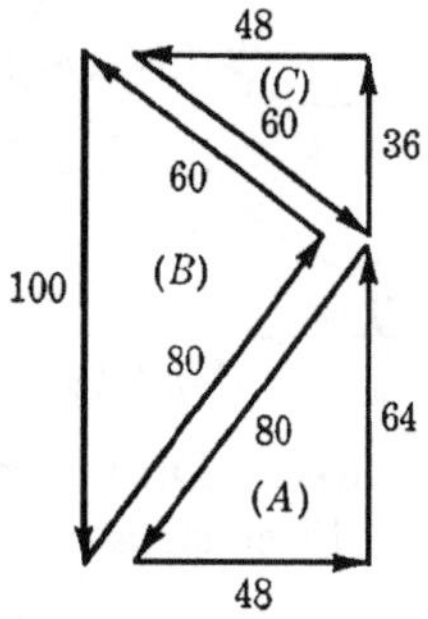

FIG. 3.43.

EXERCISES

1. A loaded sled weighs 75 lb. The coefficient of friction with a sanded sidewalk is 0.5. If the sled is to slip, how great a force must be exerted along the sled's rope inclined at an angle of 20° with the horizontal?

2. A block of weight w can be dragged along a horizontal plane by a horizontal force μw, where μ is the coefficient of friction. Show that by using a different direction for the force it is always possible to attain the same result with a force as small as $w \sin \phi$, where ϕ is the angle of friction.

3. What is the least force that will suffice to drag a 50-lb box up a plane inclined at 40° if the coefficient of friction is 0.4? How must this minimum force be directed?

4. Show that a block of weight w can be dragged up a plane inclined at an angle θ by a force of $w \sin (\theta + \phi)$, where ϕ is the angle of friction.

5. A block of weight w is kept from slipping on a plane inclined at an angle θ by a horizontal force **P**. If the coefficient of friction is μ, how large and how small can **P** be?

6. A block of weight w is kept on a plane inclined at 30° by a horizontal force. **P** is the smallest such force which will prevent downhill slipping. If the horizontal push is increased until the block is about to slip uphill, the magnitude of the force is $p + w$. Compute the coefficient of friction between block and plane.

7. Two blocks are pulled slowly and at constant speed up a plane inclined at 40° by a cord exerting a tension **T**. The blocks are joined by a cord of tension **T′**, as shown in Fig. 3.44. If the upper block weighs 10 newtons and has a coefficient of friction 0.3 while the lower block weighs 5 newtons and has a coefficient 0.1, what are the magnitudes of **T** and **T′**?

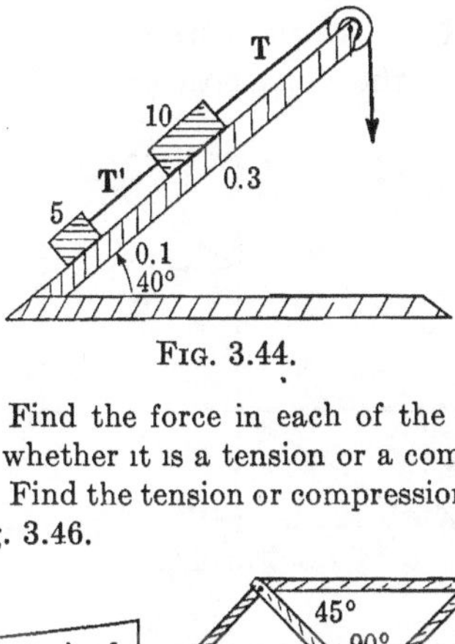

FIG. 3.44.

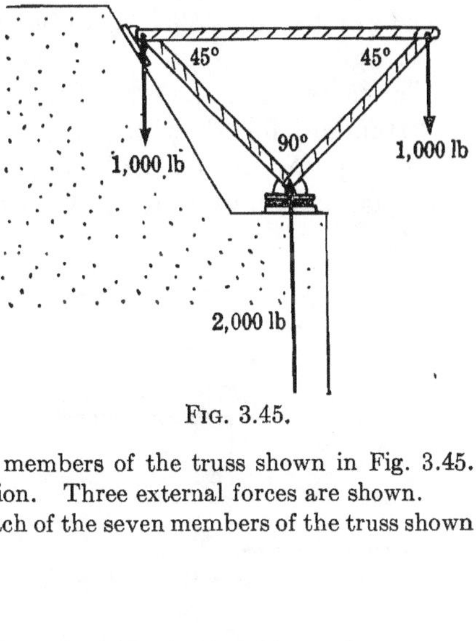

FIG. 3.45.

8. Find the force in each of the three members of the truss shown in Fig. 3.45. State whether it is a tension or a compression. Three external forces are shown.

9. Find the tension or compression in each of the seven members of the truss shown in Fig. 3.46.

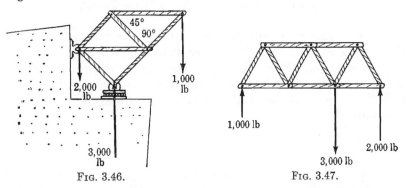

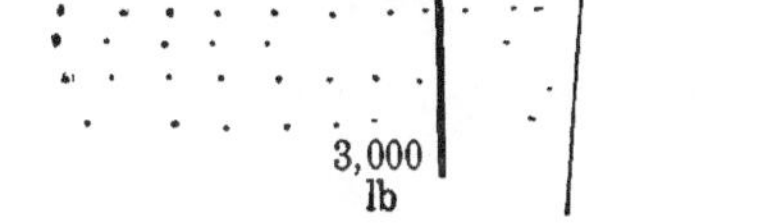

FIG. 3.46.

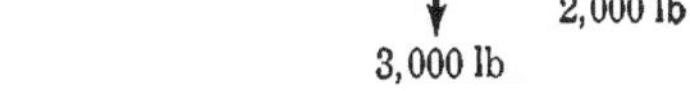

FIG. 3.47.

10. Find the force in each of the eleven members of the loaded truss shown in Fig. 3.47. For each member state whether it is under compression or tension.

CHAPTER 4

COUPLES AND MOMENTS

The preceding chapter gave an introduction to statics, but we developed no good criterion for equilibrium of nonconcurrent forces. Now we shall approach problems of a more general sort.

4.1. The Couple and Its Moment. In Sec. 3.5 the *couple* was introduced as a pair of forces (equal but opposite) which refused to be reduced to a single resultant force by a construction entirely successful in other similar cases. For the sake of simplicity let us initially represent couples in "standard form" with the points of application of the forces on a common perpendicular, as in Fig. 4.1. Now let us introduce as in Sec. 3.5 equal and opposite forces **C**, −**C** along the perpendicular. This has

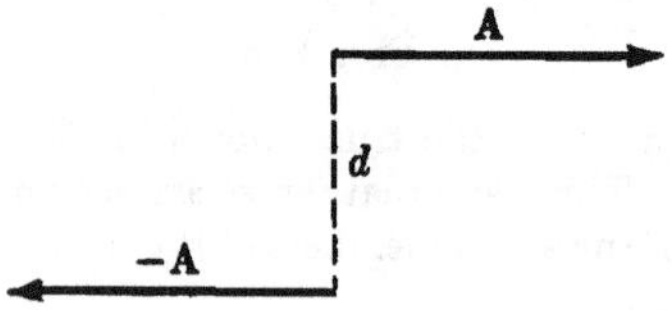

FIG. 4.1.

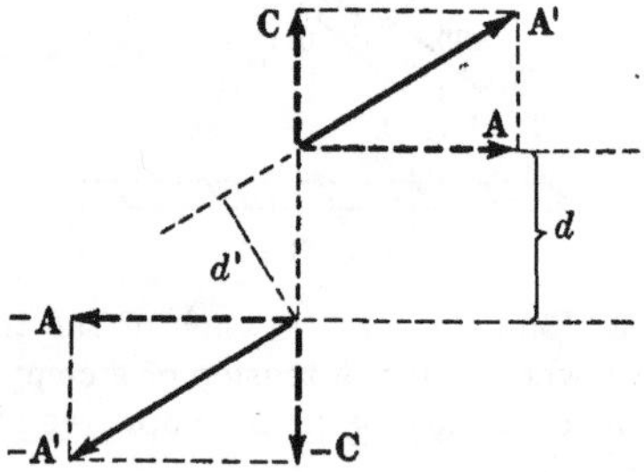

FIG. 4.2.

the effect of replacing the first couple (**A**,−**A**) by an equivalent one (**A**′,−**A**′), as shown in Fig. 4.2. These two couples have two significant things in common. First, their orientation is the same: they lie in the same plane, and they suggest rotation in the same sense (clockwise in Fig. 4.2). Second, the product of separation by magnitude is the same in each case:

$$da = d'a'. \tag{4.1}$$

These two aspects may be amalgamated by saying that the *moment of the couple* is the same in each case, the moment being a vector $\mathbf{\Gamma}$ *directed* along the normal to the plane. It has the *sense* given by a right-hand rule for the rotation suggested by the couple (compare Secs. 1.2 and 2.3). In other words, the moment vector is in the direction that a screw would follow if acted on by this couple (see Fig. 4.3). The *magnitude* of the vector is the value da, measured usually in such units as newton-meters or foot-pounds. If **K** is a unit vector normal to the plane in the proper sense, then (4.1) may be replaced by

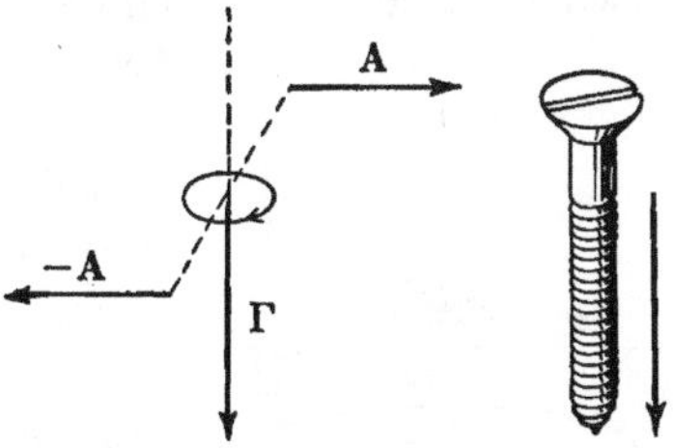

FIG. 4.3.

$$\Gamma = da\mathbf{K} = d'a'\mathbf{K}. \tag{4.2}$$

It is important to notice that $\boldsymbol{\Gamma}$ can be written in terms of a vector product:

$$\boldsymbol{\Gamma} = \mathbf{D} \times \mathbf{A}, \tag{4.3}$$

where **D**, as in Fig. 4.4, is the vector between the points of application of the forces. Observe especially that the same result is obtained if **D** is not perpendicular to **A** (that is, the couple is not in standard form). This flexible property of vector products was pointed out in Eq. (2.26). We can now write (4.2) as

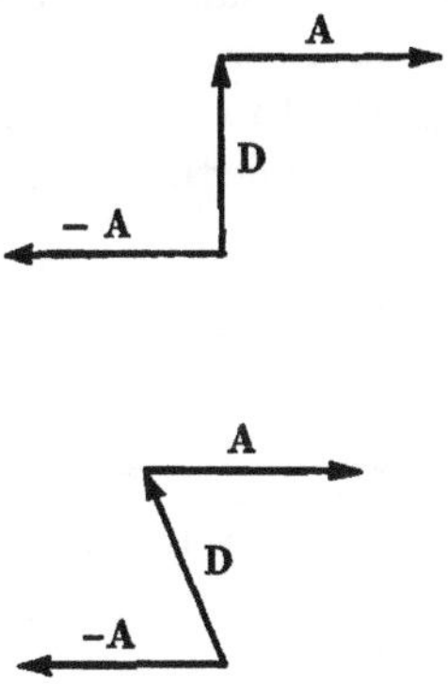

FIG. 4.4.

$$\boldsymbol{\Gamma} = \mathbf{D} \times \mathbf{A} = \mathbf{D}' \times \mathbf{A}'. \tag{4.4}$$

4.2. Equivalence of Couples. For equivalent couples related to each other in one way we have observed that the moment is the same. This is a most important observation; therefore we shall pursue the idea further. Suppose identical copies of the *same* couple occur in different places in a plane. Are they equivalent? The affirmative answer is readily demonstrated. Given the couple $(\mathbf{A}, -\mathbf{A})$, select any other point **P**. At **P** and $\mathbf{P} + \mathbf{D}$ draw copies of **A** and $-\mathbf{A}$, labeled, respectively, with primes. The resultant of $-\mathbf{A}$ and $-\mathbf{A}''$ is a force midway between, directed to the left (in terms of Fig. 4.5), and of magnitude $2a$. The resultant of **A** and $\mathbf{A}'$ is a vector to the right of magnitude $2a$, the line of action being the same. These two resultants nullify each other. Thus the couple $(\mathbf{A}, -\mathbf{A})$ is equivalent to the couple $(\mathbf{A}'', -\mathbf{A}')$.

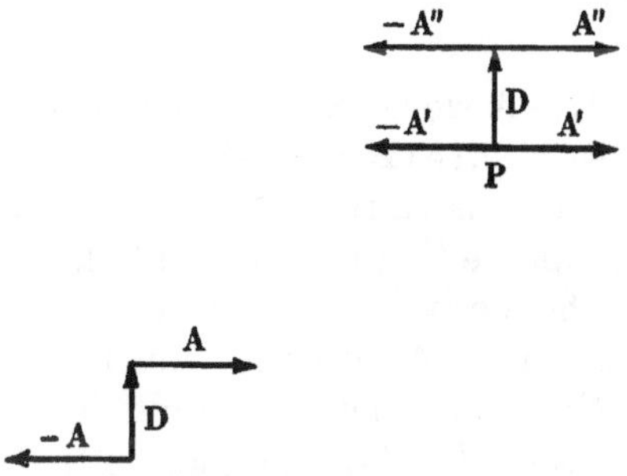

FIG. 4.5.

The result just derived may seem hard to believe. Imagine, for instance, a circular board floating in water. Suppose that the board has two light identical handles (as in Fig. 4.6) to which one may apply a twist. One of these handles is at the center O, the other at O' near the edge. Now if a twist of, say 1 ft-lb, is applied at O and then, under identical initial conditions, at O' will the results be the same? You might expect that in each case the board would tend to rotate about the handle being twisted. In practice that is partly true, but this is due merely to the difficulty of applying a perfect couple, two equal forces, to a moving axis. If this practical difficulty is overcome, then the board rotates about its center, regardless of where the couple is applied. If the handle is not at the center, however, it will travel in a circle; therefore we must either provide a moving couple or judge the experiment instantaneously.

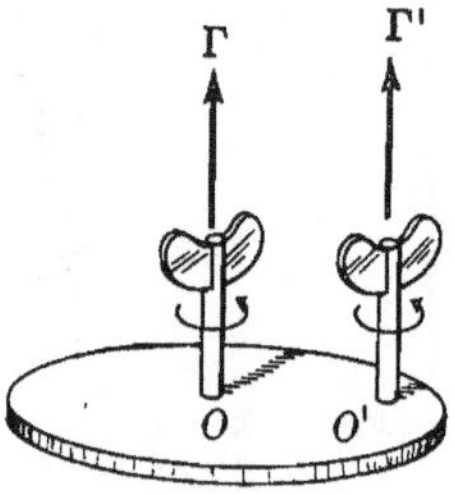

FIG. 4.6.

Now consider the question: Is it possible to replace a couple having large forces and small separation by a couple having small forces and large separation? Practical experience with levers suggests this. In Fig. 4.7, for instance, one would expect that two strong men exerting forces

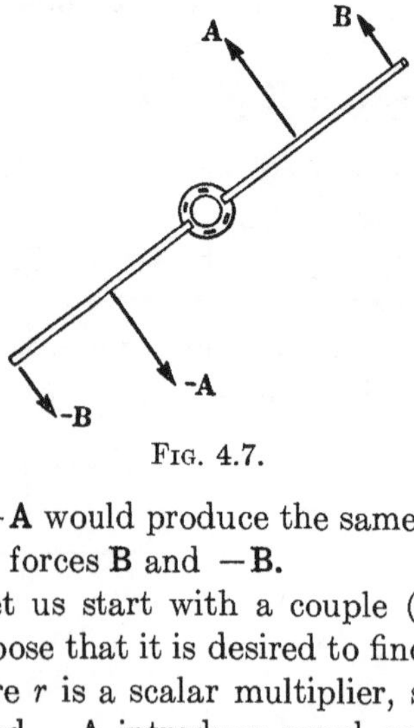

FIG. 4.7.

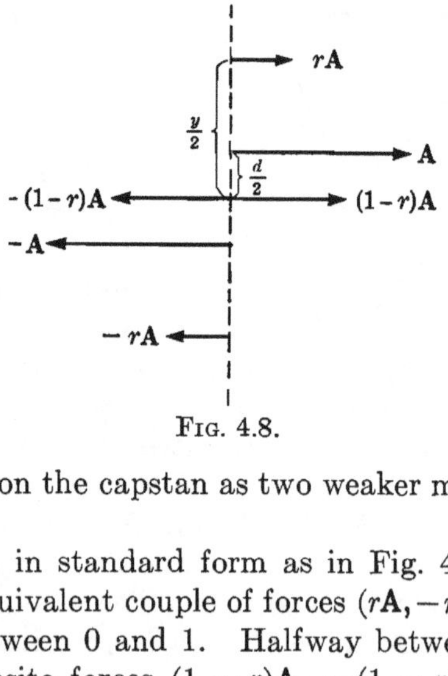

FIG. 4.8.

A, $-$**A** would produce the same effect on the capstan as two weaker men with forces **B** and $-$**B**.

Let us start with a couple (**A**, $-$**A**) in standard form as in Fig. 4.8. Suppose that it is desired to find an equivalent couple of forces (r**A**, $-r$**A**) where r is a scalar multiplier, say between 0 and 1. Halfway between **A** and $-$**A** introduce equal and opposite forces $(1 - r)$**A**, $-(1 - r)$**A**. Now construct the resultant of **A** and $-(1 - r)$**A**. It is a force r**A** located [by Eq. (3.6)] above the center by an amount $y/2$ such that

$$\frac{(1 - r)}{1} = \frac{(y/2) - (d/2)}{y/2}, \qquad \text{or} \qquad y = \frac{1}{r}\,d.$$

Similarly, the resultant of $-$**A** and $(1 - r)$**A** is a force $-r$**A** at a distance $y/2$ below the center. Thus the couple (**A**, $-$**A**) is equivalent to (r**A**, $-r$**A**), the latter forces having a separation of d/r. The moment of both couples has magnitude *da*. By successive applications of these three maneuvers (rotation, translation, and expansion), all of which leave moments unchanged, we can conclude:

(4.5) *If two coplanar couples have the same moment, they are equivalent.*

Finally, suppose that two couples have the same moment but are not coplanar. Can it be that they, too, are equivalent? Again practical experience suggests a positive answer. We unlatch a door by applying a couple to a doorknob. A parallel couple on the other knob will produce the same effect. Suppose once more that we have given a couple with forces (**A**, −**A**), and a plane parallel to that of the couple as shown in Fig. 4.9. Let **P** and **Q** be the points of application of **A** and −**A**. Let **P′** and **Q′** be their projections on the plane. The diagonals **PQ′** and **QP′** intersect at **M**. At **M** introduce equal but opposite forces 2**A** and −2**A**. The resultant of **A** and −2**A** is a force −**A** at **Q′**; the resultant of −**A** and 2**A** is a force **A** at **P′**. Our new equivalent couple is a precise copy of the given one; therefore the moments are the same.

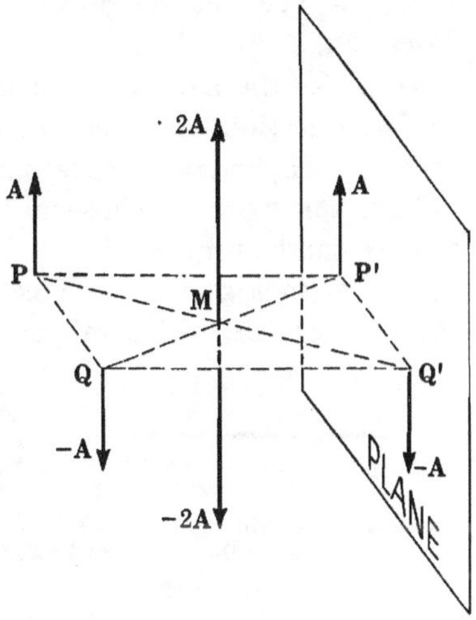

FIG. 4.9.

Now we can extend the last theorem to

(4.6) *If any two couples have the same moment, they are equivalent.*

Later on, as a sequence of Newton's second law, we shall derive the converse of this proposition.

EXERCISES

1. Figure 4.10 represents two forces lying in a plane. How far from the center *O* should two 1-lb forces be drawn to give a couple in standard position equivalent to the couple shown?

2. Given a couple in standard position: **A** acting at **O**, −**A** acting at a distance *d*. By introducing equal and opposite forces **A′** and −**A′** at both **O** and **P**, as in Fig. 4.11, show that the couple may be rotated through an angle *θ*.

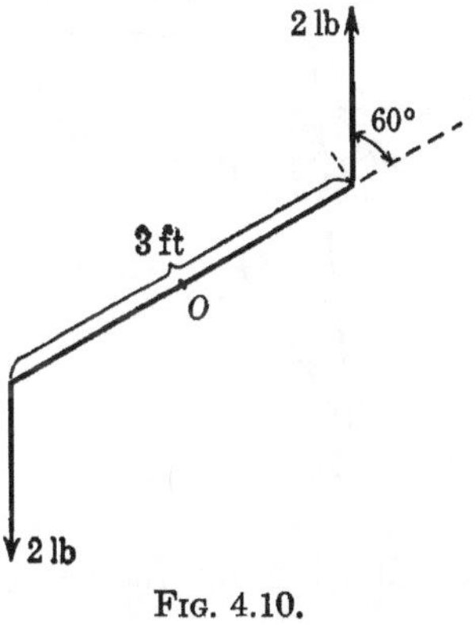

FIG. 4.10.

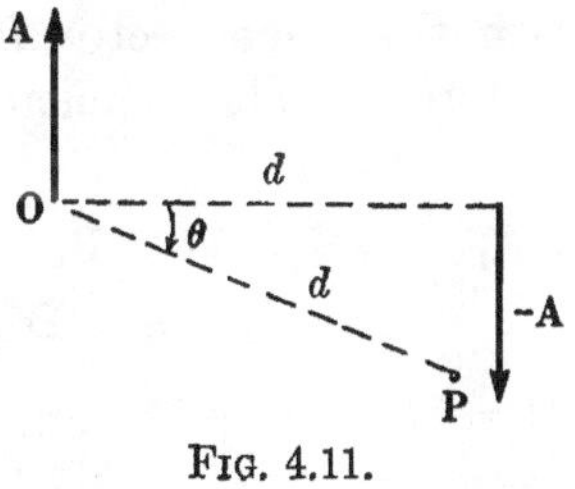

FIG. 4.11.

3. Show that the derivation based on Fig. 4.5 is valid even for the case where the point **P** is not in the plane of the forces **A** and $-\mathbf{A}$.

4.3. Addition of Couples. Since the moment of a couple is, practically speaking, its only important characteristic, *we shall represent couples by their moment vectors.* Thus instead of specifying a couple as composed of forces $(\mathbf{A}, -\mathbf{A})$ separated by d, we shall often find it convenient to call it a couple $\mathbf{\Gamma}$. The magnitude and direction of $\mathbf{\Gamma}$ have already been described.

To make the suitability of this decision to regard couples as vectors beyond question, let us consider whether couples do in fact combine like vectors. If the couples are parallel, it is obvious that the two combine to form a new couple whose moment is the sum of the other two. For the couples can be replaced by equivalent ones with common points of application, as in Fig. 4.12. Thus the two couples shown in standard form $(\mathbf{A}, -\mathbf{A})$ and $(\mathbf{B}, -\mathbf{B})$ combine to yield a couple with forces $\mathbf{A} - \mathbf{B}$ and $-(\mathbf{A} - \mathbf{B})$. The three moment magnitudes are, respectively, da, db, $d(a - b)$. Since the moment vectors of the first two are oppositely directed, we have the desired result:

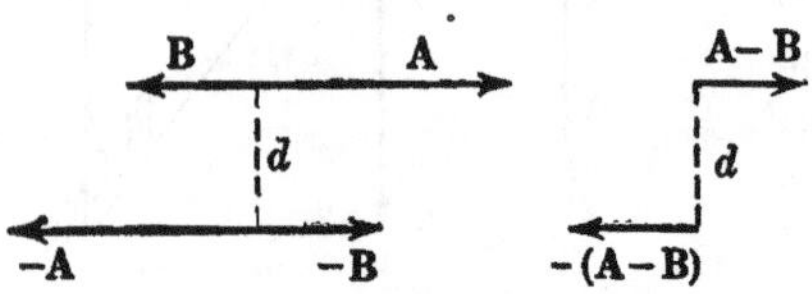

FIG. 4.12.

$$\mathbf{\Gamma}_{A+B} = \mathbf{\Gamma}_A + \mathbf{\Gamma}_B.$$

Let us now examine the more general case where the couples are not parallel. Arrange the couples in standard form so that their points of application concur on the line common to their two planes, as in Fig. 4.13. Then **A** and **B** determine a plane perpendicular to the common line and likewise $-\mathbf{A}$ and $-\mathbf{B}$ determine another plane perpendicular to the common line. Now, using Postulate (3.3), we replace **A** and **B** by their resultant **C** and $-\mathbf{A}$ and $-\mathbf{B}$ by their resultant $-\mathbf{C}$. Since **C** lies in the plane of **A** and **B**, and $-\mathbf{C}$ in the plane of $-\mathbf{A}$ and $-\mathbf{B}$, both are perpendicular to the common line, that is, the new couple is also in standard position with the same vector **D** between their forces. The moments are given by

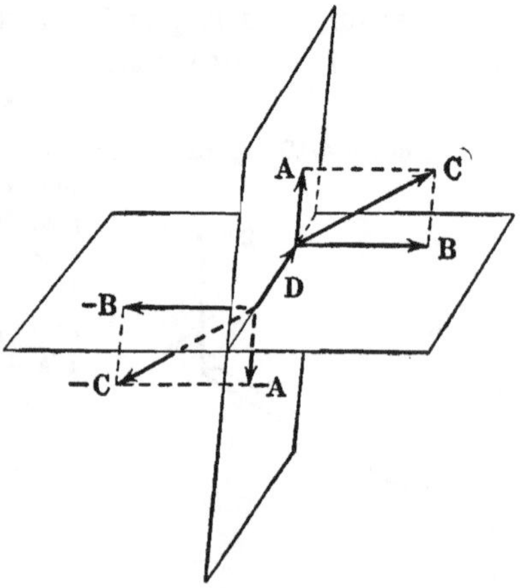

FIG. 4.13.

$$\mathbf{\Gamma}_A = \mathbf{D} \times \mathbf{A}, \qquad \mathbf{\Gamma}_B = \mathbf{D} \times \mathbf{B},$$
$$\mathbf{\Gamma}_C = \mathbf{D} \times \mathbf{C}.$$

But $\mathbf{D} \times \mathbf{C} = \mathbf{D} \times (\mathbf{A} + \mathbf{B})$, and using the distributive law for vector products,

$$\mathbf{D} \times \mathbf{C} = \mathbf{D} \times \mathbf{A} + \mathbf{D} \times \mathbf{B};$$

so

$$\mathbf{\Gamma}_C = \mathbf{\Gamma}_A + \mathbf{\Gamma}_B.$$

Our final conclusion then is this:

(4.7) *If couples are represented by their moment vectors, they can be added as vectors; i.e., a family of couples* $\mathbf{\Gamma}_1, \mathbf{\Gamma}_2, \ldots, \mathbf{\Gamma}_n$, *however located, is equivalent to a single couple* $\bar{\mathbf{\Gamma}}$ *given by*

$$\bar{\mathbf{\Gamma}} = \mathbf{\Gamma}_1 + \mathbf{\Gamma}_2 + \cdots + \mathbf{\Gamma}_n.$$

EXERCISE

Given two couples, as indicated schematically in Fig. 4.14, with

$$\mathbf{A} = 3\mathbf{I} + 4\mathbf{J} \text{ lb}, \qquad \mathbf{D} = \mathbf{I} - 2\mathbf{J} + \mathbf{K} \text{ ft},$$
$$\mathbf{A}' = 4\mathbf{I} + 3\mathbf{K}, \qquad \mathbf{D}' = 2\mathbf{J}.$$

Find the magnitude and direction cosines of the moment of a single couple equivalent to the two given couples.

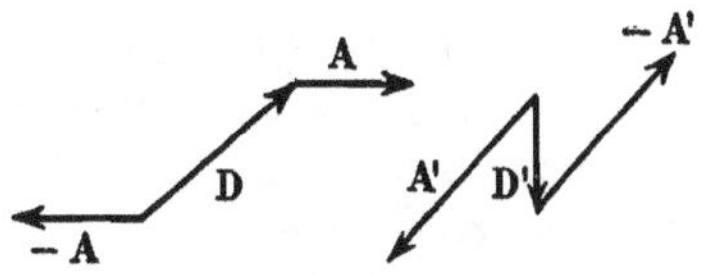

FIG. 4.14.

4.4. Moment of a Force about a Point. For any single force **F** and any reference point **O** we shall define *the moment of* **F** *about* **O** by the equation

$$\mathbf{\Gamma} = \mathbf{R} \times \mathbf{F}, \tag{4.8}$$

where **R** is the position vector with respect to **O** of a point on the line of action of **F**. This definition is quite analogous to Eq. (4.3) which expressed the moment of a couple. We shall see that it is also quite in agreement with notions about moment usually presented in courses in elementary physics. The magnitude of this vector $\mathbf{\Gamma}$ (see Fig. 4.15), by

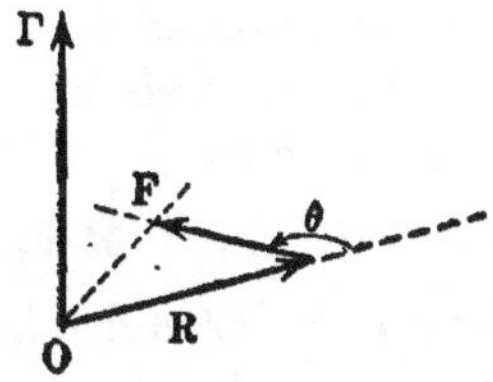

FIG. 4.15.

the definition of vector product, is equal to the magnitude of the force times its perpendicular distance from the point in question. The direction of the vector $\mathbf{\Gamma}$ is perpendicular to the plane of the point **O** and the force **F** and hence in the direction of the axis about which a force so placed would tend to cause rotation.

It is always dangerous to have one concept with two possibly different interpretations; therefore let us proceed at once to calculate the vector sum of the moments of the forces comprising a couple about an origin **O**. Given (see Fig. 4.16) a couple $(\mathbf{A}, -\mathbf{A})$ as before. Let $-\mathbf{A}$ act at the point **R**. Then **A** acts at the point $\mathbf{R} + \mathbf{D}$. The moment of **A** is $(\mathbf{R} + \mathbf{D}) \times \mathbf{A}$, that of $-\mathbf{A}$ is $\mathbf{R} \times (-\mathbf{A})$. Adding and using the rules of vector algebra we have for a sum:

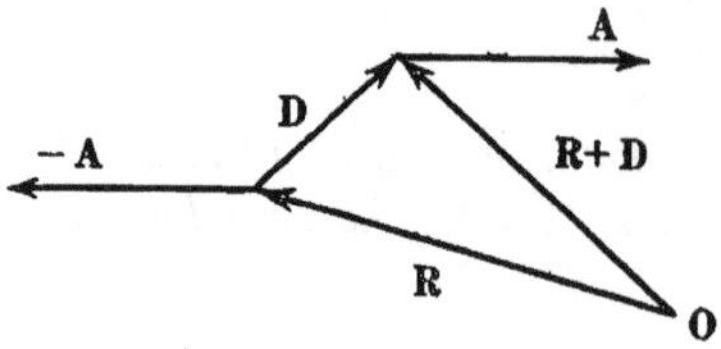

FIG. 4.16.

$$\Sigma\mathbf{\Gamma} = (\mathbf{R} + \mathbf{D}) \times \mathbf{A} + \mathbf{R} \times (-\mathbf{A}) = \mathbf{D} \times \mathbf{A}.$$

Note particularly that this sum is *independent of* **O**.

(4.9) *The vector sum of the moments (i.e., the "moment sum") about any point of the forces of a couple is equal to the moment of the couple.*

Since no confusion is likely to result we shall define *moment of a family of forces about a point* as equal to the vector sum of the moments of the separate forces. This, of course, suggests restating Proposition (4.9) as: The moment of a couple about a point is equal to its moment! Sometimes for clarity or emphasis this concept will be called the *moment sum* of the set of forces. This, of course, explains the parenthetical insertion into the statement of Proposition (4.9).

An important property of moments is crystallized in the *theorem of Varignon:*

(4.10) *The moment (about a point) of a family of concurrent forces is equal to the moment of their resultant.*

In symbols the assertion is

$$\bar{\mathbf{\Gamma}} = \Sigma\mathbf{\Gamma},$$

where $\mathbf{\Gamma}$ is the moment of a typical force in the family. It is easy to see that this theorem was essentially proved in the chapter on vector algebra (Sec. 2.4). If $\mathbf{F}_1, \mathbf{F}_2, \ldots, \mathbf{F}_n$ are forces acting at **P** as in Fig. 4.17, then the moment of the family is given by

$$\bar{\mathbf{\Gamma}} = \mathbf{P} \times \mathbf{F}_1 + \mathbf{P} \times \mathbf{F}_2 + \cdots + \mathbf{P} \times \mathbf{F}_n.$$

By the distributive property of vector multiplication this expression is equal to

$$\mathbf{P} \times (\mathbf{F}_1 + \mathbf{F}_2 + \cdots + \mathbf{F}_n).$$

But by successive application of Postulate (3.4) the sum

$$\bar{\mathbf{F}} = \mathbf{F}_1 + \mathbf{F}_2 + \cdots + \mathbf{F}_n$$

is the resultant of the set of concurrent forces.

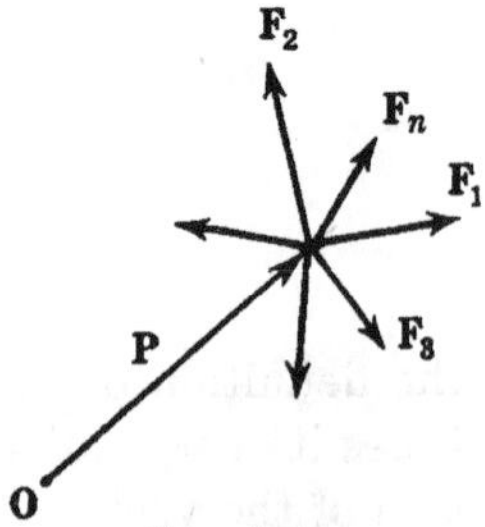

FIG. 4.17.

These concepts are particularly useful for forces in a plane; therefore our first example will be of that nature.

Example 1. Find the magnitude of the moment about the origin of a force $5\mathbf{I} + 5\mathbf{J}$ lb if it acts at the point with coordinates (2,1) ft as in Fig. 4.18.

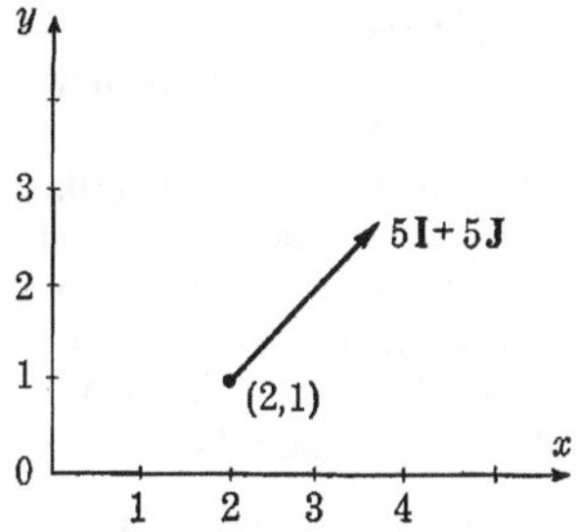

FIG. 4.18.

FIRST SOLUTION. The problem can be solved formally by vector manipulation.

$$\mathbf{R} \times \mathbf{F} = (2\mathbf{I} + \mathbf{J}) \times (5\mathbf{I} + 5\mathbf{J}) = 5\mathbf{K} \text{ ft-lb.}$$

SECOND SOLUTION. The problem can be solved in terms of the elementary idea of moment as distance times magnitude. The distance may be computed variously as a problem in analytic geometry or trigonometry. For instance, an equation of the line of action of the force is

$$y - 1 = 1(x - 2),$$

or

$$x - y - 1 = 0.$$

The distance of this line from 0 is 0.707. The force has magnitude 7.07. The product is then 5, which was the magnitude of the vector obtained in the first solution. (The student wishing to use his vector tools to the utmost will probably find the distance from 0 to the line by considering the component of **R** perpendicular to **F**.)

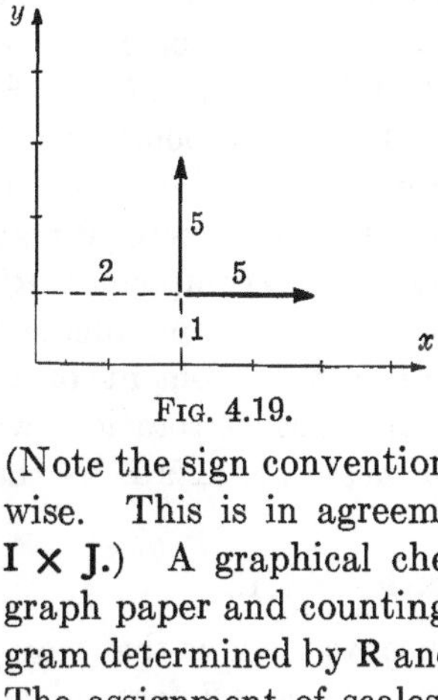

FIG. 4.19.

THIRD SOLUTION. Using Varignon's theorem, the force may be replaced by two concurrent forces $5\mathbf{I}$ and $5\mathbf{J}$ whose moments may be read off at once from Fig. 4.19 by the method used in the preceding solution.

$$\gamma = (-)1 \times 5 + (+)2 \times 5 = 5.$$

(Note the sign convention: + for counterclockwise rotation, − for clockwise. This is in agreement with our original choice of **K** as equal to $\mathbf{I} \times \mathbf{J}$.) A graphical check could be achieved by plotting to scale on graph paper and counting squares in the parallelogram determined by **R** and **F** as shown in Fig. 4.20. The assignment of scales must, of course, be kept in mind.

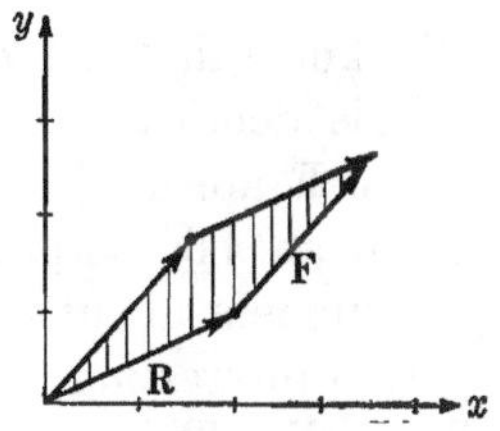

FIG. 4.20.

EXERCISES

1. Prove that the moment of a force about a point is not altered if the force is allowed to slide along its own line of action.

2. The moment of a couple is the same about any point. For a given force **F** and moment **Γ** describe the locus of origins **O** for which the moment of **F** about **O** is **Γ**.

3. Given three forces in the xy plane: $10\underline{/30°}$ at (1,0); $10\underline{/-60°}$ at (0,−2); $10\underline{/120°}$ at (0,−4). (Units are pounds and feet.) (*a*) Find the moment about the origin. (*b*) Find the moment about the point (3,0) ft.

4. Given three forces in the xy plane: $10\underline{/60°}$ at (3,2); 4**I** − 4**J** at (−7,7); and $8\underline{/135°}$ at (2,−4). (Units are newtons and meters.) Compute the moment about the origin.

5. A 60-lb force acts at the point with coordinates (8,8,−5) ft. A second point on its line of action is (10,9,−3) ft. Compute the magnitude of the moment of the force about the point (1,2,3) ft.

6. A spool of radius r and axle radius r' rests on a horizontal plane surface. The thread unwinding from the top of the spool is pulled at an angle θ above the horizontal with a force **F**. Find the moment of **F** about the line of contact with the plane (*i.e.*, about the point where the vertical plane through the thread cuts this line).

4.5. Moment of a Force about an Axis. In Sec. 4.4 it was remarked that the moment **Γ** of a force **F** about a point **O** is a vector directed along an axis about which rotation tends to take place. In mechanical work it often happens that only one particular axis is eligible to be an axis of rotation. The best possible example perhaps is a wheel with its axle set in fixed bearings. All forces applied to such a wheel may be resolved into components parallel and perpendicular to the axle. Only those components which are perpendicular will have any tendency to produce rotation. The parallel components merely conjure up equal and opposite bearing reactions. We shall then take into account only the perpendicular component when we define moment about an axis. In Fig. 4.21 force **F** acts at **R**. The axle has the direction of the unit vector **E**. **F** is resolved into components **F″** parallel to **E** and **F′** perpendicular to **E**. Let **R″** be the point on the axle nearest to **R**. Suppose that the origin is taken as any point on the axle. The vector **R** may then be thought of as resolved into components **R″** and **R′** (from **R″** to **R**), respectively, parallel and perpendicular to **E**. Since the moment of **F′** about **R″** is parallel to the axis of rotation, we shall define *moment of* **F** *about the axis* **E** by the equation

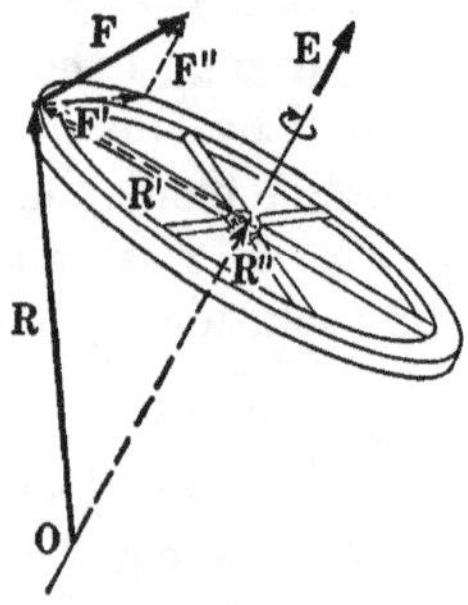

FIG. 4.21.

$$\mathbf{\Gamma}_E = \mathbf{R}' \times \mathbf{F}' = \gamma_E \mathbf{E}. \tag{4.11}$$

(We know that the vector is parallel to **E** because we made it that way.) This is identical with (4.8) except that components of **R** and **F** perpendicular to **E** are used. In the important case of plane forces the moment about an axis perpendicular to the plane is thus precisely the same as the moment about the point where the axis meets the plane.

It is interesting to find the magnitude γ_E of the vector $\mathbf{\Gamma}_E$ in terms of **R** and **F**. This might be deduced from Exercise 6, Sec. 2.7; or we may compute it directly. Recall that in Chap. 2 we arrived at formulas for components perpendicular to a unit vector:

$$(4.12) \qquad \mathbf{R}' = \mathbf{E} \times (\mathbf{R} \times \mathbf{E}), \qquad \mathbf{F}' = \mathbf{E} \times (\mathbf{F} \times \mathbf{E}).$$

If these equations are substituted in (4.11), we have rather formidable expressions which the student may wish to expand and simplify as a review exercise in vector algebra. If he does this correctly, he will arrive at

$$(4.13) \qquad \mathbf{\Gamma}_E = (\mathbf{E} \cdot \mathbf{R} \times \mathbf{F})\mathbf{E},$$

or

$$(4.14) \qquad \gamma_E = \mathbf{R} \times \mathbf{F} \cdot \mathbf{E} = \mathbf{\Gamma} \cdot \mathbf{E}.$$

Since the direction of the vector was originally confined, the scalar form (4.14) is adequate. In words, the result may be stated as follows:

(4.15) *The moment of a force about an axis is equal to the component in the direction of the axis of the moment of the force about any point on the axis.*

The sum of the moments about an axis of a set of forces will be called simply the *moment of the set of forces about that axis.* The moment of a force or couple (especially about an axis) is often called the *torque* exerted by that force or couple.

Special properties of this new concept are easily provable from results already derived:

(4.16) *The moment about any axis of the forces of a couple is equal to the component parallel to that axis of the moment of the couple.*

(4.17) *The moment about an axis of a family of concurrent forces is equal to the moment of their resultant* (*Varignon*).

(4.18) *If a force* $f_x\mathbf{I} + f_y\mathbf{J} + f_z\mathbf{K}$ *acts at the point* (x,y,z), *then the moments of the force about the coordinate axes are, respectively,*

$$\gamma_x = yf_z - zf_y, \qquad \gamma_y = zf_x - xf_z, \qquad \gamma_z = xf_y - yf_x.$$

Example. Given a force $2\mathbf{I} + 3\mathbf{J} + 4\mathbf{K}$ lb acting at the point with coordinates (3,2,0) ft. Find

a. Its moment about the origin.
b. Its moment about the coordinate axes.
c. Its moment about the line through the origin and (1,1,1).
d. Its moment about the line through (0,0,1) and (1,0,0).

SOLUTION

$$a. \quad \mathbf{\Gamma}_O = \mathbf{R} \times \mathbf{F} = \begin{vmatrix} 3 & 2 & 0 \\ 2 & 3 & 4 \\ \mathbf{I} & \mathbf{J} & \mathbf{K} \end{vmatrix} = 8\mathbf{I} - 12\mathbf{J} + 5\mathbf{K} \qquad \text{ft-lb.}$$

$$b. \quad \gamma_x = \mathbf{\Gamma}_O \cdot \mathbf{I} = 8, \qquad \gamma_y = \mathbf{\Gamma}_O \cdot \mathbf{J} = -12, \qquad \gamma_z = \mathbf{\Gamma}_O \cdot \mathbf{K} = 5.$$

c. For the line given, $\pm\mathbf{E} = \dfrac{\mathbf{I}+\mathbf{J}+\mathbf{K}}{\sqrt{3}}$. Let us arbitrarily select the plus sign.

$$\gamma = \mathbf{\Gamma}_O \cdot \mathbf{E} = \frac{8}{\sqrt{3}} - \frac{12}{\sqrt{3}} + \frac{5}{\sqrt{3}} = 0.6 \text{ ft-lb.}$$

d. Let us take our reference point on the axis as (0,0,1). Then

$$\mathbf{R} = 3\mathbf{I} + 2\mathbf{J} - \mathbf{K}, \qquad \mathbf{E} = \frac{\mathbf{I}-\mathbf{K}}{\sqrt{2}};$$

thus

$$\gamma_{\mathbf{E}} = \mathbf{R} \times \mathbf{F} \cdot \mathbf{E} = \begin{vmatrix} 3 & 2 & -1 \\ 2 & 3 & 4 \\ \dfrac{1}{\sqrt{2}} & 0 & \dfrac{-1}{\sqrt{2}} \end{vmatrix} = \frac{6}{\sqrt{2}} = 4.23 \text{ ft-lb.}$$

EXERCISES

1. Prove that the moment of a force about a line is not altered if the force is allowed to slide along its own line of action.

2. A 100-lb force acts along the line from (0,1,0) ft to (1,1,0) ft. Find its moment about the origin and about each of the coordinate axes.

3. A 100-lb force acts at the point (9,−6,3) ft. Its direction cosines are 0.667, −0.333, −0.667. Find its moment about an axis through the origin and the point (0,−8,6) ft.

4. A 5-lb force has direction cosines (0.6,0.8,0.0). A point on its line of action is (3,−2,4) ft. Find its moment about each of the following points: (0,0,0), (3,0,0), (0,−2,0), (0,0,4), (1,1,1). Find its moments about the coordinate axes.

5. A 10-lb force parallel to the positive x axis acts at the point (0,1,0) ft. Find its moment about an axis through the origin and parallel to the vector $6\mathbf{I} - 6\mathbf{J} - 3\mathbf{K}$.

6. A 100-lb force acts at the origin. Its angles with the x and y axes are, respectively, 60° and 75°. Find the magnitude of its moment about the line through (0,2,0) parallel to the x axis.

7. A force $\mathbf{F} = 7.5\mathbf{I} - 10\mathbf{J}$ acting at (−4,2) ft in the xy plane has a moment of minus $60\mathbf{K}$ ft-lb about the point with coordinates $(2,y)$ ft. Find y.

8. A rigid body is free to rotate about an axis having direction cosines 0.5, −0.5, 0.707 and passing through the point (2,1,−3). A force whose components are 10, 0, −15 in the x, y, and z directions, respectively, acts at the point (5,1,2). Find the moment of the force about the stated axis.

9. Prove Proposition (4.16).

10. Prove Proposition (4.17).

11. Prove Proposition (4.18).

12. A 10-lb force acts along the diagonal of one end of a 4-ft cubical box. Find the magnitude of the moment of the force about each edge and each vertex of the box.

4.6. A Reduction Theorem. In Sec. 3.5 it was shown that for every family of concurrent forces there is a single resultant force. This resultant is equal to the vector sum of the forces in the family. It was also shown that in special cases nonconcurrent forces may have as resultant a single force again equal to the vector sum. The line of action of this single force was uniquely specified. One very simple configuration of forces, the couple, seemed to have no single force as a resultant [Proposition (3.13)]. Furthermore, a couple can be moved anywhere without changing its effect—only its moment must be preserved [Proposition (4.6)].

In this section we shall combine previous results to show that *any* system of forces is equivalent to a simple system consisting of one force and one couple. Suppose we have given a set of forces $\mathbf{F}_1, \mathbf{F}_2, \ldots, \mathbf{F}_n$ acting at various points on a rigid body. Let us select arbitrarily a reference point **P** either on the body or on an imagined rigid extension thereof. At **P** (see Fig. 4.22) introduce equal and opposite forces $\mathbf{F}_1' = \mathbf{F}_1$ and $-\mathbf{F}_1'$. Note that the three forces $\mathbf{F}_1$, $\mathbf{F}_1'$, and $-\mathbf{F}_1'$ have the same vector sum and the same moment about *any* point as had $\mathbf{F}_1$ alone (for the contributions of the new forces just cancel). Then at **P** introduce $\mathbf{F}_2' = \mathbf{F}_2$ and also $-\mathbf{F}_2'$, etc., for all n forces. When this has been done, we have created n couples $(\mathbf{F}_1,-\mathbf{F}_1')$, $\ldots$, $(\mathbf{F}_n,-\mathbf{F}_n')$ of moments $\mathbf{\Gamma}_1, \mathbf{\Gamma}_2, \ldots, \mathbf{\Gamma}_n$ where each $\mathbf{\Gamma}_i$ is equal to the moment of $\mathbf{F}_i$ about **P**; thus if we combine the n couples into a single one $\bar{\mathbf{\Gamma}}$, we know that

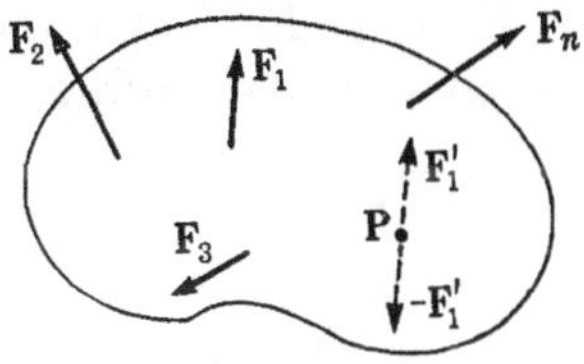

FIG. 4.22.

$$\bar{\mathbf{\Gamma}} = \Sigma\mathbf{\Gamma}, \tag{4.19}$$

that is, the moment of this single resultant couple is equal to the moment about **P** of the original set of forces. At **P** we have also created a set of n forces $\mathbf{F}_1', \mathbf{F}_2', \ldots, \mathbf{F}_n'$. They have a resultant $\bar{\mathbf{F}}$ through **P** such that

$$\bar{\mathbf{F}} = \Sigma\mathbf{F}. \tag{4.20}$$

Let us state our conclusions carefully.

(4.21) *Any set of forces* $\mathbf{F}_1, \mathbf{F}_2, \ldots, \mathbf{F}_n$ *is equivalent to a force* $\bar{\mathbf{F}}$ *at any preassigned point* **P** *together with a couple* $\bar{\mathbf{\Gamma}}$. $\bar{\mathbf{F}}$ *is equal to the vector sum of the given forces;* $\bar{\mathbf{\Gamma}}$ *is equal to the moment about* **P** *of the given set of forces (i.e., to the moment sum of the set).*

(4.22) *The moment of the new system about any point or axis is the same as that of the old system.*

This latter proposition follows from the remark made concerning the step-by-step introduction of forces during the deduction of Proposition (4.21). Let us also verify it directly. What are the moments of the systems about any point, say **O**? Let the position vector of the point of application of a typical given force $\mathbf{F}_i$ be $\mathbf{R}_i$ with respect to **O**, $\mathbf{P}_i$ with respect to **P**. For the initial system, the moment sum about **O** is

$$\mathbf{\Gamma}_O = \Sigma\mathbf{R}_i \times \mathbf{F}_i.$$

For the new system, the moment sum about **O** is

$$\mathbf{\Gamma}'_O = \bar{\mathbf{\Gamma}} + \mathbf{P} \times \bar{\mathbf{F}},$$

or since

$$\bar{\mathbf{\Gamma}} = \Sigma\mathbf{P}_i \times \mathbf{F}_i,$$
$$\mathbf{\Gamma}'_O = \Sigma(\mathbf{P}_i \times \mathbf{F}_i) + \mathbf{P} \times \Sigma\mathbf{F}_i,$$

or

$$\mathbf{\Gamma}'_O = \Sigma(\mathbf{P}_i \times \mathbf{F}_i) + \Sigma(\mathbf{P} \times \mathbf{F}_i) = \Sigma(\mathbf{P}_i + \mathbf{P}) \times \mathbf{F}_i = \Sigma\mathbf{R}_i \times \mathbf{F}_i.$$

The corresponding conclusion for moments about a line through **O** parallel to a unit vector **E** follows at once if each side of the preceding equations is multiplied by **E** (scalar product):

$$\mathbf{\Gamma}'_O \cdot \mathbf{E} = \mathbf{\Gamma}_O \cdot \mathbf{E}.$$

If the student finds these derivations obscure, he should repeat them, using actual sums for say three forces instead of the Σ notation. Each step involves only simple rules of vector algebra or direct substitutions.

Example 1. Three forces act as follows: **8I** + **6J** at (0,6,0); **4I** + **5J** + **6K** at (6,6,6); **10K** at (6,0,0), as in Fig. 4.23. Find an equivalent force (at the origin) and couple.

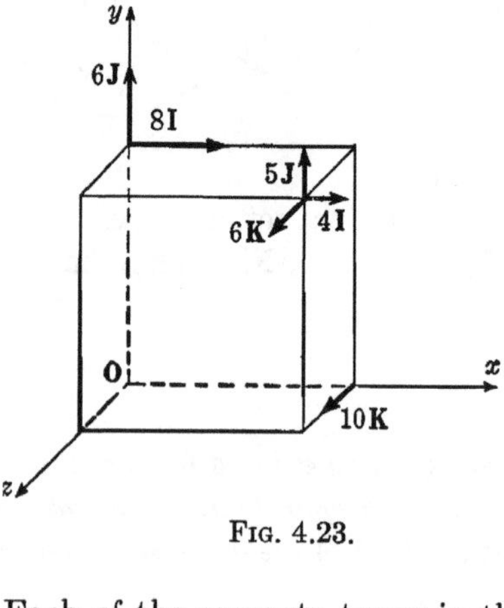

FIG. 4.23.

SOLUTION. The force at the origin $\bar{\mathbf{F}}$ will be equal to the sum of the forces listed: $\bar{\mathbf{F}} = 12\mathbf{I} + 11\mathbf{J} + 16\mathbf{K}$. The moment of the couple will be the sum of the moments about **O** of the forces listed.

$$\mathbf{\Gamma}_1 = 6\mathbf{J} \times (8\mathbf{I} + 6\mathbf{J}) = -48\mathbf{K}$$

$$\mathbf{\Gamma}_2 = \begin{vmatrix} 6 & 6 & 6 \\ 4 & 5 & 6 \\ \mathbf{I} & \mathbf{J} & \mathbf{K} \end{vmatrix} = 6\mathbf{I} - 12\mathbf{J} + 6\mathbf{K}$$

$$\mathbf{\Gamma}_3 = 6\mathbf{I} \times 10\mathbf{K} = -60\mathbf{J}.$$

Hence

$$\bar{\mathbf{\Gamma}} = 6\mathbf{I} - 72\mathbf{J} - 42\mathbf{K}.$$

Each of the separate terms in the expressions for $\mathbf{\Gamma}_i$ can be checked by looking at the figure where each force is resolved into components whose moments involve just simple multiplications.

Equivalent Systems of Forces. It is interesting to apply the reduction theorem (4.21) to general problems concerning systems of forces. Suppose that two systems of forces $\{\mathbf{F}_1, \mathbf{F}_2, \ldots, \mathbf{F}_n\}$ and $\{\mathbf{F}'_1, \mathbf{F}'_2, \ldots, \mathbf{F}'_m\}$ are being compared. Relative to a point **P** the first is equivalent, by (4.21), to $\{\bar{\mathbf{F}},\bar{\mathbf{\Gamma}}\}$ and the second to $\{\bar{\mathbf{F}}',\bar{\mathbf{\Gamma}}'\}$. If $\bar{\mathbf{F}} = \bar{\mathbf{F}}'$ and $\bar{\mathbf{\Gamma}} = \bar{\mathbf{\Gamma}}'$, then the reduced systems $\{\bar{\mathbf{F}},\bar{\mathbf{\Gamma}}\}$ and $\{\bar{\mathbf{F}}',\bar{\mathbf{\Gamma}}'\}$ are equivalent. This is a consequence of Proposition (4.6). It follows at once that the two original systems are equivalent.

(4.23) *If two systems of forces have the same vector sum and the same moment sum about a point, then they are equivalent.*

Now, conversely, suppose that the two original systems were given as equivalent. It then follows that the reduced systems are equivalent and, by Proposition (3.9), $\bar{\mathbf{F}} = \bar{\mathbf{F}}'$. Can we conclude too that $\bar{\Gamma} = \bar{\Gamma}'$? This result, quite valid, is not entirely accessible to us at this stage. It depends on the converse of Proposition (4.6) which, as stated earlier, will be deduced later from Newton's second law. Because of its utility, however, the converse is stated now:

(4.24) *If two systems of forces are equivalent, their vector sums and their moment sums about any point or axis are equal.*

EXERCISES

1. Three forces $2\mathbf{I}$, $3\mathbf{J}$, and $4\mathbf{K}$ act at one corner of a cube along its edges. These forces are equivalent to a couple $\bar{\Gamma}$ and a force $\bar{\mathbf{F}}$ at the diagonally opposite corner of the cube. Find the magnitude and the direction cosines for both $\bar{\Gamma}$ and $\bar{\mathbf{F}}$.

2. The following forces act on a rigid body: $(10\mathbf{K} - 10\mathbf{I})$ at $(1,0,0)$; $(10\mathbf{I} - 10\mathbf{J})$ at $(0,1,0)$; $(10\mathbf{J} - 10\mathbf{K})$ at $(0,0,1)$. Find their resultant.

3. A cube oriented so that its edges are parallel with the coordinate axes has one corner at the origin, as shown in Fig. 4.24. Separate forces of 10, 6, and 8 lb act at

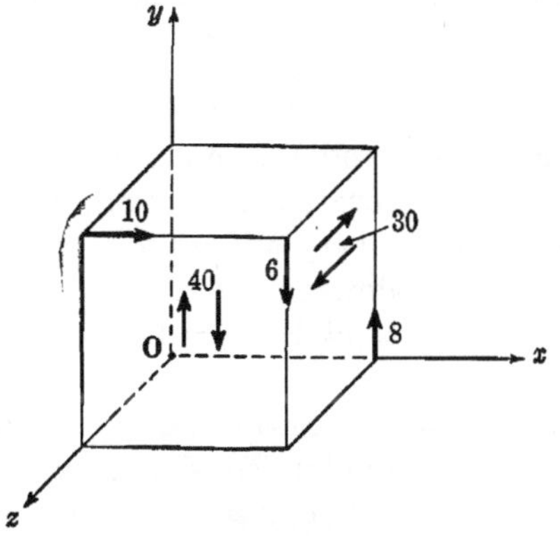

FIG. 4.24.

vertices as shown. Couples of 40 and 30 ft-lb act in the faces toward the reader. If the edges of the cube are 4 ft long, find a couple and force at the origin equivalent to the given forces.

4. In the reduction theorem (4.21) show that for a given set of forces the scalar product $\bar{\mathbf{F}} \cdot \bar{\Gamma}$ is the same for all choices of reference point $\mathbf{P}$.

4.7. Important Special Cases. We have seen that any system of forces can be reduced, for an arbitrary origin $\mathbf{O}$, to a force $\bar{\mathbf{F}}$ *and* a couple $\bar{\Gamma}$. If it happens that the following equation holds

$$\bar{\mathbf{F}} \cdot \bar{\Gamma} = 0 \qquad (4.25)$$

a reduction to a force *or* a couple is always possible. If $\bar{\mathbf{F}}$ is zero, then only the couple is left. If $\bar{\mathbf{\Gamma}}$ is zero, then $\bar{\mathbf{F}}$ alone is the resultant force. If both $\bar{\mathbf{F}}$ and $\bar{\mathbf{\Gamma}}$ are zero, then the system which they represent is equivalent to a null set of forces, and equilibrium reigns. But if neither $\bar{\mathbf{F}}$ nor $\bar{\mathbf{\Gamma}}$ is zero, then it is interesting to point out that the force $\bar{\mathbf{F}}$ at an arbitrary **P** and the couple $\bar{\mathbf{\Gamma}}$ can be replaced by an equivalent single force $\bar{\mathbf{F}}'$ suitably displaced from $\bar{\mathbf{F}}$. This situation is represented in Figs. 4.25

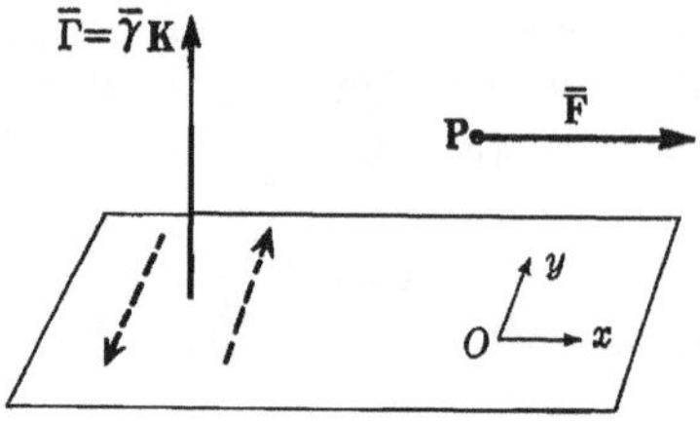

FIG. 4.25.

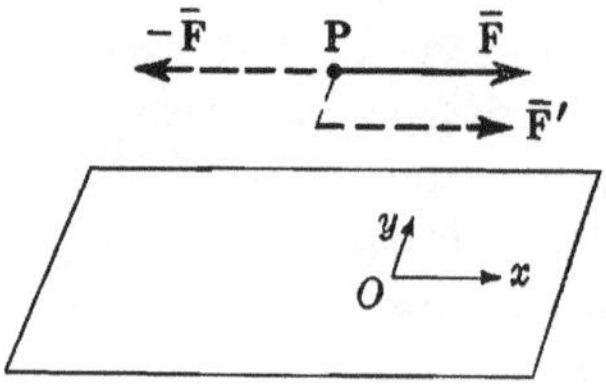

FIG 4.26.

and 4.26. Since the only significant thing about the couple $\bar{\mathbf{\Gamma}}$ is its moment, we may represent it by forces of any size we wish, as long as we take care to preserve the moment magnitude. Let us then represent the couple by two forces $(\bar{\mathbf{F}}', -\bar{\mathbf{F}})$ with $-\bar{\mathbf{F}}$ acting at **P**. The magnitude of the moment will still be equal to $\bar{\gamma}$ if we take care to have the line of action of $\bar{\mathbf{F}}'$ at a distance d from the line of action of $-\bar{\mathbf{F}}$ given by

$$d = \frac{\bar{\gamma}}{\bar{f}}, \tag{4.26}$$

as in Fig. 4.26. Since $-\bar{\mathbf{F}}$ and $\bar{\mathbf{F}}$ annul each other, it is now apparent that our original system of forces is in fact equivalent to the single force $\bar{\mathbf{F}}'$. This maneuver is often very advantageous. One form of this conclusion may be stated as follows:

(4.27) *A set of forces for which* $\bar{\mathbf{F}} \cdot \bar{\mathbf{\Gamma}} = 0$ *always has either a single force or a single couple as a resultant.*

As a first application of Proposition (4.27) suppose that all the forces under consideration lie in the xy plane. Then, if we pick our reference point **P** in this plane, $\bar{\mathbf{\Gamma}}$ is normal to the plane while of course $\bar{\mathbf{F}}$ lies in the plane; thus (4.25) is satisfied. Hence

(4.28) *A set of forces in a plane always has either a single force or a single couple as a resultant.*

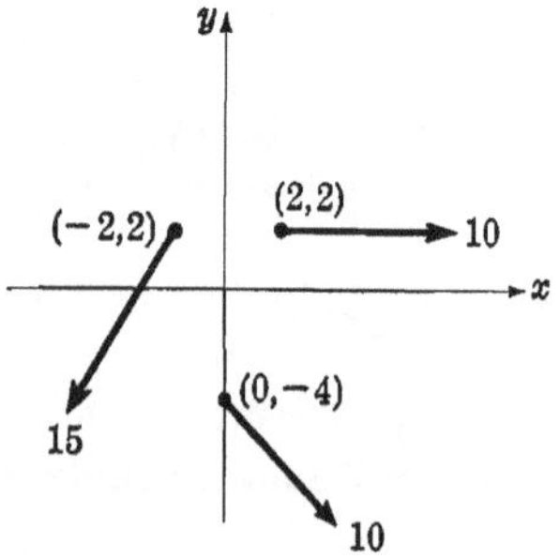

FIG. 4.27.

Example 1. Given three forces as in Fig. 4.27: $10\underline{/0°}$ lb at (2,2) ft; $15\underline{/-120°}$ at (−2,2) ft; $10\underline{/-45°}$ at (0, −4) ft.

a. Find an equivalent force (at the origin) and couple.

b. Reduce to a single force or couple.

SOLUTION. *a.* The single force at the origin is

$$\bar{\mathbf{F}} = (10 - 15 \cos 60° + 10 \cos 45°)\mathbf{I} + (-15 \cos 30° - 10 \cos 45°)\mathbf{J}$$
$$= 9.6\mathbf{I} - 20.1\mathbf{J} = 22.3\underline{/-64.5°} \text{ (lb).}$$

Now take moments about the origin to get the moment of the couple

$$\bar{\Gamma} = (-20 + 15 + 26 + 28.3)\mathbf{K} = 49.3\mathbf{K} \text{ (ft-lb).}$$

b. Now, using the method just outlined, we displace $\bar{\mathbf{F}}$ by an amount

$$d = \frac{49.3}{22.3} = 2.2 \text{ ft,}$$

where, as in Fig. 4.28, it is a suitable resultant for the given system. Note that one point on its line of action is at a distance $d/\cos 64.5° = 5.1$ ft below the origin on the y axis. This same result may be obtained without using Eq. (4.26). We wish to find a line of action for $\bar{\mathbf{F}}$ such that its moment about **O** will be equal to $\bar{\Gamma}$. Let $\mathbf{R} = x\mathbf{I} + y\mathbf{J}$ be any point on this line of action. Then

$$\mathbf{R} \times \bar{\mathbf{F}} = \bar{\Gamma}$$

or

$$(x\mathbf{I} + y\mathbf{J}) \times (9.6\mathbf{I} - 20.1\mathbf{J}) = 49.3\mathbf{K}$$

or, equating coefficients of **K**,

$$20.1x + 9.6y + 49.3 = 0$$

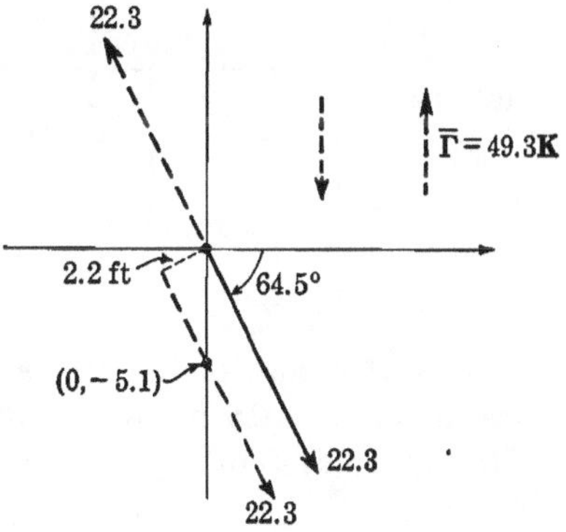

FIG. 4.28.

is an equation of the resultant. When x is set equal to zero, we get

$$y = -\frac{49.3}{9.6} = -5.1 \text{ ft}$$

as before.

A second interesting special case is that of parallel forces not necessarily confined to a plane. Suppose we have a family of forces $f_1\mathbf{J}, f_2\mathbf{J}, \ldots, f_n\mathbf{J}$, all parallel to the y axis. By (4.21) this system is equivalent to a force at the origin

$$\bar{\mathbf{F}} = (\Sigma f_i)\mathbf{J}$$

together with a couple

$$\bar{\Gamma} = \Sigma \mathbf{R}_i \times f_i\mathbf{J} = (\Sigma f_i\mathbf{R}_i) \times \mathbf{J}.$$

This last equality is justified by the laws governing multiplication of scalars and distribution with respect to addition in vector products. Since the vector product of any vector times J is perpendicular to J, it is clear that again we have $\bar{\mathbf{F}} \cdot \bar{\Gamma} = 0$; thus the conclusions of (4.27) are again valid:

(4.29) *A set of parallel forces always has either a single force or a single couple as a resultant.*

Example 2. Find the resultant of the following three parallel forces: 5J at (0,0,2); −4J at (3,0,3); and −8J at (6,0,0), as shown in Fig. 4.29.

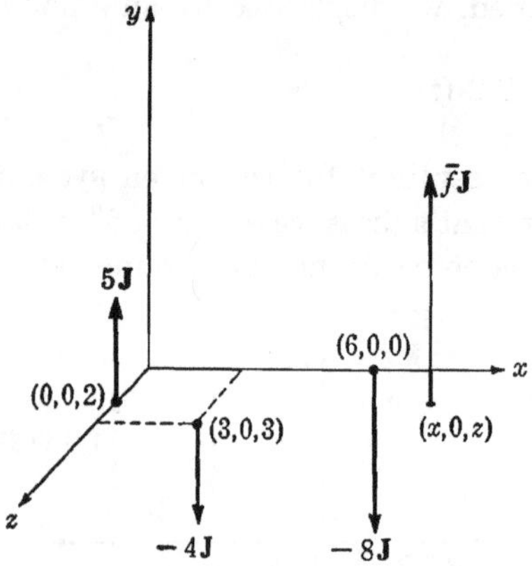

FIG. 4-29.

SOLUTION. The resultant will, by (4.21), be a force equal to the vector sum of the given forces:

$$\bar{\mathbf{F}} = (5 - 4 - 8)\mathbf{J} = -7\mathbf{J}.$$

By (4.22), the moment sum about the x axis and the z axis must be the same for the resultant as for the original system. Taking $(x,0,z)$ as a point on the resultant, we have then

$$\Sigma\gamma_x = -(5)(2) + (4)(3) = -(-7)(z),$$
$$\Sigma\gamma_z = -(4)(3) - (8)(6) = +(-7)(x).$$

Thus the resultant acts at $(\frac{60}{7},0,\frac{2}{7})$. If the vector sum of the forces had been zero, the resultant would have been a couple with moment equal to the moment sum about the origin of the given system.

EXERCISES

1. Equal forces of magnitude f act along the sides of an equilateral triangle as shown in Fig. 4.30. Construct the resultant force or couple

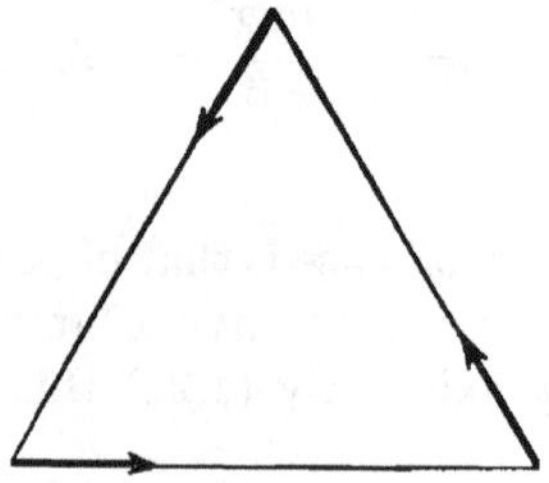

FIG. 4.30.

2. Given in the xy plane: the forces $10\underline{/-45°}$ lb at (0,3) ft, $6\underline{/-135°}$ lb at (5,5) ft, and $8\underline{/180°}$ lb at (0, −5) ft. (*a*) Reduce to a force at (5,5) and a couple. (*b*) Reduce to a single force or couple.

3. Find the resultant of the following forces (units are pounds and feet): $-6\mathbf{I}$ at (0,3,0); $7\mathbf{I}$ at (0,5,0); $5\mathbf{I}$ at (0,7,0); $10\mathbf{I}$ at (0,10,0).

4. Use the methods of this section to verify Eqs. (3.6).

5. Find the resultant of the forces shown in Fig. 4.31.

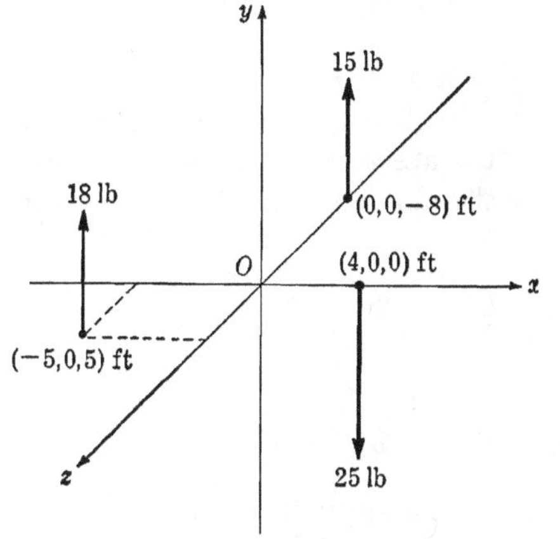

FIG. 4.31.

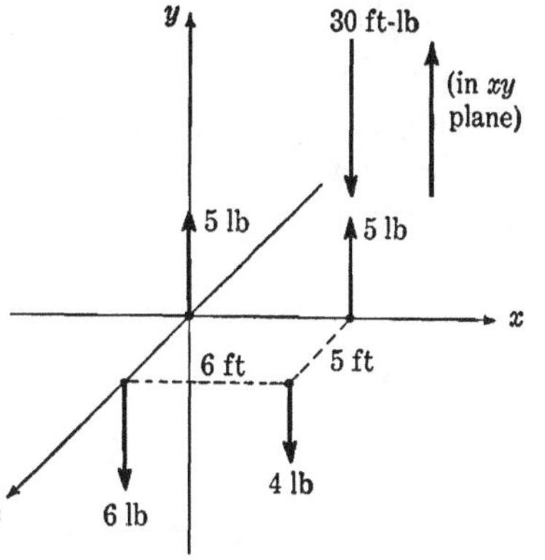

FIG. 4.32.

6. Find the resultant of the forces shown in Fig. 4.32.

7. In our main reduction theorem (4.21) **P** was *any* point. Show that **P** may always be chosen so that $\bar{\mathbf{F}}$ and $\bar{\mathbf{\Gamma}}$ are parallel (Poinsot's theorem). (HINT: Resolve $\bar{\mathbf{\Gamma}}$ into components parallel and perpendicular to $\bar{\mathbf{F}}$.)

4.8. Equilibrium with Nonconcurrent Forces. In Sec. 3.6 we adopted as a postulate the common-sense proposition that a particle or rigid body is in equilibrium if and only if the forces acting on it from the outside are equivalent to no forces. This postulate, based on Newton's treatment of mechanics and substantiated by experiment, has already served us as a means of handling problems concerning the equilibrium of particles. Now that we have discovered that any system of forces is effectively as simple as a system consisting of one force $\bar{\mathbf{F}}$ equal to the vector sum of the forces together with one couple $\bar{\mathbf{\Gamma}}$ equal to the vector sum of the moments of the forces about some point on the line of action of $\bar{\mathbf{F}}$, we can apply this same postulate to problems concerning the equilibrium of a rigid body subjected to forces not necessarily concurrent. All that we need ensure is that both $\bar{\mathbf{F}}$ and $\bar{\mathbf{\Gamma}}$ be zero. Let us state these criteria here.

(4.30) *For a rigid body to be in equilibrium, it is necessary that the vector sum of the forces acting on it be zero.*

(4.31) *For a rigid body to be in equilibrium, it is necessary that the moment about any point or axis of the set of forces acting on it be zero.*

Using Postulate (3.10) and the reduction theorem (4.21), a converse proposition might be stated. Combining these in a single statement, we have

(4.32) *A rigid body is in equilibrium if and only if the vector sum and the moment sum about any one point of the forces acting on it are both zero.*

In equation form, the condition for equilibrium is

(4.33) $$\Sigma \mathbf{F} = \mathbf{O}; \qquad \Sigma \mathbf{\Gamma} = \mathbf{O}.$$

Other special forms are possible. For instance, $\bar{\mathbf{F}}$ is zero if its x, y, and z components are zero [as already noted in (3.16)]. Similarly the vector $\bar{\mathbf{\Gamma}}$ is zero if its corresponding components are zero. We have, however, seen that these components are merely the moments about the axes; thus, along with

(4.34) $$\Sigma f_x = 0, \qquad \Sigma f_y = 0, \qquad \Sigma f_z = 0,$$

we may write

(4.35) $$\Sigma \gamma_x = 0, \qquad \Sigma \gamma_y = 0, \qquad \Sigma \gamma_z = 0.$$

Let us see how these general ideas may be applied to specific types of problems.

Parallel Forces. Suppose that the forces may all be expressed in the form $f\mathbf{J}$. Then it is clearly superfluous to use the conditions involving x and z components of the forces or y components of the moments. We are left then with the equations

(4.36) $$\Sigma f_y = 0, \qquad \Sigma \gamma_x = 0, \qquad \Sigma \gamma_z = 0.$$

The latter two equations are with respect to axes through any desired origin. The only limitation is that these axes be perpendicular to $\mathbf{J}$.

Example 1. A 100-lb uniform plank is supported horizontally at its ends, as shown in Fig. 4.33. A 200-lb load rests at a point one-third of the way from one end. What are the forces required to support the plank?

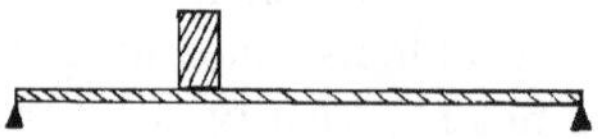

FIG. 4.33.

FIG. 4.34.

SOLUTION. As in problems involving particles, the first step is to isolate something. Suppose that we first isolate the load (see Fig. 4.34). Two forces act on it: its weight $\mathbf{W}$ (200 lb, downward) and the contact reaction $\mathbf{C}$ with the beam. The equilibrium condition $\Sigma\mathbf{F} = \mathbf{O}$ here yields

$$\mathbf{W} + \mathbf{C} = \mathbf{O} \qquad \text{or} \qquad \mathbf{C} = -\mathbf{W}.$$

Hence the contact reaction is 200 lb upward. Now isolate the beam (see Fig. 4.35). By the reaction postulate (3.1), a force equal but opposite to **C**, that is, a force equal to **W**, acts on the plank because of the load. Thus we could have just as well introduced the weight of the load as a force acting on the beam. (This device would be invalid were the beam not in equilibrium.) Another force acting on the beam is gravity. Since the plank is uniform, the weight **W**′ may be thought of as acting at its center. (Some justification for this statement will appear later.) Now consider the reactions at the ends. Let them be resolved into horizontal components **D** and **E** and vertical components **A** and **B**. By the condition $\Sigma f_x = 0$ we get $d - e = 0$, or $d = e$. Nothing further may be said. **D** and **E** might be pushes or pulls of any magnitude whatever. Since nothing in the statement of the problem suggested that the beam was under compression or tension, we shall assume that **D** = **E** = **O**.

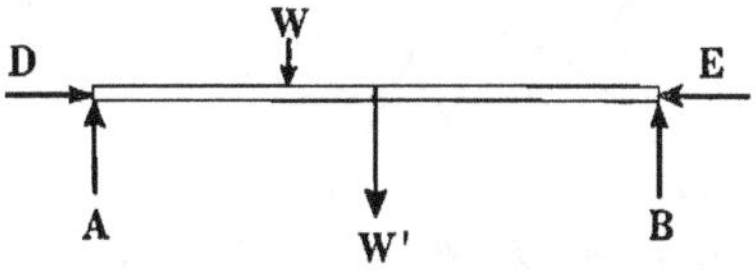

FIG. 4.35.

Then using $\Sigma f_y = 0$, we may write (referring to Fig. 4.36)

$$a - w - w' + b = 0.$$

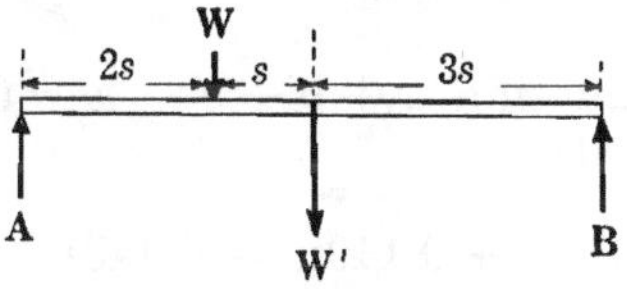

FIG. 4.36.

From this and the data of the problem we infer that

$$a + b = 300 \text{ lb}.$$

Let us now choose our z axis as perpendicular to the figure and outward through the left end of the plank. Using the condition $\Sigma\gamma_z = 0$ and denoting the length of the beam by $6s$, we get

$$(0)(a) - (2s)(w) - (3s)(w') + (6s)(b) = 0.$$

From this we conclude that $b = 116.7$ lb; so that $a = 183.3$ lb. Our choice of a z axis was arbitrary: we could just as well have chosen a parallel one through the center, other end, or even a random point of the plank. As the student gets practice in solving statics problems, he will develop facility in choosing suitable axes or points of reference. A useful check on numerical work may be obtained by substituting values in such an alternative equation. Here, for example, let us take moments about the center of the plank:

$$-(3s)(183.3) + (s)(200) + (3s)(116.7) = 0.$$

This equation is valid within the limits of accuracy of the data and of slide-rule computation.

Example 2. The position of a load **W** on a symmetrical three-legged table is shown in Fig. 4.37. Find the corresponding vertical forces transmitted by the legs.

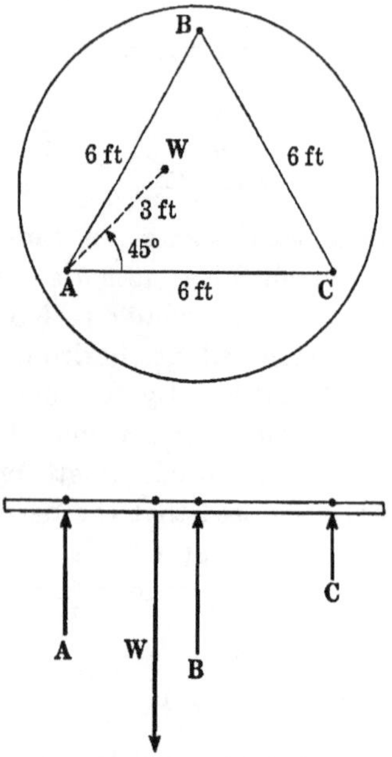

FIG. 4.37.

SOLUTION. Isolate the table. Apply the condition $\Sigma\mathbf{F} = \mathbf{O}$:

$$\mathbf{A} + \mathbf{B} + \mathbf{C} + \mathbf{W} = \mathbf{O}.$$

Apply the condition $\Sigma\gamma = 0$, taking moments about the axis **AC** in the figure,

$$-3w \sin 45° + 6b \sin 60° = 0;$$

so

$$b = 0.408w.$$

Now take moments about axis **AB**:

$$3w \sin 15° - 6c \sin 60° = 0;$$

so

$$c = 0.149w.$$

Using the first equation, $a + b + c - w = 0$, a can be found also:

$$a = w - 0.408w - 0.149w = 0.443w.$$

A check might be obtained by taking moments about **BC**.

EXERCISES

1. A rectangular table 5 ft by 3 ft has legs at each corner. It weighs 60 lb. Where is a 50-lb load placed if the loads on the legs are, respectively (reading cyclically around the table), 20, 25, 30, 35 lb?

2. A shelf 1 ft by 8 ft weighs 10 lb. It is held in horizontal position by two hinges at the ends of one long edge and by a vertical cord at one of the other corners. If a 20-lb load is hung on the fourth corner, find the tension in the cord.

3. A cubical block of edge d is subjected to forces **A, B,** and **C** as shown in Fig. 4.38. The block is also subject to two couples whose moments are normal to the faces on which they are indicated in the figure. If γ and γ' are known, find a, b, and c for equilibrium.

4. Prove that two nonparallel pairs of parallel forces in equilibrium are two couples if not all concurrent.

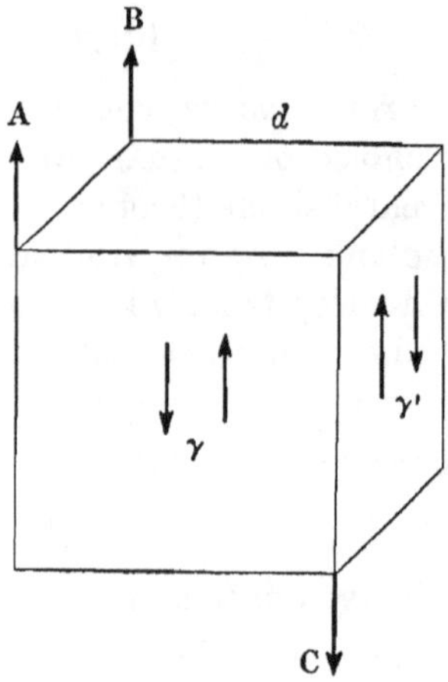

FIG. 4.38.

4.9. Equilibrium with Plane Forces. Time and time again it will be found that the forces acting on a body may be considered as lying in a single plane. For convenience, take this as the xy plane. Then each force may be expressed in the form $f_x\mathbf{I} + f_y\mathbf{J}$. For such forces the sums Σf_z, $\Sigma\gamma_x$, $\Sigma\gamma_y$ are clearly of no interest. The useful conditions of equilibrium are then

$$(4.37) \qquad \Sigma f_x = 0, \qquad \Sigma f_y = 0, \qquad \Sigma\gamma_z = 0.$$

Example 1. A metal spool consists of two disks of radius 15 in., joined by an axle of radius 9 in. The total weight is 36.8 lb. It rests on a ramp inclined at 30° to the horizontal and is held in place by a rope wrapped around the axle, coming off its upper side, and directed 20° above the ramp. If the spool is held in equilibrium, find the tension in the rope and the frictional force between spool and plane.

SOLUTION. Figure 4.39 represents the isolated spool and the forces acting on it. It is assumed that the forces are located symmetrically; so the reactions between the two disks and the ramp are replaced by single resultant forces **N** and **F** in the normal plane through the center of the spool. Resolve **T**, the tension in the rope, into components parallel and perpendicular to the ramp, and then take moments about the line of contact between spool and plane:

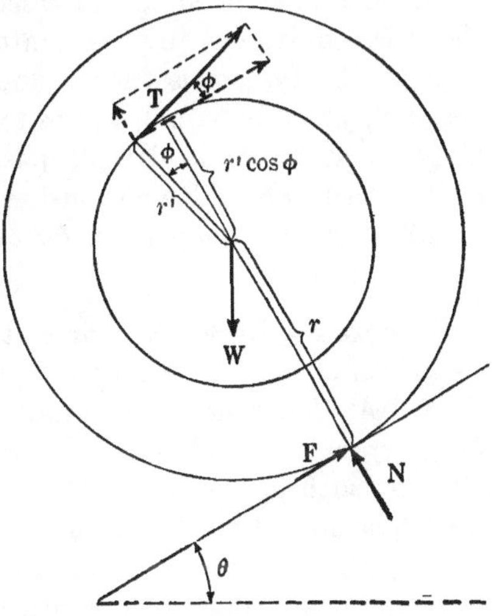

FIG. 4.39.

$$\Sigma\gamma = 0,$$

or

$$-t \cos \phi(r + r' \cos \phi) - t \sin \phi(r' \sin \phi) + w \sin \theta\, r = 0,$$

or

$$t = w \frac{r \sin \theta}{r \cos \phi + r'} = 36.8 \frac{15 \times 0.50}{14.1 + 9} = 11.9 \text{ lb.}$$

Now let us take moments about the axis of the spool, again setting the sum of these moments equal to zero,

$$-tr' + fr = 0,$$

or

$$f = t\frac{r'}{r} = 11.9 \times \frac{9}{15} = 7.2 \text{ lb.}$$

As a check let us compute the sum of the components parallel to the ramp:

$$t \cos \phi - w \sin \theta + f \overset{?}{=} 0,$$

or

$$11.9 \times 0.94 - 36.8 \times 0.50 + 7.2 \doteq 11.2 - 18.4 + 7.2 = 0.$$

Thus a check is obtained.

Three-force Problems. The two-force problem for rigid bodies was presented in Sec. 3.8. For particles, the three-force case was considered in Sec. 3.7. Suppose now that a rigid body is in equilibrium under three forces $\mathbf{F}, \mathbf{F}', \mathbf{F}''$ at points $\mathbf{P}, \mathbf{P}', \mathbf{P}''$. The points $\mathbf{P}$, $\mathbf{P}'$, and $\mathbf{P}''$ form a triangle which determines a plane of normal, say $\mathbf{N}$. If the points happened to lie on a line, one of the forces could be slid to a new point off the line except for the uninteresting case where the forces all lie along the line. In order that equilibrium obtain, the moment of $\mathbf{F}''$ about $\mathbf{PP}'$ is zero. Hence $\mathbf{F}''$ is either parallel to $\mathbf{PP}'$ or intersects it. In either case it lies in the plane of the triangle. Similarly for $\mathbf{F}'$ and $\mathbf{F}''$; therefore we infer that $\mathbf{F}$, $\mathbf{F}'$, and $\mathbf{F}''$ are *coplanar.* If they are not all parallel, two of them have lines of action intersecting at a point in the plane and are therefore equivalent [by Postulate (3.3)] to a single force through that point. The system is then reduced to two forces which, as shown in Sec. 3.8, must be equal, opposite, and with a common line of action. Consequently the third force passes through the point of intersection of the other two. The conclusion is:

(4.38) *If three nonparallel forces are in equilibrium, they are coplanar and concurrent.*

Example 2. In Sec. 3.8 some attention was given to simple structures composed of light rigid members subject only to compressions and tensions. At that stage of our study it was convenient to have all external forces specified in advance. Now we can do a more thorough piece of work on such problems, for the method of moments allows us to isolate the whole structure and to find relations between external forces.

Consider the simple truss shown in Fig. 4.40. The left ground attachment is rigid. The right contact is on rollers in order that thermal

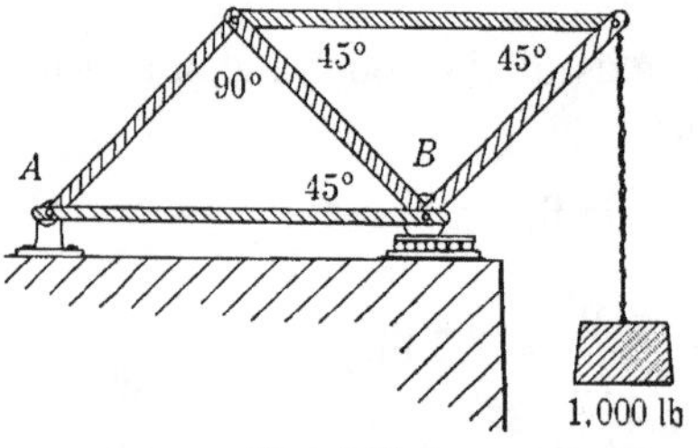

FIG. 4.40.

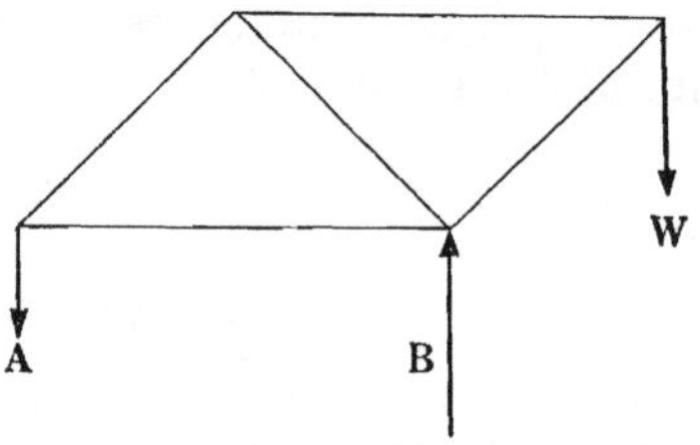

FIG. 4.41.

stresses may be minimized. First isolate the whole frame, as in Fig. 4.41. Taking moments about $\mathbf{B}$, it is clear that $\mathbf{A}$ has magnitude 500 lb, whence

B has magnitude 1,500 lb. The forces in the beams may now be determined by isolating the hinge pins in successive joints as in previous examples. This is left for the student (see Exercise 15).

EXERCISES

1. A packing box uniformly loaded is 6 ft high and 4 ft square (see Fig. 4.42). It weighs 200 lb. If the box rests on a horizontal floor against a cleat which prevents its sliding, what is the maximum perpendicular force **P** along the upper face which the box can sustain without tipping? What force must the cleat provide in this case?

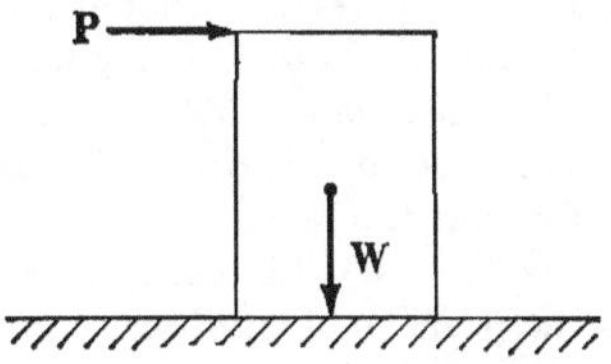

FIG. 4.42.

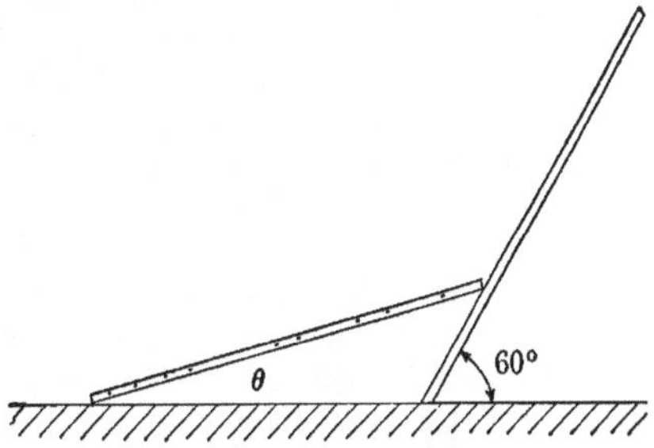

FIG. 4.43.

2. A uniform ladder rests in equilibrium with one end on the horizontal ground (coefficient of friction is 0.5) and the other end against a boarded surface (coefficient of friction is 0.3) inclined at 60° with the horizontal, as in Fig. 4.43. What is the minimum angle θ which the ladder may make, without slipping, with the ground?

3. A flat uniform board of weight w has the shape of a rectangle twice as long as it is wide. It is hung on a horizontal nail by means of a light screw eye at one corner. What must be the weight of an object hung on an adjacent corner to make the rectangle's edges inclined at 45°?

4. Each of a pair of braces for staging consists of two metal bars, one 2 ft long, the other 1.5 ft long, with a hinged joint between them. It is used, as in Fig. 4.44, on a ladder with rungs 15 in. apart. The end of the long bar has a hook to go over one round, the other bar ends in a U-shaped piece which fits over the second rung below. The load, say the weight of a 180-lb man, is supported by a bar attached to the hinges of the two braces. Find the reaction at each rung when the ladder makes an angle of 70° with the horizontal.

5. Find the tension **P** in the tie rod of the cantilever jack shown in Fig. 4.45 when the angle θ is 60° and the load is 3,000 lb.

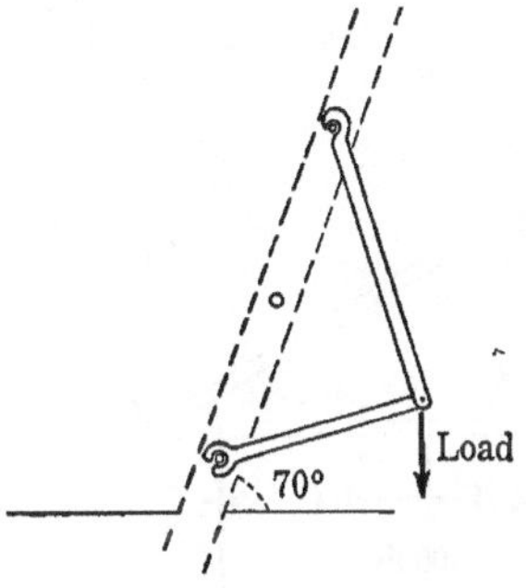

FIG. 4.44.

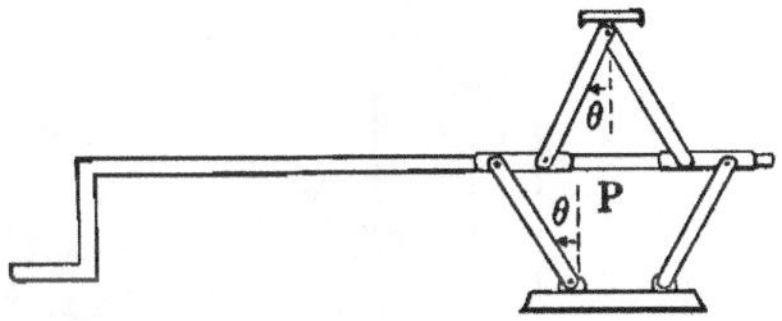

FIG. 4.45.

6. A 3-by-7 ft door weighing 80 lb is supported by two hinges 6 in. from top and bottom. (*a*) Neglecting friction, discuss the possible range of hinge reactions both in direction and magnitude. (b) Describe the locus of the points of intersection of the possible pairs of hinge forces.

7. Referring to Fig. 4.46, the lever is 17 in. long and weighs 0.5 lb. It is smoothly pivoted at a point 4 in. from one end. At B, 12 in. from the pivot, is attached a cord sustaining a tension of 1 lb. The lever is held at an angle of 45° with the horizontal by a peg A 3 in. from the pivot. What force does the peg A withstand?

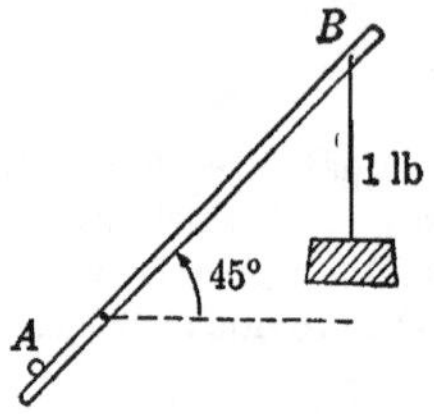

FIG. 4.46.

8. A uniform ladder 13 ft long weighing 20 lb rests against a smooth vertical wall 12 ft above a smooth horizontal floor. It is kept from slipping along the floor by means of a string running from the middle of the ladder horizontally to a hook on the wall. A 180-lb man climbs the ladder very cautiously but nevertheless the string breaks just as he reaches the half-way rung. What is the breaking strength of the string?

9. A 100-lb uniform beam is hinged at the lower end to a vertical wall at an angle of 45°. A 5-ft rope goes from the upper end of the beam to a point 3 ft higher on the wall (*i.e.*, higher than the upper end of the beam). When a load of 500 lb is attached to the upper end of the beam, (a) what is the tension in the rope and (b) what are the horizontal and vertical components of the reaction force at the hinge?

10. Two small weights, w and $2w$, connected by a light flexible cord of length r, are hung over a smooth cylinder of radius r. Find the position of equilibrium. (Find the angle θ which the radius to the smaller weight makes with the vertical.)

11. Two smooth cylinders each of weight 100 lb and radius 6 in. are connected at their centers by two cords of length 16 in., as in Fig. 4.47. They rest on a smooth horizontal plane and support a third cylinder of weight 200 lb and radius 6 in. What is the tension in each of the cords?

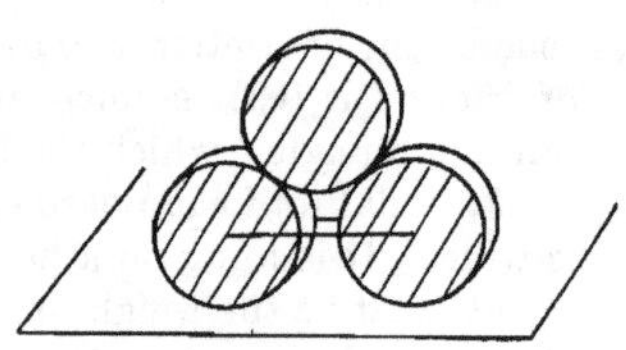

FIG. 4.47.

12. The top of a uniform 20-ft ladder weighing 50 lb rests against a smooth vertical wall at a point 16 ft from the floor. The ladder is kept from slipping by a string tied to its base and to a point on the wall 5 ft from the floor. The coefficient of friction between floor and ladder is 0.1. The string will break under a tension of 52 lb. How far may a 200-lb man ascend the ladder with safety?

13. The pulleys shown in Fig. 4.48 are frictionless and the cords are perfectly flexible and without weight. Each pulley weighs 10 lb and the load is 70 lb. How large a weight x will hold the system in equilibrium?

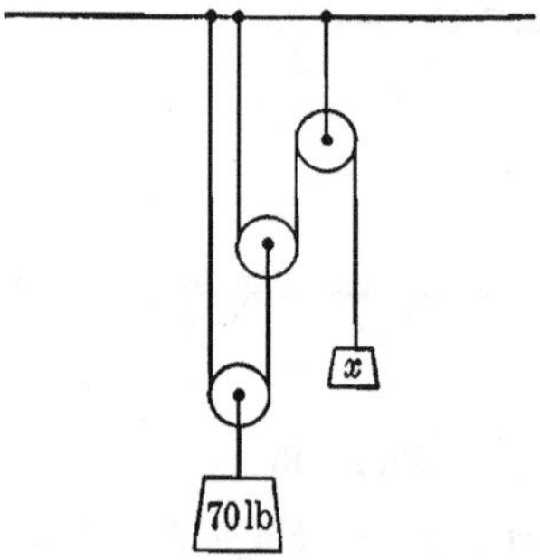

FIG. 4.48.

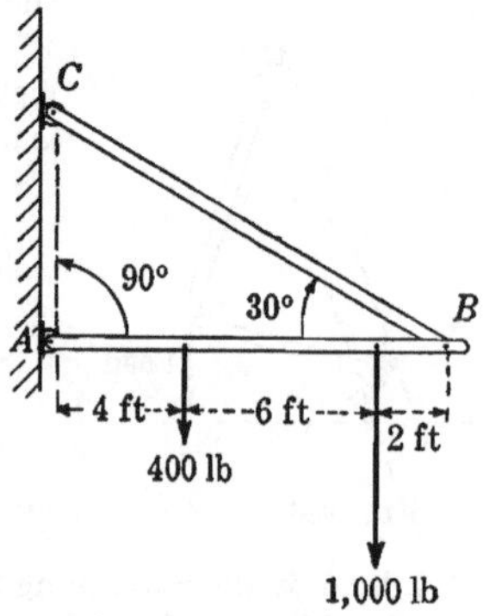

FIG. 4.49.

14. The joints of the wall bracket shown in Fig. 4.49 are smooth pins. The weights of the rods may be neglected. Find (*a*) the tension in *CB*; (*b*) the magnitude and direction of the force exerted on beam *AB* by the pin at *A*.

15. Find the forces in each of the five members of the truss described in Example 2, page 88.

16. A 6-ft square bench is supported horizontally at three corners by legs and at the fourth by a vertical rope tied to the ceiling. When a man weighing 200 lb sits on the edge of the bench 2 ft from the rope, what additional forces are sustained by the rope and each of the legs?

17. A steel hoop 4 ft in diameter and weighing 20 lb is hung as shown in Fig. 4.50 on two small smooth pegs 3 ft apart and determining a vertical line. What force is exerted on each peg?

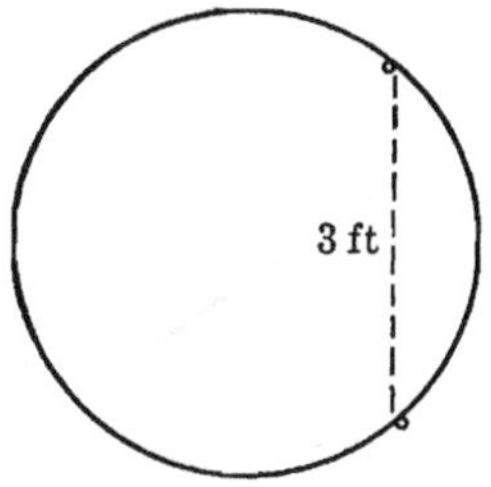

FIG. 4.50.

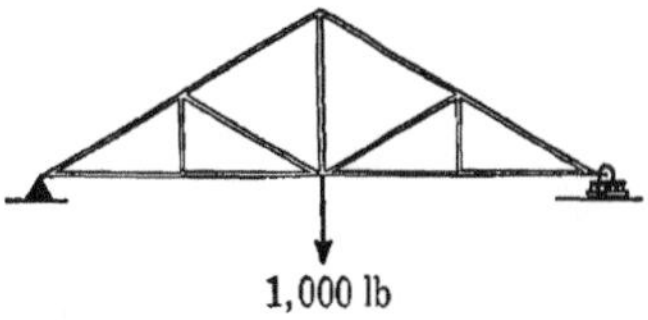

FIG. 4.51.

18. Find the force in each member of the truss shown in Fig. 4.51. Neglect weights of the beams. Each acute angle is either 30° or 60°.

19. One end of an 800-lb sign 4 ft long is hinged to a post. On the post 3 ft above the sign and at right angles to it is a horizontal bar. The other end of the sign is attached by light chains running to the ends of the bar. These chains make angles of 25° and 50°, respectively, with the plane of the sign and post as shown in Fig. 4.52. Find the tensions in the chains and the force sustained by the hinge.

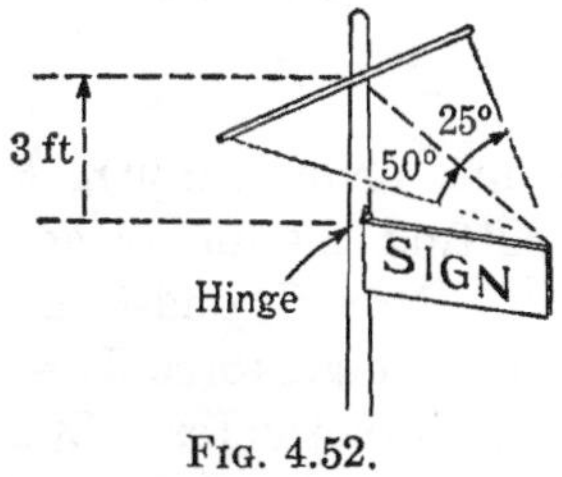

FIG. 4.52.

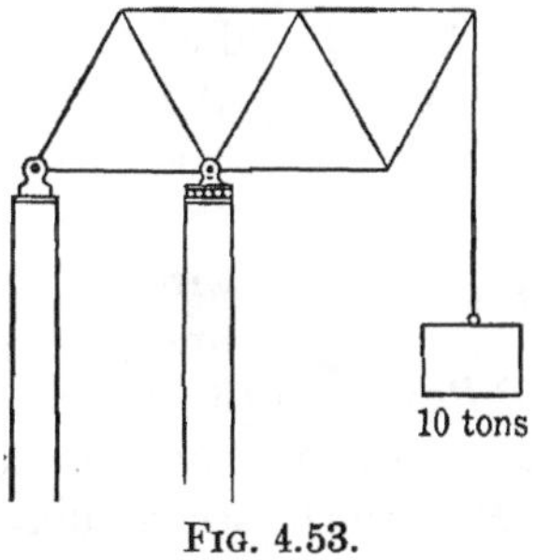

FIG. 4.53.

20. Find the forces sustained by each of the members of the truss in Fig. 4.53. Assume that the joints consist of simple frictionless pins and that the weights of the beams are to be neglected. The triangles are all equilateral.

4.10. Funicular Polygons. In this section a further graphic method for dealing with forces will be presented briefly. In Sec. 3.5 the resultant of two parallel forces was found graphically by introducing equal and opposite forces **C** and $-$**C**. This method will now be extended. Suppose that we have given, say, three forces $\mathbf{F}_1$, $\mathbf{F}_2$, $\mathbf{F}_3$, not necessarily parallel, as shown in Fig. 4.54. It is desired to find the resultant $\bar{\mathbf{F}}$. The magni-

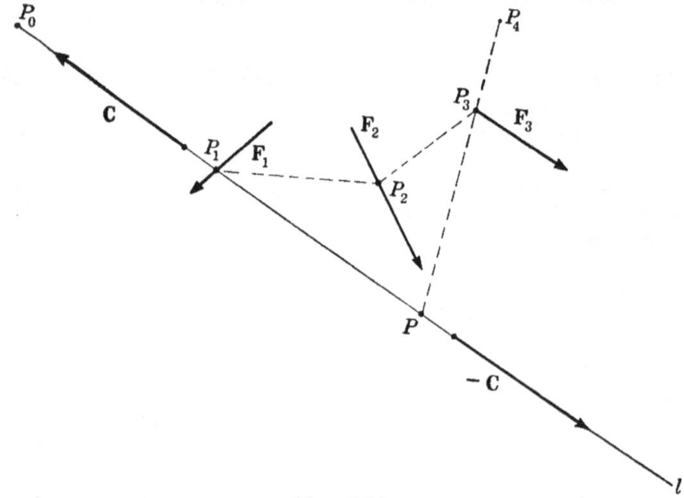

FIG. 4.54.

tude and direction of $\bar{\mathbf{F}}$ are easily found just by forming the vector sum $\bar{\mathbf{F}} = \mathbf{F}_1 + \mathbf{F}_2 + \mathbf{F}_3$, as graphed in Fig. 4.55. It remains to determine the line of action of the resultant. To do this, we draw a line l in any convenient direction cutting the line of action of $\mathbf{F}_1$ at P_1. Along this line introduce equal but opposite forces $\mathbf{C}$ and $-\mathbf{C}$. To see how $\mathbf{C}$ combines with $\mathbf{F}_1$, draw a copy of $\mathbf{C}$ in Fig. 4.55, as shown. Since $\mathbf{C}$ and $\mathbf{F}_1$ are concurrent at P_1, they are equivalent to a single force

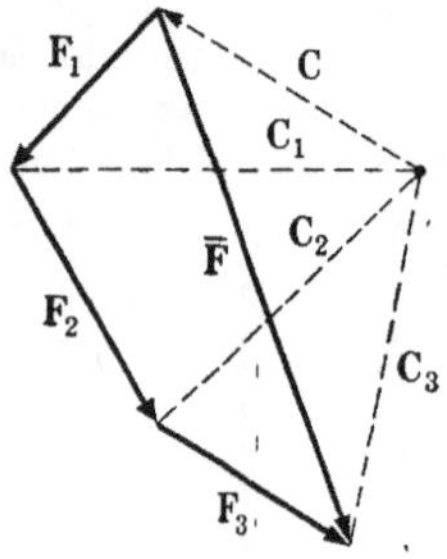

FIG. 4.55.

$$\mathbf{C} + \mathbf{F}_1 = \mathbf{C}_1$$

through the same point. Now through P_1 draw a line parallel to $\mathbf{C}_1$ cutting the line of action of $\mathbf{F}_2$ at P_2. P_2P_1 is then the line of action of $\mathbf{C}_1$. Now $\mathbf{C}_1$ and $\mathbf{F}_2$ are concurrent at P_2; therefore they are equivalent to a single force $\mathbf{C}_2 = \mathbf{C}_1 + \mathbf{F}_2$ through P_2. In the second diagram we now draw the force $\mathbf{C}_2$ as shown. Now through P_2 we can draw the line of action of $\mathbf{C}_2$ parallel to $\mathbf{C}_2$ in the auxiliary diagram and cutting the line of $\mathbf{F}_3$ at P_3. Since $\mathbf{F}_3$ and $\mathbf{C}_2$ are concurrent, their resultant is a single force $\mathbf{C}_3 = \mathbf{C}_2 + \mathbf{F}_3$ through P_3. Through P_3 we finally draw a line of action for $\mathbf{C}_3$ (parallel to $\mathbf{C}_3$ in the auxiliary diagram) cutting l at P.

We have so far shown that the original set of forces together with $\mathbf{C}$ and $-\mathbf{C}$ are equivalent to the single force $\mathbf{C}_3$ acting along P_3P together with $-\mathbf{C}$ acting along l. These two forces are concurrent at P; therefore they are equivalent to a single force $\mathbf{C}_3 - \mathbf{C}$ through P. But from the auxiliary diagram it is apparent that the following vector equation holds:

$$\mathbf{C}_3 - \mathbf{C} = \bar{\mathbf{F}}.$$

Therefore the original system is equivalent to $\bar{\mathbf{F}}$ acting at P. To complete the graphical solution, we need merely draw a vector $\bar{\mathbf{F}}$ through P. This construction could have been carried out similarly for any number of forces. Special cases will be assigned as exercises.

The polygon $P_0P_1P_2P_3P_4$ is called a *funicular polygon* or *string polygon* for the set of forces. (P_0 is a point on l and P_4 a point on PP_3 selected suitably as in Fig. 4.54.) It is so named because a light string $P_0P_1P_2P_3P_4$ fastened at P_0 and P_4 would be in equilibrium under applied forces $\mathbf{F}_1$, $\mathbf{F}_2$, $\mathbf{F}_3$.

Example 1. A rigid horizontal structure supported at the ends is subjected to vertical forces of 2 and 3 tons as shown in Fig. 4.56. Find the resultant of the five forces shown.

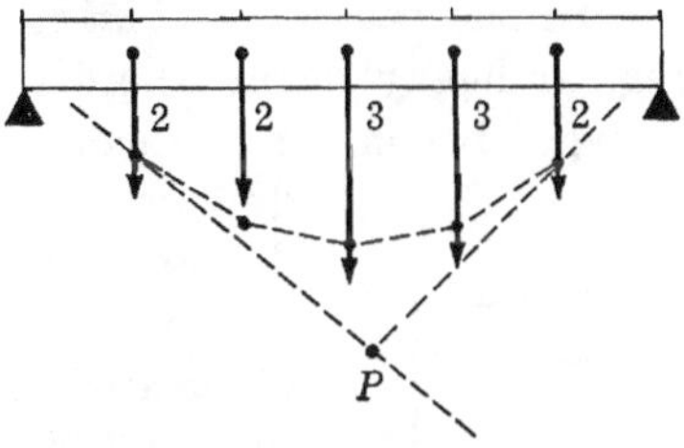

FIG. 4.56.

SOLUTION. The auxiliary vector diagram is sketched in Fig. 4.57. The construction of a point P on the 12-ton resultant is shown in Fig. 4.56.

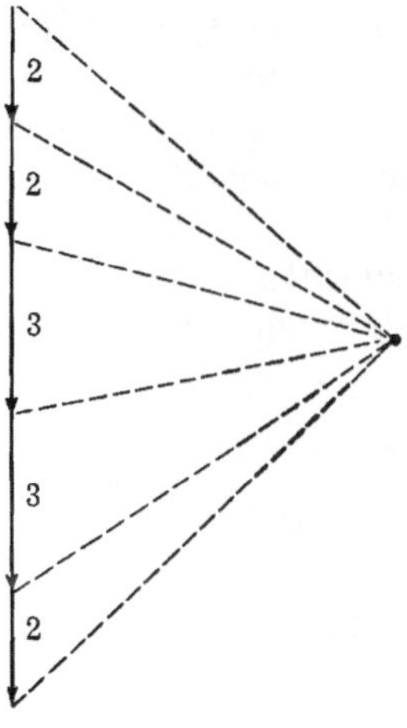

FIG. 4.57.

Example 2. The ends of a string are pegged firmly at A and B. Subject to two parallel forces **F** and **F′** making an angle of 60° with AB the string assumes the shape of Fig. 4.58. Find the ratio of the magnitudes of **F** and **F′**.

SOLUTION. The string itself is the funicular polygon for the forces **F** and **F′**; therefore let us draw the associated auxiliary polygon by constructing concentric lines parallel to the string segments, as in Fig. 4.59. Now draw a line at 60° with the middle ray. In this figure PR represents **F** and RS represents **F′**. The ratio may be determined by direct measurement in the figure.

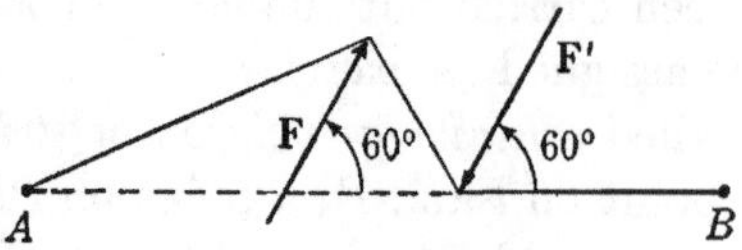

FIG. 4.58.

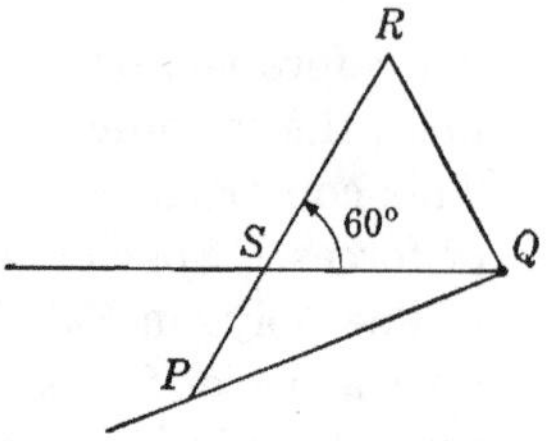

FIG. 4.59.

Continuous Loads. In the case of a continuous or distributed load, for example, an irregular heavy beam where the weight is part of the load, the funicular polygon becomes a *funicular curve*. Considering only downward parallel forces, let $q(x)$ denote force per length at a point where the coordinate is x. This is illustrated in Fig. 4.60. At x a short segment Δx is subject to a downward force Δf. Thus

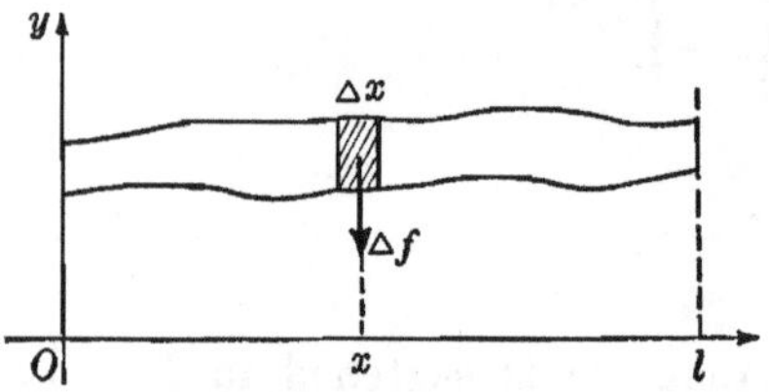

FIG. 4.60.

$$\Delta f = q(x)\Delta x. \tag{4.39}$$

Now, to find the funicular curve, we may ask: What shape would a flexible string assume if it were subject to such a load? The answer is not unique, for different horizontal tensions are possible with the same vertical load; but we can find conditions which must be satisfied. Let Fig. 4.61 represent a segment Δx of such a string. Since it is in equilibrium, we may write

$$(t + \Delta t) \sin (\theta + \Delta\theta) - t \sin \theta = q(x)\Delta x$$

or

$$\Delta(t \sin \theta) = q(x)\Delta x$$

and

$$(t + \Delta t) \cos (\theta + \Delta\theta) = t \cos \theta = h,$$

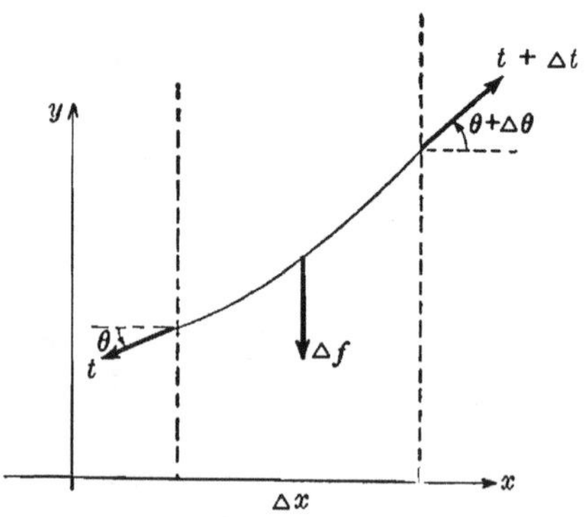

FIG. 4.61.

where h is the uniform horizontal component of the tension. Dividing the second equation by the last two members of the preceding, we get

$$\Delta(\tan\theta) = \frac{1}{h}\, q(x)\Delta x.$$

Replacing $\tan\theta$ by dy/dx, dividing by Δx and taking the limit as Δx becomes small, we arrive at

$$\frac{d^2y}{dx^2} = \frac{1}{h}\, q(x). \tag{4.40}$$

If there is a point of zero slope on the string, it makes a convenient origin. Then (4.40), integrated, yields

$$\frac{dy}{dx} = \frac{1}{h}\int_0^x q(x)dx. \tag{4.41}$$

In the case of a suspension bridge, the load of the roadbed may be much in excess of that of the cables themselves. In that case $q(x)$ is a constant q. Then

$$\frac{dy}{dx} = \frac{q}{h}\, x$$

and for the choice of axes suggested above

$$y = \frac{q}{2h}\, x^2,$$

which is a *parabola*.

The curve for a cable having no load in addition to its own weight is called a *catenary* and has the shape of a hyperbolic cosine curve.

EXERCISES

1. Draw three concurrent forces and verify by a funicular polygon that the resultant passes through the common point.

2. Use the funicular polygon to find the resultant of three parallel forces, equally spaced, having magnitudes 10, −20, 30.

3. A string $ABCDE$ carries at B, C, and D, respectively, loads of 1, 2, and 3 lb. A and E are made fast. AB is inclined at 45°, while CD is horizontal. Find the tensions in each segment and the inclinations of BC and DE.

4. Three forces act along the sides of a triangle. They are proportional to the corresponding sides and are all directed so as to produce counterclockwise rotation. Carry out a funicular polygon construction and draw what conclusions you can.

4.11. Shearing Force and Bending Moment. In dealing with solid bodies we have paid little attention to internal forces. Yet it is quite possible to isolate a portion of a body and thus bring to light the forces acting across the boundary between the isolated portion and the rest of the body. This approach will be used in the present section. It affords an interesting application of the principles of statics and at the same time gives us concepts for use in a later chapter.

This new point of view will be applied here to a very special class of problems. We shall consider the internal forces of beams. Suppose that a beam is in equilibrium subject to various external forces, such as gravity, pier reactions, and weight of loads. We shall assume that all the external forces act in the vertical plane through the beam's axis. As a boundary imagine a plane normal to the beam. The position of this plane section can be specified by giving the coordinate x of the corresponding point on an axis parallel to the beam, as in Fig. 4.62. If we isolate the portion, say to the left of the boundary, we may ask what is the resultant of the system of forces by which the right portion acts on the left portion. Such a system can always be reduced to a force $\mathbf{F}_s$ and a couple $\mathbf{\Gamma}_b$. For the cases which we are considering, $\mathbf{F}_s$ is normal to the beam and its magnitude f_s is called the *shearing force*. The magnitude of

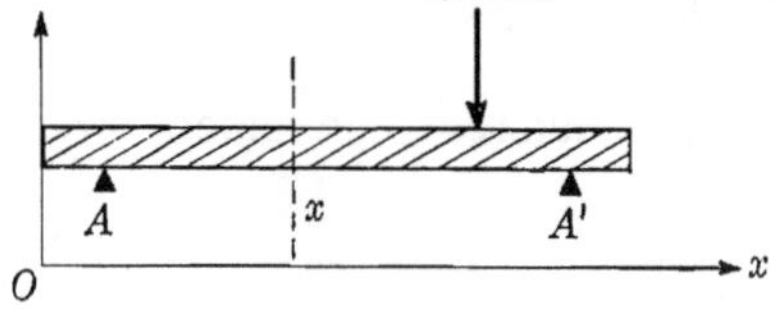

FIG. 4.62.

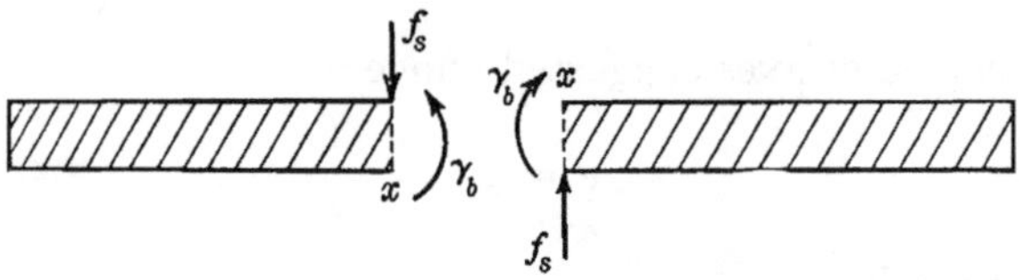

FIG. 4.63.

$\mathbf{\Gamma}_b$, γ_b, is called the *bending moment.* Figure 4.63 shows the directions which will be treated as positive for either a left or a right end isolation. Note that these are the actual directions to be expected for a small left-hand portion of a simple unloaded beam supported at its ends.

Example 1. A light uniform beam 10 ft long is held in horizontal position by simple supports (such as knife-edges) 1 ft from either end as in Fig. 4.62. It sustains a load of 1,000 lb 3 ft from one end. Find the shearing force and bending moment at the center.

SOLUTION. First we isolate the whole beam to find the forces of support at A and A'. Taking moments about A, we have

$$8a' - 6(1{,}000) = 0;$$

so

$$a' = 750 \text{ lb}, \qquad a = 250 \text{ lb}.$$

Now isolate the left half of the beam. We have for equations of equilibrium (taking moments about an axis in the plane of section in order to leave f_s out of the equation)

$$\Sigma f_v = 0: \qquad 250 - f_s = 0, \qquad f_s = 250 \text{ lb.}$$
$$\Sigma \gamma = 0: \qquad -(4)(250) + \gamma_b = 0, \qquad \gamma_b = 1{,}000 \text{ ft-lb.}$$

ALTERNATIVE SOLUTION. Let us now isolate the right half of the beam. Again we shall take moments about an axis in the plane of section.

$$f_s + 750 - 1{,}000 = 0, \qquad f_s = 250 \text{ lb,}$$
$$-\gamma_b - (2)(1{,}000) + (4)(750) = 0, \qquad \gamma_b = 1{,}000 \text{ ft-lb.}$$

The two approaches give the same answers of course. Ordinarily one should isolate the portion giving the simpler equations of equilibrium.

Example 2. Find equations for shearing force and bending moment of a uniform slender beam of mass m and length l which has simple knife-edge supports at the ends.

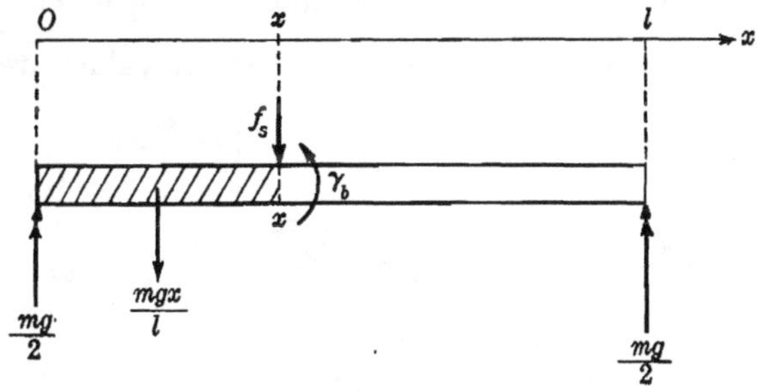

FIG. 4.64.

SOLUTION. Letting a positive x axis run along the beam as in Fig. 4.64, the possible plane sections may be described by values of x from 0 to l. Isolate the portion from 0 to x. The weight of this portion is $mg(x/l)$ acting at the middle where the coordinate is $x/2$. Each support carries half the load. The force equation of equilibrium is

$$\frac{mg}{2} - \frac{mgx}{l} - f_s = 0, \qquad f_s = \frac{mg}{2}\left(1 - \frac{2x}{l}\right).$$

The moment equation, taking moments about the right end of the isolated portion, is

$$-\frac{mg}{2}x + \frac{mgx}{l}\left(\frac{x}{2}\right) + \gamma_b = 0, \qquad \gamma_b = \frac{mgx}{2}\left(1 - \frac{x}{l}\right).$$

Graphically these results appear as in Fig. 4.65.

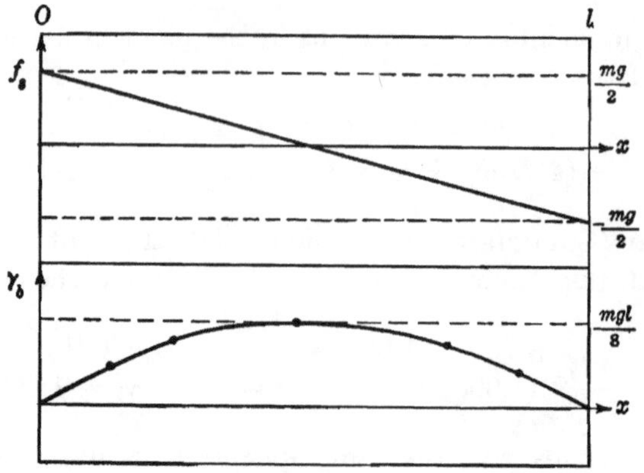

FIG. 4.65.

Interrelationships. Suppose that the weight per length (linear weight density) of a beam is $q(x)$ at the point x. Let us isolate a section of the beam carrying no additional load. Let the section extend from $x - \Delta x$ to $x + \Delta x$. For x, the shearing force and bending moment are f_s and γ_b. For the ends of this section, the approximate values are $f_s \pm \frac{df_s}{dx} \Delta x$

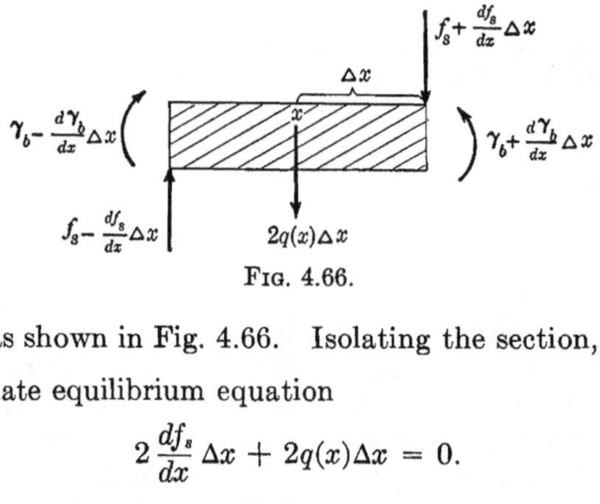

FIG. 4.66.

$\gamma_b \pm \frac{d\gamma_b}{dx} \Delta x$, as shown in Fig. 4.66. Isolating the section, we have for a first approximate equilibrium equation

$$2\frac{df_s}{dx}\Delta x + 2q(x)\Delta x = 0.$$

Dividing by Δx and taking the limit as Δx approaches zero (so that our approximate equation gets more and more exact), we get

$$\frac{df_s}{dx} = -q(x). \tag{4.42}$$

This may be checked with Fig. 4.65 where $q(x)$ is a constant and the slope is $-(mg/l)$, as predicted by the equation.

For a moment equation, taking moments around the center,

$$2\frac{d\gamma_b}{dx}\Delta x - 2f_s\Delta x = 0.$$

Dividing by Δx and taking limits as Δx approaches zero,

$$\frac{d\gamma_b}{dx} = f_s. \tag{4.43}$$

This too may be checked with Fig. 4.65.

These two results are valid except at points where concentrated loads appear. For such points, the shearing force changes instantaneously by an amount equal to the load, and the bending moment has a corresponding discontinuity in slope.

Example 3. A uniform slender beam of mass m and length l is supported as shown in Fig. 4.67. A load of $2mg$ is applied at the right end. Investigate the shearing force and bending moment.

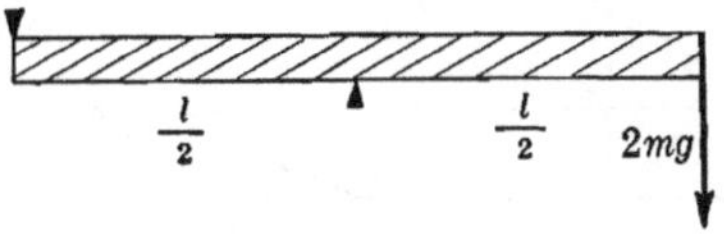

FIG. 4.67.

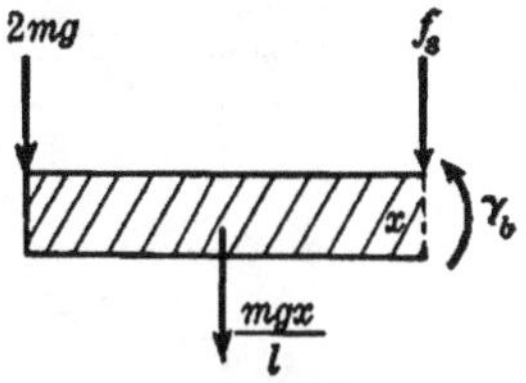

FIG. 4.68.

SOLUTION. Assigning coordinates as previously, we isolate the region from 0 to x where $x < \frac{l}{2}$. The forces on the isolated portion appear in Fig. 4.68. The equations for equilibrium are

$$2mg + \frac{mgx}{l} + f_s = 0 \qquad \text{or} \qquad f_s = -mg\left(2 + \frac{x}{l}\right).$$

$$2mgx + \frac{mgx^2}{2l} + \gamma_b = 0 \qquad \text{or} \qquad \gamma_b = -mgx\left(2 + \frac{x}{2l}\right).$$

Now, using Fig. 4.69, let us isolate the portion from 0 to x for $\frac{l}{2} < x < l$.

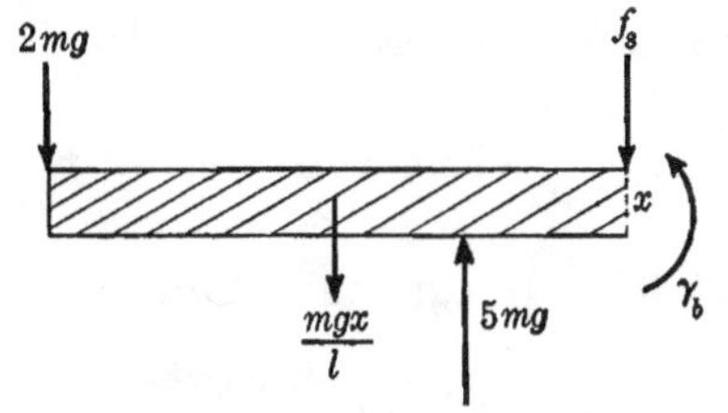

FIG. 4.69.

The equations now are

$$5mg - 2mg - \frac{mgx}{l} - f_s = 0, \qquad f_s = 3mg - \frac{mgx}{l}.$$

$$2mgx + \frac{mgx^2}{2l} - 5mg\left(x - \frac{l}{2}\right) + \gamma_b = 0,$$

or

$$\gamma_b = 3mgx - \frac{mgx^2}{2l} - \frac{5mgl}{2}.$$

The first of these equations shows that the value of f_s jumps by $5mg$ at the point of support.

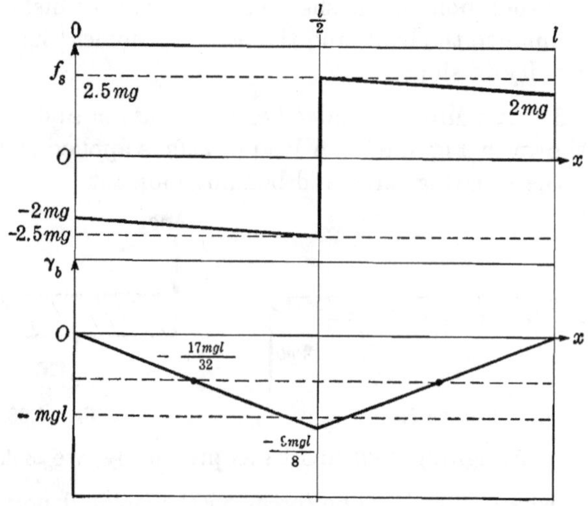

FIG. 4.70.

A graphical summary appears in Fig. 4.70.

ALTERNATIVE SOLUTION. A more analytical and somewhat shorter approach makes use of Eqs. (4.42) and (4.43). We start with

$$\frac{df_s}{dx} = -\frac{mg}{l}.$$

We integrate and use the fact that at the left support the shearing force (provided by the support) is $-2mg$. We get

$$f_s = -\frac{mg}{l}x + c, \qquad -2mg = 0 + c, \qquad f_s = -2mg - \frac{mg}{l}x.$$

Now we may use (4.43). Integrating again,

$$\gamma_b = -2mgx - \frac{mgx^2}{2l} + c'.$$

This time our boundary condition is that $\gamma_b = 0$ at the free end $x = 0$; thus

$$\gamma_b = -mgx\left(2 + \frac{x}{2l}\right)$$

as before. A similar procedure may be used for $x > \frac{l}{2}$. For at $x = l$, $f_s = 2mg$ and $\gamma_b = 0$. This time the constant of integration is given by

$$2mg = -mg + c;$$

thus

$$f_s = -\frac{mgx}{l} + 3mg.$$

Integrating again, we get

$$\gamma_b = -\frac{mgx^2}{2l} + 3mgx + c'.$$

Evaluating c',

$$0 = -\frac{mgl}{2} + 3mgl + c';$$

thus

$$\gamma_b = -\frac{mgx^2}{2l} + 3mgx - \frac{5}{2}mgl.$$

Bending Moment and Funicular Curves. As a final item let us note one interesting common ground between this section and the preceding one. From (4.43) and (4.42) together, we get

$$\frac{d^2\gamma_b}{dx^2} = -q(x). \tag{4.44}$$

This is to be compared with (4.40), an equation determining the shape of a funicular curve:

$$\frac{d^2y}{dx^2} = \frac{1}{h}q(x).$$

This comparison indicates that, except for constants, units, etc., the graph of γ_b is an inverted funicular curve. Thus in Fig. 4.65 we have a parabola—the curve which a cable with uniform horizontal loading assumes. And in Fig. 4.70 we have an inverted picture of a cable with a uniform horizontal load together with a vertical force upward.

EXERCISES

1. Plot shearing force and bending-moment curves for a uniform beam supported on two knife-edges, each a quarter length from the ends.

2. Plot shearing force and bending-moment curves for a uniform horizontal beam one end of which is set rigidly in concrete, the other end being free.

3. A light 10-ft beam rests on two simple knife-edge supports, one at the left end and the other 2 ft from the other end. A load of 1,000 lb is attached at the center of the beam, while a load of 500 lb is at the free end. Plot the shearing force and bending moment.

CHAPTER 5

MOTION OF A PARTICLE

Distance and *force* have already been introduced as logical building blocks to be used in assembling the theory of mechanics. We have reflected briefly on how numbers are assigned to these two quantities. This required both an operational procedure and an agreement on units for our measurements. As long as we were concerned with distance alone, we necessarily studied geometrical examples. In that study we implicitly accepted the postulates of Euclidean geometry, but our methods were the novel procedures of vector algebra. In our study of forces acting in space, an explicit statement of basic propositions seemed advisable. Limiting ourselves to objects no more complicated than rigid bodies, we accepted the parallelogram rule for combining concurrent forces, the principle of transmissibility, and also from Newton's famous laws certain ideas about isolation and equilibrium.

Now we shall consider a final primitive concept.

5.1. Time. The third basic ingredient of mechanics is time. Time intervals are measured by observing coincidences with some cyclic mechanism such as a clock or pendulum. Our standard unit of time, the *second*, is a specified fraction of the mean solar day. It could be defined also in terms of atomic or mechanical frequencies. In the problems which we shall consider we shall assume that time intervals are measured accurately and that such determinations are independent of the observer, no account being taken of the proper times of observers in relative motion as in relativity theory. We shall not delve into philosophical speculations concerning the nature of time, nor shall we be concerned with techniques for standardizing time measurements despite the fact that such occupations are significant and challenging. As with length we shall not deem it expedient to set up formal postulates for our use of this concept. Without any such machinery being exhibited, the reader probably would assume that we here conceive of time as smoothly flowing, uniform and irreversible, absolute and impartial. We shall denote time by the small letter t, since time is to be measured by ordinary numbers and hence is a scalar. It is convenient to think of our time measurements as being made with a stop watch which is started at the beginning of or during an experiment. Thus it will be natural to talk about $t = 0$. Such a designation will have local and temporary significance and will usually not have any such connotation as "midnight," "noon," or "dawn of history."

Chapter 1 initiated the study of "Where is the point?" This question now becomes a function of time; we shall expect that the answer may vary moment by moment. A *point* is merely a geometrical position in a reference frame, a set of coordinates such as (x,y,z), or a position vector such as **R**. When we talk about a *moving point*, we shall have in mind a continuous succession of positions, in other words a variable point whose coordinates are functions of time. It will often be convenient to use the word *particle* instead of point. Then we shall imagine not merely changing positions, but also *something* whose size is to be ignored in the discussion occupying those positions. Thus sometimes we might treat a moving baseball as a particle, its position being denoted by the position vector of its center. Under other circumstances the spin of our baseball might make a very essential contribution to its behavior. Then the particle representation would be inadequate. When we deal with the motion of a body whose physical extent is important for us, we shall regard the body as composed of many particles. These particles will not be the particles of atomic physics, but rather the arbitrarily small subdivisions, as in integral calculus, of a medium treated as continuous. The motions of these particles are interrelated. We shall discover that in important special cases the interrelationships are direct and simple.

5.2. Effective Velocity. The position vector of a moving particle or point varying with time may be considered as a vector function of the scalar time and hence may be represented thus:

$$\mathbf{R} = \mathbf{R}(t). \tag{5.1}$$

This means that for each value of t in the range of t under consideration there is a value of the vector **R**. As a special case take

$$\mathbf{R} = \mathbf{R}(t) = 2t\mathbf{I} + (t^2 - 4)\mathbf{J}. \tag{5.2}$$

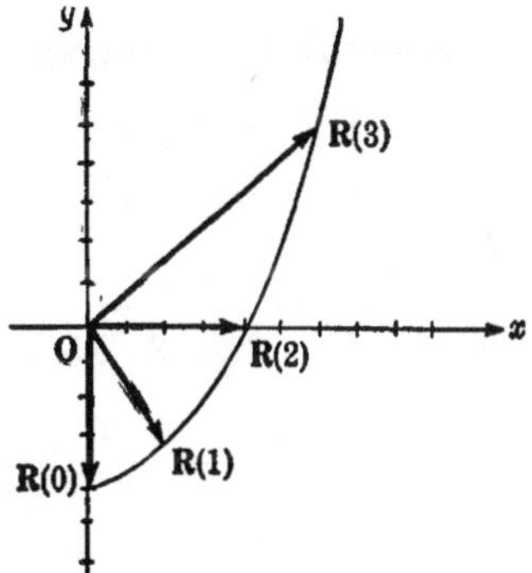

FIG. 5.1.

The path traced out by the moving point described in (5.2) and a number of typical values of **R** are shown in Fig. 5.1. From the spacing of these vectors it is apparent that the motion speeds up as time passes. One of our aims in this chapter will be to make a careful study of the rate of such movements. First, in general terms, we shall define the *effective velocity* over a given time interval.

Suppose that **R** has the value $\mathbf{R}_0$ at time $t = t_0$ and that **R** has the value

$\mathbf{R} = \mathbf{R}_0 + \Delta\mathbf{R}$ at the time $t = t_0 + \Delta t$, as in Fig. 5.2. Then the effective time rate of displacement is given by the ratio of $\Delta\mathbf{R}$ to Δt. This rather crude concept is what we shall term the *effective velocity over the time interval* Δt.

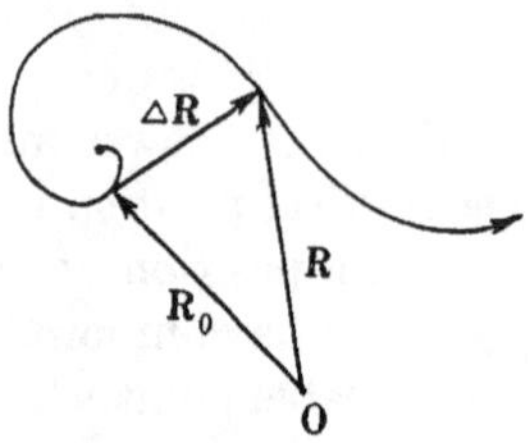

FIG. 5.2.

$$\mathbf{V}_{\text{eff}} = \frac{\Delta\mathbf{R}}{\Delta t}. \tag{5.3}$$

Clearly $\mathbf{V}_{\text{eff}}$ is a vector concept to be measured in units such as meters per second. It obviously tells nothing about what in detail has happened during the interval. Only the net result is expressed. If Δt is short and if the motion is reasonably regular, then effective velocity is a more reliable and useful concept. In Fig. 5.3 a vector $\mathbf{V}_{\text{eff}}$ is drawn for each of three time intervals. $\mathbf{V}_{\text{eff}}$ is the effective velocity for the interval t_0 to t. Since this evaluation takes no account of the arcwise nature of the displacement from $\mathbf{R}_0$ to $\mathbf{R}$, it is only mildly significant. $\mathbf{V}'_{\text{eff}}$ is a more pertinent value, for over the time interval t_0 to $t_0 + t/2$ the direction of the net displacement is more nearly that of the actual instantaneous motion. $\mathbf{V}''_{\text{eff}}$, over the interval t_0 to $t_0 + t/4$, has practically the direction of the trajectory. The limiting position $\mathbf{V}$ shown in the figure will be discussed in the next section.

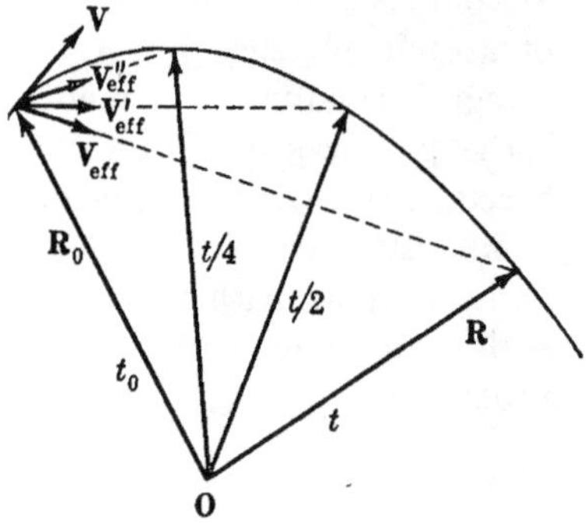

FIG. 5.3.

Example 1. Using again

$$\mathbf{R}(t) = 2t\mathbf{I} + (t^2 - 4)\mathbf{J},$$

investigate the effective velocity near $t = 2$.

SOLUTION. Let us use the time intervals 2 to t', where t' has successively the values 3, 2.5, 2.1, and $2 + \Delta t$.

$$\frac{\Delta\mathbf{R}}{\Delta t} = \frac{\mathbf{R}(3) - \mathbf{R}(2)}{1} = 2\mathbf{I} + 5\mathbf{J},$$

$$\frac{\Delta\mathbf{R}}{\Delta t} = \frac{\mathbf{R}(2.5) - \mathbf{R}(2)}{0.5} = \frac{1.0\mathbf{I} + 2.25\mathbf{J}}{0.5} = 2\mathbf{I} + 4.5\mathbf{J},$$

$$\frac{\Delta\mathbf{R}}{\Delta t} = \frac{\mathbf{R}(2.1) - \mathbf{R}(2)}{0.1} = \frac{0.2\mathbf{I} + 0.41\mathbf{J}}{0.1} = 2\mathbf{I} + 4.1\mathbf{J},$$

$$\frac{\Delta\mathbf{R}}{\Delta t} = \frac{\mathbf{R}(t + \Delta t) - \mathbf{R}(t)}{\Delta t} = \frac{2\Delta t\,\mathbf{I} + (2t\,\Delta t + \Delta t^2)\mathbf{J}}{\Delta t},$$

$$= 2\mathbf{I} + (2t + \Delta t)\mathbf{J}.$$

Example 2. The position of a point moving on the x axis is given by

$$\mathbf{R} = (t - 2t^2)\mathbf{I}.$$

What is the effective velocity for the intervals 0 to 0.25, 0.5, 1.0?

SOLUTION. $\mathbf{R}(0) = 0\mathbf{I}$; therefore $\Delta\mathbf{R} = \mathbf{R} = 0.125\mathbf{I},\ 0\mathbf{I},\ -1.0\mathbf{I}$. Dividing by Δt in each case, we have $\mathbf{V}_{\text{eff}} = 0.5\mathbf{I},\ 0\mathbf{I},\ -1.0\mathbf{I}$.

EXERCISES

1. A particle $\mathbf{R}$ travels in such a way that $\mathbf{V}_{\text{eff}}$ is constant. What is the nature of the trajectory?

2. At time t, the position of a particle $\mathbf{R}$ is given by

$$\mathbf{R} = \mathbf{R}_0 + s(t)\mathbf{E},$$

where $\mathbf{E}$ is a constant unit vector. If $\mathbf{V}_{\text{eff}}$ is to be constant, what can be said about the scalar function of time $s(t)$?

3. A particle moving counterclockwise in the circle $r = 5$ ft at a uniform speed of 10 ft/sec travels from $5\underline{/15^\circ}$ to $5\underline{/-15^\circ}$. What is the effective velocity for this transfer?

4. The position of a particle moving in the xy plane is, at time t, given by $\mathbf{R} = 6\underline{/(20t)^\circ}$ ft. Plot a graph showing the variation with time of the magnitude of the effective velocity.

5. The position of a moving particle is given by

$$\mathbf{R} = t^2\mathbf{I} + (t - 2t^2)\mathbf{J}.$$

Derive a formula for the effective velocity for the time interval from t to $t + \Delta t$.

5.3. Velocity and Derivative of a Vector. The discussion in Sec. 5.2 concerning effective velocity for diminishing time intervals suggests defining *instantaneous velocity* as the limiting value of effective velocity as the time interval approaches zero. To say that $\mathbf{V}$ is the *limit* of $\mathbf{V}_{\text{eff}}$ means that the *magnitude* and the *direction* of $\mathbf{V}_{\text{eff}}$ approach the magnitude and direction of $\mathbf{V}$ as Δt is taken continually smaller. This double convergence process is illustrated in Fig. 5.4. Here $\mathbf{V}_{\text{eff}1}$, $\mathbf{V}_{\text{eff}2}$, $\mathbf{V}_{\text{eff}3}$, . . . are a sequence of values of $\mathbf{V}_{\text{eff}}$ approaching $\mathbf{V}$. Students of the calculus will immediately discern the appropriateness of calling velocity (*i.e.*, instantaneous velocity) a derivative.

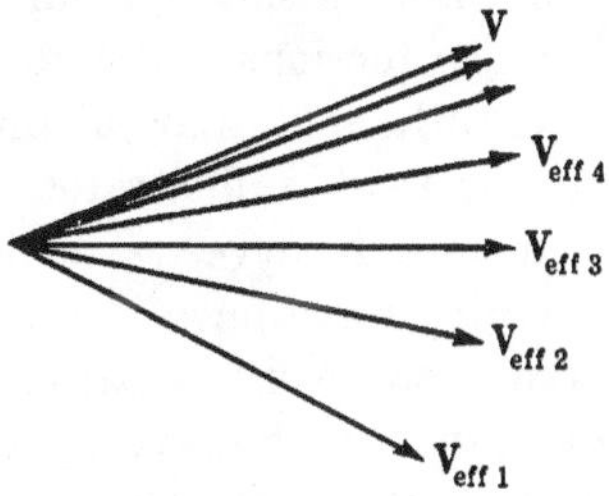

FIG. 5.4.

$$\mathbf{V} = \lim_{\Delta t \to 0} \mathbf{V}_{\text{eff}} \tag{5.4}$$

$$= \lim_{\Delta t \to 0} \frac{\Delta \mathbf{R}}{\Delta t} = \frac{d\mathbf{R}}{dt}.$$

Example 1. Uniform circular motion of period 8 sec is the basis for the following diagrams (see Fig. 5.5) in which the same scale is used for meters and meters per second.

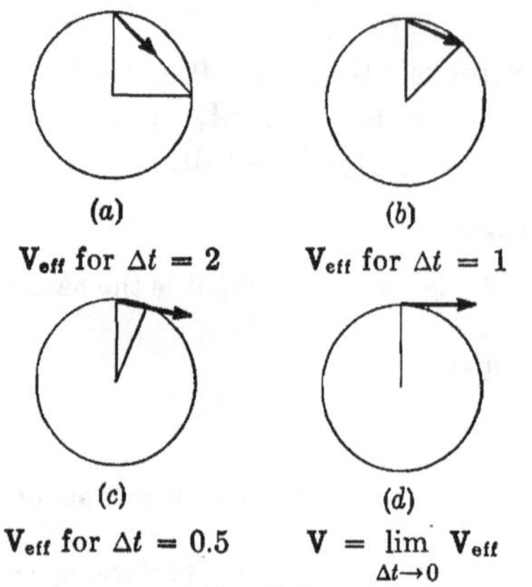

FIG. 5.5.

We shall in this section study some of the general properties of derivatives of vectors. Let us assume that **R** is a varying vector. It might, for instance, represent a velocity, a force, or a position. Suppose that **R** is a function of a scalar variable t. Usually for us this independent scalar variable will be time, but occasionally an angle or a distance will be more convenient. For any value of t, we shall define a new vector function of t, *the derivative of* **R** *with respect to* t. A defining equation has already been given in (5.4), but now our treatment is to be quite general; therefore we shall give the equation again without any reference to effective velocity:

$$(5.5) \qquad \frac{d\mathbf{R}}{dt} = \lim_{\Delta t \to 0} \frac{\mathbf{R}(t + \Delta t) - \mathbf{R}(t)}{\Delta t} = \lim_{\Delta t \to 0} \frac{\Delta \mathbf{R}}{\Delta t}.$$

Of course, this new vector is defined only for those values of t for which this limit exists. In our work in elementary mechanics we deal with vector functions whose derivatives exist everywhere that we need them.

In ordinary scalar calculus a derivative is readily illustrated as the slope of a smooth curve. The derivative of a vector function of a scalar variable is not so easily portrayed. A path diagram is, however, helpful. Let each vector $\mathbf{R}(t)$ be drawn with its initial point at an origin **O**. Then the terminal point of the vector traces out a curve as in Fig. 5.6. It should be apparent that the limit of $\Delta\mathbf{R}/\Delta t$ as Δt gets smaller and smaller is always a vector tangent to this curve at the point designated $\mathbf{R}(t)$. In summary,

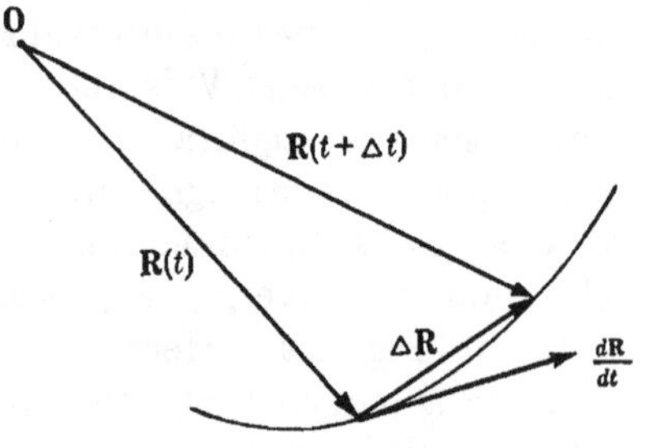

FIG. 5.6.

(5.6) *If* $\mathbf{R} = \mathbf{R}(t)$ *then* $d\mathbf{R}/dt$ *is a vector function of* t *tangent to the curve traced out by* $\mathbf{R}(t)$.

The standard rules of reckoning of scalar calculus have their counterparts in vector calculus. Such rules are justified by derivations based on theorems concerning limits such as *limit of sum equals sum of limits*, etc. These theorems may be carried over immediately from the scalar theory of real variables since each vector function is expressible in terms of three scalar functions. The details will not be included here. Only skeleton derivations of the rules will be presented.

Derivative of a Sum. Let **R** and **S** be two vector functions of t. Then

$$\frac{d}{dt}(\mathbf{R} + \mathbf{S}) = \lim_{\Delta t \to 0} \left[\frac{\mathbf{R}(t + \Delta t) + \mathbf{S}(t + \Delta t) - \mathbf{R}(t) - \mathbf{S}(t)}{\Delta t} \right]$$
$$= \lim_{\Delta t \to 0} \left[\frac{\mathbf{R}(t + \Delta t) - \mathbf{R}(t)}{\Delta t} \right] + \lim_{\Delta t \to 0} \left[\frac{\mathbf{S}(t + \Delta t) - \mathbf{S}(t)}{\Delta t} \right]$$

or, using the defining equation (5.5),

$$\frac{d}{dt}(\mathbf{R} + \mathbf{S}) = \frac{d\mathbf{R}}{dt} + \frac{d\mathbf{S}}{dt}. \tag{5.7}$$

Derivative of Product by Scalar Function. Let **R** and c be functions of t. Then

$$\frac{d(c\mathbf{R})}{dt} = \lim_{\Delta t \to 0} \left[\frac{(c + \Delta c)(\mathbf{R} + \Delta \mathbf{R}) - c\mathbf{R}}{\Delta t} \right]$$
$$= \lim_{\Delta t \to 0} \left[\frac{\Delta c}{\Delta t} \mathbf{R} + c \frac{\Delta \mathbf{R}}{\Delta t} + \Delta c \frac{\Delta \mathbf{R}}{\Delta t} \right],$$

or

$$\frac{d(c\mathbf{R})}{dt} = \frac{dc}{dt} \mathbf{R} + c \frac{d\mathbf{R}}{dt}. \tag{5.8}$$

Derivatives of Products of Vectors. Let **R** and **S** be functions of t. The derivations are left as exercises.

$$\frac{d(\mathbf{R} \cdot \mathbf{S})}{dt} = \frac{d\mathbf{R}}{dt} \cdot \mathbf{S} + \mathbf{R} \cdot \frac{d\mathbf{S}}{dt}. \tag{5.9}$$

$$\frac{d(\mathbf{R} \times \mathbf{S})}{dt} = \frac{d\mathbf{R}}{dt} \times \mathbf{S} + \mathbf{R} \times \frac{d\mathbf{S}}{dt}. \tag{5.10}$$

Components of Derivatives. Let $\mathbf{U}(t)$ be a vector function of the scalar t. Then as a consequence of the rules of vector algebra and the rules of calculus just derived we may write, assuming that **I**, **J**, and **K** are constant vectors:

$$\frac{d\mathbf{U}}{dt} = \frac{du_x}{dt} \mathbf{I} + \frac{du_y}{dt} \mathbf{J} + \frac{du_z}{dt} \mathbf{K}. \tag{5.11}$$

Applied to the case where the vector in question is a position vector, the result is

$$\mathbf{V} = \frac{dx}{dt} \mathbf{I} + \frac{dy}{dt} \mathbf{J} + \frac{dz}{dt} \mathbf{K}. \tag{5.12}$$

This equation throws considerable light on the nature of the velocity vector **V** of a moving point. Its x component is merely the velocity of the x projection of the point, and so on for the y and z components. This same principle holds for directions other than these three favored ones.

SPECIAL CONCLUSIONS. Any vector, we have seen, has direction and magnitude. As an illustration of the new ideas of this section let us look into the nature of the derivative of the following:

1. A vector whose direction does not change.
2. A vector whose magnitude does not change.

1. A variable vector of constant direction may be represented by

$$\mathbf{R} = r\mathbf{E},$$

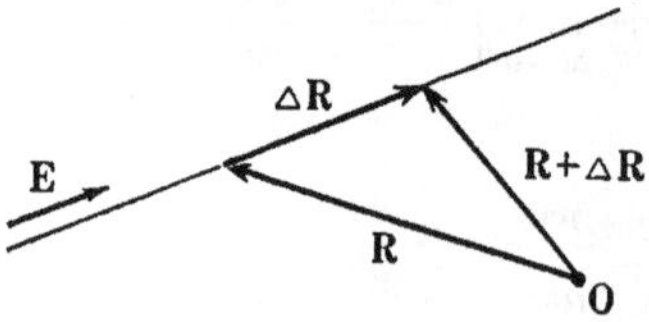

FIG. 5.7.

where **E** is a constant unit vector (see Fig. 5.7). If **E** does not vary, then

$$\Delta\mathbf{R} = \Delta r\mathbf{E};$$

therefore

(5.13) *If* **R** *is constant in direction, then* $d\mathbf{R}/dt$ *is parallel to* **R**.

This may be seen too as a quick formal conclusion from (5.8):

$$\frac{d\mathbf{R}}{dt} = \frac{dr}{dt}\mathbf{E} + r\frac{d\mathbf{E}}{dt} = \frac{dr}{dt}\mathbf{E}.$$

This follows at once from the assumptions:

$$\mathbf{R} = r\mathbf{E},$$
$$\frac{d\mathbf{E}}{dt} = \mathbf{O}.$$

2. A variable vector of constant magnitude may be represented by

$$\mathbf{R} = a\mathbf{L},$$

where a is a constant scalar and **L** a varying unit vector (see Fig. 5.8). In this interesting case the only possible path diagrams of **R** must lie on a sphere of radius a. But for any curve on a sphere, the tangent is perpendicular to the radius and hence to **R**; thus **R** and $d\mathbf{R}/dt$ are at right angles. This too may be deduced formally. First let us note, since a is constant, that

$$\frac{d(\mathbf{R}\cdot\mathbf{R})}{dt} = \frac{d(a^2)}{dt} = 0.$$

Now, using (5.9) and the commutative law for scalar products,

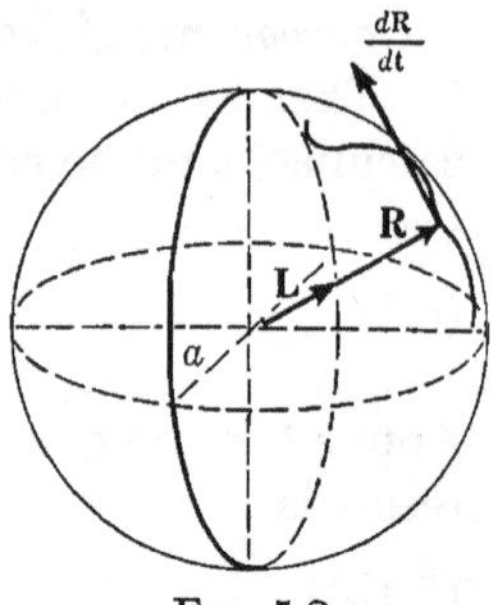

FIG. 5.8.

$$\frac{d(\mathbf{R}\cdot\mathbf{R})}{dt} = \frac{d\mathbf{R}}{dt}\cdot\mathbf{R} + \mathbf{R}\cdot\frac{d\mathbf{R}}{dt} = 2\frac{d\mathbf{R}}{dt}\cdot\mathbf{R}.$$

Combining this with the previous equation, we have (*for a vector* **R** *of constant magnitude*)

$$\frac{d\mathbf{R}}{dt} \cdot \mathbf{R} = 0. \tag{5.14}$$

In this case then **R** *and its derivative are perpendicular.*

EXERCISES

1. Use the Δ method [used for establishing (5.7) and (5.8)] to prove (5.9) and (5.10).

2. Prove that the component in the direction of a unit vector **E** of a variable vector **R** has a derivative equal to the **E** component of $d\mathbf{R}/dt$.

3. Compute in **IJK** form the derivative with respect to t of each of the following vector expressions:

(*a*) $(t\mathbf{J}) \cdot t^3(\mathbf{I} + \mathbf{J})$ (*b*) $(\sin t\,\mathbf{I}) \times (\cos t\,\mathbf{J})$ (*c*) $(2t\mathbf{J} - t^3\mathbf{K}) \times (t^2\mathbf{I} + 2t\mathbf{J})$

4. Find expressions for the velocity of each of the following points.

(*a*) $\mathbf{R} = 2t^2\mathbf{I} + 4t\mathbf{J} + 8\mathbf{K}$.

(*b*) $\mathbf{R} = 4 \sin t\,\mathbf{I} + 4 \cos t\,\mathbf{J} + t^2\mathbf{K}$.

5. The position vector of a moving particle at time t is given by

$$\mathbf{R} = \cos t\,\mathbf{I} + \sin t\,\mathbf{J} + t\mathbf{K}.$$

Find the magnitude and the direction cosines of the velocity vector at time $t = 1.0472$ sec.

6. The position of a point (x,y) ft, moving in the xy plane, is at time t given by

$$x = 4t^2, \qquad y = 6t.$$

Find analytically the direction and the magnitude of the velocity vector $\mathbf{V} = v\underline{/\theta}$ at $t = 1.0$.

7. The path of a projectile is given by

$$\mathbf{R} = v_0 t \cos \theta\,\mathbf{I} + (v_0 t \sin \theta - 16t^2)\mathbf{J},$$

where $\mathbf{V}_0 = v_0\underline{/\theta}$ is the muzzle velocity. If $v_0 = 4{,}000$ ft/sec and $\theta = 30°$, find the speed and direction of the projectile at $t = 1$, 5, 20 sec.

8. State and justify formulas for the derivative with respect to t of (*a*) $\mathbf{U} \cdot \mathbf{V} \times \mathbf{W}$ and (*b*) $\mathbf{U} \times (\mathbf{V} \times \mathbf{W})$, where **U**, **V**, and **W** are vector functions of the scalar t.

9. If **L** is the unit vector in the xy plane given by $\mathbf{L} = 1\underline{/\theta}$, where θ is a function of t, then $\mathbf{L} \cdot \mathbf{I} = \cos \theta$, $\mathbf{L} \cdot \mathbf{J} = \sin \theta$. Differentiate each of these equations with respect to t to show that

$$\frac{d\mathbf{L}}{dt} = \frac{d\theta}{dt}\mathbf{M},$$

where **M** is the variable unit vector $1\underline{/\theta + 90°}$. (NOTE: $d\theta/dt$ is expressed in radians per t interval.)

10. Two media are separated by a plane. **P** is any point on one side of the plane and **Q** any point on the other side. A particle which travels at speed v_1 in the first medium and at speed v_2 in the second medium is to go from **P** to **Q** in the shortest possible time. Show that Snell's law (sines of angles with normal to plane are proportional to speeds) is obeyed.

5.4. Relative Velocity. In our discussions of *time* and *length* it was assumed that two careful experimenters would agree in measuring either quantity. It is perhaps interesting to point out that in the theory of relativity no such assumptions are made. Even from the elementary point of view which we entertain in this course *velocity* may appear quite different to different observers. The nature of the velocity vector depends on the reference frame with respect to which displacements are measured. A ball tossed back and forth between two people on opposite sides of a train coach appears to retrace the same path over and over again. For an observer on the ground the trajectories form a zigzag pattern. A passenger in an automobile taking a curve feels pushed to the side of the vehicle. From an outside point of view, however, he is merely tending to follow a straight path instead of the sharply curved one dictated by the path of the car. We are so accustomed to considering motion relative to the surface of the earth that we seldom take account even of the diurnal rotation of our planet.

We shall now consider how apparent motions as observed with respect to different reference frames can be compared. We shall limit ourselves at present to the case where one frame does not rotate with respect to the other. Let O be the origin of the "fixed" reference frame, while O′ is origin of a second frame moving with respect to the first. Since no rotation takes place, we shall assume that the corresponding axes are always, respectively, parallel. At time t, let a particle have position vector $\mathbf{R}_1$ with respect to O and $\mathbf{R}_1'$ with respect to O′. After a time elapse Δt the position vector with respect to O is $\mathbf{R}_2$, the displacement $\Delta\mathbf{R}$ being $\mathbf{R}_2 - \mathbf{R}_1$, as shown in Fig. 5.9. But during the time interval

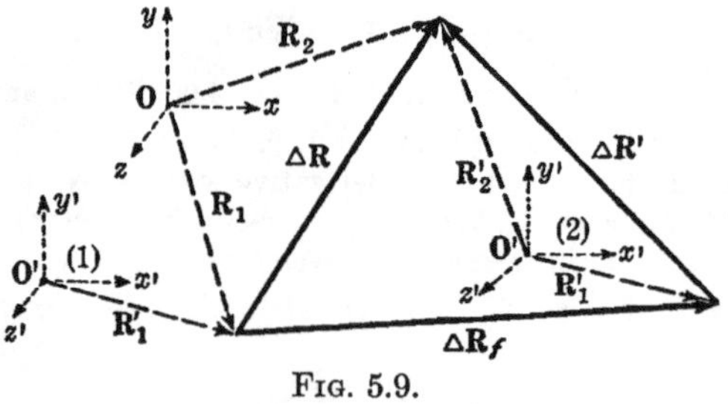

FIG. 5.9.

Δt the frame O′ has moved. This means that if our particle had remained at $\mathbf{R}_1'$ (as viewed from O′) it would have undergone a displacement $\Delta\mathbf{R}_f$ (as viewed from O). Since no rotation of the moving frame has taken place, $\Delta\mathbf{R}_f$ is also the displacement of any other point fixed in the frame, for example, of O′. Actually our particle need not merely have taken a ride on the moving frame. In Fig. 5.9 it is apparent that the new position vector $\mathbf{R}_2'$ is quite different from $\mathbf{R}_1'$. An observer at O′ would report a displacement $\Delta\mathbf{R}' = \mathbf{R}'_2 - \mathbf{R}'_1$. This is the "relative displacement" seen from the moving frame. Figure 5.9 makes it clear that the "absolute displacement" is equal to the vector sum of the "frame displacement" and the "relative displacement."

In symbols, we have then

$$\Delta\mathbf{R} = \Delta\mathbf{R}_f + \Delta\mathbf{R}'. \tag{5.15}$$

Since we are considering parallel sets of axes, $\Delta\mathbf{R}'$ has the same x, y, and z components in either frame. The three displacements entering Eq. (5.15) occurred during the same interval Δt. If we divide both members of this equation by Δt and take the limit as Δt is allowed to approach zero, we have an equation involving derivatives:

$$\frac{d\mathbf{R}}{dt} = \frac{d\mathbf{R}_f}{dt} + \frac{d\mathbf{R}'}{dt}. \tag{5.16}$$

Each of these is a velocity; therefore we rewrite (5.16) as

$$\mathbf{V} = \mathbf{V}_f + \mathbf{V}'. \tag{5.17}$$

In words we may say that the absolute velocity of the particle is equal to the vector sum of two other velocities: the velocity which the particle would share with the moving frame if it remained rigidly fixed in it and the velocity which it has relative to the moving frame. In a general case, this second vector, the relative velocity, might be described differently by observers in the two systems. As long as we limit ourselves to reference frames with parallel axes, no such ambiguity arises.

Example 1. The trail of smoke left by a steamer moving due north at 15 mph appears to an airplane pilot like an arrow pointing 30° west of north. If the true velocity of the wind is also 15 mph, what is its true direction?

SOLUTION. Take the steamer as a moving frame with velocity $\mathbf{V}_f$ north at 15 mph. The apparent velocity of the wind as seen from the steamer, $\mathbf{V}'$, has the direction of the line of smoke (*i.e.*, the wind blows toward 30° east of south). Since the absolute velocity $\mathbf{V}$ of the wind has magnitude 15 mph, the vector triangle (Fig. 5.10) relating the three velocities is isosceles; therefore the odd angle is 120°. The wind then actually blows 60° east of south (or from a point 60° west of north).

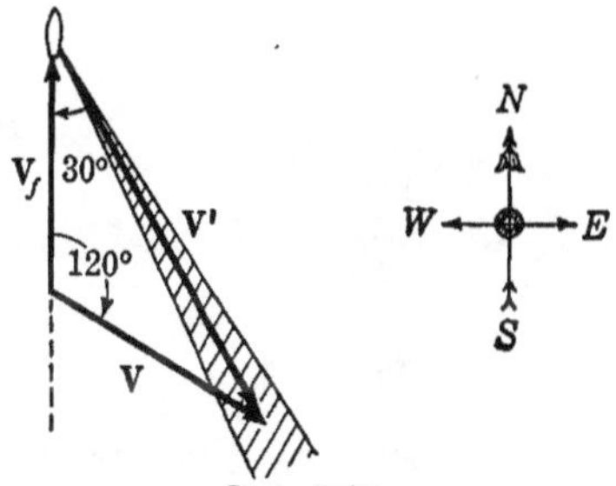

FIG. 5.10.

Example 2. An airplane points due north with an air speed of 80 mph. Due to a northwest wind the airplane's actual course is northeast. Find the actual speed of the airplane and also the speed of the wind.

SOLUTION. Of the three velocities only **V**′ is known in both direction and magnitude. (It is the velocity of the airplane relative to the air: due north at 80 mph.) $\mathbf{V}_f$ is the velocity of the air mass and it is known in direction only (a northwest wind blows southeast, as shown in Fig. 5.11). The absolute velocity **V** is known in direction only (northeast). A suitable vector diagram is in the figure. From it it is clear that

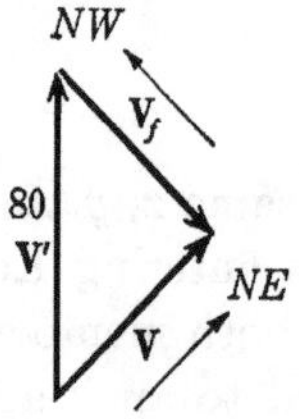

FIG. 5.11.

$$v = v_f = 80 \sin 45° = 56.6 \text{ mph.}$$

Example 3. A warship, sailing at 20 mph, sights a target ship 20 miles ahead crossing its path at right angles at 15 mph. In how long a time will their separation be a minimum if their velocities are unchanged?

SOLUTION. It is quite possible to work the problem with little reference to the methods of this section. Choosing axes, as shown in Fig. 5.12, the positions at time t are, respectively, $20t\mathbf{I}$ and $20\mathbf{I} + 15t\mathbf{J}$. The distance between them is the magnitude of the vector difference:

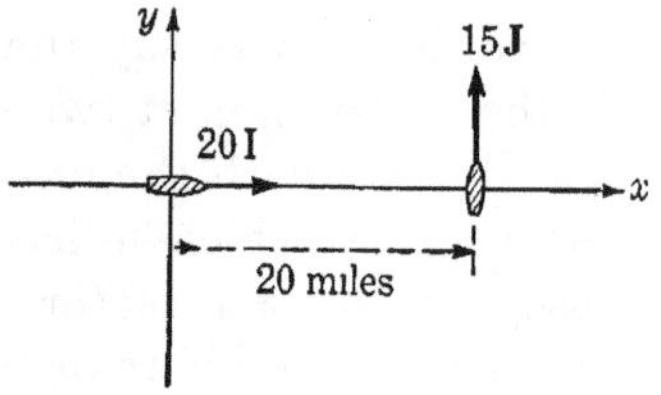

FIG. 5.12.

$$20(1 - t)\mathbf{I} + 15t\mathbf{J},$$

namely,

$$\sqrt{400(1 - t)^2 + 225t^2}.$$

If the derivative of this is set equal to zero, one finds that the minimum value occurs at $t = 0.64$ hr.

A more interesting approach is afforded by the concept of relative velocity. As seen from the ship, the target has velocity

$$\mathbf{V}' = 15\mathbf{J} - 20\mathbf{I}, \qquad v' = 25 \text{ mph.}$$

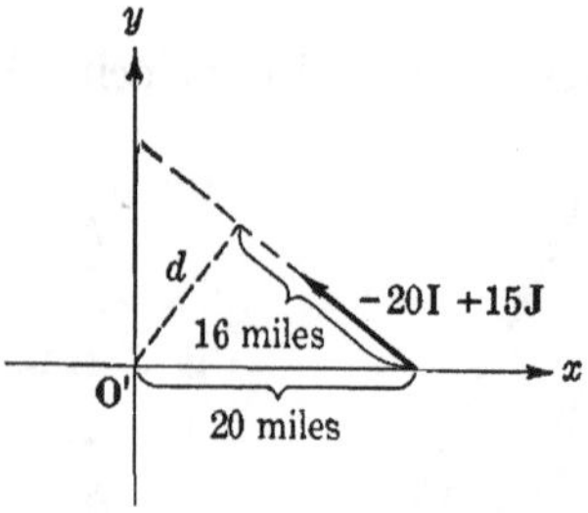

FIG. 5.13.

Regarding the ship as at the origin then the question is: Where does the course come closest to the origin? The nearest point (see Fig. 5.13) is determined by dropping a perpendicular from **O**′ to the course. The minimum distance is at once seen to be 12 miles after a relative displacement of 16 miles at 25 mph, or

$$t = \tfrac{16}{25} = 0.64 \text{ hr.}$$

EXERCISES

1. An airplane is going northeast at 100 mph. It is observed by a motorcyclist going south at 90 mph. Neglecting the difference in altitude, how fast is the distance between them increasing?

2. A bomber takes off from a base and follows a straight course to a target. Since there is a wind from the southeast, the nose of the airplane is pointed northeast instead of toward the target. It takes the bomber 1 hr to reach the target which is 200 miles from the base. Its average air speed is 195 mph. How many degrees east of the course was the airplane pointed? What was the speed of the wind?

3. A lunch box is lost from a canoe going upstream. Fifteen minutes later the canoe reverses direction and heads downstream, the effort at paddling being uniform and undiminished. The box is overtaken a mile downstream from the spot where it was dropped. What is the speed of the river?

4. A swimmer's speed in still water is 150 ft/min and the current of a river is 90 ft/min. If he swims to a point upstream and back in 5 min, what is the total distance he swam?

5. A train travels at 40 mph. How fast (relative to the train) and in what direction must a ball be thrown to travel 30 mph on a horizontal path perpendicular to the train?

6. An airplane flies north with an air speed of 129 mph and after an hour lands 75 miles due west of the starting point. Describe the wind.

7. Airplane A travels west at a speed of 150 mph. Airplane B, traveling at 250 mph, is nearest to A when it crosses A's path directly ahead of A. In what direction does B travel?

8. For a boy riding a bicycle north at 15 mph the wind apparently comes from the northwest also at 15 mph. Find in direction and magnitude the true wind velocity.

9. A man in a boat with maximum speed 20 mph sees a speedboat 10 miles away traveling 30 mph at right angles to his line of sight. By traveling at full speed how close can he get to the speedboat? What course should he choose?

10. A transport airplane traveling northeast at 150 mph is spotted 100 miles due north of a fighter which can travel 300 mph. What course should the fighter pilot be directed to take in order to overtake the transport as soon as possible and, assuming constant velocities, how long will it take him to reach the transport?

11. When a motorboat heads north at 20 mph, the apparent wind is from 30° east of north. When it turns west, the apparent wind is from 60° west of south. Find the true wind velocity in direction and magnitude.

12. A motorboat heading northwest experiences an apparent wind from the west; when it heads northeast at the same speed, the apparent wind is from the east and twice as brisk as before. Find the true wind direction.

5.5. Unit Tangent Vector. When a moving point of position vector **R** traces out a path, its velocity vector is given, as we have seen, by

$$\mathbf{V} = \lim_{\Delta t \to 0} \frac{\Delta \mathbf{R}}{\Delta t}. \tag{5.18}$$

We shall now consider the derivative of **R** with respect to a different scalar variable, namely, the positive distance s measured along the path

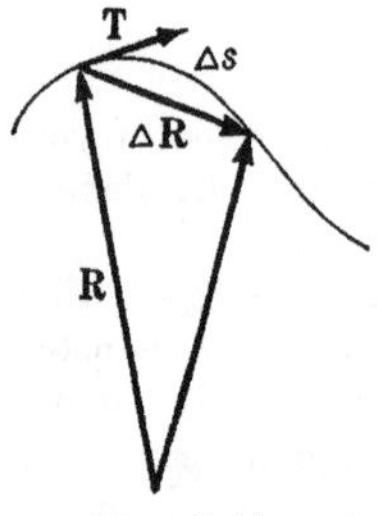

FIG. 5.14.

from any convenient fixed point on the path (see Fig. 5.14).

$$T = \lim_{\Delta s \to 0} \frac{\Delta R}{\Delta s} = \frac{dR}{ds}. \tag{5.19}$$

The *direction* of **T** is the limiting direction of ΔR, that is, tangent to the path. **T** then always points in the direction of the motion along the path. As Δs gets small, the magnitude of ΔR approaches Δs; thus **T** is a *unit vector*. This unit vector **T** may be thought of as a course indicator, always pointing out the direction to be traveled. It is a vector whose length is constant but whose direction may vary continually.

Example 1. If a point travels along the x axis in the positive direction, we have **T** = **I**. In this case it is constant in direction as well as magnitude. If the direction be reversed, **T** = −**I**.

Example 2. If a point travels counterclockwise around a circle of radius a about the origin as center in the xy plane, then at the point $R = a\underline{/\theta}$ the corresponding **T** is given by

$$T = 1\underline{/\theta + 90°}.$$

We now have two vectors, **V** and **T**, parallel to the path of a moving point at each point of the path. (Some exceptions might be made, for instance, at the point in the first example above where reversal of direction takes place.) Using a "chain rule" for differentiation exactly like that used in scalar calculus, we may write

$$V = \frac{dR}{dt} = \frac{dR}{ds}\frac{ds}{dt} = \frac{ds}{dt}T. \tag{5.20}$$

The quantity ds/dt is the positive scalar rate of travel or *speed*. We shall denote it by v, since it is equal to the magnitude of **V**.

$$V = vT; \qquad v = |V|. \tag{5.21}$$

Example 3. A moving point has coordinates $(6t,t^2,4)$. Find **T** at time $t = 4$ sec.

SOLUTION. In terms of vectors,

$$R = 6tI + t^2J + 4K.$$

Differentiating with respect to t,

$$V = 6I + 2tJ.$$

At $t = 4$,

$$V = 6I + 8J, \qquad v = 10, \qquad T = 0.6I + 0.8J.$$

Let us now see quantitatively how **T** changes in direction as a point moves along a curve. Suppose that the point moves from **P** to **P′** and that **T** meanwhile becomes **T′** (see Fig. 5.15). Let the angle between **T** and **T′**, measured in radians, be $\Delta\psi$. (It is assumed that the student is familiar with radians and knows, for instance, that an angle of 1 radian is an angle of $180/\pi$ degrees and that an angle at the center of a circle can be measured in radians in terms of the subtended arc by the formula $\theta = s/r$.) If **P′** is allowed to approach **P**, $\Delta\psi$ will, of course, get small. $\Delta\mathbf{T} = \mathbf{T}' - \mathbf{T}$ can be studied by means of the isosceles triangle determined by the unit vectors **T** and **T′**. From the diagram it is clear that

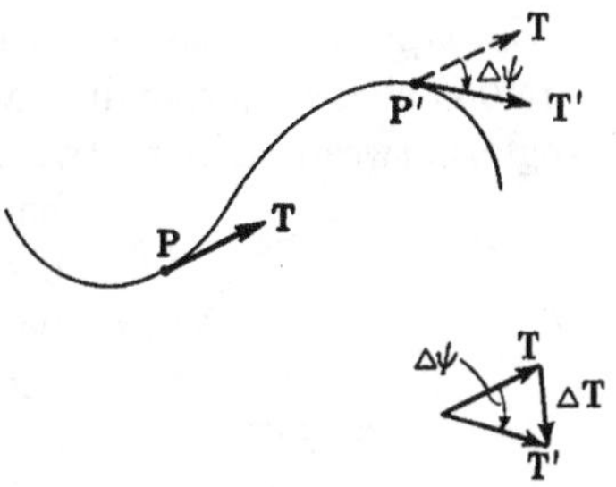

FIG. 5.15.

$$|\Delta\mathbf{T}| = 2 \sin\left(\frac{\Delta\psi}{2}\right).$$

Hence

$$\lim_{\Delta\psi\to 0} \frac{|\Delta\mathbf{T}|}{\Delta\psi} = \lim_{\Delta\psi\to 0} \frac{\sin(\Delta\psi/2)}{\Delta\psi/2} = 1.$$

Thus $d\mathbf{T}/d\psi$ is a unit vector at right angles to **T** in the direction toward which **T** turns.

This unit vector, normal to the curve and in the plane fitting it most closely (*i.e.*, the "osculating plane"), is called the *unit principal normal vector*. It is denoted by **N**.

$$\mathbf{N} = \frac{d\mathbf{T}}{d\psi}. \tag{5.22}$$

Example 4. If a point travels clockwise around a circle of radius a about the origin as center in the xy plane, then at the point $\mathbf{R} = a\underline{/\theta}$ the corresponding **N** is given by $\mathbf{N} = 1\underline{/\theta + 180°}$ (that is, $\mathbf{R} = -a\mathbf{N}$).

We have seen how **T** varies with respect to the angle measuring its orientation. It is now easy to express the rate of change of **T** with respect to displacement:

$$\frac{d\mathbf{T}}{ds} = \frac{d\mathbf{T}}{d\psi}\frac{d\psi}{ds} = \frac{d\psi}{ds}\mathbf{N}. \tag{5.23}$$

The scalar coefficient of **N** in this expression, the derivative of ψ with respect to s, is the rate with respect to displacement at which the direction of the path is changed. It is called the *curvature* and is denoted by the letter κ. As one drives along a curved road at a fixed speed, the sharper the curve, the faster one's direction changes. Thus κ is large on sharp curves and small on slow ones. In terms of κ, we may write

$$\frac{d\mathbf{T}}{ds} = \kappa\mathbf{N}. \tag{5.24}$$

Example 5. Consider a circle of radius ρ. Since the tangent to a circle is always perpendicular to the radius at the point of tangency, the angle between radii to two neighboring points is equal to the angle $\Delta\psi$ between their tangents (see Fig. 5.16). The displacement or arc length along the curve between these points is then $\rho\,\Delta\psi$. We have then

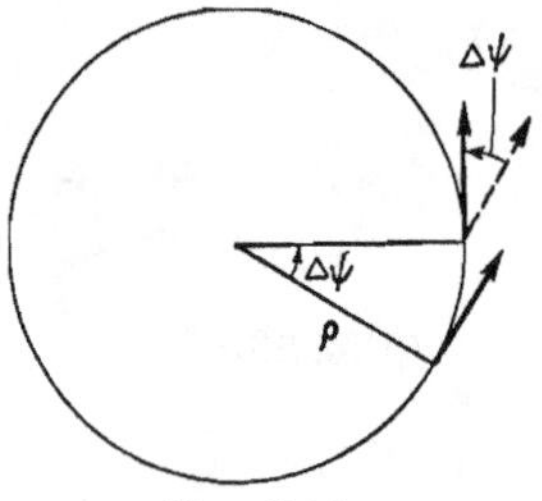

FIG. 5.16.

$$\kappa = \frac{d\psi}{ds} = \lim_{\Delta s \to 0} \frac{\Delta\psi}{\rho\,\Delta\psi} = \frac{1}{\rho}. \tag{5.25}$$

We have arrived then at the interesting conclusion that the curvature of a circle is merely the reciprocal of its radius. Thus a circle is *the* plane curve of constant curvature (a straight line being considered as part of a circle of infinite radius and hence of zero curvature). For a random curve at a random point, the reciprocal of the curvature is called the *radius of curvature*. We shall represent it by the letter ρ.

In terms of the concept described as an extension of the preceding example, Eq. (5.24) may be recast as

$$\frac{d\mathbf{T}}{ds} = \frac{1}{\rho}\mathbf{N}. \tag{5.26}$$

Let us finally compute the time derivative of **T**.

$$\frac{d\mathbf{T}}{dt} = \frac{d\mathbf{T}}{ds}\frac{ds}{dt} = v\kappa\mathbf{N} = \frac{v}{\rho}\mathbf{N}. \tag{5.27}$$

EXERCISES

1. An equation for a point moving along a cycloid is given by

$$\mathbf{R} = 5(3t - \sin 3t)\mathbf{I} + 5(1 - \cos 3t)\mathbf{J} \qquad \text{ft, sec.}$$

For what values of t does $\mathbf{T} = \mathbf{I}$? Compute **V** for this t.

2. The coordinates at time t sec of a moving particle are given in meters by

$$x = 48t, \qquad y = (\tfrac{1}{64})(4 - t^2)^2, \qquad z = 4t^2.$$

Find **T** and v at $t = 8$ sec.

3. Any derivative of **T** is a vector parallel to **N**; therefore

$$\frac{d\mathbf{T}}{d\theta} = b\mathbf{N}$$

for any scalar variable θ and some scalar constant b. For a circle of radius a, pick an origin **O** as any point on the curve. Let the x axis be a tangent to the circle at **O**.

Then the position of any point **R** on the circle can be expressed by giving the angle between **OR** and the x axis. For this θ, find b for the above formula.

4. Given $\mathbf{R} = 3t\mathbf{I} + (\frac{1}{3})t^3\mathbf{J} + t^3\mathbf{K}$. Find **T** and **N** at $t = 2$.

5. A baseball is hit directly over first base so that its position vector (taking first base as origin) is

$$\mathbf{R} = (40t - 90)\mathbf{I} + (96t - 16t^2)\mathbf{J} \qquad \text{ft.}$$

(*a*) What is the initial speed of the ball?
(*b*) Evaluate **T** for $t = 0$ and $t = 6$ sec.
(*c*) How high does the ball go?
(*d*) The right fielder catches the ball on the run at a velocity of $15\mathbf{I} + 20\mathbf{K}$ ft/sec. What is the speed of the ball relative to the fielder when he catches it? (Assume that the ball is caught at the level at which it was hit.)

6. Prove that any derivative of the "unit binormal vector" (given by $\mathbf{B} = \mathbf{T} \times \mathbf{N}$) is parallel to **N**.

5.6. Acceleration. Motion in a straight line at uniform speed has a constant velocity vector. But let either the speed or the direction vary and the velocity vector may have a nonzero derivative with respect to time. This derivative is called acceleration, denoted by **A**.

$$\mathbf{A} = \frac{d\mathbf{V}}{dt}. \tag{5.28}$$

The most interesting motions in physics are accelerated motions: the motions of falling bodies, of particles traveling in circles, and of vibrating particles. We shall shortly develop general techniques for computing acceleration. For the moment let us glance at some simpler special cases, such as the familiar ones just listed.

Example 1. Galileo discovered that in equal successive time intervals a falling body traverses distances which are proportional to the odd integers. What does this imply concerning the acceleration?

SOLUTION. The evidence is first tabulated:

From 0 to Δt distance fallen is 1
From Δt to $2\Delta t$ distance fallen is 3
From $2\Delta t$ to $3\Delta t$ distance fallen is 5, etc.

Now let us express displacements for total elapsed time.

From 0 to Δt total distance fallen is 1
From 0 to $2\Delta t$ total distance fallen is $1 + 3 = 4$
From 0 to $3\Delta t$ total distance fallen is $1 + 3 + 5 = 9$
From 0 to $4\Delta t$ total distance fallen is $1 + 3 + 5 + 7 = 16$

This suggests motion according to an equation of the form:

$$y = -bt^2 \qquad \text{or} \qquad \mathbf{R} = -bt^2\mathbf{J},$$

where b is a positive constant and **J** a fixed unit vertical vector. From this we may conclude:

$$\mathbf{V} = \frac{d\mathbf{R}}{dt} = -2bt\mathbf{J} \quad \text{and} \quad \mathbf{A} = \frac{d\mathbf{V}}{dt} = -2b\mathbf{J}.$$

Thus the evidence listed is at least consistent with the following:

(5.29) *The acceleration for a freely falling body is constant.*

Example 2. In uniform circular motion the velocity vector is constant in magnitude but varying in direction. The derivative of such a vector is perpendicular to the vector [see Eq. (5.14)]. We conclude that the acceleration is radial, toward the center of the circle. For this reason it is called *centripetal acceleration.* The magnitude of the acceleration may be easily computed in various ways, some analogous to procedures previously used. Let us do it here by observing (following Fig. 5.17) that the triangles formed by $\mathbf{V}, \mathbf{V}', \Delta\mathbf{V}$ and $\mathbf{R}, \mathbf{R}', \Delta\mathbf{R}$ are similar. Hence

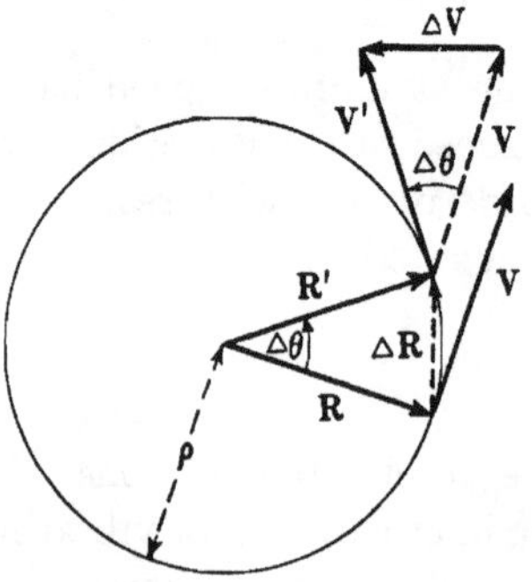

FIG. 5.17.

$$\frac{|\Delta\mathbf{V}|}{v} = \frac{|\Delta\mathbf{R}|}{\rho}$$

and consequently

$$\left|\frac{\Delta\mathbf{V}}{\Delta t}\right| = \frac{v}{\rho}\left|\frac{\Delta\mathbf{R}}{\Delta t}\right|.$$

Taking the limit as $\Delta t \to 0$,

$$(5.30) \qquad a = |\mathbf{A}| = \frac{v}{\rho}\left|\frac{d\mathbf{R}}{dt}\right| = \frac{v^2}{\rho}.$$

Example 3. Let us consider a special case of oscillation on a straight line:

$$\mathbf{R} = b \cos \omega t\, \mathbf{I}.$$

Compute the acceleration for both the extreme and the neutral positions.

SOLUTION. First we may get a general expression for the acceleration by differentiating twice:

$$\mathbf{A} = \frac{d^2\mathbf{R}}{dt^2} = -b\omega^2 \cos \omega t\, \mathbf{I}.$$

Note that this expression shows it to be a scalar (negative) multiple of $\mathbf{R}$:

$$(5.31) \qquad \mathbf{A} = -\omega^2\mathbf{R}.$$

This may at once be interpreted as a "restoring acceleration proportional to displacement." Now we may evaluate $\mathbf{A}$ for the specific cases required:

$$\mathbf{A} = +b\omega^2\mathbf{I}, \quad \text{when } \mathbf{R} = -b\mathbf{I},$$
$$\mathbf{A} = \mathbf{O}, \quad \text{when } \mathbf{R} = \mathbf{O},$$
$$\mathbf{A} = -b\omega^2\mathbf{I}, \quad \text{when } \mathbf{R} = +b\mathbf{I}.$$

Tangential and Normal Components of Acceleration. Having examined these special illustrations, let us return to the general treatment of acceleration. Using the expression $\mathbf{V} = v\mathbf{T}$,

$$\mathbf{A} = \frac{d}{dt}(v\mathbf{T}) = \frac{dv}{dt}\mathbf{T} + v\frac{d\mathbf{T}}{dt}.$$

This is a very intuitive expression for the acceleration. Here we discover explicitly that the tangential component of the acceleration vector is the *rate of increase of speed.*

$$a_T = \frac{dv}{dt}. \tag{5.32}$$

A more instructive form of the second term is easily obtained by substituting the value of $d\mathbf{T}/dt$ obtained in (5.27). For the normal component we get

$$a_N = v^2\kappa = \frac{v^2}{\rho}. \tag{5.33}$$

Note that this normal component is merely the *centripetal acceleration* which we discovered in the second example. The total acceleration then may be written

$$\mathbf{A} = a_T\mathbf{T} + a_N\mathbf{N} = \frac{dv}{dt}\mathbf{T} + \frac{v^2}{\rho}\mathbf{N}. \tag{5.34}$$

This is one of the central equations of kinematics. The student will find it instructive to interpret each of the three examples already studied in terms of this general equation. For straight-line motion, the curvature is zero. For uniform speed, a_T is zero. Let us now examine a problem which will involve somewhat fuller use of (5.34).

Example 4. The position of a moving particle is given by

$$\mathbf{R} = 2t\mathbf{I} - 3t^2\mathbf{J} + 1.5\mathbf{K} \qquad \text{ft, sec.}$$

Find v, $\mathbf{T}$, a_T, a_N for $t = 0.25$ sec.

SOLUTION. Differentiating, we obtain

$$\mathbf{V} = 2\mathbf{I} - 6t\mathbf{J} = 2\mathbf{I} - 1.5\mathbf{J}.$$

From this we deduce: $v = 2.5$ ft/sec and $\mathbf{T} = 0.8\mathbf{I} - 0.6\mathbf{J}$ at $t = 0.25$. Taking the next derivative, $\mathbf{A} = -6\mathbf{J}$. The normal and tangential accelerations may be computed thus:

$$a_T = \mathbf{A}\cdot\mathbf{T} = 3.6 \qquad \text{positive; so speed is increasing.}$$
$$a_N\mathbf{N} = \mathbf{A} - a_T\mathbf{T} = -6\mathbf{J} - 3.6(0.8\mathbf{I} - 0.6\mathbf{J}) = -2.88\mathbf{I} - 3.84\mathbf{J}.$$

The magnitude of this vector is

$$a_N = 4.8 \text{ ft/sec}^2.$$

An alternative approach to these last results is worth contemplating. From the expressions $\mathbf{V} = v\mathbf{T}$ and $\mathbf{A} = a_T\mathbf{T} + a_N\mathbf{N}$ it is clear that

$$\mathbf{V}\cdot\mathbf{A} = va_T, \qquad \mathbf{V}\times\mathbf{A} = va_N\mathbf{B}, \tag{5.35}$$

where **B** is the unit vector **T** × **N**. In this example **V** × **A** = −12**K**; therefore we have

$$a_N = \frac{12}{2.5} = 4.8 \text{ ft/sec}^2$$

as before. Note too that we can easily devise a kinematic method for computing the radius of curvature of a curve. Applying the method to our example,

$$\rho = \frac{v^2}{a_N} = \frac{6.25}{4.8} = 1.3 \text{ ft.} \tag{5.36}$$

EXERCISES

1. The position of a particle traveling along a straight line is given by

$$\mathbf{R} = 5\mathbf{J} + 0.5t^2\mathbf{I}.$$

Draw a diagram showing **R**, **V**, and **A** at $t = 0, 1, 4$ sec.

2. The position of a particle in a helical trajectory is given by

$$\mathbf{R} = 4\cos 2t\,\mathbf{I} + 4\sin 2t\,\mathbf{J} + 6t\mathbf{K} \qquad \text{m, sec.}$$

At $t = 0.785$ sec, find v, **T**, a_T, a_N, ρ.

3. The position of a particle in the xy plane is given by

$$x = 30.0t, \qquad y = -10.0t^2 \qquad \text{ft, sec.}$$

Find for $t = 2$ the speed and the normal component of acceleration.

4. A particle starts from rest and travels around a circle of radius 10 cm with a speed proportional to the time. If it takes 2 sec for the first complete revolution, what is the magnitude of the normal and tangential components of acceleration after 3 sec?

5. A particle is moving around a circle of radius 2 ft so that the distance s along the arc from a certain point on the circumference t sec after starting is $s = 0.5t^3 + t^2$. Find a_N and a_T for $t = 2$ sec.

6. The position vector of an oscillating particle is given by

$$\mathbf{R} = \sin t\,\mathbf{I} + t\mathbf{J}.$$

Find for $t = 1.571$ sec the normal and tangential components of the acceleration.

7. The distance s in centimeters from a fixed point O measured along a circle of radius 12 cm traveled at time t is given for a particle P by $s = 3t + 0.75t^2$. Compute the magnitude of the acceleration for $t = 2$ sec.

8. Given

$$v = 3s^2 - 12s,$$

where s is the distance from a fixed reference point along a curved path. For what s is the tangential component of the acceleration equal to zero?

5.7. Radial and Transverse Components. It might seem that two sets of reference vectors **I, J, K** and **T, N, B** would suffice for handling kinematic situations. On the whole this is true. When one is discussing theories of motion, one is likely to favor the "intrinsic vectors" **T, N,** and **B** which depend only on the shape of the path and the sense of motion along *it*. In solving numerical problems the "fixed vectors" **I, J,** and

K are a natural basis for analytical procedures. There are some circumstances, however, that suggest just as naturally the use of unit vectors based on the direction of a position vector; so we shall pause briefly to develop this additional machinery for *motion in the xy plane.* This will require us to study the derivatives of the unit radial vector $\mathbf{L} = 1\underline{/\theta}$. Suppose that during a time interval t to $t + \Delta t$, **L** changes in direction from **L** to **L**′ as in Fig. 5.18. Then following a pattern used more than once we may observe that the quotient of the difference $\mathbf{L}' - \mathbf{L} = \Delta\mathbf{L}$ divided by the angular displacement $\Delta\theta$ is a vector whose length approaches unity as smaller and smaller values of $\Delta\theta$ are considered, and whose direction is perpendicular in the limit to **L**. Our conclusion is that the corresponding derivative is a unit vector perpendicular to **L**. For the case where θ is increasing, this is denoted by **M** (otherwise for decreasing θ by $-\mathbf{M}$).

$$(5.37) \qquad \frac{d\mathbf{L}}{d\theta} = \frac{d}{d\theta}(1\underline{/\theta}) = 1\underline{/\theta + 90^\circ} = \mathbf{M}$$

(for increasing θ).

$$(5.38) \qquad \mathbf{M} \cdot \mathbf{M} = 1, \qquad \mathbf{M} \cdot \mathbf{L} = 0.$$

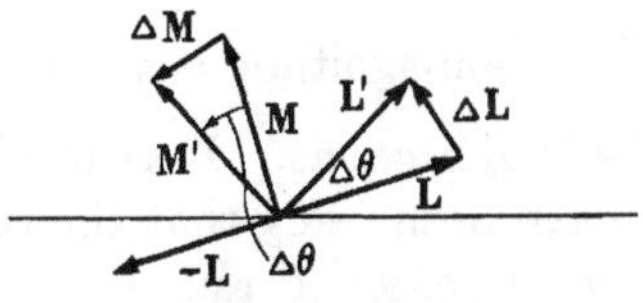

FIG. 5.18.

Note that as in the other cases we have a triad of reference unit vectors: **K, L, M** such that $\mathbf{K} \times \mathbf{L} = \mathbf{M}$, etc.

Next we must consider the derivative of **M**. Since $\mathbf{M} = 1\underline{/\theta + 90^\circ}$, it is apparent that, for increasing θ,

$$(5.39) \qquad \frac{d\mathbf{M}}{d\theta} = 1\underline{/\theta + 90^\circ + 90^\circ} = -\mathbf{L}.$$

Finally, applying the chain rule for differentiation as in similar cases previously, we get

$$(5.40) \qquad \frac{d\mathbf{L}}{dt} = \frac{d\theta}{dt}\mathbf{M}, \qquad \frac{d\mathbf{M}}{dt} = -\frac{d\theta}{dt}\mathbf{L}.$$

We are now in a position to derive expressions for velocity and acceleration in terms of the *radial unit vector* **L** and the *transverse unit vector* **M** for motion in a plane (see Fig. 5.19). Starting with the familiar relation $\mathbf{R} = r\mathbf{L}$, which we differentiate with respect to t, we obtain

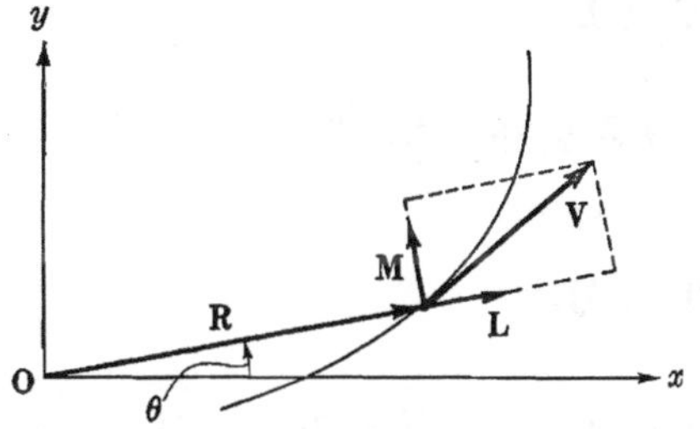

FIG. 5.19.

$$(5.41) \qquad \mathbf{V} = \frac{dr}{dt}\mathbf{L} + r\frac{d\theta}{dt}\mathbf{M}.$$

A second differentiation yields the acceleration. Since this affords

good practice in routine manipulations, only the result is stated now. The details are left as an exercise for the student.

$$\mathbf{A} = \left[\frac{d^2r}{dt^2} - r\left(\frac{d\theta}{dt}\right)^2\right]\mathbf{L} + \left(2\frac{dr}{dt}\frac{d\theta}{dt} + r\frac{d^2\theta}{dt^2}\right)\mathbf{M}. \tag{5.42}$$

Example 1. A metal collar slides outward at a uniform radial speed of 50 ft/sec along the spoke of a wheel rotating uniformly at 10 rad/sec. For the moment when its distance from the center is 4 ft, compute the magnitudes of the acceleration and the velocity.

SOLUTION. First applying (5.41),

$$\mathbf{V} = 50\mathbf{L} + 4(10)\mathbf{M}.$$

This is a vector of magnitude 64 ft/sec. Next applying (5.42),

$$\mathbf{A} = -400\mathbf{L} + 1{,}000\mathbf{M}$$

whose magnitude is about 1,080 ft/sec².

Applications. It is profitable to observe from the equations that we have been using that the rate of rotation of a position vector or the rate of increase of radial distance for a moving particle may easily be approached. First, whether the motion be plane or not, from $\mathbf{R} = r\mathbf{L}$ we deduce

$$\mathbf{V} = \frac{dr}{dt}\mathbf{L} + r\frac{d\mathbf{L}}{dt}.$$

Since $\mathbf{L}$ is a vector of constant length, we at once infer, by (5.14), that

$$\frac{d\mathbf{L}}{dt}\cdot\mathbf{L} = 0,$$

and hence

$$\frac{dr}{dt} = \mathbf{V}\cdot\mathbf{L}. \tag{5.43}$$

For the plane case it is apparent also that

$$\mathbf{L}\times\mathbf{V} = r\frac{d\theta}{dt}\mathbf{K},$$

so that

$$\frac{d\theta}{dt} = \frac{|\mathbf{V}\times\mathbf{L}|}{r}. \tag{5.44}$$

Example 2. $\mathbf{R} = 4t^2\mathbf{I} - 6t\mathbf{J}$. For $t = 2$, find $\frac{dr}{dt}, \frac{d\theta}{dt}$.

SOLUTION. Differentiating,

$$\mathbf{V} = 8t\mathbf{I} - 6\mathbf{J}.$$

At $t = 2$,

$$\mathbf{R} = 16\mathbf{I} - 12\mathbf{J}, \qquad \mathbf{L} = 0.8\mathbf{I} - 0.6\mathbf{J}, \qquad \mathbf{V} = 16\mathbf{I} - 6\mathbf{J};$$

hence

$$\mathbf{V}\cdot\mathbf{L} = 12.8 + 3.6 = 16.4,$$
$$\mathbf{V}\times\mathbf{L} = -9.6\mathbf{K} + 4.8\mathbf{K} = -4.8\mathbf{K}.$$

Thus

$$\frac{dr}{dt} = 16.4;$$
$$\frac{d\theta}{dt} = \frac{4.8}{20} = 0.24 \text{ rad/sec.}$$

Example 3. A sight which rotates about a vertical axis is used to follow a northbound airplane which passes in horizontal flight at 120 ft/sec 200 ft directly above a building 600 ft east of an observer. How fast is the distance from observer to plane increasing after one additional second? How fast is the sight being rotated at this moment?

SOLUTION. Let us pick axes as follows: **I** is east; **J** is north; **K** is up. Then

$$\mathbf{R} = 600\mathbf{I} + 120t\mathbf{J} + 200\mathbf{K}, \qquad \mathbf{V} = 120\mathbf{J},$$

and, at $t = 1$,

$$\mathbf{R} = 600\mathbf{I} + 120\mathbf{J} + 200\mathbf{K}, \qquad \mathbf{V} = 120\mathbf{J}.$$
$$\frac{dr}{dt} = \mathbf{V}\cdot\mathbf{L} = \frac{\mathbf{V}\cdot\mathbf{R}}{r} = \frac{14{,}400}{644} = 22.5 \text{ ft/sec.}$$

The change of line of sight involves the projection into the xy plane of the motion (since the axis is vertical). This means omitting 200**K** from the expression for **R**. Denoting the projected quantities with primes, we have

$$\frac{d\theta}{dt} = \left|\frac{\mathbf{V}'\times\mathbf{L}'}{r'}\right| = \left|\frac{\mathbf{V}'\times\mathbf{R}'}{r'^2}\right| = \frac{120\times 600}{612^2} = 0.192 \text{ rad/sec.}$$

EXERCISES

1. The angular position of a particle on a circle of radius 5 ft is indicated by $\theta = 3t^2$. For time $t = 0.5$ sec, compute the normal, tangential, and the total acceleration of the particle. Use Eqs. (5.41) and (5.42) with the proper correlation of **T** and **N** with **L** and **M**.

2. A wheel of radius 24 in. rolls without slipping along a level road at 8 in./sec. An insect walks outward along a spoke at the speed (relative to the wheel) of 5 in./sec. What is the actual speed of the insect at the instant when his spoke is vertical upward and his distance from the center is 1 ft?

3. A point moves along the spoke of a wheel so that its distance from the axis of the wheel is $r = 6 + 4\cos t$, r in feet, t in seconds. If the wheel rotates at 0.5 rad/sec, what is the maximum speed of the point?

4. An airplane traveling at 200 ft/sec has passed overhead at a height of 100 ft. When the line of sight becomes 30° above the horizontal, how fast is this angle diminishing and how fast is the distance to the plane increasing?

5. Derive in detail Eq. (5.42).

6. A barge is being drawn toward a wharf by a rope which is being wound up on the wharf at the rate of 5 ft/sec. If the surface of the wharf is 20 ft above the barge, how fast is the barge moving when it is 40 ft away from the wharf?

7. If $\mathbf{A} = s\mathbf{L}$, where s is a variable scalar, prove that $\mathbf{R}\times\mathbf{V}$ is a constant vector.

5.8. Rectilinear Kinematics. The basic concepts for the quantitative study of motion have so far been introduced in a general way. Our displacements, velocities, and accelerations were vectors in widely varying directions. If the motion of a particle is restricted to a straight line, say the x axis, then, as we have seen previously, **R**, **V**, and **A** may be expressed in terms of the unit vector **I**:

$$\mathbf{R} = x\mathbf{I}, \qquad \mathbf{V} = \frac{dx}{dt}\mathbf{I} = \pm v\mathbf{I}, \qquad \mathbf{A} = \pm a\mathbf{I}. \tag{5.45}$$

The plus or minus alternative is indicated because v and a previously have been magnitudes and hence positive while the derivatives of x may be of either sign. Since this distinction is easily understood, we shall in this section dispense with the minus sign, letting v be negative for motion in the negative x direction. We shall write, for the purposes of this section,

$$v = \frac{dx}{dt}, \qquad a = \frac{dv}{dt}. \tag{5.46}$$

Direction plays such a limited role in straight-line motion that it is convenient to use these scalar equations instead of the vector ones first given. The chain rule of ordinary calculus yields an alternative expression for a:

$$a = \frac{dv}{dx}\frac{dx}{dt} = v\frac{dv}{dx}. \tag{5.47}$$

The three central scalar equations so far presented are investigated in most calculus courses; so it is perhaps unnecessary to pursue them here. Considering the importance of the topic, a cursory treatment will, however, be given.

Equations (5.46) and (5.47) were presented as expressions involving derivatives. Such expressions may also be regarded as relations between differentials. Either point of view suggests the possibility of carrying out integrations. The nature of the integration depends on whether v and a happen to be regarded as functions of x or t. In the following we shall write $v(t)$ for v if it is expressed explicitly as a function of t; $v(x)$ will be used if v is a function of x. With this understanding it is easy to see that numerous possibilities arise. They are stated both in the form of simple differential equations with variables separated and in the form of definite integrals where corresponding limits of integration are employed. This means merely that at time t_0 the values x_0, v_0, and a_0 apply, while at time t the proper values are x, v, and a. This use of corresponding limits is easily seen to be equivalent to using indefinite integrals and constants of integration to be evaluated with initial or other conditions.

$$dx = v(t)dt \quad \text{or} \quad \int_{x_0}^{x} dx = \int_{t_0}^{t} v(t)dt. \tag{5.48}$$

$$dt = \frac{dx}{v(x)} \quad \text{or} \quad \int_{t_0}^{t} dt = \int_{x_0}^{x} \frac{dx}{v(x)}. \tag{5.49}$$

$$dv = a(t)dt \quad \text{or} \quad \int_{v_0}^{v} dv = \int_{t_0}^{t} a(t)dt. \tag{5.50}$$

$$v\,dv = a(x)dx \quad \text{or} \quad \int_{v_0}^{v} v\,dv = \int_{x_0}^{x} a(x)dx. \tag{5.51}$$

$$dt = \frac{dv}{a(v)} \quad \text{or} \quad \int_{t_0}^{t} dt = \int_{v_0}^{v} \frac{dv}{a(v)}. \tag{5.52}$$

$$\frac{v\,dv}{a(v)} = dx \quad \text{or} \quad \int_{x_0}^{x} dx = \int_{v_0}^{v} \frac{v\,dv}{a(v)}. \tag{5.53}$$

These long expressions assuredly are not to be memorized. The student should rather commit to memory (5.46) and (5.47). Then he should practice manipulating these expressions until he can see how (5.48) to (5.53) can be at once deduced.

Example 1. A point moves on the x axis with speed given by $v = 2x^2$. At time $t = 0$, it is at $x = 1$. Find the time required for it to reach $x = 2$ and the acceleration at $x = 2$. Units are feet, seconds, etc.

SOLUTION

$$v = \frac{dx}{dt} = 2x^2, \qquad dt = \frac{dx}{2x^2};$$

$$t = \int_1^2 \frac{dx}{2x^2} \quad \text{or} \quad t = 0.25 \text{ sec.}$$

$$a = v\frac{dv}{dx} = (2x^2)(4x) = 8x^3 = 64 \text{ ft/sec}^2.$$

Example 2. *Freely Falling Bodies.* Near the surface of the earth objects experience a downward acceleration ranging in this vicinity from 9.78 m/sec^2 in Central America to 9.82 m/sec^2 in Alaska. A "standard value," 9.80665 m/sec^2 or 32.174 ft/sec^2, rounded off to 9.81 or 32.2 will be used in problems here. At any one locality this acceleration for free fall may be considered as constant, provided that air friction can be neglected. In Exercise 1 the student will derive some formulas analogous to those used in elementary physics.

EXERCISES

1. Given the following: a is a constant; subscript 0 indicates values at time $t = 0$. Using the methods of this section verify the following equations:

$$v^2 - v_0^2 = 2a(x - x_0),$$

$$x - x_0 = v_0 t + \tfrac{1}{2}at^2,$$

$$\frac{x - x_0}{t} = v_{\text{eff}} = \frac{1}{2}(v + v_0).$$

2. A brick is dropped from the top of a high building. Ten feet below the starting point is the top of a window 10 ft high. How long does the brick spend in passing the window?

3. A man can throw a ball at 100 ft/sec. He stands on a platform 50 ft above the ground. How high above the ground can he throw the ball? With what maximum and what minimum speeds can he make the ball hit the ground?

4. A train starts from a station with a constant acceleration and reaches a speed of 60 mph in 2 min. It runs for 10 min at this speed and then reduces its speed uniformly during the next 3 min and stops at the next station. What in miles is the distance between the stations?

5. A point moves along the x axis according to the law $v = 2x + 3$ (feet, seconds). What is its acceleration when it passes through the origin? How long does it take the point to move from the origin to the point $x = 13.5$?

6. A point moves along the x axis, starting from the origin, according to the equation

$$v = \frac{2}{1 + x} \qquad \text{cm, sec.}$$

How long does it take the point to reach the position $x = 4$ cm? For what x would the acceleration be -4 cm/sec²?

7. A point starts from the origin along the positive x axis with a velocity (meters per second) inversely proportional to $x + 5$ (meters). It takes it 10 sec to go a distance of 20 m. What was the starting velocity?

8. A horse runs 10 mph on a circular mile track in the center of which is a lamppost which casts a shadow of the horse on a straight fence tangent to the track at the starting point. Find the acceleration of both horse and shadow (in miles per hour per hour) when he is $\frac{1}{8}$ mile from the starting point.

9. The acceleration (centimeters per second per second) of a particle falling vertically in a resisting medium is given in terms of the speed (centimeters per second) by

$$a = 5 - 2v.$$

If the particle falls from rest, how long in seconds will it take it to acquire a speed of 1.25 cm/sec?

10. The speed of a moving particle sliding along the x axis is given as $v = -x$ (feet, seconds). How long does it take to travel from $x = 5$ to $x = 3$? What is the acceleration at $x = 5$?

11. The acceleration of a particle moving along the x axis is given as $a = 6t - 3t^2$. At $t = 0$, the particle is at rest at $x = 1$. Find the speed at $t = 1$.

5.9. Simple Harmonic Motion. This section is devoted to a single outstandingly significant example of rectilinear motion. A more general form of the defining equation appeared in an earlier section [see Eq. (5.31)]. Limiting the motion to the x axis, we start with

$$a = -\omega^2 x. \tag{5.54}$$

This equation merely tells us that the motion is characterized by a restoring acceleration proportional to the displacement from the origin. What is the nature of the motion? This is our problem, to be solved by the methods of the preceding section.

Starting with

$$v\,dv = -\omega^2 x\,dx \qquad \text{or} \qquad \int_{v_0}^{v} v\,dv = -\omega^2 \int_{x_0}^{x} x\,dx,$$

we get

$$v^2 - v_0^2 = \omega^2 x_0^2 - \omega^2 x^2.$$

This implies that

(5.55) *The quantity* $v^2 + \omega^2 x^2$ *must be a constant for the motion governed by* (5.54).

Such an assertion immediately suggests that the motion is oscillatory, the maximum speed v_m and the maximum displacement (or amplitude) x_m being related by

$$v_m^2 = \omega^2 x_m^2.$$

Taking the position of maximum positive displacement (and hence of zero velocity) as a reference point, we have

$$v^2 = \omega^2(x_m^2 - x^2).$$

Solving for v (and picking the sign of the root to agree with that of v), we get

$$\frac{dx}{dt} = \omega\sqrt{x_m^2 - x^2},$$

or

$$\omega \int dt = \int \frac{dx}{\sqrt{x_m^2 - x^2}} + \text{const.}$$

Integration yields, letting $t = t_0$ for $x = 0$,

$$\omega(t - t_0) = \sin^{-1}\frac{x}{x_m},$$

or

(5.56) $$x = x_m \sin \omega(t - t_0).$$

The angle $-\omega t_0$ is often called the epoch angle, denoted by ϵ, and the equation (5.56) is written:

(5.57) $$x = x_m \sin(\omega t + \epsilon).$$

If ϵ happens to be chosen as $90° + \epsilon'$, the equation becomes

(5.58) $$x = x_m \cos(\omega t + \epsilon').$$

This may be compared with Example 3, Sec. 5.6. Many other equivalent forms are available and often used. In any case the *period* of an oscillation described by (5.54) is well known:

(5.59) $$\tau = \frac{2\pi}{\omega}.$$

It will pay the student to remember something equivalent to the following:

(5.60) *A motion governed by the equation* $a = -\omega^2 x$ *is a simple harmonic oscillation of period* $2\pi/\omega$.

EXERCISES

1. A point moves along the x axis according to the law $a + 4x = 0$. The largest value of x is 10. With what speed does the point go through the origin? How long does it take the point to go from $x = 2$ to $x = 6$?

2. Prove that the projection onto a diameter of a particle traveling at uniform speed around a circle is simple harmonic.

3. A point in simple harmonic motion has a period of 2 sec and an amplitude of 3 ft. What is the maximum speed? What is the maximum acceleration?

4. Discuss as fully as you can the motion of a particle subject to the relation

$$a = -6(x - 4).$$

5.10. Integral Calculus for Vectors. Up to this point we have considered only the differential calculus of vectors. To each vector function $\mathbf{R}$ of a scalar variable t we have seen how to assign, exceptional cases excepted, a new vector function, the derivative of $\mathbf{R}$ with respect to t:

$$\mathbf{V}(t) = \frac{d\mathbf{R}(t)}{dt}. \tag{5.61}$$

On the other hand, given a suitable vector function $\mathbf{V}(t)$, one can call $\mathbf{R}(t)$ an integral of $\mathbf{V}(t)$. Such integrals, as in scalar calculus, may differ by a constant (vector) of integration. Copying the usual nomenclature for the indefinite integral, we get

$$\mathbf{R}(t) = \int \mathbf{V}(t)dt. \tag{5.62}$$

Suppose that another pair of functions $\mathbf{R}'$ and $\mathbf{V}'$ are related similarly. Then we already know that

$$\frac{d}{dt}(\mathbf{R} + \mathbf{R}') = \mathbf{V} + \mathbf{V}'.$$

Consequently

$$\int(\mathbf{V} + \mathbf{V}')dt = \mathbf{R} + \mathbf{R}' = \int \mathbf{V}\, dt + \int \mathbf{V}'\, dt. \tag{5.63}$$

In a similar manner we may verify for constants c and $\mathbf{C}$ and functions u and $\mathbf{V}$

$$\begin{gathered} \int c\mathbf{V}\, dt = c\int \mathbf{V}\, dt, \qquad \int \mathbf{C}u\, dt = \mathbf{C}\int u\, dt, \\ \int \mathbf{C}\cdot\mathbf{V}\, dt = \mathbf{C}\cdot\int \mathbf{V}\, dt, \qquad \int \mathbf{C}\times\mathbf{V}\, dt = \mathbf{C}\times\int \mathbf{V}\, dt. \end{gathered} \tag{5.64}$$

Applying these conclusions, we get

$$\int \mathbf{V}\, dt = \mathbf{I}\int v_x\, dt + \mathbf{J}\int v_y\, dt + \mathbf{K}\int v_z\, dt. \tag{5.65}$$

This shows that (5.62) is equivalent to

$$x = \int v_x\, dt, \qquad y = \int v_y\, dt, \qquad z = \int v_z\, dt. \tag{5.66}$$

Proceeding from the point of view of definite integration, we may consider for a range of the scalar variable t, say from t_0 to t_1, an expression of the sort

$$\lim_{\Delta t \to 0} \Sigma \mathbf{V}(t)\Delta t,$$

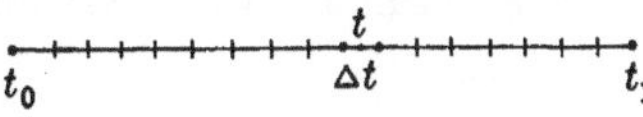

FIG. 5.20.

where it is understood that each $\mathbf{V}(t)$ is evaluated for some t in the corresponding Δt (see Fig. 5.20). One way of interpreting this limit is by resolving into components

$$\lim_{\Delta t \to 0} \Sigma \mathbf{V}(t)\Delta t = [\lim_{\Delta t \to 0} \Sigma v_x(t)\Delta t]\mathbf{I} + [\lim_{\Delta t \to 0} \Sigma v_y(t)\Delta t]\mathbf{J} + [\lim_{\Delta t \to 0} \Sigma v_z(t)\Delta t]\mathbf{K}.$$

The array on the right is immediately interpreted:

$$(5.67)\quad \lim_{\Delta t \to 0} \sum \mathbf{V}(t)\Delta t = \mathbf{I} \int_{t_0}^{t_1} v_x(t)dt + \mathbf{J} \int_{t_0}^{t_1} v_y(t)dt + \mathbf{K} \int_{t_0}^{t_1} v_z(t)dt.$$

Here the burden of proof has been shifted to the scalar point of view, but in the interest of brevity this ruse seems desirable. Needless to say the last expression suggests a symbol for our limit:

$$(5.68)\qquad \lim_{\Delta t \to 0} \sum_{t_0}^{t_1} \mathbf{V}(t)\Delta t = \int_{t_0}^{t_1} \mathbf{V}(t)dt.$$

Combining (5.67) and (5.68), one sees that definite integrals of this type must have the usual properties for scalar integrals. In particular, assuming (5.61), we have

$$(5.69)\qquad \int_{t_0}^{t_1} \mathbf{V}(t)dt = \mathbf{R}(t_1) - \mathbf{R}(t_0).$$

Example 1. *Projectile Motion.* A particle in motion near the earth is, neglecting friction, subject to a constant acceleration which we may express by

$$\mathbf{A} = \frac{d\mathbf{V}}{dt} = -g\mathbf{J}.$$

Integrating, we have

$$\mathbf{V} = \int -g\mathbf{J}\, dt + \mathbf{C}$$

or

$$\frac{d\mathbf{R}}{dt} = \mathbf{V} = -gt\mathbf{J} + \mathbf{V}_0,$$

where the constant of integration $\mathbf{C}$ is evaluated as the initial velocity $\mathbf{V}_0$. Integrating again,

$$(5.70)\qquad \mathbf{R} = \int(-gt\mathbf{J} + \mathbf{V}_0)dt + \mathbf{C}',$$

or

$$\mathbf{R} = -\tfrac{1}{2}gt^2\mathbf{J} + \mathbf{V}_0 t,$$

for if we initiate the motion at the origin it follows that $\mathbf{C}' = \mathbf{O}$. It is interesting to compare the scalar forms of this equation. Taking $\mathbf{V}_0$ in the xy plane at an elevation α we have

$$x = (v_0 \cos \alpha)t,\qquad (5.71)$$
$$y = -\tfrac{1}{2}gt^2 + (v_0 \sin \alpha)t.$$

These equations are familiar to most students of the calculus.

Example 2. A particle travels from $t = 0$ to $t = 3$ with velocity

$$\mathbf{V} = 4t\mathbf{I} - 3t^2\mathbf{J}.$$

What is the net displacement?

SOLUTION

$$\mathbf{R} = \int_0^3 \mathbf{V}\,dt = 2t^2\mathbf{I} - t^3\mathbf{J}\Big|_0^3 = 18\mathbf{I} - 27\mathbf{J}.$$

Example 3. *Centroids.* A nonkinematic example of definite integration involves the concept of centroid. Suppose that we have given a rigid body and that we divide it up, as in ordinary integral calculus, into convenient volume elements. Then from each element pick a point $\mathbf{R}$. If we use the volume of the element Δv as a scalar multiplier of $\mathbf{R}$, then add, and divide by the total volume, we get a "weighted mean" of the $\mathbf{R}$'s, where volume is the "weight function." Passing to the limit we have, by (5.68), a definite integral (divided by the volume)

$$\bar{\mathbf{R}} = \frac{1}{\text{vol}}\int_v \mathbf{R}\,dv = \frac{1}{\text{vol}}\lim_{\Delta v\to 0}\sum_v \mathbf{R}\,\Delta v.\qquad (5.72)$$

The point $\bar{\mathbf{R}}$ is called the *centroid.* The limits of the integration must be put in specifically when specific coordinates are chosen and the integration "set up" for actual computation. We indicate this part of the transaction here merely by the letter v under the integral sign. This means that if the integration is actually carried out the limits shall be so chosen as to cover the whole volume. For *our* purposes it is more important to understand the *idea* of (5.72) thoroughly than to be able to do heroic feats of integration. Computational technique is, of course, important and should be acquired in due time.

Scalar forms of (5.72) may already be familiar:

$$\bar{x} = \frac{1}{\text{vol}}\int_v x\,dv,\qquad \bar{y} = \frac{1}{\text{vol}}\int_v y\,dv,\qquad \bar{z} = \frac{1}{\text{vol}}\int_v z\,dv.\qquad (5.73)$$

The process here outlined could be applied to any other scalar function of a volume element. The mass (to be defined later) is used especially often: there, if Δm is the mass of the element of volume Δv, we should write

(5.74) $$\bar{\mathbf{R}} = \frac{1}{m}\int_m \mathbf{R}\,dm.$$

Now $\bar{\mathbf{R}}$ is called the *center of mass*. For objects of uniform density, the centroid and the center of mass coincide. Methods of computation will be given in a later chapter.

Example 4. *Impulse.* Another example of vector integration appears in the concept of impulse. It is defined by expressions of the form

$$\int_{t_0}^{t_1} \mathbf{F}(t)dt.$$

If $\mathbf{F}$ is a force varying with time, then this definite integral represents the net impulse exerted by $\mathbf{F}$ during the interval t_0 to t_1. This important concept will figure prominently in a later chapter.

EXERCISES

1. Plot for values of t from 0 to 4 two possible trajectories for which

$$\mathbf{V}(t) = 10\mathbf{I} + 2t\mathbf{J}.$$

2. Given: $\mathbf{A} = (h - t^2)\mathbf{J}$ ft/sec² and $\mathbf{V}_0 = v_0\mathbf{I}$ ft/sec. Derive an expression for $\mathbf{R}$ at time t for a particle projected from the origin at time $t = 0$. (h is a scalar constant.)

3. (*a*) Get an approximate value for $\int_0^6 (3\mathbf{I} + t\mathbf{J})dt$ by evaluating the corresponding sum using intervals Δt of length one. Illustrate with a diagram. (*b*) Check your value for part (*a*) by direct integration.

4. At time t a force is given by $\mathbf{F} = t\mathbf{I} - 10\mathbf{J}$ lb. What impulse is exerted between $t = 0$ and $t = 10$ sec?

5. What initial speed must a projectile have in order to attain an altitude of 6,400 ft (*a*) when the initial angle of elevation is 90°? (*b*) when the initial angle of elevation is 30°? (Assume gravity to be constant and friction to be negligible.)

6. The maximum range of a projectile is 2,000 yd. At what two angles of elevation will the range be 1,500 yd? (This assumes, of course, that the initial velocity always has the same magnitude.)

7. A projectile is shot uphill. Show that for maximum range the initial velocity vector should lie halfway between the vertical and the slope of the hill.

8. Use (5.72) to prove that the centroid of a body symmetrical in a point is its center.

9. If a body has a line or plane of symmetry, show that its centroid lies on this line or plane.

10. An object is composed of two parts: one of centroid $\bar{\mathbf{R}}'$ and volume v', the other of centroid $\bar{\mathbf{R}}''$ and volume v''. Prove that the centroid of the whole is

$$\bar{\mathbf{R}} = \frac{v'\bar{\mathbf{R}}' + v''\bar{\mathbf{R}}''}{v' + v''}.$$

11. Find the centroid of a set of three small identical spheres set each at a vertex of a large triangle. (Use the result of Exercise 10.)

12. A uniform wire 2 ft long is bent to form a circular arc of radius 1 ft. Where is the centroid? (HINT: Take origin at center. $dv = ra\,d\theta$, where a is area of cross section of wire and r is radius of the circle.)

13. A uniform 12-ft wire is bent to form a triangle of sides 3, 4, and 5 ft. Find the centroid.

CHAPTER 6

MOTION OF A RIGID BODY

As yet we have considered the motion of a single particle or point. While extended bodies can sometimes be considered as moving approximately like such single points, it is in general necessary to consider the motion of aggregates of particles. A swarm of unconnected or partly connected particles may move according to a very complicated pattern. Later we shall discover unifying characteristics of such motions. For the present we shall discuss the motions of aggregates in especially firm association, namely, rigid bodies (see Sec. 3.2). We shall be interested mainly in circumstances where deformations are negligible; therefore the rigid body is a practical object for our study. Wheels, pistons, cranks, spools, ladders, chairs, and vehicles may often be treated in this way.

6.1. Translation and Rotation of a Rigid Body. The motion even of a rigid body at first seems to offer a variety of complexities. It is easy to imagine twistings and spiralings which appear far from simple. In this section let us study briefly motions that are admittedly simple though distinctly important. We shall regard the motion of a rigid body as completely specified at any instant if we can compute the velocity and the position of every point of the body. In the simplest motion, *translation*, this is easily done. For *in translation, all points have identical velocities at any given time.* Suppose that **P** is a reference point in the body and **R** is any other representative point of the body (see Fig. 6.1). Then the formula for **V** at any time is simply

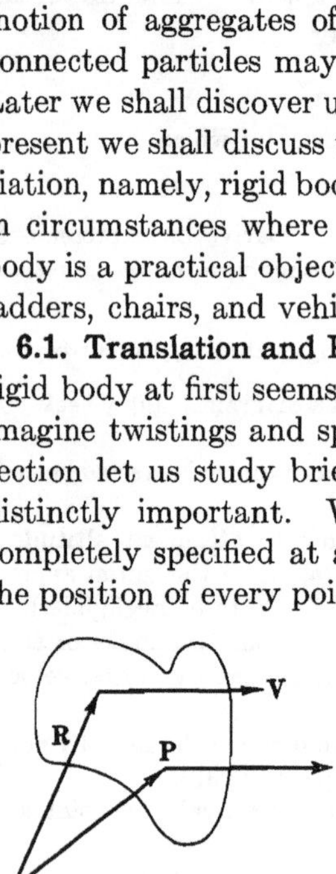

FIG. 6.1.

$$\mathbf{V} = \mathbf{V}_P. \tag{6.1}$$

Both members of this equation are functions of time; thus **V** may have any pattern already studied for a single point. Over any time interval any two points of a body in translation have the same displacement. Thus the simplifying fact of translation is that the paths traced out by different points are geometrically congruent (see Fig. 6.2). It follows that the orientation of the body is constant under translation. For instance, a steady compass needle set

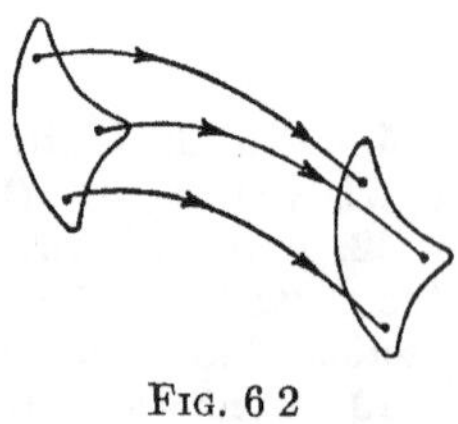
FIG. 6 2

to rotate freely about a vertical axis maintains a fixed orientation even when carried along a curved path. This is an example of curvilinear translation. More frequently encountered is motion along a straight path without change of orientation.

The second elementary motion of a rigid body is motion with one line of the body (or rigid extension thereof) fixed. Such motion is called *rotation*. For the fixed line the velocity of every point is, of course, zero. The motion of the body as a whole is best described in terms of angular displacements. Let us take the fixed line as, say, the z axis and consider the section of the body cut out by the xy plane. Let $\mathbf{P} = p\underline{/\theta}$ be a typical point of this section (see Fig. 6.3). Then θ may be thought of as a function of the time as the body rotates, it being understood that the axes do not rotate. If an angular displacement $\Delta\theta$ takes place during the time interval Δt, then the quotient $\Delta\theta/\Delta t$ is the average or *effective angular speed*. The instantaneous angular speed ω is defined by the equation

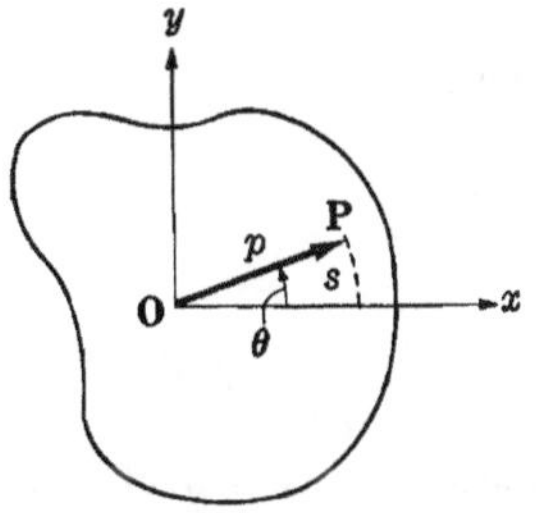

FIG. 6.3.

$$\omega = \lim_{\Delta t \to 0} \frac{\Delta\theta}{\Delta t} = \frac{d\theta}{dt}. \tag{6.2}$$

Similarly the rate of increase of angular speed, the scalar *angular acceleration*, is defined by

$$\alpha = \frac{d\omega}{dt} = \omega\frac{d\omega}{d\theta}. \tag{6.3}$$

These equations are entirely analogous to (5.46) and (5.47) concerning rectilinear motion. The corresponding variables are seen at once to be x and θ, v and ω, a and α, t and t.

Example 1. A wheel initially rotating at 120 rpm is subject to a deceleration given by $\alpha = -0.5\omega^2$. How long will it take for the wheel to halve its speed?

SOLUTION. It is given that $d\omega/dt = -0.5\omega^2$, and initially

$$\omega = 4\pi \text{ rad/sec.}$$

Integrating, we get

$$t = \int_0 dt = \int_{4\pi}^{2\pi} \frac{d\omega}{-0.5\omega^2} = \frac{2}{\omega}\Big|_{4\pi}^{2\pi} = \frac{1}{2\pi} = 0.16 \text{ sec.}$$

As is illustrated in Fig. 6.3, just as an application of the usual definition of the radian measure of an angle, $s = p\theta$. Since the perpendicular radius p is constant, successive differentiation yields similar relations between the angular velocity and the curvilinear speed of the point $\mathbf{P}$ as well as between the angular acceleration and the tangential acceleration of $\mathbf{P}$.

These equations, listed below, enable one to compute the speed and acceleration imparted to each point of a rigid body by its rotation around a fixed axis.

(6.4) $$p\frac{d\theta}{dt} = \frac{ds}{dt} \quad \text{or} \quad \omega p = v.$$

(6.5) $$p\frac{d\omega}{dt} = \frac{dv}{dt} \quad \text{or} \quad \alpha p = a_T.$$

Example 2. At a given moment a rigid body rotating about a fixed axis has an angular velocity of 2 rad/sec and an angular acceleration of 3 rad/sec². Find the magnitude of the total acceleration of a point of the body situated 20 cm from the axis of rotation.

SOLUTION

$$a_T = p\alpha = 20 \times 3 = 60 \text{ cm/sec}^2.$$

$$a_N = \frac{v^2}{\rho} = \frac{(20 \times 2)^2}{20} = 80 \text{ cm/sec}^2.$$

Thus $\mathbf{A} = 60\mathbf{T} + 80\mathbf{N}$ and $a = 100$ cm/sec².

EXERCISES

1. Prove that in any motion of a rigid body the velocities of any pair of points have equal components in the direction of the line joining them.

$$\left[\text{HINT: } \frac{d}{dt}(\mathbf{R}\cdot\mathbf{R}) = 0.\right]$$

2. At a given moment the point Q of a rigid body has velocity zero. Prove that the velocity of any other point P of the body satisfies the equation

$$\mathbf{V}_P \cdot \mathbf{P} = \mathbf{V}_P \cdot \mathbf{Q},$$

where **P** and **Q** are position vectors with respect to an arbitrary origin.

3. **M** is the mid-point of the segment **AB**, all three being points of a rigid body. **A** has velocity $10\mathbf{J}$, **B** has velocity $-4\mathbf{J}$. What is the velocity of **M**? Prove your result.

4. State and derive for θ and ω equations relating them to α and t subject to the assumption that α is constant.

5. A wheel rotates according to the pattern: $\theta + 4\alpha = 0$. Assuming that ω is equal to zero when $\theta = 1$ rad, what is the maximum angular speed, and how soon is it attained?

6. A wheel, uniformly accelerated, changes from a counterclockwise rotation at 10 rad/sec to a clockwise rotation of 10 rad/sec in 2 min. What is the angular acceleration and the effective angular speed for this time interval?

7. The angular speed of a wheel varies according to $\omega = 2\theta^{\frac{1}{2}}$. What is the time required for a displacement from $\theta = 4$ to $\theta = 9$ rad? What is the angular acceleration?

8. A wheel rotates according to the law $\alpha = 3t^2 - 2t$. If it starts rotating at 2 rad/sec, through what angle will it turn in the first 2 sec?

9. An angular rotation is subject to a deceleration given by $\alpha = -3\omega$. Through how great an angle does the wheel turn as the angular speed diminishes from 20 rad/sec to 10 rad/sec?

10. The angular speed of a rotating wheel is doubled while the wheel makes 10 revolutions. The constant angular acceleration is 30 rad/sec². What is the final angular speed?

11. A particle travels from rest about a circle of radius 3 cm at an angular speed given by $\omega = 3t$ rad/sec. Through what angle must it move before the total acceleration has magnitude 15 cm/sec²?

12. The wheel of a gyroscope which is 2 ft in radius is spinning about its fixed axis at the rate of 1,000 rpm. What is the total acceleration of a point on the outside rim of the wheel?

13. A particle travels around a circle of radius 10 ft with an angular acceleration of 3 rad/sec². At the moment when its angular speed is 2 rad/sec what are the magnitude and direction of its acceleration vector? Draw a circle to show direction.

14. A wheel of radius 6 in. rolls without slipping around the outside of a fixed circle also of radius 6 in. How many complete trips per second must it make in order that the angular speed of the wheel be 20 rad/sec?

15. A wheel of radius 1 in. rolls without slipping around the inside of a fixed circle of radius 1 ft twice a second. What is the angular speed of the small wheel?

6.2. Angular Velocity as a Vector. In the preceding section the angular speed of rotation about an axis was defined. We define now an associated *angular velocity vector* $\mathbf{\Omega}$ (see Fig. 6.4) directed along the axis of rotation (the z axis) in the sense given by the right-hand rule, and of magnitude ω; thus

$$\mathbf{\Omega} = \omega\mathbf{K}. \tag{6.6}$$

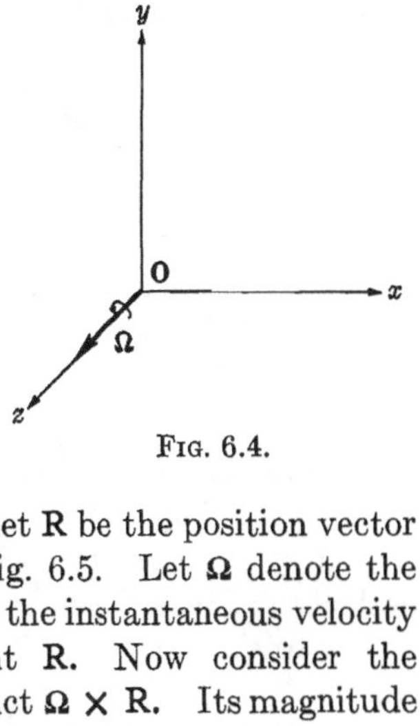

FIG. 6.4.

Just as in Sec. 5.8 we omitted the **I** in all equations, so in Sec. 6.1 it was not a disadvantage to deal with ω rather than $\mathbf{\Omega}$. But even in the simple case of a fixed axis of rotation vectors may be used to get expressions of helpful generality.

Taking our origin **O** on the axis of rotation, let **R** be the position vector of a representative point in the body as in Fig. 6.5. Let $\mathbf{\Omega}$ denote the instantaneous angular velocity. **V** will denote the instantaneous velocity of the point **R**. Now consider the vector product $\mathbf{\Omega} \times \mathbf{R}$. Its magnitude is $\omega r \sin\phi$, which we recognize as the speed of **R**. The direction of $\mathbf{\Omega} \times \mathbf{R}$, perpendicular to the plane of $\mathbf{\Omega}$ and **R**, is that of **T**, the unit tangent vector for the circular path traced out by the point **R**. Our conclusion is then

$$\mathbf{V} = \mathbf{\Omega} \times \mathbf{R}. \tag{6.7}$$

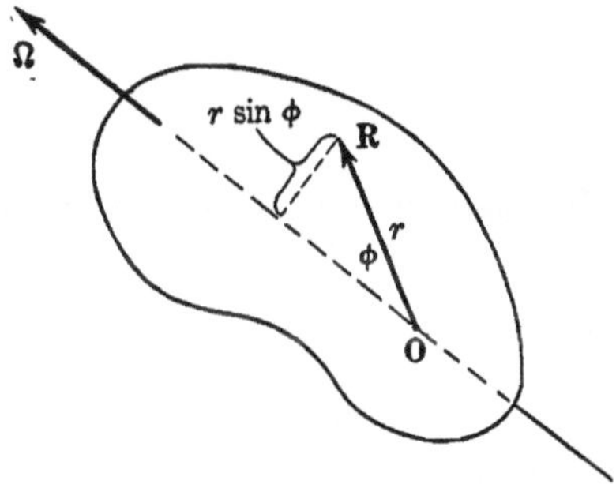

FIG. 6.5.

This is a very vital kinematic formula.

It should be understood, of course, that calling the rotation axis the z axis was merely a matter of convenience. Any fixed axis might be the rotation axis.

Vector Addition of Angular Velocities. One feels uneasy about representing quantities by vectors unless one has ascertained that, at least under favorable circumstances (such as concurrence for forces), the quantities combine like vectors—by the parallelogram rule. At first glance it is not at all obvious that angular velocities can reasonably be combined in this way. As an approach to this question let us suppose that a rigid body instantaneously has angular velocity $\mathbf{\Omega}_1 = \omega_1\mathbf{I}$ about the x axis and $\mathbf{\Omega}_2 = \omega_2\mathbf{J}$ about the y axis. This effect could, for instance, be obtained by rotating a spinning wheel and its support about an axis perpendicular to the spin axis. Let us compute the resulting behavior of the point (x,y) in the xy plane. Due to rotation about the x axis, it has an upward velocity $\omega_1 y\mathbf{K}$; due to rotation about the y axis the velocity is $-\omega_2 x\mathbf{K}$. We have already accepted the vector nature of linear velocity; so at once we add to get

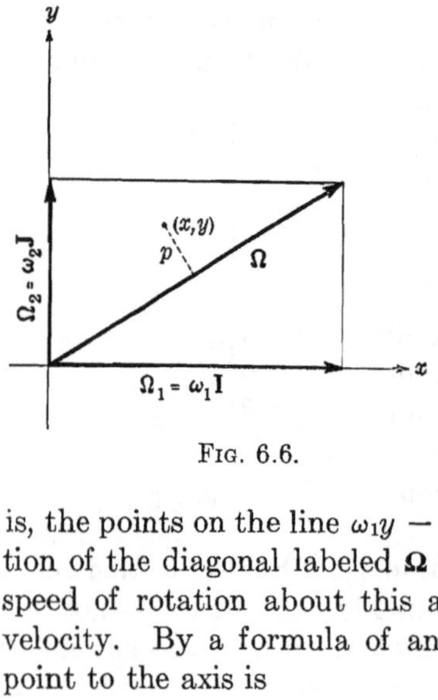

FIG. 6.6.

$$\mathbf{V} = (\omega_1 y - \omega_2 x)\mathbf{K}.$$

The speed is

$$v = \pm(\omega_1 y - \omega_2 x).$$

(The sign is taken to make v positive.) The effective axis of rotation is, of course, the locus of points for which $v = 0$; that is, the points on the line $\omega_1 y - \omega_2 x = 0$. Note well that this is the equation of the diagonal labeled $\mathbf{\Omega}$ in Fig. 6.6. Let us see, finally, for what speed of rotation about this axis our point would have the computed velocity. By a formula of analytic geometry the distance p from the point to the axis is

$$p = \frac{\omega_1 y - \omega_2 x}{\pm\sqrt{\omega_1^2 + \omega_2^2}}.$$

Just as in the preceding section the effective angular speed should be the quotient of v by p. This turns out to be

$$\omega = \sqrt{\omega_1^2 + \omega_2^2}. \tag{6.8}$$

This is the correct magnitude according to the vector configuration drawn in Fig. 6.6. Since this result is the same for any (x,y), we have in fact verified that the net result of the two angular velocities is the same instantaneously as that of the single angular velocity arrived at by adding the given ones as vectors.

The derivation just outlined brings us close to the facts but it is too long on the one hand and insufficiently general on the other. Referring now to Fig. 6.7, let us consider a general vector treatment. The equations only are given, since the main intentions of the argument are the same as before.

$$\mathbf{V} = \mathbf{V}_1 + \mathbf{V}_2 = \mathbf{\Omega}_1 \times \mathbf{R} + \mathbf{\Omega}_2 \times \mathbf{R}$$
$$= (\mathbf{\Omega}_1 + \mathbf{\Omega}_2) \times \mathbf{R}.$$

In other words the behavior of an arbitrary point **R** is precisely that which would be induced by a rotation $\mathbf{\Omega}$ given by

$$\mathbf{\Omega} = \mathbf{\Omega}_1 + \mathbf{\Omega}_2.$$

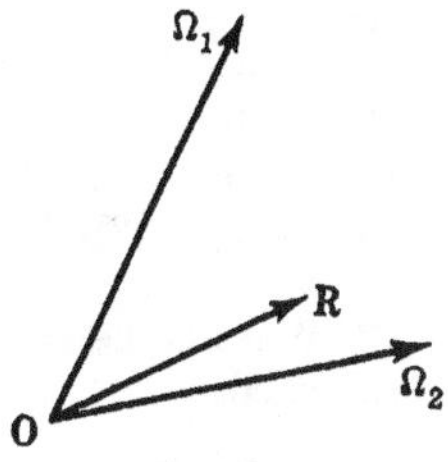

FIG. 6.7.

Example. Components of the Earth's Angular Velocity Vector. Another evidence of the vector nature of angular velocity is found in the local rotation of the earth's surface. Suppose that during the short time interval Δt the earth turns about its axis through an angle $\Delta\theta$. This means that meridian circle a in Fig. 6.8 turns into the position previously occupied by circle b. At a latitude λ how much of this rotation is experienced as a rotation? From the diagram it is clear that the direction of north (tangent to the meridian) has changed by an angle $\Delta\phi$. This is a rotation about an axis which is vertical at the point under consideration. For small enough angles, the arc Δs will do for determining the radian measure of either $\Delta\phi$ or $\Delta\theta$. Thus

$$\Delta\theta = \frac{\Delta s}{p}, \qquad \Delta\phi = \frac{\Delta s}{l} \cdot$$

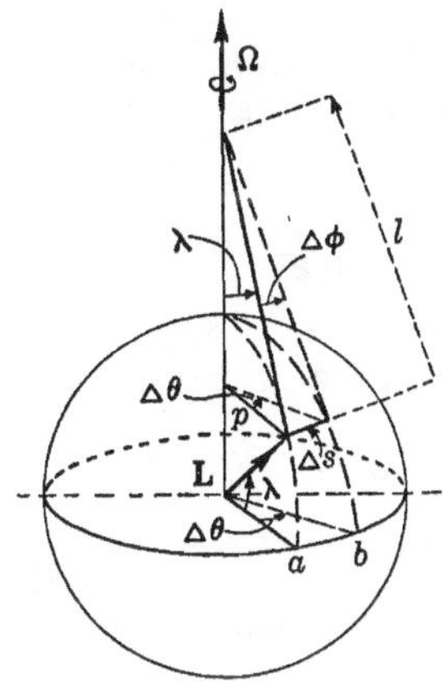

FIG. 6.8.

Hence

$$\frac{\Delta\phi}{\Delta\theta} = \frac{p}{l} = \sin\lambda = \cos(90° - \lambda).$$

Consequently

$$\frac{\Delta\phi}{\Delta t} = \frac{\Delta\theta}{\Delta t}\cos(90° - \lambda),$$

or in the limit, as Δt approaches zero,

$$\frac{d\phi}{dt} = \frac{d\theta}{dt}\cos(90° - \lambda).$$

Otherwise expressed,

(6.9) $$\omega_\lambda = \mathbf{\Omega} \cdot \mathbf{L}.$$

This is the desired result, for it shows that the local rotation is the component in that direction of the total angular velocity vector. Furthermore, this effect can be checked experimentally by means of a Foucault pendulum. The theory of this type of pendulum is given in Chap. 7.

EXERCISES

1. A rigid body rotates at 100 rad/sec about an axis with direction cosines (0.707,0, −0.707). With respect to an origin on the axis, the point **P** at a given instant has coordinates (3,4,5). Find the magnitude and direction cosines of the velocity of **P**. It is understood that the reference axes do not rotate but are fixed.

2. With respect to a fixed origin in a rigid body, point **A** of the body has coordinates (2,0,1) ft and velocity vector $-\mathbf{I} + \mathbf{J} + 2\mathbf{K}$ ft/sec. **B**, a point in the yz plane, has velocity $2\mathbf{J} + 2\mathbf{K}$ ft/sec. Find the direction cosines of the instantaneous axis of rotation, the angular speed, and the coordinates of **B**.

3. What is the angular speed due to the earth's rotation about a vertical axis of a field at latitude 45°N?

6.3. Further Conclusions about Rotation of a Rigid Body. We have already seen how for a position vector **R** the rate of change induced by rotation about a fixed axis is given by

$$\frac{d\mathbf{R}}{dt} = \mathbf{\Omega} \times \mathbf{R}. \tag{6.10}$$

This relationship has far wider application than at first appears. Let the vector **B** (drawn from **P** to **Q** in Fig. 6.9) be any vector fixed in a rigid body. Let us compute the rate of change of **B** due to rotation of the body about a fixed axis:

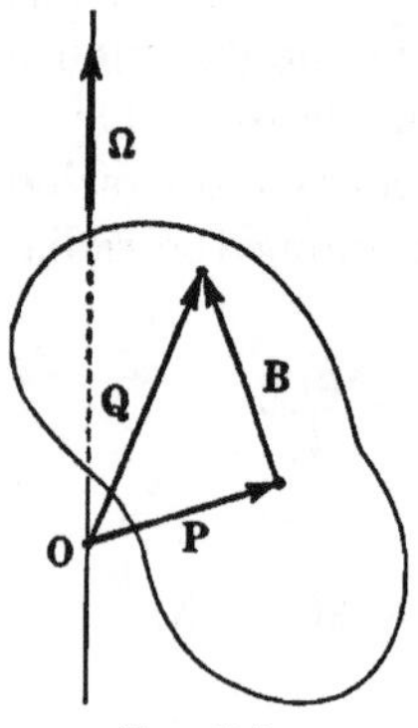

FIG. 6.9.

$$\frac{d\mathbf{B}}{dt} = \frac{d}{dt}(\mathbf{Q} - \mathbf{P}) = \frac{d\mathbf{Q}}{dt} - \frac{d\mathbf{P}}{dt}.$$

But both **P** and **Q** are vectors drawn from a point on the axis of rotation; thus (6.10) is applicable. Therefore

$$\frac{d\mathbf{B}}{dt} = \mathbf{\Omega} \times \mathbf{Q} - \mathbf{\Omega} \times \mathbf{P}.$$

Now using the distributive law for vector products, we get the desired result

$$\frac{d\mathbf{B}}{dt} = \mathbf{\Omega} \times (\mathbf{Q} - \mathbf{P}) = \mathbf{\Omega} \times \mathbf{B}.$$

(6.11) *Any vector* **B**, *constant with respect to a rigid body which is rotating with an angular velocity* **Ω**, *has induced by the rotation a rate of change given by*

$$\frac{d\mathbf{B}}{dt} = \mathbf{\Omega} \times \mathbf{B}.$$

This demonstrates how $\mathbf{\Omega} \times$ may be regarded as an *operator for differentiation.*

Acceleration Due to Rotation. As an application of (6.11) we shall find an expression for the acceleration of the point R of Fig. 6.5 for the case where $\mathbf{\Omega}$ is constant. The velocity vector V is then constant with respect to the body; thus

$$\mathbf{A} = \frac{d\mathbf{V}}{dt} = \mathbf{\Omega} \times \mathbf{V} = \mathbf{\Omega} \times (\mathbf{\Omega} \times \mathbf{R}).$$

For the sake of completeness, we shall include cases where $\mathbf{\Omega}$ is not constant. For this we need to define a *vector angular acceleration*, denoted by $\boldsymbol{\alpha}$,

$$\boldsymbol{\alpha} = \frac{d\mathbf{\Omega}}{dt}. \tag{6.12}$$

In the present case $\mathbf{\Omega}$ varies only in magnitude, since **K** is constant. Differentiating (6.6), we get

$$\boldsymbol{\alpha} = \frac{d}{dt}(\omega\mathbf{K}) = \frac{d\omega}{dt}\mathbf{K} = \alpha\mathbf{K}. \tag{6.13}$$

Now let us differentiate (6.7) in order to find an acceleration formula:

$$\mathbf{A} = \frac{d\mathbf{V}}{dt} = \frac{d}{dt}(\mathbf{\Omega} \times \mathbf{R}) = \boldsymbol{\alpha} \times \mathbf{R} + \mathbf{\Omega} \times \mathbf{V}$$

or

$$\mathbf{A} = \boldsymbol{\alpha} \times \mathbf{R} + \mathbf{\Omega} \times (\mathbf{\Omega} \times \mathbf{R}). \tag{6.14}$$

The student should convince himself that for circular motion Eq. (5.42) specializes to an equation equivalent to (6.14). In particular the second term of (6.14) is the centripetal acceleration.

Example. Precession. Figure 6.10 shows a gyroscope rotating with angular velocity

$$\mathbf{\Omega} = \omega\mathbf{E}.$$

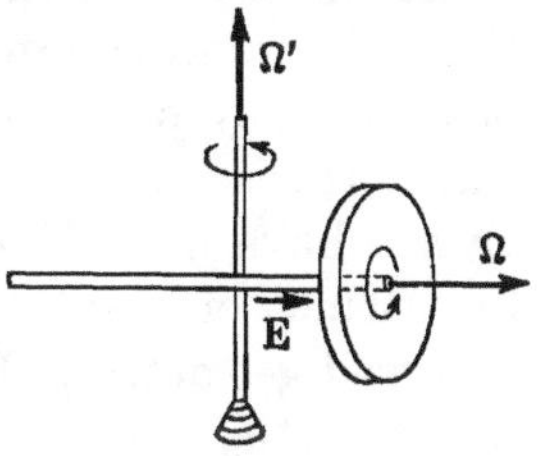

FIG. 6.10.

Suppose now that **E** rotates with an angular velocity $\mathbf{\Omega}'$. Then we have $\mathbf{\Omega}$ varying in direction. The angular acceleration, according to (6.12), is

$$\boldsymbol{\alpha} = \frac{d}{dt}(\omega\mathbf{E}) = \frac{d\omega}{dt}\mathbf{E} + \omega\frac{d\mathbf{E}}{dt}.$$

Since **E** is a vector of constant length, we can apply (6.11):

$$\frac{d\mathbf{E}}{dt} = \mathbf{\Omega}' \times \mathbf{E};$$

thus

$$\alpha = \alpha \mathbf{E} + \mathbf{\Omega}' \times \mathbf{\Omega}. \tag{6.15}$$

EXERCISES

1. A body rotates around the z axis uniformly at 20 rad/sec. Find the velocity and acceleration vectors for the point $\mathbf{I} - 2\mathbf{J} + 3\mathbf{K}$ ft.

2. A gyro rotating at a speed of 1,000 rad/sec about the x axis precesses about the y axis at 3 rad/sec. Find the angular acceleration vector.

3. For a particle in plane motion whose position vector is $\mathbf{R} = r\mathbf{L}$, show that the velocity vector may be written

$$\mathbf{V} = \frac{dr}{dt}\mathbf{L} + \mathbf{\Omega} \times \mathbf{R}.$$

4. $\mathbf{B}$ is any vector of constant length. Prove or disprove the statement: If $\mathbf{B}$ varies in direction then for an infinite number of vectors $\mathbf{\Omega}$, one can write

$$\frac{d\mathbf{B}}{dt} = \mathbf{\Omega} \times \mathbf{B}.$$

5. $\mathbf{B}$ is any vector of constant length. Prove that for the vector $\mathbf{\Omega}$ given by

$$\mathbf{\Omega} = \frac{\mathbf{B} \times (d\mathbf{B}/dt)}{\mathbf{B} \cdot \mathbf{B}},$$

it is true that $\mathbf{\Omega} \times \mathbf{B} = d\mathbf{B}/dt$.

6.4. General Motion of a Rigid Body. Thus far we have purposely considered only the simpler motions of a rigid body. Let us now turn to cases of greater generality. As a first step let us assume only that one point is held fixed during a displacement. Such is the motion of a top or gyro. As usual we shall watch the motion with respect to reference axes. The fixed point will be the origin **O**. The unit vectors along the axes are **I, J, K.** Now let us imagine a second set of unit vectors $\mathbf{I}'$, $\mathbf{J}'$, $\mathbf{K}'$, initially coincident with **I, J, K,** but rigidly attached to the body and hence moving with it. If we can analyze all possible displacements of $\mathbf{I}'$ and $\mathbf{J}'$, we shall automatically have handled the problem of the whole body, for any point of the body holds a fixed position relative to these axes. (It is not necessary to worry about $\mathbf{K}'$ separately because we always have $\mathbf{K}' = \mathbf{I}' \times \mathbf{J}'$.) Since the tips of $\mathbf{I}$, $\mathbf{J}$, $\mathbf{I}'$, and $\mathbf{J}'$ all lie in the surface of a sphere of radius 1, the problem is reduced to one of spherical geometry. The proposition to be proved is this:

(6.16) *Any possible displacement of a rigid body, one point being fixed, may be attained by a rotation about a single axis.*

To demonstrate this conclusion, let us first construct a plane through **O** bisecting $\mathbf{II}'$ and then a plane through **O** bisecting $\mathbf{JJ}'$. These planes are either identical or else they intersect in a line through **O** (as in Fig.

6.11). If they are identical, the great circles **JI** and **J′I′** intersect in a pole **P** on the sphere (see Fig. 6.12) such that a rotation through the

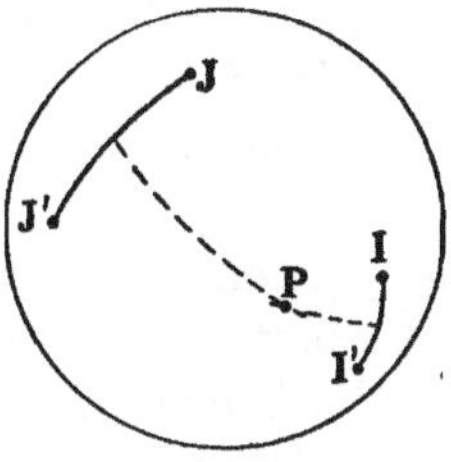

FIG. 6.11.

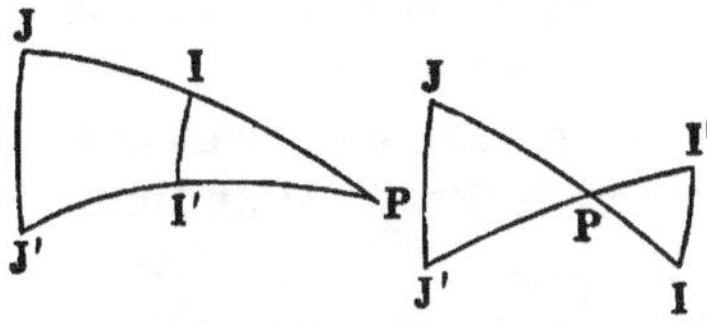

FIG. 6.12.

angle **JPJ′** (= **IPI′**) produces the desired displacement. If the two planes do intersect in a line **OP**, **P** being the intersection of the line with the sphere, then **OP** is the axis of rotation. The student should convince himself that the spherical triangles **J′I′P** and **JIP** (see Fig. 6.13) have equal sides, and hence are congruent. Consequently

$$\angle \mathbf{J'PI'} = \angle \mathbf{JPI};$$

and, subtracting $\angle \mathbf{JPI'}$ from each member,

$$\angle \mathbf{J'PJ} = \angle \mathbf{I'PI}.$$

This angle thus represents the amount of rotation about **OP** which would produce the desired displacement.

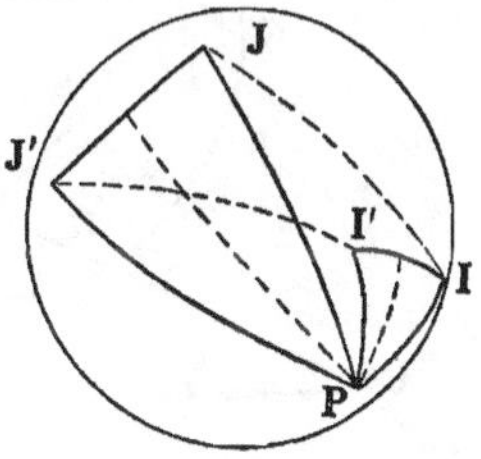

FIG. 6.13.

It is now easy to demonstrate the following:

(6.17) *Any motion of a rigid body, one point being fixed, is instantaneously a rotation about some axis through that point.*

For during any time interval Δt the net displacement $\Delta\mathbf{R}$ of any typical point on the body can, by (6.16), be analyzed in terms of an angular displacement $\Delta\theta$ about some axis having the direction of a particular unit vector **E**. As Δt is made to approach zero, let ω denote the limit of $\Delta\theta/\Delta t$. $\mathbf{\Omega}$ will denote the product of ω and the limiting value of **E**. This means that, however the rigid body may be moving, there is at any instant an angular velocity vector $\mathbf{\Omega}$ such that the velocity of any point **R** in the body is given by

$$\mathbf{V} = \mathbf{\Omega} \times \mathbf{R}. \tag{6.18}$$

Example 1. In the case of a precessing gyro, for instance, the motion might be thought of as two rotations superimposed or as a single instantaneous rotation about an axis between the spin axis and the precession axis as in Fig. 6.14.

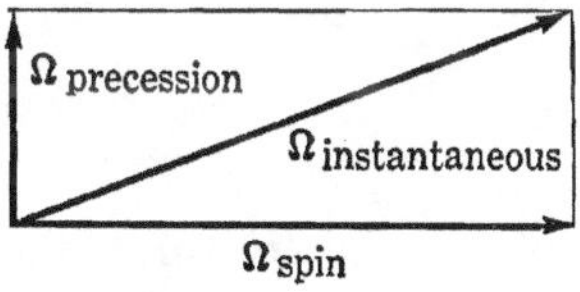

FIG. 6.14.

For our purposes the main value of (6.17) is the extension which can now be demonstrated.

(6.19) *Any motion of a rigid body can instantaneously be analyzed as a rotation superimposed on a translation.*

The worth of such a statement must be apparent; instead of confronting velocity problems associated with endless varieties of complicated motions, we can without loss concentrate on the two simplest modes already described in Sec. 6.1.

The proof of this statement is merely a combination of the results on relative motion (Sec. 5.4) and motion with one point fixed (Proposition 6.17). Given a rigid body in random motion and a fixed reference frame **OIJK** (see Fig. 6.15), pick any point **O′** in the body and take it as the origin for a new frame **I′J′K′** with axes parallel to **IJK.** Let **V′** denote the velocity of a typical point **R** in the moving body with respect to **I′J′K′** and **V** its velocity with respect to **IJK.** **R′** will denote the vector from **O′** to **R.** The velocity of **O′** relative to **IJK** is $\mathbf{V}_{O'}$; relative to **I′J′K′** it is zero [hence (6.17) may be applied in expressing **V′**]. By (5.16),

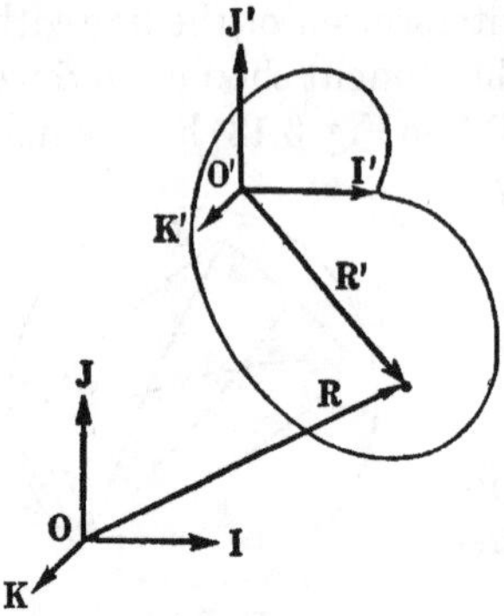

FIG. 6.15.

$$\mathbf{V} = \mathbf{V}_f + \mathbf{V}'.$$

By (6.18),

$$\mathbf{V}' = \mathbf{\Omega} \times \mathbf{R}'.$$

Our conclusion then is

(6.20) $$\mathbf{V} = \mathbf{V}_{O'} + \mathbf{\Omega} \times \mathbf{R}'.$$

The corresponding though more complex conclusion for acceleration is left for Exercise 5.

Example 2. The simplest and most vivid illustration of this important relationship is found in a rolling wheel. Pick **O′** as the center of the wheel. Then Eq. (6.20) states that the velocity pattern for points on the wheel may be constructed by superimposing and adding vectorially the velocity patterns as shown in Fig. 6.16: (*a*) for a pure translation,

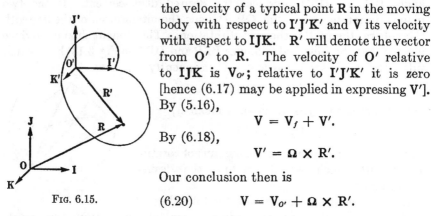

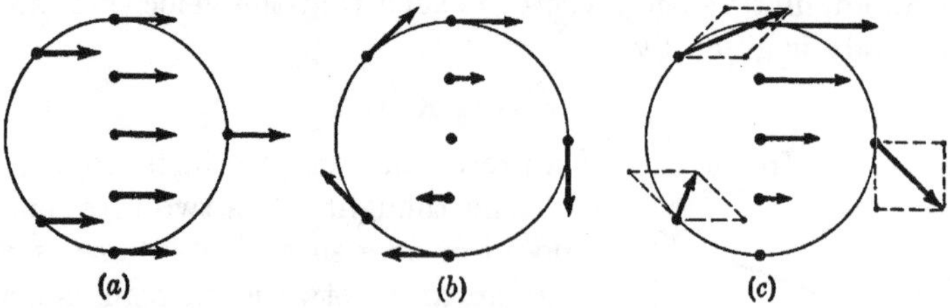

FIG. 6.16.

(*b*) for a pure rotation, and (*c*) the combination of (*a*) and (*b*) for rolling without slipping.

EXERCISES

1. Draw diagrams showing for several representative points how Eq. (6.20) adequately describes velocities of points on a wheel rolling without slipping (*a*) when **O′** is taken as the point instantaneously at the rear end of the horizontal diameter and (*b*) when **O′** is taken as the point instantaneously in contact with the ground.

2. A wheel of 30-in. diameter spins at 60 rad/sec while the vehicle advances at 30 mph. Find instantaneous velocities for points at the ends of the horizontal and vertical diameters.

3. A propeller of length 10 ft rotates at 1,000 rpm while being moved in the direction of its axis at 100 ft/sec. Find the speed of a point near the end of the propeller.

4. An automobile wheel is braked so that the velocity vector of the uppermost point is parallel to that of the lowest point and twice as large. Find the velocities of the points at the ends of a horizontal diameter.

5. Derive and interpret a formula for acceleration analogous to (6.20).

6. The center of a wheel of diameter 4 ft rotating about the z axis moves in the x direction at 20 ft/sec. At the same moment the leading point of the wheel has a speed of 35 ft/sec. What is the angular speed?

7. Use (6.20) to prove that any two points in a rigid body have equal velocity components in the direction of the angular velocity vector.

6.5. Instantaneous Axis of Rotation. We have seen that the velocities of a rigid body can at any instant be described as the sum of the velocity of a reference point **O′** of the body plus a velocity due to rotation about an axis through **O′**.

$$\mathbf{V}_R = \mathbf{V}_{O'} + \mathbf{\Omega} \times (\mathbf{R} - \mathbf{O}'). \tag{6.21}$$

In this equation **O′** is *any* reference point of the body, as in Fig. 6.17. We might wonder whether the use of another reference point might necessitate the use of a different angular velocity vector. Let us investigate this matter, choosing **O″** as a new reference point. Its velocity is given by (6.21) as

$$\mathbf{V}_{O''} = \mathbf{V}_{O'} + \mathbf{\Omega} \times (\mathbf{O}'' - \mathbf{O}'). \tag{6.22}$$

If we subtract (6.22) from (6.21), member by member, we obtain, after transposing the $\mathbf{V}_{O''}$,

$$\mathbf{V}_R = \mathbf{V}_{O''} + \mathbf{\Omega} \times (\mathbf{R} - \mathbf{O}''). \tag{6.23}$$

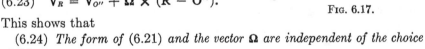

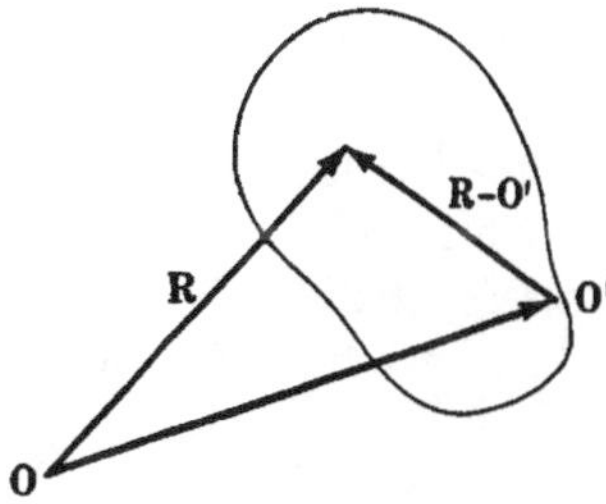

FIG. 6.17.

This shows that

(6.24) *The form of* (6.21) *and the vector* **Ω** *are independent of the choice of* **O′**.

An immediate corollary, allowing for taking components of the angular velocity vector, is

(6.25) *A rigid body has the same angular speed about any two axes in the same direction.*

The analysis of rigid-body velocities is simplified whenever one picks a reference point **C** which instantaneously is at rest. If such a point is found, then the motion is, according to (6.17), instantaneously a rotation about an axis through **C**. This axis is called the *instantaneous axis of rotation*. Such an axis will not always exist. For translation, for example, for every point **R**, $\mathbf{V}_R = \mathbf{V}_{O'}$ and $\mathbf{\Omega} = \mathbf{O}$.

Let us assume, in order to rule out translation, that $\mathbf{\Omega}$ is not a null vector and let us consider only points in a plane perpendicular to $\mathbf{\Omega}$ as in Fig. 6.18. In this plane let **R** be any typical point of the body. If in this plane there is a point **C** (of the body or an imagined rigid extension of it) which has zero velocity, we can use it in place of $\mathbf{O}''$ in (6.23) and have a velocity equation as simple as the one for rotation about a fixed axis:

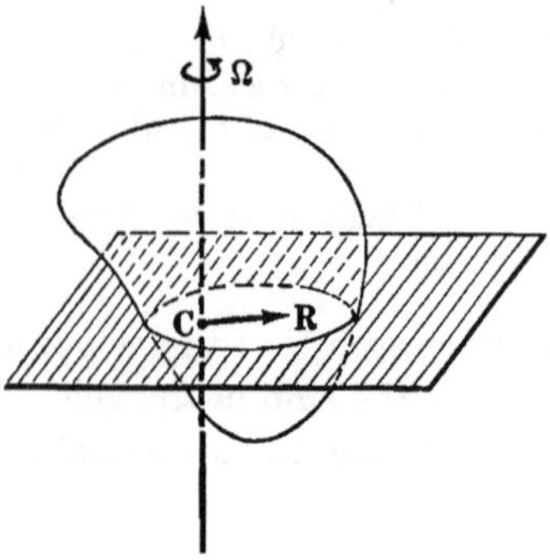

Fig. 6.18.

$$\text{(6.26)} \qquad \mathbf{V}_R = \mathbf{\Omega} \times (\mathbf{R} - \mathbf{C}).$$

Now we should like a way of finding such a point **C**; therefore we shall try to discover a formula. First take the vector product of each side of (6.26) by $\mathbf{\Omega}$:

$$\mathbf{\Omega} \times \mathbf{V}_R = \mathbf{\Omega} \times [\mathbf{\Omega} \times (\mathbf{R} - \mathbf{C})].$$

This may be simplified by using the vector identities of Chap. 2.

$$\mathbf{\Omega} \times \mathbf{V}_R = [\mathbf{\Omega} \cdot (\mathbf{R} - \mathbf{C})]\mathbf{\Omega} - (\mathbf{\Omega} \cdot \mathbf{\Omega})(\mathbf{R} - \mathbf{C}).$$

Since $\mathbf{R} - \mathbf{C}$ is normal to $\mathbf{\Omega}$, $\mathbf{\Omega} \cdot (\mathbf{R} - \mathbf{C}) = 0$. And since $\mathbf{\Omega} \neq \mathbf{O}$ we may divide by $\omega^2 = \mathbf{\Omega} \cdot \mathbf{\Omega}$. Solving for **C**,

$$\text{(6.27)} \qquad \mathbf{C} = \mathbf{R} + \frac{\mathbf{\Omega} \times \mathbf{V}_R}{\omega^2}.$$

Note that this formula is independent of $\mathbf{O}'$.

We have shown that *if* there is a point **C** of the plane at rest, it must satisfy (6.27). Let us see under what conditions $\mathbf{V}_C = \mathbf{O}$. Applying (6.21), we have for the velocity of **C**

$$\text{(6.28)} \qquad \mathbf{V}_C = \mathbf{V}_{O'} + \mathbf{\Omega} \times (\mathbf{C} - \mathbf{O}')$$

and for the velocity of a typical point **R**

$$\text{(6.29)} \qquad \mathbf{V}_R = \mathbf{V}_{O'} + \mathbf{\Omega} \times (\mathbf{R} - \mathbf{O}').$$

Subtracting member by member,

$$\mathbf{V}_C - \mathbf{V}_R = \mathbf{\Omega} \times (\mathbf{C} - \mathbf{R}).$$

Substituting (6.27), we get

$$\mathbf{V}_C - \mathbf{V}_R = \mathbf{\Omega} \times \left[\frac{(\mathbf{\Omega} \times \mathbf{V}_R)}{\omega^2}\right] = \left(\frac{\mathbf{\Omega} \cdot \mathbf{V}_R}{\omega^2}\right)\mathbf{\Omega} - \mathbf{V}_R$$

or

$$\mathbf{V}_C = \left(\frac{\mathbf{\Omega} \cdot \mathbf{V}_R}{\omega^2}\right) \mathbf{\Omega}. \tag{6.30}$$

From (6.29), taking the scalar product by $\mathbf{\Omega}$, we get

$$\mathbf{\Omega} \cdot \mathbf{V}_R = \mathbf{\Omega} \cdot \mathbf{V}_{O'}. \tag{6.31}$$

This may be substituted in (6.30) to give

$$\mathbf{V}_C = \left(\frac{\mathbf{\Omega} \cdot \mathbf{V}_{O'}}{\omega^2}\right) \mathbf{\Omega}. \tag{6.32}$$

In other terms, $\mathbf{V}_C$ is equal to the vector component of $\mathbf{V}_{O'}$ in the $\mathbf{\Omega}$ direction. It is now clear that the condition for $\mathbf{V}_C = \mathbf{O}$ is

$$\mathbf{\Omega} \cdot \mathbf{V}_{O'} = 0. \tag{6.33}$$

This is analogous to the condition $\bar{\mathbf{F}} \cdot \bar{\mathbf{\Gamma}} = 0$ which we found useful in statics. This condition may be interpreted, using (6.31), as a limitation to *plane motion:* motion instantaneously parallel to a plane having $\mathbf{\Omega}$ as normal.

For any plane motion of a rigid body which is not a translation there is then in each plane perpendicular to the angular velocity vector an *instantaneous center of rotation* **C**. Equation (6.27) tells us how to find it. From any point **R** whose velocity is known we can draw a line perpendicular to its velocity vector (see Fig. 6.19), since $\mathbf{\Omega} \times \mathbf{V}_R$ is per-

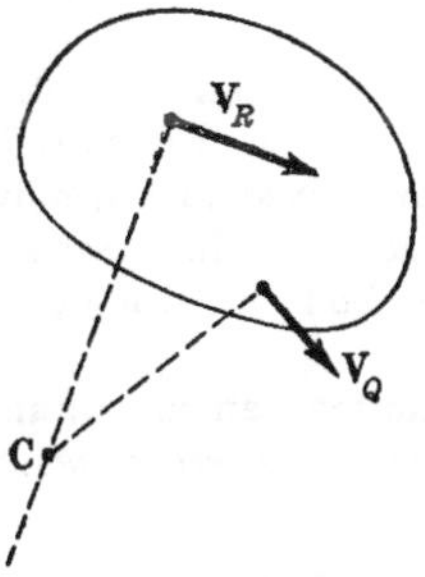

FIG. 6.19.

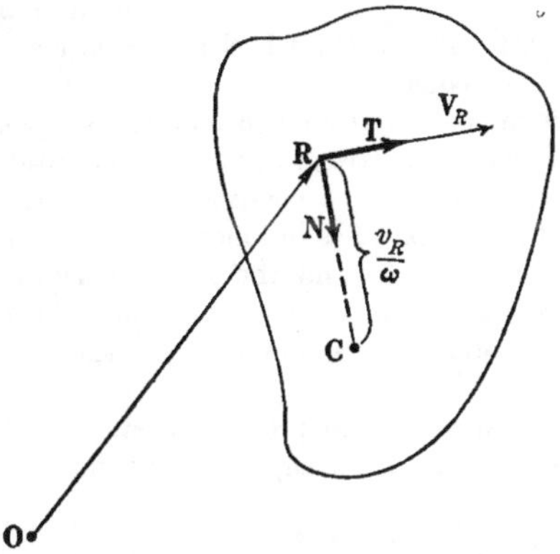

FIG. 6.20.

pendicular to $\mathbf{V}_R$. If two such lines intersect, **C** is determined. Otherwise one may measure off the distance v_R/ω from **R**. The latter interpretation appears vividly if we write (see Fig. 6.20)

$$\mathbf{V}_R = v_R\mathbf{T}, \qquad \mathbf{\Omega} = \omega\mathbf{K}, \qquad \mathbf{K} \times \mathbf{T} = \mathbf{N}.$$

Then substitution in (6.27) gives as a working formula

$$\mathbf{C} = \mathbf{R} + \frac{\omega\mathbf{K} \times v_R\mathbf{T}}{\omega^2} = \mathbf{R} + \frac{v_R}{\omega}\mathbf{N}. \tag{6.34}$$

In summary,

(6.35) *Any plane motion of a rigid body can instantaneously be analyzed as a translation or as a rotation about an instantaneous axis.*

Example. The velocity pattern for a wheel rolling without slipping in Fig. 6.16c showed clearly that the instantaneous axis of rotation is the contact axis at the ground. In the light of the ideas of this section it is interesting to note that all the velocity vectors are perpendicular to the line to this center **C** (in the plane of the wheel) and also that they are proportional to their distance from the center **C**.

EXERCISES

1. Find the instantaneous axis of rotation for the wheel of Exercise 2, Sec. 6.4.
2. Find the instantaneous center of rotation for the wheel of Exercise 4, Sec. 6.4.
3. A ladder resting on a horizontal floor and against a vertical wall makes an angle of 60° with the horizontal. If it starts to slip, where is the instantaneous axis of rotation?
4. Find the instantaneous center of rotation for the connecting rod AB in Fig. 6.21 for the position shown.

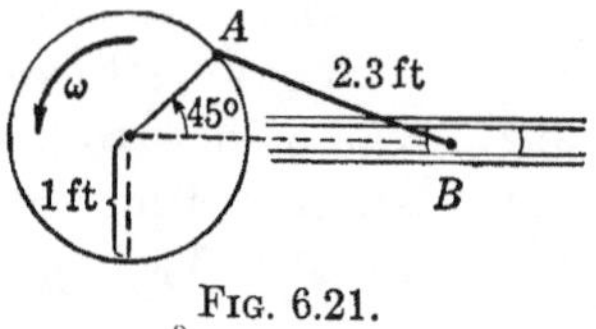

FIG. 6.21.

5. The paddle wheel of an excursion steamer rotates at 25 rpm while the ship moves at 4 mph. How far and in what direction from the axis of the wheel is the instantaneous axis of rotation?
6. The center of a wheel of radius 2 ft rotating about the z axis moves in the x direction at 10 ft/sec. The lowest point of the wheel moves twice as fast in the opposite direction. Find the instantaneous center.
7. Prove that at any given moment all possible instantaneous centers of rotation must lie on a single straight line (the instantaneous axis).
8. The loci of instantaneous axes and centers of rotation are an interesting subject often pursued in studies in kinematics. Find the locus as viewed from a fixed set of axes (*space centrode*) and the locus as viewed from axes fixed in the moving body (*body centrode*) of the center of rotation of the ladder described in Exercise 3. Note that the motion can be described as the rolling of the body centrode on the space centrode.
9. Use Eq. (6.32) to prove that any rigid body motion can instantaneously be analyzed as a rotation superimposed on translation *in the direction of the angular velocity vector*.

6.6. Motion Viewed from Moving Reference Frames. In Sec. 5.4 our discussion of relative motion was limited to the simple but important case where the moving axes remained always parallel to the fixed axes. Now that we have had some experience in dealing with rotations let us attempt a more general attack on the problem. It is still possible to resolve any displacement into two parts: a frame displacement and a relative displacement. The *frame displacement* as before is the displacement which a point would acquire by merely holding fixed coordinates in the moving frame of reference. The *relative displacement* is the apparent displacement as observed with reference to this moving frame. This is illustrated in Fig. 6.22.

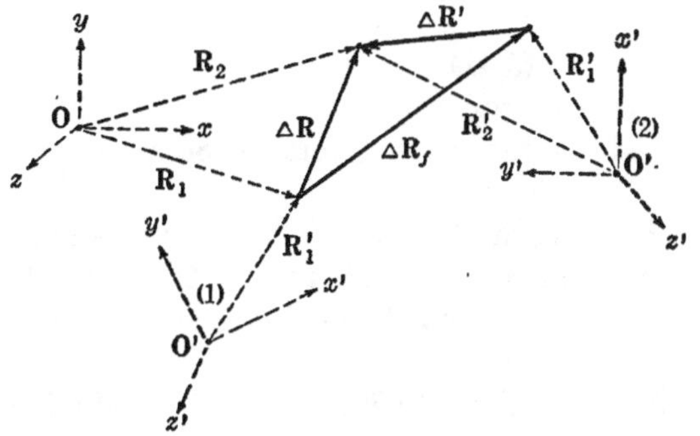

FIG. 6.22.

$$\Delta \mathbf{R} = \Delta \mathbf{R}_f + \Delta \mathbf{R}'. \tag{6.36}$$

As before, we obtain

$$\mathbf{V} = \mathbf{V}_f + \mathbf{V}'. \tag{6.37}$$

(When such a relation is used with x, y, z components, components relative to the *same* set of axes must, of course, be used for all three terms.) This time the moving frame is not necessarily in simple translation; thus $\mathbf{V}_f$ is a function of position rather than a constant. Fortunately, we can express it in a general way by applying (6.20). We merely regard the moving frame of reference as a rigid body:

$$\mathbf{V}_f = \mathbf{V}_{O'} + \mathbf{\Omega} \times \mathbf{R}'. \tag{6.38}$$

Here $\mathbf{\Omega}$ is the angular velocity vector representing instantaneously the rotation of the moving frame. The combined equation is thus

$$\mathbf{V} = \mathbf{V}_{O'} + \mathbf{\Omega} \times \mathbf{R}' + \mathbf{V}'. \tag{6.39}$$

Example 1. We have previously had occasion to consider plane motion of a particle relative to the unit vectors **L** and **M**. Regarding them as fixed in our rotating body, we have

$$\mathbf{O} = \mathbf{O}', \qquad \mathbf{V}_{O'} = \mathbf{O},$$
$$\mathbf{R} = \mathbf{R}' = r\mathbf{L}, \qquad \mathbf{V}' = \frac{d\mathbf{R}'}{dt} = \frac{dr}{dt}\mathbf{L},$$
$$\mathbf{V}_f = \mathbf{\Omega} \times \mathbf{R}',$$

or

$$\mathbf{V}_f = \omega\mathbf{K} \times r\mathbf{L} = \omega r\mathbf{M}.$$

Hence,

$$\mathbf{V} = \frac{dr}{dt}\mathbf{L} + \omega r\mathbf{M},$$

which is equivalent to (5.41).

Example 2. Taking into account the earth's daily rotation, what is the absolute speed of a car heading north at 80 mph at a point of latitude 45°N?

SOLUTION. Pick origin at center of earth, x axis along radius toward point in question, xy plane to include the North Pole. Then $\mathbf{R}' = 4{,}000\mathbf{I}$ miles, $\mathbf{V}' = 80\mathbf{J}$ mph. To find the angular velocity vector $\mathbf{\Omega}$, we observe that the angular speed is $\pi/12$ rad/hr or 0.26 rad/hr and that a unit vector in the right direction is $0.707\mathbf{I} + 0.707\mathbf{J}$. We have then

$$\mathbf{\Omega} = 0.18(\mathbf{I} + \mathbf{J}).$$

Then

$$\mathbf{V} = \mathbf{V}' + \mathbf{\Omega} \times \mathbf{R}' = 80\mathbf{J} - 720\mathbf{K},$$

which is a vector of magnitude 724 (miles per hour).

EXERCISES

1. Four airplanes leave a flying field at the equator to fly, respectively, north, east, south, and west at 100 mph. Find an absolute velocity vector for each, taking into account the earth's spin on its axis.

2. A wheel of radius 80 cm rotates at 100 rad/sec. A second wheel, mounted on the circumference of the first, has a parallel angular velocity vector. Its radius is 20 cm, and it rotates at 400 rad/sec. Let **P** be a point on the circumference of the smaller wheel. Find its speed when it is (*a*) nearest to the center of the large wheel; (*b*) farthest from the center of the large wheel. Illustrate with diagrams.

6.7. The Theorem of Coriolis. The conclusion arrived at in (6.39) was reached in a fairly careful way. Let us compare it with the result of a more headlong approach. It is obvious that $\mathbf{R} = \mathbf{O}' + \mathbf{R}'$, at any instant. Differentiating with respect to time, taking the point of view of the fixed system, we have

$$\mathbf{V} = \mathbf{V}_{O'} + \frac{d\mathbf{R}'}{dt}. \tag{6.40}$$

This, too, is a valid equation. Now let us recall the significance of $\mathbf{V}'$; it is the derivative of $\mathbf{R}'$ with respect to t as seen from the moving frame of reference:

$$\mathbf{V}' = \frac{d'\mathbf{R}'}{d't}. \tag{6.41}$$

The primes are to emphasize that the derivative is as viewed from the moving system. If we substitute (6.41) in (6.39) and compare with

(6.40), we conclude

$$\frac{d}{dt}\mathbf{R}' = \boldsymbol{\Omega} \times \mathbf{R}' + \frac{d'}{d't}\mathbf{R}'. \tag{6.42}$$

It is easy to show that this is a typical relation. Using methods quite analogous to those in Sec. 6.3, we can abstract from this specific equation the general principle epitomized in the following symbolic expression:

$$\frac{d}{dt} = \boldsymbol{\Omega}\times + \frac{d'}{d't}. \tag{6.43}$$

Such a bare expression should be fortified with words:

(6.44) *The derivative (with respect to time), viewed from a fixed frame, of any vector function of time is equal to the sum of the corresponding derivative as viewed from a moving frame plus, if the moving frame is rotating, the derivative induced by the rotation* (see 6.11).

This is too potent a conclusion to leave idle. Let us proceed to differentiate (6.39). Since $\mathbf{R}'$ and $\mathbf{V}'$ are vectors whose significance is relative to the moving frame, (6.43) will be used in computing their derivatives.

$$\mathbf{A} = \mathbf{A}_{O'} + \boldsymbol{\alpha} \times \mathbf{R}' + \boldsymbol{\Omega} \times [(\boldsymbol{\Omega} \times \mathbf{R}') + \mathbf{V}'] + \boldsymbol{\Omega} \times \mathbf{V}' + \mathbf{A}'.$$

Here we have used $\mathbf{A}'$ for $d'\mathbf{V}'/d't$. Grouping terms, we get

$$\mathbf{A} = \mathbf{A}_{O'} + \boldsymbol{\alpha} \times \mathbf{R}' + 2\boldsymbol{\Omega} \times \mathbf{V}' + \boldsymbol{\Omega} \times (\boldsymbol{\Omega} \times \mathbf{R}') + \mathbf{A}'. \tag{6.45}$$

Within this equation lies the clue to an entirely new and fascinating kinematical concept. We might, in naïve reliance on the simplicity of nature, expect that the absolute acceleration should be equal to the vector sum of the frame acceleration and the relative acceleration. This is not the case as an enumeration discloses. If our moving point remained at rest in the moving frame (that is, $\mathbf{V}' = \mathbf{O}$), it would experience the *frame acceleration* given by

$$\mathbf{A}_f = \mathbf{A}_{O'} + \boldsymbol{\alpha} \times \mathbf{R}' + \boldsymbol{\Omega} \times (\boldsymbol{\Omega} \times \mathbf{R}'). \tag{6.46}$$

This compares well with (6.14) and should compare even more favorably with the student's answer to Exercise 5, Sec. 6.4. To $\mathbf{A}_f$ and $\mathbf{A}'$ (the *relative acceleration*) must be added the so-called *Coriolis acceleration:*

$$\mathbf{A}_c = 2\boldsymbol{\Omega} \times \mathbf{V}'. \tag{6.47}$$

This concept is vital in engineering kinematics and in long-range ballistics. Observe that it is zero if there is no rotation, if the relative motion is parallel to the angular velocity, or if the point merely has its frame velocity. Full interpretation is perhaps most easily given from the dynamical point of view to be developed later; but some simple applications are in order at this time. The full equation

$$\mathbf{A} = \mathbf{A}_f + \mathbf{A}_c + \mathbf{A}' \tag{6.48}$$

is called the *theorem of Coriolis.*

Example. A particle moves with constant relative speed v' around the rim of a wheel of radius r. The wheel rotates in the opposite sense about its fixed axis at constant angular speed ω. Taking the wheel as a frame of reference, compute and diagram the components of velocity and acceleration.

SOLUTION. For the choice of axes shown in Fig. 6.23,

$$\boldsymbol{\alpha} = \mathbf{O}, \qquad \mathbf{A}_{O'} = \mathbf{O}, \qquad \mathbf{O} = \mathbf{O}', \qquad \mathbf{V}_{O'} = \mathbf{O}.$$

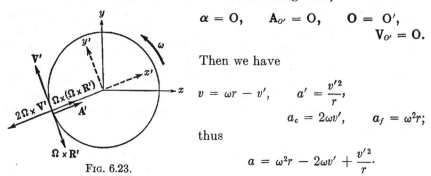

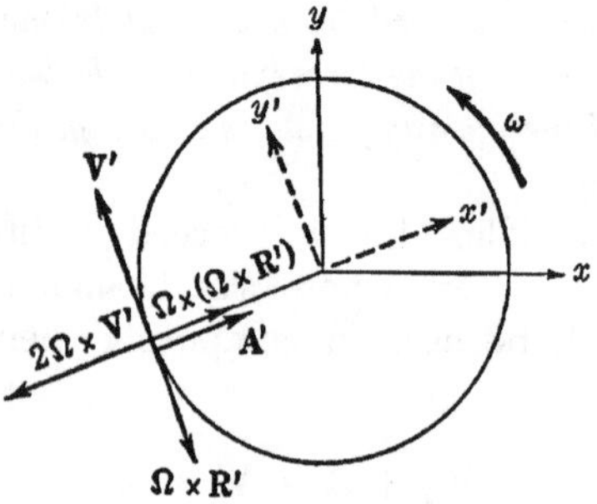

FIG. 6.23.

Then we have

$$v = \omega r - v', \qquad a' = \frac{v'^2}{r},$$

$$a_c = 2\omega v', \qquad a_f = \omega^2 r;$$

thus

$$a = \omega^2 r - 2\omega v' + \frac{v'^2}{r}.$$

As a check on this analysis observe that from the over-all view we have clockwise circular motion at a speed of $v' - \omega r$. Then the acceleration (centripetal) should be

$$\frac{(v' - \omega r)^2}{r} = \frac{v'^2}{r} - 2\omega v' + \omega^2 r,$$

as already found.

EXERCISES

1. Use the methods of this section to derive Eq. (5.42). (The first example of Sec. 6.6 may be taken as a model.)

2. To reinforce the student's comprehension of our analysis of acceleration a more formal partially analytical approach may be helpful. Let us consider the special case where the origins of the two reference frames coincide and where the moving frame rotates uniformly about an axis through the common origin. Starting with

$$\mathbf{R} = x'\mathbf{I}' + y'\mathbf{J}' + z'\mathbf{K}' = \mathbf{R}',$$

differentiate and regroup terms to show that

$$\mathbf{V} = \boldsymbol{\Omega} \times \mathbf{R}' + \mathbf{V}'$$

$$\mathbf{A} = \boldsymbol{\Omega} \times (\boldsymbol{\Omega} \times \mathbf{R}') + 2\boldsymbol{\Omega} \times \mathbf{V}' + \mathbf{A}'.$$

For instance,

$$\frac{d(x'\mathbf{I}')}{dt} = \frac{dx'}{dt}\mathbf{I}' + x'\boldsymbol{\Omega} \times \mathbf{I}', \text{ etc.}$$

3. A particle moves with constant relative speed v' outward along a spoke of a wheel rotating at uniform angular speed ω about a fixed axis. When its distance from the center is r, find expressions for the magnitude of the velocity and the acceleration. Illustrate with a diagram showing directions of the various components.

4. A particle moves with constant relative speed v' around the rim of a wheel of radius r; the wheel rolls along a straight line with uniform speed v. Taking the wheel as a frame of reference, find the Coriolis acceleration. Draw this and the other accelerations in a diagram.

5. How great is the Coriolis acceleration for an airplane traveling north and also for an airplane traveling east at 150 mph at points on the equator?

6. In what regions of the earth may the Coriolis acceleration for surface travel be vertical? Is this effect independent of the direction of travel?

7. In what regions of the earth is the horizontal component of the Coriolis acceleration a maximum for a given surface speed?

8. Prove that in the Northern Hemisphere all horizontal components of the Coriolis acceleration are to the right or to the left (state which) of the direction of travel on the surface.

9. In Fig. 6.24 the whole $x'y'$ plane rotates about the z axis counterclockwise at 2 rad/sec. A particle **P** moves clockwise at 30 ft/sec (relative to the $x'y'$ plane)

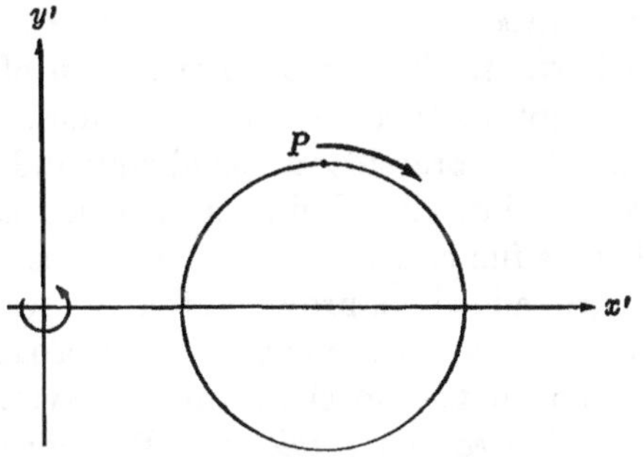

FIG. 6.24.

around the circle of radius 5 ft whose center is (12,0,0) ft. For the moment when **P** is at (12,5,0) ft, plot to scale, labeling with magnitudes, $\mathbf{V}'$, $\mathbf{V}_f$, $\mathbf{A}_f$, $\mathbf{A}_c$, $\mathbf{A}'$, $\mathbf{A}$, $\mathbf{V}$.

10. A wheel of radius 3 ft rolls without slipping along the positive x axis with angular speed 5 rad/sec. The axes $x'y'\mathbf{O}'$ are fixed on the wheel and rotate with it.

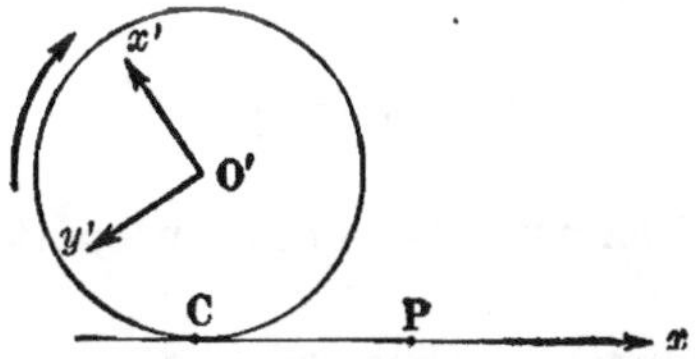

FIG. 6.25.

C is the point of contact between wheel and axis. **P** is a fixed point 4 ft from **C** at the moment shown in Fig. 6.25. Although **P** is fixed in space, it has an apparent motion as seen from the moving frame. Draw to scale and label with symbols and magnitudes the vectors $\mathbf{V}_{O'}$, $\mathbf{V}'$, $\mathbf{A}_f$, $\mathbf{A}_c$.

11. Repeat Exercise 9 with the motions unchanged but with the moving origin **O**′ at the center of the circle and with the $x'y'$ axes rotating with **P** so that its coordinates are constantly (0,5).

CHAPTER 7

PARTICLE DYNAMICS

The laws of Newton state very clearly that accelerated motion is always the result of unbalanced forces. In Chaps. 3 and 4 detailed attention has been given to sets of forces and to conditions for their equivalence. In Chaps. 5 and 6 we have devised techniques and terminology for the study of motion. It is now time to bring these two lines of study together by showing in detail the relation between accelerated motion and the forces which cause it. The science of forces and their effects is called *dynamics.*

7.1. Mass of a Particle. The important notion of mass is often used as a primitive concept in treatises on mechanics. In this course, in order that we might have practice in visualizing and using vectors at an early stage, force was introduced first and hence as a matter of convenience was taken as fundamental. This requires us to define mass in terms of force, length, and time, provided that we wish to keep the number of undefined concepts convenient. We approach this problem by first adopting as a postulate a special form of Newton's second law.

(7.1) *A particle subjected to a single force* **F** *experiences an acceleration* **A** *parallel to* **F**. *The magnitude ratio f/a is a constant for a given particle.*

This fact, experimentally verifiable, serves as the basis for the theory of this chapter. The constant ratio of force magnitude to acceleration magnitude will be called the *mass* of the particle. Since this concept represents a measure of disinclination toward acceleration, it is often called *inertial mass.*

$$m = \frac{f}{a}. \tag{7.2}$$

Another significant empirically verified property of mass will be noted at this point.

(7.3) *Two bodies having the same weight at a given locality have the same mass, and vice versa.*

We anticipated this by defining the unit of force, the newton, in terms of the weight of a standard kilogram. Since the kilogram is the unit of mass in the mks system, we can always write for a standard locality:

w (newtons) $= 9.81$ (newtons/kg) m (kg).

For a freely falling body, (7.2) applies, giving us for a standard locality:

w (newtons) $= 9.81$ (m/sec^2) m (kg).

In the English gravitational system, we may write correspondingly

w (lb) = 32.2 (lb/slug) m (slugs).

w (lb) = 32.2 (ft/sec²) m (slugs).

From the information in these equations it is apparent that the *slug* is a unit of mass given by

$$1 \text{ slug} = \frac{32.2 \times 4.45}{9.81} = 14.6 \text{ kg}.$$

Each of the four equations just listed can be expressed concisely in algebraic form:

$$w = mg \qquad \text{or} \qquad m = \frac{w}{g}. \tag{7.4}$$

These relations are in fact always valid, provided that the units of a single system of units are used. Selected sets of mechanical units are exhibited in Fig. 7.1. Other systems are quite possible; but these are

Name of system of units	Unit of force, f, w	Unit of mass, m	Acceleration of gravity, standard locality, g
mks	Newton	Kilogram	9.81 m/sec²
English (gravitational)	Pound	lb-sec²/ft, slug	32.2 ft/sec²
English (absolute)	lb_m-ft/sec², poundal	lb_m	32.2 ft/sec²
cgs (absolute)	Dyne	Gram	981 cm/sec²
cgs (gravitational)	Gram	g-sec²/cm	981 cm/sec²

FIG. 7.1.

the principal ones encountered in elementary physics. In this course we shall have little need to use "poundal," "slug," "lb_m," or the cgs units. They are included in this one section so that the student may have at least a passing acquaintance with them.

EXERCISES

1. How great a force will cause an object of mass 9.81 kg to accelerate at 1 m/sec²?

2. What is the mass of an object which experiences an acceleration of 10 ft/sec² when subjected to a force of 2 lb?

3. What acceleration will result if a force of 16.1 poundals is applied to an object of mass 2.0 lb_m?

4. Express as poundals a force of 1 newton.

5. An object of mass 1 lb_m is subjected to a force of 1 lb. What acceleration results?

6. At a standard locality two objects, respectively, of mass 1 lb_m and weight 1 lb are placed in the pans of an equal-arm balance. What occurs?

7. What in dynes is the weight of an object whose mass is 1 lb_m?
8. What in poundals is the weight of an object whose mass is 0.07 g-sec²/cm?
9. Express as dynes a force of 1 newton.

7.2. Dynamics of a Particle. From the results of the preceding section we can at once assert as the principal equation governing the motion of a particle

$$\mathbf{F} = m\mathbf{A} \qquad \text{or} \qquad \mathbf{F} = \frac{w}{g}\mathbf{A}. \tag{7.5}$$

The first form is more useful in working with absolute systems of units (for us the mks system primarily); the second for gravitational systems (mainly the English fps system). If the particle in question happens to be subjected to several forces, the single **F** of (7.5) is replaced by the resultant $\bar{\mathbf{F}}$ of the concurrent forces. How then shall we solve problems involving the motion of a single particle? In outline, the procedure is quite simple. First we isolate the particle, selecting all the forces acting on the isolated matter from the outside. Second, since for a particle these forces are necessarily concurrent, we make use of relation (7.5):

$$\bar{\mathbf{F}} = \sum \mathbf{F} = m\mathbf{A} \qquad \text{or} \qquad \bar{\mathbf{F}} = \sum \mathbf{F} = \frac{w}{g}\mathbf{A},$$

or by judicious selection of axes we may use the scalar equations equivalent to the vector ones:

$$\sum f_x = m\frac{d^2x}{dt^2}, \qquad \sum f_y = m\frac{d^2y}{dt^2}, \qquad \sum f_z = m\frac{d^2z}{dt^2}. \tag{7.6}$$

As before m may be replaced by w/g.

Example 1. A 10-lb box slides down a plane inclined at 40° even though restrained by a horizontal force of 1 lb. If the coefficient of sliding friction is 0.10, what acceleration results?

SOLUTION. Isolating the box, we find the forces portrayed in Fig. 7.2. We may choose axes as shown. (Other choices are quite as suitable.) Since d^2y/dt^2 is clearly zero, we may write

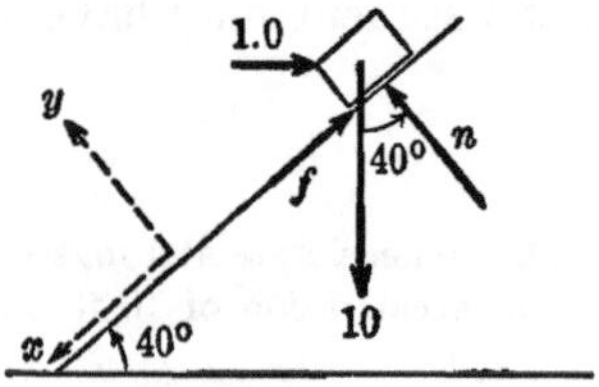

FIG. 7.2.

$$\Sigma f_y = 0,$$

or

$$-10 \cos 40° + n - 1.0 \sin 40° = 0.$$

This yields as a value for the normal force, $n = 8.31$ lb. Since the coefficient of friction is 0.1, $f = 0.83$ lb. Now using

$$\sum f_x = \frac{w}{g} a_x,$$

we have

$$10 \sin 40° - 1.0 \cos 40° - 0.83 = \frac{10}{32.2} a_x,$$

or

$$a_x = 15.6 \text{ ft/sec}^2.$$

By using the kinematical techniques of Chap. 5, many detailed questions concerning the motion could now be answered.

Example 2. A motorcyclist rides around on the inside of a vertical cylinder of radius 45 ft. The coefficient of friction is 0.5. What is the minimum "safe" speed?

SOLUTION. Isolate man and motorcycle as shown in Fig. 7.3, treating the combination as a particle. The isolating forces are the weight, the friction preventing downward slip, and the normal reaction of the wall. Choosing axes as shown in Fig. 7.3,

$$a_y = \frac{v^2}{r}, \qquad a_x = 0.$$

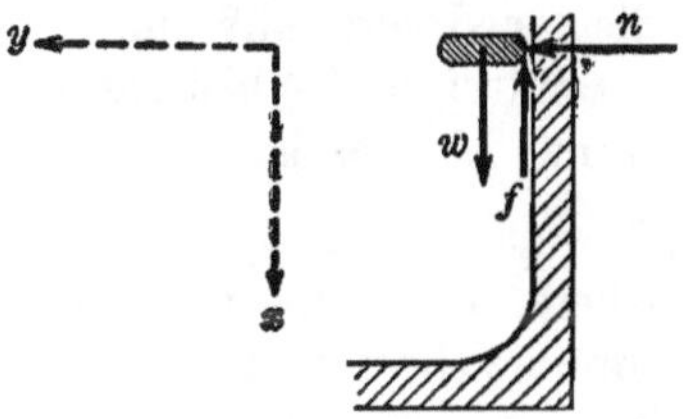

FIG. 7.3.

From Eqs. (7.6),

$$\Sigma f_x = w - f = 0.$$

But $f = \mu n$ for the critical case where slipping is imminent; thus $n = w/\mu$. Also we have

$$\sum f_y = \frac{w}{\mu} = \frac{w}{g}\frac{v^2}{r};$$

or

$$v^2 = \frac{gr}{\mu} = \frac{(32.2)(45)}{0.5};$$

or

$$v = 53.8 \text{ ft/sec (36.7 mph)}.$$

Example 3. A particle of mass 100 g starts from rest and travels around a horizontal circular track of radius 50 cm with a speed proportional to the time. If it would take 2 sec to make the first complete revolution, what horizontal force must act on it after a total time of 0.5 sec?

SOLUTION. First we compute the acceleration. We have given $v = kt$. Integrating, we get $s = 0.5kt^2$. k may be evaluated in terms of the given data:

$$k = \frac{2s}{t^2} = \frac{2(2\pi)(0.5)}{2^2} = 0.5\pi.$$

Now

$$a_T = \frac{dv}{dt} = k = 0.5\,\pi$$

$$a_N = \frac{v^2}{r} = \frac{(0.5\pi)^2 t^2}{0.5},$$

and at $t = 0.5$, $a_N = 1.23$. Consequently the magnitude of the total acceleration is given by

$$a = \sqrt{(1.57)^2 + (1.23)^2} = 2.04\ \text{m/sec}^2.$$

The force may now be computed:

$$f = ma = (0.1)(2.04) = 0.204\ \text{newton}.$$

Example 4. A bob of mass m is supported by a vertical spring of negligible mass which provides a tension $-ks$ when it is stretched downward by an amount s. With what period will the bob oscillate if it is displaced vertically and then released?

SOLUTION. When the bob is in equilibrium, the equation of equilibrium, $\Sigma f_y = 0$, is

$$+mg - ks_0 = 0,$$

where s_0 denotes the amount that the spring is stretched in order to support the bob at rest. When the bob oscillates, the equation of motion is

$$+mg - k(y + s_0) = m\,\frac{d^2(y + s_0)}{dt^2},$$

where y is the vertical displacement from equilibrium position (positive downward) or, using the previous equation,

$$-ky = m\,\frac{d^2y}{dt^2}.$$

By Proposition (5.60) this equation is recognizable as simple harmonic motion of period

$$\tau = 2\pi\sqrt{\frac{m}{k}}.$$

EXERCISES

1. A body weighing 160 lb slides on level ground and is retarded by a constant frictional force. If the initial speed of the body is 16 ft/sec and the coefficient of friction is 0.25, how long will it take the body to come to rest?

2. A weight of 3 tons is raised from the ground to a height of 80 ft in 5 sec by a constant tension in the hoisting cable. How great is this tension?

3. A 200-lb man must slide down a rope guaranteed to withstand a tension of 150 lb. How great should his acceleration be?

4. A 16-lb particle is acted on by the following forces (pounds):

$$6\mathbf{I} - 7\mathbf{J} + 3\mathbf{K}, \qquad -16\mathbf{K}, \qquad -5\mathbf{I} + 7\mathbf{J} + 10\mathbf{K}.$$

Find the acceleration.

5. An elevator weighing 2.5 tons starts from rest and descends with constant acceleration a distance of 100 ft in 10 sec. Neglecting friction, what is the tension in the cable?

6. A 150-lb man climbs a vertical rope with an acceleration of 0.4 ft/sec². Find the tension in the rope.

7. A cake of ice weighing 60 lb is pulled on level ground by a constant force of 20 lb applied at an angle of 30° above the horizontal. If the coefficient of friction between the ice and the ground is 0.1, how long will it take to move the cake of ice a distance of 300 ft starting from rest?

8. A 200-lb man can just lift a 240-lb weight when at rest on the ground. How heavy a weight can he just lift from the floor of an elevator with an upward acceleration of 8 ft/sec²? With a downward acceleration of the same magnitude? Compute both, (*a*) assuming the crucial muscles are leg muscles and (*b*) assuming the crucial muscles are arm muscles.

9. An elevator weighing 1,000 lb moves upward with uniform velocity of 12 ft/sec. If the frictional resistance is 20 lb, how far will it continue to rise if the cable is suddenly cut?

10. An automobile starting on an icy pavement takes 30 sec to attain a speed of 5 mph. What is the coefficient of friction?

11. A book rests on the level top of an automobile. The automobile starts from rest and, accelerating uniformly, attains a speed of 15 mph in 44 ft. If the book does not slip, what can be said about the coefficient of friction between book and car top?

12. A 10-lb particle traveling at 15 ft/sec is being subjected to forces whose resultant is at a given moment a 40-lb force making an angle of 30° with the tangent vector **T**. What is the radius of curvature of the path at that instant? What is the instantaneous rate of increase of speed?

13. An object of mass 2 kg is free to slide along a smooth horizontal rod. Starting from rest it is propelled by a force parallel to the rod whose magnitude is given by

$$f(t) = 5t - t^2$$

f in newtons, t in seconds. What is the speed after 5 sec?

14. An elevator is descending at 10 ft/sec when the cable breaks. On each of two sides of the car a brake is immediately applied against the shaft with a normal force of magn.tude p. If the coefficient of friction is 0.6, how great must p be in order to stop the car in 20 ft? The elevator and load weigh 1,600 lb.

15. An automobile starts from rest and travels around a circular unbanked track 400 ft in radius with a constant tangential acceleration of 2 ft/sec². After how many seconds will it start to slip if the coefficient of friction is 0.5?

16. A horizontal turntable starts from rest and accelerates according to the equation

$$\frac{d\theta}{dt} = 4t$$

(radians per second). A small eraser rests on the table at a point 18 in. from the center. It just starts to slip after 0.866 sec. What is the coefficient of friction between the eraser and the surface of the turntable?

17. A block slides down a roof inclined at an angle of 30°. It slides from rest a distance of 50 ft before leaving the roof at a speed of 20 ft/sec. What is the coefficient of friction? After falling for 2 sec, what will be its horizontal distance from the edge of the roof?

7.3. The Simple Pendulum. A simple pendulum consists of a small spherical bob of mass m attached to a light flexible inextensible string of length l whose other end is tied to a fixed point O. In equilibrium the string hangs vertically. If the bob is displaced slightly and released, an oscillation results. What is the nature of this oscillation and its period? To solve this problem, we isolate the bob in a typical position where the angular displacement is θ, as in Fig. 7.4. The forces acting on it are the pull of the cord **P** and the weight **W**. The path is necessarily circular; therefore we may write

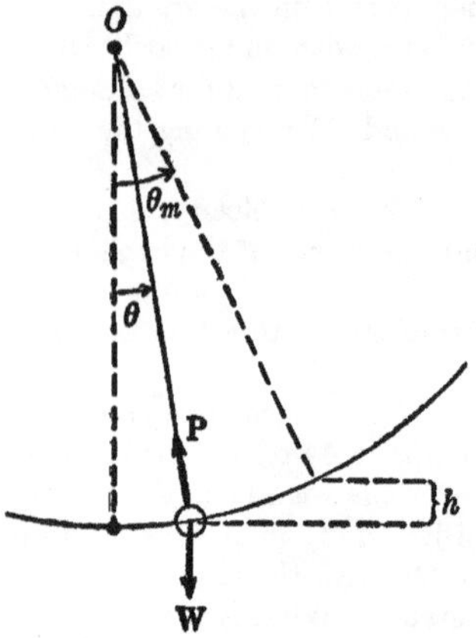

FIG. 7.4.

$$\mathbf{A} = (\alpha l)\mathbf{T} + (\omega^2 l)\mathbf{N}.$$

Taking tangential components of $\bar{\mathbf{F}} = m\mathbf{A}$, we have

$$-w \sin \theta = m\alpha l,$$

or

$$-g \sin \theta = \alpha l.$$

To find the period, we write α as $d^2\theta/dt^2$ and consider the resulting equation

$$\frac{d^2\theta}{dt^2} = -\frac{g}{l} \sin \theta.$$

It turns out that the exact integration of this equation involves non-elementary mathematics. A full analysis would reveal that the period increases slightly with amplitude. We can manage an approximate solution, however, if we agree that θ is to be kept small so that $\sin \theta$ may be replaced by θ in the equation. In that case we can apply (5.60), which identifies the motion as simple harmonic in θ with period

(7.7a) $$\tau = 2\pi \sqrt{\frac{l}{g}},$$

(7.7b) $$\tau = 2\pi \sqrt{\frac{l}{g}}\left(1 + \frac{\theta_m^2}{16}\right).$$

Formula (7.7a) is noteworthy in that it is independent of the amplitude and of the mass of the bob. Formula (7.7b) is a better approximate formula showing how the period actually does vary slightly with the amplitude θ_m.

If we go back to the original equation and this time replace α by $\omega(d\omega/d\theta)$, we get an equation which we can integrate exactly. Assuming that ω is zero when θ has its maximum value θ_m,

$$-g\int_{\theta_m}^{\theta} \sin \theta \, d\theta = l\int_0^{\omega} \omega \, d\omega.$$

Integrating,

$$g(\cos\theta - \cos\theta_m) = \tfrac{1}{2}l\omega^2.$$

Substituting v/l for ω and noting that $l\cos\theta - l\cos\theta_m$ is the vertical distance h between the two positions considered, we can easily conclude, whether θ_m is small or not:

(7.8) *The speed at any level in the path of a simple pendulum is the speed which the bob would have attained in a free fall to the same level: i.e.,*

$$v = \sqrt{2gh}.$$

EXERCISES

1. Find the maximum speed of the bob of a 2-ft pendulum released from rest at an angle of 60° with the downward vertical.

2. A pendulum bob suspended by a cord from the ceiling describes at uniform speed a horizontal circle. Show that the period is the same as that for a simple pendulum whose length is equal to the vertical distance from the circle to the ceiling.

3. A 40-lb object is suspended by a cord 10 ft long and is free to swing. What is the greatest speed with which it can swing though its lowest position if the cord will break at a tension of 80 lb?

4. Compute the period of a pendulum 1.5 m long swinging with amplitude 60°, using both forms of (7.7).

7.4. Interacting Particles. When two or more particles are in contact, their motions are interdependent. Insight into these motions can be gained by isolating the particles separately and then writing for each an equation of motion of the form $\bar{\mathbf{F}} = m\mathbf{A}$. The accelerations of the different particles may be limited by definite constraints which can be expressed mathematically. For instance, a cord joining them may be of constant length. As we shall see in the examples, such relationships together with the separate equations of motion often make possible a full solution.

Example 1. Two blocks B and C rest on an inclined plane whose angle with the horizontal is 30° as in Fig. 7.5. The weights are, respectively, 5 and 10 lb. C is smooth, but the coefficient of friction for B is 0.3. With what acceleration do the blocks slide down the incline? Find the force with which one pushes the other.

SOLUTION. First isolate B. The forces are the weight, normal and tangential reactions of the plane, and the force $\mathbf{R}$ exerted by C. Taking normal components, we get

$$-5\cos 30° + n = 0,$$

or

$$n = 4.33 \text{ lb}.$$

The coefficient of friction is known; thus we have at once $f = 1.3$ lb.

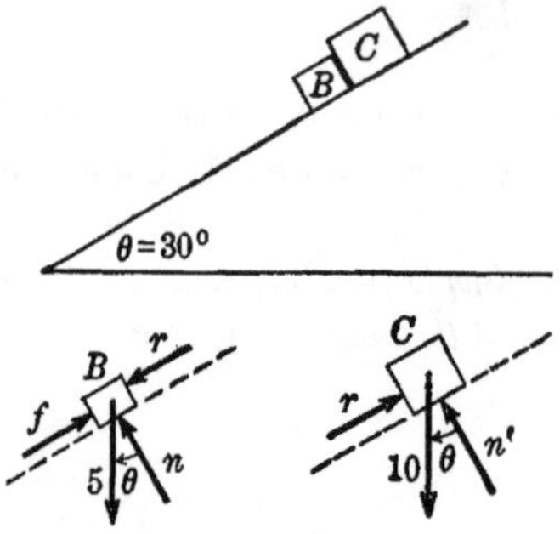

FIG. 7.5.

Now taking tangential components,

$$-1.3 + 5 \sin 30° + r = \left(\frac{5}{32.2}\right) a_T.$$

Next isolate C. The forces are the reaction to **R**, the weight, and a normal reaction **N**$'$ with the plane. Utilizing horizontal components,

$$-r + 10 \sin 30° = \left(\frac{10}{32.2}\right) a_T.$$

We have used the same acceleration symbol for both blocks since they apparently will remain in contact. Eliminating r,

$$6.2 = \left(\frac{15}{32.2}\right) a_T,$$

or

$$a_T = 13.3 \text{ ft/sec}^2.$$

Going back to the previous equations, we can solve for r:

$$r = 5 - \frac{(10)(6.2)(32.2)}{(32.2)(15)} = 0.9 \text{ lb.}$$

It is well worth noting that a general solution using letters instead of numbers is in many ways more satisfactory than a forthright numerical solution such as has been outlined above. Literal equations have the advantage that they can be checked dimensionally (in terms of length, force, and time) at any stage. For this example, literal equations might be written as follows:

$$-w \cos \theta + n = 0,$$

so

$$f = \mu w \cos \theta,$$

then

$$-\mu w \cos \theta + w \sin \theta + r = \left(\frac{w}{g}\right) a_T \qquad \text{for } B$$

and

$$-r + w' \sin \theta = \left(\frac{w'}{g}\right) a_T \qquad \text{for } C.$$

Adding member by member to eliminate r,

$$(w + w') \sin \theta - \mu w \cos \theta = \left(\frac{w + w'}{g}\right) a_T.$$

(Observe that this equation is the isolation equation for B and C together.) From the preceding equation we get

$$a_T = g\left(\sin\theta - \frac{\mu w}{w + w'}\cos\theta\right)$$

and

$$r = w'\left(\sin\theta - \frac{a_T}{g}\right) = \frac{\mu w w' \cos\theta}{w + w'}.$$

These two general answers can now be used as a source for numerical answers. Substituting the data of this example should yield the same results as before.

Example 2. Given the masses and coefficients of friction as shown in Fig. 7.6. Assume that m_3g is greater than $(\mu_1 m_1 g + \mu_2 m_2 g)$. Neglect pulley masses and frictions.

SOLUTION. Isolate the three masses separately. Denote by t the magnitude of the tension in the cord:

$$t - \mu_1 m_1 g = m_1 a_1,$$
$$m_3 g - 2t = m_3 a_3,$$
$$t - \mu_2 m_2 g = m_2 a_2.$$

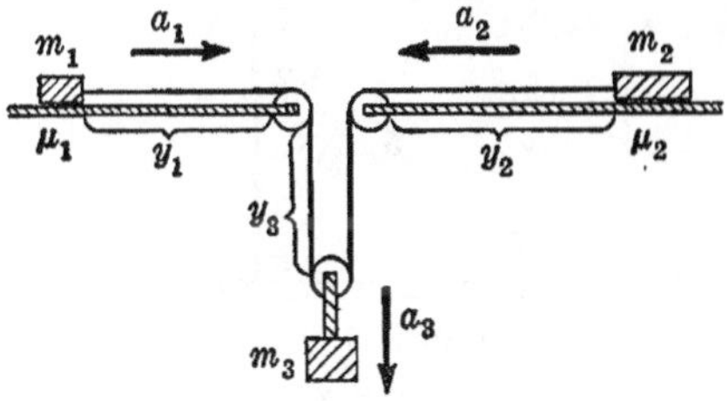

FIG. 7.6.

There are four unknown quantities: t, a_1, a_2, a_3. A fourth equation relating them is obtained by using the fact that the cord does not stretch.

$$y_1 + y_2 + 2y_3 = \text{const.}$$

Differentiating twice with respect to time,

$$-a_1 - a_2 + 2a_3 = 0.$$

Now with four equations the four unknown quantities may be determined.

EXERCISES

In each of the following ignore pulley friction and pulley inertia. Assume cords flexible and inextensible. In each case find the accelerations and tensions.

1.

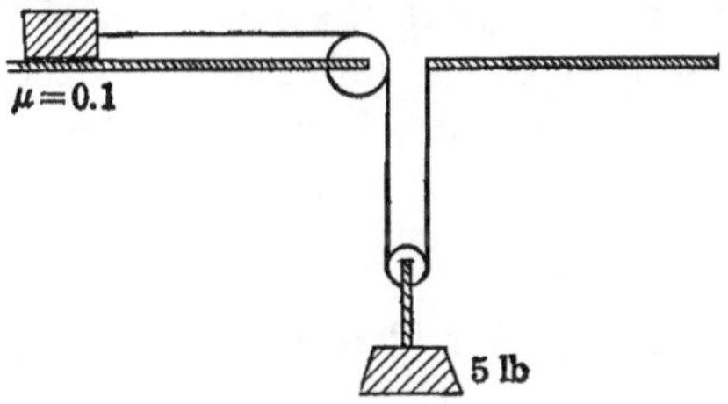

FIG. 7.7.

2.

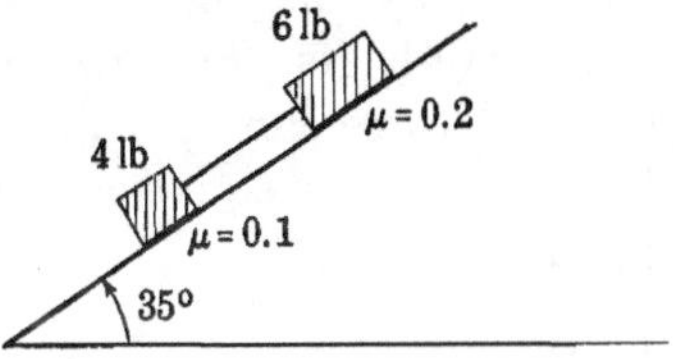

FIG. 7.8.

3.

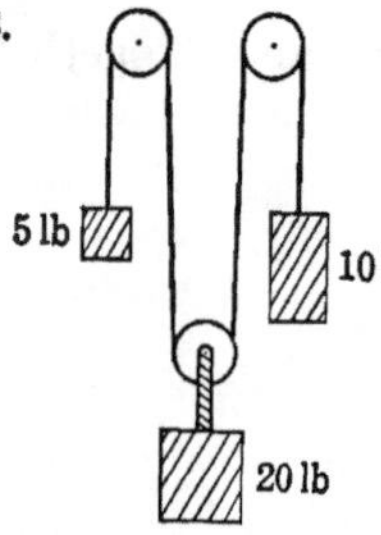

FIG. 7.9

4.

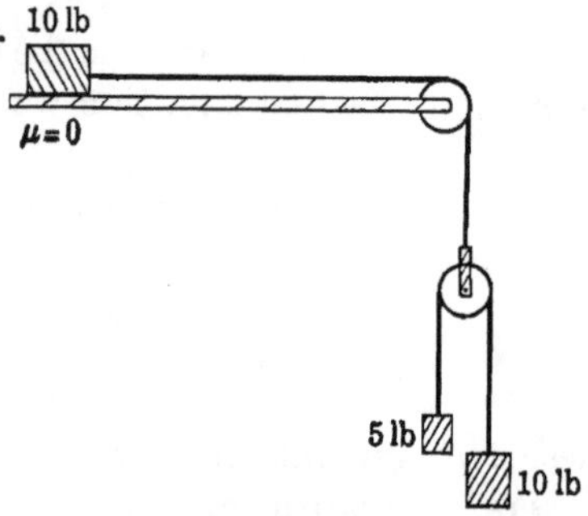

FIG. 7.10.

5.

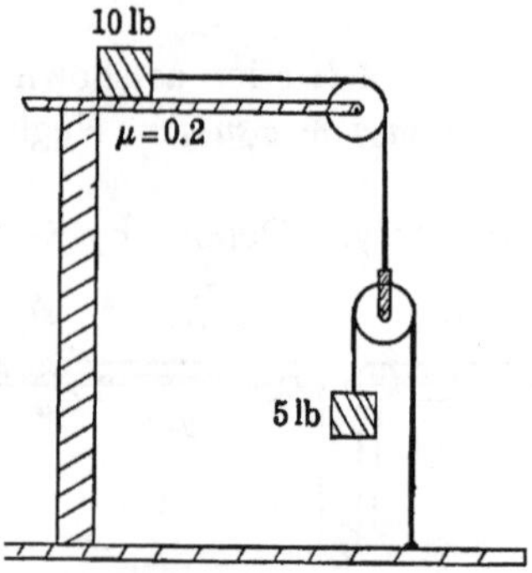

FIG. 7.11.

6.

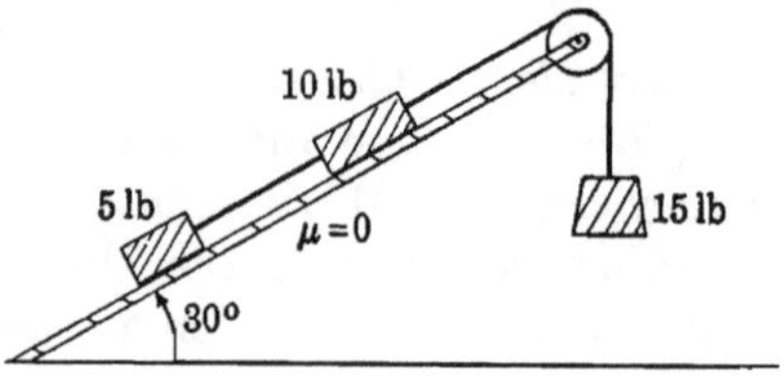

FIG. 7.12.

7.5. Aggregates of Particles. In our study of statics the objects allowed were things that could be regarded approximately as mass particles or as rigid bodies. Thus far our study of dynamics has been limited to particles either singly or in small groups. The easiest way for us to extend these results to rigid bodies is to develop a theory for large groups or aggregates of particles. Suppose that we have given a collection of particles whose masses are $m_1, m_2, \ldots, m_n$. These particles may interact. By the reaction law the forces between pairs of particles are equal and opposite. Such interaction forces will be signalized by primes and called *internal forces.* Forces acting from the outside on particles of the collection will be called *external forces.* For a typical particle, say the one with subscript i on its mass in the list above, in other words for the "ith particle," let $\bar{\mathbf{F}}_i$ denote the resultant of the external forces and let $\bar{\mathbf{F}}'_i$ be the resultant of the internal forces. Our basic dynamics equation allows us then to state, having isolated this particle,

$$\bar{\mathbf{F}}_i + \bar{\mathbf{F}}'_i = m_i\mathbf{A}_i. \tag{7.9}$$

n such equations may be written down. If we add corresponding members of these n equations, we get

$$\Sigma\bar{\mathbf{F}}_i = \Sigma m_i\mathbf{A}_i. \tag{7.10}$$

No primed forces appear because they occur in equal and opposite pairs which cancel. This equation is more easily appreciated if the notion of *center of mass* is introduced. For a system of particles, the center of mass is defined to be the point whose position vector $\bar{\mathbf{R}}$ is given by

$$\bar{\mathbf{R}} = \frac{\Sigma m_i \mathbf{R}_i}{\Sigma m_i}, \tag{7.11}$$

where $\mathbf{R}_i$ is the position vector of the *i*th particle. If this equation is differentiated twice with respect to time, we get, assuming that the masses are constant,

$$\bar{\mathbf{A}} = \frac{\Sigma m_i \mathbf{A}_i}{\Sigma m_i}. \tag{7.12}$$

This enables one to rewrite (7.11) as

$$\Sigma \bar{\mathbf{F}}_i = (\Sigma m_i)\bar{\mathbf{A}}. \tag{7.13}$$

In words we may phrase it as follows:

(7.14) *The center of mass of an aggregate of particles behaves like a single particle having the total mass of the aggregate and subjected to external forces equal to those acting on particles of the aggregate.*

Another noteworthy aspect of this result may be stated thus:

(7.15) *The effect of a force on the motion of the center of mass of an aggregate of particles is independent of the point of application of the force.*

These theorems are welcome because of their simplicity. They point out that, however chaotic the motion of an aggregate may be, there underlies a pattern as uncomplicated as the motion of a single particle.

For many practical problems it is helpful to replace (7.11) by the following scalar equations:

$$\bar{x} = \frac{\Sigma m_i x_i}{\Sigma m_i}, \qquad \bar{y} = \frac{\Sigma m_i y_i}{\Sigma m_i}, \qquad \bar{z} = \frac{\Sigma m_i z_i}{\Sigma m_i}. \tag{7.16}$$

Location of Center of Mass. For two particles of masses m_1 at $\mathbf{R}_1$ and m_2 at $\mathbf{R}_2$ the center of mass is given by

$$\bar{\mathbf{R}} = \frac{m_1\mathbf{R}_1 + m_2\mathbf{R}_2}{m_1 + m_2}. \tag{7.17}$$

It is worth noting that this may be rewritten as

$$\bar{\mathbf{R}} = \mathbf{R}_1 + \frac{m_2}{m_1 + m_2}(\mathbf{R}_2 - \mathbf{R}_1) = \mathbf{R}_2 + \frac{m_1}{m_1 + m_2}(\mathbf{R}_1 - \mathbf{R}_2). \tag{7.18}$$

This makes it clear that

(7.19) *The center of mass of a system of two particles lies on the line between them, and it divides the segment inversely as the masses.*

This approach may be easily extended to systems of more than two particles. For the center of mass of a system of n particles may be considered as the center of mass of a system of two particles: one of these being a particle of mass $m_1 + m_2 + \cdots m_{n-1}$ at the center of mass of the corresponding $n - 1$ particles; the other being the nth particle. Letting

$$\bar{\mathbf{R}}_{n-1} = \frac{m_1\mathbf{R}_1 + \cdots + m_{n-1}\mathbf{R}_{n-1}}{m_1 + \cdots + m_{n-1}},$$

we can show by direct substitution that

$$\bar{\mathbf{R}} = \bar{\mathbf{R}}_{n-1} + \frac{m_n}{\Sigma m_i}(\mathbf{R}_n - \bar{\mathbf{R}}_{n-1}). \tag{7.20}$$

The details of the substitution are left as an exercise. This result means in practice that one may find a center of mass by using (7.19) over and over. For example, consider three equal masses at the vertices of a triangle, as in Fig. 7.13. The center of mass of No. 1 and No. 2 (by 7.19) is the mid-point. Now think of the system No. 1 plus No. 2 as concentrated at this mid-point. The whole problem of three particles is thus reduced to two two-particle problems. The center of mass of the three original objects is immediately seen (by 7.19 again) to be at the point on the median of the triangle two-thirds of the way from the vertex (*i.e.*, at the centroid of the triangle itself).

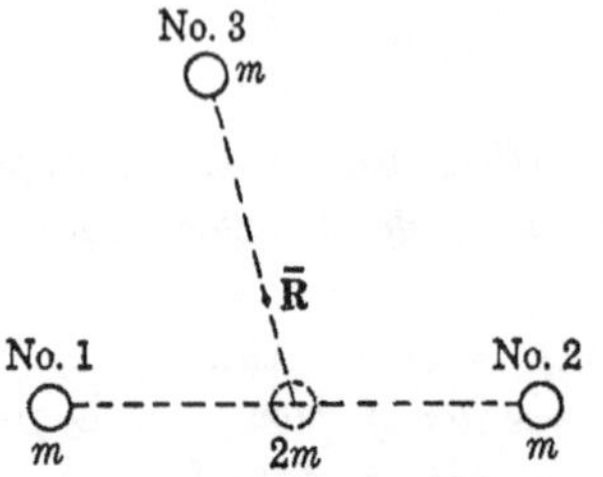

FIG. 7.13.

Center of Gravity. Consider a system of n particles in a region of uniform gravitational field where the formula for weight is

$$\mathbf{W} = m\mathbf{G},$$

where $\mathbf{G}$ normally is a vector of magnitude 9.81 newtons/kg. Then each particle of mass m_i is subject to a force $\mathbf{W}_i = m_i\mathbf{G}$. The resultant of these n forces is a single force $\bar{\mathbf{W}} = \Sigma\mathbf{W}_i$. To find its line of action, we let $\mathbf{Q}$ be any point on the line. Now take moments about the origin. The sum of the moments of the n forces must be equal to the moment of the resultant force

$$\Sigma\mathbf{R}_i \times \mathbf{W}_i = \mathbf{Q} \times \bar{\mathbf{W}},$$

or

$$\Sigma\mathbf{R}_i \times m_i\mathbf{G} = \mathbf{Q} \times (\Sigma m_i)\mathbf{G},$$

or

$$(\Sigma m_i\mathbf{R}_i) \times \mathbf{G} = \mathbf{Q} \times (\Sigma m_i)\mathbf{G},$$

or

$$(\Sigma m_i)\bar{\mathbf{R}} \times \mathbf{G} = \mathbf{Q} \times (\Sigma m_i)\mathbf{G}.$$

Canceling the scalar factor in the last equation, we get

$$\bar{\mathbf{R}} \times \mathbf{G} = \mathbf{Q} \times \mathbf{G},$$

or

$$(\mathbf{Q} - \bar{\mathbf{R}}) \times \mathbf{G} = \mathbf{O}.$$

This is equivalent to saying that $\mathbf{Q} - \bar{\mathbf{R}}$ is parallel to **G**, from which we conclude that, for some scalar constant k which acts as a parameter as **Q** is allowed to move along the line of action of $\bar{\mathbf{W}}$,

$$\mathbf{Q} = \bar{\mathbf{R}} + k\mathbf{G}.$$

Thus the line of action of the resultant is the line through the center of mass parallel to **G**. Since this would be the case also if the relative orientation of **G** could be changed, we conclude that the resultant always passes through $\bar{\mathbf{R}}$. Such a point is called the *center of gravity*. We have shown then the following statement:

(7.21) *Whenever the gravitational field may be considered as uniform, the center of gravity of an aggregate coincides with the center of mass.*

The concept of center of mass will be applied to rigid bodies in Chap. 8.

EXERCISES

1. Verify Eq. (7.20).

2. Three particles of masses 1, 2, and 3 kg, respectively, are at the vertices of an equilateral triangle of side 1 m. Find the center of mass.

3. Instantaneously the particles of Fig. 7.14 are subjected to forces as listed below.

Particle	Mass, kg	Coordinates, m	Forces, newtons
A	3	(0,1)	$-3\mathbf{J}, 2\mathbf{I} - \mathbf{J}, \mathbf{I} + \mathbf{J}$
B	1.5	(0,0)	$-2\mathbf{I}, 3\mathbf{J}$
C	0 5	(2,0)	$2\mathbf{I}, -2\mathbf{I} + \mathbf{J}, 2\mathbf{J}$

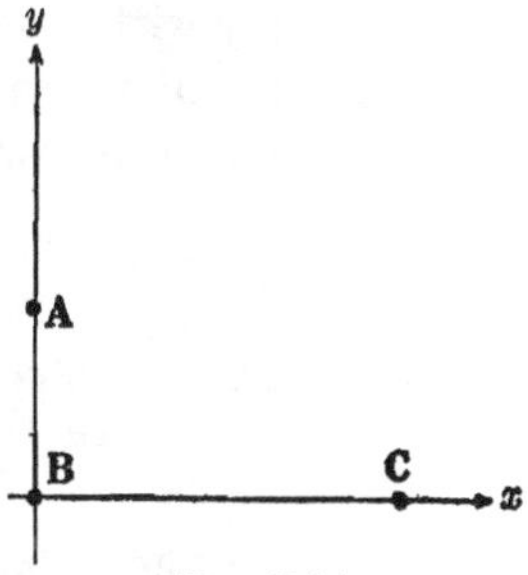

FIG. 7.14.

(*a*) Find the center of mass initially.

(*b*) Find the instantaneous acceleration of the center of mass.

4. Show that the aggregate consisting of the falling weights and pulley of Fig. 7.10 satisfies (7.13).

7.6. Dynamics in Moving Reference Frames. The basic dynamical equation

$$\bar{\mathbf{F}} = \Sigma\mathbf{F} = m\mathbf{A} \tag{7.22}$$

has meaning only in conjunction with the reference frame with respect to which **A** is reckoned. It was remarked in Sec. 3.6 that Newton's laws are not valid with respect to all frames. Frames for which they are valid are called *inertial frames*. Since a relation such as (7.22) is subject to experimental check, it seems reasonable to assume that inertial frames do exist. Let $\mathbf{O}xyz$ be such a frame and $\mathbf{O}'x'y'z'$ be a frame in motion with respect to the first frame. Let the acceleration of $\mathbf{O}'$ relative to the first frame be $\mathbf{A}_{O'}$ and the angular velocity and acceleration be $\mathbf{\Omega}$ and $\boldsymbol{\alpha}$. If a particle of mass m subject to forces of resultant $\bar{\mathbf{F}}$ has an acceleration $\mathbf{A}'$ relative to the moving frame, then, by Secs. 6.6 and 6.7, its acceleration $\mathbf{A}$ in the inertial frame is

$$\mathbf{A} = \mathbf{A}_{O'} + \boldsymbol{\alpha} \times \mathbf{R}' + 2\mathbf{\Omega} \times \mathbf{V}' + \mathbf{\Omega} \times (\mathbf{\Omega} \times \mathbf{R}') + \mathbf{A}', \tag{7.23}$$

where $\mathbf{R}'$ and $\mathbf{V}'$ give the position and velocity vectors relative to the moving frame. A somewhat better equation for our purpose is

$$\mathbf{A} = \mathbf{A}_f + \mathbf{A}_c + \mathbf{A}'. \tag{7.24}$$

It is now obvious that the equation

$$\bar{\mathbf{F}} = \Sigma\mathbf{F} = m\mathbf{A}' \tag{7.25}$$

is not valid in general. In fact we may say:

(7.26) *A frame accelerated with respect to an inertial frame is not an inertial frame.*

(7.27) *A frame rotating with respect to an inertial frame is not an inertial frame.*

Now it is often desirable to solve mechanics problems with respect to such frames of reference. In fact, any frame rigidly attached to the earth presumably has an angular velocity of approximately one revolution per day with respect to some inertial frame. The aim of this section is to point out means of adapting (7.25) for use in a noninertial frame. The expedient is direct, even naïve. First we substitute (7.24) into (7.22):

$$\Sigma\mathbf{F} = m\mathbf{A}_f + m\mathbf{A}_c + m\mathbf{A}'.$$

Next we transfer the undesirable terms from right to left:

$$\Sigma\mathbf{F} - m\mathbf{A}_f - m\mathbf{A}_c = m\mathbf{A}'.$$

Then we pretend that in addition to the usual external forces included in $\Sigma\mathbf{F}$ there are also a *frame force* $\mathbf{F}_f$ and a *Coriolis force* $\mathbf{F}_c$ given by

$$\mathbf{F}_f = -m\mathbf{A}_f, \tag{7.28}$$
$$\mathbf{F}_c = -m\mathbf{A}_c. \tag{7.29}$$

If now we reinterpret the resultant $\bar{\mathbf{F}}$ as

$$\bar{\mathbf{F}} = \Sigma\mathbf{F} + \mathbf{F}_f + \mathbf{F}_c,$$

we may write quite accurately

$$\bar{\mathbf{F}} = m\mathbf{A}'. \tag{7.30}$$

Example 1. What is the acceleration of free fall relative to a railway coach accelerated at 6 ft/sec²?

SOLUTION. Isolate a particle free to fall as shown in Fig. 7.15. The frame acceleration to the right corresponds to a frame force to the left. The resultant force $\bar{\mathbf{F}}$ determines the acceleration $\mathbf{A}'$ which is desired:

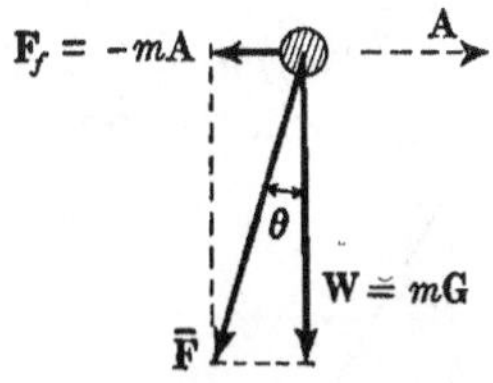

FIG. 7.15.

$$a' = \sqrt{32.2^2 + 6.0^2} = 32.8 \text{ ft/sec}^2$$

at an angle θ given by

$$\tan \theta = \frac{6.0}{32.2}, \qquad \theta = 10.6°.$$

Example 2. Whenever a particle is in motion on a rotating body, its behavior relative to that body is as if it were acted on by a Coriolis force (as well as a frame force). It is, for instance, an observable fact that rivers in the Northern Hemisphere erode their right banks more than the left. The opposite effect is found in the Southern Hemisphere. Related to this phenomenon is the tendency for water entering a sink drain to spiral clockwise in the Northern Hemisphere. Another such example is the *geostrophic wind* which tends to blow along lines of constant pressure (with the high-pressure area on the right, low-pressure area on the left, in the Northern Hemisphere) at such a speed that forces due to pressure differences are counterbalanced by Coriolis forces. When the lines of constant pressure are curved, centrifugal forces enter the picture.

Example 3. To get an idea of the magnitude of the Coriolis force, let us compute it for a 10-lb projectile traveling east horizontally at 2,000 ft/sec at a point of latitude 45° N.

SOLUTION. Pick axes locally fixed to surface of earth: x axis east, y axis north, and z axis vertical. Then $\omega = \pi/12$ rad/hr or

$$\omega = 7.27 \times 10^{-5} \text{ rad/sec.}$$

(If allowance is made for the earth's annual journey around the sun, this value must be corrected slightly.)

$$\mathbf{\Omega} = 0.707\omega(\mathbf{J} + \mathbf{K}),$$
$$\mathbf{V}' = 2{,}000\mathbf{I},$$
$$|\mathbf{F}_c| = |-2m\mathbf{\Omega} \times \mathbf{V}'| = \left|-2 \times \frac{10}{32.2} \times 7.27 \times 10^{-5} \times 2{,}000\right| = 0.09 \text{ lb.}$$

Such a force may not seem large, but it is enough to cause a trajectory to be influenced. In practical long-range ballistics the Coriolis deviation is allowed for.

Centrifugal Force. Under the category of frame forces the most familiar special case, occurring particularly for uniform rotation, is one of the form

$$-m\mathbf{\Omega} \times (\mathbf{\Omega} \times \mathbf{R}'),$$

which is called centrifugal force. Like the Coriolis force and other frame forces, this is purely fictitious. It, like the others, is merely a device to make the basic Newtonian law of motion, $\bar{\mathbf{F}} = m\mathbf{A}$, valid in a noninertial frame.

Example 4. If a railway coach takes at 60 mph a curve of radius 500 ft, at what angle will the chandeliers hang? The coach is not an inertial frame; thus the "equilibrium position" must be computed as due to both the weight and the centrifugal force:

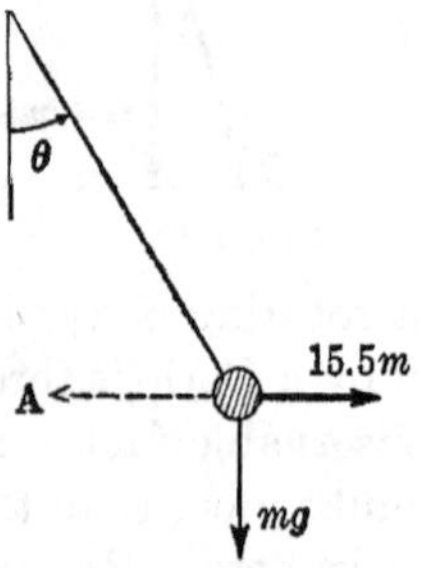

FIG. 7.16.

$$-m\omega^2 r = -m\frac{v^2}{r} = -m\frac{88^2}{500} = -15.5m.$$

The angle θ for equilibrium (see Fig. 7.16) is given by

$$\tan\theta = \frac{15.5}{32.2},$$
$$\theta = 25.7°.$$

EXERCISES

1. What is the period of a simple pendulum 24 in. long suspended from the ceiling of a railway coach traveling at 45 mph along a straight horizontal track?

2. A cannon mounted on a tank with its bore horizontal and its muzzle a distance h above the ground may be turned to fire in any direction. The muzzle speed when the tank is at rest is v_0. Suppose that the tank moves ahead at speed u. (*a*) Investigate the locus of points on the ground (assumed level) which could be hit by a projectile fired at a given moment. (*b*) If the tank continues to move at uniform speed u, how far from the tank may such a projectile land?

3. What is the period of a simple pendulum of length 24 in. (*a*) on an elevator accelerating upward at 16 ft/sec²? (*b*) on an elevator accelerating downward at 16, 32, 64 ft/sec²? (*c*) on a train accelerating at 32 ft/sec² on a straight level track?

4. A train accelerates at 8 ft/sec² uniformly along a level track. If a trainman standing on a boxcar throws a missile forward at an elevation of 30° with an initial speed of 100 ft/sec, where will the missile return to the level from which it was thrown?

5. At what angular speed will a man stick to the wall of a spinning cylindrical room of radius 10 ft if the coefficient of friction is 0.2?

6. A particle of mass m moves with constant relative speed v' around the rim of a wheel of radius r. The wheel rotates about a fixed axis at constant angular speed ω. Taking the wheel as a frame of reference, derive formulas for the magnitudes of the Coriolis force and the centrifugal force acting on the particle.

7. A particle of mass m moves with constant relative speed v' outward along a spoke of a wheel rotating about a fixed axis at constant angular speed ω. For the moment when its distance from the center is r find formulas for the magnitudes of the Coriolis force and the centrifugal force relative to a frame rigidly attached to the wheel.

7.7. Effects of the Earth's Rotation. *The Plumb Line.* It is customary to consider gravitational forces near the earth as acting in the direction of a plumb line. Let us see to what extent this direction is influenced by the centrifugal force associated with the earth's rotation. Let us suppose that at a locality of latitude λ we have a plumb bob of mass m hanging at rest at the end of a string. Relative to a frame of reference rigidly hitched to the earth at this locality (see Fig. 7.17), the bob is in equilibrium subject to three forces: the tension which just balances the apparent gravitational force, $\mathbf{T} = -m\mathbf{G}$; the purely gravitational force $m\mathbf{G}'$; and the centrifugal force $\mathbf{F}_f$ of magnitude

$$m\omega^2(\rho \cos \lambda) = m\omega^2 p$$

where ρ is the radius of the earth (considered as a sphere). Since ω^2 is so small, we shall draw approximate quantitative conclusions directly from a vector diagram relating these three forces. By inspection of Fig. 7.18 we get

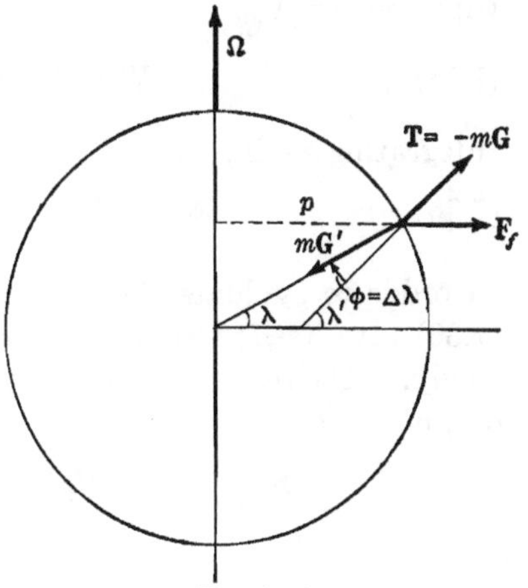

FIG. 7.17.

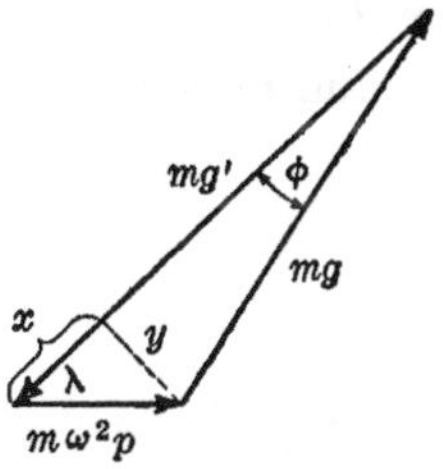

FIG. 7.18.

$$\phi = \frac{y}{mg} \qquad \text{where } y = m\omega^2 p \sin \lambda,$$

so

$$\phi = \Delta\lambda = \frac{\omega^2 \rho \sin \lambda \cos \lambda}{g}. \tag{7.31}$$

Also

$$x = m(g' - g) = m\omega^2 p \cos \lambda;$$

thus

$$\Delta g = \omega^2 \rho \cos^2 \lambda. \tag{7.32}$$

Numerical values for such effects are left for exercises.

A plumb line tends to be normal to the earth's surface (especially over oceans); therefore the conclusions just noted are qualitatively consistent with the equatorial bulge of the earth.

Effect of the Earth's Rotation on the Trajectory of a Projectile. We shall consider motion near one locality on the earth's surface. The forces acting on a projectile are the gravitational force plus centrifugal force, combined as $m\mathbf{G}$; the Coriolis force; and any further external forces of resultant $\bar{\mathbf{F}}$. Consequently,

$$\bar{\mathbf{F}} + m\mathbf{G} - 2m\mathbf{\Omega} \times \mathbf{V}' = m\mathbf{A}'. \tag{7.33}$$

Here for simplicity's sake we shall neglect air friction and other external forces except gravity. We have then

$$\mathbf{A}' = \mathbf{G} - 2\mathbf{\Omega} \times \mathbf{V}'. \tag{7.34}$$

We integrate this, assuming that the projectile initially left the origin with velocity $\mathbf{V}_0'$,

(7.35) $$\mathbf{V}' - \mathbf{V}_0' = \mathbf{G}t - 2\boldsymbol{\Omega} \times \mathbf{R}'.$$

Integrating again,

(7.36) $$\mathbf{R}' = \mathbf{V}_0't + \tfrac{1}{2}\mathbf{G}t^2 - 2\boldsymbol{\Omega} \times \int_0^t \mathbf{R}'\,dt.$$

In order to evaluate the integral in this equation, we shall substitute (7.36) into itself; but since ω^2 is very small indeed we shall do so only partly. The resulting approximate expression, good for moderate values of t, is

$$\mathbf{R}' = \mathbf{V}_0't + \tfrac{1}{2}\mathbf{G}t^2 - 2\boldsymbol{\Omega} \times \int_0^t (\mathbf{V}_0't + \tfrac{1}{2}\mathbf{G}t^2)dt,$$

or

(7.37) $$\mathbf{R}' = \mathbf{V}_0't + \tfrac{1}{2}(\mathbf{G} - 2\boldsymbol{\Omega} \times \mathbf{V}_0')t^2 - \tfrac{1}{3}(\boldsymbol{\Omega} \times \mathbf{G})t^3.$$

Numerical applications to problems involving falling particles and projectiles will be assigned as exercises.

Foucault's Pendulum. At a given point O of latitude λ let the unit vertical vector be **K** (see Fig. 7.19). Then the xy plane may be con-

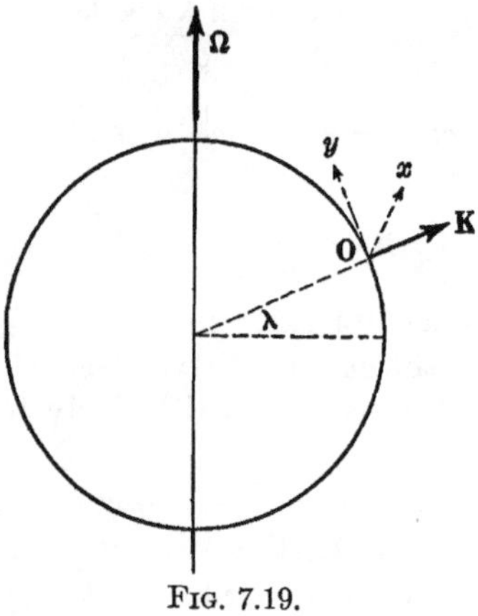

FIG. 7.19.

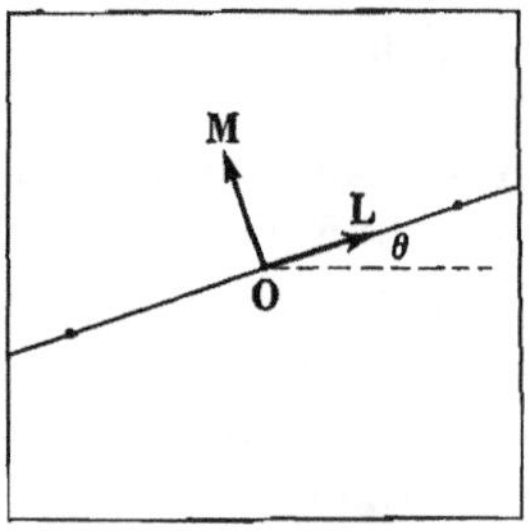

FIG. 7.20.

sidered as a tangent plane at the origin O. If a simple pendulum is set up just over O and released from rest in a displaced position of polar coordinates (r,θ), it would, were it not for the earth's rotation, describe a simple harmonic motion over the line through O at constant angle θ (see Fig. 7.20). The equation of motion would be, for a pendulum of length l,

$$-\frac{mg}{l}r = m\frac{d^2r}{dt^2},$$

or, multiplying by the unit radial vector **L**,

$$-\frac{mg}{l}\mathbf{R} = m\frac{d^2\mathbf{R}}{dt^2}. \tag{7.38}$$

The Coriolis force, acting transversely, might be expected to alter the character of the motion. Since the motion, for an inextensible string and for small displacements, is bound to be nearly plane, we shall take account only of the component parallel to the plane, *i.e.* (using Exercise 4, Sec. 2.7),

$$\begin{aligned}\mathbf{F}_{c(\text{horizontal})} &= -2m\mathbf{K} \times [(\mathbf{\Omega} \times \mathbf{V}') \times \mathbf{K}] = 2m\mathbf{K} \times [\mathbf{K} \times (\mathbf{\Omega} \times \mathbf{V}')] \\ &= 2m\mathbf{K} \times [(\mathbf{K} \cdot \mathbf{V}')\mathbf{\Omega} - (\mathbf{K} \cdot \mathbf{\Omega})\mathbf{V}'] \\ &= -2m\omega \sin\lambda(\mathbf{K} \times \mathbf{V}').\end{aligned}$$

Let us add this force to the left member of (7.38), realizing now that the oscillation will probably no longer take place along a fixed straight line.

$$-2m\omega \sin\lambda(\mathbf{K} \times \mathbf{V}') - \frac{mg}{l}\mathbf{R} = m\frac{d^2\mathbf{R}}{dt^2}.$$

Everything will now be expressed in terms of the unit radial and transverse vectors **L** and **M**. By (5.42),

$$\frac{d^2\mathbf{R}}{dt^2} = \left[\frac{d^2r}{dt^2} - r\left(\frac{d\theta}{dt}\right)^2\right]\mathbf{L} + \left[2\frac{dr}{dt}\frac{d\theta}{dt} + r\frac{d^2\theta}{dt^2}\right]\mathbf{M}.$$

Using (5.41),

$$\mathbf{K} \times \mathbf{V}' = \mathbf{K} \times \left[\frac{dr}{dt}\mathbf{L} + r\frac{d\theta}{dt}\mathbf{M}\right] = \frac{dr}{dt}\mathbf{M} - r\frac{d\theta}{dt}\mathbf{L}.$$

Substituting these expressions and equating coefficients of **M**, we get

$$-2\omega \sin\lambda\frac{dr}{dt} = 2\frac{dr}{dt}\frac{d\theta}{dt} + r\frac{d^2\theta}{dt^2}.$$

This suggests that **R** must rotate at a uniform speed

$$\frac{d\theta}{dt} = -\omega \sin\lambda. \tag{7.39}$$

Equating coefficients of **L** with this value of $d\theta/dt$ gives us

$$-2\frac{d\theta}{dt}\left(-r\frac{d\theta}{dt}\right) - \frac{gr}{l} = \frac{d^2r}{dt^2} - r\left(\frac{d\theta}{dt}\right)^2.$$

From this it is clear that if we can neglect (as previously) ω^2, the equation of motion is still (7.38) but that the plane of the oscillation rotates opposite to that of the earth at a rate $(-)\omega \sin\lambda$. This result is observable.

As originally performed by Foucault, it is one of the great historical experiments of physics, giving evidence of the rotation of the earth and also of the vector nature of angular velocity.

EXERCISES

1. An ice floe weighing 1 million tons floats in the vicinity of the North Pole moving west at 4 miles per day. Find the Coriolis force.

2. Where can the Coriolis force due to the earth's rotation be horizontal? How? Where can it be vertical? How?

3. Evaluate the Coriolis force for a 200-lb projectile fired northward at an elevation of 45° with a speed of 2,500 ft/sec at a place of latitude 45°N.

4. Because of the Coriolis force a southbound river of speed 10 ft/sec is higher at one bank than the other. The river is a mile wide. Which bank is higher and by how much? Take latitude as 50°N.

5. Show that a particle projected at 727 ft/sec on a smooth horizontal plane surface at a point of latitude 30° tends to trace out a circular arc of radius 10^7 ft.

6. If a train of mass 2,000 tons heads northeast at 60 mph on a straight level track, what is the horizontal reaction on the rails? (Latitude is 50°N.)

7. At what latitude is the direction of a plumb line most affected by the earth's rotation? How large is this maximum effect?

8. At what latitude is the magnitude of the tension in a plumb line most affected by the earth's rotation? How large is this maximum effect for a pendulum of mass 1 kg?

9. Taking your origin at the starting point (latitude λ), your y axis as vertical upward (direction of a plumb line), your x and z axes as east and south (horizontal), respectively, write three scalar equations equivalent to (7.37), expressing the position (x',y',z') of the projectile in terms of the direction cosines l, m, n of the initial velocity, the magnitude of the initial velocity v_0, and g, ω, λ, and t.

10. A particle is dropped from rest from a height of 1 mile above a point of latitude 40°N. How far from the point directly below it (plumb line) will it land? (Neglect ω^2.)

11. A bullet is fired upward at an initial speed of 1,600 ft/sec at a point of latitude 60°N. Neglecting air resistance and higher powers of the angular speed of the earth, find where the bullet will land.

12. A cannon elevated at 45° is fired first north and then south from a point of latitude 45° N. The muzzle velocity is 800 m/sec. How far from the meridian plane do the projectiles land in each case?

13. Foucault's historic pendulum experiment was performed in 1851 in Paris (48°50′N.). With what angular speed did the plane of his pendulum presumably rotate?

Could places be found where the angular speed would be twice as great? Explain.
Could places be found where the angular speed would be half as great? Explain.

CHAPTER 8

RIGID-BODY DYNAMICS

A few systematic conclusions about the dynamics of aggregates have already been introduced. These conclusions can be applied to extended bodies, for such bodies can be regarded as aggregates of particles which are tightly bound together. For our purposes at present, atoms and molecules are much too small to be of interest. The particles we speak of are merely arbitrarily small chunks which are imagined to fit together smoothly. In this way we can talk about mathematical limits as dimensions approach zero without encountering the manifold complexity which appears *physically* when dimensions approach zero. In large-scale mechanics we can properly substitute the smooth continuous pictures given us by our deceptive senses for the quite different atomic pictures which are so necessary for the study of small-scale phenomena. In this chapter we shall be concerned mainly with dynamical properties and simple motions of rigid bodies.

8.1. Center of Mass of a Rigid Body. The ideas of Sec. 7.5 can easily be applied to a rigid body. Let the body be divided into small elements. The mass of a typical element is Δm_i. The position vector of a point in this element is $\mathbf{R}_i$, as in Fig. 8.1. If the elements are small enough, the expression

$$\frac{\Sigma \, \Delta m_i \, \mathbf{R}_i}{\Sigma \, \Delta m_i}$$

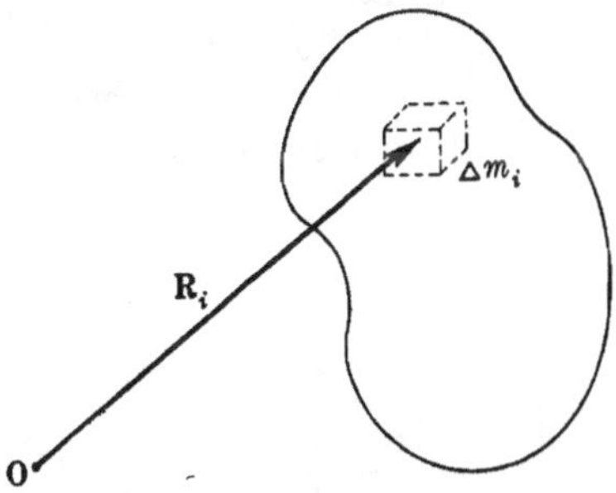

Fig. 8.1.

is a good approximation of what we would desire to call the center of mass of the body. To make the definition unique, we take the limit as the elements approach zero in size and mass. (If we let $\mathbf{R}_i$ denote the center of mass of the element, then passing to the limit is necessary only as a device for summation.) The equation is then

$$\bar{\mathbf{R}} = \lim_{\Delta m_i \to 0} \frac{\Sigma \, \Delta m_i \, \mathbf{R}_i}{\Sigma \, \Delta m_i} = \frac{1}{m} \int_m \mathbf{R} \, dm. \tag{8.1}$$

The introduction of the notation of definite integral over the whole body comes naturally from similar discussions in Sec. 5.10. m, as usual, is a symbol for the mass of the body:

$$m = \Sigma \Delta m_i = \int_m dm.$$

As usual the one vector equation is equivalent to a set of three scalar equations such as the following:

$$(8.2) \qquad \bar{x} = \frac{1}{m}\int_m x\, dm, \qquad \bar{y} = \frac{1}{m}\int_m y\, dm, \qquad \bar{z} = \frac{1}{m}\int_m z\, dm.$$

In actual numerical applications it is often convenient to express dm in some form in terms of coordinates as, for instance,

$$dm = \delta\, dx\, dy\, dz,$$

where δ is the density. Then Eqs. (8.2) become triple integrals over appropriate ranges of x, y, and z. Computations of this sort are normally performed in courses in calculus and will be omitted here. Simpler computations will be presented, however. From simple properties of the definite integral the following results (analogous to Exercise 9, Sec. 5.10) will be stated.

(8.3) *If a body of uniform density has a plane or line of symmetry, the center of mass lies on this line or plane.*

For reference we also state a conclusion already recorded in Sec. 5.10.

(8.4) *The center of mass of a solid, uniform in density, coincides with its centroid.*

Another very useful result which is an easy conclusion from elementary properties of definite integrals (already met in part in Exercise 10, Sec. 5.10) is the following:

(8.5) *If a body is composed of n parts whose centers of mass are* $\bar{\mathbf{R}}_1, \ldots, \bar{\mathbf{R}}_n$ *and whose masses are* $m_1, \ldots, m_n$, *then the center of mass of the whole is given by*

$$\bar{\mathbf{R}} = \frac{\Sigma m_i \bar{\mathbf{R}}_i}{\Sigma m_i}.$$

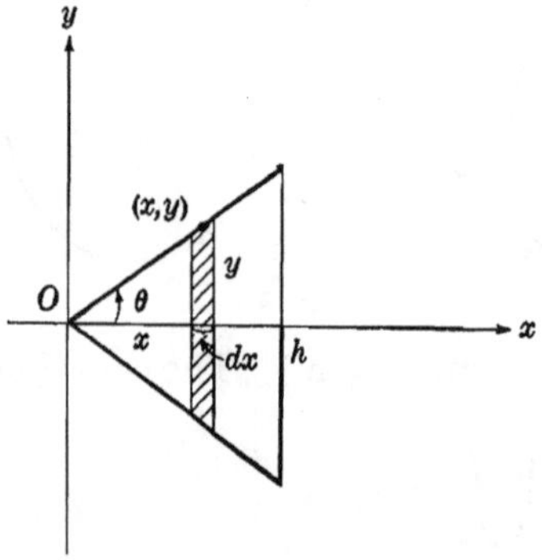

FIG. 8.2.

Example 1. Find the center of mass of a uniform solid right cone.

SOLUTION. From the symmetry, the center of mass lies on the axis (taken as x axis as shown in Fig. 8.2). It remains to compute $\bar{x}$. Take as elements disks of thickness dx and mass dm [all points in such an element have x coordinates approximately the same; thus we are in effect applying (8.5) in a limiting case, using integration for the summation]. Then

$$dm = \delta\pi\, y^2\, dx.$$

Since $y = x \tan\theta$, we have

$$\bar{x} = \frac{\delta\pi \tan^2\theta}{m}\int_0^h x^3\,dx = \frac{1}{4}\,\frac{\delta\pi\tan^2\theta}{m}\,h^4.$$

Now we compute the mass of the cone:

$$m = \delta\pi\tan^2\theta\int_0^h x^2\,dx = \tfrac{1}{3}\delta\pi\tan^2\theta\, h^3.$$

Substituting this, we get

$$\bar{x} = \tfrac{3}{4}h.$$

Theorems of Pappus. Two famous theorems are useful tools in solving for centroids or for centers of mass of uniform bodies. Given first a plane curve and an axis as in Fig. 8.3. Let the curve be rotated about the axis through an angle θ. Then a typical element of length Δs sweeps out a band of radius y whose area Δa is given by

$$\Delta a = \Delta s\, y\theta.$$

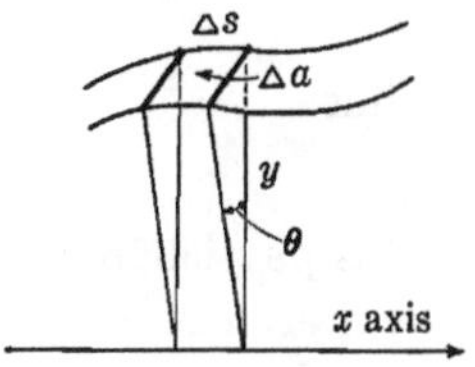

FIG. 8.3.

Summing over the whole curve and passing to the limit as Δs becomes small, we get

$$\text{Area} = \theta\textstyle\int y\,ds.$$

But, assigning uniform linear density to the original curve, its center of mass (or just its centroid) may be located by

$$\bar{y} = \frac{\int y\,ds}{l},$$

where l is the length of the curve. Our conclusion is then

$$\text{(8.6)} \qquad \text{Area} = \bar{y}\theta l.$$

Similarly, given a plane area Δa and an axis (see Fig. 8.4), a rotation about the axis through an angle θ yields an element of volume

$$\Delta v = \Delta a\, y\theta$$

for which an integration gives

$$v = \theta\textstyle\int y\,da.$$

But from

$$\bar{y} = \frac{\int y\,da}{a}$$

we get

$$\text{(8.7)} \qquad \text{Volume} = \bar{y}\theta a,$$

where a is the whole area rotated.

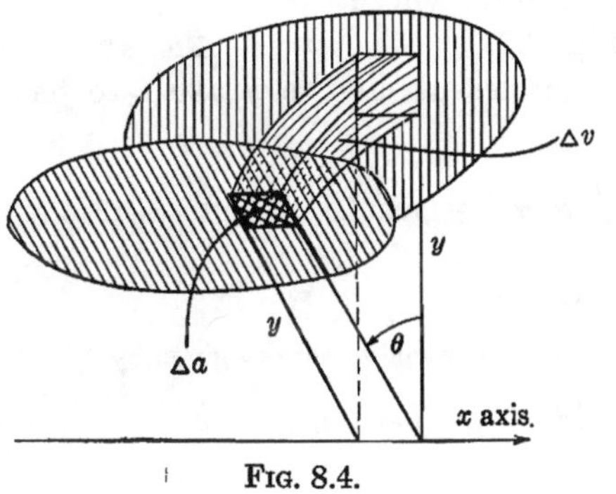

FIG. 8.4.

Equations (8.6) and (8.7) epitomize the theorems of Pappus:

(8.8) *When a homogeneous plane curve (region) is rotated about an axis in the plane, the area (volume) swept out is equal to the product of the length (area) of the curve (region) times the length of the path traced out by the centroid or center of mass of the curve (region).*

Example 2. Find the center of mass of a wire of length 8 in. bent in the shape of Fig. 8.5.

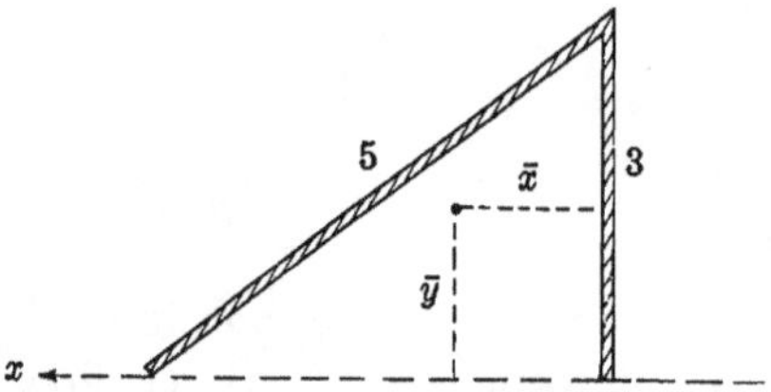

FIG. 8.5.

SOLUTION. Rotate about the x axis through an angle of 360°. The area swept out is

$$\tfrac{1}{2} \times 5 \times 2\pi \times 3 + \pi 3^2 = 24\pi.$$

Thus

$$8 \times 2\pi\bar{y} = 24\pi, \qquad \bar{y} = 1.5 \text{ in.}$$

Likewise rotating about the y axis,

$$\text{Area} = \tfrac{1}{2} \times 5 \times 2\pi \times 4 = 20\pi.$$

Thus

$$8 \times 2\pi \times \bar{x} = 20\pi, \qquad \bar{x} = 1.25 \text{ in.}$$

This particular example is inserted just to illustrate procedure. It may be more easily done by other methods (8.3 and 8.5). The two segments may be treated as particles concentrated at their centers of mass, as shown in Fig. 8.6. From this figure the results are obvious.

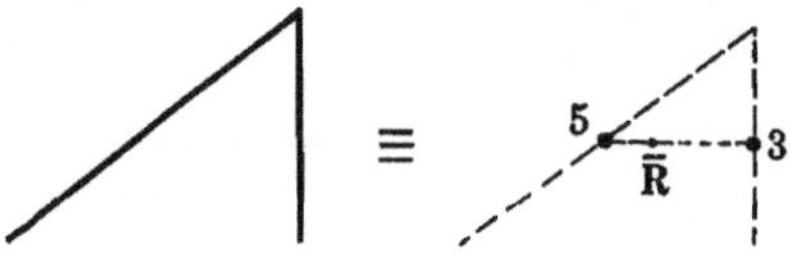

FIG. 8.6.

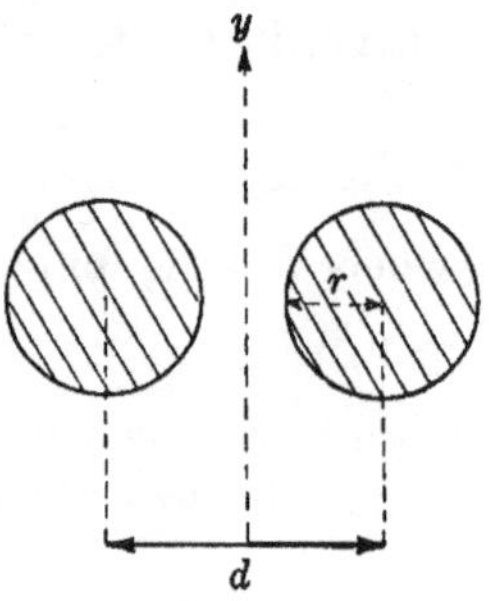

FIG. 8.7.

Example 3. Use the theorem of Pappus to compute the volume of a torus (doughnut) whose cross-sectional picture is given in Fig. 8.7.

SOLUTION. Rotating one of the circles about the y axis, we have, by (8.8),

$$\text{Volume} = 2\pi \times \frac{d}{2} \times \pi r^2 = \pi^2 d r^2.$$

EXERCISES

1. A narrow cylindrical bar of length 1 m has a variable density given by

$$\delta = 8{,}000(1 + 0.5x)\,\frac{kg}{m^3} \qquad \text{for } 0 \le x \le 1.$$

Find the center of mass.

2. A truncated cone is made of uniform material and has radii 25 cm and 40 cm. Its altitude is 40 cm. Find the center of mass.

3. Find the center of mass of a triangular frame consisting of three uniform rods whose lengths are, respectively, 5, 12, and 13 ft.

4. Find the center of mass of a triangular frame consisting of three uniform rods whose lengths are, respectively, 10, 10, and 5 ft.

5. A letter capital L is cut out of a piece of sheet metal 8 in. by 10 in. by removing a rectangle of dimensions 6 in. by 8 in. Find the center of mass.

6. Find the center of mass of a semicircular flat plate cut from uniform sheet metal.

7. Find the center of mass of a wire bent to form a semicircular arc.

8. Find the center of mass of a solid hemisphere.

9. Find the center of mass of a plane figure cut out of sheet metal having the shape of a square of side 1 ft surmounted by a semicircle of diameter 1 ft.

10. Masses of 5, 7, and 9 g are placed at points with coordinates (0,3), (0,0), and (4,0). Find the center of mass.

11. An isosceles trapezoid has bases b and $3b$. The base angles are 45°. Find the center of mass.

12. Prove that the center of mass of any uniform board cut in the shape of a triangle is the point of intersection of the medians.

8.2. Statics of a Rigid Body. In Sec. 7.5 it was shown that for an aggregate of particles the resultant of the weights passes through the center of mass as long as gravity is uniform. This fact applies to rigid bodies; therefore we may say

(8.9) *The gravitational forces on a rigid body (in a region of uniform gravity) have as resultant a single force (the weight) acting through the center of mass.*

We have assumed this to be true when dealing with symmetrical bodies in Chap. 4.

Example 1. A uniform triangular board of sides 3, 4, 5 ft is suspended by the corner having the smallest angle. What angle does the longest side make with the vertical when the board is in equilibrium?

SOLUTION. It is easy to show (using Exercise 12, Sec. 8.1) that the center of mass is at the point shown in Fig. 8.8. For equilibrium the line $\mathbf{O\bar{R}}$ must be vertical; therefore β is the desired angle. From the figure we see that

$$\tan(\alpha+\beta) = \tfrac{3}{4}, \qquad \alpha+\beta = 36.8°,$$
$$\tan\alpha = \tfrac{3}{8}, \qquad \alpha = 20.6°.$$

Thus

$$\beta = 16.2°.$$

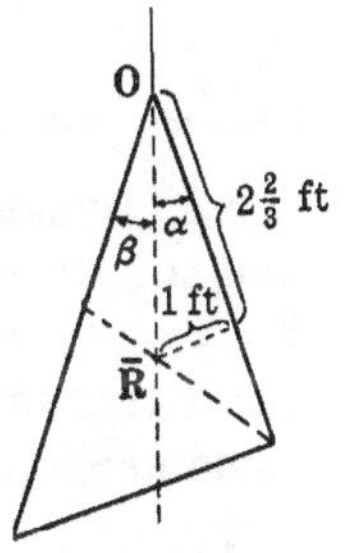

FIG. 8.8.

In physics and engineering one is likely to encounter forces whose actions are distributed over a body but which are not uniform, gravity being an example. In such cases the center of action may not be the center of mass. Such problems may be handled by replacing (4.33) by

$$\int d\mathbf{F} = \mathbf{O}, \qquad \int d\mathbf{\Gamma} = \mathbf{O}. \tag{8.10}$$

Example 2. A uniform bar of weight w and length l is supported horizontally by vertical forces **A, B** at the ends, as in Fig. 8.9. A vertical downward force in addition to gravity varies according to the rule

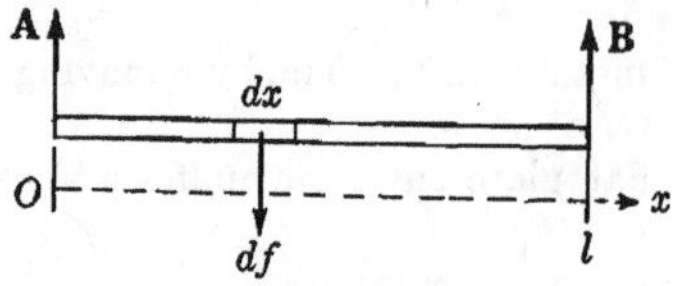

FIG. 8.9.

$$df = kx\,dx,$$

where k is a constant. Find **A** and **B**.

SOLUTION. Using (8.10),

$$a + b - w - \int_0^l kx\,dx = 0,$$

or

$$a + b = w + \tfrac{1}{2}kl^2.$$

Also

$$bl - w\frac{l}{2} - \int_0^l kx^2\,dx = 0,$$

or

$$b = \frac{w}{2} + \frac{1}{3}kl^2.$$

Whence,

$$a = \frac{w}{2} + \frac{1}{6}kl^2.$$

EXERCISES

1. A uniform triangular board weighs 10 lb. Its edges have lengths 18, 24, 30 in. It is supported, with the largest edge horizontal, by two vertical strings, one at each end of the largest edge. Find the tensions.

2. A uniform triangular plate of weight w is supported horizontally by vertical threads through the corners. The angles of the triangle are α, β, and γ. Find the tension in each of the threads.

3. A uniform bar (like the one in Fig. 8.9) is subject to a variable normal force per unit length given by

$$\frac{d\mathbf{F}}{dx} = (a + bx^2)\mathbf{J}.$$

Find the magnitude and location of the resultant.

8.3. Dynamics of a Rigid Body in Translation. In Chap. 6 rotation and translation were discussed as the principle modes of motion of a rigid body. We now turn to the dynamics of pure translation. First let us recall that in translation all points have the same velocity and hence the same acceleration:

$$\mathbf{V} = \bar{\mathbf{V}}, \qquad \mathbf{A} = \bar{\mathbf{A}}. \tag{8.11}$$

Using the results of Sec. 6.4 we might equally well describe the motion by

$$\mathbf{\Omega} = \mathbf{O}, \qquad \alpha = \mathbf{O}.$$

We might immediately consider any rigid body of mass m as an aggregate of particles and then apply earlier conclusions to the case at hand. It may, however, be more illuminating to proceed right from the beginning; thus let us now regard the body as consisting of many small elements, a typical one having mass Δm (see Fig. 8.10). Let **R** be a point within such an element. For each element Δm, **F** denotes the resultant of external forces, **F′** of internal forces. Then

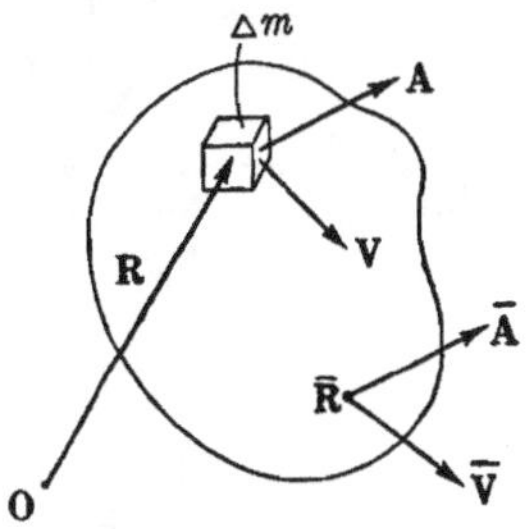

FIG. 8.10.

$$\mathbf{F} + \mathbf{F}' = \mathbf{A}\,\Delta m.$$

(Subscripts are now omitted deliberately for the sake of simplicity of notation. Any student wishing to do so is hereby authorized to insert any such trimmings.) It is to be remembered that **A** is the same for each Δm. Adding all such equations, member by member, the **F′**'s add up to zero since they are present in equal and opposite pairs, and the result is

$$\bar{\mathbf{F}} = \Sigma\mathbf{F} = \Sigma\mathbf{A}\,\Delta m = \mathbf{A}[\Sigma(\Delta m)] = m\mathbf{A} = m\bar{\mathbf{A}}. \tag{8.12}$$

This is merely a reaffirmation of the statement made previously about aggregates in general: The center of mass moves like a single particle subjected to the same external forces. Except for the emphasis on the circumstance that **A** is the same for all elements, this result makes no statement applying uniquely to translation. The negative point of view that translation is absence of rotation may be expressed by resorting to expressions involving moments. Taking moments about a random origin **O**, we get for each element

$$\bar{\mathbf{\Gamma}}_O = \Sigma\mathbf{R} \times \mathbf{F} = \Sigma\mathbf{R} \times \mathbf{A}\,\Delta m = (\Sigma\mathbf{R}\,\Delta m) \times \mathbf{A}.$$

Passing to the limit as smaller and smaller Δm's are used,

$$\bar{\mathbf{\Gamma}}_O = \Sigma\mathbf{R} \times \mathbf{F} = \left(\int_m \mathbf{R}\,dm\right) \times \mathbf{A}.$$

The notion of center of mass has again forced its way into our deliberations. Clearly this expression is simplified by rewriting as follows:

$$\bar{\mathbf{\Gamma}}_O = m\bar{\mathbf{R}} \times \mathbf{A} = \bar{\mathbf{R}} \times m\mathbf{A} = \bar{\mathbf{R}} \times \bar{\mathbf{F}}. \tag{8.13}$$

There are various ways of describing in words the results stated in Eqs. (8.12) and (8.13). One useful statement is the following:

(8.14) *For a rigid body to be in translation, the resultant of the external forces must act through the center of mass.*

A corollary is

(8.15) *If a rigid body is in translation, the moment sum of the external forces about any axis through the center of mass is zero.*

Example 1. A uniformly loaded box 8 ft high and 3 ft wide (see Fig. 8.11*a*) rests on a flatcar which accelerates at 6 ft/sec². What angle does the resultant force of reaction between box and floor make with the vertical?

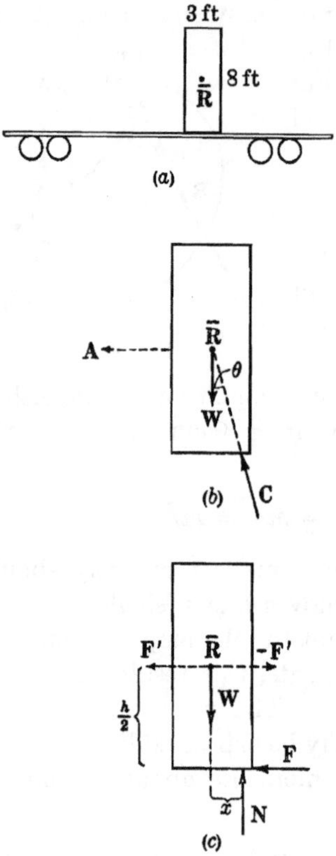

FIG. 8.11.

SOLUTION. Isolate the box (see Fig. 8.11*b*). The only forces acting are the weight of the box **W** and the reaction **C** with the floor. Since their resultant passes through the center of mass (by 8.14), **C** as well as **W** passes through $\bar{\mathbf{R}}$. Taking horizontal components,

$$c \sin \theta = \frac{w}{g} a.$$

Taking vertical components,

$$c \cos \theta - w = 0.$$

Combining the two,

$$\tan \theta = \frac{a}{g} = \frac{6}{32.2} = 0.186;$$

thus

$$\theta = 10.6°.$$

An alternative way of handling this problem is shown in Fig. 8.11*c*. Forces **F**′ and −**F**′, equal to and opposite to the frictional component **F**, are introduced at $\bar{\mathbf{R}}$. It is clear that $w = n$; thus (**W**,**N**) is a couple. By (8.15) it must be counterbalanced by an equal couple (**F**,−**F**′); therefore

$$nx = f\frac{h}{2}$$

or

$$\tan \theta = \frac{x}{h/2} = \frac{f}{w} = \frac{a}{g},$$

as before.

Example 2. For what acceleration would the box in the preceding example start to tip if it did not slip?

SOLUTION. The largest possible value of θ, if **C** is to pass through

$\bar{\mathbf{R}}$, is given by

$$\tan \theta = \frac{1.5}{4.0} = 0.375.$$

Using the result of the preceding example,

$$a = 0.375g = 12.1 \text{ ft/sec}^2.$$

EXERCISES

1. A 150-lb man stands rigidly on the platform of a truck accelerating uniformly along a straight level road. He faces the side of the road and stands with his feet 2 ft apart. The speed of the truck increases from 15 to 30 mph in 3 sec. How much of the man's weight is on his rear foot if his center of mass is 4 ft above the floor? If he were standing with his feet close together, at what angle must he lean to avoid falling?

2. A truck has a wheel base 16 ft long. When at rest, five-eighths of the weight falls on the rear wheels. At what deceleration will the weight on the front wheels be equal to that on the rear if the center of mass is 5 ft above the ground?

3. An automobile has a wheel base of length d and width b. The center of mass is at a distance h from the ground and r from the rear wheels (measured horizontally). What coefficient of friction would theoretically enable the attainment of an acceleration so great that the front wheels would rise from the road?

4. A 200-lb packing case 4 ft square and 5.3 ft high is pushed by a force **P** as shown in Fig. 8.12. When $|\mathbf{P}|$ is 40 lb, the case slides at a uniform speed. If $|\mathbf{P}|$ is increased to 100 lb, assuming the same friction, (*a*) what acceleration will result? (*b*) How far from the center will the resultant normal reaction **N** be? (*c*) For how large a value of **P** would the case start to tip?

5. A spool of rolling radius r and core radius r' rests on a horizontal table as shown in Fig. 8.13. Around the core of the spool is wrapped a thin tape. When the tape is pulled horizontally, the spool slips without rolling with an acceleration of magnitude a. What is the coefficient of friction in terms of r, r', and a?

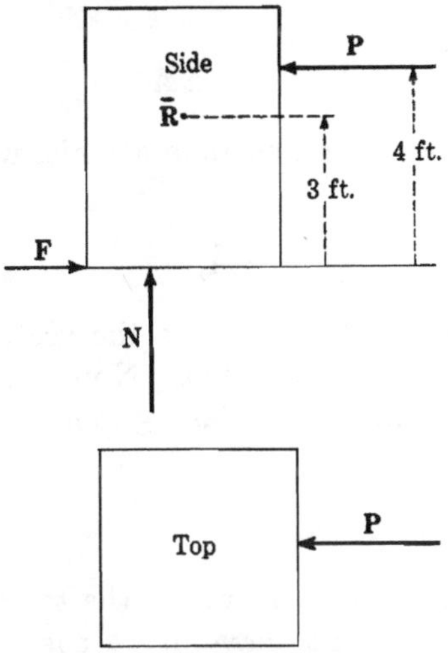

FIG. 8.12.

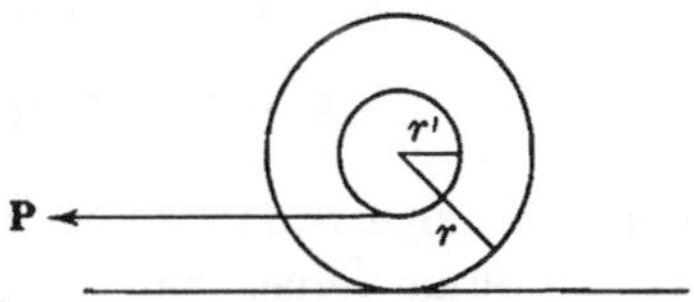

FIG. 8.13.

6. A 100-lb table is 30 in. high and 6 ft long with legs at the four corners. The table is pulled lengthwise by a symmetrically located 32 lb horizontal force at its upper edge. If the coefficient of friction is 0.1 and if the center of mass is 2 ft above the floor, how much of the weight rests on the front legs? For what acceleration would two-thirds of the weight be on these legs?

7. The runners of a sled are 18 in. apart. The center of mass of the sled together with the boy riding it is 1 ft above the ground. When the sled plus boy goes around a level unbanked curve at 30 mph, the sled starts to tip over. No slipping to the side occurs. Treating the motion as translational, find the radius of curvature of the path.

8. A 16-ft pole is dragged behind a truck. One end initially drags on the ground. The other end is fastened by a light rope 10 ft long to a point on the rear of the truck 10 ft above the ground. At what uniform acceleration would the pole and the rope form a straight line?

9. A physical pendulum is set up on a railway coach so that its plane of motion is the vertical plane in the direction of motion. If the track is straight, what angle with the vertical will specify the "equilibrium position" of the pendulum when the acceleration of the coach is a?

10. A heavy packing case 8 ft by 4 ft by 4 ft stands on the back of a truck on its square base with sides parallel to those of the vehicle. The truck accelerates down a 30° slope causing the case to tip over. If the mass of the case is uniformly distributed, state a minimum possible value for the acceleration.

8.4. Rotation of a Rigid Body. In this section we shall develop a dynamical approach to the important problem of rotation of a rigid body. Further details will appear in later sections. Suppose that we have given a rigid body free to rotate about, say, the z axis. Let us imagine the body to be divided up into pieces of mass Δm as in Fig. 8.14. Some of these pieces will be subjected to external forces of resultant **F** or internal forces of resultant **F′**. For each element

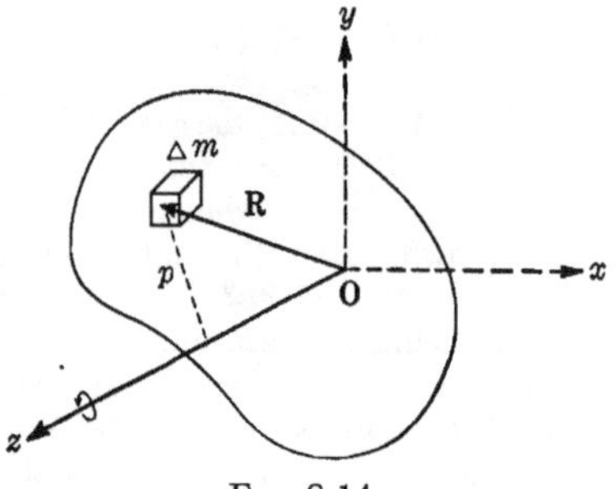

FIG. 8.14.

$$\mathbf{F} + \mathbf{F}' = \Delta m\,\mathbf{A}.$$

If we add these and take a limit, we get

$$\bar{\mathbf{F}} = m\bar{\mathbf{A}}, \tag{8.16}$$

where the left member is the vector sum of the forces applied to the body from the outside. Note that nothing is said about where the forces are applied. Taking moments about the origin, we have for each particle

$$\mathbf{R} \times \mathbf{F} + \mathbf{R} \times \mathbf{F}' = \mathbf{R} \times \Delta m\,\mathbf{A}.$$

If the sum of such equations be taken, member by member, the terms involving internal forces will disappear and we shall have, if we pass to the limit for smaller and smaller elements,

$$\sum \mathbf{\Gamma} = \int_m \mathbf{R} \times \mathbf{A}\,dm. \tag{8.17}$$

Now here in this section we are concerned only with rotation about the z axis; therefore we shall take z components of each member of the equation

$$\sum \gamma_z = \int_m \mathbf{K} \cdot \mathbf{R} \times \mathbf{A}\,dm.$$

For **A** let us substitute the expression derived in (6.14), using $\boldsymbol{\alpha} = \alpha\mathbf{K}$, $\boldsymbol{\Omega} = \omega\mathbf{K}$. The integrand then becomes

$$\mathbf{K} \cdot \mathbf{R} \times [\boldsymbol{\alpha} \times \mathbf{R} + \boldsymbol{\Omega} \times (\boldsymbol{\Omega} \times \mathbf{R})].$$

The second term in brackets is a vector in the **KR** plane; so that its scalar triple product with **K** and **R** is zero. The contribution of the first term may be written as

$$\alpha(\mathbf{K} \times \mathbf{R}) \cdot (\mathbf{K} \times \mathbf{R})$$

(interchanging · and × in a triple product). Note that the absolute value of $\mathbf{K} \times \mathbf{R}$ is equal to the perpendicular distance p of dm from the z axis. Our conclusion is then

$$\sum \gamma_z = \alpha \int_m p^2 \, dm. \tag{8.18}$$

The definite integral thus arrived at has a very special significance in mechanics. It is the *moment of inertia* of the rigid body about the z axis. Denoting it by i_z,

$$i_z = \int_m p^2 \, dm. \tag{8.19}$$

Rewriting (8.18),

$$\Sigma\gamma_z = i_z\alpha. \tag{8.20}$$

This is a rotational analog of equations of the form $\Sigma f_z = ma_z$. It provides us with a tool for solving problems involving rotation about a fixed axis. We first isolate the body, then add up moments about the axis of the isolating forces, and then finally apply (8.20) to discover the angular acceleration. This assumes optimistically that the moment of inertia is known. We shall give some study to computations of this quantity in the following sections. Sometimes it is easier to use a dynamical rather than computational solution. For instance, if we measure both the moment sum and the angular acceleration, the moment of inertia is easily found. Alternative dynamical approaches will appear as examples and exercises.

We may take the results of this section as justifying our earlier assumption (3.13) that

(8.21) *A couple is not equivalent to zero.*

For, by (8.20), a couple properly applied to a body on an axle will produce discernible angular effects. We may also take this as a means of verifying the fact [converse of (4.6)] that

(8.22) *Two equivalent couples must have equal moments.*

For two couples are called equivalent only if they always will produce the same effect on a rigid body. Equation (8.20) assures us that under certain conditions the same effect can be expected only if the moments of the couples are equal.

Example 1. A 100-lb wheel of radius 12 in. whose mass is concentrated essentially at the rim rotates about a fixed axis. When a torque of 1.2 ft-lb is applied, the wheel rotates at uniform angular speed. What angular acceleration will result if a 10-lb force is applied tangent to the rim of the wheel?

SOLUTION. In the first instance, the angular acceleration is zero; thus the moment sum is also zero. This means that in addition to the applied torque of 1.2 ft-lb there must be a frictional torque of -1.2 ft-lb. The moment of inertia is merely mr^2, since the mass is concentrated at the rim. Numerically,

$$i_z = \left(\frac{100}{32.2}\right) \times 1^2 = 3.1 \text{ ft-lb-sec}^2.$$

The 10-lb force has a moment of 10 ft-lb since the radius is 1 ft. Thus Eq. (8.20) here appears as

$$10.0 - 1.2 = 3.1\alpha,$$

or

$$\alpha = 2.84 \text{ rad/sec}^2.$$

Example 2. *Torsion Pendulum.* A torsion pendulum consists usually of a disk supported in a horizontal position by a vertical wire through its center as in Fig. 8.15. When the disk is given an angular displacement, the twisted wire provides a restoring torque proportional to the displacement,

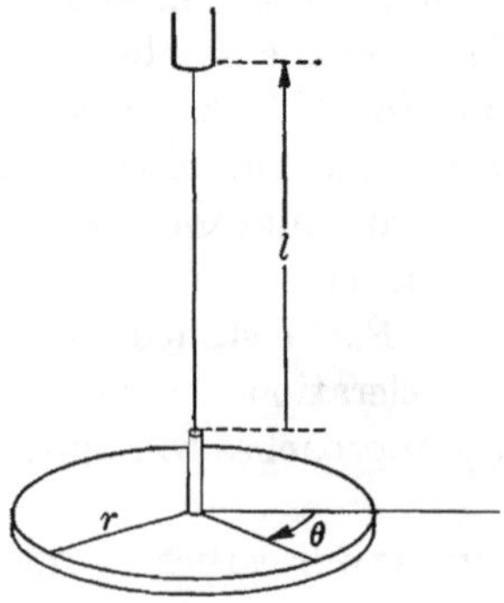

FIG. 8.15.

$$\gamma = -k\theta. \tag{8.23}$$

Applying (8.20), we have

$$-k\theta = i_z \frac{d^2\theta}{dt^2}.$$

By our study of simple harmonic motion (5.60), we recognize that the period of oscillation is

$$\tau = 2\pi \sqrt{\frac{i_z}{k}}. \tag{8.24}$$

Example 3. A wheel whose moment of inertia is 6.0 kg-m² rotates about a horizontal axis (see Fig. 8.16). The friction of the bearings produces a torque of 0.8 newton-m. The axle of the wheel has a diameter of 4 cm. A cord, wound several times around the axle, has at its free end an object of mass 5.0 kg. If this object is released from rest, how long will it take it to descend 1 m? Neglect mass and stiffness of the cord and the inertia of the axle.

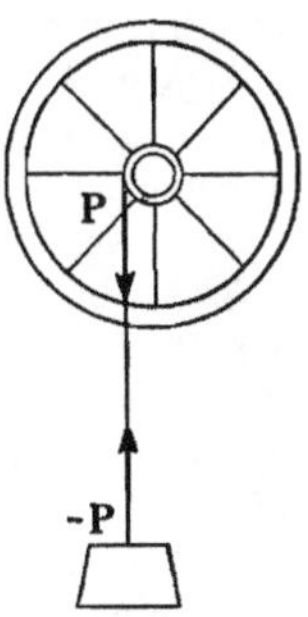

FIG. 8.16.

SOLUTION. First isolate the wheel. Let **P** be the tension produced by the cord. Let γ_f denote the magnitude of the frictional torque. Using (8.20),

$$pr - \gamma_f = i_z\alpha.$$

Now isolate the descending object:

$$mg - p = ma.$$

Assuming that the cord does not slip,

$$a = \alpha r.$$

Eliminating p, we have

$$mg - \frac{\gamma_f}{r} = \left(\frac{i}{r^2} + m\right)a.$$

Substituting numerical values,

$$5.0 \times 9.8 - \frac{0.8}{0.02} = \left(\frac{6.0}{4 \times 10^{-4}} + 5.0\right)a;$$

or

$$a = \frac{9}{1.5} \times 10^{-4}.$$

$$a = 6 \times 10^{-4}\ \text{m/sec}^2.$$

The distance s of drop and the time t are related by

$$s = \tfrac{1}{2}at^2,$$

or

$$t = \sqrt{\frac{2}{6.0 \times 10^{-4}}} = 58\ \text{sec}.$$

EXERCISES

1. A flywheel weighs 1,000 lb. Its mass may be considered as concentrated at a distance of 4 ft from the axle. Initially it is rotating at 500 rpm. A brake is applied to the outer rim at a distance of 5 ft from the axle with a normal force of 40 lb. If the coefficient of friction between brake and wheel is 0.42, how long will it take the wheel to come to rest?

2. A given wheel is free to rotate about its axis. An applied torque of 20 ft-lb is sufficient to maintain constant angular speed. A torque of 30 ft-lb produces an angular acceleration of 3 rad/sec². What applied torque is necessary to produce an angular acceleration of 6 rad/sec²?

3. A wheel and axle rigidly joined together have weight 96 lb and moment of inertia 1.33 ft-lb-sec². The diameter of the axle is 0.5 in. The axle is supported in horizontal position by bearings whose friction may be neglected. The wheel may be braked by applying a normal force to a braking block held against the axle. The coefficient of friction between block and axle is one-third. If the wheel initially rotates at 300 rpm and if the normal force used on the brake is 100 lb, how many revolutions will the wheel make before coming to a stop? How long will it take?

4. Derive a formula for the moment of inertia of the pulley in Fig. 8.17 in terms of m_1, m_2, μ, r, θ, and the acceleration a.

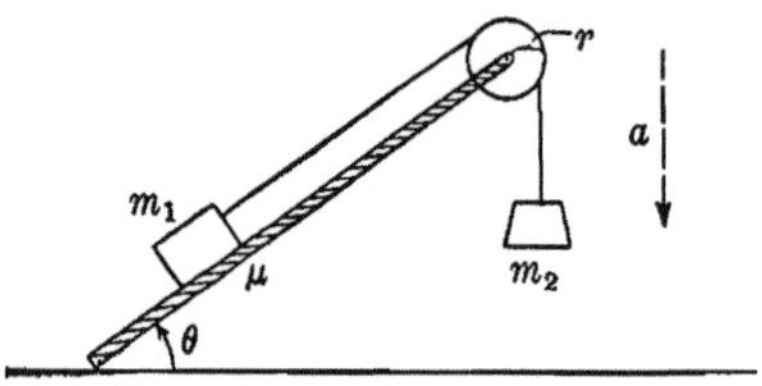

FIG. 8.17.

5. A disk is supported horizontally by a wire through its center. When a couple of 0.5 newton-m is applied, the disk is twisted through 15°. When it is released, the period of vibration is 3.5 sec. What is the moment of inertia of the disk?

6. A homogeneous disk 1 ft in diameter and 1 in. thick is suspended horizontally by a long wire through its center and it is used as a torsion pendulum. It has a period of 4 sec. If this first disk is replaced by another with the same dimensions but half the density, what period will result?

7. A double torsion pendulum as in Fig. 8.18 consists of a wire and two disks held rigidly at a fixed distance apart. The period is τ_0. When a uniform wheel of known moment of inertia i_1 is centered on the lower disk, the period is τ_1. When a symmetric wheel of unknown moment of inertia is placed on the lower disk instead of the other, the period is τ_2. Find in terms of τ_0, τ_1, τ_2, and i_1 the unknown moment of inertia.

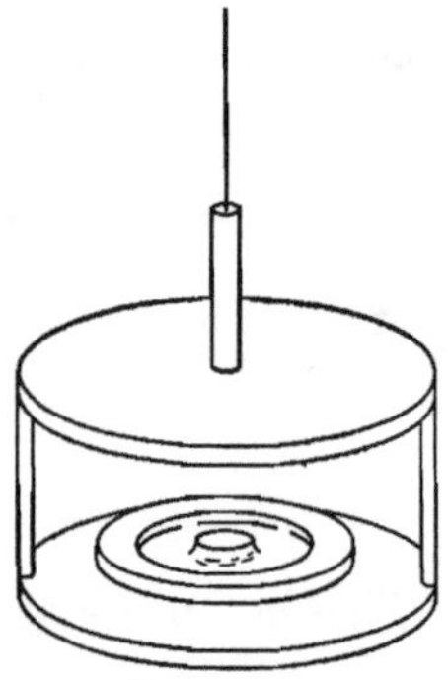
FIG. 8.18.

8.5. Moment of Inertia and Radius of Gyration.

The defining equation for moment of inertia about a particular axis of a rigid body has already been given.

$$i = \int_m p^2\,dm. \tag{8.25}$$

This quantity is a measure of rotational inertia; therefore it is of extreme importance in mechanical engineering. Dynamical methods of determining i have already been given. Another such method appears in the Sec. 8.8. This section will be devoted to mathematical methods based on the definition.

Example 1. To find the moment of inertia of a sphere about a diameter, say the x axis in Fig. 8.19.

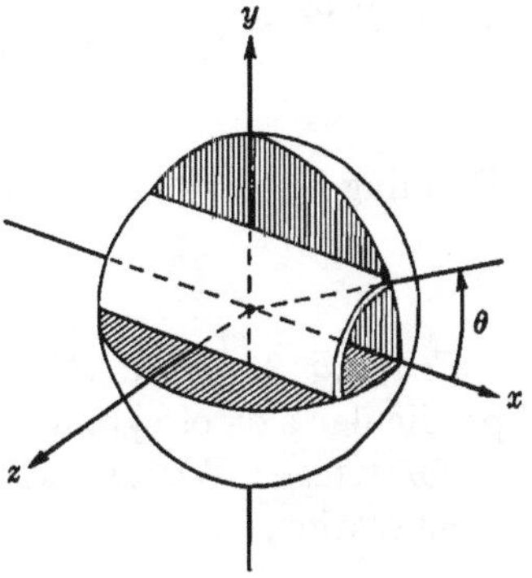

FIG. 8.19.

SOLUTION. Let us divide the sphere into elements each of which has a fixed distance from the axis, that is, into cylindrical shell elements of radius $y = r \sin\theta$ and thickness $dy = r\cos\theta\, d\theta$. The mass of such an element, taking δ as the uniform density, is

$$dm = \delta\, 4\pi x y\, dy,$$

and its moment of inertia is

$$\begin{aligned} di &= \delta\, 4\pi x y^3\, dy = 4\pi\delta r^5 \sin^3\theta \cos^2\theta\, d\theta \\ &= 4\pi\delta r^5 \cos^2\theta \sin\theta\, d\theta - 4\pi\delta r^5 \cos^4\theta \sin\theta\, d\theta. \end{aligned}$$

Integrating for θ from 0 to $\pi/2$, we get

$$i = \frac{8\pi\delta r^5}{15}.$$

The total mass m of the sphere is known:

$$m = \tfrac{4}{3}\pi\delta r^3;$$

thus i may be written

$$i = \tfrac{2}{5} m r^2.$$

Note that a sphere of mass m and radius r has the same moment of inertia as a hoop of mass m and radius $\bar{p}$ given by

$$\bar{p}^2 = \tfrac{2}{5} r^2.$$

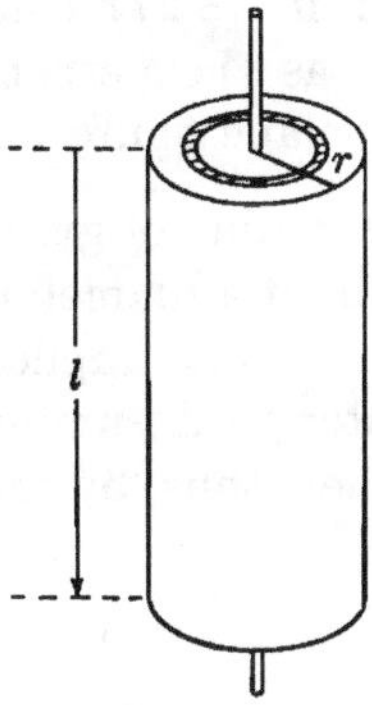

FIG. 8.20.

This convenient approach to problems of rotational inertia leads to defining the *radius of gyration* $\bar{p}$ of a rigid body about a particular axis by

$$\bar{p}^2 = \frac{i}{m} \tag{8.26}$$

or

$$m\bar{p}^2 = \int_m p^2\, dm.$$

Example 2. Find the radius of gyration of a solid cylinder about its axis (see Fig. 8.20).

SOLUTION. As in the last example let us divide the cylinder into shells of radius x, thickness dx, and hence of moment of inertia

$$di = 2\pi\delta l x^3\, dx.$$

Integrating,

$$i = 2\pi\delta l \int_0^r x^3\,dx = \tfrac{1}{2}\pi\delta l r^4.$$

Dividing by $m = \pi r^2 l\,\delta$, we get

$$\bar{p}^2 = \tfrac{1}{2}r^2.$$

Example 3. Find the radius of gyration for rotation about a perpendicular axis of symmetry of a thin uniform rod of length $2r$.

SOLUTION. We may write, canceling out factors involving density and cross section,

$$\bar{p}^2 = \frac{1}{2r}\int_{-r}^{r} x^2\,dx = \frac{1}{2r}\left[\frac{x^3}{3}\right]_{-r}^{r} = \frac{1}{3}r^2.$$

The Perpendicular-axis Theorem. Consider a plane figure lying in the xy plane as in Fig. 8.21. Its moment of inertia about the z axis may be written

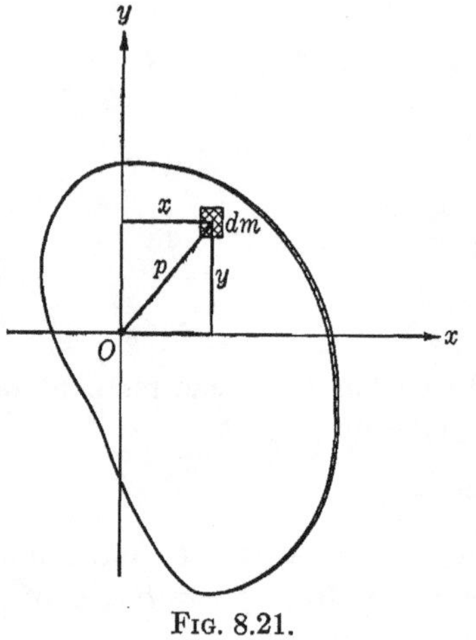

FIG. 8.21.

$$i_z = \int_m p^2\,dm = \int_m (x^2 + y^2)dm$$
$$= \int_m x^2\,dm + \int_m y^2\,dm,$$

or, since these terms are the moments of inertia about the y and x axes, respectively,

$$i_z = i_x + i_y. \tag{8.27}$$

The relationship stated in (8.27) constitutes what is known as the perpendicular-axis theorem for plane figures.

Example 4. Find the radius of gyration of a circular disk about a diameter.

SOLUTION. By the result on cylinders, $i_z = \frac{1}{2}mr^2$. (This implies that the disk lies in the xy plane with the origin at its center.) Assuming that the disk is uniform, one diameter is as good as another; thus, by the symmetry, $i_x = i_y$. Using the perpendicular axis result,

$$i_x + i_y = 2i_x = i_z;$$

or

$$i_x = \tfrac{1}{4}mr^2; \qquad \bar{p}^2 = \tfrac{1}{4}r^2.$$

Example 5. To find the radius of gyration of a plane rectangle of dimensions $2a$ by $2b$ rotated about a perpendicular axis through its center. Choosing axes as shown in Fig. 8.22, i_x is easily evaluated in terms of the previous result concerning a rod. For the whole rectangle can be thought of as composed of rods of length $2b$ laid side by side. Hence

$$i_x = \tfrac{1}{3}mb^2;$$

similarly

$$i_y = \tfrac{1}{3}ma^2.$$

By (8.27), we have

$$i_z = \frac{1}{3}\,m(a^2 + b^2), \qquad \bar{p}^2 = \frac{a^2 + b^2}{3}.$$

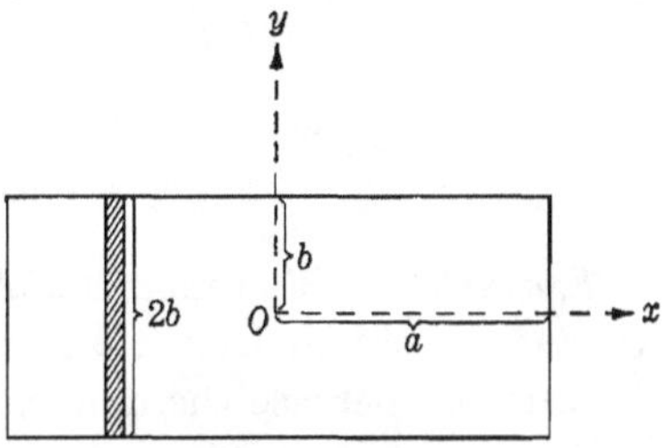

FIG. 8.22.

The Parallel-axis Theorem. In most of the examples so far we have computed moments of inertia for axes through the center of mass. For symmetrical bodies this is manifestly advantageous. We shall now introduce a theorem which enables one to use these simpler results in other circumstances without repeating computations. The statement of the result is

(8.28) *For rotation about an axis not through its center of mass, the radius of gyration $\bar{p}'$ of a rigid body is given by*

$$\bar{p}'^2 = \bar{p}^2 + d^2,$$

where $\bar{p}$ is its radius of gyration about a parallel axis through the center of mass and d is the distance between the two parallel axes.

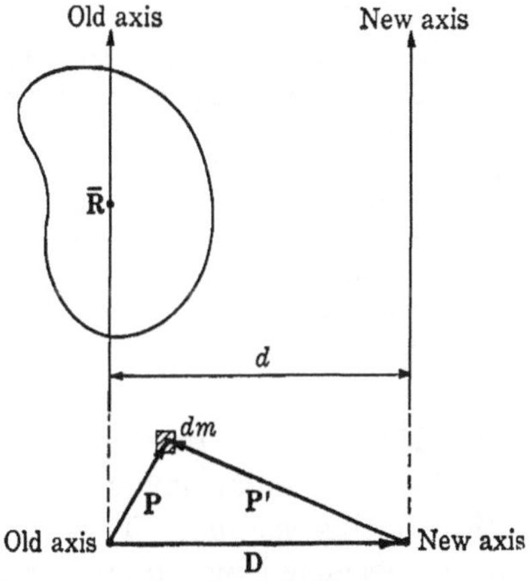

FIG. 8.23.

PROOF. For each element of mass, consider the plane through this element and perpendicular to the two axes. Let **P** and **P**′ be the vectors to the element dm from the points where the axes meet the plane and let **D** be the vector between these points in the sense shown in Fig. 8.23; so that

$$\mathbf{P}' = \mathbf{P} - \mathbf{D}.$$

This relationship is diagramed in Fig. 8.23. Then the new moment of inertia i' is given by

$$\begin{aligned} i' &= \int_m p'^2\,dm = \int_m (\mathbf{P}'\cdot\mathbf{P}')dm = \int_m (\mathbf{P}-\mathbf{D})\cdot(\mathbf{P}-\mathbf{D})dm \\ &= \int_m (\mathbf{P}\cdot\mathbf{P})dm - 2\int_m (\mathbf{P}\cdot\mathbf{D})dm + \int_m (\mathbf{D}\cdot\mathbf{D})dm \\ &= \int_m p^2\,dm - 2\mathbf{D}\cdot\int_m \mathbf{P}\,dm + d^2\int_m dm. \end{aligned}$$

Now the first term on the right is at once recognizable as i. The integral in the second term must vanish since it gives the mass times the perpendicular distance from the old axis to the center of mass. Rewriting,

$$i' = i + d^2m$$

or, dividing by m,

$$\bar{p}'^2 = \bar{p}^2 + d^2.$$

Example 6. The moment of inertia of a sphere about a diameter is $0.4mr^2$. How far from the center of the sphere must an axis be placed in order to increase the moment of inertia by 50 per cent?

SOLUTION

$$0.6mr^2 = 0.4mr^2 + md^2; \qquad 0.2r^2 = d^2;$$

thus

$$d = 0.45r.$$

EXERCISES

1. Find the moment of inertia of a uniform bar of length $4r$ and mass m about a perpendicular axis at a distance r from the center.

2. Find the radius of gyration of a circular disk of radius r about a tangent line.

3. The mass of a hoop is 5 kg. Its radius is 0.6 m. Find its moment of inertia (*a*) about a diameter; (*b*) about a tangent.

4. A half disk or semicircular plate is rotated about an axis through its center of mass and parallel to the bounding diameter. Find the radius of gyration.

5. A homogeneous plane quarter circle of radius r is rotated about a bounding diameter. Find the radius of gyration.

6. A uniform plane figure having the shape of a square surmounted by a semicircle is rotated about (*a*) the base; (*b*) the axis of symmetry. If the square has edge $2r$ and the circle has radius r, find the two radii of gyration.

7. A uniform 16-lb disk of radius 9 in. is suspended horizontally by a uniform wire attached to its center. A torque of 1 ft-lb will hold the disk turned into a position 90° from its equilibrium position. When released, it oscillates as a torsion pendulum. (*a*) Find the period. (*b*) If the mid-point of the suspending wire in part (*a*) is held fast so that the pendulum is only half as long, what will be the period? (*c*) If a thin hoop weighing 4 lb is fitted to the circumference of the disk in part (*a*), what will be the period? (The wire is full length.)

8.6. Additional Methods for Computing Moments of Inertia. It is quite possible to associate long and happily with moments of inertia without meeting explicitly the two topics of this section. They are, however, rather interesting and they will be welcomed by students who like to learn "rules of thumb" which make unnecessary tedious integrations.

The Cylinder Theorem. We shall here apply the name cylinder to any solid generated by moving a plane figure perpendicular to itself along a straight line. Thus the ordinary cylinder may be thought of as generated by moving a thin circular disk. We shall try to compute an expression for the moment of inertia about some axis (in Fig. 8.24, the y axis) perpendicular to the generators (such as the x axis in the figure) of the cylinder. Taking as an element a slice of thickness dx and mass

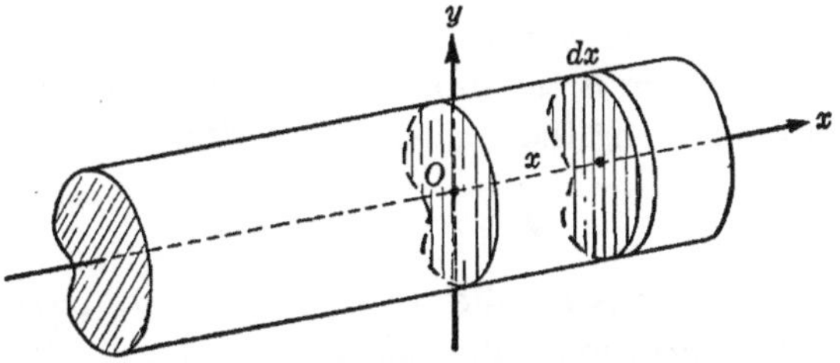

FIG. 8.24.

dm, we can write first its moment of inertia about a parallel axis through its center of mass $\bar{\mathbf{R}}$

$$di'' = \bar{p}''^2\, dm.$$

About a parallel axis, in the slice, which cuts the x axis, the moment of

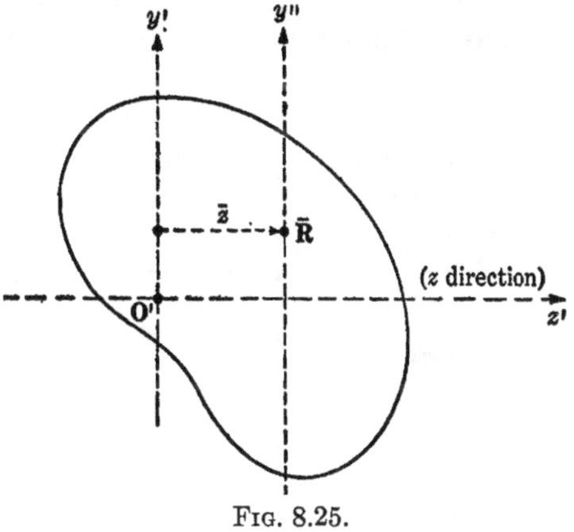

FIG. 8.25.

inertia of the slice is (see Fig. 8.25)

$$di' = \bar{p}''^2\, dm + \bar{z}^2\, dm.$$

And finally about the y axis itself:

$$di = \bar{p}''^2\, dm + \bar{z}^2\, dm + x^2\, dm.$$

This may be integrated over the whole mass.

$$i_y = \int \bar{p}''^2\, dm + \int \bar{z}^2\, dm + \int x^2\, dm.$$

Now $\bar{p}''$ and $\bar{z}$ are the same for each element; thus they may be taken outside the integration symbol:

$$i_y = m\bar{p}''^2 + m\bar{z}^2 + \int x^2\, dm.$$

Each term has its own significance. $m\bar{p}''^2$ is the moment of inertia of a disk having the shape of the slices we have taken as elements and possessing the entire mass of the cylinder. It is, however, the moment of inertia about a parallel axis through the center of mass. $m\bar{p}''^2 + m\bar{z}^2$ is the moment of inertia of such a disk located in the yz plane taken about the y axis. Finally, $\int x^2\,dm$ is the moment of inertia about the y axis of a rod of mass m lying along the x axis. We write then

$$i_{\text{cylinder}} = i_{\text{disk}} + i_{\text{rod}}. \tag{8.29}$$

In words: if a cylinder is parallel to the x axis, its moment about the y axis is the sum of (a) the moment about the y axis of the disk obtained by projecting the whole cylinder into the yz plane and (b) the moment about the y axis of the rod obtained by projecting the whole cylinder into the x axis. [Note that "y axis" may be replaced by "z axis" in the above statement. Equation (8.29) is also true for moments about the x axis; but the result is less meaty in this case.]

Example 1. Find the moment of inertia of an ordinary solid cylinder of length $2l$ and radius r about a perpendicular axis through the center (see Fig. 8.26).

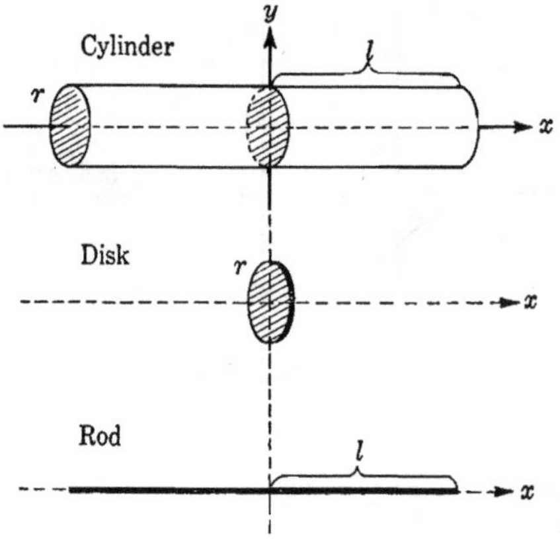

FIG. 8.26.

SOLUTION. Using the terminology of (8.29),

$$i_{\text{disk}} = \tfrac{1}{4}mr^2,$$
$$i_{\text{rod}} = \tfrac{1}{3}ml^2.$$

i_{cylinder} is the sum of these two terms.

Example 2. Find the moment of inertia of a rectangular box about an axis of symmetry.

SOLUTION. The result previously obtained about a rectangular plate can be extended to this problem. Here, however, for the present let us use the cylinder theorem (see Fig. 8.27).

$$i_{\text{disk}} = \tfrac{1}{3}mc^2, \qquad i_{\text{rod}} = \tfrac{1}{3}ma^2.$$

Hence, for the "cylinder,"

$$i_y = \tfrac{1}{3}m(a^2 + c^2);$$

similarly,

$$i_x = \tfrac{1}{3}m(b^2 + c^2).$$

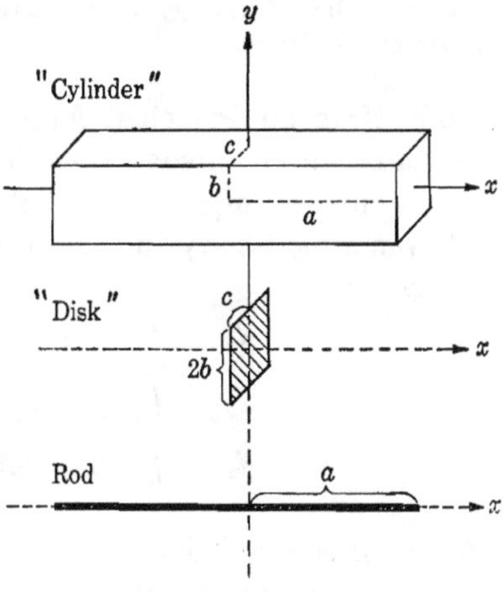

FIG. 8.27.

Routh's Rule. The results on radii of gyration for certain simple figures have been summarized by Routh in a way that is easy to remember.

(8.30) *The square of the radius of gyration for rotation about an axis of symmetry of a solid body having rectangular, elliptical, or ellipsoidal symmetry is equal to the sum of the squares of the semiaxes of symmetry perpendicular to the rotation axis divided by* 3, 4, *or* 5, *respectively.*

The student should observe that this rule includes previous results on the disk (elliptical), the sphere (ellipsoidal), the rod (rectangular), as well as for rectangular shapes. In particular the results just obtained for a solid box are given by it.

Example 3. What are the radii of gyration about the coordinate axes of the ellipsoid (see Fig. 8.28)

$$\frac{x^2}{a^2} + \frac{y^2}{b^2} + \frac{z^2}{c^2} = 1?$$

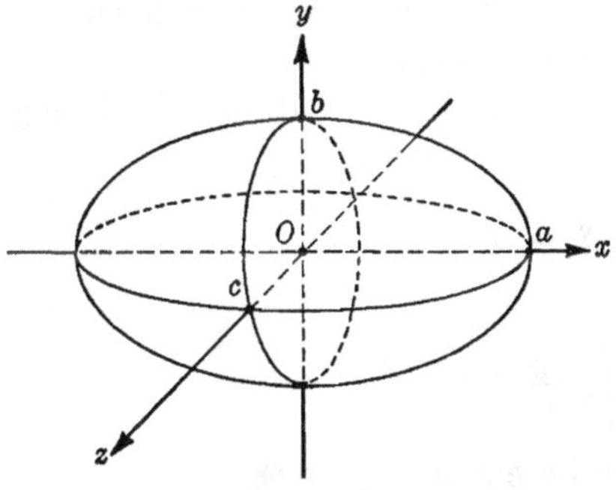

FIG. 8.28.

SOLUTION. By Routh's rule,

$$\bar{p}_x^2 = 0.2(b^2 + c^2),$$
$$\bar{p}_y^2 = 0.2(a^2 + c^2),$$
$$\bar{p}_z^2 = 0.2(a^2 + b^2).$$

For the case where $a = b = c$, this example degenerates into the sphere (previously handled).

EXERCISES

1. Find the radius of gyration of a solid cone of altitude h and radius of base r about its axis of symmetry.

2. A cube of edge s is rotated about one edge. Find the radius of gyration.

3. An elliptical disk bounded by a curve which, with respect to the axes of symmetry, has the equation

$$\frac{x^2}{a^2} + \frac{y^2}{b^2} = 1$$

is rotated about the line $x = a$. Find the radius of gyration.

4. Find the radius of gyration of a solid cone of altitude h and radius of base r about a diameter of its base.

8.7. Note on Principal Axes of Inertia. The study of moments of inertia might be pursued much further. Here we shall have to be content with a cursory inquiry into slightly more general ideas.

Given a rigid body and axes **O**xyz, we have so far defined three *moments of inertia:*

$$i_x = \int_m (\mathbf{I} \times \mathbf{R})^2 dm = \int_m (y^2 + z^2) dm,$$
$$i_y = \int_m (\mathbf{J} \times \mathbf{R})^2 dm = \int_m (z^2 + x^2) dm,$$
$$i_z = \int_m (\mathbf{K} \times \mathbf{R})^2 dm = \int_m (x^2 + y^2) dm.$$

(A vector squared denotes the scalar product with itself.) Three other inertia constants are often used. These are the *products of inertia:*

$$i_{xy} = -\int_m (\mathbf{I} \times \mathbf{R}) \cdot (\mathbf{J} \times \mathbf{R}) dm = \int_m xy\, dm,$$
$$i_{yz} = -\int_m (\mathbf{J} \times \mathbf{R}) \cdot (\mathbf{K} \times \mathbf{R}) dm = \int_m yz\, dm,$$
$$i_{zx} = -\int_m (\mathbf{K} \times \mathbf{R}) \cdot (\mathbf{I} \times \mathbf{R}) dm = \int_m zx\, dm.$$

The coordinate axes are called *principal axes of inertia relative to* **O** if these products are zero. (That is, if i_{xy} and i_{zx} are both zero, then the x axis is such an axis, etc.) It is easy to show, for instance, that a line of symmetry or a line normal to a plane of symmetry is such an axis. (In the latter case the origin is taken in the plane.)

We now consider the moment of inertia about a random axis through the origin. Let its direction be given by the unit vector

$$\mathbf{E} = l\mathbf{I} + m\mathbf{J} + n\mathbf{K}.$$

Then we have

$$i = \int_m p^2\, dm = \int_m (\mathbf{E} \times \mathbf{R})^2 dm.$$

Substituting the value for **E**, this may be expanded since

$$(\mathbf{E} \times \mathbf{R})^2 = l^2(\mathbf{I} \times \mathbf{R})^2 + m^2(\mathbf{J} \times \mathbf{R})^2 + n^2(\mathbf{K} \times \mathbf{R})^2 + 2lm(\mathbf{I} \times \mathbf{R}) \cdot (\mathbf{J} \times \mathbf{R}) + 2mn(\mathbf{J} \times \mathbf{R}) \cdot (\mathbf{K} \times \mathbf{R}) + 2nl(\mathbf{K} \times \mathbf{R}) \cdot (\mathbf{I} \times \mathbf{R}).$$

Using the values for the six inertia constants given earlier, this means

$$i = l^2 i_x + m^2 i_y + n^2 i_z - 2lm i_{xy} - 2mn i_{yz} - 2nl i_{zx}. \tag{8.31}$$

This shows how any moment of inertia is expressible in terms of the six basic inertia constants relative to a given set of axes if the axis is through the origin.

The last equation suggests that the inertia constants might be used to define a quadric surface with points at a distance from the origin correlated with radius of gyration about an axis in that direction. This suggestion leads to the fascinating theory of the *ellipsoid of inertia* which the student is encouraged to read about elsewhere.

In this course, our use of (8.31) will be brief and to the point. Picking coordinate axes in coincidence with axes of symmetry of simple bodies, we can easily compute moments of inertia about skew axes.

Example 1. Given a cylinder of length $2l$ and radius r, pick the origin at the center and the x axis along the axis of the cylinder. Then an axis through the center at an angle θ with the axis of symmetry (that is, the x axis) may be described by

$$\mathbf{E} = \cos\theta\,\mathbf{I} + \sin\theta\,\mathbf{J}.$$

All three coordinate axes are axes of symmetry; thus the products of inertia vanish giving

$$i = m\left[\cos^2\theta\,\frac{r^2}{2} + \sin^2\theta\left(\frac{l^2}{3} + \frac{r^2}{4}\right)\right].$$

Example 2. Given a cube, let us pick origin at the center and axes parallel to the edges. Then the coordinate axes are axes of symmetry and hence principal axes of inertia. Also because of the symmetry

$$i_x = i_y = i_z.$$

Using (8.31), we get

$$\begin{aligned} i &= l^2 i_x + m^2 i_y + n^2 i_z \\ &= (l^2 + m^2 + n^2) i_x \\ &= i_x. \end{aligned}$$

Thus for a uniform cube the moment of inertia is the same for any axis through the center.

EXERCISES

1. Perform in detail the vector manipulations leading to (8.31).

2. Find the radius of gyration of a disk of radius r about an axis through its center and making an angle of 45° with the normal.

3. Find the radius of gyration of a rectangle of dimensions $2a \times 2b$ about a diagonal.

4. In view of (8.31) can you extend the "cylinder theorem" (8.29) to a skew axis through the center? Reinforce your answer by details.

8.8. Physical Pendulum. Any rigid body which can be made to oscillate freely about a fixed horizontal axis may be considered as a pendulum. Figure 8.29 shows such a body displaced from equilibrium by an angle θ. Let **Q** be the point where the axis intersects the plane normal to the axis and through the center of mass $\bar{\mathbf{R}}$. Let the distance from $\bar{\mathbf{R}}$ to **Q** be written h. If the friction at the axis is negligible, then the only force having a nonzero moment about the axis is the weight. Equation (8.20) may be applied to give

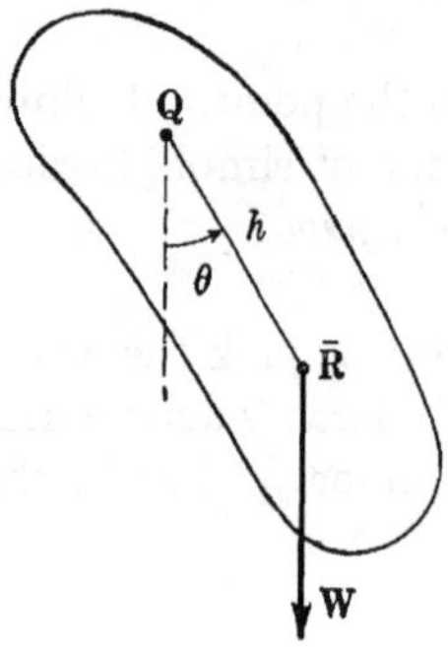

FIG. 8.29.

$$-wh \sin \theta = i_z \alpha. \tag{8.32}$$

If we replace α by $\omega(d\omega/d\theta)$, we can write, taking θ_0 as the amplitude,

$$-wh \int_{\theta_0}^{\theta} \sin \theta \, d\theta = i_z \int_0^{\omega} \omega \, d\omega. \tag{8.33}$$

Integrating,

$$wh(\cos \theta - \cos \theta_0) = \tfrac{1}{2} i_z \omega^2. \tag{8.34}$$

This is analogous to (7.8). Equations of this sort will be studied at length in the chapter on energy.

If, as in our discussion of the simple pendulum, we agree to consider only cases where θ_0 is small, Eq. (8.32) can be rewritten as

$$-wh\theta = i_z \frac{d^2\theta}{dt^2}. \tag{8.35}$$

This is an equation for simple harmonic oscillation of period given by

$$\tau = 2\pi \sqrt{\frac{i}{wh}} = 2\pi \sqrt{\frac{i}{mgh}}. \tag{8.36}$$

If we write i in terms of the radius of gyration $\bar{p}'$, an alternative expression is

$$\tau = 2\pi \sqrt{\frac{\bar{p}'^2}{gh}}. \tag{8.37}$$

By the parallel-axis theorem our formula may be written in terms of the corresponding radius of gyration about an axis through the center of mass:

$$\tau = 2\pi \sqrt{\frac{\bar{p}^2 + h^2}{gh}}. \tag{8.38}$$

From this it is apparent that the point **Q** is important only as a point in the vertical plane through $\bar{\mathbf{R}}$ and normal to the desired axis at a distance

h from $\bar{\mathbf{R}}$. Thus in Fig. 8.30, $\mathbf{Q}'$ and $\mathbf{Q}''$ are equally suitable points as are any other points on the circle of radius h about $\bar{\mathbf{R}}$. A parallel axis through any such point would give rise to an oscillation of the same period.

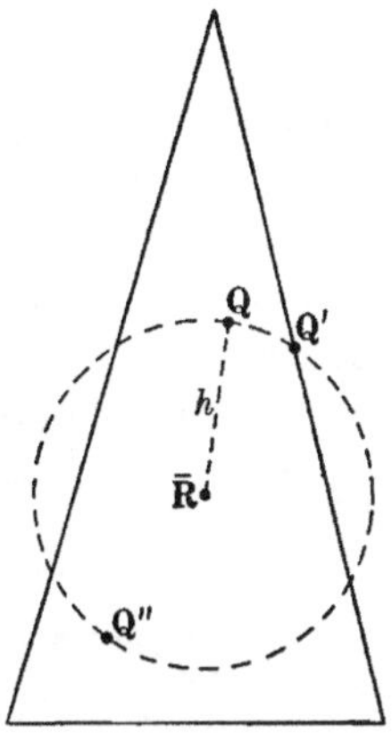

FIG. 8.30.

The behavior of a physical pendulum, for a given axis, may be summarized simply by saying "It has the same period as a simple pendulum of of length l." In this case l is called the *equivalent length* of the physical pendulum. Combining the results just obtained with those for a simple pendulum one gets as a formula for l

$$l = \frac{\bar{p}'^2}{h} = \frac{\bar{p}^2}{h} + h. \tag{8.39}$$

If we take the line $\bar{\mathbf{R}}\mathbf{Q}$ as in Fig. 8.31 as an axis, then h is the coordinate of $\mathbf{Q}$. Varying h, we should expect to get different periods. In fact, the period will reach a minimum value when l is minimum. Differentiating (8.39),

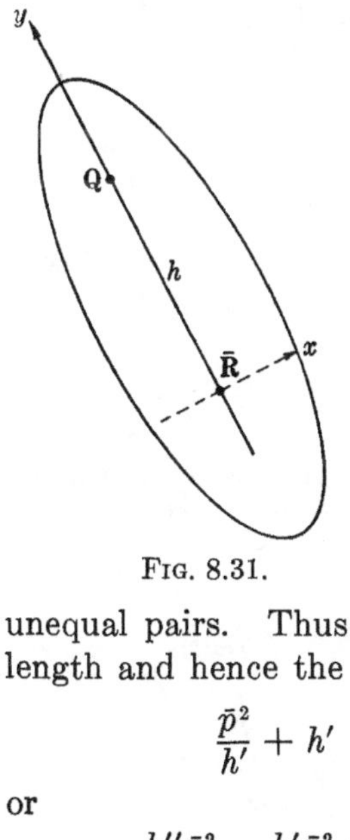

FIG. 8.31.

$$\frac{dl}{dh} = -\frac{\bar{p}^2}{h^2} + 1.$$

From this we conclude

(8.40) *For minimum period,*

$$h = \bar{p} = \tfrac{1}{2}(l_{\min}).$$

A graph of l plotted against h [using Eq. (8.39)] suggests the same result and also that for other values of l the h's (of the same sign) occur in unequal pairs. Thus in Fig. 8.32 h' and h'' have the same equivalent length and hence the same period. To find interrelations, we write

$$\frac{\bar{p}^2}{h'} + h' = \frac{\bar{p}^2}{h''} + h'',$$

or

$$h''\bar{p}^2 - h'\bar{p}^2 = h''^2h' - h'^2h''.$$

Dividing out $h'' - h'$ (since $h' \neq h''$),

$$h'h'' = \bar{p}^2. \tag{8.41}$$

It is worth pointing out that

$$h' + h'' = l, \tag{8.42}$$

as a substitution of (8.41) into (8.39) reveals.

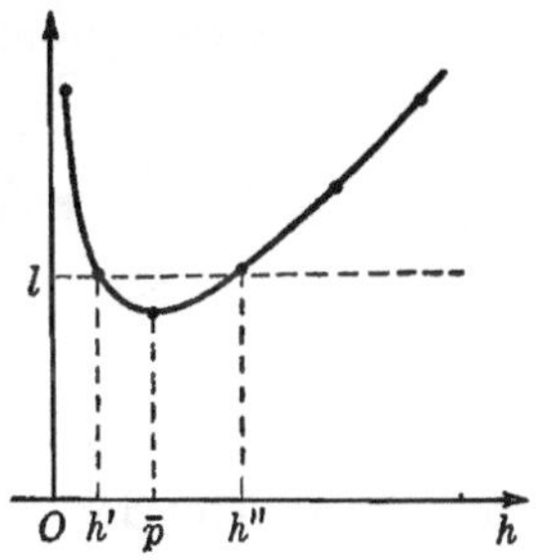

FIG. 8.32.

For any physical pendulum then, if the orientation of the horizontal axis is known, and if the desired period is greater than the minimum period, there are two circles of points in the normal plane through $\bar{\mathbf{R}}$ through which suitable axes might be constructed to yield that period. These circles have radii h' and h'' whose sum is the length of the equivalent simple pendulum and whose geometric mean is the radius of gyration for rotation about a parallel axis through the center of mass. A pair of diametrically opposite points on the two circles (separated by a distance l) are called conjugate points (for example, $\mathbf{Q}'$ and $\mathbf{Q}''$ in Fig. 8.33).

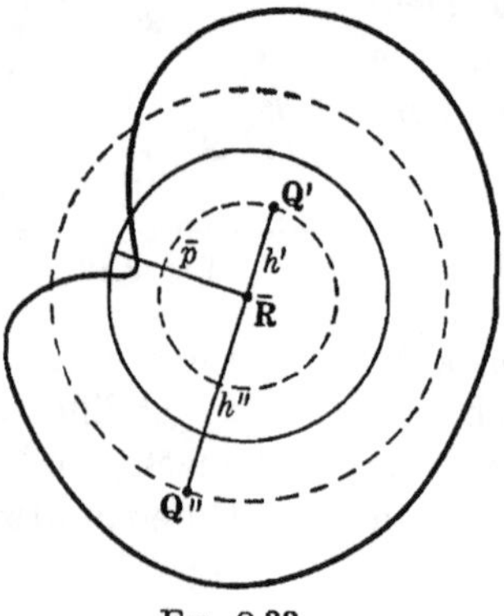

FIG. 8.33.

Example 1. A square board of length s is suspended by one corner so as to oscillate about a normal horizontal axis. Find the equivalent length.

SOLUTION. Using Routh's rule,

$$\bar{p}^2 = \frac{1}{3}\left[\left(\frac{s}{2}\right)^2 + \left(\frac{s}{2}\right)^2\right] = \frac{1}{6}s^2.$$

Now using (8.39),

$$l = \frac{\frac{1}{6}s^2}{s/\sqrt{2}} + \frac{s}{\sqrt{2}} = 0.94s.$$

Example 2. If a wheel or other mechanical object is hung on a narrow horizontal support as in Fig. 8.34 and allowed to oscillate, the period may easily be observed. The center of mass may be located by balancing; thus h may be measured. From h and τ it is easy to find the radius of gyration about a parallel axis through $\bar{\mathbf{R}}$, the center of mass of the wheel. This is a practical method for determining the moment of inertia of such an object. Numerical examples will appear among the exercises.

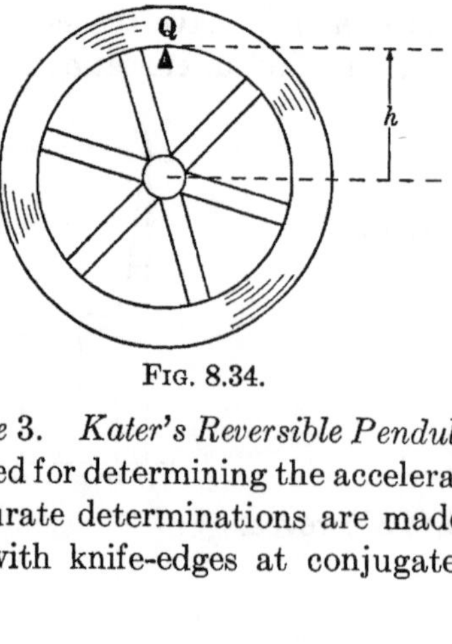

FIG. 8.34.

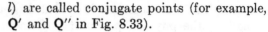

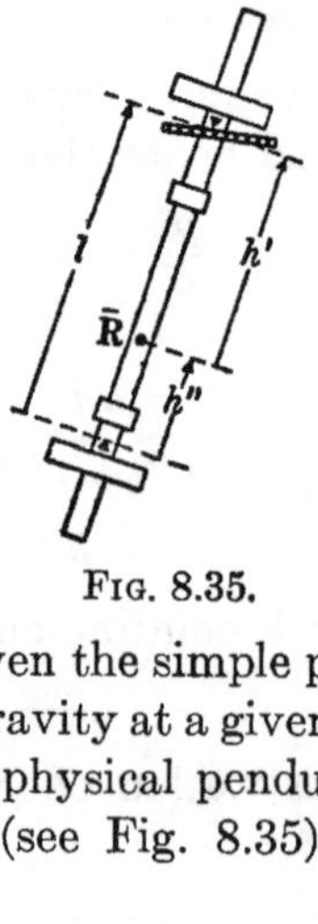

FIG. 8.35.

Example 3. *Kater's Reversible Pendulum.* Even the simple pendulum may be used for determining the acceleration of gravity at a given locality. More accurate determinations are made with a physical pendulum constructed with knife-edges at conjugate points (see Fig. 8.35). If the adjustable masses are moved to positions so that the period is the same, τ, for oscillation from either support, then g may be computed in terms of τ and the distance l between the points of support. Both τ and l may be measured with great precision. The full theory of Kater's pendulum, as this device is known, complete with corrections to allow for slight differences in periods, for the friction of the air, for various imperfections in the mounting, etc., is too extended for this treatment.

EXERCISES

1. A hoop of diameter 1 m and mass 2 kg hangs on a horizontal nail. With what period will it oscillate (*a*) in its own plane; (*b*) perpendicular to its own plane?

2. A wheel of inner diameter 6 ft 6 in. and weight 320 lb is hung on a normal horizontal knife-edge under the upper rim. The wheel oscillates in its own plane with a period of 2.93 sec. What is the moment of inertia about its axle?

3. A physical pendulum has a period of 2 sec when oscillating about one axis. It has the same period when oscillating about a second parallel axis twice as far from the center of mass. What is the radius of gyration about a parallel axis through the center of mass?

4. A thin uniform square board weighing 1 lb is pivoted about a horizontal axis perpendicular to the board at one corner. It oscillates as a pendulum. A diagonal of the square is 2 ft long. A simple pendulum having the same period must be how long?

5. A Kater's pendulum whose knife-edges are separated by 67.63 cm has a period of 1.651 sec. Find the acceleration of gravity.

6. When a physical pendulum of mass 3 kg oscillates about an axis 1 m from the center of mass, the period is 2.57 sec. What is the moment of inertia about a parallel axis 50 cm from the center of mass?

7. How far from the end of a meter stick may a pivot be placed in order that its period as a physical pendulum be 2 sec?

8. A uniform solid disk 60 cm in diameter and 1 cm thick is free to oscillate in a vertical plane about a horizontal axis at a point on its circumference. The center of the disk is displaced 3 cm from its equilibrium position, held there at rest, and then released. (*a*) What is the period of the oscillation? (*b*) What is the maximum angular speed?

9. A ring-shaped figure of outer radius 12 in. and inner radius 4 in. is cut from a uniform thin board. It is pivoted about a normal horizontal axis 8 in. from its center. With what frequency will it oscillate as a physical pendulum?

10. A uniform rod weighing 2 kg and 2 m long is suspended as a compound or physical pendulum about a point 40 cm from one end. It is given a displacement of 10° from its position of stable equilibrium and then released. (*a*) With what period will it oscillate? (*b*) What will be its maximum angular speed?

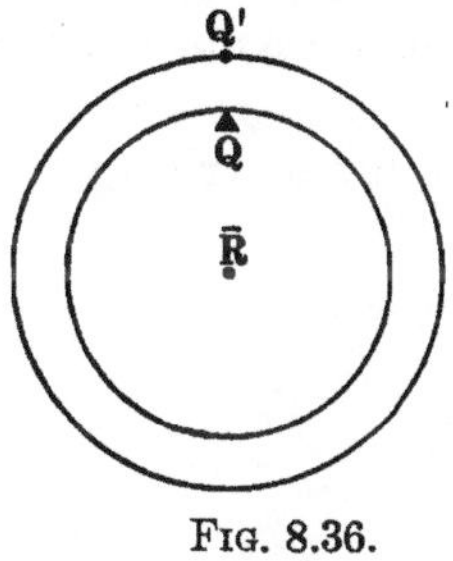

FIG. 8.36.

11. The ring shown in Fig. 8.36 weighs 200 lb, oscillates about the knife-edge at Q with a period of 3.14 sec, and has inner and outer radii of 4 and 5 ft, respectively. What is its moment of inertia about an axis through Q′ parallel to the knife-edge?

12. A uniform rod suspended from a knife-edge 4 ft from one end has the same period as a simple pendulum 8 ft long. How long is the rod?

13. Two physical pendulums designed to oscillate about a common axis are clamped together to form a new pendulum of mass m, period τ, with center of mass at a distance h from the axis. If m', h', and τ' and m'', h'', and τ'' are the corresponding values for the original pendulums taken separately, show that the new period is given by

$$\tau^2 = \frac{m'\tau'^2h' + m''\tau''^2h''}{m'h' + m''h''}.$$

14. A meter stick oscillates freely as a physical pendulum about a horizontal axis at a distance d from its center. The period is 2.156 sec. Find d.

15. A semicircular plate of radius r is cut of uniform material. It is mounted so as to be free to oscillate about a perpendicular horizontal axis through one corner. Find the period.

16. Derive Eqs. (8.41) and (8.42) algebraically by considering h' and h'' as the roots of the quadratic equation (8.39).

8.9. Dynamics of a Rigid Body in Motion Parallel to a Plane. When a rigid body rotates about a fixed axis, all velocities are parallel to any plane which has the axis as a normal. This type of motion was studied in Sec. 6.5. Algebraically the criterion may be written

$$\mathbf{K} \cdot \mathbf{V} = 0 \quad \text{and} \quad \mathbf{K} \cdot \mathbf{A} = 0, \tag{8.43}$$

if we select the xy plane as the favored one. Translation, too, may be an example of plane motion, assuming only that Eqs. (8.43) are satisfied continually. In this section we shall be considering any motion satisfying these equations. From Sec. 6.5 we may recall that there is always an instantaneous axis of rotation parallel to the z axis. As before, we shall let $\mathbf{C}$ denote the point of intersection between the axis and the reference plane. $\bar{\mathbf{R}}$ will denote the center of mass. The xy plane will be picked so that it contains $\bar{\mathbf{R}}$.

From the dynamics of aggregates we know that the basic equation

$$\Sigma \mathbf{F} = m\bar{\mathbf{A}} \tag{8.44}$$

must be satisfied. Here, as before, the left member is the vector sum of the isolating forces acting on the body. $\bar{\mathbf{A}}$ is the acceleration of the center of mass. Since the motion is plane, this vector equation is equivalent to

$$\Sigma f_x = m\bar{a}_x, \qquad \Sigma f_y = m\bar{a}_y, \qquad \Sigma f_z = 0. \tag{8.45}$$

The z components may not appear at all. If they do occur, they are merely constraining forces which ensure that the motion does not cease to be plane.

Now taking moments about the center of mass, we have, writing

$$\mathbf{R}' = \mathbf{R} - \bar{\mathbf{R}},$$

analogous to (8.17),

$$\sum \mathbf{\Gamma} = \sum \mathbf{R}' \times \mathbf{F} = \int_m \mathbf{R}' \times \mathbf{A}\, dm.$$

Substituting

$$\mathbf{A} = \bar{\mathbf{A}} + \boldsymbol{\alpha} \times \mathbf{R}' + \boldsymbol{\Omega} \times (\boldsymbol{\Omega} \times \mathbf{R}')$$

and taking scalar products with **K** gives us

$$\Sigma\gamma_z = \mathbf{K} \cdot \int \mathbf{R}'\,dm \times \bar{\mathbf{A}} + \mathbf{K} \cdot \int \mathbf{R}' \times (\boldsymbol{\alpha} \times \mathbf{R}')dm + \mathbf{K} \cdot \int \mathbf{R}' \times [\boldsymbol{\Omega} \times (\boldsymbol{\Omega} \times \mathbf{R}')]dm.$$

From the choice of origin at the center of mass, the integral in the first term is obviously zero. The integrand in the third integral is perpendicular to **K**; so that term vanishes. The second term may be rewritten as

$$\alpha \int (\mathbf{K} \times \mathbf{R}') \cdot (\mathbf{K} \times \mathbf{R}')dm = \alpha \int p'^2\,dm = \alpha \bar{\imath}_z.$$

The conclusion is, for moments about an axis through the center of mass,

$$\Sigma\gamma_z = \bar{\imath}_z \alpha. \tag{8.46}$$

Equations (8.45) and (8.46) are exactly like equations previously applied to problems of translation or rotation separately. They now may be applied to other plane motions.

Example 1. With what acceleration will a uniform solid sphere roll without slipping down a plane inclined at an angle θ with the horizontal?

SOLUTION. Isolating the sphere, the forces are the weight and the reaction of the plane, as in Fig. 8.37. This reaction force is here broken up into tangential and normal components **F** and **N**. Let the radius be r. Then

$$\bar{a}_x = r\alpha$$

since there is no slipping. The moment of inertia for the axis through the center of mass is given by

$$\bar{\imath}_z = \frac{w}{g}\bar{p}^2 = \frac{2}{5}\frac{w}{g}r^2.$$

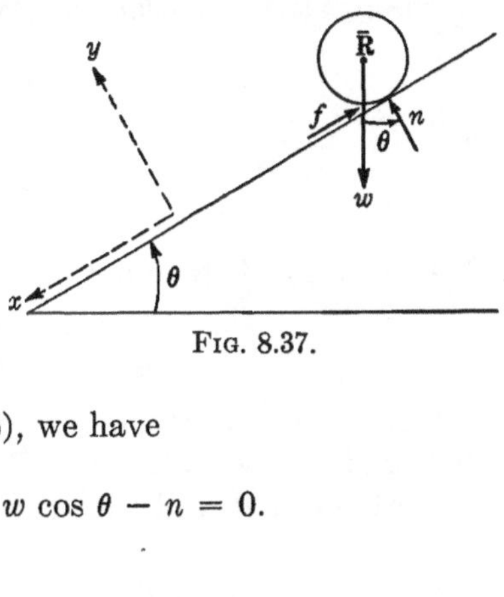

FIG. 8.37.

Applying the translation equation (8.45), we have

$$w \sin\theta - f = \frac{w}{g}\bar{a}_x, \qquad w\cos\theta - n = 0.$$

The rotation equation (8.46) gives us

$$fr = \frac{2}{5}\frac{w}{g}r^2\alpha \qquad \text{or} \qquad f = \frac{2}{5}\frac{w}{g}\bar{a}_x.$$

Combining the two, we have

$$w\sin\theta - \frac{2}{5}\frac{w}{g}\bar{a}_x = \frac{w}{g}\bar{a}_x \qquad \text{or} \qquad \bar{a}_x = \frac{5}{7}g\sin\theta.$$

Example 2. Find the coefficient μ of friction for which rolling without slipping becomes impossible in the preceding example.

SOLUTION. For rolling to take place without slipping, there is required a frictional force given by (see preceding example)

$$f = w \sin \theta - \tfrac{5}{7} w \sin \theta = \tfrac{2}{7} w \sin \theta.$$

This requires a coefficient of friction at least equal to

$$\mu = \frac{f}{n} = \frac{2}{7} \tan \theta.$$

Example 3. Find the ratio of $\bar{a}_x$ to α for the sphere of the preceding two examples when

$$\mu = k(\tfrac{2}{7} \tan \theta),$$

for some $k < 1$.

SOLUTION. In this case slipping takes place; thus

$$f = \mu n = \frac{2k}{7} \tan \theta \,(w \cos \theta).$$

Putting this for f in the translation equation, we get

$$w \sin \theta - \frac{2}{7} kw \sin \theta = \frac{w}{g} \bar{a}_x,$$

or

$$\bar{a}_x = g \sin \theta (1 - \tfrac{2}{7}k).$$

In the rotation equation we have

$$\frac{2}{7} kw \sin \theta = \frac{2}{5} \frac{w}{g} r\alpha,$$

or

$$\alpha = \frac{5 g \sin \theta k}{7r}.$$

The ratio $\bar{a}_x/\alpha$ is then not r but the following:

$$\frac{\bar{a}_x}{\alpha} = \frac{1 - (\frac{2}{7})k}{\frac{5}{7}k} r = \frac{(7 - 2k)}{5k} r.$$

Example 4. A spool of mass m, radius of gyration $\bar{p}$, outer radius r, and inner radius r' is pulled along a rough horizontal plane surface by a force $\mathbf{F}'$ exerted on a thread rolling up on the under side of the spool, as shown in Fig. 8.38. Find the acceleration and the magnitude of the frictional force $\mathbf{F}$. Assume that no slipping occurs.

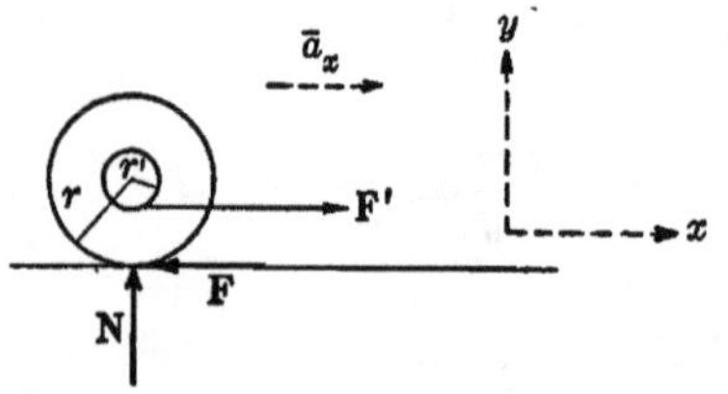

FIG. 8.38.

SOLUTION. The isolating forces are shown in the figure. The translation equation gives

$$f' - f = m\bar{a}_x.$$

The rotation equation gives

$$fr - f'r' = m\bar{p}^2\alpha,$$

or, for no slipping,

$$f - f'\frac{r'}{r} = m\frac{\bar{p}^2}{r^2}\bar{a}_x.$$

Combining the two equations to eliminate f,

$$f'\left(1 - \frac{r'}{r}\right) = \left(1 + \frac{\bar{p}^2}{r^2}\right)m\bar{a}_x.$$

This may be solved for the acceleration.

To find f, we may write, from the translation equation,

$$f = f' - m\bar{a}_x = f'\left(1 - \frac{r^2 - rr'}{r^2 + \bar{p}^2}\right) = f'\left(\frac{rr' + \bar{p}^2}{r^2 + \bar{p}^2}\right).$$

Note that the quantity in parentheses has to do only with the geometry of the spool; thus the frictional force is proportional to the applied force. This means that for f' sufficiently large, slipping will take place.

Plane Motion about Instantaneous Axis. It is interesting to see how (8.46) may be rewritten in terms of the instantaneous center **C**. Let us now use $\bar{\mathbf{R}}$ to denote the position vector of the center of mass relative to **C**. A typical force **F** acts at a point whose position vector relative to **C** is **R**, as in Fig. 8.39. As before, the point will have position vector **R**′ relative to $\bar{\mathbf{R}}$; thus

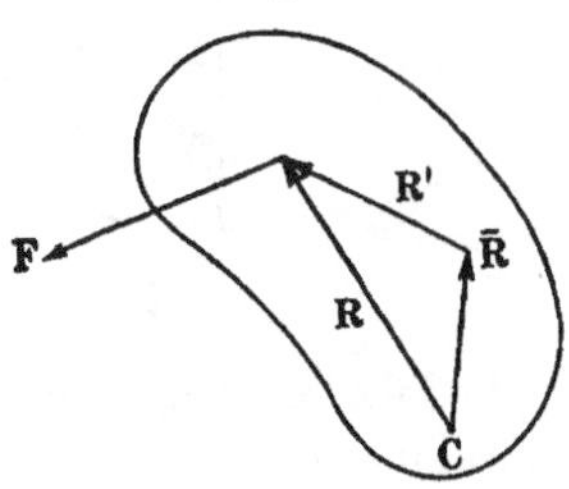

FIG. 8.39.

$$\mathbf{R} = \bar{\mathbf{R}} + \mathbf{R}'.$$

Then denoting by $\Sigma\mathbf{\Gamma}_C$ and $\Sigma\mathbf{\Gamma}$ the moment sums about **C** and $\bar{\mathbf{R}}$, respectively, and by $\bar{\mathbf{F}}$ the force sum, we have

$$\Sigma\mathbf{\Gamma}_C = \Sigma\mathbf{R}\times\mathbf{F} = \Sigma\bar{\mathbf{R}}\times\mathbf{F} + \Sigma\mathbf{R}'\times\mathbf{F} = \bar{\mathbf{R}}\times\bar{\mathbf{F}} + \Sigma\mathbf{\Gamma}.$$

Taking only the z components,

$$\Sigma\gamma_C = \mathbf{K}\cdot\bar{\mathbf{R}}\times\bar{\mathbf{F}} + \Sigma\gamma_z = \mathbf{K}\cdot\bar{\mathbf{R}}\times m\bar{\mathbf{A}} + \Sigma\gamma_z.$$

For a *homogeneous solid of revolution* (see Fig. 8.40) *rolling without slipping*, $\bar{a} = r\alpha$; thus, substituting (8.46) and using the parallel-axis theorem,

$$(8.47)\qquad \Sigma\gamma_C = (mr^2 + \bar{\imath}_z)\alpha = i_C\alpha.$$

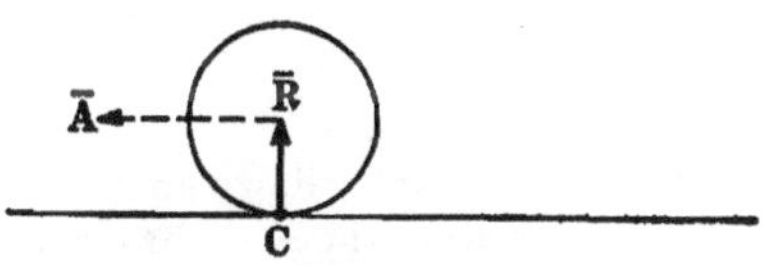

FIG. 8.40.

In the preceding equation it is understood that the subscript C indicates rotation about an axis through **C** and parallel to **K**.

Example 5. Applying this approach to the sphere of Fig. 8.37, we have

$$\sum \gamma_C = wr \sin \theta = \frac{7}{5}\frac{w}{g} r^2\alpha.$$

Hence

$$\bar{a}_x = \alpha r = \tfrac{5}{7} g \sin \theta$$

as before.

Example 6. A cylindrical rod of radius r rolls in a cylindrical trough of radius r' as in Fig. 8.41. Find the period of oscillation.

SOLUTION. First let us relate angular displacement θ of the rod with the angular displacement ϕ along the trough. If no slipping takes place the arc s' along the trough is just equal to the arc s along the sphere. We have then

$$r'\phi = s = s' = r(\theta + \phi).$$

(ϕ is added to θ in the right member to compensate for the change in direction of the normal to the trough by an angle due to its curvature.) We may write then

$$r\theta = (r' - r)\phi.$$

Hence, differentiating twice with respect to time,

$$r\alpha = r\frac{d^2\theta}{dt^2} = (r' - r)\frac{d^2\phi}{dt^2} = \bar{a}_T.$$

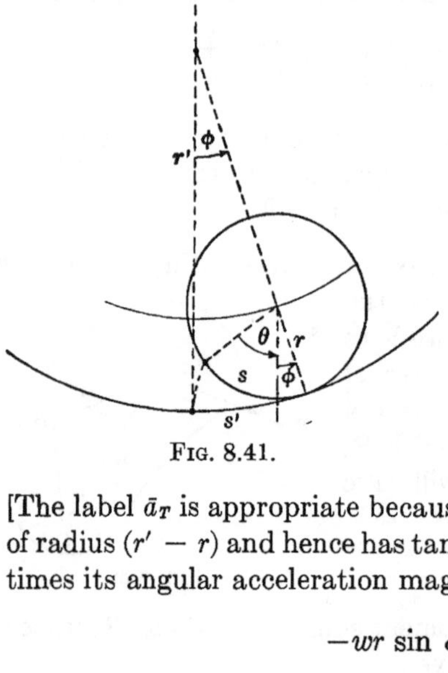

FIG. 8.41.

[The label $\bar{a}_T$ is appropriate because the center of mass travels on a circle of radius $(r' - r)$ and hence has tangential acceleration equal to this radius times its angular acceleration magnitude.] Using (8.47),

$$-wr \sin \phi = \frac{3}{2}\frac{w}{g} r^2 \frac{d^2\theta}{dt^2}.$$

Substituting the kinematical relationship just derived and replacing $\sin \phi$ by ϕ for small displacements, we have

$$-\phi = \frac{3}{2}\frac{(r' - r)}{g}\frac{d^2\phi}{dt^2}.$$

This represents a simple harmonic oscillation of period

$$\tau = 2\pi\sqrt{\frac{3(r' - r)}{2g}}.$$

EXERCISES

1. A solid cylinder and a cylindrical shell both roll without slipping down an inclined plane. What is the ratio of their accelerations? By the time the shell has rolled 10 ft, how far will the solid cylinder have rolled?

2. The center of mass of a 900-lb wheel of diameter 8 ft, rolling without slipping down a plane inclined at 30° to the horizontal, has an acceleration of 10 ft/sec². What is the radius of gyration? At least how great is the coefficient of friction?

3. The radius of gyration of a 36-lb wheel is 10 in. The rolling radius is 12 in. How long will it take the wheel to roll 32 ft from rest without slipping down a plane surface inclined at an angle of 30° with the horizontal?

4. A spool has weight w, outer radius r, inner (shaft) radius r', and radius of gyration $\bar{p}$. It is rolled without slipping along a horizontal rough plane by a horizontal thread unwinding from the upper side of the shaft. The tension in the thread is f. The spool starts from rest and after rolling a time t has acquired a spread v. Express v in terms of w, r, r', f, $\bar{p}$, and t.

5. A light flexible cord is wrapped around a narrow spool as in Fig. 8.42. The surface on which the cord is wound is 6 in. from the axis of the spool. The spool is allowed to fall from rest. The unwound portion of the cord is vertical, and the face of the spool moves in a fixed vertical plane. The spool falls 13.5 ft in 1.1 sec. Find the radius of gyration of the spool.

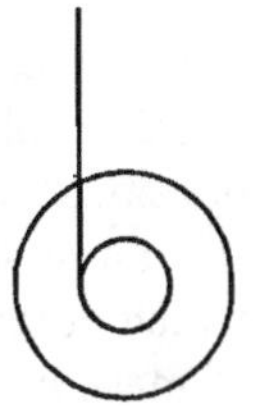

FIG. 8.42.

6. A solid steel cylinder 2 in. in diameter and 6 in. long is placed on an inclined plane with its axis horizontal. The angle of inclination of the plane is 60° with the horizontal. The coefficient of friction is 0.1. Starting from rest how long will it take the cylinder to make one complete revolution? How far will the center of the cylinder travel during this time interval?

7. A wheel rolls, slipping, along level ice. The wheel has moment of inertia 13.1 kg-m², mass 50 kg, and rolling radius 0.55 m. Initially, the wheel has an angular speed of 51 rad/sec; after 10 sec it is 11 rad/sec. The only forces acting on the wheel are gravity and the contact forces with the ice. What is the coefficient of friction?

8. A wheel has weight 400 lb, moment of inertia 320 lb-ft², diameter 2 ft. The wheel is set in motion by a horizontal force of 50 lb applied at the axis in the plane of the wheel. It rolls without slipping along a horizontal plane. Find the linear acceleration of the wheel and the frictional force at the point of contact with the plane.

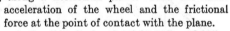

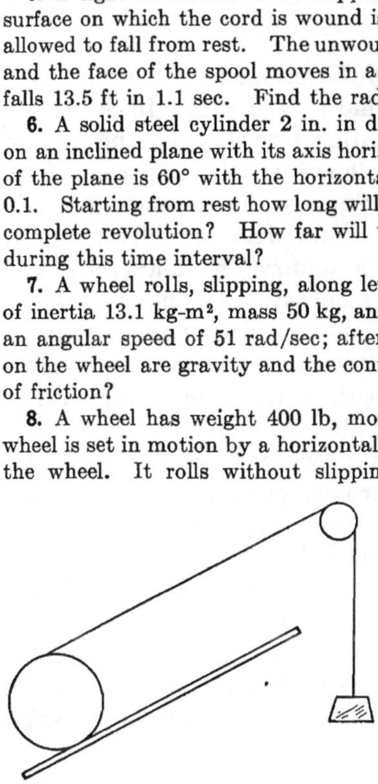

FIG. 8.43.

9. A solid cylinder of weight 20 lb and radius 6 in. has a tape wound around it, and it rests on an inclined plane with its axis horizontal. The tape passes over a smooth pulley to a 4-lb body hanging freely, as in Fig. 8.43. The inclination of the plane is 30°. Find the tension in the tape and the acceleration of the cylinder if there is no slipping.

10. A solid steel cylinder 10 cm in radius is placed with its axis horizontal on an inclined plane. The angle of inclination with the horizontal is θ. The coefficient of friction is 0.1. Find the ratio of linear to angular acceleration for the cases where θ is equal to 20°, 40°, 60°, 80°.

11. With what period will a 0.25-in. ball bearing roll in a watch glass whose radius of curvature is 6 in.?

8.10. Method of d'Alembert. *Bearing Reactions.* In Sec. 7.6 it proved to be convenient to transfer from one side of an equation to the other certain terms involving mass and accelerations. This was done to extend the applicability of a dynamics equation to a noninertial frame. A similar manipulation is often convenient, even when inertial frames are easily available. The basic dynamics equations for an aggregate of particles may be written

$$\Sigma\mathbf{F} - \Sigma m\mathbf{A} = \mathbf{O} \quad \text{or} \quad \Sigma\mathbf{F} - (\Sigma m)\bar{\mathbf{A}} = \mathbf{O}. \tag{8.48}$$

$$\Sigma\mathbf{R} \times \mathbf{F} + \Sigma\mathbf{R} \times (-m\mathbf{A}) = \mathbf{O}. \tag{8.49}$$

These equations suggest that any dynamics problem may be considered as a problem in statics, provided that to the external forces one adds for each element of mass m a force $-m\mathbf{A}$. This approach is called the method of d'Alembert.

Example 1. To illustrate the utility of this method, let us return to the problem of rotation of rigid bodies around a fixed axis. In Sec. 8.4 we obtained simple over-all conclusions relating torque about the axis and the angular acceleration. We ignored, however, the important forces which compel the axis to remain fixed. Suppose, for instance, that a bar of mass m and length $2l$ is rotated about a skew axis through its center of mass at a uniform angular velocity $\mathbf{\Omega}$. What is required of the bearing B? Of course it must provide a force to offset the weight of the bar; but we are concerned here with the forces originating with the motion. Since the center of mass is stationary, the external forces by themselves have a zero vector sum. Now let us take moments about an axis normal to the plane of the bar and the rotation axis (*i.e.*, normal to the plane of Fig. 8.44) through the bearing B. Denote the torque exerted by the bearing itself by γ_B. To this we shall add for each element of mass dm the moment of a fictitious force: $\omega^2 x\, dm$, directed outward from the axis of rotation. Now

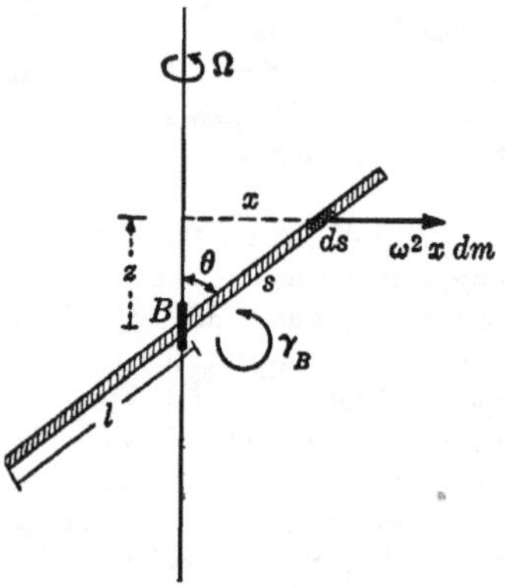

FIG. 8.44.

$$dm = \frac{m}{2l}\,ds, \qquad x = s \sin\theta, \qquad z = s\cos\theta.$$

As an application of (8.49), we may then write

$$\gamma_B - \frac{m\omega^2 \sin\theta\cos\theta}{2l}\int_{-l}^{l} s^2\,ds = 0;$$

or

$$\gamma_B = \frac{m\omega^2 \sin\theta\cos\theta\, l^2}{3}.$$

This enables us to compute the torque which the bearing must withstand for any uniform angular speed ω.

Bearing Reactions and Products of Inertia. The preceding example showed how the method of d'Alembert may be applied to a specific problem. Let us take a more general case. For a body rotating at uniform speed about a fixed z axis with the bearing at the origin (see Fig. 8.45), the moment equation (for equilibrium) at a given instant is

$$(8.50) \qquad \mathbf{\Gamma}_B - \int \mathbf{R} \times \mathbf{A}\, dm = \mathbf{O}.$$

Here $\mathbf{\Gamma}_B$ is the torque exerted by the bearing. Since we are dealing with the simple case where the rotation is uniform,

$$\mathbf{A} = \mathbf{\Omega} \times (\mathbf{\Omega} \times \mathbf{R}).$$

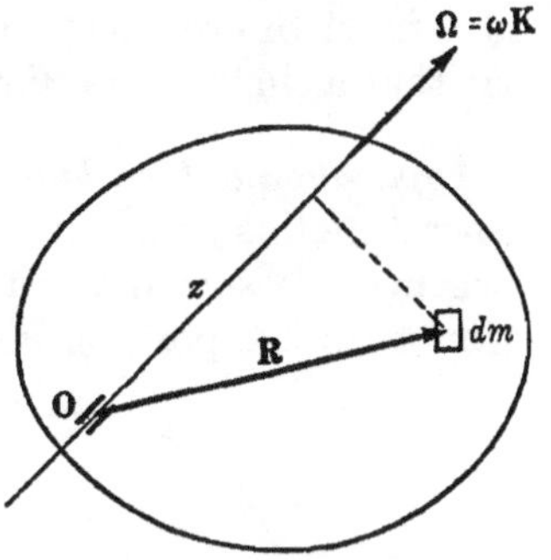

FIG. 8.45.

Hence

$$\mathbf{R} \times \mathbf{A} = \mathbf{R} \times [\mathbf{\Omega} \times (\mathbf{\Omega} \times \mathbf{R})] = \mathbf{R} \times [(\mathbf{\Omega} \cdot \mathbf{R})\mathbf{\Omega} - \omega^2\mathbf{R}]$$
$$= (x\mathbf{I} + y\mathbf{J} + z\mathbf{K}) \times \omega^2 z\mathbf{K} = \omega^2 yz\mathbf{I} - \omega^2 zx\mathbf{J}.$$

Substituting in (8.50), we have

$$(8.51) \qquad \mathbf{\Gamma}_B = \omega^2\mathbf{I}\int yz\, dm - \omega^2\mathbf{J}\int zx\, dm = \omega^2(i_{yz}\mathbf{I} - i_{zx}\mathbf{J}).$$

From this it is evident that if such bearing torques are to be avoided the products of inertia i_{yz} and i_{zx} should vanish. This is attained if the axis of rotation is a principal axis of inertia with respect to an origin taken at the bearing.

Example 2. Bearing Reactions for an Eccentric Wheel. A wheel may be set to rotate about a principal axis and yet give rise to bearing reactions associated with the motion. For uniform rotation, Eq. (8.48) becomes for Fig. 8.46

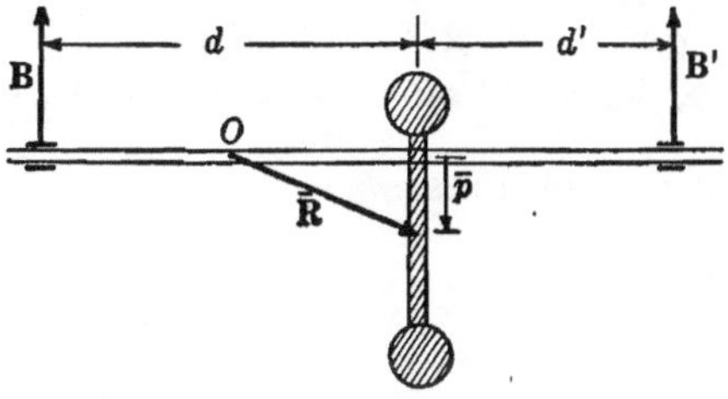

FIG. 8.46.

$$\mathbf{O} = \mathbf{B} + \mathbf{B}' + \mathbf{W} - m\mathbf{\Omega} \times (\mathbf{\Omega} \times \bar{\mathbf{R}}),$$

where $\mathbf{B}$ and $\mathbf{B}'$ are the bearing reactions and $\mathbf{W}$ is the weight. For the phase of the rotation where the center of mass is lowest,

$$0 = b + b' - w - m\omega^2\bar{p}$$
$$bd = b'd'.$$

Hence

$$b = \frac{m\omega^2\bar{p} + w}{1 + (d/d')}.$$

It should be clearly emphasized that the problems illustrated in this section can be done without the d'Alembert approach and also that this approach is by no means limited to problems involving bearing reactions. In so far as this section broadens the scope of Sec. 8.4, it should be pointed out that a similar extension might be given to Sec. 8.9.

Application to the Plane Motion of a Rigid Body. Let us consider the general motion of a rigid body parallel to the xy plane, which for convenience is assumed to pass through the center of mass $\bar{\mathbf{R}}$. Any other point then has position vector $\mathbf{R}$ expressible as

$$\mathbf{R} = \mathbf{P} + z\mathbf{K},$$

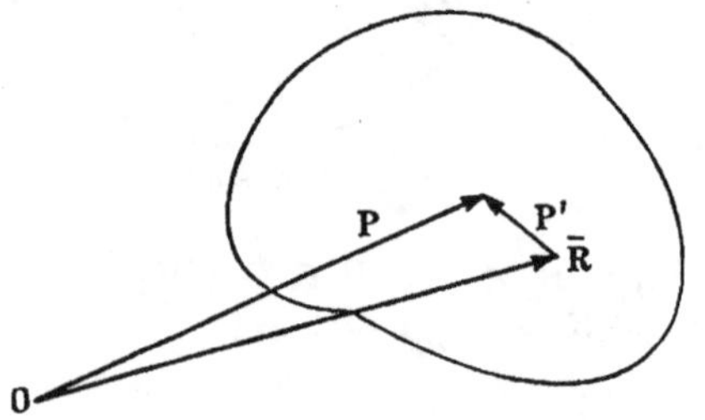

FIG. 8.47.

where $\mathbf{P} \cdot \mathbf{K} = 0$. In order to refer the motion to the center of mass, we write also (see Fig. 8.47)

$$\mathbf{P} = \bar{\mathbf{R}} + \mathbf{P}'.$$

We write Eq. (8.49) as

$$\Sigma\mathbf{R} \times \mathbf{F} - \int \mathbf{R} \times \mathbf{A}\, dm = \mathbf{O}.$$

Now

$$\begin{aligned}\mathbf{A} &= \bar{\mathbf{A}} + \boldsymbol{\alpha} \times (\mathbf{P}' + z\mathbf{K}) + \boldsymbol{\Omega} \times [\boldsymbol{\Omega} \times (\mathbf{P}' + z\mathbf{K})] \\ &= \bar{\mathbf{A}} + \boldsymbol{\alpha} \times \mathbf{P}' - \omega^2\mathbf{P}',\end{aligned}$$

and

$$\mathbf{R} = \bar{\mathbf{R}} + \mathbf{P}' + z\mathbf{K};$$

thus

$$\begin{aligned}\int \mathbf{R} \times \mathbf{A}\, dm = \bar{\mathbf{R}} \times m\bar{\mathbf{A}} &+ \bar{\mathbf{R}} \times (\boldsymbol{\alpha} \times \int \mathbf{P}'\, dm) - \bar{\mathbf{R}} \times \omega^2 \int \mathbf{P}'\, dm \\ &+ (\int \mathbf{P}'\, dm) \times \bar{\mathbf{A}} + \boldsymbol{\alpha} \int p'^2\, dm + \int \mathbf{P}' \times (-\omega^2\mathbf{P}')dm \\ &+ (\int z\, dm)\mathbf{K} \times \bar{\mathbf{A}} + \mathbf{K} \times (\boldsymbol{\alpha} \times \int \mathbf{P}'z\, dm) - \mathbf{K}\omega^2 \times \int z\mathbf{P}'\, dm.\end{aligned}$$

Now since $\mathbf{P}'$ is measured from the center of mass,

$$\int \mathbf{P}'\, dm = \mathbf{O}.$$

Since $\bar{\mathbf{R}}$ is in the xy plane,

$$\int z\, dm = 0.$$

If we assume that the normal axis through $\bar{\mathbf{R}}$ is a principal axis of inertia, then

$$\int z\mathbf{P}'\, dm = \mathbf{I}\int zx'\, dm + \mathbf{J}\int zy'\, dm = \mathbf{O}$$

(here we have merely substituted $x' = x - \bar{x}$, $y' = y - \bar{y}$). For any plane motion with a principal axis of inertia normal to the plane through the center of mass, the conclusion then is

$$\Sigma \mathbf{R} \times \mathbf{F} - \bar{\mathbf{R}} \times m\bar{\mathbf{A}} - \bar{\imath}\alpha = \mathbf{O}.$$

This indicates that to bring the external forces into equilibrium in the sense of d'Alembert's method one must add $-m\bar{\mathbf{A}}$ at the center of mass together with a couple of moment $-\bar{\imath}\alpha$ (or some forces equivalent to these).

EXERCISES

1. The top of a vertical axle is attached by a frictionless pin to a 30-in. uniform bar, as in Fig. 8.48. The higher the speed of rotation of the axle, the larger is the angle θ between the bar and the axle. For what constant speed is this angle 30°?

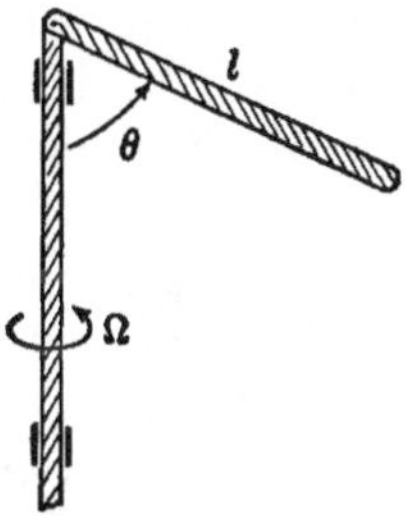

FIG. 8.48.

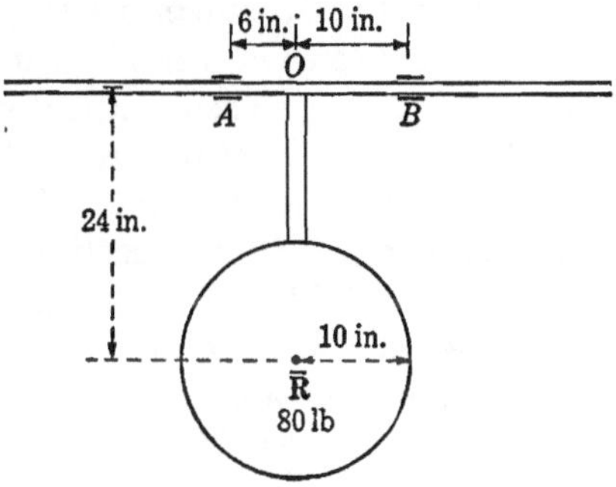

FIG. 8.49.

2. An 80-lb sphere, 10 in. in radius, is attached to a horizontal axle so that its center is 24 in. from the axle, as in Fig. 8.49. The bearings A and B are asymmetrically located as shown. The sphere rotates at 10 rad/sec. When $\bar{\mathbf{R}}$ is below O, what are the bearing forces at A and B?

3. A wheel weighs 2,100 lb. Its center of mass is 0.4 in. from its geometric axis. The wheel is mounted in two bearings A and B 5 ft apart and on opposite sides, A being 2 ft from the plane of the wheel. At 200 rpm find the forces at the bearings due to the centrifugal force.

4. The uniform bar AB in Fig. 8.50 is to rotate around the axis $A'B'$. A single bearing is to be located between A' and B', the bar being connected to it by rigid struts of negligible mass. Where should this bearing be placed so that it will need to withstand no torques due to rotation?

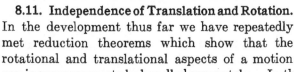

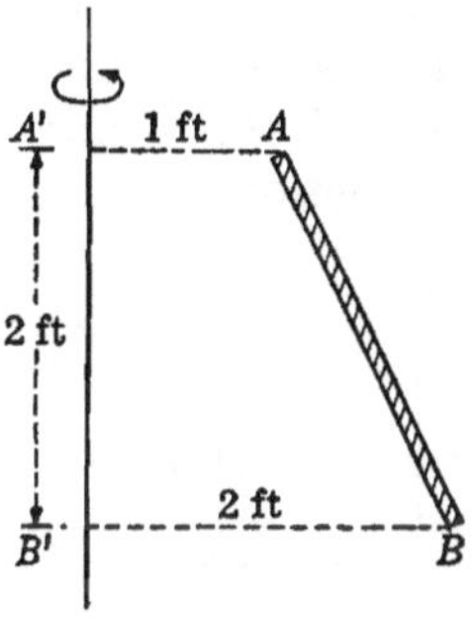

FIG. 8.50.

8.11. Independence of Translation and Rotation.

In the development thus far we have repeatedly met reduction theorems which show that the rotational and translational aspects of a motion can in many respects be handled separately. In this section some of these conclusions will be reviewed and compared.

Forces. Any system of forces may be reduced to a force $\bar{\mathbf{F}}$ and a couple $\bar{\Gamma}$, the force being at an arbitrary point. If $\bar{\mathbf{F}} \cdot \bar{\Gamma} = 0$, then the system is equivalent to an equal force at a different point (except for the case where $\bar{\mathbf{F}} = \mathbf{O}$). Diagrammatically this special case appears as in Fig. 8.51.

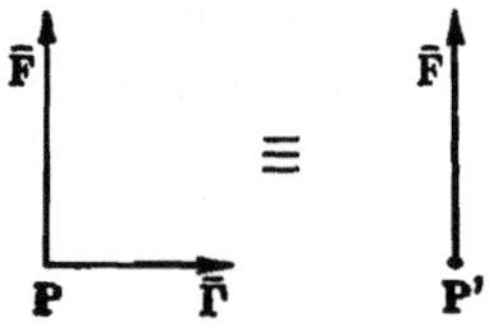

FIG. 8.51.

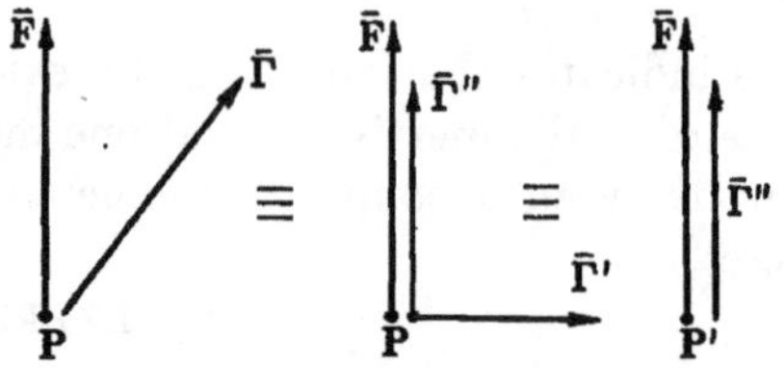

FIG. 8.52.

In the general case, by resolving $\bar{\Gamma}$ into components $\bar{\Gamma}'$ and $\bar{\Gamma}''$ perpendicular and parallel to $\bar{\mathbf{F}}$, we can use the fact that $\bar{\mathbf{F}} \cdot \bar{\Gamma}' = 0$ to replace $\bar{\mathbf{F}}$ and $\bar{\Gamma}'$ by an equal force at a new point. This reduction (already listed as an exercise) is described schematically in Fig. 8.52. This reduction is unique. That is, given a set of forces, the vectors $\bar{\mathbf{F}}$ and $\bar{\Gamma}''$ are uniquely determined, and the line on which $\mathbf{P}'$ must lie is uniquely determined. The student should convince himself of this fact.

It appears, in view of the preceding discussion, that a rigid body can, in effect, be subjected only to a push and a parallel twist in combination. (This combination is sometimes called a "wrench.") The push $\bar{\mathbf{F}}$ and the twist about a parallel axis $\bar{\Gamma}''$ represent these easily separated attributes of a system of forces.

Displacements. Any net displacement of a rigid body can be attained by superimposing a linear displacement and a rotary displacement. Since finite angular displacements do not combine as vectors, we do not follow the idea further.

Velocity Patterns. When a rigid body is in motion, one may at any moment assign to every point of the body a velocity vector. This collection of vectors at specific points is what is meant by a "velocity pattern," or, in more technical language, "velocity field." We have had reduction theorems too for velocity patterns. Our conclusion was stated in an equation of the form

$$\mathbf{V} = \mathbf{V}_{O'} + \mathbf{\Omega} \times \mathbf{R}', \tag{8.52}$$

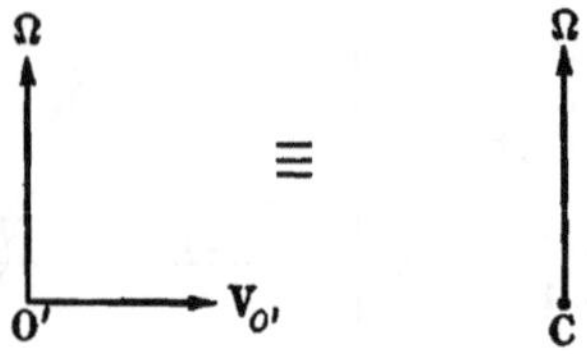

FIG. 8.53.

where $\mathbf{O}'$ is an arbitrary point of the body. In the special case where $\mathbf{\Omega} \cdot \mathbf{V}_{O'} = 0$ (plane motion), the velocity pattern may be analyzed as rotation about an instantaneous axis. Diagrammatically this special case appears as in Fig. 8.53. In the general case, by resolving $\mathbf{V}_{O'}$ into components $\mathbf{V}'_{O'}$ and $\mathbf{V}''_{O'}$ perpendicular and parallel to $\mathbf{\Omega}$, we can use the fact that $\mathbf{\Omega} \cdot \mathbf{V}'_{O'} = 0$ to find a new axis of rotation through some point **C**, as in Fig. 8.53. This reduction appears diagrammatically in Fig. 8.54. The student will wish to satisfy himself that $\mathbf{V}_C = \mathbf{V}''_{O'}$.

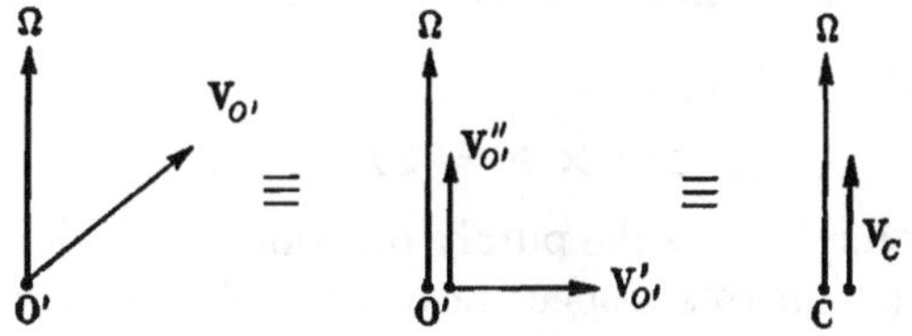

FIG. 8.54.

It appears in view of this discussion that any instantaneous velocity pattern for a rigid body can be analyzed as simple screw motion: the superposition of translation and rotation about a parallel axis. Note that in the resolution of forces and velocities rotational and translational aspects play opposite roles: $\mathbf{\Omega}$ corresponds to $\bar{\mathbf{F}}$!

Dynamics of Aggregates. In our study of systems of particles, including rigid bodies, we have seen repeatedly that translation is independent of rotation. The equation

$$\Sigma\mathbf{F} = (\Sigma m)\bar{\mathbf{A}} \tag{8.53}$$

persists in all cases. As yet it has not been pointed out as sharply that rotational dynamics is independent of translation. Relative to a fixed point **O**, the underlying dynamical relationship in rotation is

$$\Sigma\mathbf{R} \times \mathbf{F} = \Sigma\mathbf{R} \times m\mathbf{A}. \tag{8.54}$$

For rigid bodies this relationship has already appeared in the derivations of (8.13) and (8.17). Let us see what this yields relative to parallel reference frames having as origin the moving center of mass $\bar{\mathbf{R}}$ rather than the fixed point **O**. If $\mathbf{R}'$ is the position vector of a typical element of mass m relative to $\bar{\mathbf{R}}$ (see Fig. 8.55),

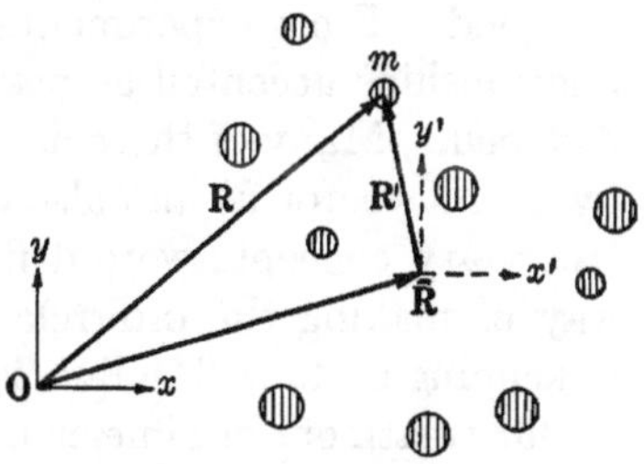

FIG. 8.55.

$$\mathbf{R} = \bar{\mathbf{R}} + \mathbf{R}',$$

and since the axes are parallel

$$\mathbf{A} = \bar{\mathbf{A}} + \mathbf{A}'.$$

Substituting into (8.54),

$$\Sigma(\bar{\mathbf{R}} + \mathbf{R}') \times \mathbf{F} = \Sigma(\bar{\mathbf{R}} + \mathbf{R}') \times m(\bar{\mathbf{A}} + \mathbf{A}').$$

But

$$\Sigma\bar{\mathbf{R}} \times \mathbf{F} = \bar{\mathbf{R}} \times (\Sigma\mathbf{F}) = \bar{\mathbf{R}} \times (\Sigma m\mathbf{A}) = \bar{\mathbf{R}} \times (\Sigma m)\bar{\mathbf{A}} = \Sigma\bar{\mathbf{R}} \times m\bar{\mathbf{A}},$$

and

$$\Sigma\bar{\mathbf{R}} \times m\mathbf{A}' = \bar{\mathbf{R}} \times \Sigma m\mathbf{A}' = \bar{\mathbf{R}} \times [\Sigma m\mathbf{A} - (\Sigma m)\bar{\mathbf{A}}] = \mathbf{O},$$

and

$$\Sigma\mathbf{R}' \times m\bar{\mathbf{A}} = (\Sigma m\mathbf{R}') \times \bar{\mathbf{A}} = [\Sigma m\mathbf{R} - (\Sigma m)\bar{\mathbf{R}}] \times \bar{\mathbf{A}} = \mathbf{O}.$$

We are left with

$$\Sigma\mathbf{R}' \times \mathbf{F} = \Sigma\mathbf{R}' \times m\mathbf{A}'. \tag{8.55}$$

This has the same form as the purely rotational equation (8.54); therefore we conclude that in this respect also rotation and translation are independent.

Plane Dynamics. In Sec. 8.9 it appeared quite clearly in Eqs. (8.44) and (8.46) that in solving practical problems it is possible to handle translational and rotational obstacles separately. The latter equation is a special consequence of (8.55).

Energy and Momentum. In succeeding chapters on momentum and energy the student will meet further evidence contributing to the general theme of this section.

EXERCISES

1. Prove that the final reduction symbolized in Fig. 8.52 is unique except that $\mathbf{P}'$ may be moved along the line of $\bar{\mathbf{F}}$.

2. Prove that in the reduction shown in Fig. 8.54 it is true that $\mathbf{V}_C = \mathbf{V}''_{O'}$.

3. Prove that Eq. (8.55) is valid even when the moving reference point is not the center of mass, provided that its acceleration is directed toward (or away from) the center of mass.

8.12. Dimensional Methods. At this point we may well pause to meditate upon the theoretical structure thus far put together. We have discussed briefly how magnitudes of length, force, and time (l, f, and t) are assigned. From experimentally verifiable properties and from intuitive relationships accepted as postulates, various new conclusions have been deduced. Many of these have involved the idea of direction (epitomized by a unit vector $\mathbf{E}$) and also certain derived concepts. These derived or secondary concepts were defined in terms of the basic quantities. One way of making the interrelationships of such a science clear, and even of keeping units well in line, is the method of dimensions.

Our treatment of dimensions will elect as *ingredients* the five symbols

$$1, \mathbf{E}, l, f, t.$$

Dimensional statements are denoted symbolically by brackets:

(8.56)

$$
\begin{aligned}
[\text{Pure number}] &= [1] \quad \text{(omitted except in the absence of everything else)}\\
[\text{Any unit vector}] &= [\mathbf{E}]\\
[\text{Length magnitude}] &= [l]\\
[\text{Force magnitude}] &= [f]\\
[\text{Time}] &= [t]
\end{aligned}
$$

In terms of these five ingredients, our three *primary concepts* are analyzed as

$$\begin{aligned}[\mathbf{R}] &= [\text{length}] = [l\mathbf{E}]\\ [\mathbf{F}] &= [\text{force}] = [f\mathbf{E}]\\ [t] &= [\text{time}] = [t]\end{aligned} \tag{8.57}$$

The *secondary concepts* can be analyzed by seeking out their definitions and then analyzing the items making up the definition. Certain algebraic identities will occur. Samples are

$$[\mathbf{E}\cdot\mathbf{E}] = [1]; \qquad [\mathbf{E}\times\mathbf{E}] = [\mathbf{E}].$$

Example 1. Velocity is defined by $\mathbf{V} = d\mathbf{R}/dt$.
Dimensionally,

$$[\mathbf{V}] = [\mathbf{R}t^{-1}] = [lt^{-1}\mathbf{E}].$$

Angle will be assigned dimension [**E**], the vector representing the axis about which the rotation takes place. This choice justifies itself when derived angular concepts are considered. A list of dimensional analyses for important derived concepts follows:

$$\begin{aligned}[\text{Angle}] &= [\mathbf{E}]\\ [\text{Area}] &= [\mathbf{R}\times\mathbf{R}] = [l^2\mathbf{E}]\\ [\text{Volume}] &= [\mathbf{R}\cdot\mathbf{R}\times\mathbf{R}] = [l^3]\\ [\text{Moment of force}] &= [\mathbf{R}\times\mathbf{F}] = [lf\mathbf{E}\times\mathbf{E}] = [lf\mathbf{E}]\\ [\text{Velocity}] &= [lt^{-1}\mathbf{E}]\\ [\text{Acceleration}] &= [lt^{-2}\mathbf{E}]\\ [\text{Angular velocity}] &= [t^{-1}\mathbf{E}]\\ [\text{Angular acceleration}] &= [t^{-2}\mathbf{E}]\\ [\text{Mass}] &= [l^{-1}ft^2]\\ [\text{Moment of inertia}] &= [lft^2]\end{aligned} \tag{8.58}$$

Any correct formula or equation should check dimensionally, that is, the dimensions of the two sides of the equation should agree.

Example 2. Let us ascertain whether $\mathbf{\Omega}\times(\mathbf{\Omega}\times\mathbf{R})$ is dimensionally an acceleration.

$$\begin{aligned}[\mathbf{\Omega}\times(\mathbf{\Omega}\times\mathbf{R})] &= [\mathbf{E}t^{-1}\times(\mathbf{E}t^{-1}\times l\mathbf{E})]\\ &= [\mathbf{E}t^{-1}\times t^{-1}l\mathbf{E}] = [lt^{-2}\mathbf{E}].\end{aligned}$$

Dimensional analysis affords a sound way of checking complicated units.

Example 3. The analysis for moment of inertia given above should make it clear that the usual unit in the mks system, the kg-m^2, is equivalent to the newton-m-sec^2. Similarly, dimensions provide a pattern for changing units from one system to another.

Example 4. Suppose that it is desired to express a velocity of 30 mph in feet per second. The dimensions of velocity are $[lt^{-1}\mathbf{E}]$ although of course only the $[lt^{-1}]$ are involved in a change of units. In the expression

$$30 \text{ mph} = 30 \times \frac{1 \text{ mile}}{1 \text{ hr}},$$

where the $\frac{1 \text{ mile}}{1 \text{ hr}}$ follows the dimensional pattern, we can substitute

$$1 \text{ mile} = 5{,}280 \text{ ft},$$
$$1 \text{ hr} = 3{,}600 \text{ sec};$$

thus,

$$30 \text{ mph} = \frac{30 \times 5{,}280}{3{,}600} \text{ ft/sec} = 44 \text{ ft/sec}.$$

Constructive Use of Dimensions. We have seen how the method of dimensions is an aid in checking equations qualitatively and in changing units systematically. Another important role which will be only hinted at here is its use as a means of discovering the forms of physical equations and interrelationships. This interesting tool is not one of the major objectives of this course, but it is too important to pass by entirely. We shall use only the ordinary scalar dimensions, omitting **E**. Easy examples are picked deliberately so that attention may be called to the procedure without an undue expenditure of time at this stage.

Example 5. Let us try to see what form the equation for the period of a simple pendulum should have. The likely variables are m, l, g; therefore we shall assume a solution of the form

$$\tau = \text{const } m^a l^b g^c.$$

Substituting dimensions,

$$[t] = [l^{-1}ft^2]^a[l]^b[lt^{-2}]^c,$$
$$[t] = [l^{-a+b+c}f^a t^{2a-2c}].$$

In order that this expression be dimensionally consistent, the following equations are satisfied:

$$0 = -a + b + c,$$
$$0 = a,$$
$$1 = 2a - 2c.$$

Solving simultaneously, $a = 0$, $c = -\frac{1}{2}$, $b = \frac{1}{2}$; thus the desired expression is

$$\tau = \text{const} \sqrt{\frac{l}{g}}.$$

Example 6. The velocity of a transverse wave along a string might be expected to depend on the mass m, the tension f, the length l. Let us seek a dimensional solution, proceeding as before,

$$\begin{aligned} v &= \text{const } m^a f^b l^c \\ [lt^{-1}] &= [l^{-1}ft^2]^a[f]^b[l]^c \\ [lt^{-1}] &= [l^{-a+c}f^{a+b}t^{2a}] \\ 1 &= -a + c \\ 0 &= a + b \\ -1 &= 2a. \end{aligned}$$

Thus $a = -\frac{1}{2}$, $b = +\frac{1}{2}$, $c = \frac{1}{2}$, giving

$$v = \text{const}\sqrt{\frac{fl}{m}}.$$

EXERCISES

1. Analyze the following dimensionally:

(*a*) Product of inertia. (*b*) $\frac{1}{2}m\mathbf{V}\cdot\mathbf{V}$.

(*c*) $\int_m \mathbf{V}\,dm$. (*d*) $\mathbf{R}\times m\mathbf{V}$.

(*e*) $m\mathbf{\Omega}\times\mathbf{\Omega}'$.

2. State units equivalent to (*a*) kg-m²/sec²; (*b*) kg-m/sec; (*c*) slug-ft²; (*d*) pdl-sec.

3. Check the following equations dimensionally:

(*a*) $\mathbf{\Gamma} = i\boldsymbol{\alpha}$. (*b*) $\mathbf{A}_c = 2\mathbf{\Omega}\times\mathbf{V}$.

(*c*) $\int\mathbf{\Gamma}\cdot\mathbf{\Omega}\,dt = \frac{1}{2}i\mathbf{\Omega}\cdot\mathbf{\Omega}$. (*d*) $\int\mathbf{\Gamma}\,dt = \int\mathbf{R}\times\mathbf{V}\,dm$.

4. An important equation in mechanics is the inverse-square law of gravitational attraction

$$f = \frac{\gamma m m'}{r^2}.$$

Find the dimensions of γ if r is a distance.

5. To how many ft-lb-sec² is a moment of inertia of 10 kg-m² equivalent?

6. A pressure of 15 lb/in.² is equivalent to how many newton/m²?

7. The velocity of a deep-water wave might be expected to depend on density, acceleration of gravity, and wavelength. Find a dimensional formula.

8. The velocity of a sound wave might be expected to depend on density; bulk modulus, β, $[fl^{-2}]$; and wavelength. Find a dimensional formula.

9. The escape speed for a projectile depends on the gravitational constant γ of Exercise 4, the mass of the earth, and the distance from the center of the earth. Find a dimensional formula for v.

10. The time for a planet to go around the sun depends on the gravitational constant γ (see Exercise 4), on the combined mass of sun and planet, and on the semimajor axis of the orbit. Find a dimensional formula for this time.

CHAPTER 9

WORK AND KINETIC ENERGY

In the preceding chapters we tackled quite a variety of problems using as our primary tool the equation $\mathbf{F} = m\mathbf{A}$. In the present chapter the new, though derived, concept of energy will be central. This concept is of unique importance in physics; yet it is often not clearly defined. Here, in the basic science of mechanics, energy will be introduced in a precise and concrete manner. First it is expedient to define the work done by a force.

9.1. Work and Power. A force is completely specified if its magnitude, direction, and point of application are known. If the point of application moves while the force is applied, the force is said to do work. For a constant force and a straight-line displacement (see Fig. 9.1), the work is equal to the scalar product of the force times the displacement:

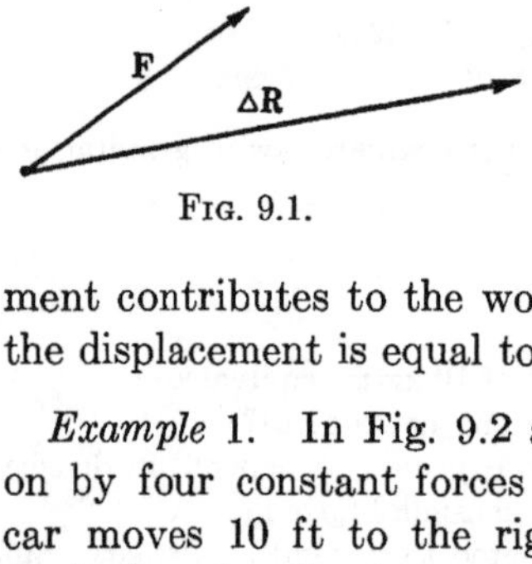

Fig. 9.1.

$$\text{Work} = \mathbf{F} \cdot \Delta\mathbf{R}. \tag{9.1}$$

In other terms we may say that only the component of force parallel to the displacement contributes to the work done: this component times the length of the displacement is equal to the work.

Example 1. In Fig. 9.2 a car free to move along fixed rails is acted on by four constant forces while the car moves 10 ft to the right. The work done by the forces is tabulated below:

Pounds	Foot-pounds
50	500
25	0
100	500
70 7	−500

The net work done by the system of four forces is +500 ft-lb.

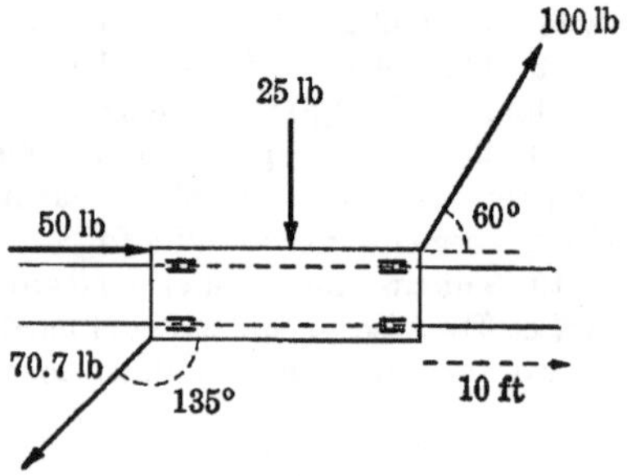

Fig. 9.2.

Let us now confront the more general situation of a variable force and a curvilinear displacement of the point of application. In Fig. 9.3 a curved path is shown along with pictures of the force at selected points. While the simple equation (9.1) does not at once apply to this more complex context, it at least does suggest our approach. Assuming that the force varies smoothly in both direction and magnitude, it is clear that for a small displacement $\Delta\mathbf{R}$ and a value of $\mathbf{F}$ associated with some point in this displacement the scalar product given by (9.1) is approximately what we should wish to call the work done during that displacement.

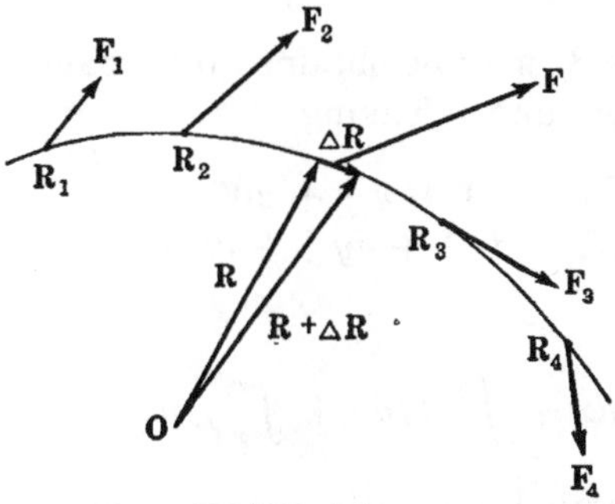

FIG. 9.3.

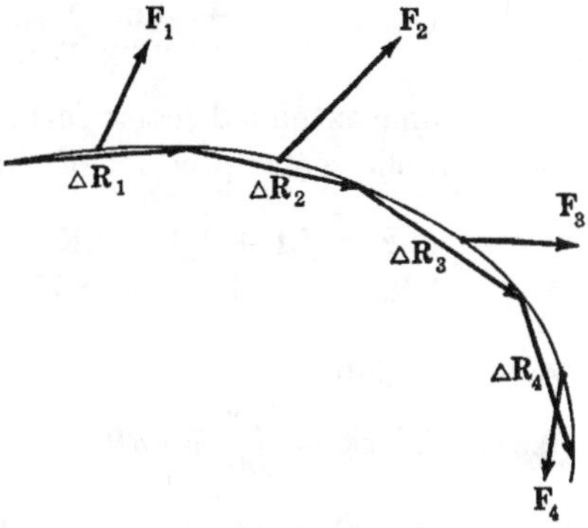

FIG. 9.4.

By approximating the whole path by a zigzag polygon consisting of successive displacements $\Delta\mathbf{R}_1, \Delta\mathbf{R}_2, \ldots$, as in Fig. 9.4, we can consider the sum of such elements of work:

$$\text{Work} \cong \mathbf{F}_1 \cdot \Delta\mathbf{R}_1 + \mathbf{F}_2 \cdot \Delta\mathbf{R}_2 + \cdots,$$

or

$$\text{Work} \cong \Sigma \mathbf{F}_i \cdot \Delta\mathbf{R}_i.$$

We should expect to get a more significant value for zigzag paths more closely fitting the curve. Consequently, it is natural to define work in this general case as the limit of such approximations as the lengths of the $\Delta\mathbf{R}$'s are made smaller and smaller.

$$\text{Work} = \lim_{|\Delta\mathbf{R}_i| \to 0} \Sigma \mathbf{F}_i \cdot \Delta\mathbf{R}_i. \tag{9.2}$$

In ordinary practical cases the limit exists. The form of the definition already suggests the ideas of integral calculus reviewed in Sec. 5.10. This limit of a sum, involving as it does a summation along a path, is called a *line integral*. It is written

$$\lim_{|\Delta\mathbf{R}_i| \to 0} \sum \mathbf{F}_i \cdot \Delta\mathbf{R}_i = \int_{\mathbf{R}_0}^{\mathbf{R}_1} \mathbf{F} \cdot d\mathbf{R}.$$

Thus

$$\text{Work} = \int_{\mathbf{R}_0}^{\mathbf{R}_1} \mathbf{F} \cdot d\mathbf{R}. \tag{9.3}$$

The $\mathbf{R}_0$ and $\mathbf{R}_1$ designate the starting and stopping points and hence set the limits for the summation. **F** may vary from point to point; therefore **F** must be regarded as a function of **R**. The significance of the line integral in terms of components is seen by expanding the scalar products:

$$(9.4)\quad \int_{\mathbf{R}_0}^{\mathbf{R}_1} \mathbf{F}\cdot d\mathbf{R} = \lim_{\Delta x_i \to 0} \sum f_{i_x}\,\Delta x_i + \lim_{\Delta y_i \to 0} \sum f_{i_y}\,\Delta y_i + \lim_{\Delta z_i \to 0} \sum f_{i_z}\,\Delta z_i = \int_{x_0}^{x_1} f_x\,dx + \int_{y_0}^{y_1} f_y\,dy + \int_{z_0}^{z_1} f_z\,dz.$$

The same extended scalar form of (9.3) may be obtained by expanding the symbolic scalar product of the integrand. Taking

$$\mathbf{F} = f_x\mathbf{I} + f_y\mathbf{J} + f_z\mathbf{K}, \qquad \mathbf{R}_1 = x_1\mathbf{I} + y_1\mathbf{J} + z_1\mathbf{K},$$
$$\mathbf{R}_0 = x_0\mathbf{I} + y_0\mathbf{J} + z_0\mathbf{K}, \qquad d\mathbf{R} = dx\,\mathbf{I} + dy\,\mathbf{J} + dz\,\mathbf{K},$$

we have again

$$(9.5)\quad \text{Work} = \int_{\mathbf{R}_0}^{\mathbf{R}_1} \mathbf{F}\cdot d\mathbf{R} = \int_{x_0}^{x_1} f_x\,dx + \int_{y_0}^{y_1} f_y\,dy + \int_{z_0}^{z_1} f_z\,dz.$$

For these scalar integrations to be carried out each integrand must be represented as a function of the corresponding independent variable. This usually requires a knowledge of equations of the path. In most of the applications considered in this chapter, the full scope of this definition of work will not be employed.

Example 2. A variable force **F** is given by

$$\mathbf{F} = 2y\mathbf{I} + xy\mathbf{J}.$$

For a straight-line displacement from the origin to the point $\mathbf{R}_1 = 2\mathbf{I} + \mathbf{J}$, what work is done?

SOLUTION. An equation of this line is $2y = x$. For points on the line, then, the force may be written

$$\mathbf{F} = x\mathbf{I} + 2y^2\mathbf{J}.$$

The work may now be computed

$$\text{Work} = \int_{0}^{\mathbf{R}_1} \mathbf{F}\cdot d\mathbf{R} = \int_0^2 x\,dx + 2\int_0^1 y^2\,dy = 2.67.$$

If several forces have the same point of application, then the net work done, that is, the algebraic sum of the work done by the individual forces, is equal to the work done by the resultant. This follows at once from the distributive law for scalar products and from the additive property of definite integrals. Thus, if $\bar{\mathbf{F}} = \Sigma\mathbf{F}$, we have

$$(9.6)\quad \Sigma\int \mathbf{F}\cdot d\mathbf{R} = \int(\Sigma\mathbf{F})\cdot d\mathbf{R} = \int \bar{\mathbf{F}}\cdot d\mathbf{R}.$$

Equation (9.5) may be thought of as a special case of this since **F** is the resultant of the three forces $f_x\mathbf{I}$, $f_y\mathbf{J}$, $f_z\mathbf{K}$.

Example 3. A block is pushed up an inclined plane by a force **F** parallel to the plane through a distance l as in Fig. 9.5. The work done by **F** is

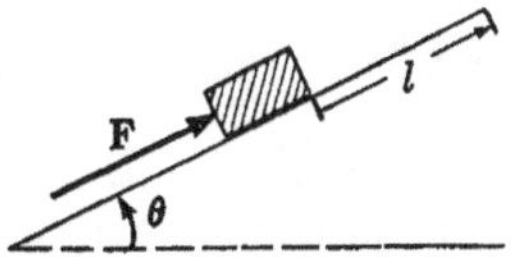

FIG. 9.5.

$$\text{Work} = fl.$$

Regarding **F** as the resultant of $f_x\mathbf{I}$ and $f_y\mathbf{J}$ and the displacement as

$$\Delta\mathbf{R} = l \cos\theta\,\mathbf{I} + l \sin\theta\,\mathbf{J},$$

$$\begin{aligned}\text{Work} &= (f_x\mathbf{I}) \cdot (l\cos\theta\,\mathbf{I} + l\sin\theta\,\mathbf{J}) + (f_y\mathbf{J}) \cdot (l\cos\theta\,\mathbf{I} + l\sin\theta\,\mathbf{J}) \\ &= (f_x\cos\theta + f_y\sin\theta)l.\end{aligned}$$

Now $f_x = f\cos\theta$ and $f_y = f\sin\theta$; thus this last expression becomes

$$\text{Work} = (f\cos^2\theta + f\sin^2\theta)l = fl$$

as before.

Example 4. *Work Done by a Constant Force.* If **F** is constant as indicated in Fig. 9.6, we have

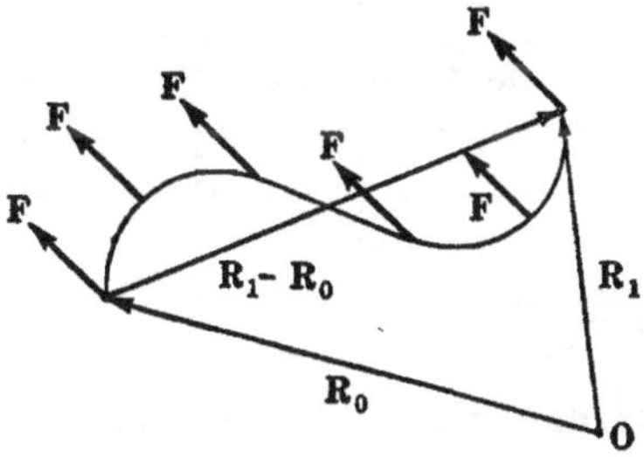

FIG. 9.6.

$$\text{Work} = \int_{\mathbf{R}_0}^{\mathbf{R}_1} \mathbf{F}\cdot d\mathbf{R} = \mathbf{F}\cdot\int_{\mathbf{R}_0}^{\mathbf{R}_1} d\mathbf{R} = \mathbf{F}\cdot(\mathbf{R}_1 - \mathbf{R}_0).$$

This means that the work done is independent of the path; one needs merely to compute the work that would be done by the force during a straight-line displacement from the initial to the final point.

Example 5. *Work Done by Gravity in a Restricted Locality on a Particle or an Aggregate of Particles.* By the last result, when a particle moves from one position to another by any path,

$$\text{Work} = \mathbf{W}\cdot(\mathbf{R}_1 - \mathbf{R}_0) = m\mathbf{G}\cdot(\mathbf{R}_1 - \mathbf{R}_0).$$

For an aggregate of particles,

$$\begin{aligned}\text{Work} &= \Sigma m\mathbf{G}\cdot(\mathbf{R}_1 - \mathbf{R}_0) \\ &= \mathbf{G}\cdot(\Sigma m\mathbf{R}_1 - \Sigma m\mathbf{R}_0) \\ &= (\Sigma m)\mathbf{G}\cdot(\bar{\mathbf{R}}_1 - \bar{\mathbf{R}}_0).\end{aligned}$$

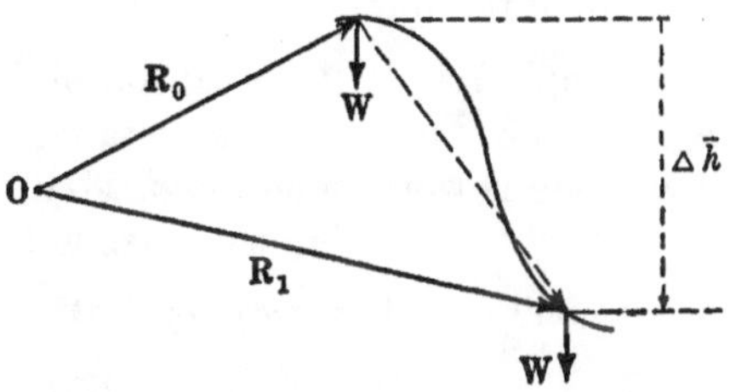

FIG. 9.7.

It is easy to calculate $\mathbf{G}\cdot(\bar{\mathbf{R}}_1 - \bar{\mathbf{R}}_0)$ as $-g\,\Delta\bar{h}$, where the latter symbol denotes the vertical displacement or increase of height of the center of mass (see Fig. 9.7). For a particle, aggregate of particles, or rigid body, then, the work done by gravity is in a restricted locality always equal to the magnitude of the weight times the vertical displacement downward.

$$\text{(9.7)} \qquad \text{Work (due to gravity)} = -w\,\Delta\bar{h}.$$

Example 6. How much work is required to lift a 400-lb flat slab of marble 6 ft square onto its edge from a horizontal position?

SOLUTION. By the result just obtained we should predict a result of 1,200 ft-lb. But let us calculate it using the ideas already introduced. Assuming that the slab does not slip, the best bet obviously is to apply a variable force **F** perpendicular to the slab (so that the whole force is tangent to its path) and at the edge (so that its magnitude may be minimum; see Fig. 9.8). Taking moments about the bottom edge, we find that **F** must be in magnitude at least equal to 200 cos θ. The corresponding displacement ds may be written $ds = 6d\theta$. Integrating,

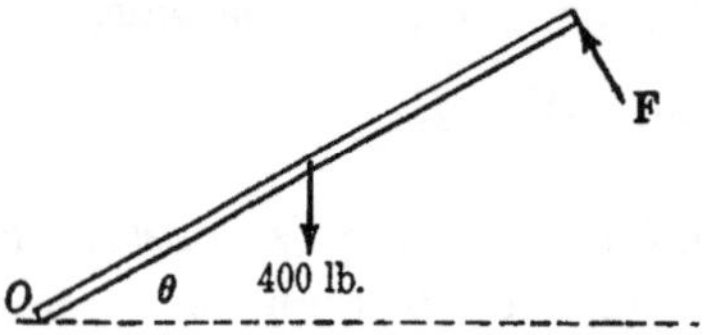

FIG. 9.8.

$$\text{Work} = 1{,}200 \int_0^{\pi/2} \cos\theta\, d\theta = 1{,}200 \Big[\sin\theta\Big]_0^{\pi/2} = 1{,}200 \text{ ft-lb.}$$

Power. The time rate of performance of work is called *power.* It is measured in foot-pounds per second (ft-lb/sec), horsepower (550 ft-lb/sec = 1 hp), or joules per second (watts).

$$\text{(9.8)} \qquad \text{Power} = \frac{d}{dt}(\text{work}) = \lim_{\Delta t \to 0} \frac{\mathbf{F} \cdot \Delta\mathbf{R}}{\Delta t} = \mathbf{F} \cdot \mathbf{V}.$$

This suggests a number of convenient alternative formulas for work:

$$\text{(9.9)} \qquad \text{Work} = \int_{t_0}^{t_1} \mathbf{F} \cdot \mathbf{V}\, dt = \int_{t_0}^{t_1} \mathbf{F} \cdot \frac{ds}{dt} \mathbf{T}\, dt = \int_{s_0}^{s_1} f_T\, ds.$$

Thus work is either the time integral of the power or the arc-length integral of the tangential component of the force.

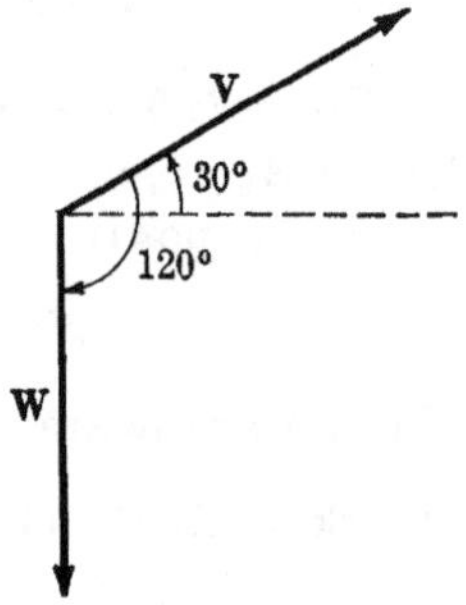

FIG. 9.9.

Example 7. A 2-ton automobile drives at 30 mph up a 30° incline for a distance of 1,000 ft. At what rate is work done by gravity?

SOLUTION. **F** · **V** in this case is (see Fig. 9.9)

$$(4{,}000 \text{ lb})(44 \text{ ft/sec}) \cos 120° = -88{,}000 \text{ ft-lb/sec} = -160 \text{ hp.}$$

EXERCISES

1. A 100-lb log is dragged at uniform speed up a 30° ramp 10 ft long by a rope making an angle of 10° above the ramp. If the coefficient of friction is 0.4, find the work done (*a*) by the friction; (*b*) by the normal reaction with the ramp; (*c*) by the force exerted by the rope; (*d*) by gravity.

2. A force with x, y, and z components of 3, 4, and 12 lb is displaced from the point (1,2,3) to the point (2,−3,1). How much work does it do?

3. If the force acting on a body at the position (x,y) m is

$$\mathbf{F} = y\mathbf{I} + 5\mathbf{J} \qquad \text{newtons,}$$

how much work is done on the body in going from (−5,0) m to (5,0) m (*a*) by a straight-line path? (*b*) by a straight-line path from (−5,0) m to (0,5) m followed by a straight-line path from (0,5) m to (5,0) m?

4. A particle moves in the xy plane from (0,2) m to (2,0) m along a straight-line path while subject to a force $\mathbf{F} = 10(\mathbf{I} + \mathbf{J})$ newtons. How much work is done by the force?

5. A block of metal 6 in. by 8 in. by 12 in. and weighing 100 lb rests on a face of least area. If the block is tipped onto a face of largest area, (*a*) what net work is done by gravity? (*b*) how much positive work must be done to get the block to tip over?

6. Find the work done in excavating a circular 10-ft well 6 ft in diameter at the top and 4 ft in diameter at the bottom. The dirt forms a conical pile 6 ft deep. Assume that a cubic foot of the soil weighs 100 lb.

7. A 10-ft chain weighing 5 lb hangs over a small pulley with 6 ft hanging down on one side. If it is released, how much work will have been done by gravity by the time the chain leaves the pulley?

8. An elevator weighing 1,700 lb is hauled up a vertical mine shaft 1,000 ft deep. The total weight of the cable used is 1,500 lb. What work is done if the cable is wound on a drum of negligible bearing friction?

9. A 3-ft 1-lb simple pendulum oscillates with an amplitude of 5°. How much work is done by gravity when it swings from its highest to its lowest point?

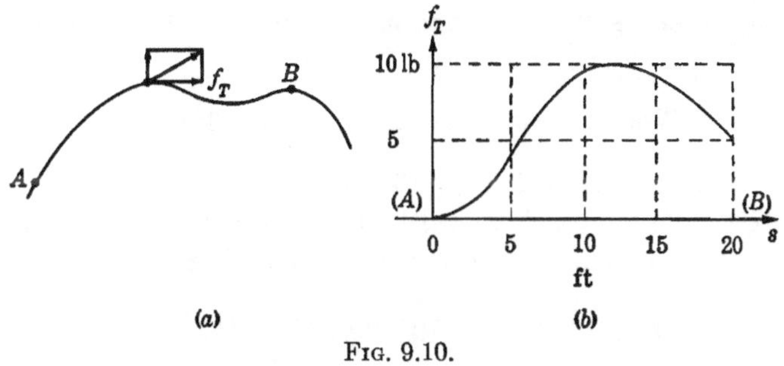

FIG. 9.10.

10. A particle is displaced a total distance of 20 ft from A to B along a curve drawn to scale above (Fig. 9.10). It is subject to a variable force whose tangential component is represented in Fig. 9.10*b*. Estimate the work done by the force.

11. A rectangular box of depth d, weight w, and specific gravity s floats at equilibrium in water. What work must be exerted to submerge the box?

9.2. Work Done by a Couple. The expression for power leads simply to a formula for work done on a rigid body by a couple. Let our couple consist of $-\mathbf{F}$ at $\mathbf{R}$ and $+\mathbf{F}$ at $\mathbf{R} + \mathbf{D}$ as in Fig. 9.11. The point $\mathbf{R}$ has velocity $\mathbf{V}_R$. Then the point $\mathbf{R} + \mathbf{D}$ has velocity

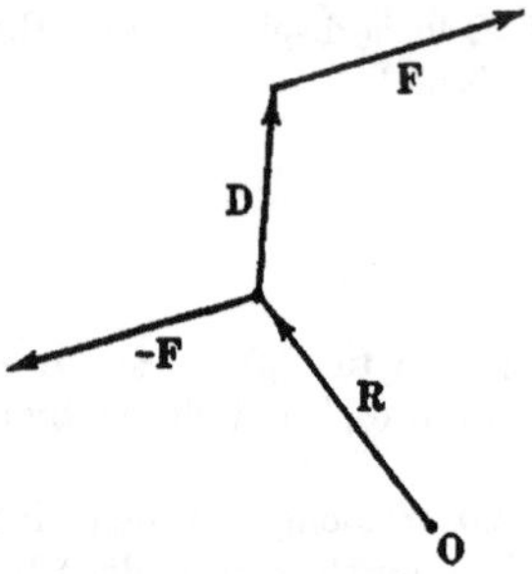

FIG. 9.11.

$$\mathbf{V}_R + \mathbf{\Omega} \times \mathbf{D}.$$

Assume that $\mathbf{\Omega} = \omega\mathbf{K}$. Then the sum of the powers exerted by these two forces is

$$\text{Power} = -\mathbf{F} \cdot \mathbf{V}_R + \mathbf{F} \cdot (\mathbf{V}_R + \mathbf{\Omega} \times \mathbf{D}),$$

or

$$(9.10) \quad \text{Power} = \mathbf{F} \cdot \mathbf{\Omega} \times \mathbf{D} = \mathbf{D} \times \mathbf{F} \cdot \mathbf{\Omega} = \mathbf{\Gamma} \cdot \mathbf{\Omega} = \gamma_z\omega.$$

Corresponding work formulas are

$$(9.11) \qquad \text{Work} = \int_{t_0}^{t_1} \mathbf{\Gamma} \cdot \mathbf{\Omega}\, dt = \int_{t_0}^{t_1} \mathbf{\Gamma} \cdot \omega\mathbf{K}\, dt = \int_{\theta_0}^{\theta_1} \gamma_z\, d\theta.$$

Example 1. A drum 2 m in diameter is used for winding up a flexible cable of length 100 m and mass 500 kg. How much work is done in the winding? The bearing friction is 50 newton-m.

SOLUTION. We can divide the work into two parts. First is the work of lifting the cable with a diminishing force always equal to the weight still hanging. This can be handled in a trice by noting that the center of mass is lifted 50 m.

$$\text{Work}_1 = 500 \times 9.8 \times 50 = 2.45 \times 10^5 \text{ joules (newton-m)}.$$

In addition there is the work against the frictional torque as the drum turns through an angle of 100 rad.

$$\text{Work}_2 = \gamma\theta = 50 \times 100 = 5 \times 10^3 \text{ joules}.$$

The total work is clearly 2.50×10^5 joules.

An alternative approach would be to represent the torque required to turn the drum in terms of the length still hanging.

$$\gamma = 50 + (5y \text{ kg})(9.8 \text{ newtons/kg})(1 \text{ m}),$$

or

$$\gamma = 50 + 49y \qquad \text{newton-m}.$$

Moreover, $d\theta = -1dy$; thus

$$\text{Work} = -\int_{100}^{0} (50 + 49y)dy = -50y - \tfrac{49}{2}y^2 \Big|_{100}^{0} = 5{,}000 + 245{,}000 = 250{,}000 \text{ joules},$$

as before.

Example 2. *Work Done by Friction.* Let us consider a solid of revolution of radius r that is rolling on a plane as shown in Fig. 9.12. Let us add two forces **F** and $-$**F** at the center. Then the original force is replaced by an uphill force **F** at the center along with a couple of moment fr. For a displacement l of the center, the work done by the force is $-fl$; by the couple, $+fr\theta$. The net work is $f(r\theta - l)$. For rolling without slipping, this is zero. If the object is rolling "too slowly" and hence slipping, the value is negative. If it is rolling "too fast" and hence slipping, the direction of each arrow must be changed and still the result is negative.

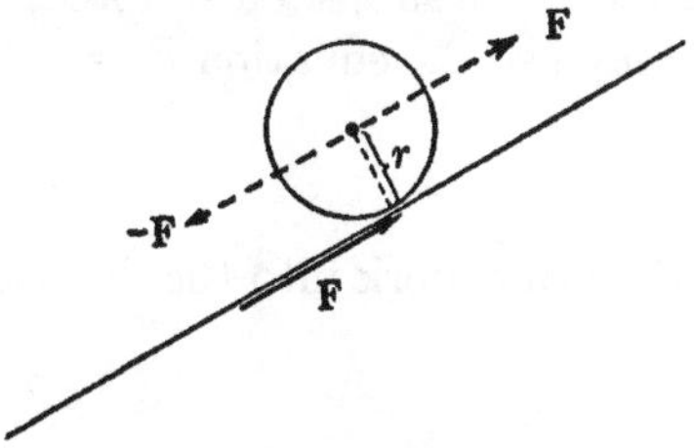

FIG. 9.12.

Example 3. Let us repeat Example 6 of the preceding section using the point of view of torques. The moment exerted by the weight, for any position θ, is

$$-(400)(3)\cos\theta.$$

Hence the applied force, wherever it is applied and whatever its direction, must have a moment

$$\gamma = 1{,}200 \cos\theta.$$

If we introduce at O equal and opposite forces **F** and $-$**F**, the work done can be analyzed as the work of a couple (as in Example 2). Thus

$$\text{Work} = \int_0^{\pi/2} \gamma\, d\theta = 1{,}200 \int_0^{\pi/2} \cos\theta\, d\theta,$$

as before.

EXERCISES

1. It requires a torque of 0.8 newton-m to hold a certain torsion pendulum twisted through an angle of 1.5 rad. How much work is done by the wire of the pendulum when it is allowed to untwist to equilibrium position?

2. The spool of Fig. 8.42 weighs 5 lb. What work is done during the descent of 13.5 ft (*a*) by the tension in the cord? (*b*) by gravity?

3. A spool (see Fig. 9.13) of outer radius 6 in. and inner radius 2 in. rolls 5 ft without slipping along a horizontal plane when a cord, unrolling from its upper edge, is pulled with a 10-lb force parallel to the plane. How much work is done by this force?

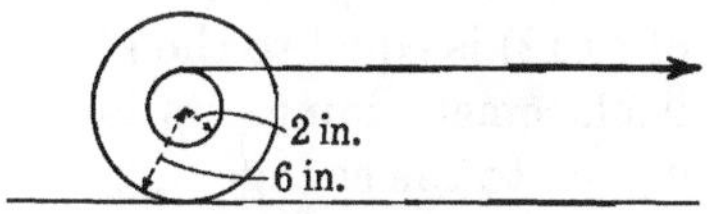

FIG. 9.13.

4. A torque of 20 ft-lb is required to keep a shaft rotating at constant angular speed. What horsepower must be exerted to keep the shaft rotating at 55 rad/sec?

5. Show that the work done by external forces on a rigid body moving parallel to the xy plane can be broken up into translational and rotational aspects thus:

$$\text{Work} = \sum \int_{\bar{\mathbf{R}}_0}^{\bar{\mathbf{R}}_1} \mathbf{F}\cdot d\bar{\mathbf{R}} + \sum \int_{\theta_0}^{\theta_1} \gamma_z\, d\theta.$$

9.3. The Work-Energy Principle for a Particle. In this section we shall investigate the dynamical significance of work. Suppose that a particle is subjected to forces whose resultant is **F**. Then, of course, we may use the equation $\mathbf{F} = m\mathbf{A}$ or

$$\mathbf{F} = m\frac{d\mathbf{V}}{dt}.$$

To bring work into the discussion, we take the scalar product with

$$d\mathbf{R} = \frac{d\mathbf{R}}{dt}\,dt = \mathbf{V}\,dt$$

and then integrate between corresponding limits

$$\int_{\mathbf{R}_0}^{\mathbf{R}_1} \mathbf{F}\cdot d\mathbf{R} = \int_{t_0}^{t_1} m\frac{d\mathbf{V}}{dt}\cdot\mathbf{V}\,dt = \int_{\mathbf{V}_0}^{\mathbf{V}_1} m\mathbf{V}\cdot d\mathbf{V}.$$

The right member is easily integrated since

$$\frac{d}{dt}(\mathbf{V}\cdot\mathbf{V}) = \frac{d\mathbf{V}}{dt}\cdot\mathbf{V} + \mathbf{V}\cdot\frac{d\mathbf{V}}{dt} = 2\mathbf{V}\cdot\frac{d\mathbf{V}}{dt};$$

so that

$$\int_{\mathbf{V}_0}^{\mathbf{V}_1} m\mathbf{V}\cdot d\mathbf{V} = \frac{1}{2}m\mathbf{V}\cdot\mathbf{V}\Big|_{\mathbf{V}_0}^{\mathbf{V}_1}.$$

Our conclusion is

(9.12) $$\int_{\mathbf{R}_0}^{\mathbf{R}_1} \mathbf{F}\cdot d\mathbf{R} = \tfrac{1}{2}m\mathbf{V}_1\cdot\mathbf{V}_1 - \tfrac{1}{2}m\mathbf{V}_0\cdot\mathbf{V}_0.$$

The left member is total work done [in view of (9.6)] on the particle during its displacement from $\mathbf{R}_0$ to $\mathbf{R}_1$. The quantity appearing twice in the right member is called the *kinetic energy, i.e.*, the energy of motion, of the particle:

(9.13) $$\text{Kinetic energy} = \text{k.e.} = \tfrac{1}{2}m\mathbf{V}\cdot\mathbf{V} = \tfrac{1}{2}mv^2.$$

Note that

(9.14) $$\text{k.e.} = \tfrac{1}{2}mv_x^2 + \tfrac{1}{2}mv_y^2 + \tfrac{1}{2}mv_z^2.$$

In terms of this concept the right member of (9.12) is equal to the kinetic energy of the particle at the end of the displacement minus its kinetic energy at the beginning of the displacement; *i.e.*, to the change in kinetic energy. This conclusion is called the *work-energy principle* for a particle.

(9.15) *The change in kinetic energy of a particle during a displacement is equal to the net work done by all the forces acting on it during this displacement.*

In short

(9.16) $$\text{Work} = \Delta(\text{k.e.}).$$

In applying this principle, a plan of attack such as the following may be used. First, isolate the body. Second, compute the work done by each of the isolating forces during the displacement in question. Third, equate the sum of these works to the final kinetic energy minus the initial kinetic energy and solve for whatever unknown there may be. In some cases the net work can best be computed by first finding the resultant force and then evaluating the work done by the resultant.

Example 1. A baseball is thrown with a speed of 100 ft/sec at an angle θ. When it reaches its maximum height of 64 ft, how fast is it traveling? Neglect air friction.

SOLUTION. The only force is the weight. The work done by this force is $-w\,\Delta h$ or

$$\text{Work} = -64w.$$

The change in kinetic energy is equal to this work:

$$\frac{1}{2}\left(\frac{w}{g}\right)v^2 - \frac{1}{2}\left(\frac{w}{g}\right)(100)^2 = -64w.$$

Hence

$$v^2 = 100^2 - 128g = 5{,}880, \qquad v = 76.7 \text{ ft/sec.}$$

Example 2. A hockey puck is projected along level ice at 60 ft/sec. If the coefficient of friction is 0.06, how far will it slide?

SOLUTION. Let the distance be s. Then

$$\Delta(\text{k.e.}) = 0 - \frac{1}{2}\left(\frac{w}{g}\right)60^2.$$

The weight and normal reaction do zero work since the displacement is horizontal and hence perpendicular to them. The work done by friction is negative:

$$\text{Work} = -0.06ws.$$

Equating these, we get

$$s = \frac{3{,}600}{0.12g} = 931 \text{ ft.}$$

Example 3. A grocer's scale descends 1 in. when a 1-lb potato is placed on it. If the potato is dropped from a height of 3 ft onto the scale, how far is the scale depressed (assuming that the energy losses of impact can be ignored)?

SOLUTION. The kinetic energy initially is zero. When the scale reaches its lowest point, the kinetic energy is again zero. Hence the net work done is zero. Let y be the amount the scale is depressed. Then the work done by gravity on the potato is $wh = 1(3 + y)$. The work done by the spring in the scale must now be computed. It presumably deflects an inch per pound, or the force is

$$f = -12y$$

and the work is

$$\text{Work} = \int_0^y f\,dy = -12\int_0^y y\,dy = -6y^2.$$

We have then

$$6y^2 - y - 3 = 0,$$

whence

$$y = 9.5 \text{ in.}$$

Example 4. A simple pendulum of mass m and length l is displaced by 90° and then released from rest. At what angle with the vertical is the tension equal to the weight?

SOLUTION. Since this problem involves the tension which does zero work, the work-energy approach can hardly be expected to provide the full solution. It is an aid, however. First isolate the bob, and use the equation $\Sigma\mathbf{F} = m\mathbf{A}$, taking components along the string for an intermediate position θ. Letting f denote the magnitude of the tension,

$$f - mg\cos\theta = m\frac{v^2}{l}.$$

The work-energy equation is

$$\tfrac{1}{2}mv^2 = mgl\cos\theta.$$

Eliminating v^2,

$$f - mg\cos\theta = 2mg\cos\theta.$$

Now let $f = mg$, and we get

$$\cos\theta = \tfrac{1}{3}, \qquad \theta = 70.5°.$$

EXERCISES

1. Starting with the definition of kinetic energy and the equation $\Sigma\mathbf{F} = m\mathbf{A}$, prove in detail the following: the rate of increase of kinetic energy of a particle is equal to the net power exerted by external forces.

2. What is the maximum kinetic energy of a simple pendulum 4 m long weighing 2.6 newtons and with an amplitude of 8°?

3. A block slides down a plane surface inclined at an angle of 30° with the horizontal. If the initial speed is 20 m/sec and the coefficient of friction 0.6, how far will it slide before coming to rest?

4. A 200-lb load on the end of a rope is hauled up vertically with an initial force of 250 lb which diminishes uniformly at the rate of a pound per foot. Find the speed after it has ascended 30 ft.

5. A block weighing 100 lb slides from rest a distance of 32 ft down a plane inclined at 60° before attaining a speed of 32 ft/sec. Find the coefficient of friction.

6. A 1,000-lb elevator breaks loose and falls from rest a distance of 16 ft, gaining a speed of 20 ft/sec. How much work was done by the friction which was the only impeding force?

7. A $\frac{1}{2}$-oz bullet traveling at 1,000 ft/sec strikes squarely a 1-in. board and emerges at 700 ft/sec. If the force of resistance is constant, how far would such a bullet penetrate into a thick block of the same material?

8. An automobile (rear-wheel drive, uniform weight distribution) starting on an icy but level pavement was able to pick up a speed of 12 mph only after it had gone 300 ft. What was the coefficient of friction between tires and ice?

9. An object is given an initial velocity of 100 ft/sec up a plane inclined at an angle θ with the horizontal. It slides a distance s up the plane before coming to a stop. If the coefficient of friction is 0.4, for what angle θ is s a minimum?

10. An object of mass m slides from the top of a sphere of radius a. Assuming that the sphere offers no resistance to the sliding of the object over its surface and that the normal force exerted by the sphere is p when the line from the center of the sphere to it makes an angle θ with the radius to the top of the sphere, for what value of θ does the following equation hold:

$$p = 0.5mg?$$

11. A boy runs and then slides a distance of 100 ft on an ice-covered lake. If he tries again with twice the initial velocity, how far will he be able to slide?

12. A spiral spring 2.5 ft long compresses an inch for each 2 lb of load. It is standing vertical and carrying a very light platform on its top when a 2-lb weight falling freely from a height of 5 ft lands on the platform. What will be the maximum compression of the spring?

13. Statement (7.8) is an important property of a simple pendulum. State a more general proposition including this as a special case, and prove it using the methods of this section.

14. A block is slid up a plane making an angle θ with the horizontal at an initial speed v_0. If the coefficient of friction is μ, with what speed will the block return to the starting point? (Assume that $\tan\theta$ is greater than μ.)

15. A 10-lb steel ball B attached by an 8-ft wire to a fixed pin A is held at rest so that the wire AB is taut and horizontal. It is then released. What angle does AB make with the horizontal when the tension in the wire is equal to twice the weight of the ball?

16. Show that for a particle subject to forces of resultant $\mathbf{F}$ the following equation holds:

$$\int_{x_0}^{x_1} f_x\,dx = \tfrac{1}{2}mv_{1x}^2 - \tfrac{1}{2}mv_{0x}^2.$$

9.4. Work and Energy for an Aggregate of Particles.

When we attempt to apply the ideas of the last section to an aggregate of particles, we find definite limitations. First, consider the matter of work. In our previous studies of aggregates, only temporary account was taken of internal forces. Their net contribution to force equations and to moment equations was zero. Suppose that two equal and opposite forces $\mathbf{F}'$ and $-\mathbf{F}'$ act, respectively, at $\mathbf{R}_1$ and $\mathbf{R}_2$, where $\mathbf{R}_1 = \mathbf{R}_2 + \mathbf{Q}$ as in Fig. 9.14. Then the total work due to these internal forces is com-

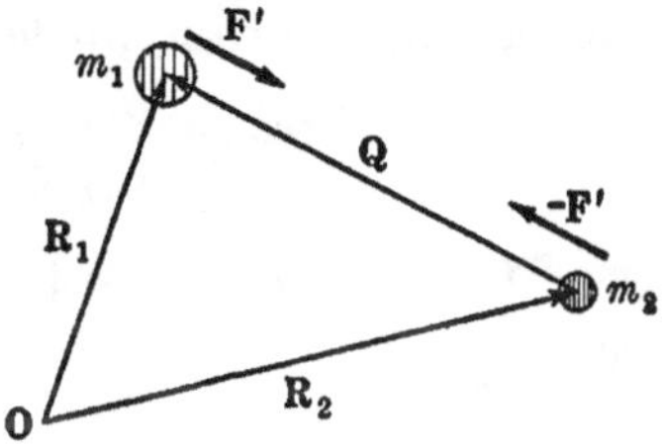

FIG. 9.14.

puted thus:

$$\text{Work}' = \int \mathbf{F}' \cdot d\mathbf{R}_1 + \int(-\mathbf{F}') \cdot d\mathbf{R}_2 = \int \mathbf{F}' \cdot (d\mathbf{R}_2 + d\mathbf{Q}) + \int(-\mathbf{F}') \cdot d\mathbf{R}_2$$

or

$$\text{Work}' = \int_{\mathbf{Q}_0}^{\mathbf{Q}_1} \mathbf{F}' \cdot d\mathbf{Q}. \tag{9.17}$$

For a typical situation where the force is one of attraction between two particles, the scalar product is easily expressed in terms of the distance q between the particles:

$$\text{Work}' = -\int_{q_0}^{q_1} f'\,dq. \tag{9.18}$$

This work is zero when the relative position of the two points is constant. Thus if two particles are joined by an inextensible cord the internal forces might be neglected, but if they are connected by an elastic cord the work done by it affects the energy equation. *When the particles are rigidly connected (as in a rigid body), the internal work is zero.*

Now suppose we have given a set of particles of which a typical one has mass m and is acted on by external forces and internal forces. During a given time interval the velocity of such a particle changes from $\mathbf{V}_0$ to $\mathbf{V}_1$. Denoting the work done during this interval by both external and internal forces by "work" we have, by (9.16),

$$\text{Work} = \tfrac{1}{2}m\mathbf{V}_1 \cdot \mathbf{V}_1 - \tfrac{1}{2}m\mathbf{V}_0 \cdot \mathbf{V}_0.$$

Such an expression can be written down for each particle of the aggregate. Summing these expressions, we get

$$\text{Total work} = \Sigma\tfrac{1}{2}m\mathbf{V}_1 \cdot \mathbf{V}_1 - \Sigma\tfrac{1}{2}m\mathbf{V}_0 \cdot \mathbf{V}_0 = \Delta(\text{k.e.}). \tag{9.19}$$

The kinetic energy of a system of particles may be related to the behavior of the center of mass. Let us consider velocities $\mathbf{V}'$ of the particles relative to the center of mass. Then

$$\mathbf{V} = \bar{\mathbf{V}} + \mathbf{V}'.$$

Consequently, for the whole system,

$$\begin{aligned}\text{k.e.} &= \Sigma\tfrac{1}{2}m(\bar{\mathbf{V}} + \mathbf{V}') \cdot (\bar{\mathbf{V}} + \mathbf{V}') \\ &= \Sigma\tfrac{1}{2}m\bar{\mathbf{V}} \cdot \bar{\mathbf{V}} + \Sigma m\mathbf{V}' \cdot \bar{\mathbf{V}} + \Sigma\tfrac{1}{2}m\mathbf{V}' \cdot \mathbf{V}'.\end{aligned}$$

Since $\bar{\mathbf{V}}$ is the same for each term in the summations, this may be factored out:

$$\text{k.e.} = \tfrac{1}{2}(\Sigma m)\bar{\mathbf{V}} \cdot \bar{\mathbf{V}} + (\Sigma m\mathbf{V}') \cdot \bar{\mathbf{V}} + \Sigma\tfrac{1}{2}m\mathbf{V}' \cdot \mathbf{V}'.$$

In the right member of this equation the first term may be called "the kinetic energy of the center of mass": it is the energy of a single particle at the center of mass and having the whole mass of the system. The second term is equal to zero, for

$$\sum m\mathbf{V}' = \frac{d}{dt}\left(\sum m\mathbf{R}'\right) = \frac{d}{dt}\left[\sum m\mathbf{R} - \left(\sum m\right)\bar{\mathbf{R}}\right].$$

The third term may be called "the kinetic energy relative to the center of mass." The conclusion may be written, for an aggregate,

$$\text{k.e.} = \tfrac{1}{2}(\Sigma m)\bar{v}^2 + \Sigma(\tfrac{1}{2}mv'^2). \tag{9.20}$$

Example 1. Two objects of mass 1 and 3 kg are connected by a light inextensible cord passing over a frictionless light pulley. If these are released at the same level, how fast will the system be going after a displacement of 50 cm?

SOLUTION. Only gravity does work. We could measure this in terms of the displacement of the center of mass. It is probably quicker to do it for the objects separately.

$$\text{Work} = 1(-0.5)9.8 + 3(0.5)9.8 = 9.8 \text{ joules.}$$

Since the cord does not stretch, the speeds of the two particles are equal:

$$\text{k.e.} = \tfrac{1}{2}(1 + 3)v^2.$$

Using (9.19),

$$2v^2 = 9.8, \qquad v = 2.2 \text{ m/sec.}$$

Example 2. A 12-lb 6-ft chain rests with 4 ft held on a horizontal table top, the two remaining feet hanging over the smooth edge. If the coefficient of friction is 0.3, with what speed will the last link leave the table if the chain is released?

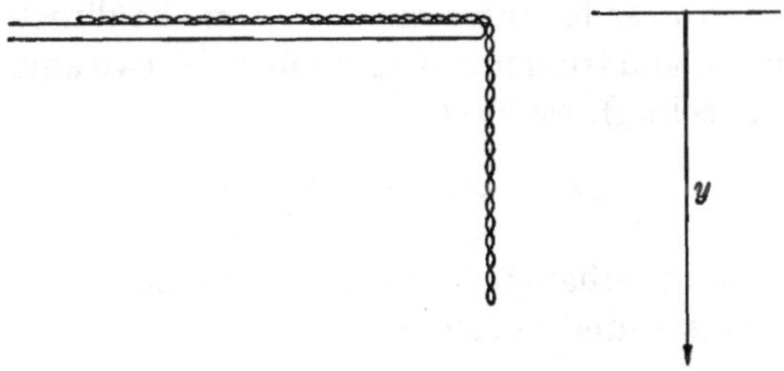

FIG. 9.15.

SOLUTION. Initially, the center of mass is given by (see Fig. 9.15)

$$\bar{y} = \frac{2(0) + 1(1)}{3},$$

that is,

$$\bar{y} = 0.33 \text{ ft} \qquad \text{or} \qquad 4 \text{ in.}$$

When the last link is leaving the table,

$$\bar{y} = 3 \text{ ft.}$$

The work done by gravity is then

$$12(3 - \tfrac{1}{3}) = 32 \text{ ft-lb.}$$

The work done by friction during a displacement dy is, when y represents the length of the hanging portion,

$$-0.3\left(\frac{6-y}{6}\right)12dy.$$

During the whole displacement it is

$$-0.6\int_2^6 (6-y)dy = -0.6\left[6y - \frac{y^2}{2}\right]_2^6 = -4.8 \text{ ft-lb.}$$

The work energy equation then gives

$$32 - 4.8 = \frac{1}{2}\left(\frac{12}{32.2}\right)v^2,$$

from which

$$v = 12.1 \text{ ft/sec.}$$

As in nearly all cases there are advantages for a purely literal solution, substituting numerical values in the last step. Here we have used a numerical approach in order to keep energy magnitudes and units in sight. A literal approach will be used in an alternative solution.

ALTERNATIVE SOLUTION. Just as a check let us compute the preceding result from the methods of Chap. 7. Isolating the overhanging portion of the chain, the forces are weight and tension. Isolating the portion on the table, the forces having components in the direction of the acceleration are tension and friction. Combining the two equations of motion (the tensions canceling), we have

$$w' - \mu w'' = \frac{w' + w''}{g}a.$$

The weights of the overhanging and remaining portions for a given position y may be substituted as follows:

$$\left(\frac{y}{l}\right)w - \mu\frac{(l-y)}{l}w = \frac{w}{g}v\frac{dv}{dy}.$$

Integrating this equation,

$$\frac{g}{l}\int_{l/3}^{l}[(1+\mu)y - \mu l]dy = \int_0^v v\,dv.$$

Solving for v^2,

$$v^2 = \frac{4gl}{9}(2-\mu).$$

Note that v does not depend on the density of the chain. Now we may put in numerical values.

$$v = \tfrac{2}{3}\sqrt{gl(2-\mu)} = \tfrac{2}{3}\sqrt{32.2(6)(2-0.3)} = 12.1 \text{ ft/sec.}$$

EXERCISES

1. Two particles, of mass 0.5 kg each, are initially at rest on a smooth horizontal table. Initially they are separated by a distance of 1 m. The magnitude of the force of attraction between them is given by

$$f = \frac{0.1}{q^2} \qquad \text{newtons}$$

(q is the separation in meters). What speed does each have by the time the separation is reduced to 10 cm?

2. Neglecting friction and inertia of the pulley, find (in Fig. 9.16), (*a*) the velocity after w_2 has moved from rest a distance of 50 cm; (*b*) the tension in the cord if w_1 is an object of mass 1 kg and w_2 of mass 0.5 kg.

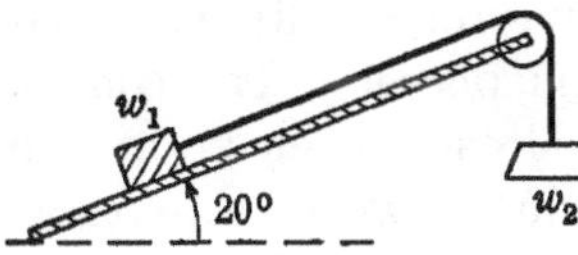

FIG. 9.16.

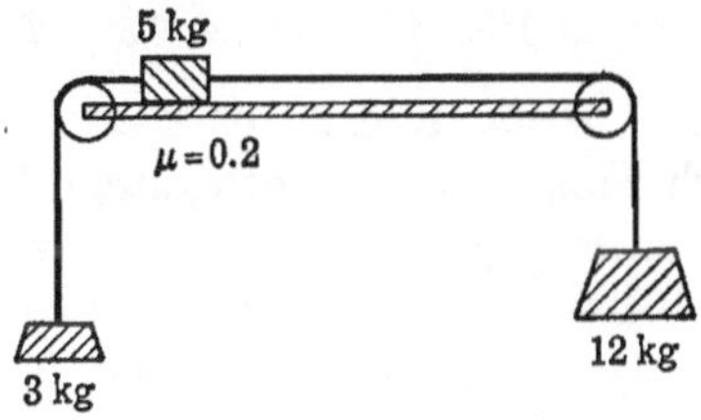

FIG. 9.17.

3. Find the speed after a displacement of 25 cm for the system shown in Fig. 9.17. The inertia and friction of the pulleys may be neglected. The system starts from rest.

4. A 28-ft chain weighing 11 lb is held on a 30° smooth roof with 14 ft hanging over the edge as in Fig. 9.18. If it is released, with what speed will the last link leave the edge?

5. A chain of length l on a smooth horizontal table has an initial overhang y_0 when the chain is at rest. It is released and the last link leaves the table with speed v_0. Show that y_0 is given by

$$y_0 = l\sqrt{1 - \frac{2v_0^2}{v_1^2}},$$

where v_1 is the speed which the whole chain would acquire in a free fall from rest through a distance equal to its length.

6. A chain 5 ft long is held on a rough horizontal table, half of it hanging over the smooth edge. If it is released, with what speed will the last link leave the table? (The coefficient of friction is 0.5.)

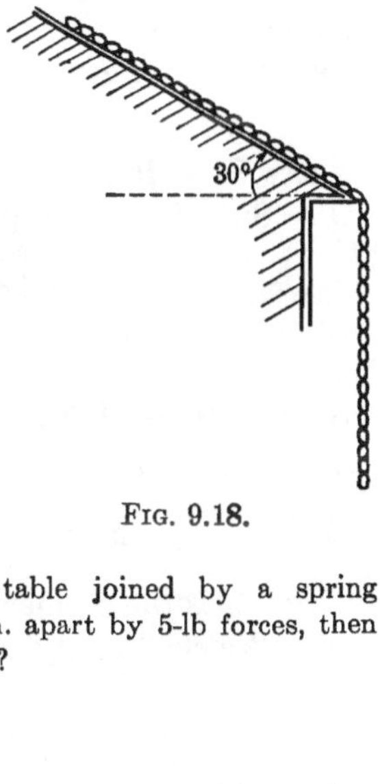

FIG. 9.18.

7. Two 1-lb blocks of wood rest on a smooth table joined by a spring whose unstretched length is 12 in. They are held 24 in. apart by 5-lb forces, then released. What is their speed when they are 18 in. apart?

8. A 1-lb block (see Fig. 9.19) is placed on the smooth sloping face of a right triangular 45° prism which weighs 4 lb. The prism rests on a smooth horizontal plane. If the initial position of the block is 12 in. above the plane, how fast will the prism be moving by the time the block reaches the end of the slope?

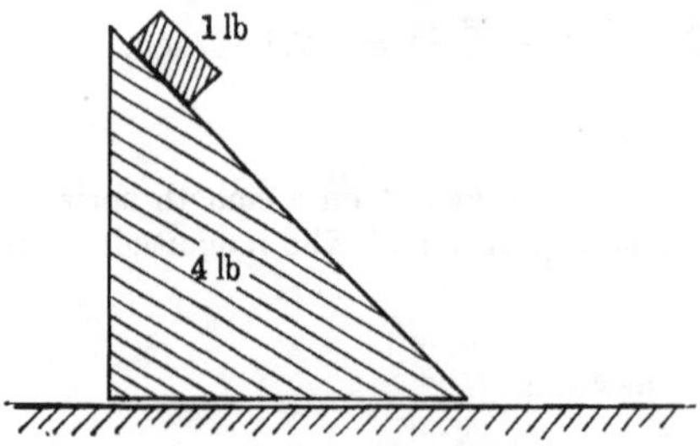

FIG. 9.19.

9. Show that the kinetic energy relative to the center of mass of an aggregate consisting of two particles can be written

$$\tfrac{1}{2}\mu(\mathbf{V}_2 - \mathbf{V}_1) \cdot (\mathbf{V}_2 - \mathbf{V}_1),$$

where μ stands for the reduced mass given by

$$\mu = \frac{m_1 m_2}{m_1 + m_2}.$$

10. Show that the kinetic energy of a system of two particles can be expressed as

$$\frac{1}{2}\frac{m_1 m_2}{\mu}\bar{\mathbf{V}} \cdot \bar{\mathbf{V}} + \frac{1}{2}\mu(\mathbf{V}_2 - \mathbf{V}_1) \cdot (\mathbf{V}_2 - \mathbf{V}_1),$$

where μ is as defined in Exercise 9 and $\bar{\mathbf{V}}$ is the velocity of the center of mass.

9.5. Kinetic Energy of a Rigid Body. By using a limiting process which replaces sums with integrals we have repeatedly extended results derived for aggregates of particles to rigid bodies. The conclusions of Sec. 9.4 may be used similarly. It has already been pointed out that with a single rigid body internal forces do no work; thus they can be ignored as far as mechanical energy problems are concerned.

We shall now analyze the kinetic energy of a rigid body. As a first step we may write

$$\text{(9.21)} \qquad \text{k.e.} = \tfrac{1}{2}\int_m \mathbf{V} \cdot \mathbf{V}\, dm = \tfrac{1}{2}\int_m v^2\, dm.$$

Let $\mathbf{O}'$ be a particular point of the rigid body. We shall use it as a reference point. Then

$$\mathbf{V} = \mathbf{V}_{O'} + \mathbf{\Omega} \times \mathbf{R}',$$

where $\mathbf{R}' = \mathbf{R} - \mathbf{O}'$; that is, $\mathbf{R}'$ is the position vector of dm relative to $\mathbf{O}'$. Substituting in (9.21), we get

$$\text{k.e.} = \tfrac{1}{2}\int_m \mathbf{V}_{O'} \cdot \mathbf{V}_{O'}\, dm + \int_m \mathbf{V}_{O'} \cdot \mathbf{\Omega} \times \mathbf{R}'\, dm + \tfrac{1}{2}\int_m (\mathbf{\Omega} \times \mathbf{R}') \cdot (\mathbf{\Omega} \times \mathbf{R}')dm.$$

In each integral $\mathbf{V}_{O'}$ and $\mathbf{\Omega}$ are independent of dm; thus we have, after simplifying the last integral in a manner used before in Secs. 8.4 and 8.9,

$$\text{(9.22)} \qquad \text{k.e.} = \tfrac{1}{2}mv_{O'}^2 + \mathbf{V}_{O'} \cdot \mathbf{\Omega} \times \int_m \mathbf{R}'\, dm + \tfrac{1}{2}i_{O'}\omega^2,$$

where $i_{O'}$ is the moment of inertia about an axis parallel to $\mathbf{\Omega}$ and through $\mathbf{O}'$. We shall apply this in turn to a few important special cases.

Case I. *Instantaneous Rotation with One Fixed Point.* Pick **O**′ as the fixed point. (If a whole axis is fixed, it may be any point on the axis.) Then $\mathbf{V}_{O'} = \mathbf{O}$, yielding

$$\text{k.e.} = \tfrac{1}{2}i\omega^2. \tag{9.23}$$

Using (8.31), one may easily show that for coordinate axes instantaneously coinciding with principal axes of inertia, (9.23) may be rewritten

$$\text{k.e.} = \tfrac{1}{2}i_x\omega_x^2 + \tfrac{1}{2}i_y\omega_y^2 + \tfrac{1}{2}i_z\omega_z^2. \tag{9.24}$$

The details are left as an exercise.

Case II. *Translation.* Pick **O**′ as a point of the body. Since $\mathbf{\Omega} = \mathbf{O}$, we have

$$\text{k.e.} = \tfrac{1}{2}mv^2. \tag{9.25}$$

Case III. *Plane Motion in Terms of Instantaneous Center.* Pick **O**′ as the instantaneous center **C**. Then $\mathbf{V}_{O'} = \mathbf{O}$, giving

$$\text{k.e.} = \tfrac{1}{2}i_C\omega^2. \tag{9.26}$$

Case IV. *Any Motion in Terms of an Arbitrary* **O**′. Let **O**′ be any point of the body. The integral in the middle term of (9.22) may be appraised:

$$\int_m \mathbf{R}'\,dm = m\bar{\mathbf{R}}'.$$

($\bar{\mathbf{R}}'$ is the vector from **O**′ to the center of mass.) Now (9.22) may be rewritten

$$\text{k.e.} = \tfrac{1}{2}mv_{O'}^2 + \tfrac{1}{2}i_{O'}\omega^2 + m\mathbf{\Omega} \times \bar{\mathbf{R}}' \cdot \mathbf{V}_{O'}. \tag{9.27}$$

Case V. *Any Motion in Terms of the Center of Mass.* Pick **O**′ as the center of mass $\bar{\mathbf{R}}$. Then the integral $\int \mathbf{R}'\,dm$ is equal to zero. Thus

$$\text{k.e.} = \tfrac{1}{2}m\bar{v}^2 + \tfrac{1}{2}\bar{i}\omega^2. \tag{9.28}$$

This clear-cut separation of the kinetic energy of a rigid body into a translational term [analogous to (9.25)] and a rotational term [analogous to (9.23)] is quite in line with the discussions of Sec. 8.11. The corresponding result for work was given in Exercise 5, Sec. 9.2.

EXERCISES

1. Compute the kinetic energy of a 2-lb 2-in. uniform sphere rolling without slipping at 2 ft/sec (*a*) using (9.26); (*b*) using (9.28).

2. A uniform rod 2 m long rotates at 3 rad/sec about a perpendicular axis 40 cm from one end. Compute the kinetic energy (*a*) using (9.23); (*b*) using (9.27), with **O**′ as an end of the rod (do it once for each end); (*c*) using (9.28).

3. A skidding 30-in. 40-lb wheel rotates at 40 rad/sec while traveling at 30 ft/sec. If the radius of gyration about the axis of the wheel is 12 in., what is the kinetic energy?

4. What solids of revolution have, for rolling without slipping, rotational kinetic energy which is 40, 50, and 100 per cent of the translational kinetic energy?

5. A car door weighing 60 lb, 2 ft by 4 ft, closes at 0.8 rad/sec while the car advances at 45 mph. The hinges are at the forward edge of the door. Compute the kinetic energy of the door for the moment when it is open at a 45° angle.

6. A rigid body moves with one point fixed. Instantaneously, the axis of rotation has direction cosines l, m, and n. (a) Derive an expression for the kinetic energy in terms of $\omega_x, \omega_y, \omega_z, i_x, i_y, i_z, i_{yz}, i_{zx}, i_{xy}$. (b) Verify (9.24).

9.6. Work-Energy Problems for a Rigid Body. Regarding the rigid body, as usual, as merely an aggregate of particles where the members are very firmly linked, we may apply (9.19)

$$\text{Total work} = \Delta(\text{k.e.}). \tag{9.29}$$

Sections 9.1 and 9.2 have provided us with ways of computing work and Sec. 9.5 has given us ways of computing the kinetic energy. We can now illustrate the practical combination of these ideas.

Example 1. How far must a cylindrical shell roll without slipping down a plane inclined at 20° in order to attain a speed of 10 ft/sec?

SOLUTION. The kinetic energy is, since $\bar{v} = r\omega$, $\bar{p} = r$,

$$\text{k.e.} = \tfrac{1}{2}m\bar{v}^2 + \tfrac{1}{2}\bar{i}\omega^2 = m\bar{v}^2.$$

The only work done is by gravity:

$$\text{Work} = wh = mgs \sin \theta,$$

where s is the distance traveled along the plane and θ its inclination to the horizontal. Equating work and energy,

$$s = \frac{\bar{v}^2}{g \sin \theta}$$

or

$$s = \frac{100}{32.2 \times \sin 20°} = 9.1 \text{ ft}.$$

The work-energy relationship was originally obtained in Sec. 9.3 by integrating the equation $\mathbf{F} = m\mathbf{A}$. We shall now obtain some special results by integrating separately the equations of motion already derived for rigid bodies.

Translational Energy of a Rigid Body. In the case of a rigid body, we know already that

$$\Sigma \mathbf{F} = m\bar{\mathbf{A}}.$$

Multiplying by $d\bar{\mathbf{R}}$ and integrating, using the substitution

$$\bar{\mathbf{A}} \cdot d\bar{\mathbf{R}} = \bar{\mathbf{V}} \cdot d\bar{\mathbf{V}},$$

$$\sum \int_{\bar{\mathbf{R}}_0}^{\bar{\mathbf{R}}_1} \mathbf{F} \cdot d\bar{\mathbf{R}} = m \int_{\bar{\mathbf{V}}_0}^{\bar{\mathbf{V}}_1} \bar{\mathbf{V}} \cdot d\bar{\mathbf{V}} = \tfrac{1}{2}m\bar{v}_1^2 - \tfrac{1}{2}m\bar{v}_0^2. \tag{9.30}$$

This shows that by assigning all external forces and all mass to the center of mass of a body we may deal with translational energies quite apart from rotation.

Example 2. Consider, for instance, as in Fig. 9.20 a solid of revolution of radius r rolling and slipping down a plane inclined at an angle ϕ. After a linear displacement s the linear speed is $\bar{v}$. If the initial linear speed was zero, the translational-energy equation is

$$(w \sin \phi - f)s = \tfrac{1}{2}m\bar{v}^2.$$

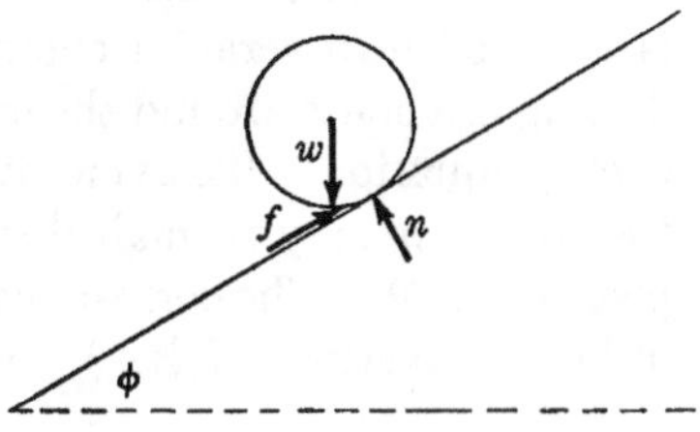

FIG. 9.20.

Rotational Energy of a Rigid Body in Plane Motion. A rigid body in motion parallel to the xy plane satisfies

$$\Sigma\gamma_z = \bar{\imath}_z\alpha.$$

Multiplying by $d\theta$ and integrating,

$$\sum \int_{\theta_0}^{\theta_1} \gamma_z \, d\theta = \bar{\imath}_z \int_{\omega_0}^{\omega_1} \omega \, d\omega = \tfrac{1}{2}\bar{\imath}_z\omega_1^2 - \tfrac{1}{2}\bar{\imath}_z\omega_0^2. \tag{9.31}$$

This shows that by considering rotational motion about an axis through the center of mass perpendicular to the plane of motion, we may deal with rotational energies quite apart from translation. It should be emphasized that the sum of (9.30) and (9.31) member by member is merely a form of (9.29).

Example 3. Referring to the body in Fig. 9.20 again, if initially the angular speed is zero and if it is ω after an angular displacement of θ, then the rotational-energy equation is

$$fr\theta = \tfrac{1}{2}\bar{\imath}\omega^2.$$

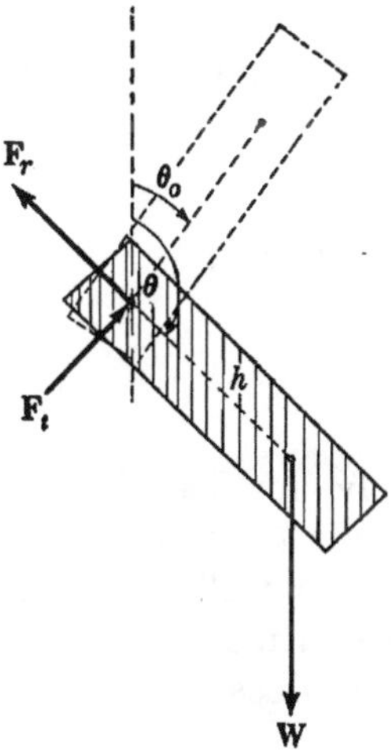

FIG. 9.21.

Example 4. *Bearing Reactions for a Physical Pendulum.* A physical pendulum is released from rest at an angle θ_0 with the vertical. Express the angular speed in terms of the angle θ. Investigate the bearing reaction.

SOLUTION. The center of mass travels along a circle of radius h (see Fig. 9.21). The work done by gravity is

$$\text{Work} = wh(\cos \theta_0 - \cos \theta).$$

The kinetic energy is

$$\text{k.e.} = \frac{1}{2}\,i\omega^2 = \frac{1}{2}\frac{w}{g}(\bar{p}^2 + h^2)\omega^2.$$

We conclude then

$$\omega^2 = \frac{2gh}{\bar{p}^2 + h^2} (\cos \theta_0 - \cos \theta).$$

Note that ω is maximum when $\cos \theta = -1$, or when $\theta = 180°$, as would be expected. For convenience, the bearing reaction force in Fig. 9.21 is resolved into a radial component $\mathbf{F}_r$ and a transverse component $\mathbf{F}_t$. Taking moments around the center of mass, we can get a rotational work-energy equation. To avoid difficult work integrations, one may evaluate the work for only a small displacement. Here let us allow a small displacement $d\theta$. The corresponding work done by $\mathbf{F}_t$ is $f_t h\, d\theta$. The change in kinetic energy is $d(\frac{1}{2}\bar{\imath}\omega^2)$. Our rotational equation is then

$$f_t h\, d\theta = d\left(\frac{1}{2}\bar{\imath}\omega^2\right) = \bar{\imath}\omega\, d\omega = \frac{w}{g}\bar{p}^2 \left[\frac{gh}{\bar{p}^2 + h^2} \sin \theta\, d\theta\right].$$

Hence

$$f_t = w\left[\frac{\bar{p}^2}{\bar{p}^2 + h^2}\right] \sin \theta.$$

The magnitude of $\mathbf{F}_r$ may be computed easily by using radial components of $\Sigma\mathbf{F} = m\bar{\mathbf{A}}$:

$$f_r + w \cos \theta = \frac{w}{g}\omega^2 h.$$

Since ω^2 has already been found for any θ, the computation is immediate. A similar approach might have been used for finding f_t. In the above computation of f_t, differentials were used. Some students will take more comfort in an approach based on derivatives. It is easy to show that the work-energy equation is equivalent to

$$\text{Power} = \frac{d}{dt}\,(\text{k.e.}) \tag{9.32}$$

(Exercise 1, Sec. 9.3). In the rotational aspect of this example we have (relative to the center of mass)

$$\text{Power} = f_t h\omega.$$

$$\frac{d}{dt}\left(\frac{1}{2}\bar{\imath}\omega^2\right) = \frac{1}{2}\bar{\imath}\frac{d}{dt}\left[\frac{2gh}{\bar{p}^2 + h^2}(\cos \theta_0 - \cos \theta)\right];$$

so

$$\frac{d}{dt}\,(\text{k.e.}) = \frac{\bar{\imath}gh}{\bar{p}^2 + h^2} \sin \theta \frac{d\theta}{dt}.$$

Now using (9.32), canceling ω and $d\theta/dt$, we can solve for f_t as before.

Example 5. A spool of mass m, moment of inertia $\bar{\imath}$, outer radius r, and inner radius r' rolls on a horizontal plane without slipping when pulled with a horizontal force $\mathbf{P}$ acting at the upper surface of the inner circumference as in Fig. 9.22. What angular speed does it acquire in turning through an angle θ? How large may **P** be without causing slipping?

SOLUTION. For no slipping, only **P** actually does work. We shall, however, first write the rotation and translation equations separately.

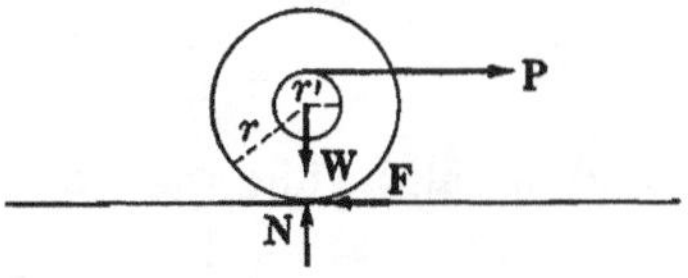

FIG. 9.22.

Rotation: $(pr' + fr)\theta = \frac{1}{2}\bar{\imath}\omega^2.$
Translation: $(p - f)r\theta = \frac{1}{2}m\bar{v}^2$
$= \frac{1}{2}mr^2\omega^2.$

Adding the two, we get the over-all energy equation:

$$p(r + r')\theta = \tfrac{1}{2}mr^2\omega^2 + \tfrac{1}{2}\bar{\imath}\omega^2.$$

This may be solved for ω^2:

$$\omega^2 = \frac{2p(r + r')\theta}{mr^2 + \bar{\imath}}.$$

Now eliminate θ and ω^2. This may be done, for instance, by dividing the rotation equation by the translation equation, member by member. Solving the result for p,

$$p = f\left[\frac{\bar{\imath} + mr^2}{\bar{\imath} - mrr'}\right].$$

The maximum value for f is $\mu w = \mu mg$; thus p may, without causing slipping, have any value less than

$$\mu mg\left[\frac{\bar{\imath} + mr^2}{\bar{\imath} - mrr'}\right].$$

Example 6. A 20-ft ladder rests against a vertical wall with its base on horizontal ice. Initially a rope from base to wall holds it at an angle $\theta_0 = 20°$ with the vertical. The rope breaks and the ladder slides in a vertical plane. Neglecting all friction, find

a. The angular speed at the moment when the ladder ceases to touch the wall.

b. The angular speed as the ladder strikes the ice.

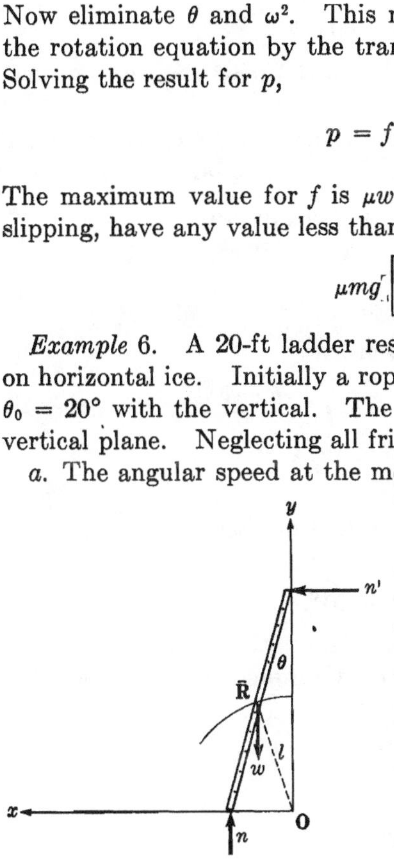

FIG. 9.23.

SOLUTION. *a*. We shall assume that the ladder can be treated as a uniform bar of length $2l$ and mass m. As long as the ladder is in contact with both the horizontal and vertical surfaces, its center of mass describes a circle of radius l (see Fig. 9.23) and we may write $\bar{v} = l\omega$. For any position θ,

$$\text{Work} = wl(\cos\theta_0 - \cos\theta),$$

and

$$\text{k.e.} = \tfrac{1}{2}m\bar{v}^2 + \tfrac{1}{2}\bar{I}\omega^2 = \tfrac{1}{2}ml^2\omega^2 + \tfrac{1}{6}ml^2\omega^2.$$

Equating the two, we get

$$\omega^2 = \frac{3g}{2l}(\cos\theta_0 - \cos\theta).$$

This is valid while the ladder touches the wall. The moment when the ladder leaves the wall can be identified as the moment when the normal reaction n' becomes zero or as the moment when the horizontal component of $\bar{v}$ becomes a maximum. Now (see Fig. 9.24)

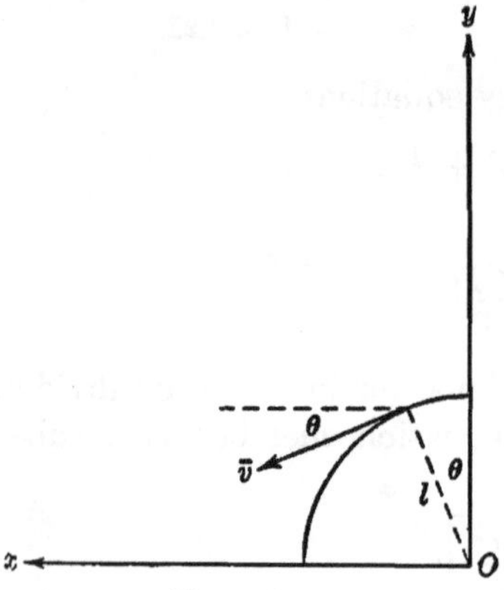

FIG. 9.24.

$$\bar{v}_x = \bar{v}\cos\theta = \omega l\cos\theta;$$

thus

$$\bar{v}_x^2 = \omega^2 l^2 \cos^2\theta$$
$$= \frac{3gl}{2}(\cos^2\theta\cos\theta_0 - \cos^3\theta).$$

Differentiating with respect to θ and setting the result equal to zero, we have

$$\cos\theta\sin\theta\,(-2\cos\theta_0 + 3\cos\theta) = 0.$$

The maximum comes then for

$$\cos\theta = \tfrac{2}{3}\cos\theta_0.$$

The corresponding angular speed is given by

$$\omega^2 = \frac{3g}{2l}\left(\cos\theta_0 - \frac{2}{3}\cos\theta_0\right) = \frac{g\cos\theta_0}{2l}.$$

For the values given in this example,

$$\omega = \sqrt{\frac{(32.2)(0.94)}{20}} = 1.23 \text{ rad/sec}$$

at

$$\theta = \cos^{-1}\left(\tfrac{2}{3}\cos\theta_0\right) = 51°.$$

To check on the angle at which the ladder leaves the wall, let us evaluate n' in terms of θ. First we determine α by differentiating the equation for ω^2 with respect to t.

$$2\omega\alpha = \frac{3g}{2l}\sin\theta\,\omega,$$

or

$$\alpha = \frac{3g}{4l}\sin\theta.$$

Now taking x components of $\Sigma\mathbf{F} = m\bar{\mathbf{A}}$, we have (see Fig. 9.25)

$$n' = \frac{w}{g}(\alpha l \cos\theta - \omega^2 l \sin\theta).$$

Substituting values for α and ω^2, we get

$$n' = \frac{3w}{4}\sin\theta\,(3\cos\theta - 2\cos\theta_0).$$

For the θ found above where $\cos\theta = \frac{2}{3}\cos\theta_0$, we have $n' = 0$, as was expected.

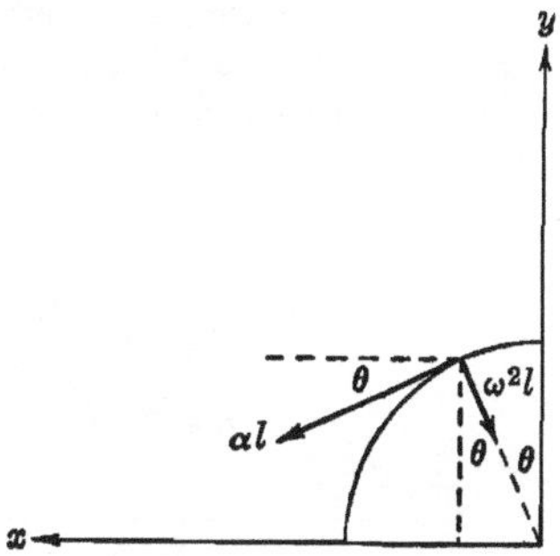

FIG. 9.25.

b. Once the ladder is free of the wall (after $\theta = 51°$), we have a new dynamical setup (see Fig. 9.26). Only the forces n and w now act. Our initial conditions for the new problem are $\theta_1 = 51°$, $\omega_1 = 1.23$ rad/sec.

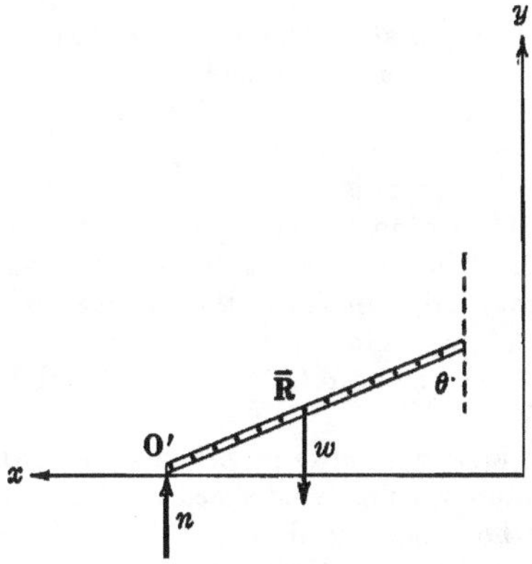

FIG. 9.26.

Also

$$\bar{v}_{x_1} = (1.23)(10)(\cos 51°) = 7.7 \text{ ft/sec},$$
$$\bar{v}_{y_1} = -(1.23)(10)(\sin 51°) = -9.6 \text{ ft/sec}.$$

Since there is no horizontal force, $\bar{v}_x$ remains constant. Since $\mathbf{V}_{O'}$ is horizontal, we conclude from

$$\bar{\mathbf{V}} = \mathbf{V}_{O'} + \mathbf{\Omega} \times (\mathbf{O'\bar{R}})$$

that

$$\bar{v}_y = -\omega l \sin\theta.$$

For the remaining displacement, $\theta = 51°$ to $\theta = 90°$, we have

$$\text{Work} = wl\cos\theta_1,$$
$$\Delta\,\text{k.e.} = \tfrac{1}{2}m(\bar{v}^2 - \bar{v}_1^2) + \tfrac{1}{2}\bar{I}(\omega^2 - \omega_1^2),$$

or

$$\Delta\,\text{k.e.} = \tfrac{1}{2}m\omega^2 l^2 \sin^2 90° - \tfrac{1}{2}m(9.6)^2 + \tfrac{1}{2}\bar{I}(\omega^2 - \omega_1^2)$$

(replacing $\bar{v}^2 - \bar{v}_1^2$ by $\bar{v}_y^2 - \bar{v}_{y_1}^2$, since the x component is constant). Equating work to energy change,

$$mgl\cos\theta_1 = \tfrac{1}{2}m\omega^2 l^2 - \tfrac{1}{2}m(9.6)^2 + \tfrac{1}{6}m\omega^2 l^2 - \tfrac{1}{6}ml^2(1.23)^2.$$

From this we compute ω as 2.0 rad/sec.

EXERCISES

1. A semicircular track of radius 6 in. is set up in a vertical plane. A 1-in. steel ball bearing is placed on the track at a point where its tangent is inclined at 45°. It rolls without slipping. What is the maximum linear speed?

2. A wheel of mass m, radius r, and radius of gyration p is set to roll on its axle (radius r') down a plane inclined at θ (see Fig. 9.27). No slipping takes place. Find the angular speed acquired in a displacement s along the plane.

FIG. 9.27.

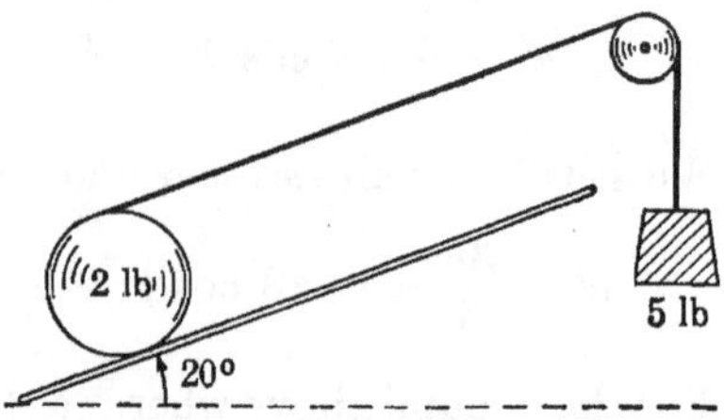

FIG. 9.28.

3. A 2-lb homogeneous cylinder of radius 2 in. is drawn up a plane inclined at 20° by a tape wrapped around it and passing over a light frictionless pulley to a 5-lb weight (see Fig. 9.28). Assuming that the cylinder does not slip, what speed has it acquired after moving 2 ft?

4. A wheel is caused to rotate about its fixed horizontal axis by a light flexible cord wrapped around the axle of the wheel and attached to a 640-lb load. The moment of inertia of the wheel is 2 slug-ft². The radius of the axle is 2 in. If the 640-lb load descends from rest a distance of 10 ft, its speed becomes how great?

5. A flexible chain 10 m long of linear density 0.5 kg/m is wound around a uniform solid cylinder of mass 5.0 kg and radius 20 cm. The cylinder is equipped with bearings so that it can rotate about its horizontal axis. The bearing friction constitutes a constant torque of 0.40 newton-m impeding rotation. Initially, the cylinder is at rest and the unwound portion of the chain is 1 m long. How fast will the cylinder be rotating after 5 m of the chain is unwound (*i.e.*, when the total portion unwound is 5 m), if the chain does not slip on the cylinder?

6. A wheel of radius r, radius of gyration p, and mass m is propelled by an axial couple of moment γ. If it starts from rest and does not slip, what speed will it acquire after a displacement s? How large may γ be without causing slipping if the coefficient of friction is μ?

7. A uniform rod weighing 20 lb is pivoted about a point 2 ft from its center. The length of the rod is 8 ft. The rod, initially at rest in a horizontal position, is released and swings freely about the pivot. After it has moved through an angle of 30°, what are the vertical and horizontal components of the bearing reactions?

8. A uniform bar 16 ft long and weighing 40 lb is pivoted about a horizontal axis at a point 4 ft from the center. If it falls from rest when horizontal, find the radial and transverse components of the bearing reactions when the angle is 45°.

9. A 10-lb uniform disk 2 ft in diameter is pivoted about a normal horizontal axis at the circumference. It is released from rest at its highest position. What is the maximum speed attained? What is the bearing reaction when the diameter through the pivot is horizontal?

10. A uniform rod 3 ft long is placed with one end on a smooth horizontal table and it is allowed to fall from rest. Initially it is inclined at 60° with the horizontal. What is the speed of the center of mass at the moment when the rod becomes horizontal?

11. A uniform rod initially standing vertically on end on a horizontal table tips and falls. It does not slip until its inclination is 45°. What is the coefficient of friction?

12. A tripod consisting of three uniform legs 6 ft long hinged freely at the top is placed on perfectly smooth ice with the legs vertical. They slip outward, and the tripod flattens. With what speed does the top hit the ice?

13. A rigidly attached smooth post stands vertically on a laboratory table. Beside it is placed vertically a uniform rod a meter long. The top of the rod is hinged flexibly to a light ring which slides freely on the post. The bottom of the rod rests on the smooth table. The rod slips and falls, its ring sliding down the post. (*a*) At what angle of inclination does the ring withstand no force due to the rod? (*b*) At what angle of inclination does the rod cease to press down on the table?

14. A uniform 2-lb bar 12 in. long is held vertically at rest against the interior of a smooth sphere of radius 10 in. It is then released. When the upper end crosses the horizontal equator of the sphere, (*a*) what is the speed of the center? (*b*) what are the reaction forces at the ends?

15. An 8-ton trailer, uniformly loaded, is 40 ft by 10 ft wide. It is attached to a 4-ton tractor by a single central pivot. The tractor has brakes and chains for all wheels. The effective coefficient of friction is 0.4. The trailer has no chains; so

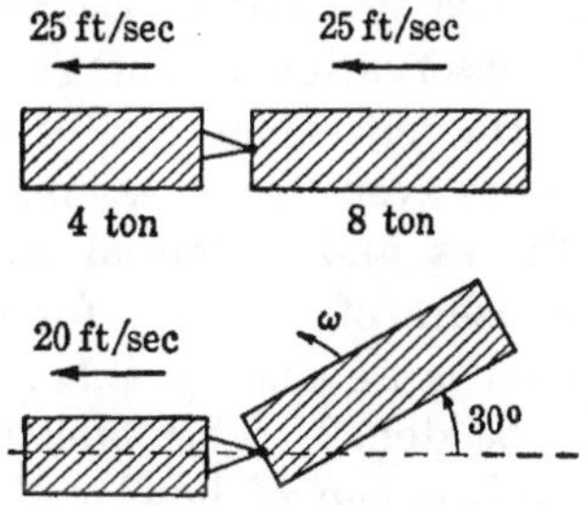

FIG. 9.29.

for it the friction is negligible. After riding steadily along a level icy road at 25 ft/sec, the tractor's brakes are locked with the result that the speed diminishes to 20 ft/sec while traveling 12 ft. The trailer, skidding, swings about its pivot, getting 30° out of line in the 12-ft displacement of the tractor (see Fig. 9.29). Find its angular speed at this moment. Assume that braking is maximum. Neglect lateral skidding of tractor.

CHAPTER 10

POTENTIAL ENERGY AND VIRTUAL WORK

In the last chapter energy was introduced as an adjunct of Newtonian mechanics. This same point of view will lead us in the present chapter to a conclusion concerning the conservation of mechanical energy. This result is a single special case of a principle which plays a dominant role in physics: the law of conservation of energy. According to this law, energy may change its form, but is neither created nor destroyed. Properly interpreted this applies even to nuclear reactions.

10.1. Conservative Forces and Potential Energy. Energy is sometimes described as a measure of capacity for doing work. Associated with a particle in motion is an energy $\frac{1}{2}mv^2$. In what sense can the particle cause work to be done? This question can be answered by considering the converse problem of how to deprive the particle of its energy. This can be accomplished by applying a suitable force to the particle and letting it do work. When the particle is brought to rest, the net work done by this force is, by the work-energy principle, equal to $-\frac{1}{2}mv^2$. But by the reaction postulate (3.1) we know that the force gave rise to an equal and opposite companion force. This force, exerted by the particle on whatever was stopping it, did work equal to $+\frac{1}{2}mv^2$. In this sense the kinetic energy is a precise appraisal of the work which the particle can stimulate.

A particle may also have a capacity for causing work to be done because of its position or state. An example is the driving weight of a "grandfather's clock." When the clock is wound, the weight is in such a position that the work of running the clock can be done. Such stored energy is usually called *potential energy.* In this case it is associated with the gravitational pull on the weight. In a spring clock a potential energy is stored in the spring: it is associated with the torque exerted by the spring. Energy may also be stored in electrical and magnetic as well as mechanical devices.

Not all forces can reasonably be thought of as generators of potential energy. Only forces which can do positive as well as negative work are suitable. That rules out frictional forces which cannot do positive work. Another necessary characteristic is uniqueness. If potential energy is to be a useful index of capacity to do work, each position or state of the body having the energy must correspond to a unique value of the potential energy, independent of the method of computation. The concept of *conservative force* will now be defined precisely. It will then be shown that such a force is suitable for use in discussions of potential energy.

Given a force **F**, defined for all positions which may be occupied by the particle or body under consideration, then **F** is said to be a *conservative force* if the net work done by it for a displacement around every closed path is zero. Two symbolic statements follow:

$$\int_{\mathbf{R}_0}^{\mathbf{R}_0} \mathbf{F} \cdot d\mathbf{R} = 0 \qquad \text{or} \qquad \oint \mathbf{F} \cdot d\mathbf{R} = 0. \tag{10.1}$$

A conservative force must satisfy our first criterion of being able to do positive as well as negative work. Since the net work is zero, there are only two alternatives: either it always does zero work or it does work of both signs. If it does zero work, it is of only trivial interest from the energy standpoint. An example of such a force is the normal reaction between a rolling object and an inclined plane. This kind of force is called a constraint. It clearly could not contribute to potential energy. If, on the other hand, a conservative force does negative work during part of a displacement, it must do positive work during another part in order that the net work be zero.

Example 1. Any constant force is conservative. For, as was shown in Example 4, Sec. 9.1, the work done by such a force is a multiple of the net displacement. (The net displacement for a closed path is obviously zero.) In particular, *weight* is a conservative force for any locality.

Example 2. An elastic force obeying a form of Hooke's law, $\mathbf{F} = -k\mathbf{R}$, is conservative. ($k$ is a constant.) For

$$\begin{aligned}\oint (-k\mathbf{R}) \cdot d\mathbf{R} &= \oint (-kr\mathbf{L}) \cdot (dr\,\mathbf{L} + r\,d\theta\,\mathbf{M}) \\ &= \oint -\,kr\,dr = -k\frac{r^2}{2}\bigg|_{r_0}^{r_0} = 0.\end{aligned}$$

Further examples will be investigated in Chap. 13.

We can now define potential energy for any conservative force. Let there be given a body or particle subjected to a conservative force **F**. Let **B** be designated as a base point or reference point. This choice is arbitrary; therefore in practice it is selected on the grounds of expediency. Then at position **R** the particle or body is said to possess by virtue of **F** *potential energy relative to* **B** equal to minus the work done by **F** in a displacement from **B** to **R**.

$$\text{p.e.} = -\int_{\mathbf{B}}^{\mathbf{R}} \mathbf{F} \cdot d\mathbf{R}. \tag{10.2}$$

We can now check on the second criterion for a suitable force: is the potential energy relative to **B** unique, or does it depend on the path taken from **B** to R? In Fig. 10.1 two routes for the displacement are shown.

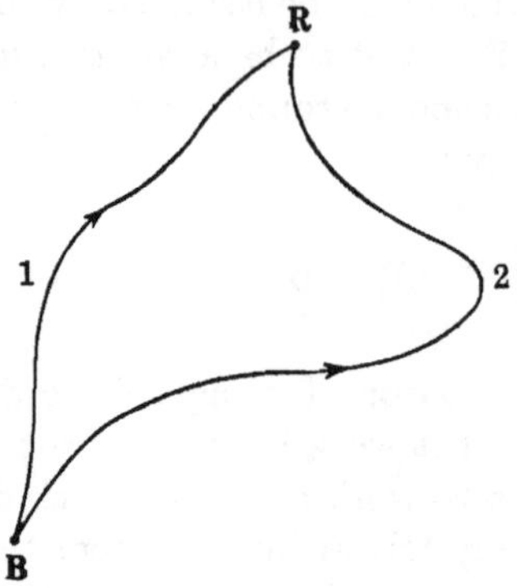

FIG. 10.1.

We need merely use (10.1) together with underlying properties of any integration to show that

$$(10.3) \qquad \int_{\mathbf{B}}^{\mathbf{R}} \mathbf{F} \cdot d\mathbf{R}_1 = \int_{\mathbf{B}}^{\mathbf{R}} \mathbf{F} \cdot d\mathbf{R}_2.$$

This follows from the identity

$$(10.4) \qquad \int_{\mathbf{B}}^{\mathbf{R}} \mathbf{F} \cdot d\mathbf{R} = - \int_{\mathbf{R}}^{\mathbf{B}} \mathbf{F} \cdot d\mathbf{R}$$

and the following form of (10.1):

$$(10.5) \qquad \int_{\mathbf{B}}^{\mathbf{R}} \mathbf{F} \cdot d\mathbf{R}_1 + \int_{\mathbf{R}}^{\mathbf{B}} \mathbf{F} \cdot d\mathbf{R}_2 = 0.$$

(The excursion **B-1-R-2-B** is a closed path.)

This result may be stated in more general terms:

(10.6) *The work done by a conservative force during a displacement from one point to another is independent of the path taken between these two points.*

Example 3. When the force in question is the weight of a body (or aggregate of particles), the potential energy is expressible in terms of the height of the center of mass above the level of the base point **B** (see Fig. 10.2).

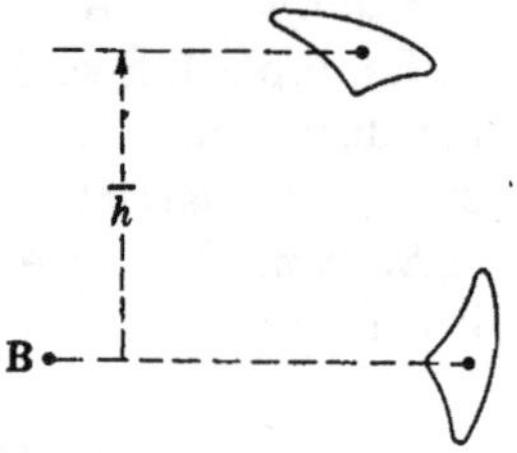

FIG. 10.2.

$$(10.7) \qquad \text{p.e.} = w\bar{h}.$$

This follows from (9.7).

Example 4. When the force is that of a spring obeying Hooke's law, with the base point at the unstretched position, the potential energy is given by

$$(10.8) \quad \text{p.e.} = - \int_{\mathbf{B}}^{\mathbf{R}} \mathbf{F} \cdot d\mathbf{R} = - \int_{\mathbf{B}}^{\mathbf{R}} (-k\mathbf{R}) \cdot d\mathbf{R} = \int_0^r kr\, dr = \tfrac{1}{2}kr^2.$$

EXERCISES

1. Compute $\oint \mathbf{F} \cdot d\mathbf{R}$ for the force of friction when a 10-lb object is constrained to slide around a circle of radius 10 in. on a horizontal table when the coefficient of friction is 0.4. The circuit is accomplished at uniform speed in 3 sec.

2. Show that Δ(p.e) is independent of the base point **B**.

3. An object hangs at the end of a vertical spring which obeys Hooke's law. Taking the equilibrium position as base point, find a formula for potential energy taking account of both gravity and spring.

4. A system of particles consists of n objects of masses $m_1, m_2, \ldots, m_n$. Show that the potential energy relative to gravity of the subsystem $m_1, m_2, \ldots, m_k$, plus the potential energy of the subsystem $m_{k+1}, m_{k+2}, \ldots, m_n$ is equal to the potential energy of the whole system.

10.2. Law of Conservation of Mechanical Energy. The concept of potential energy is primarily useful as a means of dodging explicit computation of work. Since the force is to be conservative, by (10.6) the work for a displacement as in Fig. 10.3 from $\mathbf{R}_0$ to $\mathbf{R}_1$ can be evaluated by changing the route to include $\mathbf{B}$.

$$\int_{\mathbf{R}_0}^{\mathbf{R}_1} \mathbf{F} \cdot d\mathbf{R} = \int_{\mathbf{R}_0}^{\mathbf{B}} \mathbf{F} \cdot d\mathbf{R} + \int_{\mathbf{B}}^{\mathbf{R}_1} \mathbf{F} \cdot d\mathbf{R},$$

or

$$\int_{\mathbf{R}_0}^{\mathbf{R}_1} \mathbf{F} \cdot d\mathbf{R} = (\text{p.e.})_0 - (\text{p.e.})_1, \tag{10.9}$$

that is,

$$\text{Work} = -\Delta(\text{p.e.}).$$

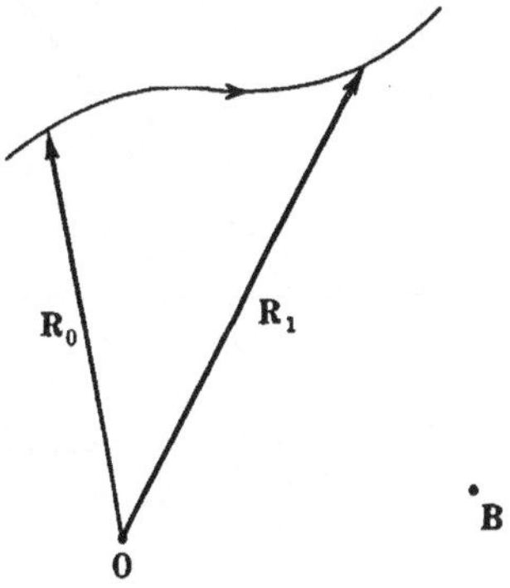

FIG. 10.3.

In words, we have shown that

(10.10) *The work done by a conservative force is equal to the loss in potential energy of the object on which the force acts.*

Example 1. A spring initially a foot long stretches an inch when a 2-lb force is applied. The constant k appearing in (10.8) is then $k = 24$ lb/ft. The potential energy formula then is

$$\text{p.e.} = 12r^2.$$

Let us now compute the work done by the spring as it contracts from 16 to 14 in.:

$$\text{Work} = 12(r_0^2 - r_1^2) = 12[(\tfrac{1}{3})^2 - (\tfrac{1}{6})^2] = 1 \text{ ft-lb}.$$

Let us now combine (10.9) with the work-energy principle:

$$\Delta(\text{k.e.}) = \text{work} = -\Delta(\text{p.e.}), \tag{10.11}$$

or

$$\Delta(\text{k.e.} + \text{p.e.}) = 0. \tag{10.12}$$

This is a symbolic statement of one of the best known propositions of mechanics:

(10.13) *If a particle, system of particles, or rigid body is subject to a conservative force only, then the sum of kinetic plus potential energies is a constant.*

This is immediately extended to the case where several conservative forces act in concert; then the potential energy is the sum of the separate potential energies.

Example 2. A bead slides from rest down a smooth curved wire (see Fig. 10.4) in the vertical xy plane from (x,y) ft to the origin. What speed does it have at the origin?

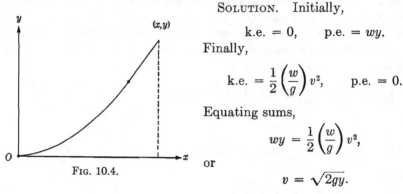

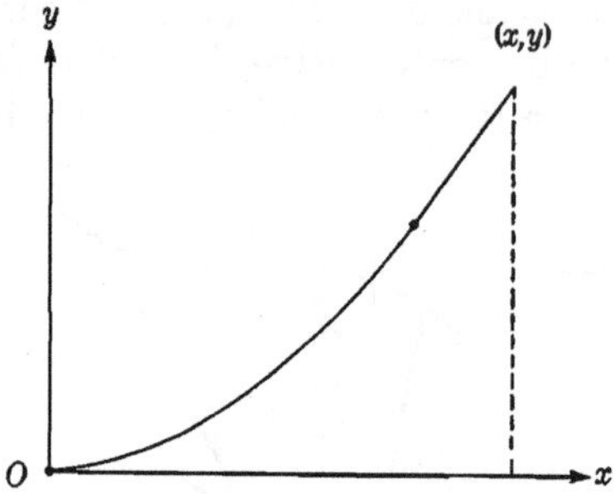

FIG. 10.4.

SOLUTION. Initially,

$$\text{k.e.} = 0, \qquad \text{p.e.} = wy.$$

Finally,

$$\text{k.e.} = \frac{1}{2}\left(\frac{w}{g}\right)v^2, \qquad \text{p.e.} = 0.$$

Equating sums,

$$wy = \frac{1}{2}\left(\frac{w}{g}\right)v^2,$$

or

$$v = \sqrt{2gy}.$$

Example 3. Equation (8.34) may be considered as an example of the conservation of energy.

EXERCISES

1. A ball bearing of radius 0.500 in. rolls without slipping down a curved chute through a vertical drop of 20 ft. What angular speed does it attain?

2. A uniform disk of diameter 68 cm and weight 7.2 newtons is free to oscillate as a physical pendulum about a horizontal axis normal to the disk through a point 34 cm from the center. What angular speed must the disk receive at its equilibrium position if it is to make a complete revolution?

3. A spool consists of two 1-lb disks of radius 9 in. joined at the center by a short light axle of radius $\frac{1}{4}$ in. A string is wound many times around the axle, its free end being tied to a hook on the ceiling. The spool is allowed to fall, the string unwinding as it falls. What angular speed is acquired after a fall of 8 ft?

4. A sphere of radius r is placed on the top of a rough stationary horizontal cylinder of radius r'. The sphere is released. It rolls without slipping, leaving the cylinder at a point whose angular distance from the top is ϕ. Find ϕ.

5. A "parabolic spring" has a characteristic given by

$$f = kx^2.$$

From what height h above the spring should an object of mass m be dropped onto the spring in order that the dynamic deflection so obtained will be twice the static deflection (obtained when the object is supported in equilibrium by the spring)?

10.3. Oscillations of a Rigid Body. In this section the methods developed thus far will be applied to the problem of oscillations of a rigid body. Usually these oscillations will be small and simple harmonic. Such problems may be attacked by the methods of Chap. 8, but energy methods will now be emphasized. One approach is to differentiate an energy equation to get an equation of motion which can be recognized as simple harmonic. This is a natural step, since our original energy equations were reached by integrating $\mathbf{F} = m\mathbf{A}$. This often involves approximations for small angles:

$$\sin\theta \to \theta. \tag{10.14}$$

Also

$$1 - \cos\theta = 2\sin^2\frac{\theta}{2} \to 2\left(\frac{\theta}{2}\right)^2 = \frac{\theta^2}{2};$$

thus

$$\cos\theta \to 1 - \frac{\theta^2}{2} \to 1. \tag{10.15}$$

Another approach is to assume that the motion is simple harmonic and then to determine the period τ by the property

$$\tau = \frac{2\pi(\text{amplitude})}{(\text{max speed})}. \tag{10.16}$$

This property is easily verified from the elementary theory of simple harmonic motion such as is given in Sec. 5.9.

Example 1. Let us first return to the cylindrical rod rolling in a cylindrical trough. The problem is to find the period of the oscillation.

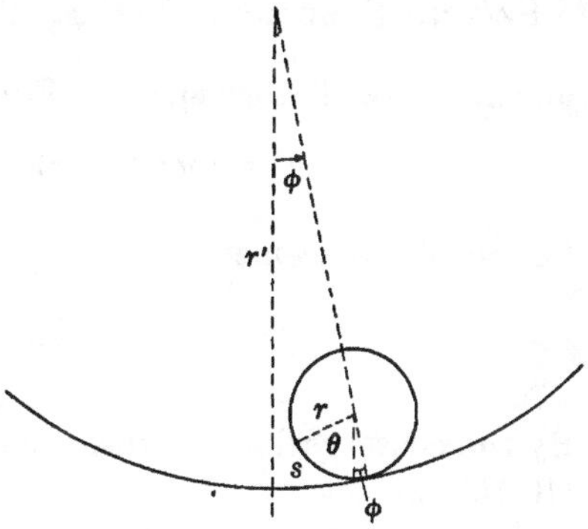

FIG. 10.5.

FIRST SOLUTION. Since $\theta = \frac{s}{r} - \phi$ (see Fig. 10.5) and $s = \phi r'$, we have

$$\omega = \left(\frac{r' - r}{r}\right)\frac{d\phi}{dt}.$$

The kinetic energy is easily expressed:

$$\text{k.e.} = \tfrac{1}{2}m\bar{v}^2 + \tfrac{1}{2}\bar{\imath}\omega^2.$$

Now

$$\bar{\imath} = \frac{1}{2}mr^2 \qquad \text{and} \qquad \bar{v} = (r' - r)\frac{d\phi}{dt};$$

thus

$$\text{k.e.} = \frac{1}{2}m\left[(r' - r)^2\left(\frac{d\phi}{dt}\right)^2 + \frac{1}{2}r^2\left(\frac{r' - r}{r}\right)^2\left(\frac{d\phi}{dt}\right)^2\right];$$

or

$$\text{k.e.} = \frac{3}{4}m(r' - r)^2\left(\frac{d\phi}{dt}\right)^2.$$

The potential energy relative to the lowest position is

$$\text{p.e.} = mg(r' - r)(1 - \cos \phi).$$

By the law of conservation of energy,

$$\frac{3}{4} m(r' - r)^2 \left[\frac{d\phi}{dt}\right]^2 + mg(r' - r)(1 - \cos \phi) = \text{const.}$$

Now differentiating with respect to t and dividing out common factors,

$$\frac{3}{2}(r' - r)\frac{d^2\phi}{dt^2} + g \sin \phi = 0.$$

For small oscillations, using (10.14), we have a simple harmonic motion of period

$$\tau = 2\pi \sqrt{\frac{3(r' - r)}{2g}}$$

as before (Example 6, Sec. 8.9).

SECOND SOLUTION. Let ϕ_m denote the amplitude and $\left[\frac{d\phi}{dt}\right]_m$ the maximum oscillatory speed. For maximum displacement,

$$\text{p.e.} = mg(r' - r)(1 - \cos \phi_m), \qquad \text{k.e.} = 0.$$

For zero displacement,

$$\text{p.e.} = 0, \qquad \text{k.e.} = \frac{3}{4} m(r' - r)^2 \left[\frac{d\phi}{dt}\right]_m^2.$$

By the conservation law these maximum values may be equated. Using (10.15), we get

$$g\left(\frac{\phi_m^2}{2}\right) = \frac{3}{4}(r' - r)\left[\frac{d\phi}{dt}\right]_m^2.$$

If this is rearranged in the shape of (10.16), we have

$$\tau = 2\pi \frac{\phi_m}{\left[\frac{d\phi}{dt}\right]_m} = 2\pi \sqrt{\frac{3(r' - r)}{2g}}.$$

Example 2. The center of mass of a weighted solid of revolution of radius r is at a distance h from its center. The radius of gyration about an axis through the center of mass is $\bar{\rho}$. When the solid is displaced slightly from equilibrium position on a horizontal plane surface, it oscillates. Find the period if there is no slipping.

FIRST SOLUTION. The potential energy (see Fig. 10.6) for the displaced position is (relative to the equilibrium position)

$$\text{p.e.} = mgh(1 - \cos\theta).$$

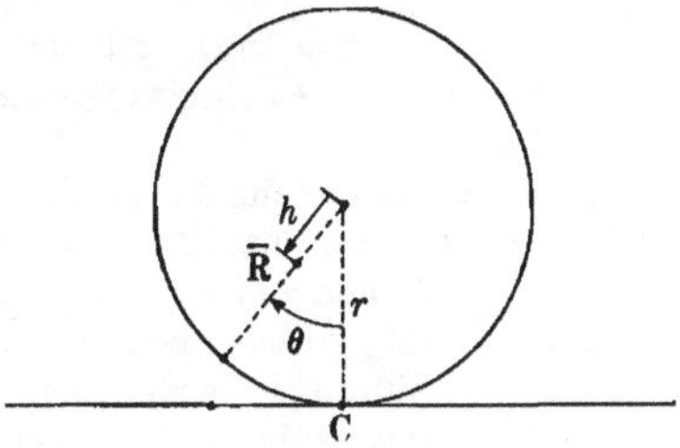

FIG. 10.6.

The kinetic energy may be computed with reference to the point of contact. The moment of inertia may be evaluated in terms of the distance $\bar{\mathbf{R}}\mathbf{C}$. Since θ is to be small, we shall use the approximate value $r - h$ for this distance:

$$\text{k.e.} = \tfrac{1}{2}m[\bar{p}^2 + (r - h)^2]\omega^2.$$

By the conservation law we have

$$\text{p.e.} + \text{k.e.} = mgh(1 - \cos\theta) + \tfrac{1}{2}m[\bar{p}^2 + (r - h)^2]\omega^2 = \text{const.}$$

Take the derivative with respect to time.

$$mgh\sin\theta\,\omega + m[\bar{p}^2 + (r - h)^2]\omega\frac{d^2\theta}{dt^2} = 0.$$

With $\sin\theta$ replaced by θ for small oscillations, we have simple harmonic motion of period

$$\tau = 2\pi\sqrt{\frac{\bar{p}^2 + (r - h)^2}{gh}}.$$

SECOND SOLUTION. For maximum displacement,

$$\text{p.e.} = mgh(1 - \cos\theta_m), \qquad \text{k.e.} = 0.$$

For zero displacement,

$$\text{p.e.} = 0, \qquad \text{k.e.} = \tfrac{1}{2}m[\bar{p}^2 + (r - h)^2]\omega_m^2.$$

Using the approximation $1 - \cos\theta_m = \frac{\theta_m^2}{2}$, we get for the conservation equation,

$$gh\theta_m^2 = [\bar{p}^2 + (r - h)^2]\omega_m^2.$$

From this we get as before

$$\tau = \frac{2\pi\theta_m}{\omega_m} = 2\pi\sqrt{\frac{\bar{p}^2 + (r - h)^2}{gh}}.$$

EXERCISES

1. A uniform cylindrical shell of radius r rests on a cylindrical surface of radius r'. Use the methods of this section to compute the period with which it will oscillate if no slipping takes place. Use both methods explicitly.

2. With what period will a bead oscillate at the bottom of a smooth vertical semicircular wire of radius r?

3. Half a solid uniform cylinder (*i.e.*, cross section is a semicircle) of radius r is placed on a concave cylindrical surface of radius r'. Compute the period with which it will rock.

4. A uniform rectangular plank 6 in. by 2 in. by 4 ft balances, wide face horizontal, across a cylinder of diameter 1 ft. Find the period of the tipping.

5. A 150-lb man and a 10-lb rocking chair have a center of mass 15 in. off the floor and a radius of gyration about an axis through the center of mass is also 15 in. If the radius of curvature of the rockers is 4 ft, what is the period of rocking?

6. With what period will the bar of Exercise 14, Sec. 9.6, oscillate about its equilibrium position?

7. A uniform bar of length d has at one end a screw eye through which passes a taut perfectly smooth horizontal wire. With what period will the bar oscillate (*a*) in the vertical plane including the wire? (*b*) in the vertical plane normal to the wire?

10.4. The Principle of Virtual Work. The concepts of work and energy can be very useful in statics problems. Suppose that we have given a system of interacting particles and rigid bodies. Each member of the system may be subject to three kinds of forces.

Internal Forces. These are, as before, forces of interaction between members. They occur in equal but opposite pairs. When the system is displaced, each pair may do work if the distance between the points of application can vary. For interconnections such as hinges, inextensible taut strings, and smooth sliding contacts the net work done by each such pair of forces is zero.

Constraints. A constraint is a force of interaction between a member of the system and an external object directly limiting the motion of the member. Constraints restrict the geometrical character of the motion of the system. Examples are the *normal* reaction of a wire on a bead which is constrained to slide on the wire, the force exerted by a hinge which binds a member of the system to an external object, forces exerted by bearings which constrain a rigid body to have one fixed axis. For a displacement of the system, a constraint does zero work, for it is always normal to the path of its point of application. Now the force of reaction between a member of the system and an external object may involve friction. Such a tangential component will be considered as a force in the next category.

Applied Forces. Applied forces are external forces other than constraints. They include pushes and pulls, weight, and frictional forces. An applied force may do and usually does do positive work when the system experiences a displacement.

If our system of interacting particles and rigid bodies is in static equilibrium, we naturally do not expect any work to be done. If there are no constraints, the system could, of course, be in a state of unaccelerated translation even when the forces are in equilibrium. In such a case, it would be possible to compute a rate of doing work, *i.e.*, the power, for each force. But we shall not be concerned with *actual* motion or actual work in this section. What is proposed is this: We shall *imagine* various possible sets of infinitesimal displacements of the parts of the system, taking care that we consider only displacements that do not violate the limitations imposed by the constraints. Such hypothetical displacements are usually called *virtual displacements.* The work which would be done by the forces, treated as constant, during such a virtual displacement is called *virtual work.*

Example 1. Consider the system in equilibrium shown in Fig. 10.7. A 100-lb load is hung at one end of a light bar. At a distance s from this end is a horizontal pivot At the other end, a distance s' from the pivot, is applied a force **F** normal to the bar. In this case certain constraints at the pivot ensure that the only possible motion of the bar is about one fixed axis. One virtual displacement consistent with the constraints for this system would be a small rotation in either direction. This would involve a displacement of the point of application of **F** equal to $s' \Delta\theta$ and in a direction opposite to **F**. The 100-lb object would have a displacement $s \Delta\theta$ in a direction making an angle θ with the vertical. The virtual work associated for this displacement with **F** is $-fs' \Delta\theta$; with **W**, it is $100s \cos \theta \, \Delta\theta$.

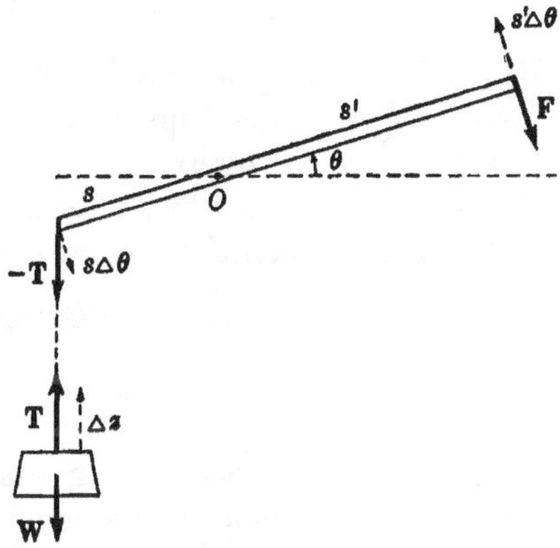

FIG. 10.7.

Let the system now be thought of as divided into small elements. When the system undergoes its displacement consistent with the constraints, a typical element has its displacement $\Delta\mathbf{R}_i$. We shall compute for each element the virtual work. Since for a single element the forces are concurrent, it is clear that, denoting internal forces by primes,

$$\Sigma\mathbf{F}_i \cdot \Delta\mathbf{R}_i + \Sigma\mathbf{F}'_i \cdot \Delta\mathbf{R}_i = \bar{\mathbf{F}}_i \cdot \Delta\mathbf{R}_i,$$

where $\bar{\mathbf{F}}_i$ is the resultant of all forces acting on the element. If the element is in equilibrium, then $\bar{\mathbf{F}}_i$ is equal to a null vector. Such an equation can be written for each element, and these equations may be added member by member. Internal forces involved in no expansion or contraction of the system do no *net* work. Similarly the constraints do no work. Our conclusion is this:

(10.17) *If a system of particles and rigid bodies is in equilibrium, the virtual work associated with the applied forces for any virtual displacement consistent with the constraints is zero.*

Internal forces involved in expansions or contractions must be treated here as applied forces.

Example 2. Referring again to Fig. 10.7, since the system is given in equilibrium, we conclude immediately that the sum of the virtual works is zero:

$$-fs'\,\Delta\theta + 100s\cos\theta\,\Delta\theta = 0;$$

thus

$$f = 100\frac{s}{s'}\cos\theta.$$

It should perhaps be noted that another type of virtual displacement is consistent with the constraints. The bar could be left fixed with the 100-lb load raised by an amount Δz. In this case work would be done by the internal tension (treated as constant) in the cord supporting the load. Call this **T**. Then the virtual work equation is

$$-100\Delta z + t\,\Delta z = 0;$$

or

$$t = 100 \text{ lb}.$$

Let us now consider the converse proposition. Suppose that for every set of virtual displacements consistent with the constraints, it turns out that the virtual work of the applied forces is zero. Is the system then in equilibrium? Suppose the contrary. Then acceleration takes place, and the system acquires kinetic energy. But the initial actual infinitesimal displacements are a perfectly good set of virtual displacements; thus by our hypothesis the net work is zero. By the work-energy principle then no kinetic energy may be acquired; thus the system is in equilibrium, contrary to our assumption. We conclude then:

(10.18) *If the virtual work associated with all possible virtual displacements (consistent with the constraints) of a system of particles and rigid bodies is zero, then the system must be in equilibrium.*

One of the advantages of this criterion for equilibrium is that only the applied forces have to be studied. The constraints or "hidden forces" as they used to be called can be ignored.

Example 3. A freely jointed symmetrical framework such as is shown in Fig. 10.8 is supported at A and withstands a force **W** at the other end. The frame is maintained in rigid form because of a crossbar BD. The problem is to find the force exerted by the strut BD.

SOLUTION. As the problem stands, there are no useful displacements consistent with the constraints. We remedy this by imagining that the strut BD is removed, the frame being kept in place by forces of magnitude f at B and D. From the geometry of the situation, the point of application of $\mathbf{W}$ is given by

$$y = 8d \cos \theta$$

and the point D is given by

$$x = d \sin \theta.$$

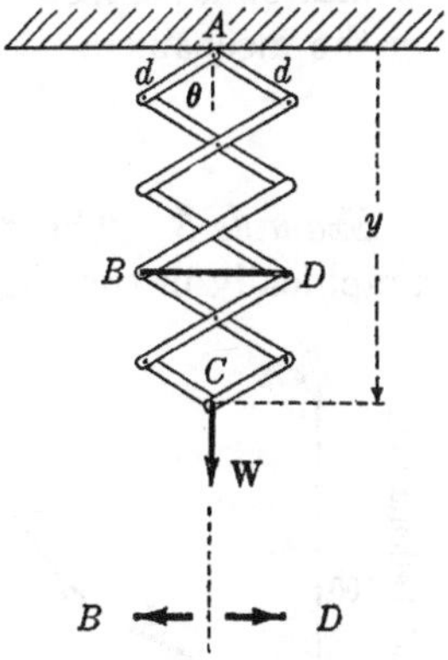

FIG. 10.8.

B is symmetrically located. For our virtual displacement, let x be increased by Δx. The corresponding change in y is Δy. The total virtual work is expressible as

$$w \,\Delta y + 2f \,\Delta x = 0.$$

A relationship between Δy and Δx can be obtained by finding dy and dx in terms of $d\theta$:

$$\Delta y = dy = -8d \sin \theta \, d\theta$$
$$\Delta x = dx = d \cos \theta \, d\theta$$

which gives

$$w(-8d \sin \theta \, d\theta) + 2f(d \cos \theta \, d\theta) = 0.$$

Hence

$$f = 4w \tan \theta.$$

The principle of virtual work is most impressive when dealing with hidden or complex mechanisms where frictional effects are negligible.

Example 4. Consider, for instance, a set of scales for weighing express packages. The inner mechanism is concealed, but it presumably consists of levers and pivots. The forces then are constraints. If when the platform is depressed a millimeter the beam is raised 50 mm, what force on the beam will provide equilibrium when a 160-lb man steps on the platform? Here, aside from the constraints, only two forces are involved. The weights of various parts of the mechanism are already balanced; therefore the sum of their virtual works will be zero for any suitable virtual displacement. The two remaining forces have virtual displacements which are in a ratio depending on the geometry of the mechanism. Writing the work equation as

$$f_1 \,\Delta y_1 + 160 \Delta y_2 = 0,$$

we can express the original evidence as

$$\Delta y_1 = -50 \Delta y_2.$$

From the two equations we compute f_1 as 3.2 lb.

The ratio of displacements might be available as the slope, at a particular point, of a curve which is a summary of the characteristic geometry of the mechanism.

$$\frac{\Delta y_1}{\Delta y_2} = \frac{dy_1}{dy_2}.$$

Example 5. The displacement geometry of a wire cutter is recorded graphically in the Fig. 10.9. What is the minimum force which will be exerted at the knife when a force of 60 lb is used on the handle?

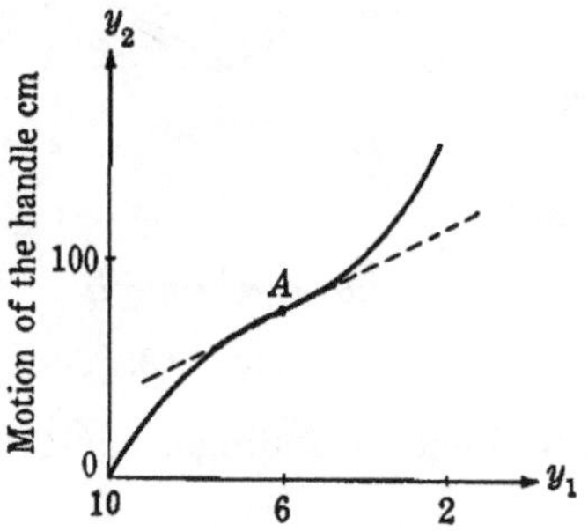

FIG. 10.9.

SOLUTION. The knife force is smallest for a fixed applied force when the slope is minimum. This occurs at A, and is numerically about $\frac{4}{9}$. Allowing for the difference in scales,

$$-\frac{dy_2}{dy_1} = \frac{4}{9} \times \frac{20 \text{ cm}}{(2.54 \text{ cm/in.})(\frac{1}{16} \text{ in.})} = 56.$$

From this ratio the virtual work equation yields

$$f_2 = 56 \times 60 = 3{,}360 \text{ lb}.$$

EXERCISES

Use the principle of virtual work in solving:

1. A beam 20 ft long, weighing 100 lb, hinged at the base, center of mass 8 ft from the base, is held at an angle of 20° with the horizontal by a horizontal rope through the upper end. Find the tension in the rope.

2. Referring to Fig. 10.10, find the force in BD if A is a fixed point and the force at D is normal to AD. (The figure represents a vertical plane.)

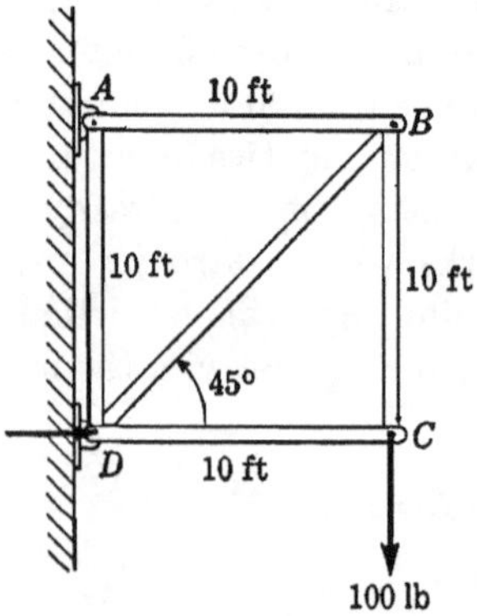

FIG. 10.10.

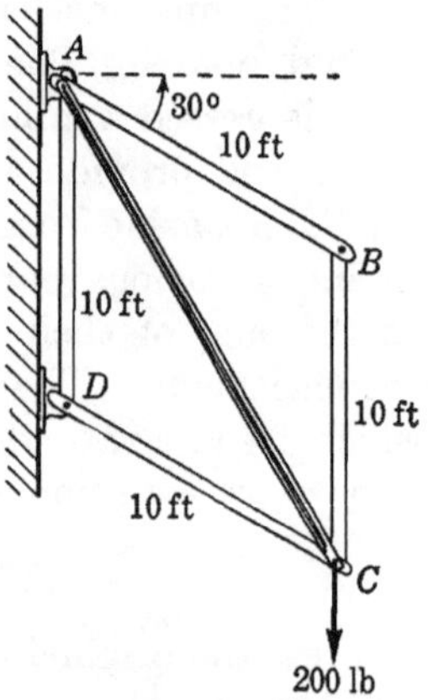

FIG. 10.11.

3. Referring to Fig. 10.11, find the force in AC if A is a fixed point and the force at D is normal to AD. (The figure represents a vertical plane.)

4. Find the tension in the support AB of the stepladder shown in Fig. 10.12. The floor is smooth.

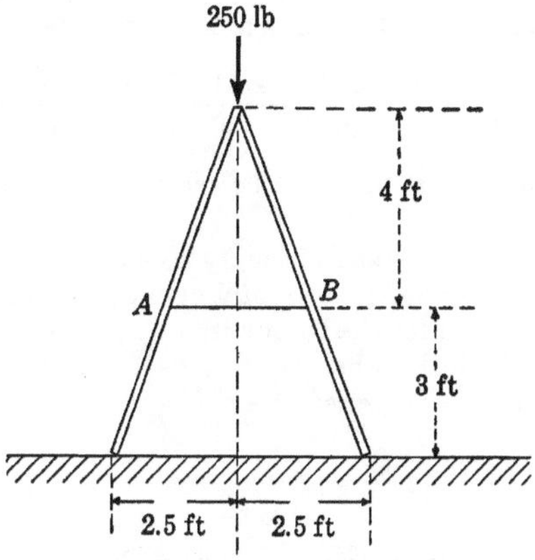

FIG. 10.12.

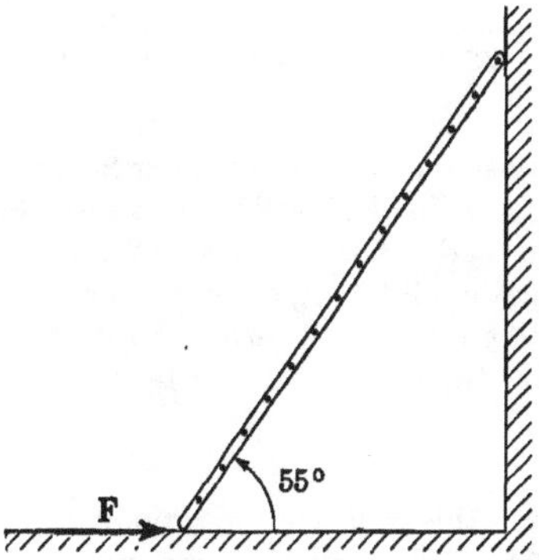

FIG. 10.13.

5. In Fig. 10.13 the floor is rough. The ladder is 20 ft long and uniform. It weighs 70 lb. The ladder is in equilibrium. Find the frictional force **F**. Assume that the wall is smooth.

6. Four 6-ft rods are hinged smoothly to form a rhombus $ABCD$ as in Fig. 10.14. Rod AD is fixed in a horizontal position. Angle BAD is 60°. A 500-lb load is attached at C. A strut DB keeps the frame rigid. Neglecting the weights of the frame, find the force exerted by the strut DB.

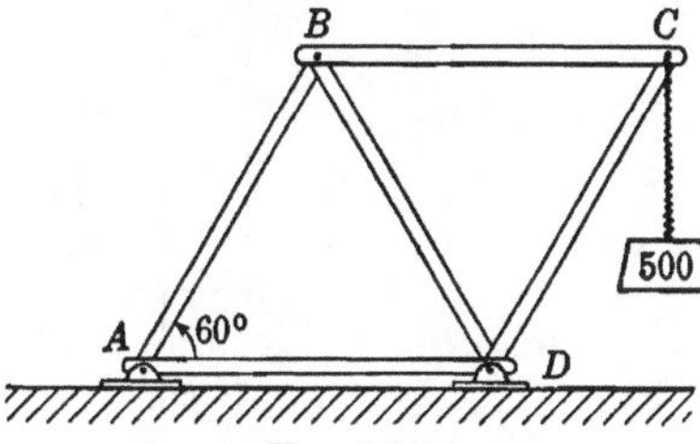

FIG. 10.14.

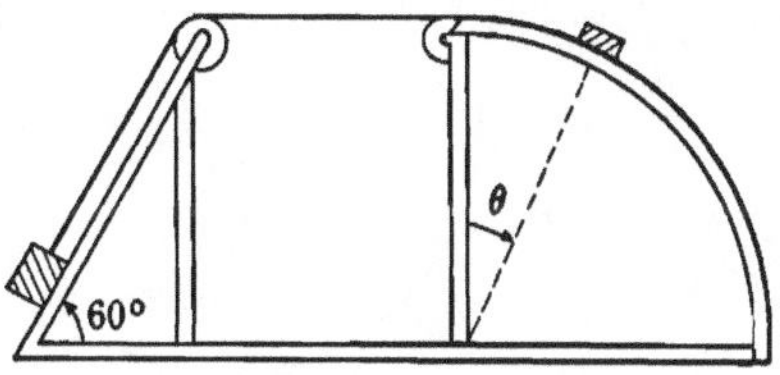

FIG. 10.15.

7. Frictionless pulleys are attached to the tops of two smooth tracks, one of which is plane and inclined at an angle of 60° while the other is cylindrical (see Fig. 10.15). A cord passes over the pulleys and between two objects which slide on the tracks The object on the plane weighs 0.5 lb; that on the cylinder weighs 1 lb. The radius of the cylinder drawn to the second object makes an angle θ with the vertical. Find the value of θ for which the system is in equilibrium.

8. Solve Exercise 5, Sec. 4.9.

9. Solve Exercise 11, Sec. 4.9.

10. Solve Exercise 13, Sec. 4.9.

11. The knife of a metal shear (see Fig. 10.16) is driven by the vertical displacement

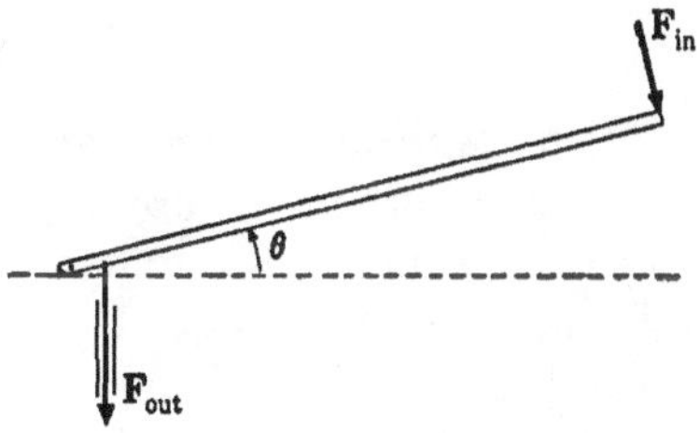

FIG. 10.16.

of a pin set rigidly in the 18-in. handle 1 in. from the center of the pivot. The input force is normal to the handle. Find the output force in terms of θ and f_{in}.

12. The jaws of a lever wrench have a separation x varying with the separation x' of the handles as recorded in the following table. The units are centimeters.

x	3 20	2.71	2 22	1 93	1 49	1 23	0 97	0 71	0 51	0 29	0 13	0 00
x'	22 8	21.8	20 6	19 7	18 4	17 4	16 4	15 3	14.0	12 7	11 8	10.1

If the handles are closed with a force of 20 lb, what force can be exerted on a sphere of diameter 2 mm? of diameter 25 mm?

13. A load of weight w is suspended by a long tape of length y_0 and thickness b. The load is hoisted by winding up the tape around a horizontal cylinder of radius a. Initially all the tape is out. Find an expression for the torque which must be applied to the cylinder in terms of the angle θ by which it has been turned. (HINT: First show that the amount of tape still hanging after an angle θ is

$$y = y_0 - a\theta - \frac{b}{4\pi}\theta^2.$$

From this evaluate the ratio of $\Delta\theta$ and Δy.)

14. A thin rope is wound up on an eccentric drum (radius a, axis at distance h from the center as in Fig. 10.17) thereby hoisting a load of weight w. Find the torque to be exerted on the drum as a function of θ.

15. A smooth hemispherical cup has radius r. A needle of length $2l(l < r)$ is placed in the cup. Show that its only equilibrium positions are horizontal.

16. A *bifilar suspension* is shown in Fig. 10.18. It consists of two strings of length l supporting a bar of weight w horizontally. In equilibrium position the strings are separated by a distance $2r$. When a small vertical torque $\mathbf{\Gamma}$ is applied, the bar rotates through an angle θ about a vertical axis of symmetry to a new equilibrium position. If l is much larger than r and if θ is small, show that

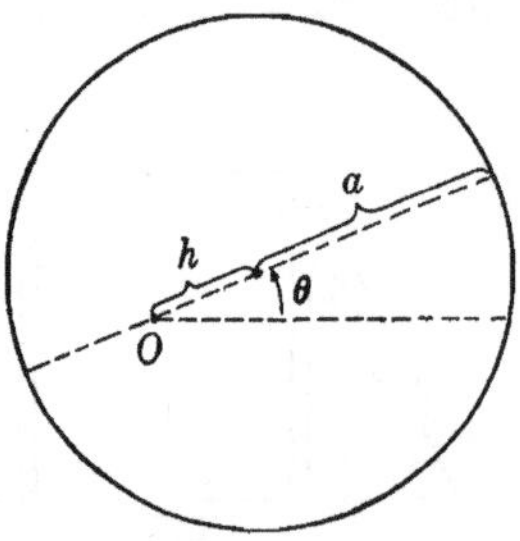

FIG. 10.17.

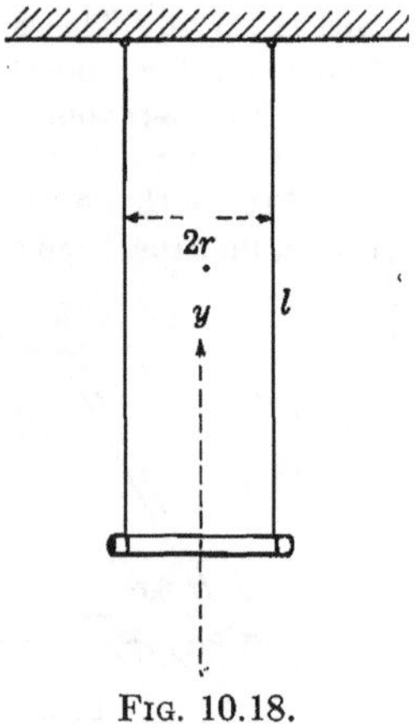

FIG. 10.18.

$$\gamma = \frac{wr^2 \sin\theta}{l}.$$

10.5. Potential Energy and Equilibrium. The concept of potential energy can be applied usefully to problems in equilibrium. Suppose that a system is in equilibrium subject to (*a*) conservative forces and (*b*) constraints. If the system is allowed any virtual displacement, we know that the virtual work done is zero. Let us see what sort of potential energy change is associated with this virtual work. If $\mathbf{F}_i$ is a typical conservative force and $\Delta\mathbf{R}_i$ the corresponding virtual displacement, then we may write, from (10.9),

$$\Delta(\text{p.e.})_i = -\mathbf{F}_i \cdot \Delta\mathbf{R}_i. \tag{10.19}$$

Such an equation may be written for each conservative force. Adding, member by member,

$$\Delta(\text{p.e.}) = \Sigma\Delta(\text{p.e.})_i = -\Sigma\mathbf{F}_i \cdot \Delta\mathbf{R}_i = 0. \tag{10.20}$$

The criterion for equilibrium then may be described as follows.

(10.21) *A system acted on by conservative forces and constraints is in equilibrium if and only if the potential energy change associated with every virtual displacement consistent with the constraints is zero.*

In many practical problems, the virtual displacement of the system can be described in terms of a single coordinate, say θ. Then this criterion for equilibrium can be stated succinctly thus

$$\frac{d(\text{p.e.})}{d\theta} = 0. \tag{10.22}$$

Example 1. Let us apply (10.22) to the example considered previously of a weighted solid of revolution (see Fig. 10.6). Taking potential energy as zero when θ is zero, we have for a potential energy formula:

$$\text{p.e.} = mgh(1 - \cos\theta).$$

Then

$$\frac{d(\text{p.e.})}{d\theta} = mgh \sin\theta.$$

This derivative is equal to zero for $\theta = 0°$ and also for $\theta = 180°$. These, of course, are the obvious equilibrium positions.

Equation (10.22) points out that a point of equilibrium might be a point of maximum potential energy, minimum potential energy, or neither. These possibilities are illustrated by points c, a, and b, respectively, in Fig. 10.19. In the neighborhood of a maximum, the potential energy is smaller than at the equilibrium point. This must correspond to an increase in kinetic energy if the forces are conservative and if the system was in equilibrium at the maximum point. Such a point is called a point of *unstable equilibrium*.

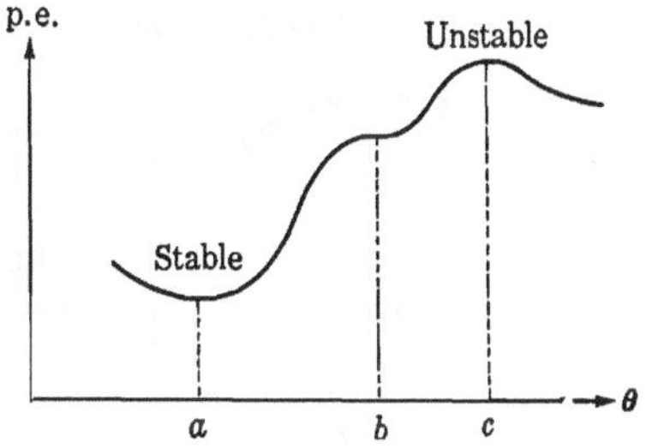

FIG. 10.19.

(10.23) *Unstable equilibrium:* $\dfrac{d(\text{p.e.})}{d\theta} = 0$; *p.e. a maximum.*

Similarly in the neighborhood of a minimum the potential energy is larger than at the minimum. Hence the kinetic energy should tend to be smaller rather than larger. Hence we have a point of *stable equilibrium.*

(10.24) *Stable equilibrium:* $\dfrac{d(\text{p.e.})}{d\theta} = 0$; *p.e. a minimum.*

Example 2. Referring again to the body of Fig. 10.6, we may test for maximum or minimum potential energy by evaluating the second derivative:

$$\frac{d^2(\text{p.e.})}{d\theta^2} = mgh \cos \theta.$$

For $\theta = 0°$, this is positive; hence it is a minimum, and the equilibrium is *stable.* For $\theta = 180°$, the second derivative is negative; hence the potential energy is maximum, and the equilibrium is *unstable.*

The mechanism of stability or instability can be visualized in terms of the forces involved when the equilibrium position is deserted. For a displacement in the **T** direction, by passing to a limit in (10.19), we may write

$$-\frac{d(\text{p.e.})}{ds} = f_s. \qquad (10.25)$$

Thus when the potential energy is increasing, the force is a restoring force, tending to cause a return to the equilibrium position. This is a sign of stability. When the potential energy is decreasing, f_s is positive; therefore the equilibrium is unstable.

EXERCISES

1. Solve Exercise 7 of the previous section by the method of this section. Test for stability.

2. Solve Exercise 15 of the previous section by the method of this section. Test for stability.

3. A plank of length l and thickness h balances in equilibrium across a horizontal cylinder of radius r. Under what conditions is equilibrium stable?

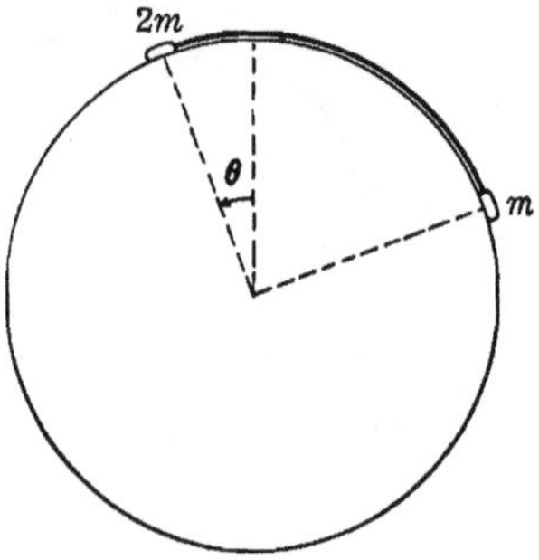

FIG. 10.20.

4. A cylindrical can is made of uniform tin. It has a bottom but no top. It rests in stable equilibrium on top of a sphere. If the can is 10 in. high and 8 in. in diameter, how small may the sphere be?

5. A smooth cylinder is fixed with its axis horizontal. Two particles of masses m and $2m$ are joined by a cord whose length is equal to one-quarter of the circumference of the cylinder. If the cord is laid across the cylinder as shown in Fig. 10.20, what is the equilibrium position? Is it stable?

6. Two beads, of masses $3m$ and $2m$, are on a smooth circular wire of radius r which is standing in a vertical plane. The beads are joined by a cord of length r. Find an equilibrium position for the beads, assuming the cord to be taut. Test for stability.

7. A smooth cylinder of diameter d has its axis horizontal. Two boards of width d are hinged together at one edge lengthwise. This book-shaped combination is placed over the cylinder as shown in Fig. 10.21. Write an equation which the angle θ between a board and the vertical must satisfy for equilibrium. Show that the equilibrium is stable.

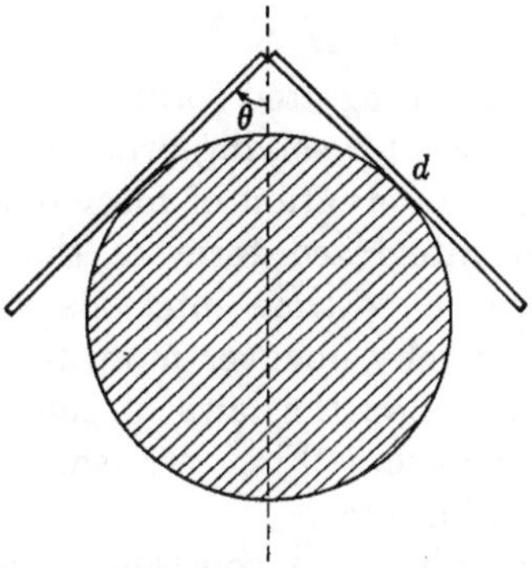

FIG. 10.21.

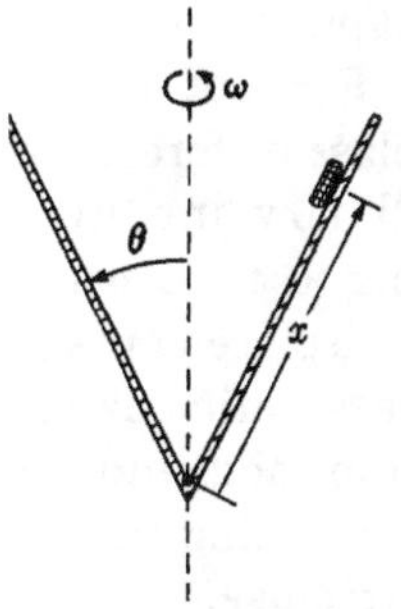

FIG. 10.22.

8. A smooth cone rotates at ω rad/sec about its vertical axis as shown in Fig. 10.22. If the vertex angle of the cone is 2θ, how far from the apex will a small button rest in equilibrium relative to the cone? Test for stability. It is assumed, of course, that for each position x the button is given the same angular speed ω about the axis of the cone; so that slipping may take place only in the x direction.

CHAPTER 11

IMPULSE AND MOMENTUM

In Chaps. 9 and 10 we saw how an integrated form of the dynamics equation $\mathbf{F} = m\mathbf{A}$ led to important tools for solving problems and, for a special class of forces, to the law of conservation of mechanical energy. We shall now investigate another integrated form of that equation, evaluating the persistence of forces over time intervals rather than through displacements. We shall thereby uncover more tools and also some conservation laws of wider validity: the laws of conservation of momentum and moment of momentum. First we shall deliberate briefly concerning the time integral of a force.

11.1. Impulse. As in elementary physics a constant force $\mathbf{F}$ acting for a time interval $t_1 - t_0$ is said to exert an impulse $\mathbf{P}$ equal to the product of the force by the length of the interval:

$$\mathbf{P} = \mathbf{F}(t_1 - t_0). \tag{11.1}$$

Impulse is a vector concept. In this simple case it has the direction of the force $\mathbf{F}$. When $\mathbf{F}$ is variable, one needs a more careful definition of impulse. This can be approached by dividing the time interval under consideration into subintervals as is suggested by the diagram of the time axis in Fig. 11.1. Suppose that at some instant during the interval Δt_i the force function $\mathbf{F}$ has the value $\mathbf{F}_i$. Then a reasonable approximation to the net impulse exerted ought to be given by the sum of the impulses which would have been exerted had each $\mathbf{F}_i$ remained constant during Δt_i:

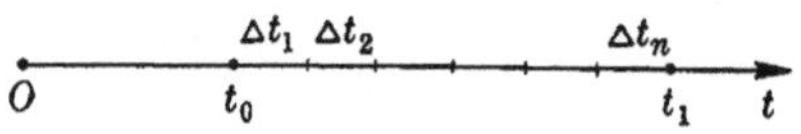

FIG. 11.1

$$\mathbf{P} = \Sigma \mathbf{F}_i \, \Delta t_i.$$

By taking smaller and smaller subdivisions of the time interval during which the variable force acts, we get approximations which are more and more significant since more details are utilized. It is thus fairly natural to define impulse for a variable force as the limit, if it exists, of such summations.

$$\mathbf{P} = \lim_{\Delta t \to 0} \sum \mathbf{F}_i \, \Delta t_i = \int_{t_0}^{t_1} \mathbf{F} \, dt. \tag{11.2}$$

The **P** defined by this equation has a direction determined by the mean (using time as a basis for averaging) of the forces **F** during the time interval.

Let us observe that the component of the impulse vector in any direction is merely the impulse which is associated with the component in the same direction of the variable force. Thus for any constant direction specified by the unit vector **E**,

$$\mathbf{P}_E = (\mathbf{P} \cdot \mathbf{E})\mathbf{E} = \mathbf{E} \int_{t_0}^{t_1} (\mathbf{F} \cdot \mathbf{E})dt. \tag{11.3}$$

In particular, taking **E** successively as **I**, **J**, and **K**,

$$\mathbf{P} = \mathbf{I} \int_{t_0}^{t_1} f_x\, dt + \mathbf{J} \int_{t_0}^{t_1} f_y\, dt + \mathbf{K} \int_{t_0}^{t_1} f_z\, dt = p_x\mathbf{I} + p_y\mathbf{J} + p_z\mathbf{K}. \tag{11.4}$$

Note, too, that

(11.5) *The impulse exerted by the resultant of a number of concurrent forces is equal to the sum of the impulses exerted by the forces taken separately.*

This follows at once from additive properties of integrals:

$$\int_{t_0}^{t_1} \left(\sum \mathbf{F}_i\right) dt = \sum \int_{t_0}^{t_1} \mathbf{F}_i\, dt.$$

Example. A force is given by

$$\mathbf{F} = 2t\mathbf{I} - 10\mathbf{J} + 3t^2\mathbf{K}.$$

Express the net impulse exerted by **F**, since $t = 0$ as a function of t.

SOLUTION

$$\begin{aligned}\mathbf{P} &= \int_0^t \mathbf{F}\, dt = \mathbf{I} \int_0^t 2t\, dt + \mathbf{J} \int_0^t (-10)dt + \mathbf{K} \int_0^t 3t^2\, dt \\ &= t^2\mathbf{I} - 10t\mathbf{J} + t^3\mathbf{K}.\end{aligned}$$

The visualization of any concept expressible as an integral is likely to be aided by the use of graphs. The variation of impulse components with time can be thought of in terms of the area under the force-component curves as in Fig. 11.2.

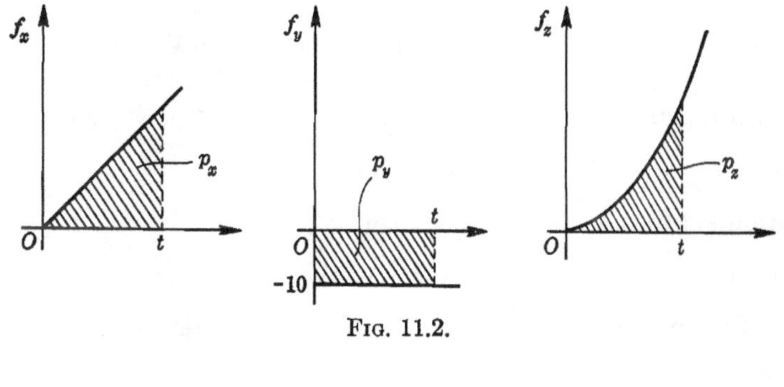

FIG. 11.2.

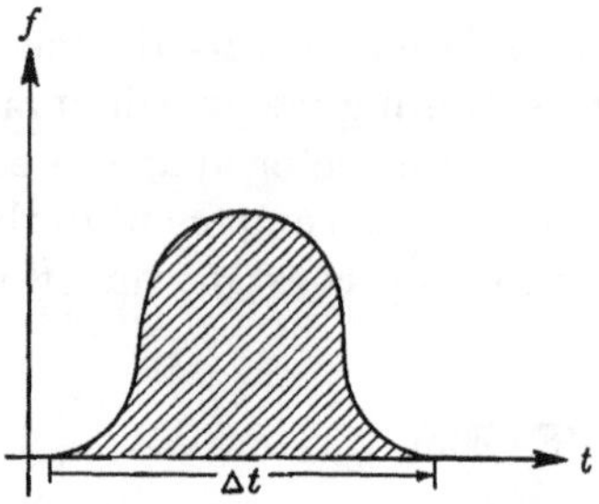

FIG. 11.3.

In practical problems impulses often occur for which the force pattern is unknown. For instance, when a bat hits a ball the exact nature of the force is hard to determine. Its magnitude might vary according to a graph such as Fig. 11.3. In an impact the duration Δt of the pulse might be extremely short; therefore, presumably, the force is correspondingly large. The impulse-momentum approach often allows us to forget our ignorance of forces by concentrating on the observable effects of the impulses.

EXERCISES

1. A 15-lb force is applied for 2.4 sec in a direction parallel to the vector $9\mathbf{I} - 12\mathbf{J} + 20\mathbf{K}$. Compute the z component of the impulse.

2. An impulse of 500 newton-sec is due to a force whose graph is given in Fig. 11.3. If the total duration is 1,000 microseconds (μsec), what is the average magnitude of the force?

3. The magnitude of a force as a function of time is shown in Fig. 11.4. Compute the magnitude of the total impulse.

4. The profile of a force is the complete arch of a sine curve (sine x, $0 \le x \le \pi$). If the total duration of the pulse is 500 μsec and the magnitude of the impulse is 100 lb-sec, how large does the force get?

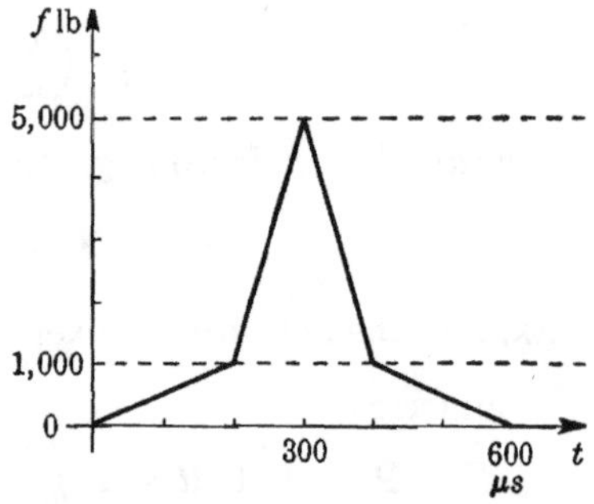

FIG. 11.4.

11.2. The Impulse-Momentum Principle for a Single Particle. To evaluate the dynamical effect of an impulse on a particle of mass m, we need only integrate the equation $\Sigma\mathbf{F} = m\mathbf{A}$ with respect to time.

$$\int_{t_0}^{t_1} \left(\sum \mathbf{F}\right) dt = \int_{t_0}^{t_1} m \frac{d\mathbf{V}}{dt}\, dt = m \int_{\mathbf{V}_0}^{\mathbf{V}_1} d\mathbf{V}$$

or

$$\sum \mathbf{P} = \sum \int_{t_0}^{t_1} \mathbf{F}\, dt = m\mathbf{V}_1 - m\mathbf{V}_0. \tag{11.6}$$

The right member of this equation is called the *change in momentum.*

$$\text{Momentum} = m\mathbf{V}. \tag{11.7}$$

Equation (11.6) may be written succinctly as

$$\Sigma\mathbf{P} = \Delta(m\mathbf{V}). \tag{11.8}$$

This is the impulse-momentum principle. In words:

(11.9) *The change of momentum of a particle during a time interval is equal to the net impulse exerted by the external forces during this interval.*

Example 1. A block slides for 5 sec down a plane inclined at 40°, the coefficient of friction being 0.4. How much does the speed increase?

SOLUTION. The procedure is rather simple—and distinctly similar to techniques used many times before. First, we isolate the block as in Fig. 11.5. The external forces are the weight w, the normal reaction n, and the friction f. We now compute the net impulse exerted by these forces. In the y direction the net impulse is zero, since $w \cos \theta = n$. In the x direction the net impulse is given by

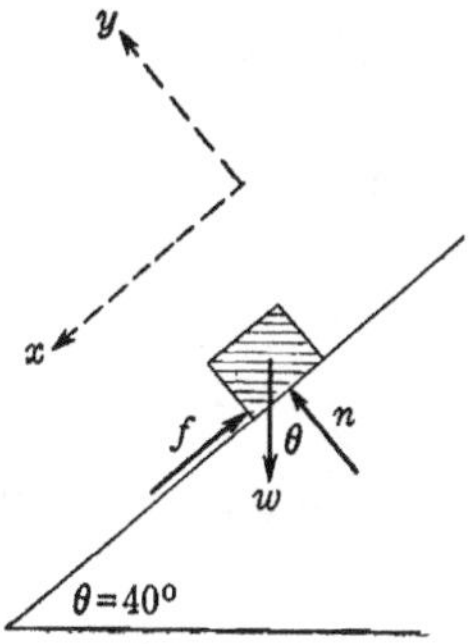

FIG. 11.5.

$$p_x = (w \sin \theta - f)t = w(\sin \theta - \mu \cos \theta)t.$$

This may be set equal to the x component of the change in momentum:

$$w(\sin \theta - \mu \cos \theta)t = \Delta(mv) = \frac{w}{g}(\Delta v),$$

whence,

$$\begin{aligned} \Delta v &= g(\sin \theta - \mu \cos \theta)t \\ &= 32.2(0.337)(5.0) = 54 \text{ ft/sec.} \end{aligned}$$

Example 2. A baseball weighing 9 oz originally traveling at 120 ft/sec across home plate leaves the bat at 160 ft/sec at an angle of 45° with the horizontal directly over the first-base line. Find the impulse in magnitude and direction.

SOLUTION. Taking home plate as origin and the base lines as x and y axes, the initial velocity is

$$\mathbf{V}_0 = 120(-0.7\mathbf{I} - 0.7\mathbf{J}).$$

The final velocity is

$$\mathbf{V} = 160(0.7\mathbf{I} + 0.7\mathbf{K}).$$

We have then

$$\begin{aligned} \mathbf{P} = \Delta(m\mathbf{V}) &= m \times 0.7[160(\mathbf{I} + \mathbf{K}) - 120(-\mathbf{I} - \mathbf{J})] \\ &= \left(\frac{9}{16 \times 32}\right)(0.7)(280\mathbf{I} + 120\mathbf{J} + 160\mathbf{K}) \\ &= 4.2(0.81\mathbf{I} + 0.35\mathbf{J} + 0.46\mathbf{K}) \qquad \text{lb-sec.} \end{aligned}$$

This shows that the impulse was 4.2 lb-sec in the direction of the unit vector appearing in parentheses.

The concept of momentum makes it possible for us to rephrase our basic dynamics equation in a form closer to Newton's second law (3.8):

$$\sum \mathbf{F} = \frac{d}{dt}(m\mathbf{V}). \tag{11.10}$$

Example 3. An object of mass m traveling at velocity $\mathbf{V}_0$ strikes a smooth plane surface whose normal makes an acute angle θ with $\mathbf{V}_0$. The object is deflected by the surface and travels along it as shown in Fig. 11.6. Find the impulse exerted and the final speed.

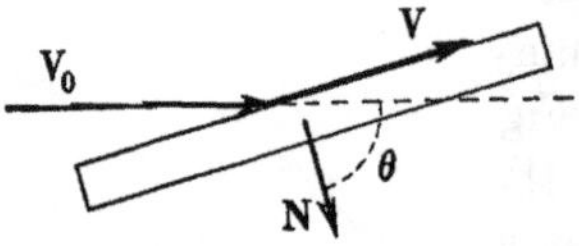

FIG. 11.6.

SOLUTION. Since the surface is smooth, the impulse is normal to the plane:

$$\mathbf{P} = -p\mathbf{N}.$$

The change in momentum may be written

$$m(\mathbf{V} - \mathbf{V}_0) = -p\mathbf{N}.$$

To solve for p, take the scalar product with $\mathbf{N}$:

$$m(\mathbf{V} \cdot \mathbf{N} - \mathbf{V}_0 \cdot \mathbf{N}) = -p(\mathbf{N} \cdot \mathbf{N}).$$

Clearly $\mathbf{V} \cdot \mathbf{N} = 0$; thus

$$p = m\mathbf{V}_0 \cdot \mathbf{N} = mv_0 \cos \theta.$$

To evaluate $\mathbf{V}$, consider the vector product with $\mathbf{N}$:

$$m(\mathbf{V} \times \mathbf{N} - \mathbf{V}_0 \times \mathbf{N}) = -p(\mathbf{N} \times \mathbf{N}).$$

This simplifies to

$$v = v_0 \sin \theta.$$

We see here how impact with a smooth surface cannot change the tangential component of velocity.

EXERCISES

1. The resultant force acting on a 100-lb particle is given at time t by

$$\mathbf{F} = 3t^2\mathbf{I} - 7\mathbf{K} \quad \text{lb}.$$

When $t = 0$, the velocity is $5\mathbf{J}$ ft/sec. What is the velocity when $t = 2$ sec?

2. An object of weight 32 lb is subjected to a force

$$\mathbf{F} = 3t^2\mathbf{I} - 10\mathbf{J} \quad \text{lb}.$$

Initially, the velocity is $-8\mathbf{I} + 5\mathbf{K}$ ft/sec. What is the velocity after 3 sec?

3. A sled reaches the bottom of a hill at 40 ft/sec and coasts across a level field for 3.5 sec before coming to rest. What was the coefficient of friction?

4. A particle of weight 2 lb initially has velocity $33\mathbf{I} - 56\mathbf{J}$ ft/sec. A force given by $32t\mathbf{I} + 42t^2\mathbf{J}$ poundals acts on the particle for 2 sec. (*a*) What impulse is exerted by the force during this time interval? (*b*) What work is done by the force during this interval?

5. A ball weighing 9 oz travels at 75 mph. What net sudden impulse will change its direction by 30°, leaving its speed unchanged?

6. The initial velocity of a 9-oz ball is east and horizontal at 75 mph. A variable force whose magnitude is plotted in Fig 11.7 and whose direction is always north and horizontal is applied. Find for $t = 3$ sec the speed and direction cosines of the ball's motion.

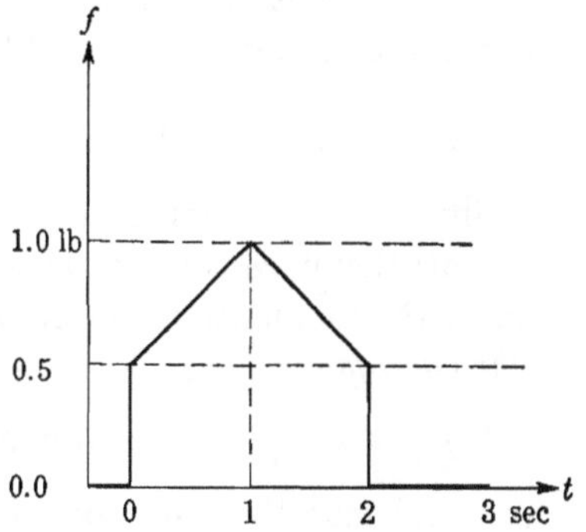

FIG. 11.7.

7. A 9-oz baseball is to be suspended by a piece of twine whose breaking tension is 6 lb. How long must the twine be in order that it shall not break when the ball is given a sudden horizontal impulse of 1.7 lb-sec?

8. A 10-lb body moving in a straight line received an impulse during a certain interval of 5 lb-sec in the line of its motion. If the work done by the force in this interval was 60 ft-lb, what was the final speed?

9. When a simple pendulum is deflected "statically" by a horizontal force on the bob, the deflection (if small) is proportional to the force:

$$\theta = kf.$$

When it is deflected "ballistically" by a quick horizontal impulse on the bob, the deflection (if small) is proportional to the impulse:

$$\theta = k'p.$$

Demonstrate both of these statements, and evaluate the ratio $k'\tau/k$, where τ is the period of the pendulum.

10. If the same powder charge (and hence the same energy) is always used in a certain gun while projectiles of different mass may be used, how does the recoil (reaction to impulse) vary with the projectile mass? (The force acting on the projectile during its trip along the gun barrel may be taken as constant.)

11. A spherical particle of mass m strikes a hard smooth surface at speed v with an angle of incidence (*i.e.*, angle with normal) of θ. It rebounds according to the *law of regular reflection* (making equal angles with the normal). (*a*) Prove that the speed of the rebound is v. (*b*) Derive a formula for the magnitude of the impulse exerted by the surface.

12. A simple pendulum of weight w and length l hangs at rest. It receives a horizontal impulse of such magnitude that it whirls through a complete vertical circle of radius l. (*a*) Find a minimum value for the impulse. (*b*) Find the instantaneous tension in the cord. (*c*) Find the speed at the top of the circle if the impulse was minimum.

11.3. The Impulse-Momentum Principle for an Aggregate of Particles. When dealing with an aggregate of particles, we distinguish between the effects of internal and of external forces. Suppose that a typical particle of mass m_i and initial velocity $\mathbf{V}_{0i}$ is acted on during a given time interval by external forces whose resultant impulse is $\mathbf{P}_i$ and internal forces whose resultant impulse is $\mathbf{P}_i'$. Then the final velocity $\mathbf{V}_i$ is determined by Eq. (11.6):

$$\mathbf{P}_i + \mathbf{P}_i' = m_i\mathbf{V}_i - m_i\mathbf{V}_{0_i}. \tag{11.11}$$

Let such an equation be written down for each of the particles. Then if corresponding members are added, one gets

$$\Sigma\mathbf{P}_i + \Sigma\mathbf{P}_i' = \Sigma m_i\mathbf{V}_i - \Sigma m_i\mathbf{V}_{0_i}.$$

The internal forces act in equal and opposite pairs during the given time interval; therefore their impulses add up to zero. Let us call the vector sum of the moments of the individual particles by the name *momentum of the aggregate:*

$$\text{Momentum} = \Sigma m_i\mathbf{V}_i. \tag{11.12}$$

Our conclusion then may be stated as follows:

(11.13) *The change of momentum during a time interval of an aggregate of particles is equal to the sum of the impulses exerted by external forces.*

Example 1. Initially, three pool balls of mass m have velocities, respectively, $2(\mathbf{I} + \mathbf{J})$ m/sec, **O**, **O**. After the first has hit the second and the second has hit the third, the velocities are (not necessarily in the same order): $0.5(-\mathbf{I} - \mathbf{J})$, $0.4(\mathbf{I} - \mathbf{J})$, and $0.1(-2\mathbf{I} - \mathbf{J})$ m/sec. What resultant impulse was exerted on the balls by the cushions during this time interval? Neglect frictional forces.

SOLUTION. The final momentum, since the masses are equal, is m times the sum of the stated velocities or

$$m(-0.3\mathbf{I} - 1.0\mathbf{J}).$$

The initial momentum was $m(2\mathbf{I} + 2\mathbf{J})$. The change in momentum is then $m(-2.3\mathbf{I} - 3.0\mathbf{J})$. If m is expressed in kilograms, then this is equal to the net external impulse in newton-seconds.

Example 2. A chain 9 ft long weighs 18 lb. It is held up vertically so that the bottom link touches the floor and is then allowed to drop. What is the total force on the floor when the last link hits? Neglect rebounds.

SOLUTION. Isolating the whole chain of length l and mass m, the external forces are the total weight w downward and the upward force f of the floor. Let y be the length already on the floor. Then consider the momentum change for a time Δt during which an additional length Δy reaches the floor at speed v. During this time interval the piece of length Δy ceases to move. This means a momentum change of

$$-\frac{m}{l}\,\Delta y\, v.$$

The momentum of the chain still in the air increases, however, because the speed has increased with an acceleration g. This momentum change is approximately

$$+m\left(1 - \frac{y}{l}\right) g \, \Delta t.$$

The corresponding impulse is $(w - f)\Delta t$ (where now f actually denotes the *average* force). Equating, dividing by Δt, and taking limits as Δt approaches zero,

$$m\left(1 - \frac{y}{l}\right) g - \frac{mv^2}{l} = w - f,$$

or

$$f = \frac{mv^2}{l} + \frac{y}{l} mg.$$

The speed v, since every link falls with an acceleration g, is given by

$$v^2 = 2gy.$$

The conclusion is then

$$f = 3\frac{y}{l} w.$$

This result is based on the implicit assumption that the links are very tiny; for otherwise each link would produce its own separate impulse and the net impulse would not be so simple. For the moment when $y = l$, we get

$$f = 3w = 54 \text{ lb.}$$

Example 3. Water under an absolute pressure p flowing steadily and smoothly at speed v through a horizontal pipe of cross-sectional area a has its direction changed by an angle θ (see Fig. 11.8). Neglecting friction and assuming homogeneity of flow, what net force must be provided by the walls of the pipe?

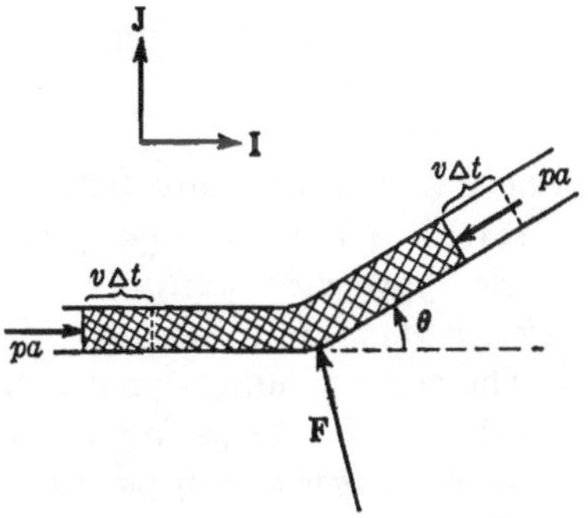

FIG. 11.8.

SOLUTION. A sample of the water may be regarded as an aggregate of particles. Let us isolate a section bounded by normal planes and including the corner. Consider this section as it advances during an interval Δt. During this interval in effect a segment of length $v \, \Delta t$ has been transferred from the pipe before the corner to the pipe after the corner. This segment has mass

$$m = va\,\delta\,\Delta t$$

and the corresponding change in momentum is given by

$$\begin{aligned}\Delta(m\mathbf{V}) &= v^2 a\,\delta\,\Delta t(\cos\theta\,\mathbf{I} + \sin\theta\,\mathbf{J} - \mathbf{I}) \\ &= v^2 a\,\delta\,\Delta t[(\cos\theta - 1)\mathbf{I} + \sin\theta\,\mathbf{J}].\end{aligned}$$

The impulses due to pressure on the normal bounding planes are

$$pa\mathbf{I}\,\Delta t + pa(-\cos\theta\,\mathbf{I} - \sin\theta\,\mathbf{J})\Delta t.$$

Let $\mathbf{F}$ denote the unknown force; then the impulse-momentum equation is

$$\mathbf{F}\,\Delta t + pa[(1 - \cos\theta)\mathbf{I} - \sin\theta\,\mathbf{J}]\Delta t = v^2 a\,\delta\,\Delta t[(\cos\theta - 1)\mathbf{I} + \sin\theta\,\mathbf{J}].$$

The conclusion is then

$$\mathbf{F} = (v^2\,\delta + p)a[(\cos\theta - 1)\mathbf{I} + \sin\theta\,\mathbf{J}].$$

The magnitude of the vector in brackets is $\sqrt{2(1 - \cos\theta)}$; thus

$$f = \sqrt{2}\,(v^2\,\delta + p)a\,\sqrt{(1 - \cos\theta)}.$$

Observe that when the liquid is at rest, the force associated with p is the same; thus the additional force due solely to the change in momentum is

$$f' = \sqrt{2}\,v^2\,\delta a\,\sqrt{(1 - \cos\theta)}.$$

It often happens that one has little interest in the individual motions of the members of an aggregate. In such a case information concerning the over-all motion may be desirable. It is then most convenient to study the behavior of the center of mass. From the familiar equation

$$(\Sigma m)\bar{\mathbf{R}} = \Sigma m\mathbf{R}$$

one obtains, by differentiating with respect to t,

$$(\Sigma m)\bar{\mathbf{V}} = \Sigma m\mathbf{V}. \tag{11.14}$$

The statement in words follows:

(11.15) *The momentum of an aggregate is equal to the momentum of a single hypothetical particle having the whole mass of the aggregate and the velocity of the center of mass.*

The corresponding dynamical result might be phrased thus:

(11.16) *The change in momentum during a time interval of the center of mass of an aggregate of particles is equal to the sum of the impulses exerted on the aggregate by external forces.*

It is to be understood that the "momentum of the center of mass" is a technical term having to do with the hypothetical particle of (11.15). In symbolic form our proposition is

$$\Sigma\mathbf{P} = (\Sigma m)\bar{\mathbf{V}} - (\Sigma m)\bar{\mathbf{V}}_0. \tag{11.17}$$

EXERCISES

1. A rocket ship of gross weight 5 tons is traveling at 500 ft/sec. Approximately how large a rocket charge should be fired at right angles to the ship's trajectory in order to change the course of the ship by 5°? (The firing speed is 2,500 ft/sec.)

2. A pile of 10 balls each weighing 75 g is scattered by a blow from a 2-kg block traveling at 12 m/sec. If the block is brought to rest by the blow, what is the resulting speed of the center of mass of the original aggregate of balls after the impact?

3. The upper end of a 10-m chain of linear density 0.5 kg/m is held at rest 20 m above a horizontal floor. If the chain is released, what total force will it exert on the floor at the moment when its middle link strikes?

4. Bullets from a machine gun strike a heavy steel target at the rate of three per second. The rebound is negligible. Each bullet weighs 40 g. The speed is 600 m/sec. Find the average force exerted by the target.

5. Water from a fire hose with a nozzle 2 in. in diameter strikes a plate-glass window at an angle of 65° with the normal and is deflected parallel to the glass. What force does the window sustain if the water is delivered at 600 gal/min?

6. Wooden spools weighing 15 g are carried at 4 m/sec by a horizontal conveyor belt. The coefficient of friction is 0.2. There are about 80 spools per meter of belt. The spools are taken off the belt by a smooth vertical vane which makes an angle of 30° with the direction of motion of the conveyor. If most of the spools leave the belt in a line parallel to the vane, (*a*) what is the speed of departure? (*b*) what force does the vane sustain? (HINT: The motion of spools relative to the belt must, in general, be normal to the smooth vane; hence the friction force also may be considered as normal to the vane.)

11.4. Conservation of Momentum. If an aggregate of particles is subject to no external forces during a given time interval, the change in momentum during that interval must be zero. This corollary of (11.13) is called the *law of conservation of momentum.*

(11.18) *The momentum of an aggregate is constant when there is no net external impulse.*

It immediately follows that

(11.19) *The center of mass of an aggregate which is subject to no external forces travels in a straight line at constant velocity.*

Example 1. A 2-kg sphere with a velocity of $3\mathbf{I} - 4\mathbf{J}$ m/sec collides with a 3-kg sphere of velocity $-\mathbf{I} + \mathbf{J}$ m/sec. After the collision the 3-kg sphere has velocity $\mathbf{I} + \mathbf{J}$ m/sec. Find the new velocity of the 2-kg sphere.

SOLUTION. By the conservation law the total momentum after impact is equal to that before.

$$2(3\mathbf{I} - 4\mathbf{J}) + 3(-\mathbf{I} + \mathbf{J}) = 2(v_x\mathbf{I} + v_y\mathbf{J}) + 3(\mathbf{I} + \mathbf{J}).$$

Equating x and y components,

$$6 - 3 = 2v_x + 3 \quad \text{or} \quad v_x = 0 \text{ m/sec},$$
$$-8 + 3 = 2v_y + 3 \quad \text{or} \quad v_y = -4 \text{ m/sec}.$$

Example 2. When an artillery shell explodes in mid-air, the velocity of the center of mass is unchanged since the only impulses are internal.

Example 3. Two blocks, of mass 3 and 5 kg, are tied together with a spring compressed between. If the blocks are released, the spring expands, obeying Hooke's law. Its force initially is 8 newtons and after expanding 4 cm the force is 4 newtons. What is the velocity of the 3-kg block at that moment?

SOLUTION. The spring obeys Hooke's law: thus $f = -ky$. The work done as it expands is

$$\int_{y_0}^{y} f\,dy = -\frac{1}{k}\int_{f_0}^{f} f\,df = \frac{1}{2k}(f_0^2 - f^2)$$
$$= \frac{1}{2k}(f_0 + f)(f_0 - f)$$
$$= \frac{1}{2}(f_0 + f)(y - y_0)$$
$$= \frac{1}{2}(8 + 4)(0.04) = 0.24 \text{ joules.}$$

The kinetic energy attained may be written, using the conservation of momentum law, $mv + m'v' = 0$,

$$\frac{1}{2}mv^2 + \frac{1}{2}m'v'^2 = \frac{1}{2}mv^2 + \frac{1}{2}m'\left(\frac{-mv}{m'}\right)^2$$
$$= \frac{1}{2}mv^2\left(1 + \frac{m}{m'}\right) = \frac{3}{2}\left(1 + \frac{3}{5}\right)v^2 = 2.4v^2.$$

Finally, by the work-energy principle, these may be equated:

$$2.4v^2 = 0.24 \qquad \text{or} \qquad v = 0.32 \text{ m/sec.}$$

EXERCISES

1. A single freight car coasting at 4 ft/sec bumps into and is coupled to a car twice as heavy which initially is at rest. What is their common speed after the impact?

2. A 2-kg sphere of velocity $3\mathbf{I} - 4\mathbf{J}$ m/sec has its velocity exactly reversed by collision with a moving 4-kg sphere. What change in velocity does the latter undergo?

3. A 2-lb duck flying at 40 ft/sec is struck from the side by 2 oz of shot traveling at 800 ft/sec. How much is the path deflected if the shot lodges in the bird?

4. Two objects A and B are initially at rest a meter apart. They attract each other with a force inversely proportional to the square of the distance between them. The initial value of this force is 0.4 newton. The masses of A and B are, respectively, 300 g and 600 g. When the distance between the objects has decreased to 50 cm, how fast will A be moving?

5. Two particles having momenta $m_1\mathbf{V}_1$ and $m_2\mathbf{V}_2$ collide and stick together. The resulting velocity of the coalesced pair is $\mathbf{V}$. Show that the energy lost in the collision is expressible as

$$\tfrac{1}{2}\mu(\mathbf{V}_2 - \mathbf{V}_1)\cdot(\mathbf{V}_2 - \mathbf{V}_1),$$

where μ is the *reduced mass* of the aggregate, given by

$$\mu = \frac{m_1 m_2}{m_1 + m_2}.$$

6. A rocket of gross mass m and initial velocity $\mathbf{V}_0$ emits a charge of mass m' at relative velocity $\mathbf{V}'$. In order that the rocket undergo a velocity change $\Delta\mathbf{V}$, show that $\mathbf{V}'$ must be given by

$$\mathbf{V}' = \left(1 - \frac{m}{m'}\right)\Delta\mathbf{V}.$$

7. A rocket of instantaneous gross mass m emits a continuous blast of gases at relative velocity $\mathbf{V}'$ and at a rate $(-dm/dt)$. Show that the acceleration of the rocket is given by

$$\frac{d\mathbf{V}}{dt} = \frac{1}{m}\left(\frac{dm}{dt}\right)\mathbf{V}'.$$

(HINT: Replace m' in Exercise 6 by $-\Delta m$, and use limiting process.)

8. A rocket of net mass $\bar{m}$ and propellant mass m'' is coasting in interstellar space at speed v_0. If the relative escape speed of the rocket's gases is v', show that the maximum increase in speed to be gotten from the remaining fuel is given by

$$\Delta v = v' \ln\left(1 + \frac{m''}{\bar{m}}\right).$$

(HINT: Use an integrated form of the result of Exercise 7.)

9. Two smooth uniform solid spheres of unequal mass collide in such a way that their line of centers at the moment of contact is parallel to the x axis. After the rebound the total kinetic energy is the same as it was before the collision. Show that the x component of the relative velocity merely reversed in sign during the collision.

11.5. Angular Impulse and Moments of Momentum. If a force acts during a time interval, it is said, as we have seen in Sec. 11.1, to exert an impulse. Similarly, if a couple $\mathbf{\Gamma}$ acts during an interval, it is said to exert an *angular impulse*, defined analogously:

$$\text{Angular impulse} = \int_{t_0}^{t_1} \mathbf{\Gamma}\, dt. \tag{11.20}$$

Relative to any origin **O**, this definition may be applied to any force **F** acting at a point of position vector **R**. For, as we learned much earlier, this force is equivalent to an equal force at **O** together with a couple $\mathbf{\Gamma} = \mathbf{R} \times \mathbf{F}$. For any such force, then we write

$$\text{Angular impulse} = \int_{t_0}^{t_1} \mathbf{R} \times \mathbf{F}\, dt = \int_{t_0}^{t_1} \mathbf{\Gamma}\, dt. \tag{11.21}$$

Likewise, relative to any axis, say the z axis, we may discuss the angular impulse exerted about that axis:

$$\text{Angular impulse} = \int_{t_0}^{t_1} \mathbf{K} \cdot \mathbf{R} \times \mathbf{F}\, dt = \int_{t_0}^{t_1} \gamma_z\, dt. \tag{11.22}$$

In the case of sudden impact, the duration of the angular impulse is likely to be very brief. In such a case **R** may vary negligibly during the interval. Then

$$\int_{t_0}^{t_1} \mathbf{\Gamma}\, dt = \int_{t_0}^{t_1} \mathbf{R} \times \mathbf{F}\, dt = \mathbf{R} \times \int_{t_0}^{t_1} \mathbf{F}\, dt = \mathbf{R} \times \mathbf{P}.$$

or

(11.23) *A very brief angular impulse exerted by a force* **F** *is equal (essentially) to the moment of the linear impulse exerted by* **F**.

Let us now investigate the dynamical effect of angular impulses. In earlier discussions of aggregates, we used an equation of the form

$$\sum \mathbf{R} \times \mathbf{F} = \sum \mathbf{R} \times m \frac{d\mathbf{V}}{dt}, \tag{11.24}$$

where the left member includes only moments of *external forces*. Let us observe that

$$\frac{d}{dt}\left(\sum \mathbf{R} \times m\mathbf{V}\right) = \sum \mathbf{V} \times m\mathbf{V} + \sum \mathbf{R} \times m \frac{d\mathbf{V}}{dt}; \tag{11.25}$$

thus (11.24) can be written

$$\sum \mathbf{R} \times \mathbf{F} = \frac{d}{dt}\left(\sum \mathbf{R} \times m\mathbf{V}\right). \tag{11.26}$$

This will be recognized as another form of (8.54). The quantity $\mathbf{R} \times m\mathbf{V}$ is clearly the moment about **O** of the momentum vector $m\mathbf{V}$; therefore it is called *moment of momentum*. As an incidental result we may then state:

(11.27) *The moment of momentum of an aggregate of particles has a time rate of increase equal to the moment of the external forces.*

Now let (11.26) be integrated relative to time:

$$\int_{t_0}^{t_1} \left(\sum \mathbf{R} \times \mathbf{F}\right) dt = \left(\sum \mathbf{R} \times m\mathbf{V}\right)_{\text{at } t_1} - \left(\sum \mathbf{R} \times m\mathbf{V}\right)_{\text{at } t_0}$$

or

$$\sum \int_{t_0}^{t_1} \mathbf{R} \times \mathbf{F}\, dt = \Delta\left(\sum \mathbf{R} \times m\mathbf{V}\right). \tag{11.28}$$

In words, it may be stated:

(11.29) *The change during a time interval in moment of momentum of an aggregate of particles is equal to the net angular impulse exerted by the external forces during this interval.*

An immediate special case is the *law of conservation of moment of momentum.*

(11.30) *The moment of momentum about a fixed point* **O** *is constant as long as the net external angular impulse about* **O** *is zero.*

Example. Ballistic Pendulum. The velocity of a bullet is often found by firing it into a heavy pendulum whose deflection can readily be measured (see Fig. 11.9). The bullet and the pendulum bob may be taken as a two-particle aggregate. The only external forces at the instant of impact are gravity and the tension in the string, neither of which has a moment about the point of support **O**. Consequently, moment of momentum is conserved. Taking magnitudes only,

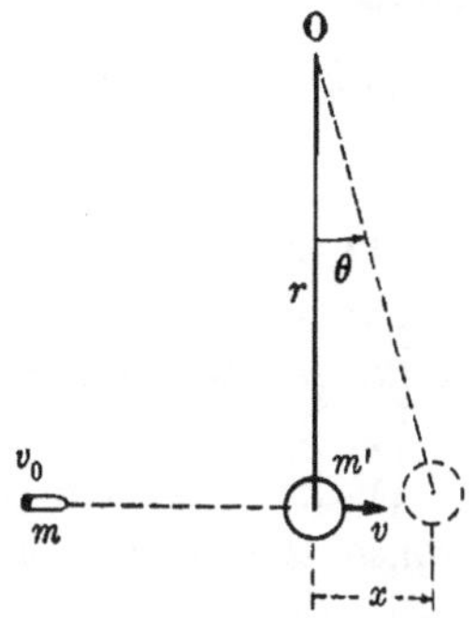

FIG. 11.9.

$$rmv_0 = r(m + m')v.$$

This equation could, of course, have been deduced equally well from the linear momentum relationships. We have then v_0 in terms of v:

$$v_0 = \left(1 + \frac{m'}{m}\right) v.$$

The joint speed v of the particles after impact may be computed in terms of the angular displacement θ by energy methods:

$$\tfrac{1}{2}(m + m')v^2 = (m + m')gr(1 - \cos\theta).$$

In practice, it is usually more feasible to measure the horizontal displacement x rather than the angle θ. Using the approximation, for small θ, given in Sec. 10.3,

$$1 - \cos\theta = \frac{\theta^2}{2} = \frac{x^2}{2r^2}.$$

We have then

$$v^2 = \frac{gx^2}{r};$$

thus, assuming that m' is much larger than m, we get as a working formula

$$v_0 = \frac{m'}{m}\sqrt{\frac{g}{r}}\,x.$$

It should be pointed out that by taking components in, say, the z direction, one may obtain results analogous to (11.29) and (11.30) for moments about an axis.

Thus far in this section moments have been taken about a point **O** (or an axis) fixed in an inertial frame of reference. Other points might be used. For instance, using the center of mass of the aggregate as reference point, we may write instead of (11.24) a form of (8.55):

$$\sum \mathbf{R}' \times \mathbf{F} = \sum \mathbf{R}' \times m\frac{d\mathbf{V}'}{dt}. \tag{11.31}$$

Pursuing the same sort of argument as before, we arrive at, instead of (11.28),

$$\sum \int_{t_0}^{t_1} \mathbf{R}' \times \mathbf{F}\, dt = \Delta\left(\sum \mathbf{R}' \times m\mathbf{V}'\right). \tag{11.32}$$

Our main propositions can be rephrased for this case as follows:

(11.33) *The change during a time interval in moment of relative momentum about the center of mass of an aggregate of particles is equal to the net angular impulse about the center of mass exerted by external forces during this interval.*

(11.34) *The moment of relative momentum about the center of mass is constant as long as the net external angular impulse about the center of mass is zero.*

This latter pair of theorems will be especially useful for rigid bodies.

EXERCISES

1. A rod of length r hangs vertically from a horizontal pivot through one end. A force of constant magnitude f is applied at the other end and is maintained normal to the rod while it rotates through a small angle θ. Taking the angular speed as ω during this displacement, find (*a*) the angular impulse and (*b*) the moment about the pivot of the linear impulse regarding this net impulse as acting at the point of initial application. Show that the ratio of these two is $\theta \cdot \sin \theta$.

2. Proposition (11.23) was derived for angular impulses exerted about a point. State and prove correspondingly a proposition for angular impulses about an axis.

3. Regard the planets, moons, asteroids, comets, etc., around our sun as an aggregate of particles. Assume that each particle experiences a force of attraction toward each of the others and toward the sun. Show that the moment of momentum about the sun is constant.

4. A ballistic pendulum consists of a 10-kg bob on a 3-m rope. A 50-g bullet aimed 15° below the horizontal strikes the pendulum and produces a deflection of 35°. Find the velocity of the bullet.

5. The position, mass, and velocity of three particles is given below:

R, m	m, kg	**V**, m/sec
O	2	**I** − 4**J** + 2**K**
5**I**	3	3**J** − **K**
2**I** − 4**J**	5	−**I** + **J** − **K**

Compute the following: (*a*) the momentum of the aggregate; (*b*) the velocity of the center of mass; (*c*) the position of the center of mass; (*d*) the moment of momentum about the origin; (*e*) the moment of relative momentum about the center of mass.

6. Show that Proposition (11.33) is valid relative to a point Q (not the center of mass), provided that the acceleration vector for Q is directed toward (or away from) the center of mass throughout the interval.

11.6. Momentum Relationships of a Rigid Body. Since we can regard a rigid body as an aggregate of particles in a limiting sense, the equations of the preceding sections can easily be adjusted to apply. From (11.13) and (11.17), we get

$$\sum \mathbf{P} = \sum \int_{t_0}^{t_1} \mathbf{F}\, dt = \Delta\left(\int \mathbf{V}\, dm\right) = m\bar{\mathbf{V}}_1 - m\bar{\mathbf{V}}_0. \tag{11.35}$$

From (11.28) and (11.33), we get for moments about the origin

$$\sum \int_{t_0}^{t_1} \mathbf{\Gamma}\, dt = \Delta\left(\int \mathbf{R} \times \mathbf{V}\, dm\right) \tag{11.36}$$

and for moments about the center of mass

$$\sum \int_{t_0}^{t_1} \mathbf{\Gamma}\, dt = \Delta\left(\int \mathbf{R}' \times \mathbf{V}'\, dm\right). \tag{11.37}$$

In applying these angular results, we shall limit ourselves to special classes of problems.

First, let us assume that the rigid body is constrained to rotate around a fixed z axis. Substituting $\mathbf{V} = \mathbf{\Omega} \times \mathbf{R}$ and taking only the z components of the angular impulses, we get, from (11.36),

$$\sum \int_{t_0}^{t_1} \gamma_z\, dt = \Delta\left[\int \mathbf{K} \cdot \mathbf{R} \times (\mathbf{\Omega} \times \mathbf{R}) dm\right]. \tag{11.38}$$

The right member may be simplified in a manner which we have met before (*e.g.*, in Sec. 8.4):

$$\sum \int_{t_0}^{t_1} \gamma_z\, dt = \Delta(i_z\omega). \tag{11.39}$$

The quantity $i_z\omega$ is usually called the *angular momentum* of the body about the z axis. This conclusion is then very much analogous to (11.9).

(11.40) *The change during a time interval in the angular momentum of a rigid body free to rotate about a fixed axis is equal to the net angular impulse about that axis exerted by the external forces during this interval.*

Example 1. A wheel is mounted rigidly on a horizontal axle at whose ends are bearings. The wheel and axle together have a moment of inertia of 4.2 ft-lb-sec². The axle is 2 in. in diameter. A rope is wound several times around the axle. When the end of the rope is pulled, the wheel rotates. If the rope does not slip, what speed will the wheel attain if the rope is pulled with a 40-lb force for 3 sec?

SOLUTION. The moment about the axle is $\frac{40}{12} = 3.33$ ft-lb, and hence the angular impulse is 10 ft-lb-sec. By (11.40), this must equal the angular momentum attained:

$$i\omega = 10,$$

or

$$\omega = \frac{10}{i} = \frac{10}{4.2} = 2.38 \text{ rad/sec}.$$

Now limiting ourselves to any motion of a rigid body parallel to the xy plane, we have from (11.37), by similar arguments, for moments about an axis through the center of mass and perpendicular to the xy plane

$$(11.41) \qquad \sum \int_{t_0}^{t_1} \gamma_z \, dt = \Delta(\bar{\imath}_z \omega).$$

(11.42) *The change during a time interval in the angular momentum (about a normal axis through the center of mass) of a rigid body in motion parallel to a fixed plane is equal to the net external angular impulse about that axis during that interval.*

Example 2. A sphere of mass m and radius r (see Fig. 11.10) rolls and slips from rest down a plane inclined at θ acquiring a linear speed $\bar{v}$ in t sec. Find the angular speed acquired and also the frictional force.

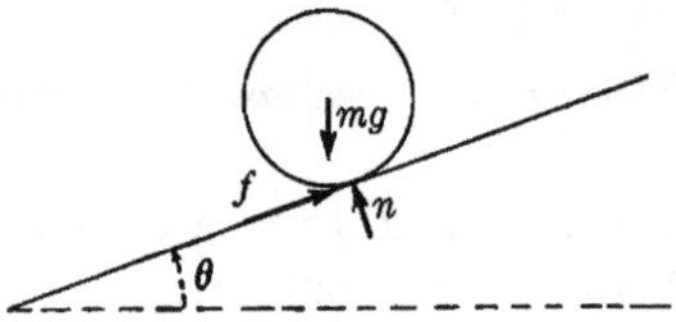

FIG. 11.10

SOLUTION. The linear impulse equation is

$$(mg \sin \theta - f)t = m\bar{v}.$$

The angular impulse equation is

$$frt = i\omega.$$

From the first,

$$f = mg \sin \theta - \frac{m\bar{v}}{t}.$$

Substituting in the second,

$$\omega = \frac{frt}{i} = \frac{m(gt \sin \theta - \bar{v})r}{0.4mr^2} = \frac{2.5(gt \sin \theta - \bar{v})}{r}.$$

Example 3. A sphere such as is used in bowling is given a linear speed v_0 along a horizontal plane with which it has a coefficient of friction μ. Initially, the angular speed is zero. How long before it rolls without slipping?

SOLUTION. In general, one may say that the same constant external force f (the force of friction) provides a negative linear impulse to slow down the translation of the ball and a positive angular impulse to speed up the rotation until the critical ratio $v/\omega = r$ is reached. The linear impulse equation is

$$mv - mv_0 = -ft.$$

The angular impulse equation is

$$frt = \tfrac{2}{5}mr^2\omega.$$

Writing $f = \mu mg$ and $v = \omega r$, we may solve for t:

$$t = \frac{2v_0}{7\mu g}.$$

Example 4. A disk of radius r and mass m is mounted on a smooth horizontal pivot **O** on its edge as in Fig. 11.11. A sudden impulse **P**, horizontal and in the plane of the disk, sets the disk in motion. Find the initial angular speed and the resulting impulse **P′** at the pivot.

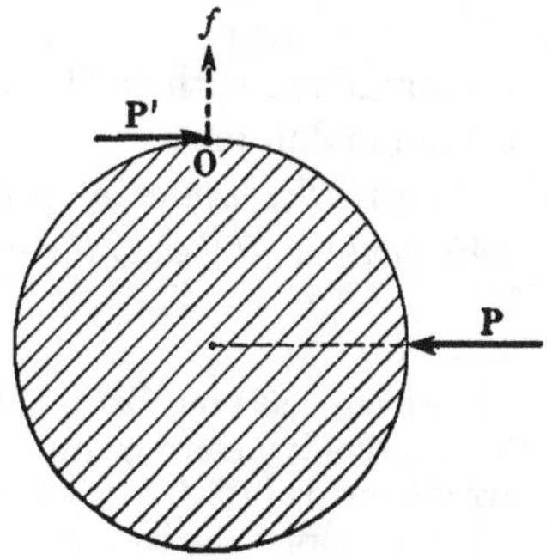

FIG. 11.11.

SOLUTION. Using (11.23) and (11.40), we have, taking moments about the axis at **O**,

$$pr = i\omega = \tfrac{3}{2}mr^2\omega;$$

thus

$$\omega = \frac{2}{3}\frac{p}{mr}.$$

The instantaneous velocity of the center of mass is then

$$\bar{v} = r\omega = \frac{2}{3}\frac{p}{m}.$$

Now, using (11.35),

$$p - p' = m\bar{v} = \tfrac{2}{3}p;$$

thus

$$p' = \tfrac{1}{3}p.$$

Note that the pivot has to provide an additional centripetal force

$$f = m\omega^2 r = m\,\frac{4p^2r}{9m^2r^2} = \frac{4p^2}{9mr}.$$

Center of Percussion. Starting with any rigid body mounted to rotate freely about a horizontal pivot **O**, that is, a body suitable for use as a physical pendulum, let us consider the problem of eliminating the bearing impulse **P′** which occurred in the last example. Let a sudden horizontal impulse **P** (in the normal plane containing the center of mass) act on the body at **Q**, at a distance y from **O** along the line **O$\bar{\mathbf{R}}$** (see Fig. 11.12). If **Q** is located in such a way that the bearing impulse **P′** is zero, then **Q** is called the *center of percussion* relative to the axis at **O**.

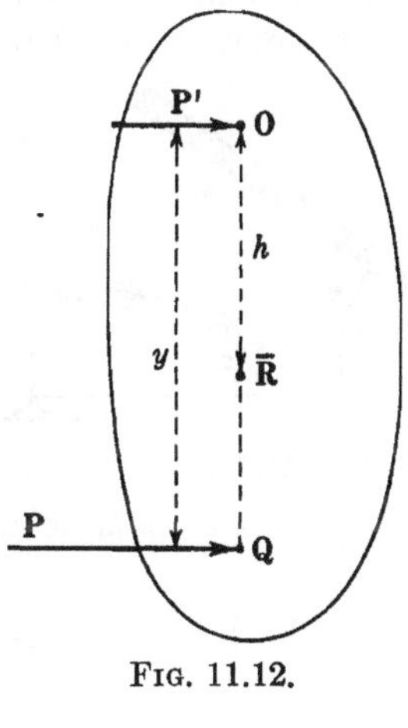

FIG. 11.12.

The angular impulse equation, for moments about the pivot, is

$$py = i\omega.$$

The linear impulse equation is

$$p + p' = m\bar{v} = m\omega h.$$

Now eliminating ω and setting p' equal to zero,

$$y = \frac{i}{mh}.$$

A comparison with (8.39) shows that y is equal to the *equivalent length* l of the pendulum.

(11.43) *The center of percussion of a physical pendulum is located an equivalent length below the axis of rotation.*

EXERCISES

1. An airplane propellor is 8 ft long and weighs 220 lb. Assuming that the mass of the propellor is uniformly distributed along its length, find what constant torque would give it a speed of 1,800 rpm 1 min after starting from rest.

2. A uniform spherical shell mounted on a diametrical axis has radius 0.26 m and mass 2.4 kg. A torque given by

$$\gamma = 4.8t^{\frac{1}{2}} \qquad \text{newton-m}$$

is applied. How long must it act to achieve a speed of 100 rad/sec?

3. A spool has moment of inertia i and radius r. Its weight is w. A long, light, thin, flexible tape is wound around the spool, the free end being fastened to the ceiling. The spool is released from rest with the tape taut and is allowed to fall, the tape unrolling. Find the time required for the descending spool to acquire a speed v. Find an expression for the impulse exerted by the tension in the tape during this time.

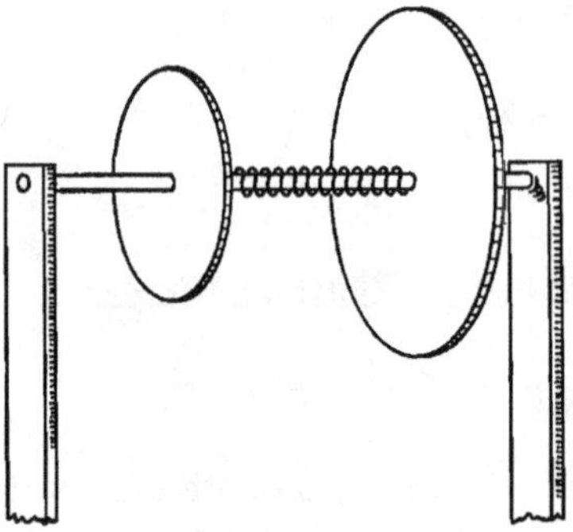

FIG. 11.13.

4. A smooth axle is set rigidly in horizontal position. Two wheels, of moment of inertia i_1 and i_2, respectively, turn freely about this axle as shown in Fig. 11.13. They are connected by a spring which provides a torque γ proportional and opposite to the angle θ through which one disk is rotated relative to the other. Initially, the relative displacement is θ_m and the torque γ_m with both wheels at rest. Then they are released. Show that when the spring reaches its unstrained position, the angular velocity of the first wheel is

$$\omega_1 = \sqrt{\frac{i_2\gamma_m\theta_m}{i_1(i_1 + i_2)}}.$$

5. A uniform rod of length l and mass m is pivoted at one end as in Fig. 11.14. When released from rest at an angle θ_1 with the horizontal, it falls from rest. The other end strikes a fixed object when the rod is horizontal and rebounds to an angle θ_2. Show that the impulse **P** has magnitude

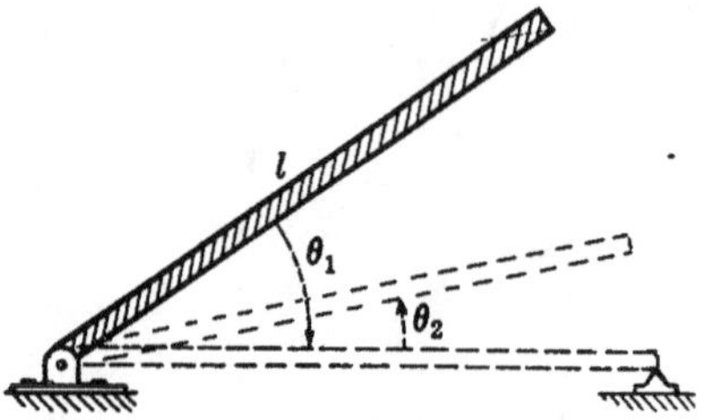

FIG. 11.14.

$$p = m\sqrt{\frac{gl}{3}}\,(\sqrt{\sin\theta_1} + \sqrt{\sin\theta_2}).$$

6. A uniform rod lying on ice receives at one end a normal horizontal blow of impulse p. Show that the point of impact has an instantaneous speed four times as great as would have been the case if the blow had been at the center.

7. A uniform meter stick is free to rotate in a horizontal plane about a pivot at a distance d above the center. When it is struck a horizontal blow at a point at a distance d below the center, no horizontal pivot reaction results. Find d.

8. A plane rigid body of mass m free to move in the xy plane is set initially with its center of mass $\bar{\mathbf{R}}$ at the origin as in Fig. 11.15. At the point corresponding to $(0, -d)$ a sudden blow of impulse $p\mathbf{I}$ is delivered. Show that the instantaneous speed of the point $\mathbf{Y}:(0,y)$ is given by

$$v = \frac{p}{m}\left[\frac{\bar{\imath} - mdy}{\bar{\imath}}\right],$$

$\bar{\imath}$ being the moment of inertia about the normal axis through the center of mass.

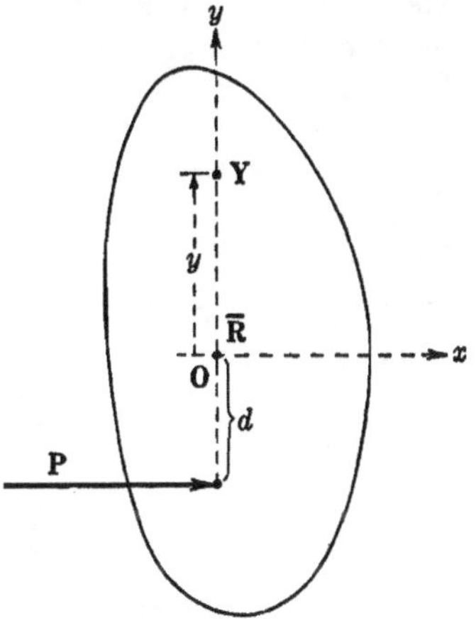

FIG. 11.15.

9. A wheel lies flat on a horizontal table. When a spoke receives a sharp normal horizontal blow at a distance 24 in. from the center of the wheel, the wheel makes a small angular displacement, having apparently as center of rotation a point 20 in. beyond the center of the wheel. What is the approximate radius of gyration (about a normal axis through the center of the wheel)?

10. An airplane about to land at 90 mph loses a wheel (initially unspinning) which rolls along the ground. The rolling radius is 18 in. By the time the wheel stops slipping its angular speed is 55 rad/sec. Find the radius of gyration.

11. A steel pulley 2 ft in diameter slips off its fixed axle while rotating at 36 rad/sec. It travels along a concrete floor rolling and slipping. When slipping stops, the speed of rotation has diminished to 16 rad/sec. Find the radius of gyration of the pulley.

12. A rigid body is in motion parallel to the xy plane. Show that the moment of momentum about the z axis can always be expressed as the sum of the angular momentum about a parallel axis through the center of mass plus the moment about the z axis of the momentum $m\bar{\mathbf{V}}$ of the center of mass.

11.7. Coefficient of Restitution. When a uniform solid spherical ball strikes at right angles a fixed smooth plane surface such as a wall or floor, the process of collision may be studied in terms of the impulses generated. Isolating the ball, we may say that the wall exerts an impulse $\mathbf{P}$ while the ball is being brought to rest. High-speed photographs show that a golf ball undergoes flattening when subjected to such an impulse. Ordinarily, the ball does not remain at rest, although one made of putty might. Usually, there is a rebound, and the ball tends to regain its shape. This requires a brief period of acceleration while the ball is still in contact with the barrier. Let the impulse exerted by the barrier during this period be indicated by $\mathbf{P}'$. Now $\mathbf{P}'$ may be zero, as in the case of the putty, or it may be practically equal to $\mathbf{P}$ as in the case of a good rubber ball (or it might even be greater than **P** in case it is properly charged with an explosive). Ordinarily, **P**′ is somewhere between zero and **P**. Since the surface is smooth and the collision is normal, **P**′ will have the same direction as **P**; thus we may write

$$\mathbf{P}' = e\mathbf{P}, \tag{11.44}$$

where ordinarily $0 \leqq e \leqq 1$. For spheres, e is nearly a constant and is called the *coefficient of restitution*. Note that (11.44), together with the assumption that e is a constant, constitutes a minor postulate based, as in earlier more significant cases, on empirical evidence. If **U** is the velocity of approach (see Fig. 11.16) and **V** the velocity of rebound, we have as impulse-momentum equations:

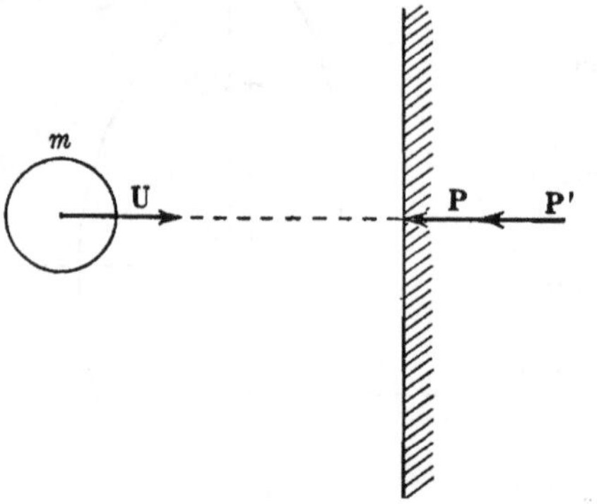

FIG. 11.16.

$$O - m\mathbf{U} = \mathbf{P},$$
$$m\mathbf{V} - O = \mathbf{P}';$$

so

$$m\mathbf{V} = e(-m\mathbf{U}),$$

or

$$\mathbf{V} = -e\mathbf{U}. \tag{11.45}$$

Except for the change in direction, then, the coefficient of restitution appears as the ratio of velocity after and before impact. If at the moment of collision the barrier happens to be moving in the direction of **U** or **P**, the velocities in (11.45) are replaced by relative velocities. The details of this deduction are left as an exercise.

Let us now consider a less special example of impact from the point of view of restitution. Consider two smooth spheres in collision. Let their line of centers at the moment of collision have a direction designated by the unit vector **I** as in Fig. 11.17. Before impact the velocities are, respectively, **U** and **U**′. The center of mass must have a constant velocity $\bar{\mathbf{U}}$ throughout. After impact the velocities are **V** and **V**′. At one moment of closest approach the spheres have a common normal velocity component $\bar{\mathbf{U}} \cdot \mathbf{I} = \bar{u}_x$. The impulse before this moment is **P** and after this moment it is **P**′. We assume that (11.44) still holds. Isolating the bodies separately and applying the impulse-momentum equation, we have

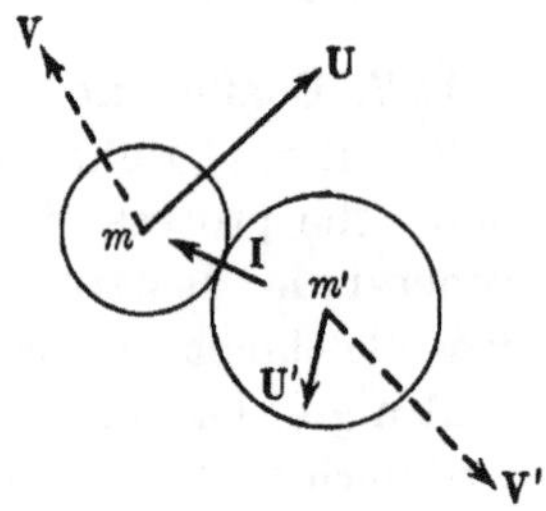

FIG. 11.17.

$$m\bar{\mathbf{U}} - m\mathbf{U} = \mathbf{P}, \qquad m'\bar{\mathbf{U}} - m'\mathbf{U}' = -\mathbf{P},$$
$$m\mathbf{V} - m\bar{\mathbf{U}} = \mathbf{P}', \qquad m'\mathbf{V}' - m'\bar{\mathbf{U}} = -\mathbf{P}'.$$

Taking the scalar products with **I**, these equations become

$$m\bar{u}_x - mu_x = p, \qquad m'\bar{u}_x - m'u'_x = -p,$$
$$mv_x - m\bar{u}_x = p', \qquad m'v'_x - m'\bar{u}_x = -p'.$$

Using the relationship $p' = ep$,

$$v_x - \bar{u}_x = e(\bar{u}_x - u_x), \qquad v'_x - \bar{u}_x = e(\bar{u}_x - u'_x).$$

Separating terms in $\bar{u}_x$,

$$\bar{u}_x(1 + e) = v_x + eu_x = v'_x + eu'_x.$$

Rearranging terms in the last two members,

$$v_x - v'_x = -e(u_x - u'_x), \tag{11.46}$$

or

$$(\mathbf{V} - \mathbf{V}') \cdot \mathbf{I} = -e(\mathbf{U} - \mathbf{U}') \cdot \mathbf{I}.$$

The essence of this result may be summarized as follows:

(11.47) *When two smooth spheres collide, the impact being in the direction of the x axis, the x component of their relative velocity reverses signs and is diminished by a factor equal to the coefficient of restitution.*

It is interesting although not surprising to observe how symmetrical is the motion relative to the center of mass in the situation just described. Rearranging the equations before (11.46), we have

$$v_x - \bar{u}_x = -e(u_x - \bar{u}_x), \qquad v'_x - \bar{u}_x = -e(u'_x - \bar{u}_x). \tag{11.48}$$

This should be compared with both (11.46) and (11.45). The latter comparison shows that both spheres behave as if they were bouncing off a wall of normal **I** which moves with the center of mass.

Let us finally seek a formula for the energy loss when a pair of spheres collides. By (9.20), we know that the kinetic energy of the system is equal to the kinetic energy associated with the center of mass plus the kinetic energy of relative motion. Since the center of mass maintains the same velocity throughout in the case of two colliding spheres, only the relative velocity need be considered. Since all the y and z components are unchanged by the collision, we have only x terms:

$$-\Delta\ \text{k.e.} = \tfrac{1}{2}m(u_x - \bar{u}_x)^2 + \tfrac{1}{2}m'(u'_x - \bar{u}_x)^2 - \tfrac{1}{2}m(v_x - \bar{u}_x)^2 - \tfrac{1}{2}m'(v'_x - \bar{u}_x)^2.$$

Using (11.48), this becomes

$$-\Delta\ \text{k.e.} = [\tfrac{1}{2}m(u_x - \bar{u}_x)^2 + \tfrac{1}{2}m'(u'_x - \bar{u}_x)^2](1 - e^2).$$

Now

$$u_x - \bar{u}_x = u_x - \frac{mu_x + m'u'_x}{m + m'} = \frac{m'}{m + m'}(u_x - u'_x);$$

and

$$u'_x - \bar{u}_x = u'_x - \frac{mu_x + m'u'_x}{m + m'} = \frac{m}{m + m'}(u'_x - u_x).$$

Using these expressions, we get

$$-\Delta \text{ k.e.} = \frac{1}{2}\left(\frac{mm'}{m + m'}\right)(u_x - u'_x)^2(1 - e^2). \tag{11.49}$$

A collision where there is no energy loss is called *perfectly elastic.* Here $e = 1$. A collision where the energy loss is maximum is called *inelastic.* Here $e = 0$. The student should compare (11.49) with Exercise 5, Sec. 11.4.

The theory of restitution has been developed here for spheres only. In simple problems involving symmetrical bodies other than spheres, we shall assume that Eqs. (11.44) and (11.46) are valid. Detailed analysis of these extensions will not be given here.

Example 1. When two smooth spheres collide, their line of centers is parallel to the x axis. Just before collision their velocities were

$$\mathbf{U} = 10\mathbf{I} - 5\mathbf{J} \text{ cm/sec} \quad \text{and} \quad \mathbf{U}' = 5\mathbf{J} \text{ cm/sec}.$$

If the coefficient of restitution is 0.5 and if the mass of the first is twice that of the second, what is the velocity of the second right after the collision?

SOLUTION. The restitution equation (11.46) is here

$$v_x - v'_x = -\tfrac{1}{2}(10 - 0) = -5.$$

The x components in the conservation of momentum equation gives

$$10(2m) = 2mv_x + mv'_x.$$

Solving simultaneously,

$$v'_x = 10 \text{ cm/sec}, \qquad v'_y = u'_y = 5 \text{ cm/sec};$$

thus

$$\mathbf{V}' = 10\mathbf{I} + 5\mathbf{J} \quad \text{cm/sec}.$$

Example 2. A uniform bar 3 ft long and weighing 5 lb is pivoted at one end, as shown in Fig. 11.18. It swings from rest in a horizontal position striking squarely a 5-lb uniform solid spherical ball of diameter 1 ft when the bar is vertical. The ball is initially at rest. The point of contact is 6 in. from the end of the bar. The coefficient of restitution is 0.5. Find for the moment immediately after impact (*a*) the initial speed of the ball; (*b*) the impulse given the bar at the bearing.

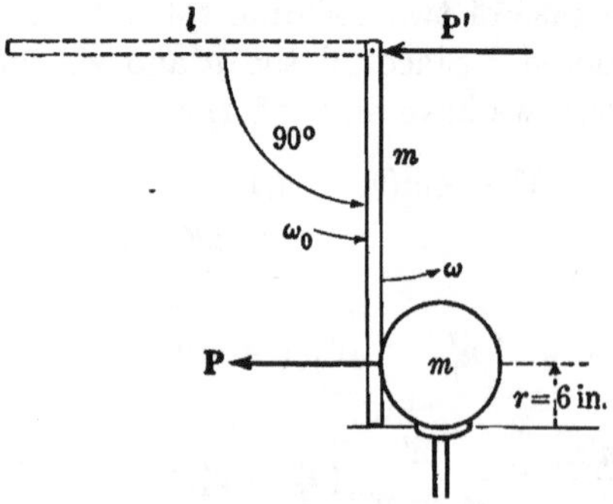

FIG. 11.18.

SOLUTION. Let ω_0 be the angular speed just before impact. Then the conservation of energy principle enables us to find ω_0.

$$\tfrac{1}{2}(\tfrac{1}{3}ml^2)\omega_0^2 = \tfrac{1}{2}mgl;$$

thus

$$\omega_0 = \sqrt{\frac{3g}{l}} = 5.7 \text{ rad/sec.}$$

Let **P** and **P**′ be the impulses at ball and bearing, respectively. Then the impulse-momentum principle gives

$$-p - p' = m\frac{l}{2}(\omega - \omega_0),$$

where ω is the new angular speed of the bar. For the ball (same mass) the same principle gives

$$p = mv.$$

By the conservation of moment of momentum we may write

$$(\tfrac{1}{3}ml^2)\omega_0 = (\tfrac{1}{3}ml^2)\omega + mv(l - r).$$

The restitution relationship is

$$\omega(l - r) - v = -e\omega_0(l - r).$$

Eliminating ω between the last two equations, we get

$$v = \frac{\omega_0(1 + e)l^2(l - r)}{4l^2 - 6lr + 3r^2} = \frac{5.7(1.5)(9)(2.5)}{27.75} = 6.9 \text{ ft/sec.}$$

Eliminating ω from the linear impulse equation, we get

$$p' = mv\left(\frac{l - 3r}{2l}\right) = \frac{5(6.9)(1.5)}{(32.2)(6)} = 0.27 \text{ lb-sec.}$$

EXERCISES

1. A spherical particle strikes a fixed plane wall with an angle of incidence (*i.e.*, with normal) of θ_1. Using only (11.44) and the laws of impulse and momentum, derive an expression for tan θ_2 (where θ_2 is the angle between normal and velocity after impact) in terms of θ_1 and e [and μ in (*b*)], (*a*) assuming that the wall is smooth; (*b*) assuming that the wall is rough (coefficient of friction = μ) and that slipping is imminent during the whole contact.

2. A spherical particle strikes perpendicularly at a speed u a massive smooth wall which is receding at a constant speed u'. The coefficient of restitution is e. Using only (11.44) and the laws of impulse and momentum, derive an expression for the speed of the particle after impact.

3. A number of identical perfectly elastic spheres are lined up almost touching as in Fig. 11.19. Another such sphere traveling at speed v along the same line

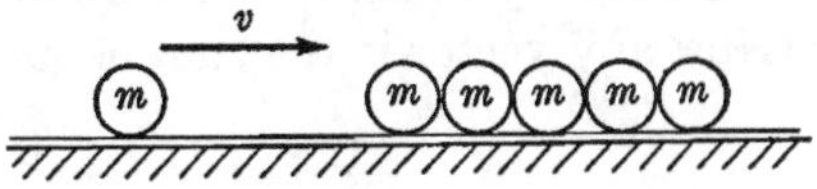

FIG. 11.19.

strikes the end of the column. Show that after the full impact the sphere on the opposite end has acquired the speed v while all the others are at rest.

4. Two spheres of identical radius but different mass roll on a horizontal plane surface. The first, of mass 200 g, is traveling with a velocity of 80 cm/sec in the x direction. It is struck by the other whose mass is 150 g and which has a velocity of 60**J** cm/sec. The line of centers is parallel to **J** at the impact. Find both velocities right after impact if the coefficient of restitution is 0.6.

5. Two spheres are to collide head-on with a relative speed v. The sum of the masses of the two spheres is m. The coefficient of restitution is e. Show that the maximum energy is lost in the collision if the spheres have equal masses.

6. A ball is dropped from a height h onto a hard pavement. On the second rebound the ball reaches a height h'. Express the coefficient of restitution in terms of h and h'.

7. A 2-lb particle and a 3-lb particle collide head-on in such a way that the 2-lb particle is stopped "dead" while the 3-lb particle has its velocity just reversed in direction. Find the coefficient of restitution.

8. An object weighing 100 lb and traveling 100 ft/sec collides head-on with a 20-lb object traveling at 300 ft/sec. The lighter object rebounds at 200 ft/sec. Find the final speed of the first object, the energy lost in collision, and the coefficient of restitution.

9. A 10-ft plank weighing 60 lb is balanced in a horizontal position by pivots at its middle as in Fig. 11.20. A 20-lb steel ball is dropped from a height of 9 ft to strike the plank near one end. The coefficient of restitution is 0.2. Find the initial angular speed of the plank and the new velocity of the ball.

10. A 10-lb board 16 in. square is suspended from one edge about which it is free to rotate. With what horizontal velocity must a baseball weighing 9 oz strike this target in the center (as in Fig. 11.21) in order to make it rotate through 180°? The coefficient of restitution is $\frac{1}{3}$.

FIG. 11.20.

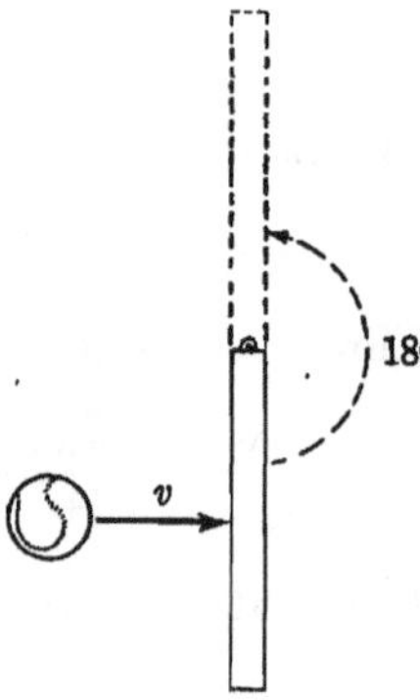

FIG. 11.21.

11.8. Note on Gyroscopic Phenomena. Suppose that we have given a rigid body with one point fixed at the origin **O**. By (6.17), the motion of the body at any instant is characterized by an angular velocity vector **Ω**. Let us first compute the moment of momentum relative to **O**.

$$\int_m \mathbf{R} \times \mathbf{V}\, dm = \int_m \mathbf{R} \times (\mathbf{\Omega} \times \mathbf{R})dm.$$

We shall try to express this quantity in terms of x, y, and z components. Now any vector is the sum of such components, thus

$$\mathbf{U} = (\mathbf{U} \cdot \mathbf{I})\mathbf{I} + (\mathbf{U} \cdot \mathbf{J})\mathbf{J} + (\mathbf{U} \cdot \mathbf{K})\mathbf{K}.$$

Here, likewise,

$$\int \mathbf{R} \times \mathbf{V}\, dm = [\int \mathbf{I} \cdot \mathbf{R} \times (\mathbf{\Omega} \times \mathbf{R}) dm]\mathbf{I} + [\int \mathbf{J} \cdot \mathbf{R} \times (\mathbf{\Omega} \times \mathbf{R}) dm]\mathbf{J} + [\int \mathbf{K} \cdot \mathbf{R} \times (\mathbf{\Omega} \times \mathbf{R}) dm]\mathbf{K}.$$

In each integrand on the right, interchange the first $\times$ with the $\cdot$. Also replace $\mathbf{\Omega}$ by

$$\omega_x \mathbf{I} + \omega_y \mathbf{J} + \omega_z \mathbf{K}.$$

We may write the result as follows:

$$\begin{aligned}\int \mathbf{R} \times \mathbf{V}\, dm = {} & [\omega_x \int (\mathbf{I} \times \mathbf{R}) \cdot (\mathbf{I} \times \mathbf{R}) dm + \omega_y \int (\mathbf{I} \times \mathbf{R}) \cdot (\mathbf{J} \times \mathbf{R}) dm \\ & + \omega_z \int (\mathbf{I} \times \mathbf{R}) \cdot (\mathbf{K} \times \mathbf{R}) dm]\mathbf{I} \\ & + [\omega_x \int (\mathbf{J} \times \mathbf{R}) \cdot (\mathbf{I} \times \mathbf{R}) dm + \omega_y \int (\mathbf{J} \times \mathbf{R}) \cdot (\mathbf{J} \times \mathbf{R}) dm \\ & + \omega_z \int (\mathbf{J} \times \mathbf{R}) \cdot (\mathbf{K} \times \mathbf{R}) dm]\mathbf{J} \\ & + [\omega_x \int (\mathbf{K} \times \mathbf{R}) \cdot (\mathbf{I} \times \mathbf{R}) dm + \omega_y \int (\mathbf{K} \times \mathbf{R}) \cdot (\mathbf{J} \times \mathbf{R}) dm \\ & + \omega_z \int (\mathbf{K} \times \mathbf{R}) \cdot (\mathbf{K} \times \mathbf{R}) dm]\mathbf{K}.\end{aligned}$$

The integrands are now in a form which we can identify as moments of inertia and products of inertia:

$$(11.50) \qquad \int_m \mathbf{R} \times \mathbf{V}\, dm = [i_x\omega_x - i_{xy}\omega_y - i_{zx}\omega_z]\mathbf{I} + [-i_{xy}\omega_x + i_y\omega_y - i_{yz}\omega_z]\mathbf{J} + [-i_{zx}\omega_x - i_{yz}\omega_y + i_z\omega_z]\mathbf{K}.$$

An expression of this sort can be expressed more elegantly in matrix or tensor form, but such techniques will be considered as beyond the scope of this treatment.

If principal axes of the body are chosen as coordinate axes, some simplification obviously results:

$$(11.51) \qquad \int \mathbf{R} \times \mathbf{V}\, dm = i_x\omega_x \mathbf{I} + i_y\omega_y \mathbf{J} + i_z\omega_z \mathbf{K}.$$

Steady Precession of a Top or Gyro. Consider as a special case a uniform solid of revolution such as a top or gyro which rotates about an axis of symmetry and at the same time precesses about a vertical axis. Let the coordinate axes be chosen thus: axis of spin is x axis; y axis is normal to the x axis and in the same vertical plane (as in Fig. 11.22). Then the moment of momentum vector may be instantaneously expressed in terms of the angular velocity of spin ω_s and of precession ω_p. The total angular velocity is

$$\mathbf{\Omega} = \mathbf{\Omega}_s + \mathbf{\Omega}_p.$$

(A special case of this was previously

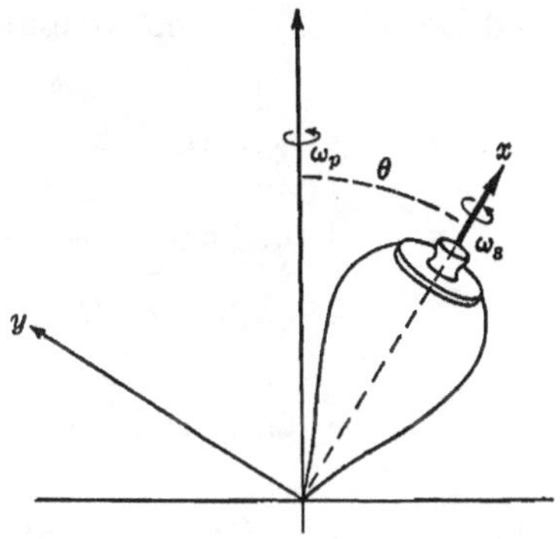

FIG. 11.22.

considered in Fig. 6.14.) The components of the angular velocity may be expressed as follows:

$$\omega_x = \omega_s + \omega_p \cos \theta,$$
$$\omega_y = \omega_p \sin \theta,$$
$$\omega_z = 0.$$

(One might regard the whole component ω_x as the component of spin. In that case the following development would be carried out in terms of ω_x rather than ω_s.) Using (11.51), we get

$$\int \mathbf{R} \times \mathbf{V}\, dm = i_x(\omega_s + \omega_p \cos \theta)\mathbf{I} + i_y(\omega_p \sin \theta)\mathbf{J}. \tag{11.52}$$

Now relative to a fixed frame coinciding instantaneously with the rotating frame described above, the dynamical equation [generalization of (11.26)]

$$\mathbf{\Gamma} = \frac{d}{dt}\left(\int \mathbf{R} \times \mathbf{V}\, dm\right) \tag{11.53}$$

is valid. This derivative may most easily be computed by use of the operation (6.43)

$$\frac{d}{dt} = \mathbf{\Omega} \times \quad + \frac{d'}{d't}.$$

Assuming that the spin is uniform,

$$\mathbf{\Gamma} = \frac{d}{dt}\left(\int \mathbf{R} \times \mathbf{V}\, dm\right) = \mathbf{\Omega}_p \times \left(\int \mathbf{R} \times \mathbf{V}\, dm\right).$$

This already brings to light the startling fact that the torque required for such a steady precession is normal to both the precession and the moment of momentum vector.

Now let us substitute

$$\mathbf{\Omega}_p = \omega_p(\cos \theta\, \mathbf{I} + \sin \theta\, \mathbf{J})$$

and Eq. (11.52). The computation is as follows:

$$\mathbf{\Gamma} = \omega_p \begin{vmatrix} \cos \theta & \sin \theta & 0 \\ i_x(\omega_s + \omega_p \cos \theta) & i_y(\omega_p \sin \theta) & 0 \\ \mathbf{I} & \mathbf{J} & \mathbf{K} \end{vmatrix}$$
$$= (i_y\omega_p^2 \sin \theta \cos \theta - i_x\omega_p\omega_s \sin \theta - i_x\omega_p^2 \sin \theta \cos \theta)\mathbf{K}$$
$$= \omega_p\omega_s \sin \theta \left[(i_y - i_x)\frac{\omega_p}{\omega_s} \cos \theta - i_x\right]\mathbf{K}$$
$$= (\mathbf{\Omega}_s \times \mathbf{\Omega}_p)\left[(i_y - i_x)\frac{\omega_p}{\omega_s} \cos \theta - i_x\right].$$

$$\mathbf{\Gamma} = (\mathbf{\Omega}_p \times i_x\mathbf{\Omega}_s)\left[1 + \left(1 - \frac{i_y}{i_x}\right)\frac{\omega_p}{\omega_s} \cos \theta\right]. \tag{11.54}$$

In many important applications it happens that either $\theta = 90°$ or $\omega_s \gg \omega_p$. Then we may use

$$\mathbf{\Gamma} = \mathbf{\Omega}_p' \times i_s\mathbf{\Omega}_s, \tag{11.55}$$

where now i_s is used to denote the moment of inertia about the axis of spin.

EXERCISES

1. For coordinates relative to axes instantaneously coincident with principal axes of inertia, show that the kinetic energy of a rigid body moving with one point fixed is equal to one-half the scalar product of moment of momentum and angular velocity.

2. A rigid body moves with one point fixed. Choose coordinate axes fixed in the body along principal axes. Show from (11.51) and (11.53) that one may deduce the following (*Euler's equations of motion*):

$$\gamma_x = i_x \frac{d\omega_x}{dt} + (i_z - i_y)\omega_y\omega_z,$$

$$\gamma_y = i_y \frac{d\omega_y}{dt} + (i_x - i_z)\omega_z\omega_x,$$

$$\gamma_z = i_z \frac{d\omega_z}{dt} + (i_y - i_x)\omega_x\omega_y.$$

3. Use Euler's equations (Exercise 2) to establish the constancy of kinetic energy for a rigid body in motion with one point fixed and with external forces having zero moment about the fixed point. [HINT: Multiply each equation by the proper component of $\mathbf{\Omega}$, add, and integrate. Compare with (9.24).]

4. A top consists of a thin disk 12 cm in diameter weighing 200 g together with a pin of negligible mass mounted normal to the disk through its center. The point of the pin is 3 cm from the disk. The top spins with the point fixed and precesses at an angular speed of 2 rad/sec, while the pin makes an angle of 20° with the vertical. Find the rate of spin.

CHAPTER 12

MECHANICAL VIBRATIONS IN ONE DIMENSION

A full study of oscillations would include a large part of the subjects of acoustics, electrical and radio engineering, and even of atomic theory. Uncontrolled oscillations may result in bridge failures, in howling amplifiers, or in noisy motors. We already have investigated important cases of small oscillations: pendulums of various sorts and other special cases of simple harmonic motion. Thus far no account has been taken of the effect of friction; yet we realize that all mechanical motion is, to some extent, dissipative. The oscillations thus far considered have not been driven; thus problems of resonance have not arisen. These topics will be touched on in this chapter.

12.1. Dynamical Analogues of Electric Circuits. An exhaustive study even of mechanical vibrations would demand too much time and too much mathematics for this course. As an introduction to the subject, we shall analyze the one-dimensional behavior of an oscillator consisting of a uniform spring, a bob, and a damper. We shall assume that the three functions of these elements can be separated one from another. Thus the system will be described by three numbers, assumed constant. These three numbers are called the compliance, the mass, and the mechanical resistance of the system. They are denoted by c, m, and r; and they are associated primarily with the spring, the bob, and the damper, respectively, as is indicated in Fig. 12.1.

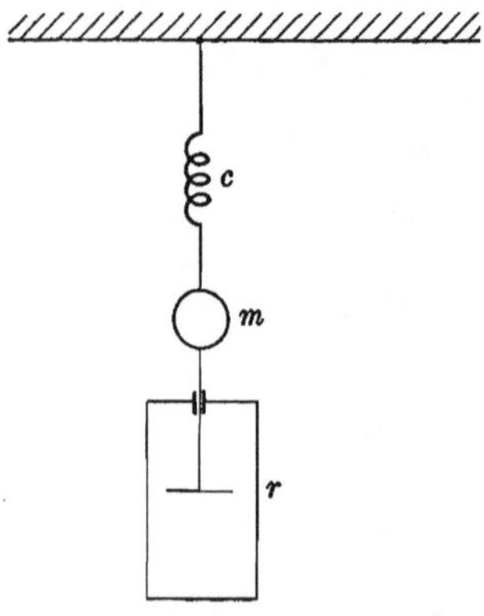

Fig. 12.1.

Since this is a course in mechanics, we shall not study electrical oscillations. But it is, nevertheless, a fact that the study of electrical oscillations is very highly developed and rather well known. In an elementary physics course one usually studies alternating-current theory to some extent. Topics in electrical transients may be included, too. For instance, the voltage pattern for a charging or discharging capacitor may be familiar to readers of this text. Much use is often made of the language and methods of electrical theory in dealing with other kinds of oscillations. This approach has been particularly fruitful in the field of acoustics. The topics in this chapter will be developed as analogies with electrical situations. An electrical analogue of Fig. 12.1 is shown in Fig. 12.2. The compliance c corresponds to the capacitance C, the mass m to the inductance L, and the mechanical resistance r to the electrical resistance R. Any constant applied force f (such as weight in Fig. 12.1) corresponds to a constant applied electromotive force E. A displacement s of the mechanical system, measuring the amount that the spring is contracted or stretched from its equilibrium position, corresponds to the charge Q on the capacitor.

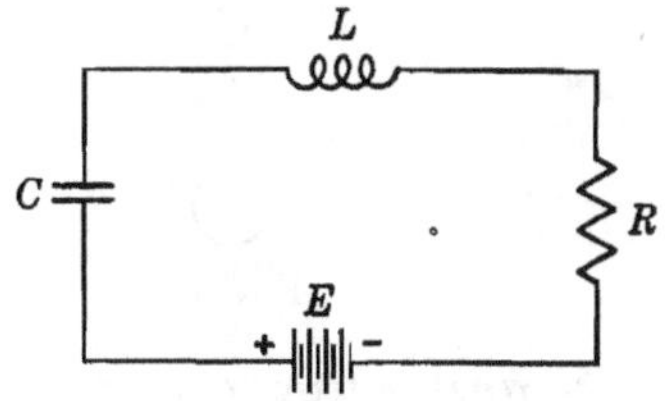

FIG. 12.2.

Letting the electric potentials across capacitor, inductor, and resistor be E_C, E_L, E_R, basic electrical equations are

$$C = \frac{Q}{E_C}, \qquad L = \frac{E_L}{dI/dt}, \qquad R = \frac{E_R}{I}.$$

The equations serve as guides for setting up the mechanical analogues. The *compliance* c of a spring is defined as the ratio of stretch to tension:

$$c = \frac{s}{f_c}. \tag{12.1}$$

The effective *mass* of the moving parts is defined as the ratio of resultant force acting on the bob to the acceleration:

$$m = \frac{f_m}{dv/dt}. \tag{12.2}$$

The *mechanical resistance* of the damper may be defined as the ratio of damping force to velocity:

$$r = \frac{f_r}{v}. \tag{12.3}$$

We assume that for a given system c, m, and r are constants. In the first two cases this involves nothing new, for we have dealt only with linear springs and constant masses. In the case of r, it implies that frictional resistance is proportional to the first power of the speed. Actual physical behavior is usually more complicated, but for moderate speed in liquids or gases this assumption gives fairly good results.

EXERCISES

1. What are the dimensions of mechanical resistance and compliance?

2. What in terms of c' and c'' is the compliance of the system of springs shown in Fig. 12.3?

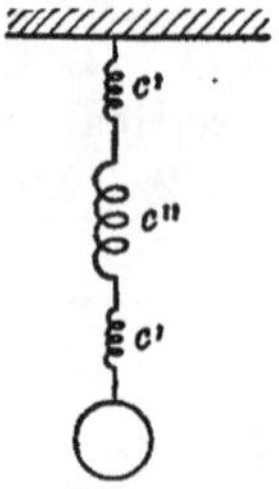

FIG. 12.3.

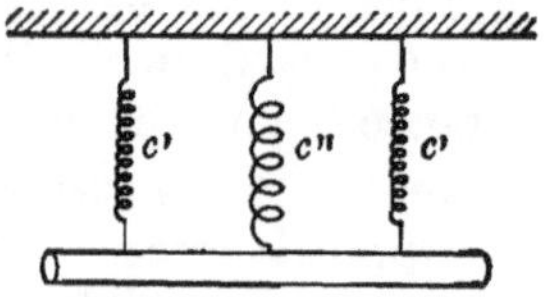

FIG. 12.4.

3. What in terms of c' and c'' is the compliance of the system of springs shown in Fig. 12.4?

4. What in terms of c' and c'' is the compliance of the system of springs shown in Fig. 12.5?

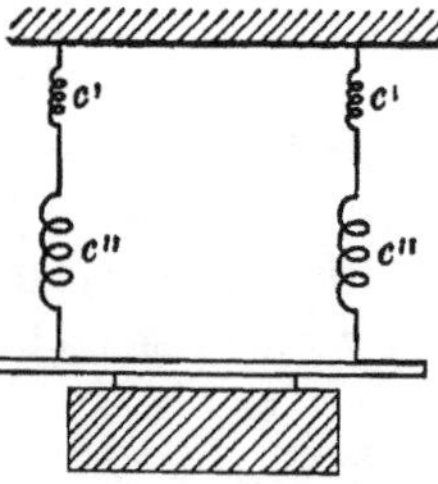

FIG. 12.5.

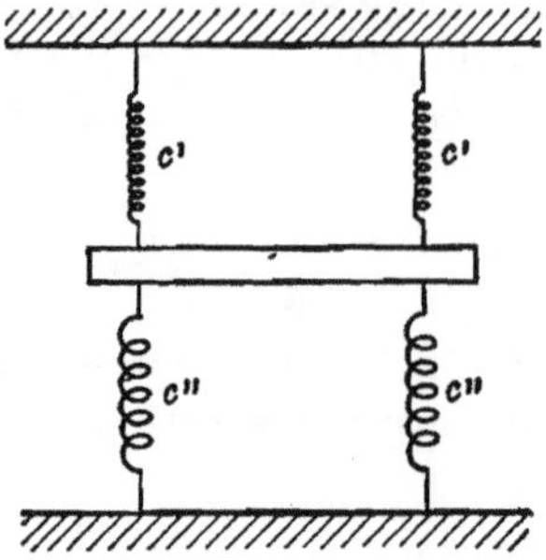

FIG. 12.6.

5. What in terms of c' and c'' is the compliance of the system of springs shown in Fig. 12.6?

6. A spring balance has a 6-in. scale reading from 0 to 60 lb. What is the compliance of the spring? What work must be done in applying a 60-lb force to the balance?

7. Plot a graph of the potential energy stored in the spring of Exercise 6 as a function of the displacement x ranging from 0 to 6 in.

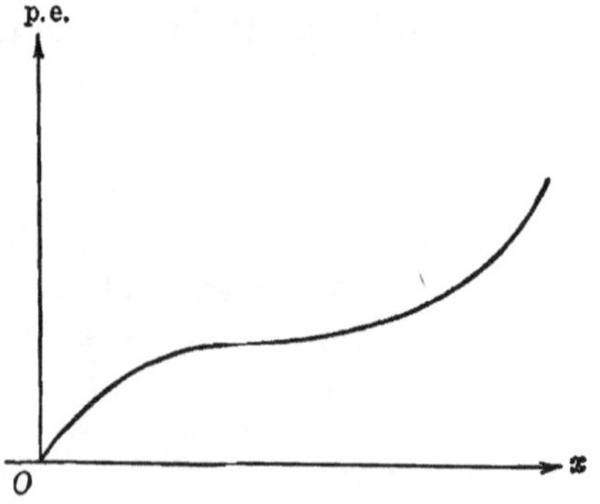

FIG. 12.7.

8. The potential energy stored in a spring of variable compliance varies with displacement, as shown in Fig. 12.7. Plot a graph showing approximately the behavior of the compliance as a function of x.

12.2. Effective Mass of a Simple Oscillator. When the system shown in Fig. 12.1 is oscillating, the bob and the damper always have identical velocities; therefore we should expect that the effective oscillatory mass m would include the masses of these parts. For the spring, the situation is less clear. The upper end of the spring has zero velocity, the lower end moves with the bob, and all intermediate values are found at intermediate points. To find the effective mass contribution of the spring, let us analyze its kinetic energy. Assuming that the spring is quite uniform, the ratio (see Fig. 12.8) y'/y is constant for any state of stretch that the spring is in:

$$y' = ky.$$

Consequently, differentiating,

$$v' = kv.$$

For an element of length dy, the kinetic energy is

$$d(\text{k.e.}) = \frac{1}{2}\left(\frac{m'}{y}\,dy'\right)v'^2,$$

where m' is the mass of the spring. Substituting the two preceding equations and integrating,

$$\text{k.e.} = \frac{m'v^2}{2y^3}\int_0^y y'^2\,dy' = \frac{1}{2}\left(\frac{m'}{3}\right)v^2.$$

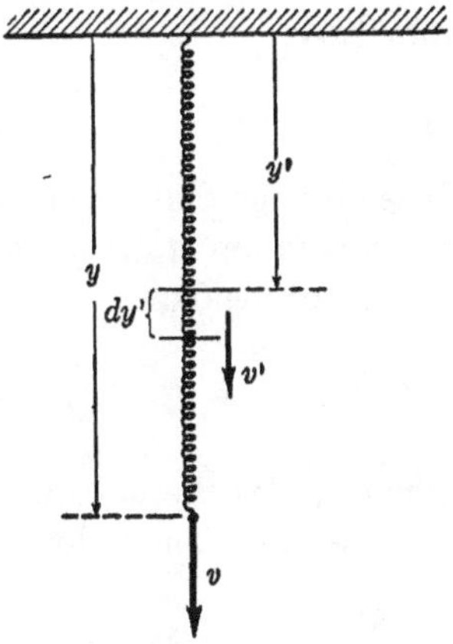

FIG. 12.8.

Thus the effective mass m of the whole system is given by

(12.4) $$m = m_{\text{bob}} + m_{\text{damper}} + \tfrac{1}{3}(m_{\text{spring}}).$$

12.3. Undamped Free Vibration. In our earlier study of simple harmonic motion, the special case of bob and spring without resistance was solved (Example 4, Sec. 7.2). For the sake of completeness a similar situation is examined here, with emphasis on energy relationships. When the system (see Fig. 12.9) is in equilibrium, the weight mg of the bob is just balanced by an extension of the spring which we denote by s_0. The letter x will signify the displacement away from the equilibrium position. The energy of the spring when stretched by $s_0 + x$ is equal to the work done in the stretching:

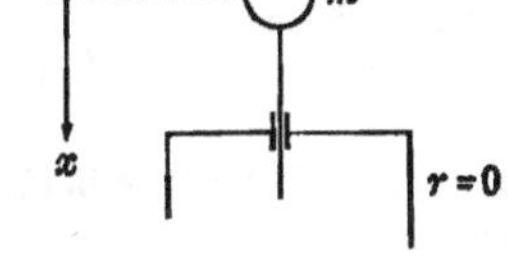

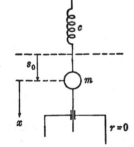

FIG. 12.9.

$$\int_0^{s_0+x} f\,ds = \frac{1}{c}\int_0^{s_0} s\,ds + \frac{1}{c}\int_{s_0}^{s_0+x} s\,ds$$
$$= \frac{1}{2}\left(\frac{1}{c}\right)s_0^2 + \frac{1}{2}\left(\frac{1}{c}\right)x^2 + \frac{s_0}{c}x$$
$$= \frac{1}{2}\left(\frac{1}{c}\right)(s_0^2 + x^2) + mgx.$$

The potential energy due to gravity may be written $-mgx$. By the law of conservation of energy, the sum of the two potential energies plus the kinetic energy is constant.

$$\frac{1}{2}mv^2 + \frac{1}{2}\left(\frac{1}{c}\right)(s_0^2 + x^2) = \text{const.}$$

Since s_0 is a constant of the system, we can conclude also

$$\frac{1}{2}mv^2 + \frac{1}{2}\left(\frac{1}{c}\right)x^2 = \text{const.} \tag{12.5}$$

Similarly,

$$\tfrac{1}{2}mv^2 + \tfrac{1}{2}cf^2 = \text{const.} \tag{12.6}$$

It is obvious that v has a maximum value (v_{max}) when x is zero, and that x is maximum (x_{max}) when v is zero. Equating the energy sums for these two cases yields

$$\frac{1}{2}mv_{max}^2 = \frac{1}{2}\left(\frac{1}{c}\right)x_{max}^2 = \frac{1}{2}cf_{max}^2, \tag{12.7}$$

where f_{max} is the maximum amount by which the tension of the spring exceeds mg. The following are immediate consequences:

$$x_{max} = \sqrt{mc}\, v_{max}, \tag{12.8}$$

$$f_{max} = \sqrt{\frac{m}{c}}\, v_{max}, \tag{12.9}$$

$$f_{max}x_{max} = mv_{max}^2. \tag{12.10}$$

The electrical analogues of these last three equations are useful in connection with "tank circuits."

Using (10.16), the period of the oscillation can be identified as

$$\tau = 2\pi \frac{x_{max}}{v_{max}},$$

or

$$\tau = 2\pi\sqrt{mc}. \tag{12.11}$$

EXERCISES

1. Referring to Fig. 12.10, the bob weighs 10 lb, and the weight of the spring is negligible. A force of 10 additional pounds will draw the mass downward 2 in. It is then released. Friction may be ignored. (*a*) How much energy was stored in the spring just before release? (*b*) With what period will it oscillate? (*c*) What will be the maximum speed?

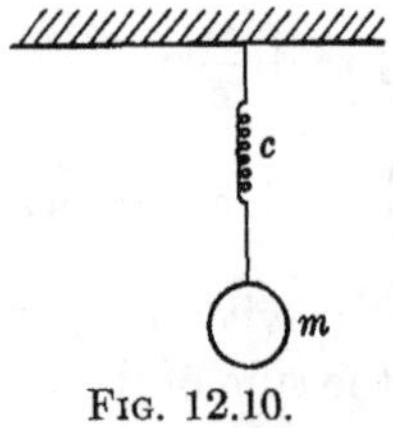

FIG. 12.10.

2. Refer to Fig. 12.10. The maximum speed of the bob is 26 cm/sec. When the displacement is 5 cm, the speed is only 24 cm/sec. What is the period of the oscillation? What is the amplitude of the oscillation?

3. Refer to Fig. 12.10. The maximum total tension in the spring is to be 25.0 lb and the corresponding maximum displacement from equilibrium position is to be 7.0 in. If the period is to be 0.935 sec, find the required mass and compliance.

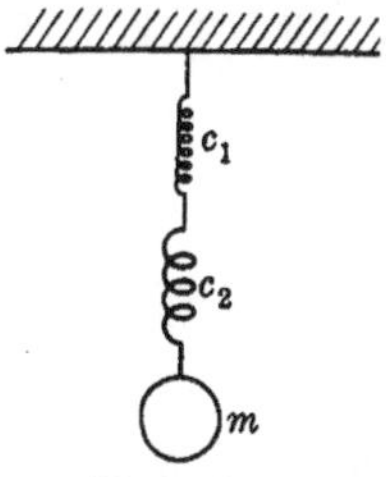

FIG. 12.11.

4. Referring to Fig. 12.11, the data are as follows:
c_1: 1-in. stretch for 5 lb additional tension
c_2: 1-in. stretch for 10 lb additional tension
m: Weight of bob is 16 lb, weight of springs may be neglected

(*a*) What is the period of oscillation?

(*b*) If the bob is displaced by 6 in. from the equilibrium position and then released, what is the maximum speed the bob will attain?

5. The 10-lb weight in Fig. 12.12 is suspended between two stretched springs. The top spring has a constant of 5 lb/in.; the bottom spring has a constant of 10 lb/in. (*a*) What work must be done to displace the mass upward by 1 in.? (*b*) downward by 1 in.? (*c*) With what period will it oscillate?

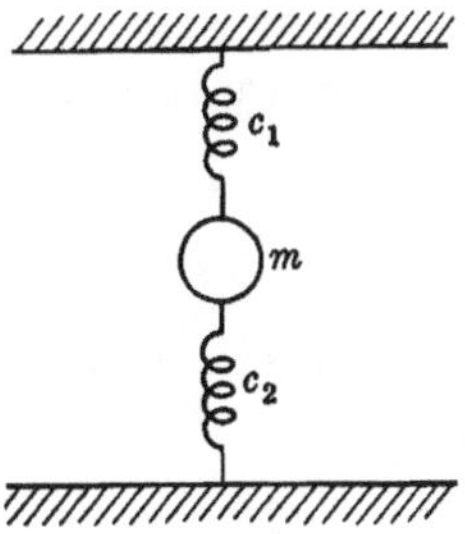

FIG. 12.12.

6. A 200-g sphere is supported by two vertical springs (as in Fig. 12.12). The compliances are

$$c_1 = 0.010 \text{ m/newton}, \qquad c_2 = 0.015 \text{ m/newton}.$$

When the sphere is at equilibrium, the tension in the lower spring is f. (*a*) What force will displace the sphere vertically 3 cm from equilibrium position? (*b*) With what period will it oscillate if released?

7. Let k denote the ratio of angular displacement to torque and i the moment of inertia of a torsion pendulum. Assuming that friction is negligible, derive the formulas

$$\theta_{\max} = \sqrt{ik}\,\omega_{\max},$$

$$\text{Torque}_{\max} = \sqrt{\frac{i}{k}}\,\omega_{\max},$$

$$\tau = 2\pi\sqrt{ik}.$$

12.4. Mechanical Resistance and Terminal Speed. The preceding section handled a special case of Fig. 12.1: the damper was omitted, and we had $r = 0$. This time the spring is omitted as in Fig. 12.13, or, we might say, the spring has infinite compliance. In this special case, no oscillation takes place. The mass falls subject to the pull of gravity impeded by the frictional resistance to the damper. The faster it falls, the greater is this retarding force. If space permits, a balance will eventually be realized; the friction will practically offset the weight, and the speed of fall will be essentially constant. This limiting speed is called the *terminal speed*, v_t. To check on this speed, we set up and integrate the equation of motion. First we have

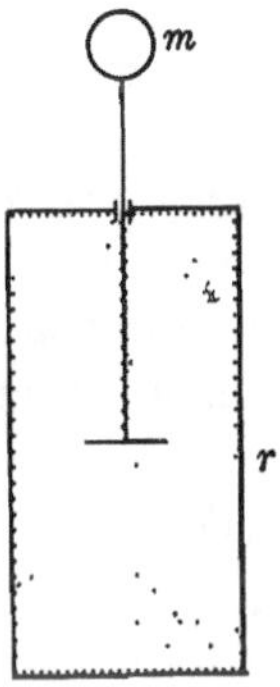

FIG. 12.13.

$$w - rv = m\frac{dv}{dt}, \tag{12.12}$$

or

$$-\frac{r}{m}\,dt = \frac{-r\,dv}{w - rv}.$$

This yields, upon integration,

$$-\frac{r}{m}t = \ln(w - rv) + \text{const.}$$

Let v_0 be the initial speed; then the constant of integration is evaluated as

$$\text{const} = -\ln(w - rv_0).$$

The preceding equation may then be rewritten as

$$v - v_0 = \left(\frac{w}{r} - v_0\right)(1 - e^{-(r/m)t}). \tag{12.13}$$

This equation shows that the terminal speed is that given by $rv = w$,

$$v_t = \frac{w}{r}, \tag{12.14}$$

and that v approaches v_t *exponentially* (see Fig. 12.14). Thus the terminal speed theoretically is approached, but never attained.

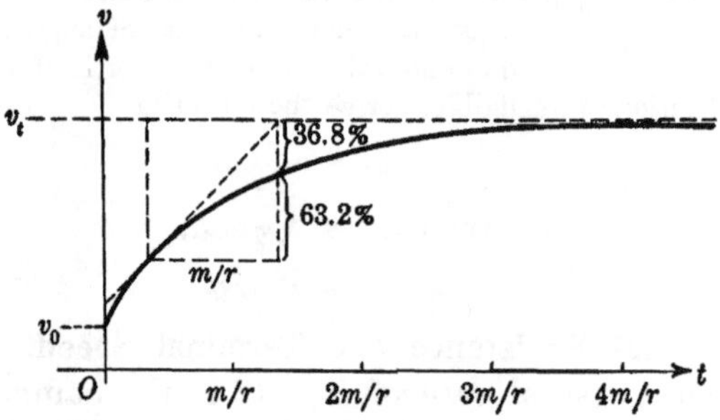

FIG. 12.14.

The statement "v starts at v_0 and approaches v_t exponentially" describes a sort of situation occurring widely in physics and other sciences. The time required (see Exercise 1) for the variable to get from its current value to a value 63.2 per cent nearer the final value is called the *time constant* of the exponential (the reciprocal of e is 0.368). For the case under discussion, the time constant τ_e is given by

$$\tau_e = \frac{m}{r} = \frac{v_t}{g}. \tag{12.15}$$

It should be emphasized that the equations of this section were derived for a body falling in a resisting medium, for in Eq. (12.12) w represents the only force besides friction. The method, however, can be adapted very easily to other situations. The basic procedure is merely to set up an equation of motion analogous to (12.12), and then to integrate, evaluating constants of integration in terms of initial conditions or other specified conditions.

EXERCISES

1. Suppose that $y(t)$ approaches a limit $y(\infty) = a$ exponentially, that is, that y can be expressed thus:

$$y(t) = a + be^{-(t/\tau_e)},$$

where a and b are constants and τ_e is the time constant. At any time t, $y(t)$ is the "current value." Prove that in one time constant, y will get 63.2 per cent of the way toward its limit, *i.e.*, that

$$y(t + \tau_e) - y(t) = 0.632[y(\infty) - y(t)].$$

2. At the point where $t = t'$, a tangent is drawn to the graph of

$$y(t) = a + be^{-(t/\tau_e)}.$$

Show that this tangent cuts the line $y = a$ at the point where

$$t = t' + \tau_e.$$

3. Check Eq. (12.14) dimensionally.

4. A raindrop has a terminal speed of 25 ft/sec. If the resistance is proportional to the speed, (*a*) how long would it take such a drop, starting from rest, to acquire a speed of 15 ft/sec? (*b*) how far from rest will such a drop fall in 2 sec?

5. A man and his parachute weigh 150 lb. Fifteen feet per second will be considered a safe landing speed. The material of the parachute, tested in a 15 mph wind blast, creates a force of $\frac{1}{2}$ lb/ft². The resistance is proportional to the speed. (*a*) What should be the minimum diameter of the parachute? (*b*) How much of a drop is necessary for acquiring a speed of 12 ft/sec?

6. (*a*) A 320-lb canoe maintains a speed of 7.5 mph when pulled by a steady force of 5.5 lb. If the force is removed, what will be the speed of the canoe after 10 sec? (Assume that the resistance is proportional to the speed.) (*b*) How far will the canoe glide during the time interval specified in part (*a*)?

7. Repeat Exercise 6, using the assumption that the resistance is proportional to the *square* of the speed.

8. For a body of weight w falling in a resisting medium with resistance proportional to the *square* of the speed

$$f_r = r'v^2$$

show that the terminal speed is

$$v_t = \sqrt{\frac{w}{r'}}.$$

12.5. Mechanical Analogue of a Capacitor.

When a system is light, its behavior may sometimes be predicted by neglecting the mass. This is particularly feasible when the motion is slow. Figure 12.15 represents a light spring with heavy damping. The restoring force of the spring just

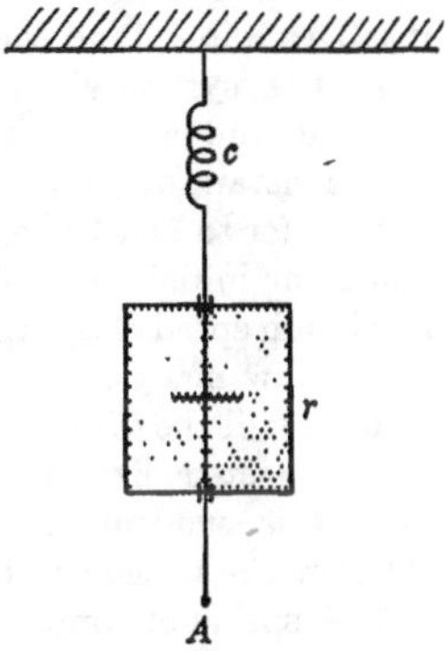

FIG. 12.15.

offsets the drag of the damper when no other force is applied. The force equation is

$$-r\frac{dx}{dt} - \frac{x}{c} = 0, \tag{12.16}$$

or

$$\frac{dx}{x} = -\frac{dt}{rc}.$$

If the initial displacement is x_0, the return toward equilibrium position is given by

$$x = x_0 e^{-(t/rc)}. \tag{12.17}$$

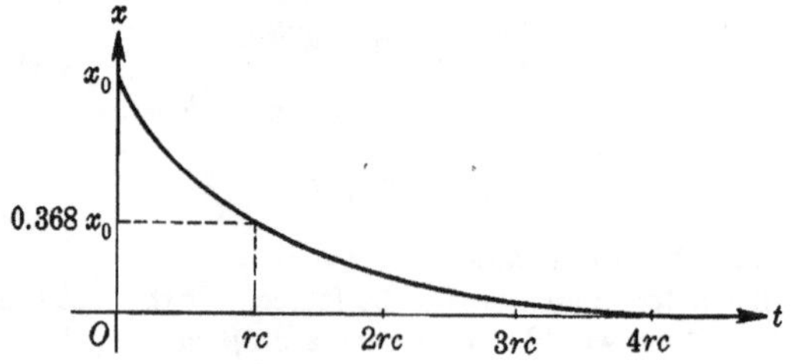

FIG. 12.16.

This is diagramed in Fig. 12.16. The time constant for this exponential is rc.

$$\tau_e = rc. \tag{12.18}$$

The electrical analogy of a discharging condenser should be obvious. The equation for charging is left as an exercise.

EXERCISES

1. In the highly damped system discussed in the preceding section, the damper is held at rest at a displacement of 15 in. by a tension of 1 lb and then released. In 3 sec it moves 3 in. Find the resistance constant r.

2. In a system similar to the one just described, the damper is held at rest, is released, and in 10 sec is halfway back toward the equilibrium position. What is the time constant of the exponential?

3. Refer to Fig. 12.15. If r has the value 300 kg/sec, if c has the value 0.05 sec²/kg, and if the initial displacement from the equilibrium position is 0.25 m, (*a*) what is the maximum speed of return (assuming that the damper is held at rest and then released)? (*b*) in how many seconds will the speed be half of its maximum? (*c*) in how many seconds will the displacement be 0.125 m?

4. A system like the one in Fig. 12.15 is initially in equilibrium. A downward force f is suddenly applied at A. (*a*) Plot the velocity as a function of time. (*b*) Plot the tension in the spring as a function of time.

5. A spring of compliance 0.05 ft/lb has a damper of resistance 40 lb-sec/ft. The system is initially at rest in equilibrium, as shown in Fig. 12.15. A sudden downward force of 40 lb is applied. How long will it take to get halfway to its new equilibrium position?

6. In Exercise 5 how long before the rate of energy storage in the spring is a maximum?

12.6. Free Damped Vibration. We now consider the general case (see Fig. 12.17) where r, m, and c have arbitrary values. The equation of motion

$$mg - \frac{1}{c}(s_0 + x) - r\frac{dx}{dt} = m\frac{d^2x}{dt^2}$$

becomes, since $mg = s_0/c$,

$$\frac{d^2x}{dt^2} + \frac{r}{m}\frac{dx}{dt} + \frac{1}{mc}x = 0. \tag{12.19}$$

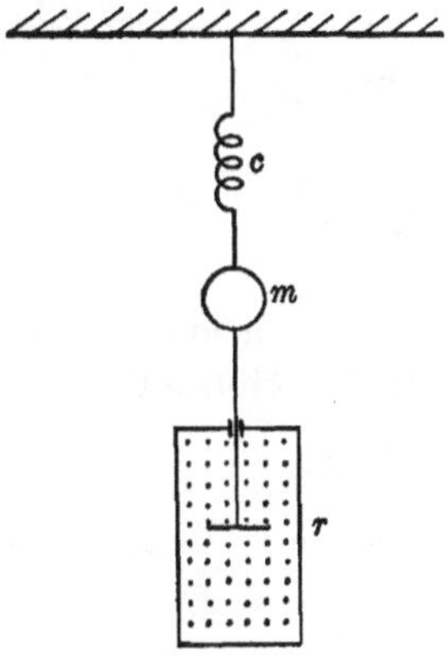

FIG. 12.17.

This is a standard second-order linear homogeneous differential equation, and it is easy to find functions $x(t)$ which satisfy it. A student who has had a course covering such solutions may wish to pass over some of the following.

We observe that the second derivative of the function

$$xe^{rt/2m}$$

is related to Eq. (12.19) for

$$\frac{d^2}{dt^2}(xe^{rt/2m}) = \left(\frac{d^2x}{dt^2} + \frac{r}{m}\frac{dx}{dt} + \frac{r^2}{4m^2}x\right)e^{rt/2m}. \tag{12.20}$$

With this in mind we get a simpler equation by multiplying (12.19) by $e^{rt/2m}$ and subtracting from (12.20). We get

$$\frac{d^2}{dt^2}(xe^{rt/2m}) + \left(\frac{1}{mc} - \frac{r^2}{4m^2}\right)xe^{rt/2m} = 0. \tag{12.21}$$

The nature of the solutions of this equation depends on the relative importance of the resistance r; we therefore consider three cases separately. These cases depend on the quantity in parentheses

$$\frac{1}{mc} - \frac{r^2}{4m^2}.$$

Note that for a critical value of r (called the *critical damping resistance* r_c) this quantity is equal to zero. It is easy to solve for r_c:

$$r_c = 2\sqrt{\frac{m}{c}}. \tag{12.22}$$

In this section we shall limit our discussion to what is called *underdamp-*

ing, determined by

$$r < r_c. \tag{12.23}$$

This hypothesis allows us to write (12.21) in the familiar form.

$$\frac{d^2y}{dt^2} + \omega^2 y = 0, \tag{12.24}$$

where

$$y = xe^{rt/2m}$$

$$\omega = \sqrt{\frac{1}{mc} - \frac{r^2}{4m^2}}. \tag{12.25}$$

This equation we know to represent a simple harmonic motion of period $2\pi/\omega$. Hence the general solution of (12.21) may be written

$$xe^{rt/2m} = a \sin (\omega t + \epsilon), \tag{12.26}$$

where a and ϵ are constants. The displacement x is then given in full by

$$x = ae^{-(rt/2m)} \sin \left(\sqrt{\frac{1}{mc} - \frac{r^2}{4m^2}}\, t + \epsilon\right). \tag{12.27}$$

This is the product of a sine of period

$$\tau = \frac{2\pi}{\sqrt{(1/mc) - (r^2/4m^2)}} \tag{12.28}$$

by a damping exponential of time constant

$$\tau_e = \frac{2m}{r}. \tag{12.29}$$

Such a function of t is known as a *damped oscillation*. In the solution of problems *where the damping is slight*, it is often expedient to neglect r in computing ω. The displacement is then regarded as the product of an *undamped* sinusoid by a damping exponential.

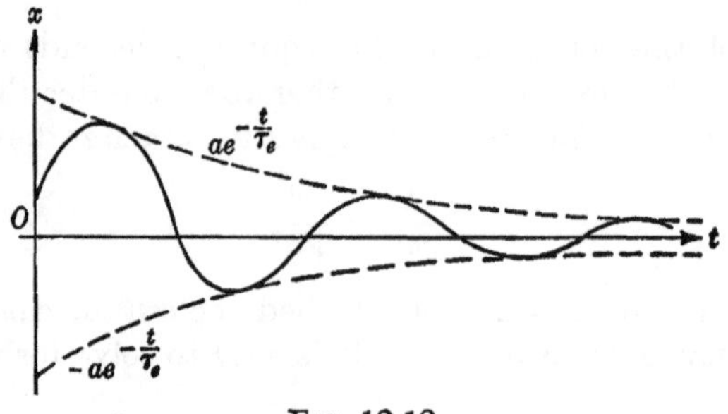

FIG. 12.18.

The graph of Eq. (12.27) is a sine curve oscillating between two damping exponentials as shown in Fig. 12.18.

EXERCISES

1. If the mass m in the underdamped system of the preceding section is started at rest with an initial displacement x_0, show that the constants in Eq. (12.27) have the values

$$a = \frac{x_0}{\sqrt{1 - \rho^2}}, \qquad \epsilon = \tan^{-1} \frac{-\rho}{\sqrt{1 - \rho^2}},$$

where ρ is the ratio of the resistance r to the critical resistance r_c.

2. (*a*) Show that the zeros of a damped oscillation occur every half period. (*b*) Show that the peaks of a damped oscillation occur every half period, but that the separations of peaks and zeros are not quarter periods.

3. Let x_n and x_{n+1} denote two successive peak values of a damped oscillation. Treat them both as positive quantities. The quantity

$$\lambda = \ln \left(\frac{x_n}{x_{n+1}} \right)$$

is called the *logarithmic decrement per half period.* Prove that (*a*) $\lambda = \tau/2\tau_e$ (hence λ is independent of n); (*b*) for small λ, $x_{n+1} = x_n e^{-\lambda} = x_n(1 - \lambda)$.

4. The turning points of a particle in damped oscillation are recorded by taking readings on a single scale. Three successive scale readings are s_1, s_2, s_3. Show that the equilibrium position is given by the scale reading

$$s_0 = \frac{s_1 s_3 - s_2^2}{s_1 - 2s_2 + s_3}.$$

5. Three successive excursions on a ballistic galvanometer were read as +20.4, −18.9, +19.0. The equilibrium position would not be exactly zero, since the scale was slightly off center. Give corrected values for the three excursions.

6. Three successive deflections of a ballistic galvanometer are +25.4, −25.0, +24.6. (*a*) What approximately is the logarithmic decrement per half period? (*b*) After how many complete oscillations will the deflection be less than 50 per cent of the initial deflection?

7. Equation (12.28) shows that the period τ of a damped oscillation is longer than the corresponding undamped period τ_0. Show that

$$\frac{\tau}{\tau_0} = \sqrt{1 + \frac{\lambda^2}{\pi^2}}.$$

8. Show that the constants of Exercise 1 may be written as

$$a = x_0 \sqrt{1 + \frac{\lambda^2}{\pi^2}}, \qquad \epsilon = \tan^{-1} \frac{-\lambda}{\pi}.$$

9. A damped harmonic oscillation has period 0.5 sec and logarithmic decrement (per half period) of 0.025. The effective mass is 1 kg. (*a*) What is the compliance of the spring? (*b*) What is the resistance?

10. Each successive excursion of the system in Exercise 6, Sec. 12.3, is nine-tenths as long as the previous one. What is the resistance?

12.7. Critical Damping and Overdamping. When a speedy return to equilibrium is desired, the system may be adjusted for critical damping. In this case the resistance satisfies $r = r_c$, and $\omega = 0$. No oscillation takes place. A typical displacement curve is shown in Fig. 12.19. The case of critical damping will here be considered as the limit, as ω becomes small, of underdamping cases. This can be handled easily if we use a different form of our underdamped equation. Equation (12.27) may be written

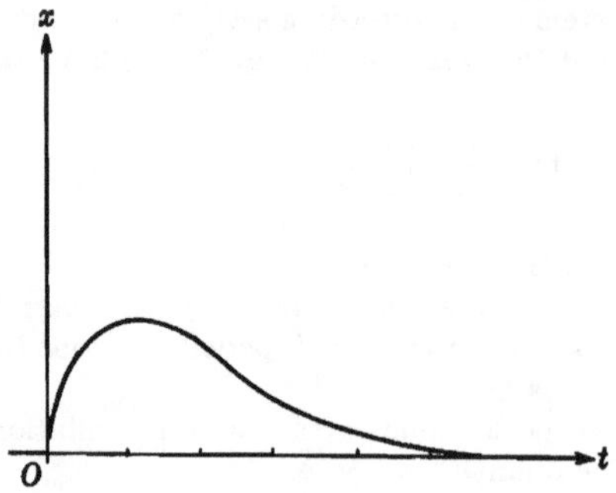

FIG. 12.19.

$$x = e^{-(t/\tau_e)}(b \sin \omega t + d \cos \omega t). \tag{12.30}$$

The constants of integration b and d, or *arbitrary constants* as they are often called, can be evaluated in terms of initial conditions. If the initial displacement was x_0 and the initial velocity v_0, we find at once that

$$d = x_0. \tag{12.31}$$

Now differentiate (12.30) with respect to t:

$$\frac{dx}{dt} = e^{-(t/\tau_e)}(\omega b \cos \omega t - \omega d \sin \omega t) - \frac{1}{\tau_e} x.$$

Substituting the initial values,

$$v_0 = \omega b - \frac{x_0}{\tau_e}$$

or

$$b = \frac{v_0 + (x_0/\tau_e)}{\omega}. \tag{12.32}$$

We may then write (12.30) as

$$x = e^{-(t/\tau_e)} \left[\frac{v_0 + (x_0/\tau_e)}{\omega} \sin \omega t + x_0 \cos \omega t \right]. \tag{12.33}$$

This equation is useful in dealing with underdamped problems where initial conditions are known.

To get an equation for critical damping, we now take limits as ω approaches zero. We use the facts that

$$\lim_{\omega \to 0} \cos \omega t = 1$$

and

$$\lim_{\omega \to 0} \frac{\sin \omega t}{\omega} = \lim_{\omega \to 0} \left(\frac{\sin \omega t}{\omega t} \right) t = t.$$

We get then as a *critical damping equation*

$$x = e^{-(t/\tau_e)}\left[\left(v_0 + \frac{x_0}{\tau_e}\right)t + x_0\right]. \tag{12.34}$$

Note that x is now the product of a linear function of t by an exponential whose time constant is

$$\tau_e = \frac{2m}{r_c} = \sqrt{mc}. \tag{12.35}$$

Further properties of Eq. (12.34) are investigated in Exercises 1 and 2.

Overdamping. When the resistance in a system such as we have discussed is excessive, the behavior becomes sluggish and, for most purposes, less interesting. The forces of spring and friction may be so large that inertia forces are negligible. In that case an approximate picture of what happens may be obtained by neglecting the mass and proceeding as in Sec. 12.5. If a more exact analysis is desired, Eq. (12.21) may again be integrated. Now that

$$r > r_e \tag{12.36}$$

we have

$$\frac{r^2}{4m^2} - \frac{1}{mc} > 0;$$

so the equation has the form

$$\frac{d^2y}{dt^2} = w^2y$$

the general solution of which is

$$y = ae^{wt} + be^{-wt}.$$

Substituting

$$w = \sqrt{\frac{r^2}{4m^2} - \frac{1}{mc}}, \qquad y = xe^{rt/2m},$$

and then solving for x yields

$$x = ae^{-\left(\frac{r}{2m} - \sqrt{\frac{r^2}{4m^2} - \frac{1}{mc}}\right)t} + be^{-\left(\frac{r}{2m} + \sqrt{\frac{r^2}{4m^2} - \frac{1}{mc}}\right)t}. \tag{12.37}$$

As before, the constants a and b depend on initial conditions. If the initial speed and displacement are v_0 and x_0, they may be evaluated as

(12.38)

$$a = \frac{x_0}{2} + \frac{v_0 + (r/2m)x_0}{2\sqrt{(r^2/4m^2) - (1/mc)}}; \qquad b = \frac{x_0}{2} - \frac{v_0 + (r/2m)x_0}{2\sqrt{(r^2/4m^2) - (1/mc)}}.$$

The exponents in Eq. (12.37) are always negative; therefore the function x is always the sum of two decreasing exponentials of different time constants. The second term has the smaller time constant; thus the first term is the last to die out. It is important that the first term dies out most quickly when $w = 0$, that is, when the damping is critical.

EXERCISES

1. We have seen that for critical damping the displacement from equilibrium is given as

$$x = l(t)e^{-(t/\sqrt{mc})},$$

where $l(t)$ is a linear function of t. Let t_0 be the value of t for which $l(t) = 0$. Show that x has a maximum (or minimum) for

$$t = t_0 + \sqrt{mc}.$$

2. Assuming that x_0 is positive in Exercise 1, (*a*) what positive values of v_0 would give rise to a *maximum* value of x for a positive t? (*b*) what negative values of v_0 would give rise to a *minimum* value of x for a positive t?

3. A damped harmonic oscillation has period 1.3 sec and logarithmic decrement 1.95 (per half period). The effective mass of the system is 1 kg. (*a*) What is the compliance of the spring? (*b*) What is the resistance constant? (*c*) With the same mass and spring, what resistance constant would provide critical damping?

4. A mass suspended by a spring and equipped with a damping device is free to oscillate vertically as in Fig. 12.17. The data are:

Mass: 32.2 lb

Spring: 3 lb tension produces 1 in. extension

Resistance: Proportional to speed

Assume that the displacement is zero and the speed 12 ft/sec at time $t = 0$. Plot displacement against time for the first 2 sec of motion for each of the following values of the resistance constant:

(*a*) $r = 0$. (*b*) $r = 1.5$ lb-sec/ft.
(*c*) $r = 12$ lb-sec/ft. (*d*) $r = 20$ lb-sec/ft.

5. Referring still to Fig. 12.17, at time $t = 0$ the 1-lb bob goes through equilibrium position with a speed of 3 ft/sec. The spring is such that a force of 8.75 lb produces an extension of 8.5 in. Find the time and magnitude of the first excursion of the bob if (*a*) $r = 0.1r_{\text{critical}}$; (*b*) $r = r_{\text{critical}}$.

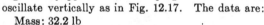

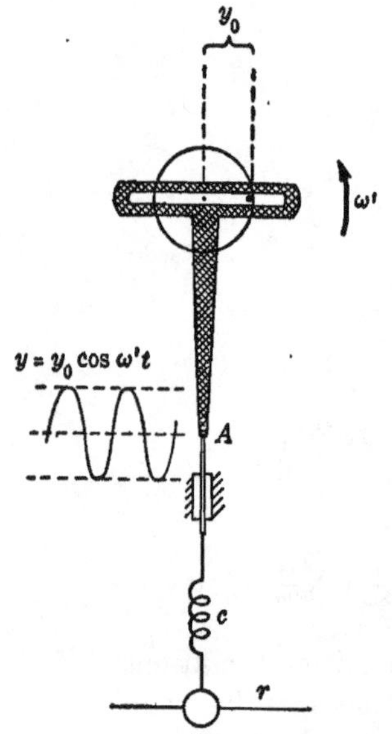

FIG. 12.20.

12.8. Damped Vibrations with a Driving Force. A simple system made up of mass, spring, and damper shows remarkable and important properties when driven by a periodic force. We shall continue to illustrate phenomena by single examples. Here we imagine the spring of the preceding section to be attached to a gadget (see Fig. 12.20) which impresses a displacement

$$y = y_0 \cos \omega' t \tag{12.39}$$

on the upper end of the spring. A sinusoidal drive is used because it is typical of periodic disturbances prevalent in machinery, and also because other periodic functions can be studied in terms of sines and cosines by means of Fourier analysis.

In Eq. (12.39) the coordinate y is considered as positive downward. The coordinate x is measured from the equilibrium position corresponding to $y = 0$. In writing the equations of motion, we use the same terminology as before

$$m \frac{d^2x}{dt^2} = mg - \frac{1}{c}(s_0 + x - y) - r\frac{dx}{dt},$$

or

$$\frac{d^2x}{dt^2} + \frac{r}{m}\frac{dx}{dt} + \frac{x}{mc} = \frac{y_0}{mc}\cos \omega' t. \tag{12.40}$$

Since y/c is the effective force applied to the mass, we write

$$\frac{y_0}{c} = f_0. \tag{12.41}$$

This shows that the same performance would follow if a force

$$f = f_0 \cos \omega' t \tag{12.42}$$

were applied to the bob.

The general solution to (12.40) has two parts:

$$x = x_{\text{transient}} + x_{\text{steady state}}. \tag{12.43}$$

The transient part of the solution is the so-called complementary function, the general solution of the related homogeneous equation

$$\frac{d^2x}{dt^2} + \frac{r}{m}\frac{dx}{dt} + \frac{x}{mc} = 0.$$

Using the result (12.27) of the preceding section, we get

$$x_{\text{transient}} = ae^{-(rt/2m)} \sin\left(\sqrt{\frac{1}{mc} - \frac{r^2}{4m^2}}\,t + \epsilon\right). \tag{12.44}$$

(It is, of course, assumed here that the resistance is less than critical.) The arbitrary constants a and ϵ cannot be determined until the whole solution x has been formulated.

The steady-state part of the solution is the oscillation generated by the driving force. It is a particular integral of the main equation (12.40). We shall try to fit the following form to that equation:

$$x_{\text{steady state}} = b \sin \omega' t + d \cos \omega' t. \tag{12.45}$$

Substituting (12.45) in (12.40), we get

$$-b\omega'^2 \sin \omega' t - d\omega'^2 \cos \omega' t + \frac{rb\omega'}{m} \cos \omega' t$$
$$- \frac{rd\omega'}{m} \sin \omega' t + \frac{b}{mc} \sin \omega' t + \frac{d}{mc} \cos \omega' t = \frac{f_0}{m} \cos \omega' t.$$

In order that this equation hold for all t, the coefficients of sine and cosine separately must agree:

$$-b\omega'^2 - \frac{rd\omega'}{m} + \frac{b}{mc} = 0,$$

and

$$-d\omega'^2 + \frac{rb\omega'}{m} + \frac{d}{mc} = \frac{f_0}{m}.$$

These two equations may be solved for b and d as follows:

(12.46)
$$b = \frac{f_0 r}{\omega' \left[r^2 + \left(\omega' m - \frac{1}{\omega' c} \right)^2 \right]}$$
$$d = \frac{f_0 \left(\frac{1}{\omega'^2 c} - m \right)}{\left[r^2 + \left(\omega' m - \frac{1}{\omega' c} \right)^2 \right]}.$$

Equation (12.45) with constants as in (12.46) is a particular integral of (12.40).

12.9. Mechanical Impedance. The ungainly expressions (12.46) derived in the preceding section are conveniently abbreviated according to the pattern used in electrical theory. For each ω', the system is said to have a *mechanical reactance* r' given as

(12.47)
$$r' = \omega' m - \frac{1}{\omega' c}$$

and a *mechanical impedance* whose magnitude z is given by

(12.48)
$$z^2 = r^2 + \left(\omega' m - \frac{1}{\omega' c} \right)^2 = r^2 + r'^2.$$

Actually it is very useful to deal with z as a complex number, as is usually done in electrical work. In this limited treatment, only the magnitude will be introduced. Note that the frequency for which the reactance is zero is the natural undamped frequency determined by Eq. (12.11).

In terms of reactance and impedance, the coefficients of the steady-state equation are

$$b = \frac{f_0 r}{\omega' z^2}, \tag{12.49}$$

$$d = \frac{-f_0 r'}{\omega' z^2}$$

so the equation becomes

$$x_{\text{steady state}} = \frac{f_0}{\omega' z^2}(r \sin \omega' t - r' \cos \omega' t); \tag{12.50}$$

or, using a little trigonometry,

$$x_{\text{steady state}} = \frac{f_0}{\omega' z} \sin \left(\omega' t - \tan^{-1} \frac{r'}{r}\right). \tag{12.51}$$

Resonance. It appears then from Eqs. (12.43), (12.44), and (12.51) that when a sinusoidal force is applied to a spring-mass system having resistance, the displacement consists of two separate patterns of behavior superimposed. The transient pattern has the characteristics of a free damped oscillation; but the steady-state behavior reflects the frequency of the driving force. The amplitude of this steady-state displacement depends on the impedance of the system at the driving frequency. In many problems of engineering design, it is essential to know under what conditions this amplitude will become large. From Eq. (12.51) it should be clear that this amplitude will be maximum when $\omega'^2 z^2$ is a minimum. Using Eq. (12.48), we find the derivative with respect to ω', set it equal to zero, and solve for the critical value. This is a standard calculus problem, and the conclusion is this: The steady-state amplitude is maximum when

$$\omega' = \sqrt{\frac{1}{mc} - \frac{r^2}{2m^2}}. \tag{12.52}$$

This condition of maximum amplitude is called *resonance.* Note that for small r this is essentially equal to the value for a free vibration [compare Eq. (12.28)]. In fact, for really small r, both values are approximately the same as the undamped value: $1/\sqrt{mc}$.

For resonance with *low resistance,* then

$$\omega' = \frac{1}{\sqrt{mc}}, \tag{12.53}$$

or

$$\omega' m = \frac{1}{\omega' c},$$

or

$$r' = 0,$$

or

$$z = r.$$

For small r it is interesting to compute the *magnification factor* at resonance:

$$\text{Magnification factor} = \frac{\text{output amplitude}}{\text{input amplitude}} = \frac{f/\omega' z}{y_0} = \frac{f/\omega' r}{fc},$$

or

$$\text{Magnification factor} = \frac{1}{r\omega' c} = \frac{\omega' m}{r}. \tag{12.54}$$

In electrical analogues this factor is called the Q of the circuit. For a high Q circuit the resonant response is sharp and often violent.

Phase Relationships. In the preceding discussions the input displacement was

$$y = y_0 \cos \omega' t.$$

The corresponding output displacement (12.51) may be written

$$x_{\text{steady state}} = \frac{f}{\omega' z} \cos\left(\omega' t - \tan^{-1}\frac{r'}{r} - 90°\right). \tag{12.55}$$

The speed of displacement is obtained by differentiating (12.51):

$$v_{\text{steady state}} = \frac{f}{z} \cos\left(\omega' t - \tan^{-1}\frac{r'}{r}\right). \tag{12.56}$$

At *resonance*, we may observe that the output speed is *in phase* with the input displacement, while the output displacement lags by 90° (that is, the peak values of $x_{\text{steady state}}$ occur one quarter period later than those of y). The reactance r' [see Eq. (12.47)] is positive for frequencies greater than the resonance value and negative for frequencies smaller than the resonance value. For small r, then, if the frequency is reduced, the angle whose tangent is r'/r approaches $-90°$; thus y and $x_{\text{steady state}}$ are nearly in phase for low frequencies. Similarly, we can deduce that for high frequencies $x_{\text{steady state}}$ lags y by 180°. These phase relationships are verified by experiment. A student familiar with complex impedances in electrical work will readily translate these results.

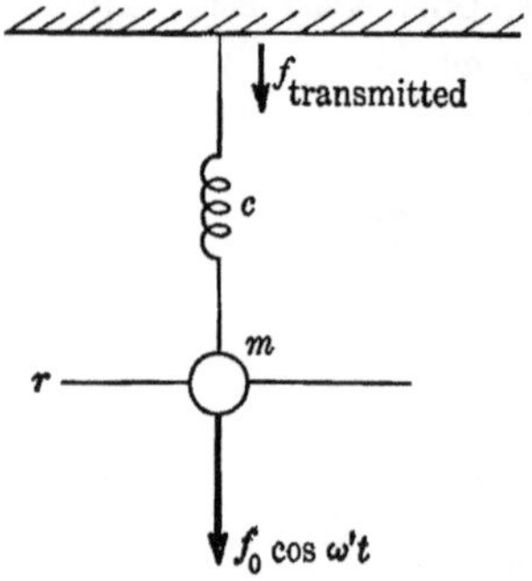

FIG. 12.21.

Mechanical Isolation. In practical engineering it is frequently desirable to keep forced oscillations well away from resonance. In mounting electric motors, for instance, spring or rubber supports are used to prevent the transmission of vibration. If a vibrating mass is subjected to a periodic force (see Fig. 12.21)

$$f_0 \cos \omega' t,$$

the equation of motion is as given by Eqs. (12.40) and (12.41), and the steady-state displacement is given by (12.51): a sine of amplitude

$$\frac{f_0}{\omega' z}.$$

The maximum periodic force transmitted to the rigid support is merely the maximum displacement from equilibrium divided by the compliance of the spring; therefore the ratio of maximum transmitted force to maximum applied force is easily computed:

$$\frac{f_{\text{transmitted}}}{f_{\text{applied}}} = \frac{x_{\max}}{cf_0} = \frac{f_0}{\omega' zcf_0} = \frac{1}{\omega' cz}. \tag{12.57}$$

If the resistance is small and the mass and frequency fixed, it is possible to control the ratio (12.57) by adjusting c. Numerical examples are given as exercises.

EXERCISES

1. What are the dimensions of mechanical impedance?

2. (See Fig. 12.20.) Data: A force of 1 lb produces an elongation of 1 in. in the spring. When A is held fixed, the free period of oscillation is 3.142 sec. It takes 20 complete oscillations for the amplitude in the free oscillation to reach 37 per cent of the initial displacement. The wheel rotates with angular speed ω' and imparts to A a simple harmonic motion of amplitude $y_0 = 1$ ft. Find the steady-state amplitude of the displacement of the mass when (*a*) $\omega' = 0.2$ rad/sec; (*b*) $\omega' = 2.0$ rad/sec.

3. A periodic force

$$f = f_0 \cos \omega' t$$

is applied to an object of mass 0.72 kg suspended by a simple spring. The spring will stretch 1 cm under a force of 60 newtons. When $\omega' = 100$ rad/sec and $f_0 = 6.5$ newtons, the steady-state amplitude is 0.5 cm. (*a*) What value of ω' will produce resonance? (*b*) What is the resistance r? (*c*) What would be the amplitude of the oscillation at resonance?

4. Show that the magnification factor to be expected from a low-r system operated at resonance is equal to

$$\frac{r_{\text{critical}}}{2r}.$$

5. Express the magnification factor to be expected from a low-r system operated at resonance entirely in terms of the logarithmic decrement per half period of the undriven system.

6. For the case where r is negligible, show that the ratio of the transmitted to applied force will be less than k when the springs are so chosen that the natural period τ will satisfy

$$\tau > \tau' \sqrt{\frac{1+k}{k}},$$

where τ' is the period of the applied force.

7. An electric motor and the platform on which it is mounted weigh together 500 lb. At 600 rpm, a force

$$f_0 \cos 20\pi t$$

is effectively applied to the system. To isolate the vibration, the platform is supported on four like coil springs (see Fig. 12.22). The maximum force transmitted to the floor for steady state is not to be more than 10 per cent of the maximum impressed force f_0. What is the minimum permissible compliance for each of the four springs? (Neglect damping.)

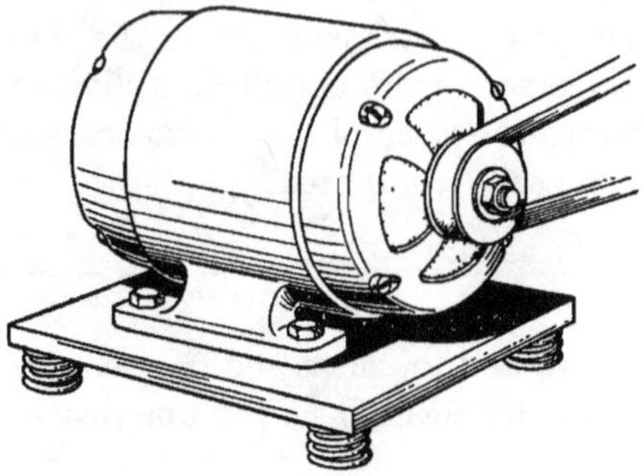

FIG. 12.22.

8. An electric motor weighing 200 lb is suspended by vertical springs which stretch 6 in. when the motor is attached. (*a*) If the flywheel had its center of gravity off center, for how many rpm would resonance be expected? (*b*) For steady state, what fraction of the vibrational force is transmitted to the ceiling when the motor is operated at 600 rpm?

9. What phase relationships will exist between the input displacement y and the output speed for very low and for very high frequencies?

CHAPTER 13

MOTION IN A CONSERVATIVE FORCE FIELD

Thus far we have concerned ourselves mainly with specific applied forces acting on idealized objects. In much of the remaining work we shall emphasize properties that can be associated with the very space in which events happen. Gravitational forces are an example. Any object near the earth is apparently subject to a downward pull. This pull obviously depends on no actual contact. Even the moon is held in its orbit by just such a force. We feel confident in predicting that a rocket will experience gravitational forces corresponding to various positions near the earth. The force then is a *function of position.*

Much of the subject matter of this chapter could have been presented earlier. It is set apart here both to provide an illustration of the manner in which methods from several other chapters may be applied and also to introduce the point of view of *fields.*

13.1. The Nature of a Field. By now we are quite in the habit of describing the position of a point by coordinates: (x,y,z), $\mathbf{R}$, or (r,θ,z). Each point in a region of space may have characteristics of various sorts. For instance, height above the floor is a scalar characteristic of every point in a room. Since to each point in the room is assigned a number (say the number of inches above the floor), we say that height is a *scalar function of position.* It is a function having a scalar value for every point in a region. The region and function together are sometimes called a *scalar field.* Other examples of scalar point functions are temperature, $\mathbf{A} \cdot \mathbf{R}$ for a constant vector $\mathbf{A}$, and gravitational potential. The functions with which we shall deal in this context are usually continuous, varying smoothly from point to point in the regions where they are used.

In an entirely similar manner a function which assigns a unique vector to each point of a region is called a *vector function of position* and the function and region together constitute a *vector field.* Examples of vector point functions have been encountered several times. Gravitational fields of force are clearly vector fields. The position vector $\mathbf{R}$ with respect to a specific origin is a simple vector function of position.

Example. The unit radial vector $\mathbf{L}$ may be thought of as a vector function of position assigning to each point a vector drawn away from the

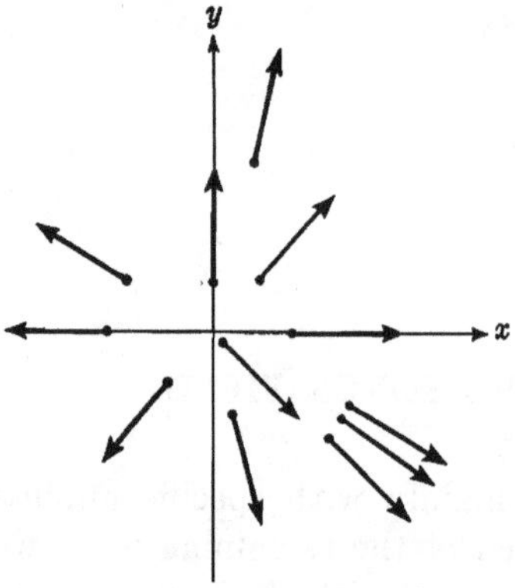

FIG. 13.1.

origin. This is sketched for a few points in the xy plane in Fig. 13.1. Note that this function is not defined at the origin.

EXERCISES

1. For several points in the xy plane draw to scale vectors illustrating each of the following functions of position:

(*a*) $\mathbf{L} + \mathbf{I}$. (*b*) $0.5\mathbf{R}$.

(*c*) $\mathbf{K} \times \mathbf{R}$. (*d*) $-\frac{1}{r^2}\mathbf{L}$.

13.2. Directional Derivatives for Scalar Fields. Let us suppose that we are concerned with a scalar function of position $\varphi(\mathbf{R})$. Then we may often need to know how decidedly the function varies in the vicinity of any interesting point. This involves the simple but important concept of directional derivative.

Imagine that you pick a direction determined by a unit vector

$$\mathbf{T} = l\mathbf{I} + m\mathbf{J} + n\mathbf{K}.$$

Call a line in that direction the s axis and move in that direction, noting variations in φ. The values encountered might be plotted as a graph to show φ as a function of s as in Fig. 13.2. The derivative of φ with respect to s at a given point as usual is equal to the slope of the tangent to the

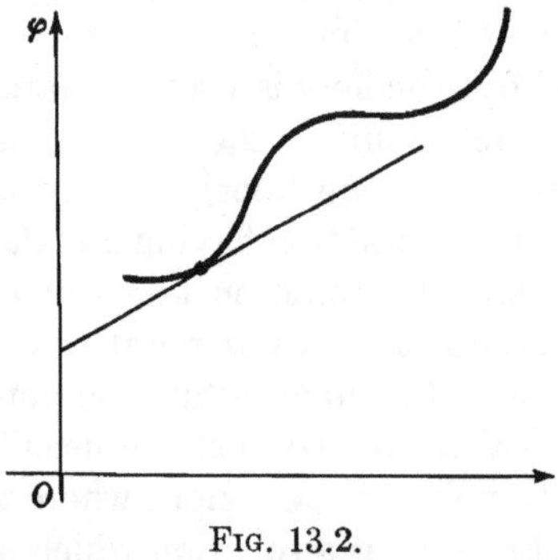

FIG. 13.2.

curve at the corresponding point. This derivative is the *directional derivative* for the $\mathbf{T}$ direction. Directional derivatives for the x, y, and z directions are customarily denoted by

$$\frac{\partial\varphi}{\partial x}, \frac{\partial\varphi}{\partial y}, \frac{\partial\varphi}{\partial z}$$

and are called *partial derivatives*, the implication being that y and z do not vary when $\partial\varphi/\partial x$ is being evaluated, etc. It should be observed that no mention has been made of the *existence* of these derivatives. In the cases we consider, differentiability may be assumed.

Directional derivatives offer a convenient language for dealing with small changes in a scalar function φ. For instance, if φ is known at (x,y,z), then at $(x + \Delta x,y,z)$ the value $\varphi + \Delta\varphi$ can be estimated (see Fig. 13.3) to be *approximately*

$$(13.1) \qquad \varphi + \Delta\varphi = \varphi + \frac{\partial\varphi}{\partial x}\,\Delta x.$$

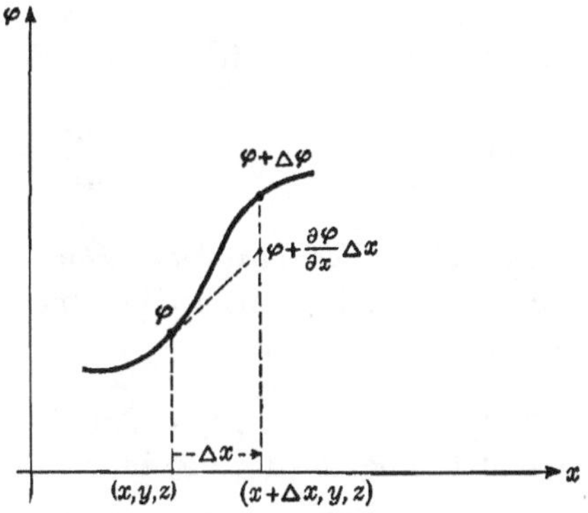

FIG. 13.3.

Similar approximate expressions for small changes in φ for y or z displacements will be used. The estimate of (13.1) is absolutely correct when φ varies uniformly with x. When this is not the case, we can take comfort in the fact that conclusions based on such an approximation usually become more reliable as one takes the limit as Δx becomes small. In this treatment the emphasis will be on ideas rather than rigor: we wish to use mathematical language without undertaking lengthy justifications. Naturally, the student will wish to reinforce his confidence and comprehension by detailed study of these methods in mathematical courses.

It is easily possible to express directional derivatives for the s direction in terms of those for the x, y, and z directions. Regard a small displacement in the s direction as a vector

$$\Delta\mathbf{R} = \Delta x\,\mathbf{I} + \Delta y\,\mathbf{J} + \Delta z\,\mathbf{K} = \Delta s(l\mathbf{I} + m\mathbf{J} + n\mathbf{K}).$$

The net displacement $\Delta\mathbf{R}$ could just as well have been carried out in three steps: $\Delta x\,\mathbf{I}$ followed by $\Delta y\,\mathbf{J}$ followed by $\Delta z\,\mathbf{K}$. Then the corresponding change in φ too may be calculated approximately in steps: the x step increases φ by $\frac{\partial\varphi}{\partial x}\Delta x$, the y step increases φ by $\frac{\partial\varphi}{\partial y}\Delta y$, and the z step increases φ by $\frac{\partial\varphi}{\partial z}\Delta z$. We have then approximately

$$(13.2) \qquad \Delta\varphi = \frac{\partial\varphi}{\partial x}\,\Delta x + \frac{\partial\varphi}{\partial y}\,\Delta y + \frac{\partial\varphi}{\partial z}\,\Delta z.$$

If we divide through by Δs and take the limit as Δs becomes small, we arrive at

$$(13.3) \qquad \frac{d\varphi}{ds} = \frac{\partial\varphi}{\partial x}\,l + \frac{\partial\varphi}{\partial y}\,m + \frac{\partial\varphi}{\partial z}\,n.$$

It is useful to interpret the right side of (13.3) as the scalar product of two vectors: the unit vector **T** in the s direction and the following vector, $\nabla\varphi$ (∇ is read as "del" or "nabla").

$$\nabla\varphi = \frac{\partial\varphi}{\partial x}\mathbf{I} + \frac{\partial\varphi}{\partial y}\mathbf{J} + \frac{\partial\varphi}{\partial z}\mathbf{K}. \tag{13.4}$$

This allows us to write, instead of (13.3),

$$\frac{d\varphi}{ds} = \mathbf{T}\cdot\nabla\varphi. \tag{13.5}$$

Directional derivatives for vector fields are discussed in the next chapter. No new complications are involved since any vector can be expressed in terms of three scalars.

Example. If $\varphi(x,y,z) = 3xy + x^2z + yz$, find the directional derivative at the point $(2,0,-2)$ in the direction $\mathbf{T} = 0.8\mathbf{I} - 0.6\mathbf{K}$.

SOLUTION. We shall use (13.3). This requires us to find $\frac{\partial\varphi}{\partial x}, \frac{\partial\varphi}{\partial y}, \frac{\partial\varphi}{\partial z}$. Now $\frac{\partial\varphi}{\partial x}$ is a directional derivative for displacements along a line parallel to the x axis, that is, along a line for which y and z do not vary. So in finding $\frac{\partial\varphi}{\partial x}$, we treat y and z as constants. Similarly for the other coordinates

$$\frac{\partial\varphi}{\partial x} = 3y + 2xz = -8,$$

$$\frac{\partial\varphi}{\partial y} = 3x + z = 4,$$

$$\frac{\partial\varphi}{\partial z} = x^2 + y = 4.$$

Now using (13.3),

$$\frac{d\varphi}{ds} = (0.8)(-8) + (0.0)(4) - (0.6)(4) = -8.8.$$

EXERCISES

1. Find the directional derivative at (x,y,z) parallel to $\mathbf{I} - \mathbf{J} - \mathbf{K}$ of the scalar point function $x + xy + xyz$.

2. If $\varphi(\mathbf{R}) = \mathbf{R}\cdot\mathbf{R}$, evaluate the directional derivative parallel to **R** at a point where $|\mathbf{R}| = r$.

3. If $\varphi(\mathbf{R}) = \mathbf{A}\cdot\mathbf{R}$, where **A** is a constant vector, show that the directional derivative for displacements parallel to the unit vector **T** is always equal to $\mathbf{A}\cdot\mathbf{T}$.

4. Show that $\nabla(\mathbf{R}\cdot\mathbf{R}) = 2\mathbf{R}$.

5. The scalar function $\varphi(x,y,z) = x^2y + y^2z + z^2x$ obviously has the value 3 at $(1,1,1)$. Use the methods of this section to evaluate it approximately at $(1.02,1.00,0.99)$.

13.3. The Notion of Gradient. In the preceding section we started with a scalar function of position $\varphi(\mathbf{R})$, and we were led to a related vector function of position $\nabla\varphi$. From (13.5) we can deduce important properties of this function. Using the definition of scalar product, we have (see Fig. 13.4)

$$\frac{d\varphi}{ds} = \mathbf{T} \cdot \nabla\varphi = |\nabla\varphi| \cos \theta. \tag{13.6}$$

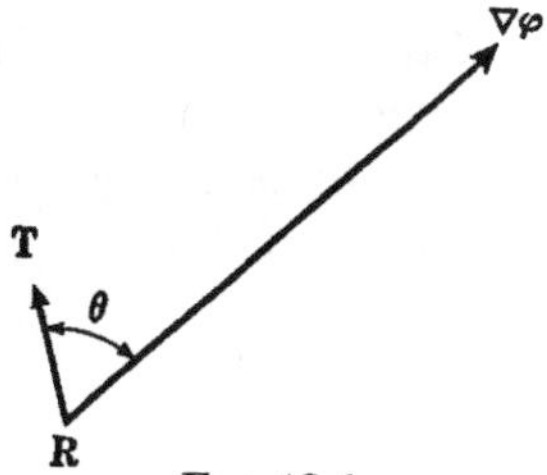

FIG. 13.4.

If, for a particular point $\mathbf{R}$, we pick $\mathbf{T}$ in the direction of $\nabla\varphi$, we get the largest possible value of $d\varphi/ds$. We can then describe the vector $\nabla\varphi$ as follows:

(13.7) $\nabla\varphi$ *has the* direction *for which the directional derivative is maximum. It has the* magnitude *of this maximum directional derivative.*

Thus $\nabla\varphi$ is a function of position which at each point indicates in direction and magnitude the way in which φ varies with position. This function is called the *gradient of* φ, denoted by **grad** φ.

$$\mathbf{grad}\ \varphi = \nabla\varphi = \frac{\partial\varphi}{\partial x}\mathbf{I} + \frac{\partial\varphi}{\partial y}\mathbf{J} + \frac{\partial\varphi}{\partial z}\mathbf{K}. \tag{13.8}$$

We may now restate (13.5) in words:

(13.9) *The directional derivative of a scalar point function is merely the component in that direction of the gradient.*

$$\frac{d\varphi}{ds} = \mathbf{T} \cdot \nabla\varphi = \mathbf{T} \cdot (\mathbf{grad}\ \varphi). \tag{13.10}$$

For brevity we shall use the symbol ∇ for gradient.

The locus of points for which a scalar point function is constant is called a *level surface.* In Fig. 13.5, a plane picture is given. The curved lines are the intersections of the plane with level surfaces. At a typical point R the vector $\nabla\varphi$ is shown. Its direction is, of course, normal to the level surface, since the rate of change with displacement is maximum in that direction. A familiar example of these ideas is found in contour maps. Here the scalar function is height above sea level. The level surfaces are the lines of constant altitude. The gradient is steepest where the lines

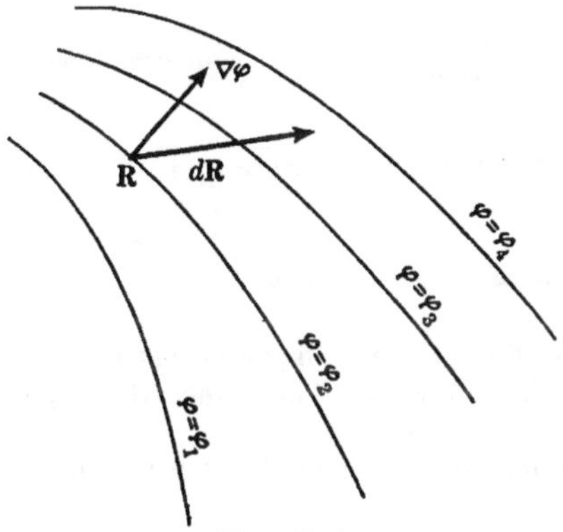

FIG. 13.5.

are closest together. Weather maps show level lines of a different sort, representing constant pressure loci.

Example. The relationship between directional derivative and gradient is illustrated by the slopes of a simple roof. The roof surface itself may be thought of as a graph of the scalar function altitude. This function is defined for points in the horizontal plane under the roof. Fig-

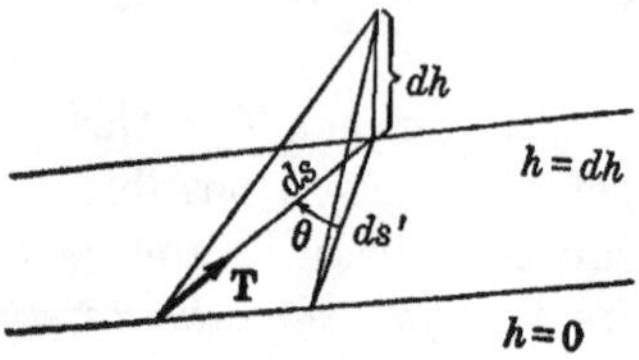

FIG. 13.6.

ure 13.6 shows two level lines: one for height zero, the other for height dh. A displacement ds' normal to these gives the direction of the gradient. A displacement ds in a direction **T** at an angle θ with the normal is obviously related to ds' by the equation

$$\frac{ds'}{ds} = \cos\theta.$$

We have then for our directional derivative in the **T** direction

$$\frac{dh}{ds} = \frac{dh}{ds'}\frac{ds'}{ds} = \frac{dh}{ds'}\cos\theta = |\nabla h|\cos\theta = \mathbf{T}\cdot\nabla h.$$

EXERCISES

1. Plot level lines in the xy plane for $\varphi(x,y) = 2x + y$. Compute and draw vectors equal to the gradient at (0,0), (0,1), (0,−1).

2. Draw several level curves for $\varphi(x,y) = \frac{100}{x^2 + y^2}$. Compute and draw vectors equal to the gradient at (5,0), (0,10).

3. Compute $\nabla\varphi$, where (*a*) $\varphi = \frac{\gamma m'm}{r}$; (*b*) $\varphi = r$; (*c*) $\varphi = \sqrt{x^2 + y^2 + z^2}$.

4. The scalar point function

$$\varphi(x,y,z) = xy^2z^3$$

has the value 1 at the point (1,1,1). Consider the surface of all points in space having $\varphi = 1$. What are the direction cosines of the normal to that surface at the point (1,1,1)?

5. At the point $\mathbf{R} = \mathbf{J} + 2\mathbf{K}$, what is the maximum rate of change with displacement of

$$\varphi(\mathbf{R}) = xy^2z^3?$$

6. Elevation is a scalar function of position. Figure 13.7 is a topographic map; level lines are drawn. From the figure, find ∇h at the points A and B.

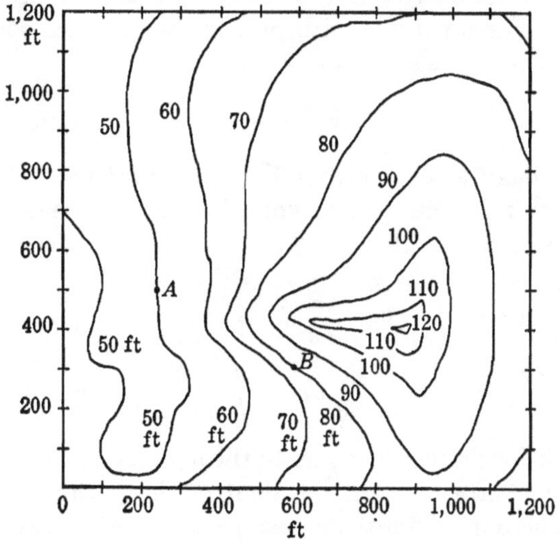

FIG. 13.7.

13.4. Conservative Force Fields. As an example of a *vector* field we shall in this chapter consider cases where the function of position is a force. We have already seen that with a *conservative* force $\mathbf{F}(\mathbf{R})$ there is associated a scalar function of position, the potential energy. Applying (10.9) to a small displacement $\Delta\mathbf{R}$, we get

$$\Delta(\text{p.e.}) = -\Delta(\text{work}) = -\mathbf{F}\cdot\Delta\mathbf{R}.$$

Now if $\Delta\mathbf{R}$ is a displacement in the $\mathbf{T}$ direction, we may write

$$\Delta\mathbf{R} = \Delta s\,\mathbf{T}.$$

Hence

$$\Delta(\text{p.e.}) = -\mathbf{F}\cdot\mathbf{T}\,\Delta s.$$

Dividing by Δs and taking the limit as Δs becomes small, we have a directional derivative of this scalar function of position

$$\frac{d(\text{p.e.})}{ds} = -\mathbf{F}\cdot\mathbf{T}. \tag{13.11}$$

From (13.10) we have then

$$-\mathbf{F}\cdot\mathbf{T} = \mathbf{T}\cdot\nabla(\text{p.e.}). \tag{13.12}$$

Since this is true for any choice of $\mathbf{T}$, we arrive at the very important equation

$$\mathbf{F}(\mathbf{R}) = -\nabla(\text{p.e.}). \tag{13.13}$$

It should be recalled that these relationships have been met before in (10.25).

There is an interesting converse to the result just derived. Suppose that we have a force varying with position with which some scalar function φ is associated in such a way that

$$\mathbf{F}(\mathbf{R}) = \nabla\varphi.$$

Is this fact enough to ensure that **F** is conservative? We shall make a formal check on this point. The work done by **F** for a displacement from $\mathbf{R}_1$ to $\mathbf{R}_2$ is equal to

$$\int_{\mathbf{R}_1}^{\mathbf{R}_2} \mathbf{F}\cdot d\mathbf{R} = \int_{\mathbf{R}_1}^{\mathbf{R}_2} \nabla\varphi\cdot\frac{d\mathbf{R}}{ds}\,ds = \int_{\mathbf{R}=\mathbf{R}_1}^{\mathbf{R}=\mathbf{R}_2} \mathbf{T}\cdot\nabla\varphi\,ds$$
$$= \int_{\mathbf{R}=\mathbf{R}_1}^{\mathbf{R}=\mathbf{R}_2} \frac{d\varphi}{ds}\,ds = \int_{\mathbf{R}=\mathbf{R}_1}^{\mathbf{R}=\mathbf{R}_2} d\varphi = \varphi(\mathbf{R}_2) - \varphi(\mathbf{R}_1).$$

Thus the work done is merely equal to the net change in φ for the two positions. Consequently, it is independent of the path; therefore **F** is conservative. These important conclusions are recapitulated thus:

(13.14) *A force field is conservative if and only if it is expressible as the gradient of a scalar field.*

A second criterion for conservative fields is too important to be omitted although a full treatment will not be given until later [see (15.33)]. If **F** is conservative, we have, by (13.14),

$$f_x = \frac{\partial\varphi}{\partial x},$$
$$f_y = \frac{\partial\varphi}{\partial y},$$
$$f_z = \frac{\partial\varphi}{\partial z}.$$

It follows that (since order of partial differentiations is unimportant for decent functions—this is shown in calculus courses):

$$\frac{\partial f_x}{\partial y} = \frac{\partial^2\varphi}{\partial y\,\partial x} = \frac{\partial^2\varphi}{\partial x\,\partial y} = \frac{\partial f_y}{\partial x}; \tag{13.15}$$

thus

$$\frac{\partial f_x}{\partial y} = \frac{\partial f_y}{\partial x},$$

and similarly

$$\frac{\partial f_y}{\partial z} = \frac{\partial f_z}{\partial y},$$
$$\frac{\partial f_z}{\partial x} = \frac{\partial f_x}{\partial z}.$$

A converse theorem can be shown to hold. Thus we may say

(13.16) **F** *is a conservative force if and only if Eqs.* (13.15) *are valid.*

EXERCISES

1. Show that

$$\mathbf{F} = u(x)\mathbf{I} + v(y)\mathbf{J} + w(z)\mathbf{K}$$

is a conservative force.

2. Which of the following forces are conservative?

(*a*) $x^2y\mathbf{I} + y^2x\mathbf{J}$. (*b*) $y^2x\mathbf{I} + x^2y\mathbf{J}$.

(*c*) $\mathbf{F}(\mathbf{R}) = \dfrac{k\mathbf{R}}{\mathbf{R}\cdot\mathbf{R}}$, where k is a constant.

3. Show that $\mathbf{F}(\mathbf{R}) = \dfrac{-k\mathbf{L}}{\mathbf{R}\cdot\mathbf{R}}$ is conservative (k is a constant, **L** the unit radial vector).

4. In the xy plane a force field is defined by

$$\mathbf{F}(x,y) = x^2\mathbf{J} \qquad \text{newtons, m.}$$

(*a*) What total work is done by the field during displacement along straight lines around the square described by (0,0) to (0,1) to (1,1) to (1,0) to (0,0)?

(*b*) If a 2-kg particle subject to this variable force is released at $(0,-2)$m with a velocity of 4**I** m/sec, with what speed will it reach the x axis?

5. A particle of mass m is attracted toward a fixed point **O** by a force inversely proportional to the cube of its distance from **O**. From an initial distance r_1 it is launched with an initial velocity $\mathbf{V}_0$ directly away from **O**. Derive a formula for the maximum distance r_2 away from **O** attained by the particle.

13.5. Field Strength and Potential. The actual force experienced by a particle in a gravitational field depends on the mass of the particle. Thus the force itself is not really a property just of the field. It is perhaps more appropriate to talk about the *field strength* of a field. *Gravitational field strength,* denoted here by $\mathfrak{F}$, is defined as the ratio of force to mass. It is a vector which has the direction of the force.

$$\mathfrak{F}(\mathbf{R}) = \frac{\mathbf{F}(\mathbf{R})}{m}. \tag{13.17}$$

This is a satisfactory concept since for different small particles the ratio has the same value at the same point:

$$\mathfrak{F}(\mathbf{R}) = \mathbf{A} = \frac{\mathbf{F}(\mathbf{R})}{m} = \frac{\mathbf{F}'(\mathbf{R})}{m'} = \mathbf{A}'. \tag{13.18}$$

Gravitational potential is similarly defined as the ratio of potential energy to mass:

$$\text{pot.} = \frac{\text{p.e.}}{m}. \tag{13.19}$$

From (13.13) we deduce at once for a conservative field

$$\mathfrak{F}(\mathbf{R}) = -\nabla(\text{pot.}). \tag{13.20}$$

The law of conservation of mechanical energy immediately yields this result

$$\text{pot.} + \frac{v^2}{2} = \text{const.} \tag{13.21}$$

In case of superimposed fields, field strengths are added vectorially while potentials are added as ordinary numbers. For complicated cases, the use of potentials is thus especially advantageous. In this course it will for the most part be convenient to work with particular force fields and potential energies rather than with field strength and potential. In electrical and magnetic work, the other choice is usually made.

EXERCISES

1. What, in newtons per kilogram, is the gravitational field strength at the earth's surface?

2. How fast must a 9-oz baseball be thrown to attain a height of 150 ft (assume that the ball is released at a height of 6 ft) (*a*) thrown vertically? (*b*) at an angle of 45°?

3. In a constant force field where

$$\mathbf{F}(\mathbf{R}) = 3\mathbf{I} - 7\mathbf{K} \quad \text{lb}$$

a 6-lb object is projected from the origin with a speed of 6 ft/sec. A little later the particle passes through the point (2,0,0) ft. (*a*) Find a formula for potential relative to the origin. (State units.) (*b*) What is the speed of the particle at (2,0,0)?

4. A 5-kg particle is subject to a force

$$\mathbf{F}(\mathbf{R}) = -k\mathbf{R} \quad \text{newtons} \quad \text{for } \mathbf{R} \text{ in meters,}$$

where k is a constant. Find a formula for potential relative to the origin.

5. Relative to the earth's surface, what is the gravitational potential at an elevation of 1,000 m?

13.6. The Inverse-square Gravitational Field. According to Newton's law of universal gravitation (1672), between any two mass particles there is a force of attraction proportional to the product of the masses and inversely proportional to the square of the distance of separation. Referring to Fig. 13.8, the force on the particle of mass m is given by

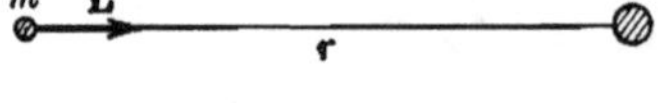

FIG. 13.8.

$$\mathbf{F} = \frac{\gamma m m'}{r^2}\mathbf{L}, \tag{13.22}$$

where γ is the gravitational constant, experimentally determined, having the value 6.67×10^{-11} in the mks system. Similarly, if we isolate the other mass, it is subject to a force

$$\mathbf{F}' = -\frac{\gamma m m'}{r^2}\mathbf{L}. \tag{13.23}$$

To make sure that this force is conservative, let us derive a work formula, using the following equations developed somewhat earlier:

$$d\mathbf{R} = d(r\mathbf{L}) = dr\,\mathbf{L} + r\,d\mathbf{L},$$
$$\mathbf{L}\cdot\mathbf{L} = 1, \qquad \mathbf{L}\cdot d\mathbf{L} = 0.$$
$$\int_{\mathbf{R}_1}^{\mathbf{R}_2} \mathbf{F}'\cdot d\mathbf{R} = -\gamma mm' \int_{\mathbf{R}_1}^{\mathbf{R}_2} \frac{\mathbf{L}\cdot(dr\,\mathbf{L} + r\,d\mathbf{L})}{r^2}$$
$$= -\gamma mm' \int_{r_1}^{r_2} \frac{dr}{r^2} = \gamma mm'\left[\frac{1}{r_2} - \frac{1}{r_1}\right].$$

This value is independent of the path; therefore the force is conservative.

Now let us concentrate on the one object, of mass m. The gravitational field strength at a distance r from this object is given as

$$\mathfrak{F} = \frac{\mathbf{F}'}{m'} = -\frac{\gamma m}{r^2}\mathbf{L}. \tag{13.24}$$

Relative to a point far away from the object ($r = \infty$) the potential is easily computed:

$$\text{pot.} = -\int_{\infty}^{\mathbf{R}} \mathfrak{F}\cdot d\mathbf{R} = \gamma m \int_{\infty}^{\mathbf{R}} \frac{\mathbf{L}\cdot d\mathbf{R}}{r^2} = \gamma m \int_{\infty}^{r} \frac{dr}{r^2} = -\gamma m\left[\frac{1}{r}\right]_{\infty}^{r}$$

or

$$\text{pot.} = -\frac{\gamma m}{r}. \tag{13.25}$$

The attraction between extended bodies may be computed by means of integral calculus. A body is thought of as an aggregate of elements of mass dm. The corresponding field strength at $\mathbf{P}$ has an x component equal to (referring to Fig. 13.9)

$$d\mathfrak{F}\cdot\mathbf{I} = -\frac{\gamma\cos\theta\,dm}{r^2}.$$

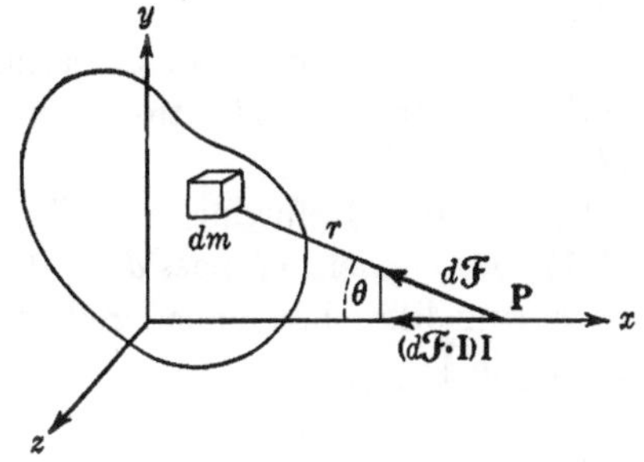

FIG. 13.9.

When the integrations are carried out, one for each component, the magnitude and direction are determined. The integrations are often tedious and only a few of them will be examined in this course. They are standard exercises in courses in the calculus. Instead of the three integrations just suggested, one may integrate once to find the potential and then use (13.20) for computing field strength.

Example 1. A uniform ring has radius a and mass m (see Fig. 13.10). Find the field strength at a point on its axis at a distance x from its plane.

SOLUTION. From the symmetry it is clear that the y and z components are zero; therefore only one integration is necessary to find the field strength. An element of mass determined by the angle $d\alpha$ is

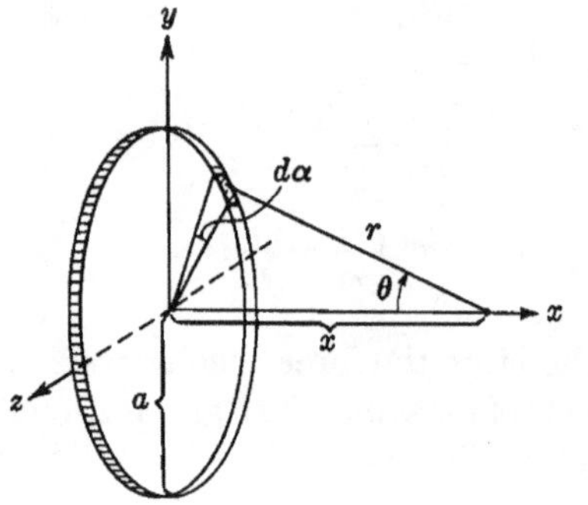

FIG. 13.10.

$$dm = \frac{m}{2\pi a}\, a\, d\alpha.$$

Its contribution to the x component of field strength is

$$d\mathfrak{F} \cdot \mathbf{I} = -\frac{\gamma m \cos\theta}{2\pi r^2}\, d\alpha.$$

The integration is trivial, since r and θ are the same for each value of α.

$$\mathfrak{F} \cdot \mathbf{I} = -\frac{\gamma m \cos\theta}{2\pi r^2}\int_0^{2\pi} d\alpha = -\frac{\gamma m \cos\theta}{r^2}.$$

So

$$\mathfrak{F} = -\frac{\gamma m \cos\theta}{r^2}\mathbf{I} = -\frac{\gamma m x}{r^3}\mathbf{I} = -\frac{\gamma m x}{(x^2 + a^2)^{\frac{3}{2}}}\mathbf{I}.$$

ALTERNATIVE SOLUTION. The potential may be written down by inspection, using (13.25),

$$\text{pot.} = -\frac{\gamma m}{r} = -\frac{\gamma m}{\sqrt{x^2 + a^2}}.$$

We may now use (13.20)

$$\mathfrak{F} = \nabla\left(\frac{\gamma m}{\sqrt{x^2 + a^2}}\right) = -\frac{\gamma m x}{(x^2 + a^2)^{\frac{3}{2}}}\mathbf{I},$$

as before.

Example 2. A uniform spherical shell has mass m and radius a. What is the gravitational situation at a point whose distance from the center is $x(>a)$?

SOLUTION. Referring to Fig. 13.11, our element of mass dm will be a ring like that considered in Example 1:

$$dm = \frac{m}{4\pi a^2}(2\pi a \sin\alpha)(a\, d\alpha).$$

Its potential is

$$d(\text{pot.}) = -\frac{\gamma\, dm}{r}.$$

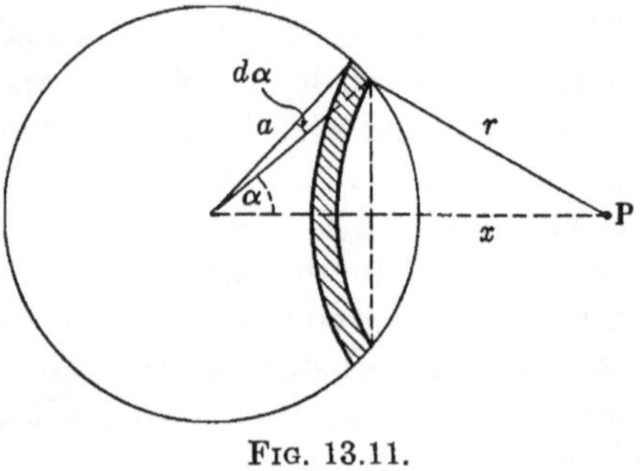

FIG. 13.11.

Now

$$a^2 + x^2 - 2ax \cos \alpha = r^2.$$

Differentiating and dividing by 2,

$$ax \sin \alpha \, d\alpha = r \, dr;$$

therefore

$$\text{pot.} = \frac{-\gamma m}{2ax} \int_{x-a}^{x+a} dr = \frac{-\gamma m}{2ax} (2a) = \frac{-\gamma m}{x}.$$

This shows that *the gravitational attraction exerted at an external point by a uniform spherical shell would be unchanged if the body were compressed to a point at the center.*

Since a uniform solid sphere can be regarded as an aggregate of concentric uniform shells, the same result is valid:

(13.26) *A uniform solid sphere exerts gravitational attraction at external points just as if it were a particle at its own center.*

Example 3. A uniform spherical shell has mass m and radius a. What is the gravitational situation at a point whose distance from the center is $x(\leqq a)$?

SOLUTION. Proceeding as before, we get

$$\text{pot.} = \frac{-\gamma m}{2ax} \int_{a-x}^{a+x} dr = \frac{-\gamma m}{2ax} (2x) = -\frac{\gamma m}{a}.$$

This shows that *within a uniform spherical shell the gravitational potential is constant.* This means that the gradient is zero; therefore the *field strength is zero.* Now imagine a point within a uniform *solid* sphere at some distance x from the center. It is then attracted toward the center by a sphere of radius x and is uninfluenced by the outer shell of inner radius x.

EXERCISES

1. Obtain a formula for gravitational field strength exerted by a uniform disk of mass m and radius a at a point at a distance x from its center on a normal axis through the center. (Do not hesitate to use tables of integrals.)

2. Show that the gravitational field strength within a solid uniform sphere varies directly as the distance from the center.

3. The diameter of the moon is 2,163 miles. Its mass is 0.0123 times that of the earth. What is the acceleration of gravity on the moon?

4. What is the ratio of the sun's pull on the moon to that of the earth? (Take the distances from the earth as 92.3 million and 239,000 miles. The mass of the sun is about 332,000 times that of the earth.)

5. Between two identical lead spheres (sp. gr. = 11.3) in contact the gravitational force is 1 newton. Find the diameter.

13.7. The Earth's Gravitational Field. Let us now apply the ideas of the preceding section to motion of a particle in the neighborhood of the earth. Let m denote the mass of the earth and ρ the radius (see Fig. 13.12). Then a particle at a point with position vector **R** (relative to the center of the earth) experiences a force toward the center. The equation

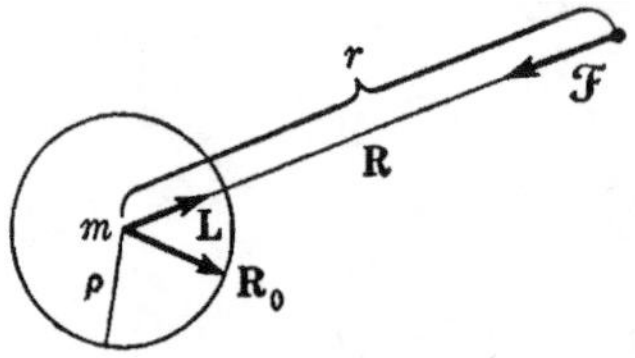

FIG. 13.12.

$$\mathfrak{F} = -\frac{\gamma m}{r^2}\mathbf{L}$$

applies. The mass of the earth is not a convenient constant to keep in mind; therefore let us use the fact that at the surface of the earth $\mathfrak{F}$ has magnitude g:

$$\frac{\gamma m}{\rho^2} = g.$$

Hence

(13.27) $$\mathfrak{F} = -\frac{g\rho^2}{r^2}\mathbf{L}.$$

It is convenient in many cases to consider the earth's surface as a reference level for potential and potential energy. Following the pattern of integration used previously,

$$\text{pot.} = -\int_{\mathbf{R}_0}^{\mathbf{R}} \mathfrak{F}\cdot d\mathbf{R} = g\rho^2\int_\rho^r \frac{dr}{r^2} = -g\rho^2\left[\frac{1}{r}\right]_\rho^r$$

or

(13.28) $$\text{pot.} = g\rho^2\left(\frac{1}{\rho} - \frac{1}{r}\right) = \frac{g\rho}{r}(r - \rho).$$

Example. With what speed must a projectile be launched vertically from the surface of the earth to attain a height of 1,000 miles? (Neglect air friction.)

SOLUTION. Using the law of conservation of energy (13.21),

$$\text{pot.} + \frac{v^2}{2} = \text{const},$$

we have at the earth's surface, pot. $= 0$, and at the peak of the trajectory, $v = 0$; thus

$$0 + \frac{v^2}{2} = \frac{g\rho}{r}(r - \rho) + 0,$$

or

$$v^2 = \frac{2g\rho(r-\rho)}{r} = \frac{(2)(32.2)}{(5{,}280)}\frac{(3{,}960)}{(4{,}960)}1{,}000;$$

hence

$$v^2 = 9.73 \qquad \text{and} \qquad v = 3.1 \text{ mps}.$$

EXERCISES

1. At what distance from the surface of the earth would one's "weight" be one-half its usual value?

2. How much work would be required to take a 1-lb object at the surface of the earth and remove it from the earth's gravitational field?

3. With what speed must a projectile be fired vertically from the earth in order that it never return? Neglect friction. ($\rho = 3{,}958.8$ miles.)

4. With what speed would an object falling freely from an infinite distance strike the earth?

5. A projectile is fired vertically with a speed of 1 mps. How high will it rise, (*a*) assuming gravity to be constant? (*b*) allowing for the decrease of gravitational attraction away from the earth?

6. Using the formula for potential with respect to the earth's surface, derive the usual p.e. $= wh$ by making suitable approximations. For how large values of h is this formula correct within 1 per cent?

7. What would be the diameter of a planet having the same average density as the earth but on whose surface the acceleration due to gravity is 4.9 m/sec^2?

8. (*a*) Compute the mass of the earth in kilograms. (*b*) What is the specific gravity of the earth?

9. Suppose that a rocket, 100,000 miles from the center of the earth, has exhausted its fuel. If it is heading outward radially, what minimum speed would prevent its falling back toward the earth?

10. If the sun's mass and diameter exceed those of the earth by factors 3.3×10^5 and 1.1×10^2, respectively, what speeds must particles have initially to attain heights of 10,000 miles in solar prominences? What speed would be required for escape from the sun?

13.8. Motion of a Particle in a Central Force Field.

It was remarked in the preceding section that a particle near the earth experiences a force toward the center of the earth. This is an example of a *central* field of force. Other examples will be encountered later. The force may be one of attraction or of repulsion and its behavior is limited only by the fact that it is a central function of position. Thus the conclusions which we draw are of very broad application.

Since the position vector **R** and the strength $\mathfrak{F}$ are parallel, we may write (see Fig. 13.13)

$$\mathbf{R} \times \mathfrak{F} = \mathbf{R} \times \mathbf{A} = \mathbf{O}.$$

It is now easy to show that the moment about the center **O** of the velocity **V** is a constant vector **H**, for its derivative is null:

$$\frac{d}{dt}(\mathbf{R} \times \mathbf{V}) = \mathbf{V} \times \mathbf{V} + \mathbf{R} \times \mathbf{A} = \mathbf{O}.*$$

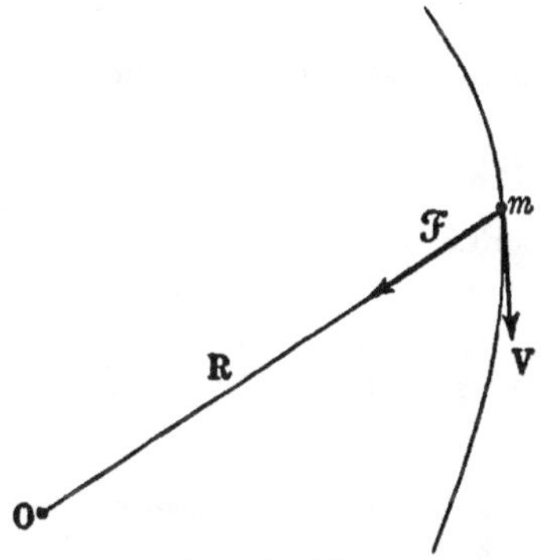

FIG. 13.13.

* The student should note that this conclusion may be obtained equally well from Eq. (11.26).

Hence

$$\mathbf{R} \times \mathbf{V} = \mathbf{H}. \tag{13.29}$$

If **H** happens to be a zero vector, the path goes directly through **O**, for in that case **R** and **V** are parallel. If **H** is not a zero vector, we can at least observe that *the path of the particle lies in a plane* for both **R** and **V** are perpendicular to **H**.

A second conclusion concerning central force motion of a particle is this: The rate at which the position vector **R** sweeps out area in the plane of the motion is constant; this is known as the *law of areas.* To prove it, we seek an expression for the rate of area sweeping. Observe that for a very small displacement $d\mathbf{R}$ the area swept out is essentially that of a triangle bounded by vectors **R**, $d\mathbf{R}$, and $\mathbf{R} + d\mathbf{R}$ (see Fig. 13.14). Now recall that the area of a triangle is half the magnitude of the cross product of two of the bounding vectors.

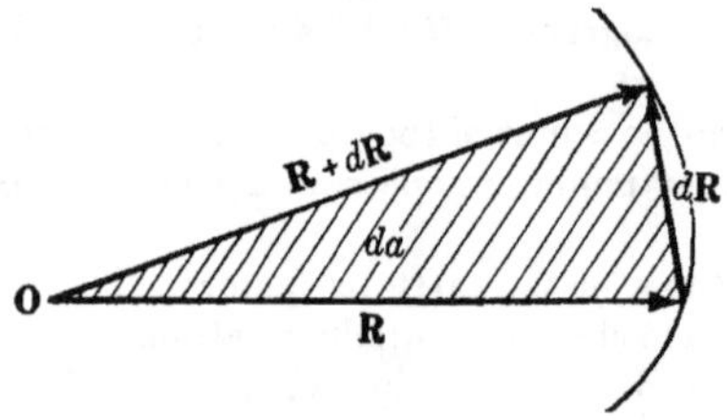

FIG. 13.14.

$$da = \tfrac{1}{2}|\mathbf{R} \times d\mathbf{R}|. \tag{13.30}$$

If this equation be divided, member by member, by dt, we have the desired result:

$$\frac{da}{dt} = \frac{1}{2}\left|\mathbf{R} \times \frac{d\mathbf{R}}{dt}\right| \tag{13.31}$$
$$= \frac{1}{2}|\mathbf{R} \times \mathbf{V}| = \frac{1}{2}|\mathbf{H}| = \frac{1}{2}h.$$

A useful and easily remembered property of central force motion is *Newton's theorem.* It has been shown that

$$|\mathbf{R} \times \mathbf{V}| = h.$$

This may be rewritten (see Fig. 13.15) as

$$rv \sin \psi = h.$$

Let p denote the perpendicular distance from **O** to the tangent to the trajectory, that is, $p = r \sin \psi$. We have then

$$pv = h. \tag{13.32}$$

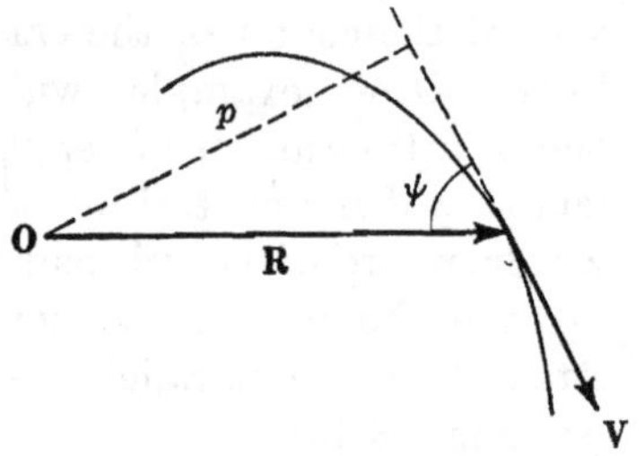

FIG. 13.15.

EXERCISES

In the first three of these exercises consider the motion of a particle of mass m attracted toward a fixed point O by a force proportional to the distance:

$$\mathfrak{F} = -n^2\mathbf{R}.$$

1. Prove that the field is conservative.

2. Prove that the potential energy of the particle (with respect to O) when at a distance r from O is $\frac{1}{2}n^2mr^2$.

3. Prove that

$$v^2 + n^2r^2 = \text{const.}$$

4. Prove that the angular momentum of a particle subject to a central force field is constant.

13.9. Planetary Motion. After arduous study of observed data Kepler, in the early seventeenth century, enunciated three conclusions about the motion of planets.

I. *The orbit of a planet is an ellipse with the sun as focus.*

II. *The area swept out by the radius from the sun to the planet is traversed at a constant rate.*

III. *The square of the time in which a planet traces out its orbit is proportional to the cube of its mean distance from the sun.*

Newton used these results in arriving at the law of gravitation. In this course we shall reverse the order and see how Kepler's laws are a consequence of the law of gravitation.

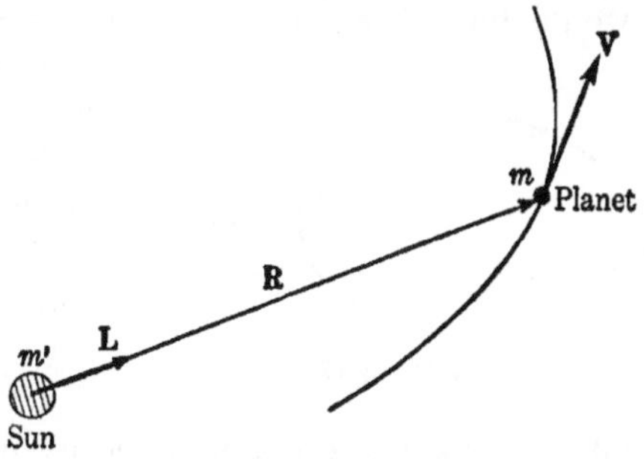

FIG. 13.16.

Proof of the First Law. (See Fig. 13.16.) Since the force is central,

$$\mathbf{H} = \mathbf{R} \times \mathbf{V}. \tag{13.33}$$

We shall analyze this in terms of unit radial and transverse vectors, substituting

$$\mathbf{R} = r\mathbf{L}$$

and

$$\mathbf{V} = \frac{dr}{dt}\mathbf{L} + r\frac{d\theta}{dt}\mathbf{M}.$$

As a result of this substitution we get, writing $\mathbf{L} \times \mathbf{M} = \mathbf{K}$,

$$\mathbf{H} = r^2\frac{d\theta}{dt}\mathbf{K} \qquad \text{or} \qquad h = r^2\frac{d\theta}{dt}. \tag{13.34}$$

Now we shall use the fact that the field is an inverse-square one:

$$\mathfrak{F} = \mathbf{A} = -\frac{\gamma m'}{r^2}\mathbf{L}$$

or, substituting k for $\gamma m'$,

$$\frac{d\mathbf{V}}{dt} = -\frac{k}{r^2}\mathbf{L}. \tag{13.35}$$

Equations (13.34) and (13.35) represent in useful form the information available about central forces and about gravitation. To get something which we can integrate, we multiply (13.35) vectorially by **K** and then substitute (13.34); thus

$$\frac{d\mathbf{V}}{dt} \times \mathbf{K} = -\frac{k}{r^2}\mathbf{L} \times \mathbf{K} = -\frac{k}{h}\frac{d\theta}{dt}(\mathbf{L} \times \mathbf{K}).$$

Since $\mathbf{L} \times \mathbf{K} = -\mathbf{M}$, the right member is equal to $\frac{k}{h}\frac{d\mathbf{L}}{dt}$. Now integrating, we have,

$$\mathbf{V} \times \mathbf{K} = \frac{k}{h}(\mathbf{L} + \mathbf{E}). \qquad (13.36)$$

The vector **E** (see Fig. 13.17) comes in as a constant of integration. It would have been more natural perhaps to write $(k/h)\mathbf{L} + \mathbf{C}$, where **C** is a constant of integration. In that case **E** is equal to $(h/k)\mathbf{C}$.

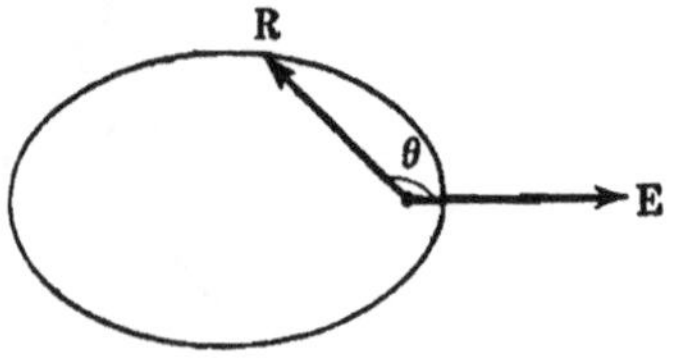

FIG. 13.17.

It is now easy to eliminate **V** from (13.33) and (13.36) in order to arrive at an equation for orbits. From (13.33) we conclude, by multiplying by **K**,

$$\mathbf{R} \times \mathbf{V} \cdot \mathbf{K} = h;$$

an equal expression is obtained by multiplying (13.36) by $\mathbf{R} = r\mathbf{L}$,

$$\mathbf{R} \cdot \mathbf{V} \times \mathbf{K} = \frac{k}{h} r(\mathbf{L} \cdot \mathbf{L} + \mathbf{L} \cdot \mathbf{E}).$$

Now $\mathbf{L} \cdot \mathbf{L} = 1$ and $\mathbf{L} \cdot \mathbf{E} = e \cos \theta$ where $e = |\mathbf{E}|$ and θ is the angle between the fixed vector **E** and the variable vector **L**. We can write then

$$h^2 = kr(1 + e \cos \theta).$$

This means that a polar coordinate equation of such an orbit is

$$r = \frac{h^2/k}{1 + e \cos \theta}. \qquad (13.37)$$

A student well versed in analytic geometry will recognize this as an equation of a conic with focus at the origin, with eccentricity e, and with semi-latus rectum equal to h^2/k. Since planetary orbits are obviously closed, parabolas and hyperbolas can be ruled out. The orbit then has to be an ellipse as is claimed in Kepler's first law. Later we shall use the results of this derivation for other situations, some of which will require conics other than ellipses.

Proof of the Second Law. The second law is precisely the law of areas derived for all central force fields.

Proof of the Third Law. The period τ of a planet's description of its orbit may be expressed as the area of the orbit divided by the constant rate at which area is swept out. That rate is given in (13.31) as $0.5h$.

$$\tau = \frac{\text{area}}{0.5h}. \tag{13.38}$$

We can use the equation of the orbit to relate h to the mean distance. The mean distance a is defined as the average of the maximum and minimum distances (see Fig. 13.18):

$$a = \tfrac{1}{2}(r_2 + r_1).$$

These extreme differences may be found by putting $\theta = 0°$, $180°$ in (13.37),

$$r_1 = \frac{h^2/k}{1 + e}, \qquad r_2 = \frac{h^2/k}{1 - e},$$

$$a = \left(\frac{h^2}{k}\right)(1 - e^2)^{-1}$$

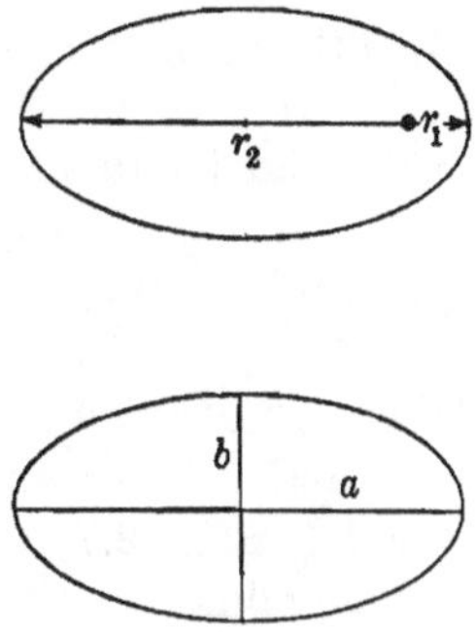

FIG. 13.18.

so that

$$h = \sqrt{ak(1 - e^2)}. \tag{13.39}$$

The area of the ellipse is πab (b is the semiminor axis) or $\pi a^2 \sqrt{1 - e^2}$; thus (13.38) becomes

$$\tau = \frac{\pi a^2 \sqrt{1 - e^2}}{0.5\sqrt{ak(1 - e^2)}} = \frac{2\pi a^{\frac{3}{2}}}{k^{\frac{1}{2}}}$$

or

$$\frac{\tau^2}{a^3} = \frac{4\pi^2}{k} = \frac{4\pi^2}{\gamma m'}. \tag{13.40}$$

The right member is the same for every planet; thus the law is proved. The discussion thus far has postulated an unaccelerated sun. Modifications will be suggested in a later section.

EXERCISES

The earth's eccentricity is 0.0167, and the mean distance from the sun is 92.9 million miles.

1. What is the ratio of the maximum to the minimum speed of the earth in its orbit?

2. Saturn takes 29.5 years to complete its orbit. What is its mean distance from the sun?

3. For how many days in the year is the earth's distance from the sun greater than the mean distance?

4. The number of days spent by the planetoid Eros in each quadrant of its elliptical orbit are, respectively, as follows: 138.0, 183.6, 183.6, 138.0. Find the eccentricity of the orbit and the mean distance from the sun. (Take the corresponding distance for the earth as 92.9 million miles.)

13.10. Energy Criteria for Orbits in an Inverse-square Field. The potential energy of a particle of mass m moving freely under the gravitational influence of a spherical mass m' taken with respect to a point at infinity is

$$\text{p.e.} = -\frac{\gamma m m'}{r} = -\frac{km}{r}. \tag{13.41}$$

Since a field of this type is conservative, the total energy (kinetic plus potential) is constant.

$$\text{t.e.} = \text{k.e.} + \text{p.e.} = \frac{1}{2}mv^2 - \frac{km}{r} = \text{const.} \tag{13.42}$$

Note that for this total energy to be zero,

$$v = v_c = \sqrt{\frac{2\gamma m'}{r}} = \sqrt{\frac{2k}{r}}. \tag{13.43}$$

This *critical speed* is the *escape speed, i.e.*, the speed which would enable the particle to escape from the influence of the field (compare Exercises 3 and 4, Sec. 13.7).

To evaluate v, we square (13.36) of the preceding section.

$$(\mathbf{V} \times \mathbf{K}) \cdot (\mathbf{V} \times \mathbf{K}) = v^2 = (1 + 2\mathbf{L} \cdot \mathbf{E} + \mathbf{E} \cdot \mathbf{E})\frac{k^2}{h^2},$$

or

$$v^2 = \frac{k^2}{h^2}[2(1 + \mathbf{L} \cdot \mathbf{E}) + e^2 - 1].$$

According to (13.37), $1 + \mathbf{L} \cdot \mathbf{E} = \dfrac{h^2}{kr}$; therefore

$$v^2 = \frac{k^2}{h^2}\left(\frac{2h^2}{kr} + e^2 - 1\right) = v_c^2 + \frac{k^2}{h^2}(e^2 - 1). \tag{13.44}$$

Hence,

$$\text{t.e.} = \frac{1}{2}m\left[\frac{2k}{r} + \frac{k^2}{h^2}(e^2 - 1)\right] - \frac{km}{r},$$

or

$$\text{t.e.} = \frac{1}{2}m\frac{k^2}{h^2}(e^2 - 1). \tag{13.45}$$

The following conclusions may now be drawn:

If $v > v_c$, then t.e. > 0, $e > 1$, and the orbit is hyperbolic.
If $v = v_c$, then t.e. $= 0$, $e = 1$, and the orbit is parabolic.
If $v < v_c$, then t.e. < 0, $e < 1$, and the orbit is elliptic.

EXERCISES

1. A comet has speed 5×10^4 m/sec when at a distance 2×10^{11} m from the sun (mass 2×10^{30} kg). Will the orbit be elliptic, parabolic, or hyperbolic?

2. What are the maximum and minimum speeds of a parabolic comet whose nearest approach to the sun is 1 million miles?

13.11. A Property of Planetary Kinetic Energy. In this section we shall endure a rather arduous calculation for the sake of a result interesting in its own right and also important in certain applications. First, let us note that the kinetic energy of a particle in plane motion can easily be expressed as the sum of a radial term and a transverse term. For

$$\mathbf{V} = \frac{dr}{dt}\mathbf{L} + r\omega\mathbf{M};$$

therefore

$$\mathbf{V}\cdot\mathbf{V} = \left(\frac{dr}{dt}\right)^2 + (r\omega)^2.$$

Thus

$$\text{k.e.} = \frac{1}{2}m\mathbf{V}\cdot\mathbf{V} = \frac{1}{2}m\left(\frac{dr}{dt}\right)^2 + \frac{1}{2}m(r\omega)^2.$$

Writing

$$(13.46) \qquad (\text{k.e.})_r = \frac{1}{2}m\left(\frac{dr}{dt}\right)^2, \qquad (\text{k.e.})_t = \frac{1}{2}m(r\omega)^2,$$

we shall compare the average values of (k.e.) and $(\text{k.e.})_t$.

First we look at $(\overline{\text{k.e.}})$, defined as

$$(13.47) \qquad (\overline{\text{k.e.}}) = \frac{m}{2\tau}\int_0^\tau v^2\,dt,$$

where τ is the time over which the averaging takes place. For us it will be the period of orbital motion. From (13.34) we get

$$(13.48) \qquad dt = \frac{r^2}{h}\,d\theta$$

and using (13.37),

$$(13.49) \qquad dt = \frac{(h^3/k^2)d\theta}{(1 + e\cos\theta)^2}.$$

In Sec. 13.10 a formula for v^2 was obtained equivalent to

$$(13.50) \qquad v^2 = \frac{k^2}{h^2}(1 + 2e\cos\theta + e^2).$$

Now let (13.49) and (13.50) be substituted in (13.47):

$$(\overline{\text{k.e.}}) = \frac{hm}{2\tau}\int_0^{2\pi}\frac{(1 + 2e\cos\theta + e^2)}{(1 + e\cos\theta)^2}\,d\theta,$$

or

$$(\overline{\text{k.e.}}) = \frac{hm}{2\tau}\int_0^{2\pi}\left[1 + \frac{e^2\sin^2\theta}{(1 + e\cos\theta)^2}\right]d\theta.$$

Integrating by parts and simplifying this reduces to

$$(\overline{\text{k.e.}}) = \frac{hm}{2\tau}\int_0^{2\pi}\frac{d\theta}{1 + e\cos\theta}.$$

A good table of integrals[1] will finally enable us to conclude

$$\overline{(\text{k.e.})} = \frac{hm}{2\tau}\frac{2\pi}{\sqrt{1-e^2}} = \frac{\pi hm}{\tau\sqrt{1-e^2}}.$$

Using the fact that for an ellipse

$$b = a\sqrt{1-e^2},$$

we may write

$$\overline{(\text{k.e.})} = \frac{\pi hma}{\tau b}. \tag{13.51}$$

The other average is easier to compute:

$$\overline{(\text{k.e.})}_t = \frac{m}{2\tau}\int_0^\tau (r\omega)^2 dt.$$

As in (13.48)

$$r^2\omega = h;$$

therefore

$$\overline{(\text{k.e.})}_t = \frac{hm}{2\tau}\int_0^\tau \omega\, dt = \frac{hm}{2\tau}\int_0^{2\pi} d\theta.$$

Hence

$$\overline{(\text{k.e.})}_t = \frac{\pi hm}{\tau}. \tag{13.52}$$

The main result of this section, valid for any elliptical motion due to an inverse-square law, is contained in the following equation:

$$\frac{\overline{(\text{k.e.})}_t}{\overline{(\text{k.e.})}} = \frac{b}{a}. \tag{13.53}$$

EXERCISES

1. Show that the average kinetic energy of a planet is given by the formula

$$\overline{(\text{k.e.})} = \frac{1}{2}m\left(\frac{h}{b}\right)^2.$$

2. Use Newton's law for central force motion to prove that the actual kinetic energy of a planet at the ends of the minor axes of its orbit is equal to the average kinetic energy for the whole orbit.

3. What are the dimensions of h and k?

13.12. Mechanics of the Bohr Hydrogen Atom. In many branches of physics it has been found natural and advantageous to explain phenomena in terms of mechanical models. It is not always possible to devise simple models which lead to results verified by experiment. The Bohr theory of the atom was an unusual success, particularly for simpler

[1] For example, *Handbook of Physics and Chemistry*, Chemical Rubber Publishing Company; or B. O. Peirce, *A Short Table of Integrals*, Ginn.

atoms, because of its simplicity and because of the remarkable agreement between spectrographic data and the results of the theory. Modern theories of the atom are more complex, but the simple model is still very helpful. According to this theory the hydrogen atom consists of a "sun" (proton) having a positive electrical charge of 1.60×10^{-19} coulomb and a "planet" (electron) having an equal negative charge. The mass of the proton is roughly 1,800 times that of the electron; therefore we shall assume the proton to be at rest with the electron coursing about it.

Using Coulomb's law, the force of attraction is (in newtons)

$$\mathbf{F} = \frac{-q^2}{4\pi\epsilon_0 r^2}\mathbf{L} = m\frac{d\mathbf{V}}{dt}, \tag{13.54}$$

where q is the electronic charge and ϵ_0 the permittivity of free space (8.854×10^{-12} farad/m). This falls at once into the framework of our planetary motion studies.

$$\frac{d\mathbf{V}}{dt} = -\frac{k}{r^2}\mathbf{L}, \tag{13.55}$$

where

$$k = \frac{q^2}{4\pi\epsilon_0 m}.$$

By Sec. 13.9 then, we say immediately that Kepler's laws are obeyed by the electron in its travels around the proton. The difficulty with this model thus far is that such an atom is a miniature antenna and should, according to the classical theory, radiate energy. This would be at the expense of potential energy: the electron would spiral into the nucleus.

The first step in the Bohr solution is to suppose that the electron may travel in certain *permissible* orbits without radiating. These orbits are described by *quantum conditions.* We shall here take the liberty of stating these conditions in a form that fits the discussion of Sec. 13.11. Ordinarily action or angular momentum are quantized. We shall describe orbits as permissible if their *average kinetic energies* satisfy the following two equations. (Only one quantum number was used in the original theory.)

$$\overline{(\text{k.e.})} = \frac{nh}{2\tau}, \tag{13.56}$$

$$\overline{(\text{k.e.})}_t = \frac{n_t h}{2\tau}, \tag{13.57}$$

where n and n_t (not greater than n) are integers known, respectively, as *principal quantum number* and *azimuthal quantum number.* τ is the period of the electron in its orbit. h is Planck's constant (6.62×10^{-34} joule-sec). From the results of Sec. 13.11, it is apparent that only those ellipses are permissible orbits for which

$$\frac{b}{a} = \frac{n_t}{n} = \sqrt{1 - e^2}. \tag{13.58}$$

Consequently, only certain values of the eccentricity are possible (see Exercise 3), and the axes of the orbits are in whole number ratios.

The total energy associated with a given orbit is, by (13.45),

$$(\text{t.e.}) = \frac{1}{2} m \frac{k^2}{h^2} (e^2 - 1) = -\frac{1}{2} m \frac{k^2}{h^2} \cdot \frac{n_t^2}{n^2}.$$

Now

$$(\overline{\text{k.e.}})_t = \frac{n_t h}{2\tau} = \frac{\pi h m}{\tau}$$

(from Sec. 13.11); thus, substituting for k its value in (13.55), we have

$$(\text{t.e.})_n = \frac{-mq^4}{8\epsilon_0^2 h^2 n^2}. \tag{13.59}$$

Observe that this value depends on the principal quantum number, but not the azimuthal.

There are then, according to the Bohr theory, strictly defined permissible orbits in which an electron can remain with constant total energy. The second step in the Bohr theory is the assumption as to what takes place when an electron changes its orbit. When an electron passes from one permissible orbit to another of lower energy, radiation takes place

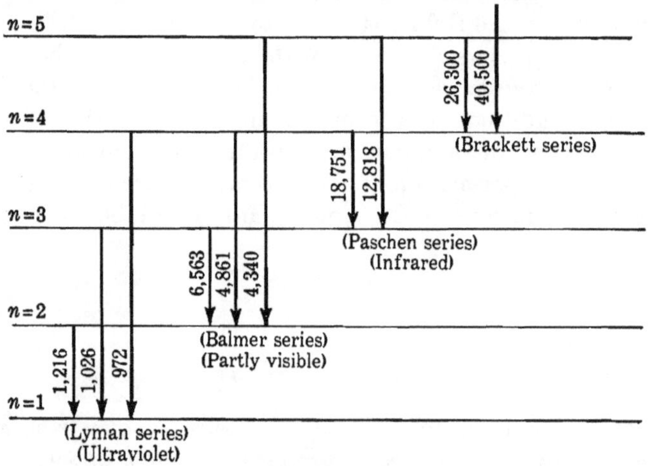

(Wavelengths in angstrom units)

FIG. 13.19.

at a frequency ν such that the energy loss is precisely $h\nu$. It is possible to compute the values of orbital energy to considerable accuracy, and hence to predict those frequencies at which radiation may occur. These computed frequencies check remarkably well with the lines of the hydrogen spectrum. Figure 13.19 shows the relationship between electron transitions for orbits of low quantum number and wavelengths of lines in the hydrogen spectrum. [One angstrom unit (1 A) is equal to 1×10^{-10} m.]

The discovery of the Balmer series, the conclusion that frequencies in such a series can be expressed in the form

$$\nu = \text{const}\left(\frac{1}{n^2} - \frac{1}{n'^2}\right),$$

and the theoretical confirmation by means of the Bohr theory make a fascinating story. The student is referred to any good elementary text on atomic physics for information of this sort.

EXERCISES

Constants

Mass of electron	9.11×10^{-31} kg
Mass of proton	1.67×10^{-27} kg
Velocity of light (c)	2.998×10^{8} m/sec

1. Show that the semiaxes of an electron orbit of principal quantum number n and azimuthal quantum number n_t are

$$a = \frac{n^2 h^2 \epsilon_0}{\pi m q^2}, \qquad b = \frac{n n_t h^2 \epsilon_0}{\pi m q^2}.$$

2. Compute a in meters for $n = 1$.

3. Complete the following table, where n is the principal quantum number, n_t is the azimuthal quantum number, e is the eccentricity of the orbit, a, b are the semimajor and semiminor axes of the orbit, and a_1, b_1 are these semiaxes for the case $n = 1$.

Orbit	n	n_t	e^2	a/a_1	b/b_1
i	1	1	0	1	1
ii	2	1			
iii	2	2			
iv	3	1			
v	3	2			
vi	3	3			

4. Sketch to scale for a fixed center the six orbits described in Exercise 3.

5. According to the Bohr theory, radiation takes place at frequency ν given by

$$h\nu = \frac{hc}{\lambda} = (\text{t.e.})' - (\text{t.e.})$$

when an electron goes from an orbit of energy (t.e.)′ to one of energy (t.e.). What should be the wavelength λ of radiation resulting from a transition (*a*) from orbit v to orbit ii (notation of Exercise 3)? (*b*) from orbit ii to orbit i (notation of Exercise 3)?

6. Show that the period of revolution of an electron in the hydrogen atom is given by

$$\tau = \frac{4n^3h^3\epsilon_0^2}{mq^4}.$$

7. The mechanical frequency of revolution for principal quantum number n can be computed from the preceding result. Call it f. The frequency of radiation for a transition to the orbit with principal quantum number equal to $n - 1$ is given by the procedure of Exercise 5. Call it ν. Find the ratio f/ν. What is its limit for large n?

13.13. Bombardment of Heavy Nuclei by α Particles. The kinetic theory of gases shows atoms to behave like elastic spheres of radius approximately 10^{-10} m. This also is the order of magnitude of inner Bohr orbits. To see how large a part of this space is devoid of mass, attempts were made to probe the atom. Rutherford used α particles the mass of which (6.64×10^{-27} kg) is too great to permit deflections by electrons in the orbits. It was observed that some of these particles when shot through gold foil were deflected through large angles, indicating collision with a massive nucleus. It is our aim to calculate the nearest approach to the center of the atom in terms of the amount that the projectile is deflected. The α particle consists of two protons and two neutrons; therefore its charge is $+2q$. The nucleus of the target atom has a positive charge also denoted by zq, where z is the atomic number (see Fig. 13.20). Using Coulomb's law, the equation of motion is

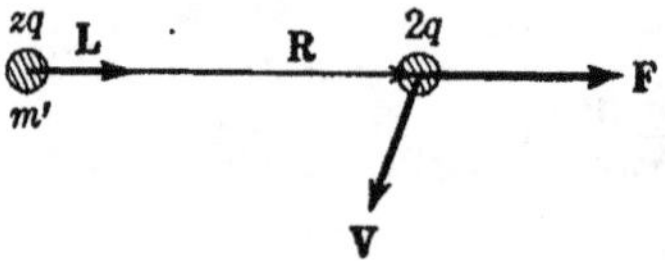

FIG. 13.20.

$$\mathbf{F} = \frac{2zq^2}{4\pi\epsilon_0 r^2}\mathbf{L} = m\frac{d\mathbf{V}}{dt}.$$

This is a force of repulsion, but the equation can again be put in the form

$$\frac{d\mathbf{V}}{dt} = -\frac{k}{r^2}\mathbf{L}, \qquad k = -\frac{zq^2}{2\pi\epsilon_0 m}. \tag{13.60}$$

Consequently, the orbit is a conic with the target as focus. From the speed equation

$$v^2 = \frac{k^2}{h^2}\left(\frac{2h^2}{kr} + e^2 - 1\right)$$

it is apparent that $e > 1$, since k is negative. The orbit then is *hyperbolic*. Note that the firing speed, taken for $r = \infty$, is

$$v_0 = \frac{-k}{h}\sqrt{e^2 - 1}. \tag{13.61}$$

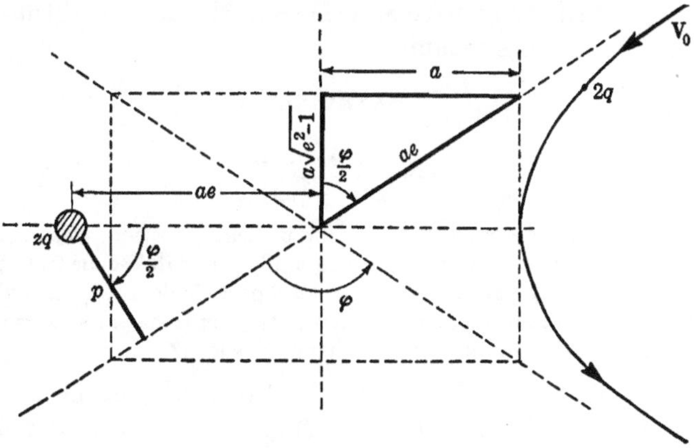

FIG. 13.21.

From the geometry of the hyperbola, it is clear that (see Fig. 13.21)

$$\sqrt{e^2 - 1} = \text{ctn}\,\frac{\varphi}{2}, \tag{13.62}$$

where φ is the angle of deflection, and that

$$p = ae\cos\frac{\varphi}{2} = a\sqrt{e^2 - 1}.$$

By Newton's law for central forces,

$$h = pv_0 = av_0\sqrt{e^2 - 1}. \tag{13.63}$$

Eliminating h between (13.61) and (13.63), we get

$$a = -\frac{k}{v_0^2}; \tag{13.64}$$

hence, substituting the value for k in (13.60),

$$a = +\frac{zq^2}{2\pi\epsilon_0 m v_0^2}. \tag{13.65}$$

The distance of nearest approach to the nucleus is (see Fig. 13.21)

$$d = a + ae = a\left(1 + \csc\frac{\varphi}{2}\right). \tag{13.66}$$

As φ approaches 180°, d approaches a minimum. Actual angles of scattering up to 150° were observed when α particles of speed $0.064c$ (c denotes speed of light) were used with gold ($z = 79$). For these values,

$$d = \frac{zq^2[1 + \csc(\varphi/2)]}{2\pi\epsilon_0 m v_0^2}$$

$$= \frac{79(1.6 \times 10^{-19})^2(1 + 1.04)}{2\pi(8.854 \times 10^{-12})(6.64 \times 10^{-27})(0.064)^2(9 \times 10^{16})}$$

$$= 3.0 \times 10^{-14}\text{ m}.$$

This result showed the relative emptiness of the atom and thus made the Bohr theory seem more tenable.

EXERCISES

1. Prove that

$$\tan\frac{\varphi}{2} = \frac{zq^2/4\pi\epsilon_0 p}{\frac{1}{2}mv_0^2}.$$

2. In the numerical case worked out in the preceding section, what is the speed of the α particle at the point of deepest penetration? After its escape from the nucleus?

3. What is the eccentricity of the orbit of an α particle deflected through 90°?

4. A hyperbolic comet passes close enough to the sun to have its course changed by 60°. What is the maximum percentage change in speed?

13.14. The Two-body Problem. In the examples of central fields examined thus far the center was assumed to be a fixed point. This assumption was justified by the comparatively large mass of the sun, the hydrogen nucleus, and the gold nucleus. We now consider, particularly for the gravitational case, the consequences of removing this restriction. This constitutes the famous "problem of two bodies," which was solved by Newton. The system of two particles is subjected to no external forces; therefore the center of mass $\bar{\mathbf{R}}$ experiences no acceleration. Let $\bar{\mathbf{R}}$ be the origin (see Fig. 13.22). Then the equations of motion are

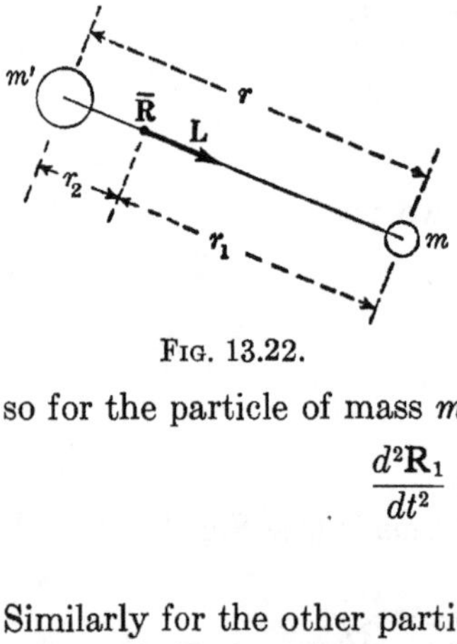

FIG. 13.22.

$$\frac{d\mathbf{V}_1}{dt} = -\frac{\gamma mm'}{mr^2}\mathbf{L}$$

and

$$\frac{d\mathbf{V}_2}{dt} = \frac{\gamma mm'}{m'r^2}\mathbf{L}$$

where

$$r = r_1 + r_2 = r_1 + \frac{m}{m'}r_1;$$

so for the particle of mass m, for instance,

$$\frac{d^2\mathbf{R}_1}{dt^2} = -\frac{\gamma m'}{\left[1+\frac{m}{m'}\right]^2 r_1^2}\mathbf{L}.$$

Similarly for the other particle. Hence,

(13.67) *Each of the particles describes a conic with* $\bar{\mathbf{R}}$ *as focus.*

In contemplating planetary motion, we are more interested in motion with respect to the sun:

$$\frac{d\mathbf{V}}{dt} = \frac{d}{dt}(\mathbf{V}_1 - \mathbf{V}_2) = \frac{d\mathbf{V}_1}{dt} - \frac{d\mathbf{V}_2}{dt} = -\frac{\gamma(m+m')}{r^2}\mathbf{L}. \tag{13.68}$$

This is to be compared with previous result (13.35):

$$\frac{d\mathbf{V}}{dt} = -\frac{\gamma m'}{r^2}\mathbf{L} = -\frac{k}{r^2}\mathbf{L}.$$

It is apparent that Kepler's third law must now be written with $k = \gamma(m + m')$.

$$\frac{\tau^2}{a^3} = \frac{4\pi^2}{k} = \frac{4\pi^2}{\gamma(m + m')}. \tag{13.69}$$

In the case of the Bohr hydrogen atom, a similar adjustment is made. From

$$\frac{d\mathbf{V}_1}{dt} = -\frac{q^2}{4\pi\epsilon_0 m r^2}\mathbf{L}$$

and

$$\frac{d\mathbf{V}_2}{dt} = \frac{q^2}{4\pi\epsilon_0 m' r^2}\mathbf{L}$$

we get

$$\frac{d\mathbf{V}}{dt} = \frac{d\mathbf{V}_1}{dt} - \frac{d\mathbf{V}_2}{dt} = -\frac{q^2}{4\pi\epsilon_0 r^2}\left(\frac{1}{m} + \frac{1}{m'}\right)\mathbf{L} = -\frac{q^2}{4\pi\epsilon_0 r^2}\left(\frac{1}{\mu}\right)\mathbf{L},$$

where μ is the *reduced mass* of the satellite. μ should be substituted for m in the formulas derived for the hydrogen atom. The theory of α particle scattering for light nuclei would be equally appropriate here. The other examples have been elected because of their relative simplicity.

EXERCISES

1. If the mass of the earth were equal to that of the sun, the relative orbit being as at present, how long would a year be?

2. Compute the reduced mass of the planetary electron in the hydrogen atom.

3. Two particles have masses m_1 and m_2. Their center of mass has velocity $\bar{\mathbf{V}}$. Prove that

$$\frac{\bar{\mathbf{V}}}{\mu} = \frac{\mathbf{V}_1}{m_2} + \frac{\mathbf{V}_2}{m_1}.$$

4. Two particles collide elastically (coefficient of restitution is 1). The x axis is normal to the surface of contact. Show that the amount of energy gained by one particle and lost by the other is equal to $2\mu\bar{v}_x(v_{2_x} - v_{1_x})$, where $\bar{v}_x$ is the x component of the velocity of the center of mass.

CHAPTER 14

DEFORMABLE BODIES IN EQUILIBRIUM

If an ideal rigid body is in equilibrium, its shape and size remain the same regardless of what the applied forces may be. Any actual body behaves differently. A loaded cable stretches, a loaded beam bends, a body under pressure shrinks. When forces are applied, both the size and shape may be altered. The changes bear a direct relation to the forces involved. When the forces are removed, the distortion often disappears. This is called *elastic* behavior. Many materials exhibit this behavior within limits. When the *elastic limit* is reached, shape and size are not restored by the removal of the forces. For elastic behavior a very simple sort of relationship is found experimentally to hold. This important phenomenon was announced in 1676 by Robert Hooke. His conclusion was that *the force is proportional to the stretch.* In this chapter we shall make a study of elastic behavior. A central feature will be *Hooke's law: The stress is proportional to the strain.* The terms *stress* and *strain* will be defined in the following sections. The subject of elasticity is a large one, and many of its parts can best be pursued by the use of mathematical methods not assumed for this course. Since a selection must be made, methods and results will be presented which are important and which also fit in with the procedures in other parts of the course. As a mathematical preliminary we shall resume the study of directional derivatives.

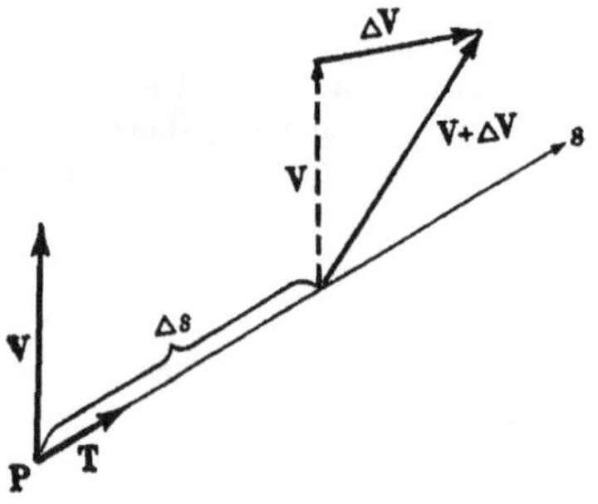

FIG. 14.1.

14.1. Directional Derivatives for Vector Fields. Let **V** be a vector function of position. At any point **P** and for any direction given by the unit vector **T**, we may consider the directional derivative of **V**. It is easily defined (see Fig. 14.1) as

$$\frac{d\mathbf{V}}{ds} = \lim_{\Delta s \to 0} \frac{\Delta \mathbf{V}}{\Delta s}.$$

To suggest how it may be evaluated, let us express **V** in terms of its components and then differentiate term by term:

$$\mathbf{V} = v_x\mathbf{I} + v_y\mathbf{J} + v_z\mathbf{K},$$

$$\frac{d\mathbf{V}}{ds} = \frac{dv_x}{ds}\mathbf{I} + \frac{dv_y}{ds}\mathbf{J} + \frac{dv_z}{ds}\mathbf{K}.$$

This effectively reduces the problem to one of computing three directional derivatives for the scalars v_x, v_y, v_z. Using (13.5),

$$\frac{d\mathbf{V}}{ds} = (\mathbf{T} \cdot \nabla v_x)\mathbf{I} + (\mathbf{T} \cdot \nabla v_y)\mathbf{J} + (\mathbf{T} \cdot \nabla v_z)\mathbf{K}. \tag{14.1}$$

This equation shows how the derivative often may be computed, component by component. Abbreviating the right member, the following expression is commonly used:

$$\frac{d\mathbf{V}}{ds} = (\mathbf{T} \cdot \nabla)\mathbf{V}. \tag{14.2}$$

It should be clearly understood that the right member of (14.2) is merely an abbreviation for the right member of (14.1). The same sort of abbreviation is used even when $\mathbf{T}$ is replaced by a vector whose magnitude is not 1.

Example. Find the directional derivative at $\mathbf{R} = 3\mathbf{I} - 2\mathbf{K}$ in the direction of $\mathbf{A} = 4\mathbf{J} + 3\mathbf{K}$ of the variable vector

$$\mathbf{V} = 3xz\mathbf{I} + 2xy\mathbf{J} + y^2\mathbf{K}.$$

SOLUTION. Here $\mathbf{T} = \dfrac{\mathbf{A}}{a} = 0.8\mathbf{J} + 0.6\mathbf{K}.$

The computation proceeds thus:

$$\begin{aligned} \nabla(3xz) &= 3z\mathbf{I} + 3x\mathbf{K}, & \mathbf{T} \cdot \nabla(3xz) &= 1.8x = 5.4, \\ \nabla(2xy) &= 2y\mathbf{I} + 2x\mathbf{J}, & \mathbf{T} \cdot \nabla(2xy) &= 1.6x = 4.8, \\ \nabla(y^2) &= 2y\mathbf{J}, & \mathbf{T} \cdot \nabla(y^2) &= 1.6y = 0. \end{aligned}$$

(The values for x and y are those given in the specification of $\mathbf{R}$: $x = 3$, $y = 0$, $z = -2$.) Thus

$$\frac{d\mathbf{V}}{ds} = (\mathbf{T} \cdot \nabla)\mathbf{V} = 5.4\mathbf{I} + 4.8\mathbf{J}.$$

EXERCISES

1. Find the directional derivative of

$$\mathbf{B} = xy\mathbf{I} + y^2\mathbf{J} + xz^3\mathbf{K}$$

at the point

$$\mathbf{R} = \mathbf{I} + 2\mathbf{J} + 3\mathbf{K}$$

in the direction of

$$\mathbf{A} = 2\mathbf{I} - \mathbf{J} + 2\mathbf{K}.$$

2. If $\mathbf{A} = a_x\mathbf{I} + a_y\mathbf{J} + a_z\mathbf{K}$ and similarly $\mathbf{B} = b_x\mathbf{I} + b_y\mathbf{J} + b_z\mathbf{K}$, where b_x, b_y, b_z are scalar functions of x, y, and z, express completely in scalar symbols the x component of the vector $(\mathbf{A} \cdot \nabla)\mathbf{B}$.

3. Write out the x, y, and z components of the vector $(\mathbf{V} \cdot \nabla)\mathbf{V}$, where

$$\mathbf{V} = v_x\mathbf{I} + v_y\mathbf{J} + v_z\mathbf{K}.$$

14.2. Simple Strains. Strain may be defined as relative distortion. In this section we shall introduce a few simple special cases.

Stretched Rod. Consider a homogeneous solid cylindrical rod as is shown in Fig. 14.2. Let its original length be l and its original radius be r. When the rod is stretched, l increases by an amount Δl. The *longitudinal strain* in this case is

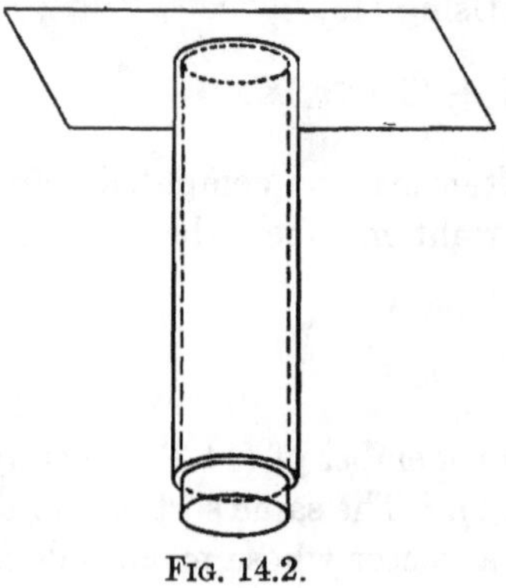

FIG. 14.2.

(14.3) $$e_l = \frac{\Delta l}{l}.$$

The radius is likely to change also. For a stretch Δr is negative; therefore the corresponding *radial strain* e_r is negative.

(14.4) $$e_r = \frac{\Delta r}{r}.$$

The positive ratio of lateral to longitudinal strain (when no external lateral forces are applied), here given by $-\frac{e_r}{e_l}$, is known as *Poisson's ratio:*

(14.5) $$\sigma = -\frac{e_r}{e_l}.$$

The value of σ is usually between 0.30 and 0.40. (When lateral forces are applied to keep $e_r = 0$, the strain is called a *simple* extension.)

Let us now see how the volume v of the rod has changed. Assuming, as must be true for elastic behavior of most solids, that the strains are small, we have

$$v = \pi r^2 l$$
$$\Delta v = 2\pi r l\, \Delta r + \pi r^2\, \Delta l,$$

and hence that the *volume strain* or *cubical dilatation* as it is called is

(14.6) $$e_v = \frac{\Delta v}{v} = 2e_r + e_l.$$

Using (14.5), this may be written

(14.7) $$e_v = e_l(1 - 2\sigma).$$

Simple Shear. Suppose that a homogeneous cubical block has one pair of opposite faces pushed out of line without changing the planes or areas of another pair of opposite faces. One of these faces is shown in Fig. 14.3. It is distorted into a rhombus. The angle ϕ by which the third pair of opposite faces is tipped is a measure of the *shearing strain*

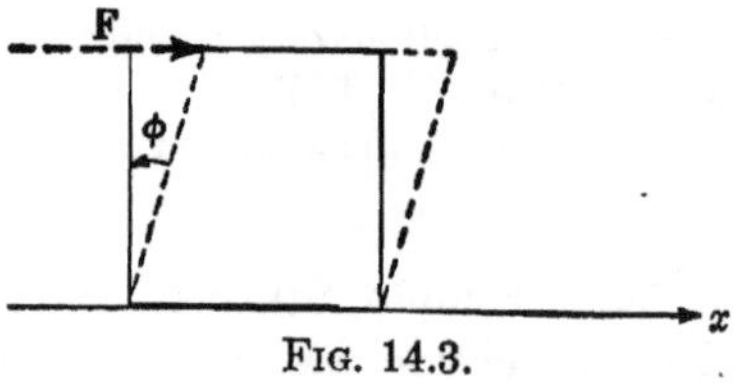

FIG. 14.3.

(14.8) $$e_s = \phi.$$

In the next section we shall take a more general approach to deformations.

EXERCISES

1. An isotropic rectangular beam has length l, breadth b, and depth h. It is stretched a little longitudinally until the new length is $l + \Delta l$. Poisson's ratio is σ. Find an expression for the fractional decrease in area of cross section.

2. A rod of Poisson's ratio 0.3 is stretched until its length is increased by 0.5 per cent. What is the percentage decrease in density?

3. A $\frac{1}{4}$-in. section of a $\frac{1}{2}$-in. rivet (shaded) in Fig. 14.4 is distorted in a shear so that the top face is 0.001 in. out of line with the bottom face. What is its shearing strain?

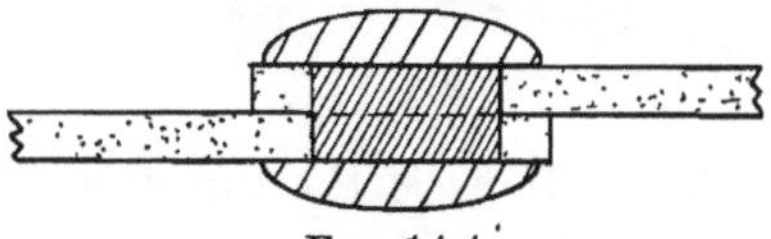

FIG. 14.4.

4. A thin cylindrical pipe of radius r and length l has one end firmly fastened. The other end is twisted through an angle θ. What is the shearing strain? (HINT: To get a rectangle to work with, imagine the cylinder slit and unrolled.)

14.3. Small Distortion of a Deformable Body. If a body is subject to forces in equilibrium, the distortion which ensues can be described in terms of the small displacement of each point. In the distortions which we shall ordinarily consider, straight line segments in the body before distortion will be straight line segments after distortion. Thus we shall be particularly interested in the way in which a line segment alters its direction or length. We shall assume, in any case, that the distortions are "smooth," so that derivatives will exist and be continuous.

As usual, let **R** denote the position of an arbitrary point and let **H** be its displacement. Then **H** is a vector function of position. We shall concentrate on a directed line segment from **R** to **R** + Δ**R**. In Fig.

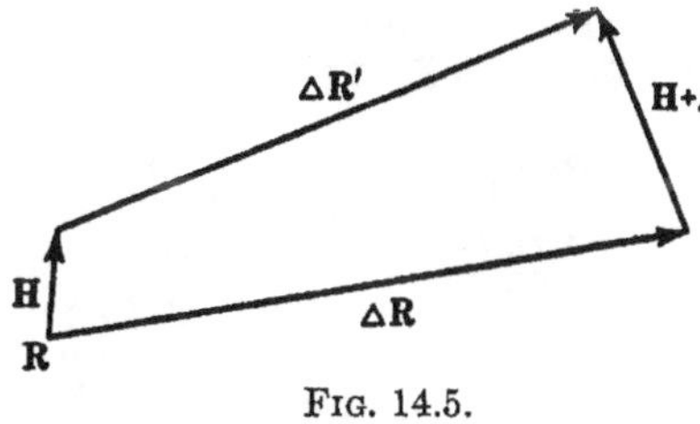

FIG. 14.5.

14.5, Δ**R** is the original directed segment. The displacement of the initial end is **H**, and that of the terminal end is **H** + Δ**H**. From the diagram we may write

$$\Delta\mathbf{R}' = \Delta\mathbf{R} + \mathbf{H} + \Delta\mathbf{H} - \mathbf{H} = \Delta\mathbf{R} + \Delta\mathbf{H}.$$

The equation

$$\Delta\mathbf{R}' = \Delta\mathbf{R} + \Delta\mathbf{H} \tag{14.9}$$

is diagramed separately in Fig. 14.6. This diagram might be interpreted as representing displacements relative to **R**. This is a reasonable view to take, for one may just as well pick as origin a point which we hold fixed during the distortion. Since the distortion is small, $|\Delta\mathbf{H}|$ is much smaller than Δs, Δs being the length of $\Delta\mathbf{R}$. We shall assume the validity of the substitution

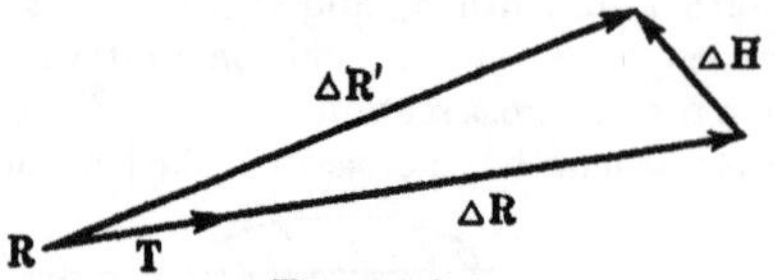

FIG. 14.6.

$$\Delta\mathbf{H} = \frac{d\mathbf{H}}{ds}\Delta s, \tag{14.10}$$

where $d\mathbf{H}/ds$ is the directional derivative at **R** in the direction of the vector $\Delta\mathbf{R}$. This assumption is justified if Δs is sufficiently small or if the distortion is in fact a "homogeneous" one, sending straight lines into straight lines. Then, using the methods of Sec. 14.1, we can compute:

$$\Delta\mathbf{H} = (\mathbf{T}\cdot\nabla)\mathbf{H}\,\Delta s \tag{14.11}$$

and

$$\Delta\mathbf{R}' = \Delta s[\mathbf{T} + (\mathbf{T}\cdot\nabla)\mathbf{H}]. \tag{14.12}$$

Analytic expressions for the displacement may be written down at once. If

$$\mathbf{H} = \xi\mathbf{I} + \eta\mathbf{J} + \zeta\mathbf{K},$$
$$\mathbf{T} = l\mathbf{I} + m\mathbf{J} + n\mathbf{K},$$

we have

$$\frac{\Delta\mathbf{H}}{\Delta s} = \frac{d\mathbf{H}}{ds} = (\mathbf{T}\cdot\nabla)\mathbf{H} \tag{14.13}$$

or

$$\begin{aligned}\frac{\Delta\mathbf{H}}{\Delta s} &= (\mathbf{T}\cdot\nabla\xi)\mathbf{I} + (\mathbf{T}\cdot\nabla\eta)\mathbf{J} + (\mathbf{T}\cdot\nabla\zeta)\mathbf{K}\\ &= \left(l\frac{\partial\xi}{\partial x} + m\frac{\partial\xi}{\partial y} + n\frac{\partial\xi}{\partial z}\right)\mathbf{I} + \left(l\frac{\partial\eta}{\partial x} + m\frac{\partial\eta}{\partial y} + n\frac{\partial\eta}{\partial z}\right)\mathbf{J}\\ &\qquad + \left(l\frac{\partial\zeta}{\partial x} + m\frac{\partial\zeta}{\partial y} + n\frac{\partial\zeta}{\partial z}\right)\mathbf{K}.\end{aligned}$$

One aspect of the distortion which we are considering is the longitudinal strain (relative change in length) or the *extension* of the segment. Denoting extension for the **T** direction by e_T, we have

$$e_T = \frac{|\Delta\mathbf{R}'| - \Delta s}{\Delta s} = \frac{|\Delta\mathbf{R}'|}{\Delta s} - 1. \tag{14.14}$$

In the limit, the extension at **R** is then

$$e_T = \left|\frac{d\mathbf{R}'}{ds}\right| - 1.$$

To evaluate e_T, we must find the magnitude of the vector

$$(14.15)\quad \Delta\mathbf{R}' = \Delta s\left\{\left[l\left(1+\frac{\partial\xi}{\partial x}\right)+m\frac{\partial\xi}{\partial y}+n\frac{\partial\xi}{\partial z}\right]\mathbf{I} + \left[l\frac{\partial\eta}{\partial x}+m\left(1+\frac{\partial\eta}{\partial y}\right)+n\frac{\partial\eta}{\partial z}\right]\mathbf{J} + \left[l\frac{\partial\zeta}{\partial x}+m\frac{\partial\zeta}{\partial y}+n\left(1+\frac{\partial\zeta}{\partial z}\right)\right]\mathbf{K}\right\}.$$

In evaluating this magnitude, we merely add the squares of the components and take the square root, just as usual. We do, however, neglect the squares of derivatives in comparison with 1 because of our assumption that $\Delta\mathbf{H}$ is small in comparison with $\Delta\mathbf{R}$.

$$|\Delta\mathbf{R}'|^2 = \Delta s^2\left(l^2+2l^2\frac{\partial\xi}{\partial x}+2lm\frac{\partial\xi}{\partial y}+2ln\frac{\partial\xi}{\partial z} + m^2+2ml\frac{\partial\eta}{\partial x}+2m^2\frac{\partial\eta}{\partial y}+2mn\frac{\partial\eta}{\partial z} + n^2+2nl\frac{\partial\zeta}{\partial x}+2nm\frac{\partial\zeta}{\partial y}+2n^2\frac{\partial\zeta}{\partial z}\right).$$

Now $l^2 + m^2 + n^2 = \mathbf{T}\cdot\mathbf{T} = 1$. Using the binomial theorem to take the square root, thus,

$$(1+a)^{\frac{1}{2}} = 1 + \tfrac{1}{2}a + \text{terms of higher power in } a$$

and neglecting higher powers of the derivatives, we have

$$(14.16)\quad |\Delta\mathbf{R}'| = \Delta s\left[1+l^2\frac{\partial\xi}{\partial x}+m^2\frac{\partial\eta}{\partial y}+n^2\frac{\partial\zeta}{\partial z} + lm\left(\frac{\partial\xi}{\partial y}+\frac{\partial\eta}{\partial x}\right)+mn\left(\frac{\partial\eta}{\partial z}+\frac{\partial\zeta}{\partial y}\right)+nl\left(\frac{\partial\zeta}{\partial x}+\frac{\partial\xi}{\partial z}\right)\right].$$

From this we get for the extension,

$$(14.17)\quad e_T = \frac{|\Delta\mathbf{R}'|}{\Delta s} - 1 = l^2\frac{\partial\xi}{\partial x}+m^2\frac{\partial\eta}{\partial y}+n^2\frac{\partial\zeta}{\partial z} + lm\left(\frac{\partial\xi}{\partial y}+\frac{\partial\eta}{\partial x}\right)+mn\left(\frac{\partial\eta}{\partial z}+\frac{\partial\zeta}{\partial y}\right)+nl\left(\frac{\partial\zeta}{\partial x}+\frac{\partial\xi}{\partial z}\right).$$

EXERCISES

1. (*a*) Evaluate each of the nine coefficients $\frac{\partial\xi}{\partial x}$, $\frac{\partial\xi}{\partial y}$, etc., in (14.13) for the case where the displacement is, instead of a deformation, a rigid rotation through a *small* angle θ about the z axis. Let $\Delta\mathbf{R}$ be the position vector $x\mathbf{I} + y\mathbf{J}$. (*b*) Use (14.17) to evaluate e_T for the displacement described in part (*a*).

14.4. Coefficients of Extension and Shear. In discussing distortions it is customary to list, separately, the components in the different coordinate directions. In Eq. (14.17) we may find the x, y, *and* z *coefficients of extension*, e_{xx}, e_{yy}, e_{zz}, by replacing **T** by **I, J,** and **K** successively. When **T** is replaced by **I,** l, m, and n become 1, 0, and 0; thus we get approximately

$$e_{xx} = \frac{\partial \xi}{\partial x}, \qquad e_{yy} = \frac{\partial \eta}{\partial y}, \qquad e_{zz} = \frac{\partial \zeta}{\partial z}. \tag{14.18}$$

Another aspect of distortion concerns angles between reference directions. Thus the *coefficients of shear* e_{xy}, e_{yz}, e_{zx} are defined by

$$\begin{aligned} e_{xy} &= 0.5 \cos (\mathbf{I}',\mathbf{J}'), \\ e_{yz} &= 0.5 \cos (\mathbf{J}',\mathbf{K}'), \\ e_{zx} &= 0.5 \cos (\mathbf{K}',\mathbf{I}'), \end{aligned} \tag{14.19}$$

where $(\mathbf{I}',\mathbf{J}')$ stands for the angle after distortion between segments originally in the x and y directions, and similarly for $(\mathbf{J}',\mathbf{K}')$ and $(\mathbf{K}',\mathbf{I}')$. (Sometimes these coefficients of shear are defined as exactly equal to the cosines.)

To get information concerning these directions, let $\Delta\mathbf{R}$ be replaced by **I, J, K** successively. Applying Eq. (14.15), we have

$$\begin{aligned} \mathbf{I}' &= 1\left[1\left(1 + \frac{\partial \xi}{\partial x}\right)\right]\mathbf{I} + \left[1\left(\frac{\partial \eta}{\partial x}\right)\right]\mathbf{J} + \left[1\left(\frac{\partial \zeta}{\partial x}\right)\right]\mathbf{K}, \\ \mathbf{J}' &= \frac{\partial \xi}{\partial y}\mathbf{I} + \left(1 + \frac{\partial \eta}{\partial y}\right)\mathbf{J} + \frac{\partial \zeta}{\partial y}\mathbf{K}, \\ \mathbf{K}' &= \frac{\partial \xi}{\partial z}\mathbf{I} + \frac{\partial \eta}{\partial z}\mathbf{J} + \left(1 + \frac{\partial \zeta}{\partial z}\right)\mathbf{K}. \end{aligned} \tag{14.20}$$

Now each of these vectors is practically a unit vector. Discarding higher powers of the derivatives, we have, in fact,

$$|\mathbf{I}'| = 1 + \frac{\partial \xi}{\partial x}, \qquad |\mathbf{J}'| = 1 + \frac{\partial \eta}{\partial y}, \qquad |\mathbf{K}'| = 1 + \frac{\partial \zeta}{\partial z}.$$

Let us proceed with the evaluation

$$\begin{aligned} 2e_{xy} = \cos (\mathbf{I}',\mathbf{J}') &= \frac{\mathbf{I}' \cdot \mathbf{J}'}{|\mathbf{I}'||\mathbf{J}'|} \\ &= \frac{\left(1 + \frac{\partial \xi}{\partial x}\right)\left(\frac{\partial \xi}{\partial y}\right) + \left(\frac{\partial \eta}{\partial x}\right)\left(1 + \frac{\partial \eta}{\partial y}\right) + \left(\frac{\partial \zeta}{\partial x}\right)\left(\frac{\partial \zeta}{\partial y}\right)}{\left(1 + \frac{\partial \xi}{\partial x}\right)\left(1 + \frac{\partial \eta}{\partial y}\right)} \end{aligned}$$

Neglecting higher powers of the derivatives, $\left(1 + \frac{\partial \xi}{\partial x}\right)^{-1} = 1 - \frac{\partial \xi}{\partial x}$, etc., and we get

$$2e_{xy} = \left(1 - \frac{\partial \eta}{\partial y}\right)\left(\frac{\partial \xi}{\partial y}\right) + \left(1 - \frac{\partial \xi}{\partial x}\right)\left(\frac{\partial \eta}{\partial x}\right) = \frac{\partial \xi}{\partial y} + \frac{\partial \eta}{\partial x},$$

$$e_{xy} = 0.5\left(\frac{\partial \xi}{\partial y} + \frac{\partial \eta}{\partial x}\right). \tag{14.21}$$

Likewise

$$e_{yz} = 0.5\left(\frac{\partial \eta}{\partial z} + \frac{\partial \zeta}{\partial y}\right),$$

$$e_{zx} = 0.5\left(\frac{\partial \zeta}{\partial x} + \frac{\partial \xi}{\partial z}\right).$$

Application to Longitudinal Strain. In terms of these elementary coefficients of extension and shear, we may rewrite our general expression (14.17) for extension in the **T** direction:

$$e_T = l^2 e_{xx} + m^2 e_{yy} + n^2 e_{zz} + 2mne_{yz} + 2nle_{zx} + 2lme_{xy}. \tag{14.22}$$

This equation is analogous to (8.31) for moments of inertia, and it leads to the theory of a strain ellipsoid analogous to the ellipsoid of inertia.

Application to Angular Strain. The angular distortion for any two directions may be ascertained in terms of these coefficients by applying (14.15) successively to the two corresponding unit vectors

$$\mathbf{T}_1 = l_1\mathbf{I} + m_1\mathbf{J} + n_1\mathbf{K},$$
$$\mathbf{T}_2 = l_2\mathbf{I} + m_2\mathbf{J} + n_2\mathbf{K}.$$

We get

$$\mathbf{T}_1' = \left[l_1(1 + e_{xx}) + m_1\frac{\partial \xi}{\partial y} + n_1\frac{\partial \xi}{\partial z}\right]\mathbf{I} + \cdots \text{ (terms in } \mathbf{J} \text{ and } \mathbf{K}),$$

$$\mathbf{T}_2' = \left[l_2(1 + e_{xx}) + m_2\frac{\partial \xi}{\partial y} + n_2\frac{\partial \xi}{\partial z}\right]\mathbf{I} + \cdots \text{ (terms in } \mathbf{J} \text{ and } \mathbf{K}).$$

Now

$$\cos(\mathbf{T}_1',\mathbf{T}_2') = \frac{\mathbf{T}_1' \cdot \mathbf{T}_2'}{|\mathbf{T}_1'||\mathbf{T}_2'|} = \frac{\mathbf{T}_1' \cdot \mathbf{T}_2'}{(1 + e_{T_1})(1 + e_{T_2})},$$

where e_{T_1} and e_{T_2} are given by (14.22). The result is, grouping the factors for ease in writing,

$$\begin{aligned}[\cos(\mathbf{T}_1',\mathbf{T}_2') - \cos(\mathbf{T}_1,\mathbf{T}_2)](1 + e_{T_1})(1 + e_{T_2}) \\ = 2(l_1l_2e_{xx} + m_1m_2e_{yy} + n_1n_2e_{zz}) + 2e_{xy}(l_1m_2 + m_1l_2) \\ + 2e_{yz}(m_1n_2 + n_1m_2) + 2e_{zx}(n_1l_2 + l_1n_2).\end{aligned} \tag{14.23}$$

Application to Volume Strain. Finally, let us see what happens to the volume of a small cubical figure when it experiences a small strain. Let the cube be aligned with the axes, its dimensions being Δx, Δy, Δz. Then the volume $v = \Delta x\, \Delta y\, \Delta z$. After deformation, the edges are

$$\Delta x(1 + e_{xx}), \qquad \Delta y(1 + e_{yy}), \qquad \Delta z(1 + e_{zz})$$

and the volume is approximately

$$v' = \Delta x\, \Delta y\, \Delta z(1 + e_{xx})(1 + e_{yy})(1 + e_{zz}).$$

Multiplying out and discarding higher powers in the e's, we have for the cubical dilatation

$$e_v = \frac{v' - v}{v} = e_{xx} + e_{yy} + e_{zz}. \tag{14.24}$$

We have seen, then, how three main aspects of strain (changes in length, angle, and volume) are expressible in terms of the six elementary coefficients of extension and shear.

Significance of the Coefficients. Since e_{xx}, e_{yy}, e_{zz} were defined as extensions in the coordinate directions, their significance in terms of simple strains is obvious. Each is a measure of stretch (either positive or negative) in these directions. The relationship of coefficients of shear to simple shear may be less apparent. Consider a strain in which all displacement is parallel to the xy plane, the origin being kept fixed. Suppose that the square **OABC** (see Fig. 14.7) is deformed into the rhombus **OA′B′C′**. This is an example of what is called a *pure shear*. In terms of our previous terminology, referring to Fig. 14.7 (somewhat idealized to clarify the example),

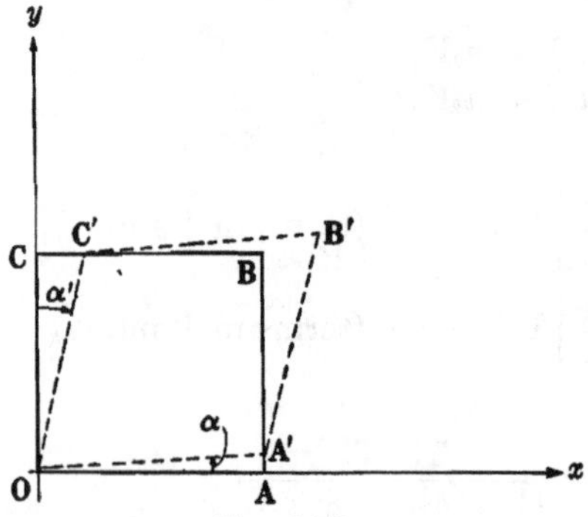

FIG. 14.7.

$$|\mathbf{OA}| = \Delta x, \qquad |\mathbf{AA'}| = \Delta\eta,$$
$$|\mathbf{OC}| = \Delta y, \qquad |\mathbf{CC'}| = \Delta\xi.$$

Hence, for small strains, we have

$$\alpha = \tan \alpha = \frac{\Delta\eta}{\Delta x} = \frac{\partial\eta}{\partial x},$$
$$\alpha' = \tan \alpha' = \frac{\Delta\xi}{\Delta y} = \frac{\partial\xi}{\partial y}.$$

(The last equality in each case follows since straight lines are deformed into straight lines.) Now how are α and α' related to ϕ of Fig. 14.3? Since the whole body may be rotated through an angle $-\alpha$ without further distortion, it is apparent that

$$e_s = \phi = \alpha + \alpha' = \frac{\partial\eta}{\partial x} + \frac{\partial\xi}{\partial y} = 2e_{xy}. \tag{14.25}$$

Thus we see that the three coefficients of shear are measures of shearing strains associated with the three coordinate planes.

Pure Shear and Coefficients of Extension. If an x extension and a y compression are combined, a square figure with the x and y axes as diagonals is distorted into a rhombus as shown in Fig. 14.8. This, too,

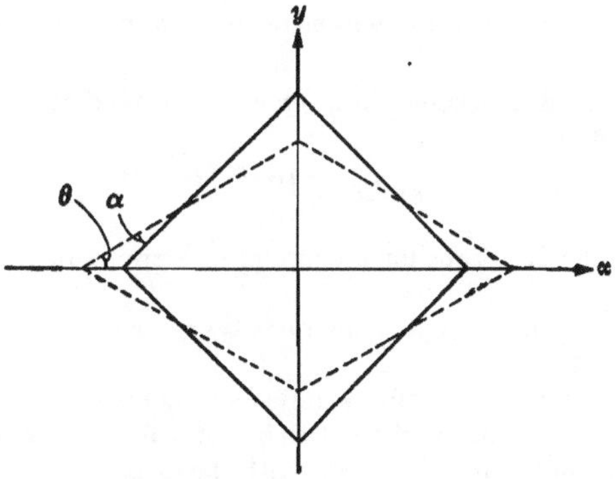

FIG. 14.8.

will be a *pure shear*, provided that the area does not change. This requires

$$(1 + e_{xx})(1 + e_{yy}) = 1,$$

or

$$e_{xx} = -e_{yy}.$$

The angle α is determined by

$$\tan \alpha = \tan (45^\circ - \theta);$$

thus

$$\tan \alpha = \tan (45^\circ - \theta) = \frac{1 - \tan \theta}{1 + \tan \theta},$$

or

$$\alpha = \frac{1 - \dfrac{1 - e_{xx}}{1 + e_{xx}}}{1 + \dfrac{1 - e_{xx}}{1 + e_{xx}}} = e_{xx};$$

thus

(14.26) $$\alpha = e_{xx} = -e_{yy}.$$

EXERCISES

1. A small displacement parallel to the xy plane carries each point (x,y) into a point (x',y') given by

$$x' = a_{11}x + a_{12}y,$$
$$y' = a_{21}x + a_{22}y.$$

Evaluate the six coefficients of extension and shear for this displacement in terms of the four coefficients a_{ij}.

2. A small displacement parallel to the xy plane carries each point (x,y) into a point (x',y') given by

$$x' = 1.005x - 0.002y,$$
$$y' = 0.006x + 0.995y.$$

For what directions $\mathbf{T} = 1\underline{/\theta}$ is the extension maximum? For what directions is it minimum?

3. (*a*) Show that the displacement in Exercise 1 has maximum and minimum extensions for directions θ such that

$$\tan 2\theta = \frac{a_{12} + a_{21}}{a_{11} - a_{22}}.$$

(*b*) Show that the directions for maximum and minimum extensions are at right angles.

4. What is the percentage change in density associated with the displacement described in Exercise 2?

5. A solid, homogeneous rectangular sample is stretched parallel to one set of edges until the extension is e. What is the extension of a line segment on one face of the sample if its direction makes an angle of 45° with the direction of stretch? The answer will be in terms of Poisson's ratio σ.

6. A plane square figure has one diagonal compressed with a strain $-e$ and the other stretched by a strain $+e'$. By what angles are the sides of the square distorted?

14.5. Superposition of Small Displacements. In our study of small displacements associated with distortion, we surely are not interested in pure translation; therefore let us assume that the origin is a fixed point of the body. We may then write $\mathbf{R}$ instead of $\Delta\mathbf{R}$ in (14.15). In scalar rather than vector form, this becomes (writing x for $l\,\Delta s$, etc.)

$$\begin{aligned} x' &= \left(1 + \frac{\partial \xi}{\partial x}\right) x + \frac{\partial \xi}{\partial y} y + \frac{\partial \xi}{\partial z} z, \\ y' &= \frac{\partial \eta}{\partial x} x + \left(1 + \frac{\partial \eta}{\partial y}\right) y + \frac{\partial \eta}{\partial z} z, \\ z' &= \frac{\partial \zeta}{\partial x} x + \frac{\partial \zeta}{\partial y} y + \left(1 + \frac{\partial \zeta}{\partial z}\right) z. \end{aligned} \tag{14.27}$$

This set of equations for small strains represents an example of a non-degenerate *linear homogeneous transformation*. The inverse transformation is of the same type; thus it is easy to show that it sends straight lines into lines, planes into planes, parallel lines into parallel lines, etc. The proofs of these statements are omitted. Suppose that a second transformation follows:

$$\begin{aligned} x'' &= \left(1 + \frac{\partial \xi'}{\partial x'}\right) x' + \frac{\partial \xi'}{\partial y'} y' + \frac{\partial \xi'}{\partial z'} z', \\ y'' &= \frac{\partial \eta'}{\partial x'} x' + \left(1 + \frac{\partial \eta'}{\partial y'}\right) y' + \frac{\partial \eta'}{\partial z'} z', \\ z'' &= \frac{\partial \zeta'}{\partial x'} x' + \frac{\partial \zeta'}{\partial y'} y' + \left(1 + \frac{\partial \zeta'}{\partial z'}\right) z'. \end{aligned}$$

Substituting for x', y', z', but discarding higher powers of the derivatives, we get

$$x'' = \left(1 + \frac{\partial \xi}{\partial x} + \frac{\partial \xi'}{\partial x'}\right) x + \left(\frac{\partial \xi}{\partial y} + \frac{\partial \xi'}{\partial y'}\right) y + \left(\frac{\partial \xi}{\partial z} + \frac{\partial \xi'}{\partial z'}\right) z,$$
$$y'' = \left(\frac{\partial \eta}{\partial x} + \frac{\partial \eta'}{\partial x'}\right) x + \left(1 + \frac{\partial \eta}{\partial y} + \frac{\partial \eta'}{\partial y'}\right) y + \left(\frac{\partial \eta}{\partial z} + \frac{\partial \eta'}{\partial z'}\right) z,$$
$$z'' = \left(\frac{\partial \zeta}{\partial x} + \frac{\partial \zeta'}{\partial x'}\right) x + \left(\frac{\partial \zeta}{\partial y} + \frac{\partial \zeta'}{\partial y'}\right) y + \left(1 + \frac{\partial \zeta}{\partial z} + \frac{\partial \zeta'}{\partial z'}\right) z.$$

Thus the displacement resulting from two successive small displacements is characterized by constants which are the sums of those for the two original displacements taken separately. In particular

$$(14.28) \qquad \begin{aligned} e''_{xx} &= e_{xx} + e'_{xx}, \\ e''_{xy} &= e_{xy} + e'_{xy}, \text{ etc.} \end{aligned}$$

This result is particularly useful in reverse: a complex displacement may often be analyzed as compounded of simpler ones.

EXERCISES

1. Show that deformation equations for a *simple homogeneous extension* in the x direction may be written

$$x' = x(1 + e), \quad y' = y, \quad z' = z,$$

where e is the longitudinal strain. Write corresponding equations for ξ, η, ζ.

2. Show that deformation equations for a *uniform dilatation* may be written

$$x' = x(1 + e), \quad y' = y(1 + e), \quad z' = z(1 + e),$$

where e is the longitudinal strain in each of the coordinate directions. Write corresponding equations for ξ, η, ζ.

3. Show that deformation equations for a *simple shear* such as is shown in Fig. 14.3 may be written

$$x' = x + ey, \quad y' = y, \quad z' = z,$$

where e is equal to the angle ϕ which measures the strain. Write corresponding equations for ξ, η, ζ.

4. Show that deformation equations for a *pure shear* in terms of axes as in Fig. 14.8 may be written

$$x' = x(1 + e), \quad y' = y(1 - e), \quad z' = z,$$

where the measure ϕ of the corresponding simple strain is $\phi = 2e$. Write corresponding equations for ξ, η, ζ.

5. Show that deformation equations for a *pure shear* in terms of axes as in Fig. 14.7 may be written

$$x' = x + ey,$$
$$y' = ex + y,$$
$$z' = z,$$

where $e = \alpha = \alpha'$.

6. Show by rotating axes through 45° that the strains of Exercises 4 and 5 are equivalent.

7. A plane square figure has its diagonals stretched with extensions e_{xx} and e_{yy} (the coordinate axes are taken as the diagonals). Use the main result of this section to show that this distortion may be regarded as a uniform dilatation (in x and y directions only) with

$$e_v = e_{xx} + e_{yy}$$

superimposed on a pure shear corresponding to a simple shear of amount

$$\phi = e_{xx} - e_{yy}.$$

8. Use the main result of this section to show that a simple shear like that of Fig. 14.3 may be regarded as a pure shear (see Exercise 5 above) and a rotation through an angle $-e$. (Exercise 1, Sec. 14.3 was concerned with such a rotation.)

14.6. Rotation and Pure Strain. In discussing homogeneous strains, we were careful to eliminate translations by choosing a fixed origin. We have not yet eliminated the possibility of small rotations. A small rigid rotation would be just such a small displacement as we have discussed, and yet it would involve no distortion. Let us see what equations for such a displacement would look like. Any instantaneous rotation during a time Δt can be described by

$$\mathbf{V} = \mathbf{\Omega} \times \mathbf{R}, \qquad \text{where } \mathbf{\Omega} = \omega \mathbf{E},$$

or

$$\frac{\Delta \mathbf{R}}{\Delta t} = \frac{\Delta \theta}{\Delta t} (\mathbf{E} \times \mathbf{R}).$$

Let us write $\Delta\theta\,\mathbf{E} = \theta_1\mathbf{I} + \theta_2\mathbf{J} + \theta_3\mathbf{K}$.
We get

$$\Delta \mathbf{R} = \begin{vmatrix} \theta_1 & \theta_2 & \theta_3 \\ x & y & z \\ \mathbf{I} & \mathbf{J} & \mathbf{K} \end{vmatrix}. \tag{14.29}$$

Multiplying out and equating x, y and z components, we have

$$\begin{aligned} x' - x = \xi = \Delta x &= \quad\cdots\quad - \theta_3 y + \theta_2 z, \\ y' - y = \eta = \Delta y &= \theta_3 x \quad\cdots\quad - \theta_1 z, \\ z' - z, = \zeta = \Delta z &= -\theta_2 x + \theta_1 y \quad\cdots \end{aligned}$$

We shall now be able to recognize a *small rotation* by the skew-symmetric array of coefficients. (Taking main diagonal, dotted above, as axis of symmetry, symmetrically situated coefficients are equal but opposite in sign.)

It is now instructive to rearrange terms in the displacement equations (14.27) thus

$$\Delta x = x' - x = \xi = \frac{\partial \xi}{\partial x} x + \frac{1}{2}\left(\frac{\partial \xi}{\partial y} + \frac{\partial \eta}{\partial x}\right) y + \frac{1}{2}\left(\frac{\partial \xi}{\partial z} + \frac{\partial \zeta}{\partial x}\right) z + \frac{1}{2}\left(\frac{\partial \xi}{\partial y} - \frac{\partial \eta}{\partial x}\right) y + \frac{1}{2}\left(\frac{\partial \xi}{\partial z} - \frac{\partial \zeta}{\partial x}\right) z.$$

Similarly

$$\eta = \frac{1}{2}\left(\frac{\partial \eta}{\partial x} + \frac{\partial \xi}{\partial y}\right) x + \frac{\partial \eta}{\partial y} y + \frac{1}{2}\left(\frac{\partial \eta}{\partial z} + \frac{\partial \zeta}{\partial y}\right) z + \frac{1}{2}\left(\frac{\partial \eta}{\partial x} - \frac{\partial \xi}{\partial y}\right) x + \frac{1}{2}\left(\frac{\partial \eta}{\partial z} - \frac{\partial \zeta}{\partial y}\right) z.$$

$$\zeta = \frac{1}{2}\left(\frac{\partial \zeta}{\partial x} + \frac{\partial \xi}{\partial z}\right) x + \frac{1}{2}\left(\frac{\partial \zeta}{\partial y} + \frac{\partial \eta}{\partial z}\right) y + \frac{\partial \zeta}{\partial z} z + \frac{1}{2}\left(\frac{\partial \zeta}{\partial x} - \frac{\partial \xi}{\partial z}\right) x + \frac{1}{2}\left(\frac{\partial \zeta}{\partial y} - \frac{\partial \eta}{\partial z}\right) y.$$

If we let

$$\theta_1 = \frac{1}{2}\left(\frac{\partial \zeta}{\partial y} - \frac{\partial \eta}{\partial z}\right),$$

$$\theta_2 = \frac{1}{2}\left(\frac{\partial \xi}{\partial z} - \frac{\partial \zeta}{\partial x}\right), \qquad (14.31)$$

$$\theta_3 = \frac{1}{2}\left(\frac{\partial \eta}{\partial x} - \frac{\partial \xi}{\partial y}\right),$$

it is apparent, by use of the superposition property of Sec. 14.5, that the displacement equation may be analyzed into a rotation with Eqs. (14.30) together with a symmetrical transformation (taking what is left of the rearranged equations) as follows:

$$\begin{aligned} \xi &= e_{xx}x + e_{xy}y + e_{zx}z, \\ \eta &= e_{xy}x + e_{yy}y + e_{yz}z, \\ \zeta &= e_{zx}x + e_{yz}y + e_{zz}z. \end{aligned} \qquad (14.32)$$

Equations (14.32) represent a small homogeneous displacement free from both rotation and translation. It is a *pure strain*.

The general conclusions achieved thus far are then:

(14.33) *Any small homogeneous displacement of a body may be analyzed into a rigid-body displacement plus a pure strain.*

(14.34) *Any pure homogeneous strain is determined uniquely by the six coefficients of shear and extension.*

This last statement, in view of the superposition possibility, is equivalent to resolving any such strain into three simple extensions plus three simple shears.

Note that for a *pure strain*,

$$(14.35)\qquad \frac{\partial \xi}{\partial y} = \frac{\partial \eta}{\partial x} = e_{xy}, \qquad \frac{\partial \eta}{\partial z} = \frac{\partial \zeta}{\partial y} = e_{yz}, \qquad \frac{\partial \zeta}{\partial x} = \frac{\partial \xi}{\partial z} = e_{zx}.$$

EXERCISES

1. In a pure strain a typical point (x,y,z) is distorted to (x',y',z') given by

$$\begin{aligned} x' &= 1.052x - 0.008y + 0.004z, \\ y' &= -0.008x + 0.967y, \\ z' &= 0.004x \qquad\qquad + 1.009z. \end{aligned}$$

Evaluate the six coefficients of extension and shear.

14.7. Principal Strains. We have considered in some detail the nature of strain and the way in which complex situations may be analyzed in terms of simple ones. Several of our conclusions could have been reached more quickly if the mathematics of transformations could have been assumed. In this section a result will be pointed out which has counterparts and generalizations all through mathematics and mathematical physics. No proof will be given.

Consider a solid sphere within the body with center at the origin. Let this be subject to a small homogeneous pure strain. Since parallel lines in the body before deformations are parallel afterwards, it is not surprising that the sphere is deformed into an ellipsoid. Its axes are the *principal axes of strain.* If they are taken as coordinate axes, the coefficients of shear are zero.

(14.36) *Relative to principal axes a pure strain may be analyzed as three simple extensions superimposed.*

The equations (14.32) now take the form

$$(14.37)\qquad \begin{aligned} \xi &= e'_{xx}x, \\ \eta &= \qquad e'_{yy}y, \\ \zeta &= \qquad\qquad e'_{zz}z. \end{aligned}$$

For these axes e'_{xx}, e'_{yy}, and e'_{zz} are called principal strains.

Since volume dilatation is manifestly independent of axes, we have it as an invariant

$$e_{xx} + e_{yy} + e_{zz} = e'_{xx} + e'_{yy} + e'_{zz}.$$

A pure strain is sometimes defined as a deformation for which there are three mutually perpendicular directions such that a position vector in each one of these directions is deformed into a vector in the same direction. Such vectors are called proper vectors (eigenvectors) of the deformation. The corresponding factors of multiplication $1 + e'_{xx}$, $1 + e'_{yy}$, and $1 + e'_{zz}$ are called proper values (eigenvalues). This terminology is mentioned, not because it is essential to the course, but because the words are bandied about so freely nowadays that an early contact with them may be of some slight value.

Principal Axes in the Plane. To make these concepts seem more concrete, let us consider briefly the plane case. Suppose that a figure confined to the xy plane is given a pure strain described by the equations

$$x' = a_{11}x + a_{12}y = (1 + e_{xx})x + e_{xy}y,\qquad (14.38)$$
$$y' = a_{12}x + a_{22}y = e_{xy}x + (1 + e_{yy})y.$$

Let us explore this question: For what angles θ (given by)

$$\tan\theta = \frac{y}{x} \qquad (14.39)$$

is a position vector $\mathbf{R} = r\underline{/\theta}$ transformed into a vector $\mathbf{R}' = r'\underline{/\theta}$ in the same direction? Algebraically the condition may be stated thus:

$$\frac{y}{x} = \tan\theta = \frac{a_{12}x + a_{22}y}{a_{11}x + a_{12}y} = \frac{y'}{x'},$$

or, equivalently,

$$\tan\theta = \frac{a_{12} + a_{22}\tan\theta}{a_{11} + a_{12}\tan\theta}.$$

This gives us a quadratic equation in $\tan\theta$:

$$a_{11}\tan\theta + a_{12}\tan^2\theta = a_{12} + a_{22}\tan\theta$$

$$\tan^2\theta - \left(\frac{a_{22} - a_{11}}{a_{12}}\right)\tan\theta - 1 = 0. \qquad (14.40)$$

This quadratic equation always has two real roots which determine directions. Suppose that $\tan\theta_1$ and $\tan\theta_2$ are such roots. Then

$$(\tan\theta - \tan\theta_1)(\tan\theta - \tan\theta_2) = 0$$

must be a factored form of our quadratic. Let us multiply out and compare coefficients:

$$\tan^2\theta - (\tan\theta_1 + \tan\theta_2)\tan\theta + \tan\theta_1\tan\theta_2 = 0.$$

Comparing, we get for the sum of the roots

$$\tan\theta_1 + \tan\theta_2 = \frac{a_{22} - a_{11}}{a_{12}}, \qquad (14.41)$$

and for their product

$$\tan\theta_1\tan\theta_2 = -1. \qquad (14.42)$$

The last equation tells us that the two directions are perpendicular. It is equivalent to $\mathbf{E}_1 \cdot \mathbf{E}_2 = 0$, where

$$\mathbf{E}_1 = \cos\theta_1\mathbf{I} + \sin\theta_1\mathbf{J},$$
$$\mathbf{E}_2 = \cos\theta_2\mathbf{I} + \sin\theta_2\mathbf{J}.$$

This shows us that in the plane case at least the *principal axes* are suitable coordinate axes. The roots of (14.40) tell us how to find these axes. A slightly different approach may be found at once. Since our directions are perpendicular,

$$\tan(\theta_1 + \theta_2) = \tan(90° + 2\theta) = -\operatorname{ctn} 2\theta$$

(where θ is the more suitable choice of the two angles selected). Using simple trigonometric identities,

$$-\operatorname{ctn} 2\theta = \tan(\theta_1 + \theta_2) = \frac{\tan\theta_1 + \tan\theta_2}{1 - \tan\theta_1 \tan\theta_2}.$$

Now substituting (14.41) and (14.42),

$$\operatorname{ctn} 2\theta = \frac{a_{11} - a_{22}}{2a_{12}} \tag{14.43}$$

or

$$\tan 2\theta = \frac{2a_{12}}{a_{11} - a_{22}} = \frac{2e_{xy}}{e_{xx} - e_{yy}}. \tag{14.44}$$

This last equation is particularly useful since it gives us *both* axes; for 2θ and $2\theta + 180°$ have the same tangent. Hence θ and $\theta + 90°$ are both roots.

If you are an avid student of analytical geometry, you will wish to pursue the matter further, showing that the principal axes discovered here by proper vectors are in fact the axes of symmetry of an ellipse into which the circle $x^2 + y^2 = r^2$ is deformed. Equation (14.44) should also be compared with Exercise 3, Sec. 14.4.

EXERCISES

1. In a plane strain the principal axes bisect the angles formed by the coordinate axes. Show that the strain is a uniform plane dilatation.

2. For a plane strain characterized by $e_{xx} = 0.0050$, $e_{yy} = 0.0020$, $e_{xy} = 0.0015$, find the principal axes of strain.

14.8. Pure Plane Homogeneous Strains. Let us collect for special attention the plane form of some of our conclusions. Suppose that the strain is characterized by the three coefficients e_{xx}, e_{yy}, e_{xy}. The extension or longitudinal strain e_T in the direction of a unit vector **T** was given by (14.22). The plane version (with $\mathbf{T} = l\mathbf{I} + m\mathbf{J}$) is

$$e_T = l^2 e_{xx} + m^2 e_{yy} + 2lm e_{xy}. \tag{14.45}$$

To get a formula for the shear or angular distortion suffered by a vector in the **T** direction, we may apply (14.13), which may be written here, using the notation of Fig. 14.9, as

$$(14.46)\qquad \frac{\mathbf{H}}{r} = \left(l\frac{\partial \xi}{\partial x} + m\frac{\partial \xi}{\partial y}\right)\mathbf{I} + \left(l\frac{\partial \eta}{\partial x} + m\frac{\partial \eta}{\partial y}\right)\mathbf{J}.$$

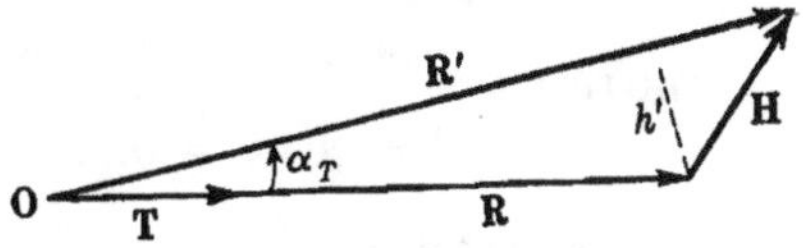

FIG. 14.9.

Now the angle α_T is approximately h'/r rad, where h' is the component of **H** perpendicular to **T**, or

$$\alpha_T\mathbf{K} = \mathbf{T}\times\frac{\mathbf{H}}{r} = \left[l^2\frac{\partial \eta}{\partial x} - m^2\frac{\partial \xi}{\partial y} + ml\left(\frac{\partial \eta}{\partial y} - \frac{\partial \xi}{\partial x}\right)\right]\mathbf{K}.$$

But, substituting the coefficients of extension and shear, we may write

$$(14.47)\qquad \alpha_T = (l^2 - m^2)e_{xy} + lm(e_{yy} - e_{xx}).$$

If we use **T** in terms of polar coordinates, $\mathbf{T} = 1\underline{/\theta}$, the relation becomes

$$(14.48)\qquad \alpha_T = \tfrac{1}{2}[2\cos 2\theta\; e_{xy} + \sin 2\theta\,(e_{yy} - e_{xx})].$$

Relative to principal axes, these general strain equations are simply

$$(14.49)\qquad e_T = l^2e'_{xx} + m^2e'_{yy},$$
$$(14.50)\qquad \alpha_T = lm(e'_{yy} - e'_{xx}).$$

Example 1. Suppose that a homogeneous pure plane strain is characterized by

$$e_{xx} = 0.0020,\qquad e_{yy} = -0.0010,\qquad e_{xy} = 0.0010.$$

Find the principal axes and the principal strains.

SOLUTION. To find the principal axes, we use (14.44) which gives

$$\tan 2\theta = \tfrac{2}{3},\qquad 2\theta = 33.7^\circ \quad\text{or}\quad 213.7^\circ,$$
$$\theta = 16.8^\circ \quad\text{or}\quad 106.8^\circ.$$

To find the principal strains, we first need some sines and cosines which, with slide-rule accuracy, are

$$\cos 16.8^\circ = 0.96 = \sin 106.8^\circ,$$
$$\sin 16.8^\circ = 0.29 = -\cos 106.8^\circ.$$

Substituting in (14.45),

$$e'_{xx} = (0.96)^2(0.002) + (0.29)^2(-0.001) + (0.96)(0.29)(0.002) = 0.0022,$$
$$e'_{yy} = (-0.29)^2(0.002) + (0.96)^2(-0.001) + (-0.29)(0.96)(0.002) = -0.0013.$$

Example 2. Work backwards to get original data from principal strains of Example 1.

SOLUTION

$$l = \cos\theta = 0.96, \qquad m = \sin\theta = -0.29;$$

thus, using (14.49),

$$e_T = (0.96)^2(0.0022) + (0.29)^2(-0.0013) = 0.0021 - 0.0001 = 0.0020.$$

Now taking

$$\theta = 90^\circ - 16.8^\circ = 73.2^\circ,$$
$$l = \cos 73.2^\circ = 0.29,$$
$$m = \sin 73.2^\circ = 0.96,$$
$$e_{T'} = (0.29)^2(0.0022) + (0.96)^2(-0.0013) = 0.0002 - 0.0012 = -0.0010.$$

Both of these results check with the original data. Finally, using (14.50),

$$e_s = lm(e'_{yy} - e'_{xx}) = (0.96)(-0.29)(-0.0035) = 0.0010,$$

which is the correct value for e_{xy}.

EXERCISES

These exercises all have to do with pure plane homogeneous strain.

1. Use (14.49) to verify that maximum and minimum extensions occur in the directions of the principal axes.

2. In what directions relative to the principal axes are vectors subject to the greatest or least shearing strains?

3. In what directions relative to the principal axes is the extension equal to one-half the volume dilatation?

4. If $e_{xx} = -0.0020$, $e_{yy} = 0.0060$, $e_{xy} = -0.0035$, what is the maximum (or minimum) shearing strain?

5. If principal strains are $e'_{xx} = 0.004$, $e'_{yy} = -0.002$, what are the extension and shearing strains for a vector $\mathbf{T} = 1/\underline{20^\circ}$?

14.9. Stress. When a body is in a state of strain due to external forces, a pattern of internal forces will result. The body is thus said to be in a state of stress. Stress is measured as force per area. In Fig. 14.10 is shown an element of area Δa with unit normal $\mathbf{N}$. Let the force acting across the area be $\Delta\mathbf{F}$. That is, if we isolate the part of the body on the $-\mathbf{N}$ side of Δa, we consider the force exerted across Δa by the part of the body on the $+\mathbf{N}$ side of Δa. The *mean stress* $\bar{\mathbf{S}}$ [or $\bar{\mathbf{S}}(\mathbf{N})$ if we wish to emphasize its dependence on the orientation of the area] across Δa is defined by

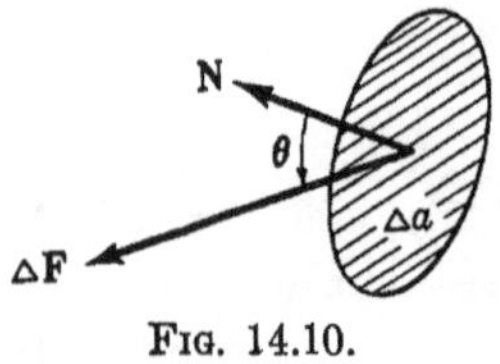

FIG. 14.10.

$$\bar{\mathbf{S}}(\mathbf{N}) = \bar{\mathbf{S}} = \frac{\Delta\mathbf{F}}{\Delta a}. \tag{14.51}$$

If the angle θ between **N** and Δ**F** is zero, the stress is called a *traction*. If θ is 180°, the stress is called a *pressure*. If $\theta = 90°$, the stress is called a *shearing stress*. *Stress at a point in a given direction* may be defined as the limit, as Δa becomes small, of the stress across Δa.

$$\mathbf{S}(\mathbf{N}) = \mathbf{S} = \frac{d\mathbf{F}}{da}. \tag{14.52}$$

One of the simplest kinds of stress is hydrostatic pressure. The stress at a point in an ideal fluid is always a *uniform pressure*. More about this will be studied in the chapter on hydromechanics. Other simple cases will be considered now.

Simple Traction. Consider a narrow cylindrical rod being stretched by a force **F**. Let us consider the stress across a plane section. Assuming uniformity, we shall assign a single stress **S** to the whole area a. Neglecting other forces, it is apparent for equilibrium that **S** is parallel

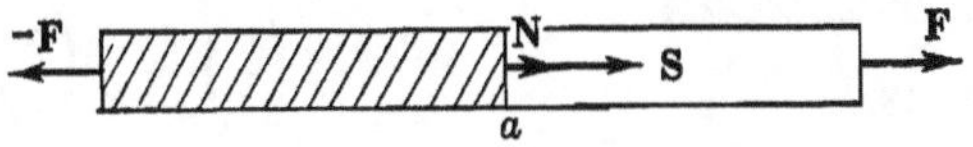

FIG. 14.11.

to **N** (in Fig. 14.11). The equation of equilibrium for the shaded portion is

$$\mathbf{S}a - \mathbf{F} = \mathbf{O};$$

thus

$$\mathbf{S} = \frac{\mathbf{F}}{a}.$$

To emphasize that stress at a point varies with direction, let us consider the same rod but a different plane of section, tilted at an angle θ, as in

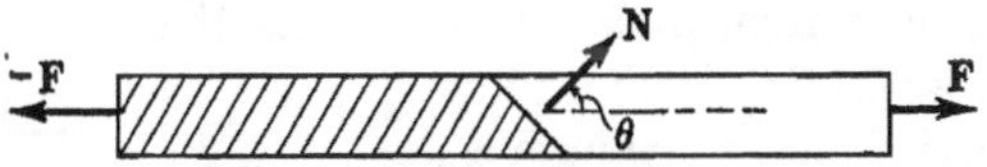

FIG. 14.12.

Fig. 14.12. The area is now $a \sec \theta$. So the net stress is

$$\mathbf{S}_\theta = \frac{\mathbf{F}}{a} \cos \theta.$$

It is interesting to resolve this stress into tangential (shearing) and normal (tractive) components.

$$s_t = |\mathbf{S}_\theta| \sin \theta = \frac{|\mathbf{F}|}{a} \sin \theta \cos \theta,$$

$$s_n = |\mathbf{S}_\theta| \cos \theta = \frac{|\mathbf{F}|}{a} \cos^2 \theta.$$

Both are zero for $\theta = 90°$. s_t is maximum for $\theta = 45°$; s_n is maximum for $\theta = 0°$.

Simple Shearing Stress. To produce a simple shear (Fig. 14.13), a couple ($\mathbf{F}, -\mathbf{F}$) is needed. Then to restore equilibrium a countercouple ($\mathbf{G}, -\mathbf{G}$) is required. If the dimensions of the square block shown in Fig. 14.13 are b, b, h, then for equilibrium

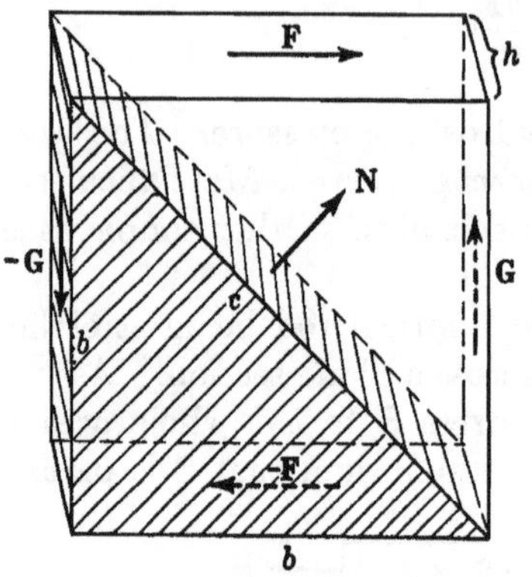

FIG. 14.13.

$$f = g.$$

This means that the tangential stresses have the same magnitude f/bh. Now let us find the stress across the diagonal plane of dimensions c, h. Isolating the shaded half of the cube, we see that for equilibrium the tangential components of the forces across this plane must add up to

$$f\left(\frac{b}{c}\right) - g\left(\frac{b}{c}\right) = 0.$$

The normal components add up to

$$f\left(\frac{b}{c}\right) + g\left(\frac{b}{c}\right) = 2f\left(\frac{b}{c}\right).$$

The corresponding normal stress has magnitude

$$\frac{2f(b/c)}{ch} = 2\,\frac{f}{bh}\left(\frac{b^2}{c^2}\right).$$

Since $c = \sqrt{2}b$, we have again a stress of magnitude f/bh. Thus *equal tangential stresses on perpendicular surfaces indicate a normal traction of the same magnitude across a set of planes at* 45°.

Similarly, let us compute the stress across the other diagonal plane, diagramed in cross section in Fig. 14.14. Isolating the shaded half, the tangential force across the plane is clearly zero. The normal force is equal to $-2f(b/c)$, and the stress again has the same magnitude. This shows that *the simple shearing stress with which we started might equally well have been described as the result of a compression of one diagonal and an equal traction along the other.* The corresponding situation for strain was shown in Fig. 14.8.

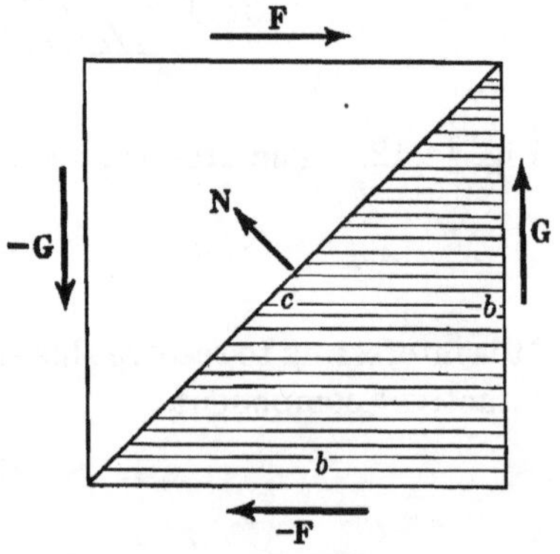

FIG. 14.14.

EXERCISES

1. A disk of radius r and thickness h centered in the xy plane is subjected to compression forces $-\mathbf{G}$ and $\mathbf{G}$ at the ends of the x diameter and tensile forces $\mathbf{F}$ and $-\mathbf{F}$ at the ends of the y diameter. Compute in terms of f, g, r, h, and θ the normal and tangential components of stress for a plane section through the origin making an angle θ with the x axis.

2. A wire 1 mm in diameter holds a load of 150 lb. Find the magnitude and direction of the total stress for a cross section whose normal makes an angle of 30° with the wire. What are the normal and tangential components of this stress?

3. Compute the normal and tangential stress components across the diagonal planes in a rectangular block like that of Fig. 14.13 except that the dimensions are b, d, h ($b \neq d$). Assume that the two couples are in equilibrium.

14.10. Components of Stress. At any point in a strained solid let us denote by **X**, **Y**, and **Z** the stresses across areas whose normals are, respectively, **I**, **J**, and **K**. Now for a random direction given by

$$\mathbf{N} = l\mathbf{I} + m\mathbf{J} + n\mathbf{K}$$

what is the stress **S** across an area having **N** as normal? It is the aim of this section to show how the components of **S** may be expressed in terms of those of **X**, **Y**, and **Z**. At the point in question draw coordinate axes and consider the small tetrahedron cut off by a plane of normal **N** at a small distance h from the origin. The outward unit normals for the four faces are (see Fig. 14.15), respectively, $-\mathbf{I}$, $-\mathbf{J}$, $-\mathbf{K}$, and **N**. The corresponding areas are, respectively, a_x, a_y, a_z, and a. Let us isolate this part of the body. For equilibrium the vector sum of the forces must be zero. Neglecting the weight (depends on volume which may be neglected since limit vol/a as $h \to 0$ is 0),

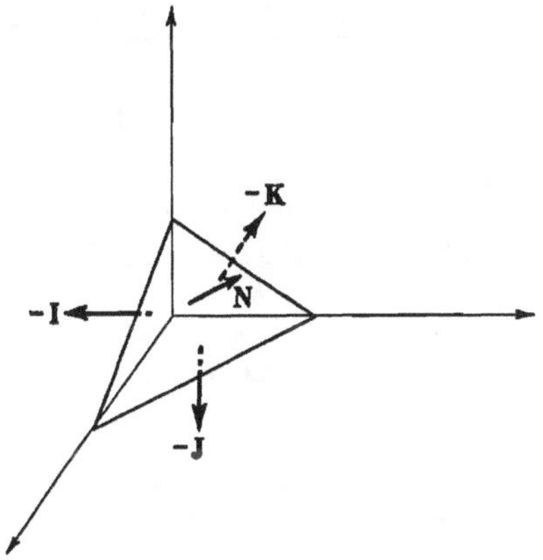

FIG. 14.15.

$$(14.53) \qquad -\mathbf{X}a_x - \mathbf{Y}a_y - \mathbf{Z}a_z + \mathbf{S}a = \mathbf{O}.$$

The minus signs go back to the definition of stress from which it is apparent that

$$(14.54) \qquad \mathbf{S}(-\mathbf{N}) = -\mathbf{S}(\mathbf{N}).$$

Now a_x, a_y, a_z are the projections of a onto the coordinate planes; thus

$$a_x = al, \qquad a_y = am, \qquad a_z = an.$$

Hence

$$(14.55) \qquad \mathbf{S} = l\mathbf{X} + m\mathbf{Y} + n\mathbf{Z}.$$

In order for **S** to represent the stress at the given point, we must take the limit as the plane approaches the origin. The equations are unchanged thereby. The corresponding three scalar equations are

$$
\begin{aligned}
s_x &= lx_x + my_x + nz_x,\\
s_y &= lx_y + my_y + nz_y,\\
s_z &= lx_z + my_z + nz_z.
\end{aligned}
\tag{14.56}
$$

Thus at any point the stress is determined uniquely by the *nine components of stress*

$$x_x,\ x_y,\ x_z,\ y_x,\ y_y,\ y_z,\ z_x,\ z_y,\ z_z.$$

We shall soon see that the coefficients of (14.56) are symmetrical in the same sense that those for a pure strain are. Consider a small box within the body, the edges being aligned with the axes and the dimensions Δx, Δy, Δz (see Fig. 14.16). Take the center of the box as temporary origin. We shall treat the force across each face as if it acted at the mean position, *i.e.*, the center of that face. The box is subject to forces as follows:

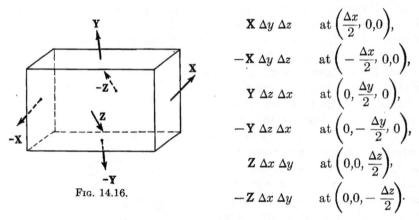

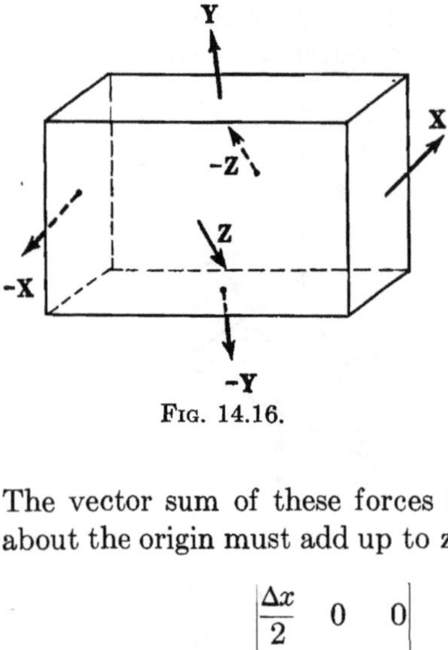

FIG. 14.16.

$$
\begin{aligned}
&\mathbf{X}\,\Delta y\,\Delta z && \text{at}\left(\frac{\Delta x}{2}, 0,0\right),\\
&-\mathbf{X}\,\Delta y\,\Delta z && \text{at}\left(-\frac{\Delta x}{2}, 0,0\right),\\
&\mathbf{Y}\,\Delta z\,\Delta x && \text{at}\left(0, \frac{\Delta y}{2}, 0\right),\\
&-\mathbf{Y}\,\Delta z\,\Delta x && \text{at}\left(0, -\frac{\Delta y}{2}, 0\right),\\
&\mathbf{Z}\,\Delta x\,\Delta y && \text{at}\left(0,0, \frac{\Delta z}{2}\right),\\
&-\mathbf{Z}\,\Delta x\,\Delta y && \text{at}\left(0,0, -\frac{\Delta z}{2}\right).
\end{aligned}
$$

The vector sum of these forces is zero. For equilibrium the moments about the origin must add up to zero. For the first force, the moment is

$$\Delta y\,\Delta z\begin{vmatrix}\frac{\Delta x}{2} & 0 & 0\\ x_x & x_y & x_z\\ \mathbf{I} & \mathbf{J} & \mathbf{K}\end{vmatrix} = (x_y\mathbf{K} - x_z\mathbf{J})\left(\frac{\Delta x}{2}\,\Delta y\,\Delta z\right).$$

For the second force,

$$\Delta y\,\Delta z\begin{vmatrix}-\frac{\Delta x}{2} & 0 & 0\\ -x_x & -x_y & -x_z\\ \mathbf{I} & \mathbf{J} & \mathbf{K}\end{vmatrix} = (x_y\mathbf{K} - x_z\mathbf{J})\left(\frac{\Delta x}{2}\,\Delta y\,\Delta z\right).$$

Treating the other forces similarly, adding, setting the sum equal to zero, dividing by Δx, Δy, Δz, and taking the limit as the sides of the box approach zero in length,

$$\mathbf{I}(y_z - z_y) + \mathbf{J}(z_x - x_z) + \mathbf{K}(x_y - y_x) = \mathbf{O}.$$

Or

$$y_z = z_y, \qquad z_x = x_z, \qquad x_y = y_x. \tag{14.57}$$

Thus only six quantities are required to specify the stress in any direction at a point.

Let us use this result to derive a stress analogue of a strain equation which proved to be very useful. Equation (14.22) gave us the extension e_T associated with any direction **T**. The corresponding stress concept would be the component s_N of stress normal to a plane having unit normal **N**. This is a simple vector problem

$$s_N = \mathbf{S} \cdot \mathbf{N} = s_x l + s_y m + s_z n.$$

Using (14.56) and (14.57), we get for *normal stress*

$$s_N = l^2 x_x + m^2 y_y + n^2 z_z + 2lm x_y + 2mn y_z + 2nl z_x. \tag{14.58}$$

The *tangential stress* is easily computed from

$$s_t = |\mathbf{N} \times \mathbf{S}|. \tag{14.59}$$

EXERCISES

1. Write for a *plane stress* ($z_z = y_z = z_x = 0$) in terms of x_x, y_y, x_y, and θ formulas for normal and tangential stresses s_N and s_t across a plane whose normal **N** is in the xy plane: $\mathbf{N} = 1\underline{/\theta}$.

2. At a given point, the three stresses **X**, **Y**, and **Z** are given by

$$\begin{aligned} \mathbf{X} &= 40{,}000(2\mathbf{I} - \mathbf{J} + \mathbf{K}) \\ \mathbf{Y} &= 30{,}000(\mathbf{I} + 2\mathbf{J} - \mathbf{K}) \\ \mathbf{Z} &= 50{,}000(-\mathbf{I} - \mathbf{J} + 2\mathbf{K}) \end{aligned}$$

(units are pounds per square inch). What normal stress is experienced across an area normal to the vector $3\mathbf{I} - 4\mathbf{K}$?

14.11. Principal Stresses. Just as with strains, it is possible to pick three mutually perpendicular directions for which the stress is parallel to the direction. These are called *principal axes of stress.* We shall prove neither this result nor the following:

(14.60) *Any state of stress may be analyzed as three tractions (or pressures) along the principal axes of stress.*

Relative to principal axes, the stress is specified by only three quantities called *principal stresses:* x'_x, y'_y, z'_z.

The discussion has considered stresses at a point. When the same state of stress exists throughout a body, the stress is called *homogeneous.*

Application to Plane Stresses. In the case of plane stress in the xy plane, (14.56) may be written

$$s_x = lx_x + mx_y, \qquad (14.61)$$
$$s_y = lx_y + my_y.$$

The question may be asked: For what unit normal vector $\mathbf{N} = l\mathbf{I} + m\mathbf{J}$ is the corresponding stress vector $\mathbf{S} = s_x\mathbf{I} + s_y\mathbf{J}$ parallel to $\mathbf{N}$? Such directions are principal directions and the stresses are *principal stresses.* Following the same algebra used for (14.38), we conclude that principal directions are given for $\mathbf{N} = 1\underline{/\theta}$ such that

$$\tan 2\theta = \frac{2x_y}{x_x - y_y}. \qquad (14.62)$$

The same argument shows that two mutually perpendicular directions are obtained.

The plane form of (14.58) is

$$s_N = l^2x_x + m^2y_y + 2lmx_y. \qquad (14.63)$$

The plane form of (14.59) is

$$s_t = (l^2 - m^2)x_y + lm(y_y - x_x). \qquad (14.64)$$

These results should be compared with the corresponding strain equations (14.45) and (14.47).

Relative to principal axes, the equations are

$$s_N = l^2x'_x + m^2y'_y, \qquad (14.65)$$
$$s_t = lm(y'_y - x'_x). \qquad (14.66)$$

EXERCISES

1. A plane sample is subjected to two normal stresses as follows: in the x direction a compression of 4,000 lb/in.² and in the y direction a traction of 2,000 lb/in.² Find the normal and tangential stresses for sections bisecting the angles between axes.

2. A plane stress is characterized by $x_x = -3{,}000$ lb/in.², $y_y = 6{,}000$ lb/in.², $x_y = -2{,}000$ lb/in.² Find the maximum and minimum values of normal stress and tangential stress.

3. Principal stresses are given as $x_x = 4{,}000$ lb/in.², $y_y = 3{,}000$ lb/in.², $z_z = -4{,}000$ lb/in.² Find the normal stress across an area whose unit normal vector is $0.8\mathbf{I} + 0.6\mathbf{J}$.

14.12. Hooke's Law. The basic experimental fact relating stress and strain was stated, though not precisely, at the beginning of this chapter. For any choice of axes, we have seen that strain can be expressed in terms of six coefficients and that the stress also can be expressed in terms of six components. A generalized form of Hooke's law says that the six stresses depend linearly on the six strains. The mathematical expression of this assertion involves thirty-six constants of the body, the c_{ij} of the following:

$$\begin{aligned}
x_x &= c_{11}e_{xx} + c_{12}e_{yy} + c_{13}e_{zz} + c_{14}e_{yz} + c_{15}e_{zx} + c_{16}e_{xy},\\
y_y &= c_{21}e_{xx} + c_{22}e_{yy} + c_{23}e_{zz} + c_{24}e_{yz} + c_{25}e_{zx} + c_{26}e_{xy},\\
z_z &= c_{31}e_{xx} + c_{32}e_{yy} + c_{33}e_{zz} + c_{34}e_{yz} + c_{35}e_{zx} + c_{36}e_{xy},\\
y_z &= c_{41}e_{xx} + c_{42}e_{yy} + c_{43}e_{zz} + c_{44}e_{yz} + c_{45}e_{zx} + c_{46}e_{xy},\\
z_x &= c_{51}e_{xx} + c_{52}e_{yy} + c_{53}e_{zz} + c_{54}e_{yz} + c_{55}e_{zx} + c_{56}e_{xy},\\
x_y &= c_{61}e_{xx} + c_{62}e_{yy} + c_{63}e_{zz} + c_{64}e_{yz} + c_{65}e_{zx} + c_{66}e_{xy}.
\end{aligned} \tag{14.67}$$

It does not, however, take a table of 36 constants to predict the elastic behavior of a material. An analysis of work-energy relations into which we shall not go shows that the coefficient array is symmetrical (that is, $c_{ij} = c_{ji}$). So in any case not more than (18 + 3) or 21 constants are needed.

We shall agree to deal with *isotropic bodies, i.e.*, bodies in which elastic behavior is the same for all directions. This choice rules out considerations of problems involving anisotropic crystals, although the crystalline aspects of most metal samples are lost because of the random arrangement. For isotropic bodies, principal axes of stress and principal axes of strain coincide, as one would expect. Using principal axes as coordinate axes, the equations (14.67) are replaced by

$$\begin{aligned}
x_x &= c_{11}e_{xx} + c_{12}e_{yy} + c_{12}e_{zz},\\
y_y &= c_{12}e_{xx} + c_{11}e_{yy} + c_{12}e_{zz},\\
z_z &= c_{12}e_{xx} + c_{12}e_{yy} + c_{11}e_{zz}.
\end{aligned} \tag{14.68}$$

The *two constants* c_{11} and c_{12} suffice to describe the elastic properties of a homogeneous isotropic material. The details for other axes will not be given here.

14.13. Elastic Moduli. We shall apply the simplified stress-strain equations (14.68) to some special cases. First, the stretched rod. Here, taking the x axis along the rod, x_x is the only nonzero stress component and $e_{yy} = e_{zz} = -\sigma e_{xx}$. Thus, if the stretching force is f and the area of cross section a, the first two of these equations become, respectively,

$$\begin{aligned}
\frac{f}{a} &= c_{11}e_{xx} - 2c_{12}\sigma e_{xx},\\
0 &= c_{12}e_{xx} - c_{11}\sigma e_{xx} - c_{12}\sigma e_{xx}.
\end{aligned}$$

We conclude from the second equation that *Poisson's ratio*, σ, is expressible as

$$\sigma = \frac{c_{12}}{c_{11} + c_{12}}. \tag{14.69}$$

Now *Young's modulus*, ψ (usually denoted by E or Y), is defined by

$$\psi = \frac{f/a}{e_{xx}}. \tag{14.70}$$

Therefore the first equation yields

$$\psi = c_{11} - 2\sigma c_{12}, \tag{14.71}$$

and substituting (14.69)

$$\psi = \frac{(c_{11} - c_{12})(c_{11} + 2c_{12})}{(c_{11} + c_{12})}. \tag{14.72}$$

If now we solve (14.69) and (14.72) for c_{11} and c_{12}, we can replace the constants of (14.68) by expressions in ψ and σ which have more familiar physical significance. The results are

$$\begin{aligned} c_{11} &= \frac{(1 - \sigma)\psi}{(1 + \sigma)(1 - 2\sigma)}, \\ c_{12} &= \frac{\sigma\psi}{(1 + \sigma)(1 - 2\sigma)}. \end{aligned} \tag{14.73}$$

Next let us consider a uniform compression:

$$x_x = y_y = z_z = -p,$$
$$e_{xx} = e_{yy} = e_{zz}.$$

Now (14.68) gives us

$$-p = (c_{11} + 2c_{12})e_{xx}.$$

Now the *bulk modulus* β is defined by

$$\beta = \frac{p}{-(\Delta v/v)}. \tag{14.74}$$

By (14.24)

$$\frac{\Delta v}{v} = 3e_{xx};$$

thus we get

$$\beta = \frac{c_{11} + 2c_{12}}{3}. \tag{14.75}$$

From this, using (14.73), we can at once express β in terms of ψ and σ

$$\beta = \frac{\psi}{3(1 - 2\sigma)}. \tag{14.76}$$

This last relationship may be interpreted less formally. A uniform dilatation (negative compression) may be considered as three equal simple extensions superimposed. Suppose that each face of a cube is pulled normally, as in Fig. 14.17, the stress being of magnitude s. Such a pull in, say, the x direction causes a stretch in the x direction, but at the same time it causes contractions in the y and z directions. When three such pulls are superimposed, the y and z pulls reduce the effectiveness of the x pull. For the x direction, the modified equation is

$$s - 2\sigma s = \psi e_{xx}.$$

Replacing $s/3e_{xx}$ by β, we have

$$3\beta(1 - 2\sigma) = \psi,$$

as before.

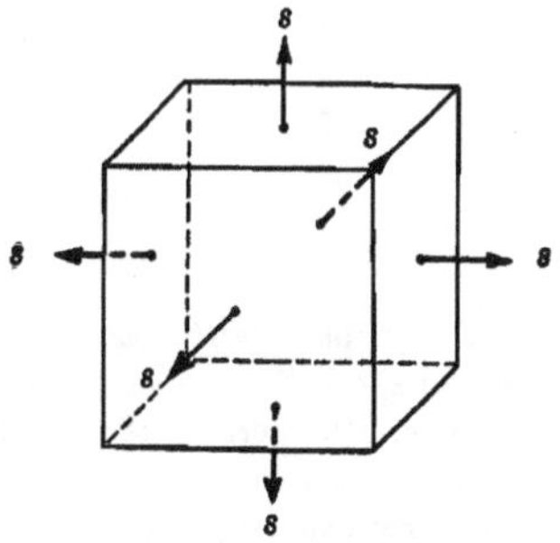

FIG. 14.17.

It remains to consider the *modulus of shear*, μ. It is defined in terms of a simple shear as the ratio of shearing stress s to the angle ϕ of the shear.

$$\mu = \frac{s}{\phi}. \tag{14.77}$$

To bring this within the scope of Eqs. (14.68), where principal axes are used, we shall regard the distortion as due to numerically equal traction and pressure along the diagonals (as was exhibited in Sec. 14.9). We shall also use (14.25) and (14.26). The stresses are (see Fig. 14.18)

$$x_x = s, \qquad y_y = -s,$$

and the strains are

$$e_{xx} = \frac{\phi}{2}, \qquad e_{yy} = -\frac{\phi}{2}.$$

Substituting in (14.68), we have

$$s = c_{11}\frac{\phi}{2} - c_{12}\frac{\phi}{2},$$

$$-s = c_{12}\frac{\phi}{2} - c_{11}\frac{\phi}{2}.$$

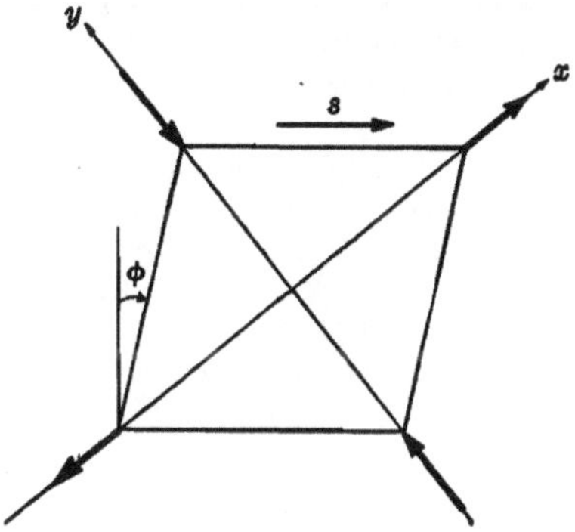

FIG. 14.18.

Consequently,

$$\mu = \frac{c_{11} - c_{12}}{2}. \tag{14.78}$$

In terms of ψ and σ,

$$\mu = \frac{\psi}{2(1 + \sigma)}. \tag{14.79}$$

The constants ψ and μ are easily measured for many materials. Formulas for β and σ in terms of ψ and μ are thus clearly desirable. These are left as exercises:

$$\beta = \frac{\psi\mu}{3(3\mu - \psi)},$$

$$\sigma = \frac{\psi - 2\mu}{2\mu}.$$

EXERCISES

1. A copper wire has diameter 2 mm, length 1 m, Young's modulus 1.2×10^{11} newtons/m^2, and Poisson's ratio 0.4. If it holds a load of 80 newtons, how much is its length increased? How much is its diameter diminished? (State answer as percentages.)

2. From the data of Exercise 1, what would you expect for values of the modulus of shear? of the bulk modulus?

3. Derive formulas for β and σ in terms of ψ and μ.

4. Derive formulas for ψ and σ in terms of β and μ.

5. A rod is found to have Young's modulus 1.8×10^{11} newtons/m^2 and modulus of shear 0.7×10^{11} newtons/m^2. Find Poisson's ratio and the bulk modulus for this material.

6. A uniform rod hangs vertically from one end. Show that under its own weight it stretches an amount equal to $\delta g l^2/2\psi$. δ is density, g acceleration of gravity, l the length, and ψ Young's modulus.

7. A cubical copper block 5 cm across rests on a firm table and supports a load of 500 newtons. What lateral forces are required to keep the block from dilating slightly? Use constants of Exercise 1.

8. A uniform metal rod of length l, area of cross section a, and Young's modulus ψ is rigidly clamped at both ends. The center of the rod is forcibly moved a distance ϵ toward one end, compressing one half and stretching the other. Find a formula for the work done.

9. Change in length due to temperature change is studied by means of a coefficient of linear expansion defined as the ratio of extension to increase in temperature.

A weight of 40 lb is hung on a wire 0.040 in. in diameter, 20 ft long, with Young's modulus 2.8×10^7 lb/in.^{2} and linear coefficient of 6.2×10^{-6} per °F. If the temperature falls 100°F after the weight is hung, what is the net change in length?

10. A cylinder of diameter 2 in. and length 10 in. is held rigidly in place so that its length is constant. There is no stress at 80°F. What pull is exerted at 40°F? Use the constants of the preceding exercise.

14.14. Twisted Rods. The modulus of shear was defined in terms of a cubical element. The same formula

$$\mu = \frac{s}{\phi} \tag{14.80}$$

can be used for any rectangular sample undergoing a simple shear as in Fig. 14.19, since it could be cut up into a large number of small cubical elements undergoing the same strain and stress. In spite of this possibility, the range of usefulness of this particular modulus may still seem limited. It can be used effectively, however, in dealing with a most important example of a deformed body, the twisted rod. The theory of this example will be outlined briefly.

Suppose that a uniform cylindrical body of length l and radius a, as is shown in Fig. 14.20, has one end anchored and that a torque γ is applied at the other end. An angular displacement θ at that end will result. From the dimensions of the rod together with γ and θ the modulus of shear may be determined. Let us conceive of the cylinder as being made

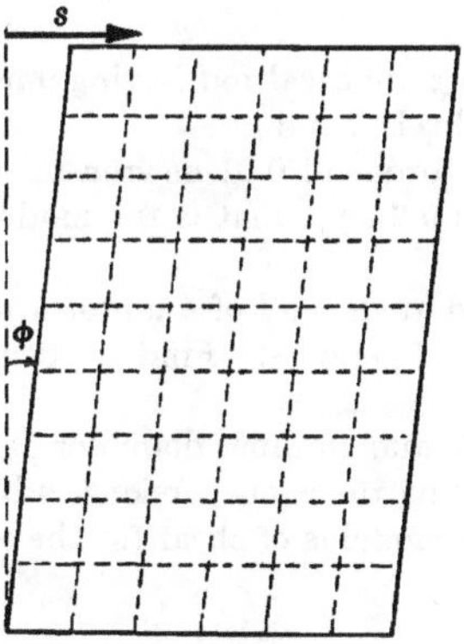

FIG. 14.19

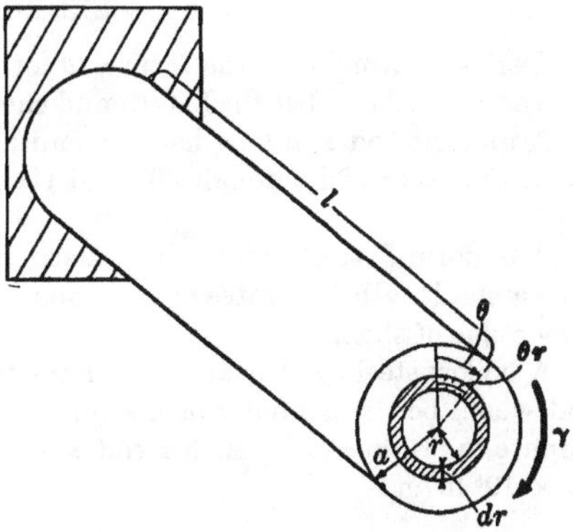

FIG. 14.20.

up of numerous coaxial cylindrical shells, a typical one having radius r and thickness dr. If such a shell were slit down one side and unrolled, a rectangular sheet would result. When twisted, assuming that a simple shear takes place, it would be deformed into a parallelogram similar to Fig. 14.19. From the geometry of this shell it is apparent that

$$\phi = \frac{\theta r}{l}.$$

From (14.80) the corresponding shearing stress is

$$s = \frac{\mu\theta r}{l}.$$

Since the rod and the deformation are uniform, this stress consists of tangential forces adding up to df distributed over the area $2\pi r\,dr$ of the end of the shell.

$$s = \frac{df}{2\pi r\,dr}.$$

The torque associated with this df is

$$d\gamma = r\,df = 2\pi s r^2\,dr = \frac{2\pi\mu\theta}{l}\,r^3\,dr.$$

Thus we have, adding the necessary torques over all the shells from $r = 0$ to $r = a$,

$$\gamma = \int_0^a d\gamma = \frac{2\pi\mu\theta}{l}\int_0^a r^3\,dr,$$

or

(14.81) $$\gamma = \frac{\pi\mu\theta a^4}{2l}.$$

EXERCISES

1. Derive a formula for the ratio γ/θ for a hollow cylindrical rod having inner and outer radii a' and a. Let the length and shear modulus be l and μ.

2. A uniform rod 1 m long has one end fixed. A torque of 0.01 newton-m suffices to turn the other end through 60°. If the radius is 0.2 cm, what is the modulus of shear?

3. A uniform disk of radius r and mass m fastened at the end of a uniform wire of radius a and length l operates as a torsion pendulum of period τ. Find a formula for the modulus of shear.

4. A hollow steel rod has an outer diameter of 2 in. and an inner diameter of $1\frac{7}{8}$ in. What would be the diameter of a solid steel rod having the same torsional stiffness? Compute the ratio γ/θ for such a rod 8 ft long if the modulus of shear for the steel is 11.5×10^6 lb/in.^{2}

14.15. Deflections of Beams. In Sec. 4.11 we evaluated shearing force and bending moment for beams having various loads. As a final exercise in elasticity, we shall consider the shape of a beam under such loads.

We assume that the beam, initially straight, has only very slight curvature even when deflected by a load. And we assume that the stiffness of the beam is solely dependent on stretching and compressing of elastic fibers running parallel to the beam itself.

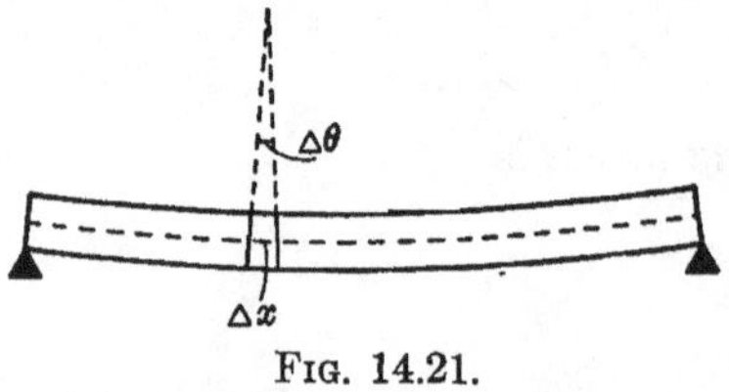

FIG. 14.21.

If Fig. 14.21 represents a beam bent under its own weight, then a plane intermediate layer called the *neutral layer* (shown in cross section by the dotted line) is assumed to retain its initial length. Layers above this are compressed; those below are stretched. The stresses associated with these strains are the source of bending moments. To see this quantitatively, let us look at a segment of length Δx in the unstrained beam. It is bounded by planes normal to the beam, both before and after we assume the distortion. Initially then it is a rectangular box, but after strain it becomes slightly wedge-shaped. The nature of this distortion is shown in Fig. 14.22, where the neutral layer and the original size of the section are shown by the dotted lines. Since we are isolating the segment

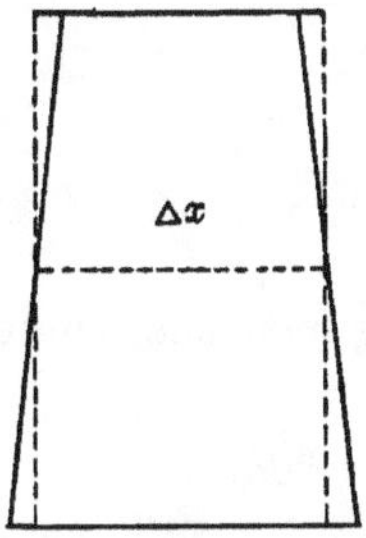

FIG. 14.22.

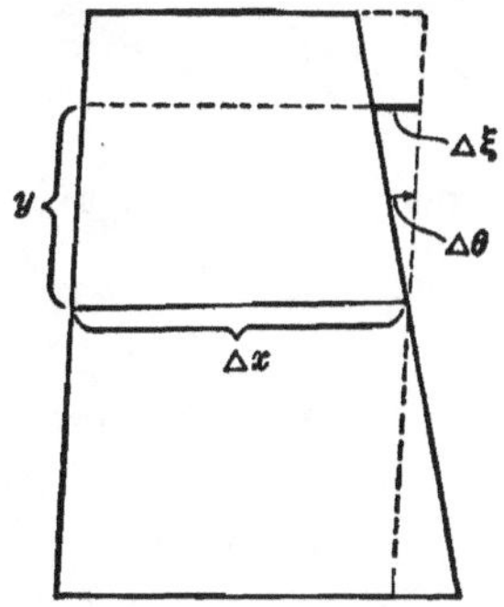

FIG. 14.23.

of length Δx, let us consider the distortion relative to its left plane of section as in Fig. 14.23. Originally the other plane was parallel. Now it is tilted by an angle $\Delta\theta$. Calling $-\Delta\xi$ the contraction of fibers in the layer of coordinate y, we can express $\Delta\theta$ as

$$\Delta\theta = \frac{-\Delta\xi}{y}$$

or, since the neutral layer is normal to the plane of section, its change in slope (and hence in angle for such small angles) is

$$\Delta\left(\frac{dy}{dx}\right) = \Delta\theta = \frac{-\Delta\xi}{y}.$$

But $\Delta\xi/\Delta x$ represents the longitudinal strain for fibers at a distance y from the neutral layer; therefore

$$\text{Strain} = \frac{-y\Delta(dy/dx)}{\Delta x}.$$

In the limit, for smaller and smaller Δx,

$$\text{Strain} = -y\,\frac{d^2y}{dx^2}.$$

Now let us consider a cross section of the beam (see Fig. 14.24). It is assumed symmetric (to avoid complex bending). The z axis shows the neutral layer. The locus of O for successive normal planes is the *neutral axis*. If da is an element of area of coordinate y, the compressive force across it is, by the definition of Young's modulus, equal to

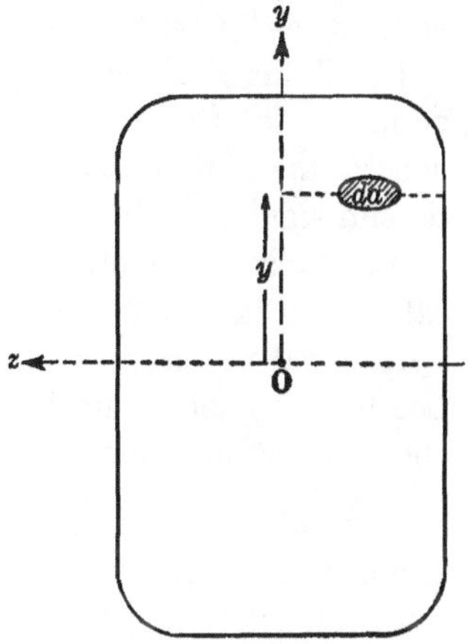

FIG. 14.24.

$$df = -\psi(\text{strain})da,$$

or

$$df = \psi \frac{d^2y}{dx^2} y \, da.$$

Its moment about the z axis is

$$d\gamma_b = y \, df = \psi \frac{d^2y}{dx^2} y^2 \, da.$$

The total moment may be found by summing over the whole area:

$$\gamma_b = \int_a y \, df = \psi \frac{d^2y}{dx^2} \int_a y^2 \, da. \tag{14.82}$$

Since the quantity $\int_a y^2 \, da$ bears much resemblance to the defining expression for *moment of inertia*, the same term is often used in this context, especially by engineers. Here we shall call it *second moment of area*, but to emphasize the similarity we shall denote it by i'.

$$i' = \int_a y^2 \, da. \tag{14.83}$$

We shall deal with symmetric beams under no tension or compression for which it is safe to take the neutral layer as a central one. Equation (14.82) may now be written

$$\gamma_b = \psi i' \frac{d^2y}{dx^2}. \tag{14.84}$$

This is an equation that must be obeyed by the neutral axis of a symmetric beam, if our assumptions about its elastic behavior are justified. It is called the *differential equation for the bending of beams.*

In solving problems, we must integrate (14.84) twice if we are to get an equation for the curve formed by the neutral axis. The evaluation of constants of integration depends on boundary conditions. If a beam has its end rigidly set in horizontal position, we may write $dy/dx = 0$ for the value of x at that point. For symmetric loading, it is often convenient to take the origin at the center of the beam. Then a boundary condition is $dy/dx = 0 = y$ at $x = 0$. When there are concentrated loads so that the bending-moment equation changes, one may use the fact that the slope of the beam is the same at such a point when approached from either side.

Example 1. What is the second moment of area of a cylindrical beam?

SOLUTION. All the techniques for moment of inertia and radius of gyration calculations may be used for area moments of inertia, substituting area for mass. Thus for a circular disk about a diameter,

$$i = \tfrac{1}{4}mr^2,$$
$$i' = \tfrac{1}{4}(\pi r^2)r^2.$$

Example 2. Find an equation for a uniform beam of weight w and length l supported at its ends.

SOLUTION. Since symmetry is assured, let us take origin at the center. Then isolating the beam at the left of x (see Fig. 14.25), we have for a

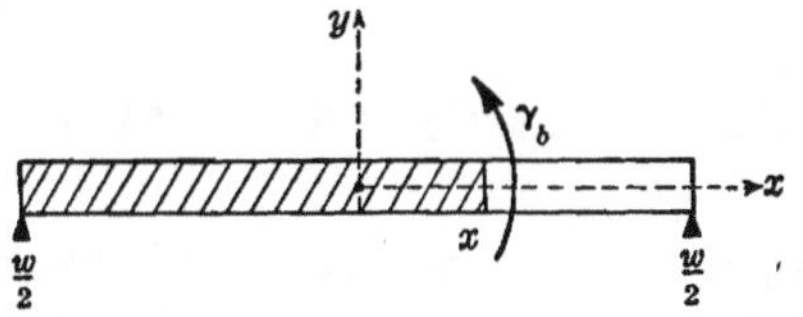

FIG. 14.25.

moment equation of equilibrium

$$-\frac{w}{2}\left(x+\frac{l}{2}\right)+\left[\frac{x+(l/2)}{l}\right]w\left[\frac{x+(l/2)}{2}\right]+\gamma_b=0,$$

or

$$\gamma_b=\frac{wl}{8}-\frac{wx^2}{2l}.$$

Now using (14.84),

$$\frac{wl}{8}-\frac{wx^2}{2l}=\psi i'\frac{d^2y}{dx^2}.$$

Integrating,

$$\frac{wlx}{8}-\frac{wx^3}{6l}+c=\psi i'\frac{dy}{dx}.$$

Since the slope is zero at the center, $c = 0$. Integrating again,

$$\frac{wlx^2}{16}-\frac{wx^4}{24l}+c'=\psi i'y.$$

Since the origin is at the center, $c' = 0$. To find the deflection at the center due to the bending, we merely evaluate y for $x = l/2$:

$$\psi i'y=\frac{wl(l/2)^2}{16}-\frac{w(l/2)^4}{24l}=\frac{5wl^3}{384}.$$

EXERCISES

1. A uniform rectangular beam of length l, breadth b, and depth d rests horizontally on simple supports at its ends. A load w, large in comparison with the weight of the beam, is placed at its center. Find a formula for the deflection at the center.

2. A wood cylinder 20 ft long and 4 in. in diameter rests horizontally on supports at its ends. If the specific gravity is 0.6 and Young's modulus (longitudinally) is 1.5×10^6 lb/in.^{2}, find how much it will sag under its own weight.

3. A uniform beam is free at one end but the other is set horizontally in concrete. Find an equation for its shape as it bends under its own weight.

4. A beam of length l is free at one end but the other is set horizontally in concrete. Find an equation for its shape as it bends under a concentrated heavy load w at its free end.

5. Rewrite Eq. (14.81) in terms of the second moment of area i'. Do the same for your result for Exercise 1, Sec. 14.14.

CHAPTER 15

MECHANICS OF AN IDEAL FLUID

In the preceding two chapters forces and displacements have been studied from the point of view of vector fields. Gravitational potential provided an example of a scalar field. In this chapter we shall continue our study of deformable bodies by considering the special case for which the only possible stress is pressure. Pressure will be treated as a scalar function of position. We shall also deal with limited dynamical situations. In the flow patterns which result, we shall find further examples of vector fields. A fluid in motion will be treated as a continuous medium. Instead of studying individual objects we shall be concerned with typical elements (in the sense of the calculus) to which elementary mechanical principles may be applied. Our aim will be to deduce a few of the important equations of hydrodynamics.

15.1. Pressure. At a point in a fluid the pressure is defined except for sign as the normal component of the stress across any element of area. Approaching the subject directly let us take a small element of area Δa of normal $\mathbf{N}$ across which a force $\Delta \mathbf{F}$ acts as in Fig. 15.1. The average pressure for this orientation is then

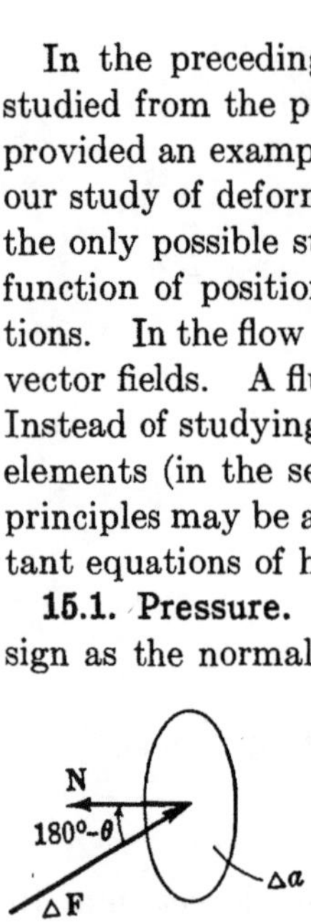

FIG. 15.1.

$$(15.1) \qquad \bar{p}(\mathbf{N}) = -\frac{\Delta \mathbf{F}}{\Delta a} \cdot \mathbf{N}.$$

Taking the limit as Δa becomes small, we get the pressure, still dependent on $\mathbf{N}$, as

$$(15.2) \qquad p(\mathbf{N}) = -\frac{d\mathbf{F}}{da} \cdot \mathbf{N}.$$

For an *ideal fluid*, the angle θ between force and normal is 180°:

$$(15.3) \qquad p(\mathbf{N}) = \left|\frac{d\mathbf{F}}{da}\right|.$$

Now let us verify the fact that for an ideal fluid $p(\mathbf{N})$ is the same for every $\mathbf{N}$. This might be done formally by writing the ideal fluid condition into Eq. (14.55). The substitutions would be

$$-\mathbf{X} = p(\mathbf{I})\mathbf{I}, \qquad -\mathbf{Y} = p(\mathbf{J})\mathbf{J}, \qquad -\mathbf{Z} = p(\mathbf{K})\mathbf{K}, \qquad -\mathbf{S} = p(\mathbf{N})\mathbf{N}.$$

The result of the substitution would be

$$p(\mathbf{N})(l\mathbf{I} + m\mathbf{J} + n\mathbf{K}) = lp(\mathbf{I})\mathbf{I} + mp(\mathbf{J})\mathbf{J} + np(\mathbf{K})\mathbf{K}.$$

Equating x coefficients, y coefficients, and z coefficients, we get

$$p(\mathbf{N}) = p(\mathbf{I}) = p(\mathbf{J}) = p(\mathbf{K}). \tag{15.4}$$

Since **N** is arbitrary, we conclude that *pressure in an ideal fluid is a function of position, independent of orientation.* Thus we shall write p instead of $p(\mathbf{N})$.

As an alternative demonstration let us isolate a cylindrical portion of the fluid as shown in Fig. 15.2. Let one end be terminated by a normal

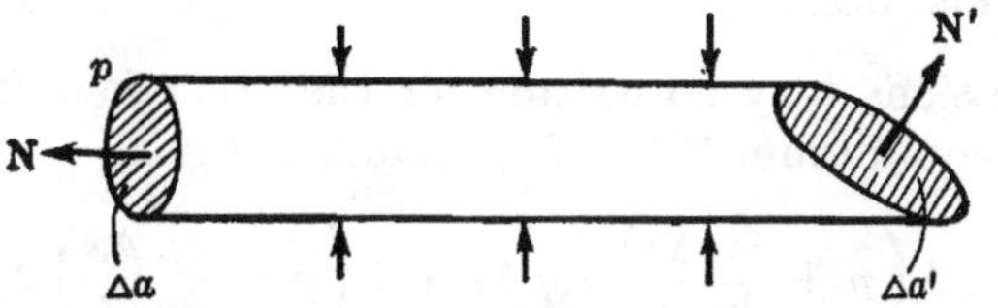

FIG. 15.2.

section of normal **N** and the other by a skew section of normal **N′**. The area of the first end is Δa, of the second $\Delta a'$. The density is δ. The mean length is Δl; therefore the mass is $\delta\,\Delta l\,\Delta a$. Taking components parallel to the axis of the cylinder, we have

$$p(\mathbf{N})\Delta a + p(\mathbf{N}')\Delta a'\,(\mathbf{N}'\cdot\mathbf{N}) - \delta\,\Delta l\,\Delta a\,\mathbf{G}\cdot\mathbf{N} = -\delta\,\Delta l\,\Delta a\,\mathbf{A}\cdot\mathbf{N}.$$

Here **G** is the acceleration of gravity vector, and **A** is the acceleration vector. Pressure forces on the lateral surface of the cylinder do not appear in this equation, since they must be normal (in as much as the fluid is ideal). Now divide by Δa, and take the limit as both Δa and Δl approach zero. We get

$$p(\mathbf{N}) + p(\mathbf{N}')\frac{\Delta a'}{\Delta a}(\mathbf{N}'\cdot\mathbf{N}) = 0.$$

Since

$$-(\mathbf{N}'\cdot\mathbf{N})\Delta a' = \Delta a,$$

we have

$$p(\mathbf{N}) = p(\mathbf{N}'). \tag{15.5}$$

15.2. Equilibrium. It is well known that pressure differences can cause a fluid to flow as, for instance, in a fire hose. Let us see how a fluid in equilibrium can be characterized. Select a point **O** in a fluid, and consider a small rectangular element of volume $\Delta x\,\Delta y\,\Delta z$ and center **O** as shown in Fig. 15.3. We shall let this volume approach zero; thus we shall assume that the gravitational field strength (or other field strength) $\mathfrak{F}$ and the density δ are constant over the isolated region. If p is the pressure at **O**, then the average pressure on the faces having normals **I** and $-$**I**, are respectively [approximately, compare (13.1)],

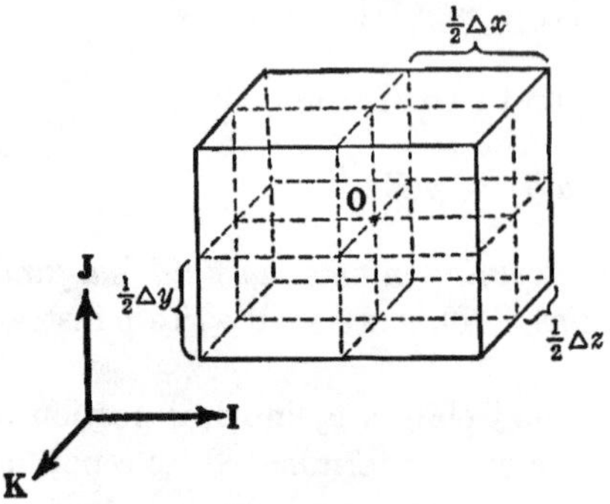

FIG. 15.3.

$$\left(p + \frac{\partial p}{\partial x}\frac{\Delta x}{2}\right)$$

and

$$\left(p - \frac{\partial p}{\partial x}\frac{\Delta x}{2}\right).$$

Similar expressions may be written for the other four faces. Now the condition for equilibrium $\Sigma\mathbf{F} = \mathbf{O}$ becomes

$$\begin{aligned}\mathfrak{F}\,\delta\,\Delta x\,\Delta y\,\Delta z - \mathbf{I}\left(p + \frac{\partial p}{\partial x}\frac{\Delta x}{2}\right)\Delta y\,\Delta z + \mathbf{I}\left(p - \frac{\partial p}{\partial x}\frac{\Delta x}{2}\right)\Delta y\,\Delta z \\ -\mathbf{J}\left(p + \frac{\partial p}{\partial y}\frac{\Delta y}{2}\right)\Delta z\,\Delta x + \mathbf{J}\left(p - \frac{\partial p}{\partial y}\frac{\Delta y}{2}\right)\Delta z\,\Delta x \\ -\mathbf{K}\left(p + \frac{\partial p}{\partial z}\frac{\Delta z}{2}\right)\Delta x\,\Delta y + \mathbf{K}\left(p - \frac{\partial p}{\partial z}\frac{\Delta z}{2}\right)\Delta x\,\Delta y = \mathbf{O};\end{aligned}$$

or, dividing by $\Delta x\,\Delta y\,\Delta z$ and taking the limit as Δx, Δy, and Δz approach zero (so that our approximations become better), we get at **O**

$$\mathfrak{F}\,\delta - \frac{\partial p}{\partial x}\mathbf{I} - \frac{\partial p}{\partial y}\mathbf{J} - \frac{\partial p}{\partial z}\mathbf{K} = \mathbf{O},$$

or

$$\mathfrak{F}\,\delta - \nabla p = \mathbf{O}. \tag{15.6}$$

This equation must be valid at each point within a fluid at equilibrium. This result means essentially that a fluid is at equilibrium when forces associated with pressure differences are exactly equal to and opposite to the forces of other origin. The force associated with pressure differences is opposite to the gradient: the trend is toward the lower pressure.

Now this derivation leaves much to be desired in the way of rigor. Calling $p + \dfrac{\partial p}{\partial x}\dfrac{\Delta x}{2}$ an average value over a whole face when we have reason to expect it to be only approximate at the center of the face may seem too sanguine. Of course, our aim is to give intuitive derivations rather than rigorous proofs. It is not assumed that the student has either background or, at the moment, the time for a sounder treatment. As soon as he is able, mathematically, to handle a more thorough presentation, he is encouraged to seek it out and to ponder it. It is hoped that the present approach will both make available important results and methods at an early stage and also provide practical motivation for further study of a more demanding sort.

Some of the objections to the preceding derivation may be avoided by using a different shaped figure. Suppose we isolate a cylindrical element with center **O** and with an arbitrarily small cross-sectional area Δa. Let this cylinder at first be parallel to the x axis as in Fig. 15.4. Now the

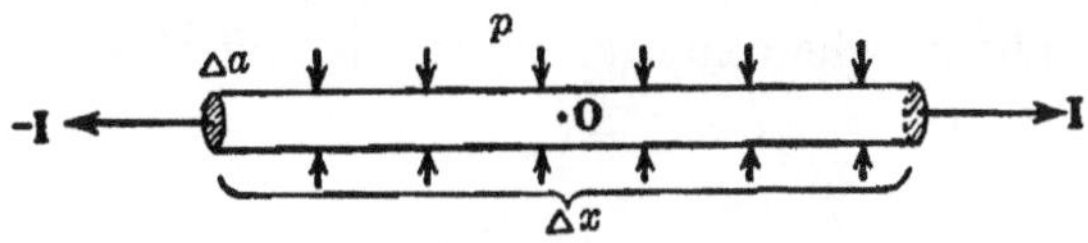

FIG. 15.4.

problem appears one-dimensional rather than three-dimensional, and Eq. (13.1) is a one-dimensional tool. The x equation of equilibrium gives us

$$(\mathfrak{F} \cdot \mathbf{I})\delta\, \Delta x\, \Delta a - \left(p + \frac{\partial p}{\partial x}\frac{\Delta x}{2}\right)\Delta a + \left(p - \frac{\partial p}{\partial x}\frac{\Delta x}{2}\right)\Delta a = 0;$$

or, dividing by $\Delta a\, \Delta x$ and taking the limit as Δx and Δa approach zero [the ratio between Δa and $(\Delta x)^2$ being constant, if you wish], we get

$$\frac{\partial p}{\partial x} = (\mathfrak{F} \cdot \mathbf{I})\delta.$$

Similarly, if we take cylinders in the y and z directions, we have

$$\frac{\partial p}{\partial y} = (\mathfrak{F} \cdot \mathbf{J})\delta, \qquad \frac{\partial p}{\partial z} = (\mathfrak{F} \cdot \mathbf{K})\delta.$$

Now multiplying the first equation by **I**, the second by **J**, the third by **K** and adding corresponding members, we get

$$\frac{\partial p}{\partial x}\mathbf{I} + \frac{\partial p}{\partial y}\mathbf{J} + \frac{\partial p}{\partial z}\mathbf{K} = \delta(\mathfrak{F} \cdot \mathbf{I})\mathbf{I} + \delta(\mathfrak{F} \cdot \mathbf{J})\mathbf{J} + \delta(\mathfrak{F} \cdot \mathbf{K})\mathbf{K}$$

or, as before,

$$\nabla p = \delta\,\mathfrak{F}.$$

This time the averaging difficulty may seem to have been dodged by making the faces so very small. But, if for a given pressure field it is possible to pick Δa small enough to make our approximations satisfactory, then clearly the cube of Fig. 15.3 can be picked with all its faces more than adequately small. We may conclude then that while demonstrations of this sort are not thorough proofs, they are instructive derivations of valid relationships.

Example 1. The field strength of terrestrial gravitation may be expressed for J vertical downward

$$\mathfrak{F} = g\mathbf{J}.$$

We may at once conclude:

$$\frac{\partial p}{\partial x} = \frac{\partial p}{\partial z} = 0$$

(for equilibrium), while

$$\frac{\partial p}{\partial y} = \delta g.$$

In the case of a liquid where the density is constant, this last equation may be integrated to give

$$p = p_0 + \delta g y. \tag{15.7}$$

Ordinarily the origin is taken at a free surface of the fluid so that the constant of integration p_0 is barometric pressure.

Example 2. If the body forces are negligible, the pressure is constant; for its maximum directional derivative is zero.

Center of Pressure. The total force exerted across a plane boundary by a fluid is given by

$$\mathbf{F} = \mathbf{N} \int_a p \, da, \tag{15.8}$$

where **N** is the unit outward normal vector for the plane. If we take two axes in this plane, the resultant force is located by moment equations. If $(\bar{x},\bar{y})$ is the point where the resultant acts in this plane,

$$\begin{aligned} \bar{x}f &= \int_a xp \, da, \\ \bar{y}f &= \int_a yp \, da. \end{aligned} \tag{15.9}$$

$(\bar{x},\bar{y})$ is called the *center of pressure.* In practice one side of the boundary is often exposed to the atmosphere; therefore the net pressure $p' = p - p_0$ is used instead of p.

Suppose that the y axis is vertical downward as in Fig. 15.5 and that the pressure varies only with the depth as in Eq. (15.7). Then if the breadth b also can be expressed in terms of y, $da = b(y)dy$; thus we have

$$\begin{aligned} f &= \int_0^h p'(y)b(y)dy, \\ \bar{y}f &= \int_0^h yp'(y)b(y)dy. \end{aligned} \tag{15.10}$$

The x coordinate of the center of pressure may be found similarly.

Example 3. A dam has the shape of a trapezoid (as in Fig. 15.5). It is 40 ft deep, 70 ft wide at the top, and 50 ft wide at the bottom. How far from the top is the center of net pressure if the water just reaches the top of the dam?

SOLUTION. Since the sides are straight, we can express b in terms of y without taking account of the slopes of the sides.

$$b = 70 - \frac{70 - 50}{40} y = 70 - 0.5y.$$

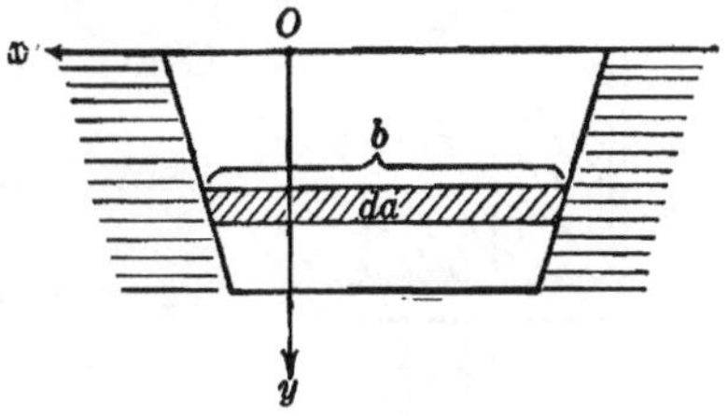

FIG. 15.5.

Using Eq. (15.7), and the fact that

$$\delta g = 62.4 \text{ lb/ft}^3,$$

we have

$$p' = p - p_0 = 62.4y.$$

These expressions may be substituted in (15.10) to determine $\bar{y}$. We get

$$f = \tfrac{1}{2}(62.4) \int_0^{40} (140y - y^2)dy = \tfrac{1}{2}(62.4)(1{,}600)(70 - \tfrac{40}{3}),$$

$$\bar{y}f = \tfrac{1}{2}(62.4) \int_0^{40} (140y^2 - y^3)dy = \tfrac{1}{2}(62.4)(1{,}600)(40)(\tfrac{140}{3} - \tfrac{40}{4});$$

so

$$\bar{y} = \frac{(40)(36.7)}{56.7} = 25.9 \text{ ft}.$$

Equipotential Surfaces. If $\mathfrak{F}$ is conservative,

$$\mathfrak{F} = -\nabla \text{ pot.} = \frac{1}{\delta} \nabla p.$$

If δ is constant, we may rewrite the equation as

$$\nabla \left(\frac{p}{\delta} + \text{pot.}\right) = \mathbf{0}.$$

This may be integrated at once to yield

$$\frac{p}{\delta} + \text{pot.} = \text{const.}$$

The interpretation is immediate:

(15.11) *Free surfaces (p constant) are equipotential surfaces.* For a fluid at rest on the earth, then, a free surface is approximately spherical.

An accelerated fluid may be treated by these hydrostatics methods, provided that suitable fictitious forces are introduced.

Example 4. Consider as in Fig. 15.6 a fluid rotating in a cylinder after steady state has been reached. There are now two body forces (per unit mass):

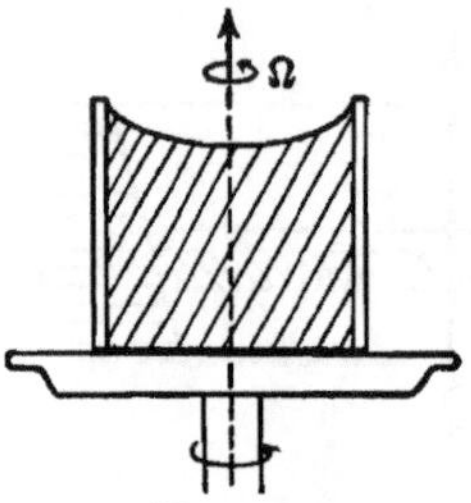

FIG. 15.6.

Gravitational: $-\nabla gy.$

Centrifugal: $\nabla \frac{\omega^2 r^2}{2}.$

The field strength $\mathfrak{F}$ is now

$$\mathfrak{F} = \nabla\left(-gy + \frac{\omega^2 r^2}{2}\right).$$

By the preceding result, the free surface is one for which the potential is constant; so its equation is

$$+gy - \frac{\omega^2 r^2}{2} = \text{const}, \qquad \text{parabolic.}$$

EXERCISES

1. Assuming air of constant temperature (so that Boyle's law is valid), use the equation for hydrostatic equilibrium to derive the law of Halley for the variation of atmospheric pressure with height y:

$$p = p_0 e^{-(\delta_0/p_0)gy}.$$

2. Use the result of Exercise 1 to predict air pressure at a height of 4,000 m when the barometer on the ground reads 76. (Specific gravity of air is 0.0012.)

3. Find the force exerted against a vertical rectangular dam 60 ft long, when the water is 60 ft deep.

4. A trapezoidal dam similar to the one in Fig. 15.5 has upper length b_1, lower length b_2, and depth h. Find the *net* force due to pressure against it in terms of the density δ of the fluid.

5. A dam is shaped like an inverted triangle (as in Fig. 15.7) of base b and depth h. Find the depth of the center of *net* pressure.

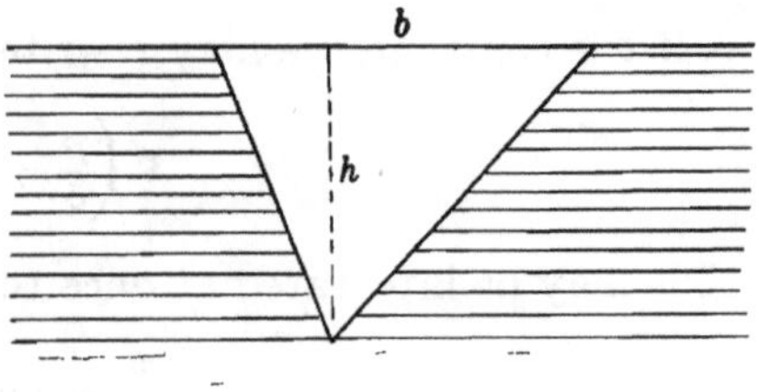

FIG. 15.7.

15.3. The Gradient Theorem. If we compare the hydrostatic equation for equilibrium

$$\mathfrak{F}\,\delta - \nabla p = 0$$

with the general equation

$$\Sigma \mathbf{F} = 0,$$

previously used, we can conclude that *the net compressive force per volume is equal to minus the pressure gradient.* This interpretation of ∇p will enable us to derive intuitively a very important mathematical conclusion of considerable generality and usefulness.

Suppose that we are interested in a region of a fluid having a well-defined boundary. Let the region be divided up into small cubical elements as is suggested by Fig. 15.8. A typical element of volume Δv is subject to a net compressive force

$$-\nabla p \, \Delta v.$$

If we isolate two adjoining elements such as those of volumes Δv and $\Delta v'$ in the figure, the net compressive force is

$$-\nabla p \, \Delta v - \nabla p' \, \Delta v'$$

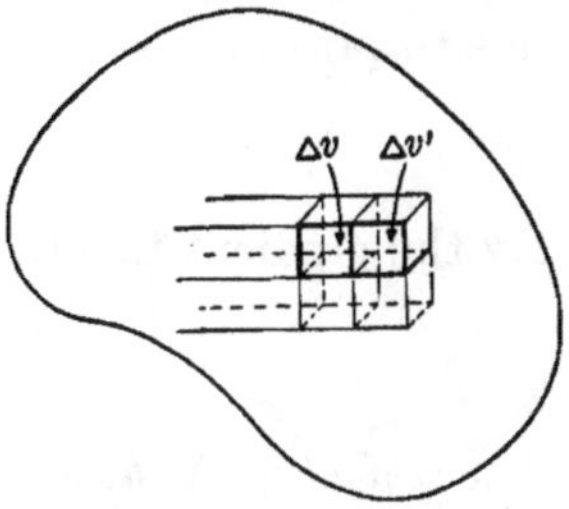

FIG. 15.8.

because the forces across their common boundaries just cancel. Adding such terms for *all* the elements, we get

$$-\Sigma \nabla p \, \Delta v$$

as the net compressive force for the whole isolated region. Taking the limit of such sums as the elements are made arbitrarily small, we get as the net compressive force:

$$-\int_v \nabla p \, dv.$$

Isolating the whole region, we can also express the net compressive force in terms of the forces across the boundary of the region. For each element of area Δa, the net compressive force is

$$-\mathbf{N} p \, \Delta a.$$

Adding up over the whole boundary area, we get

$$-\Sigma \mathbf{N} p \, \Delta a,$$

and taking the limit of such sums as the Δa's become arbitrarily small, we have as the net compressive force for the whole region

$$-\int_a \mathbf{N} p \, da.$$

We have found two ways of expressing mathematically the net compressive force for a region. Equating them we arrive at a formula which may be used for any suitable scalar function of position p:

$$\int_v \nabla p \, dv = \int_a \mathbf{N} p \, da. \tag{15.12}$$

For any such scalar φ, the integral over the area of a region of the vector $\mathbf{N}\varphi$, where $\mathbf{N}$ is the unit normal vector (outward), is equal to the integral over the volume enclosed by the area of the gradient of the scalar function. This is the *gradient theorem*.

Archimedes' Principle. As an application of the gradient theorem let us consider the celebrated principle of Archimedes. Consider a random object submerged in a nonviscous fluid. The *buoyant force* is the net force due to pressure:

$$\int_a -\mathbf{N}p\, da.$$

By the gradient theorem, this is equal to

$$-\int_v \nabla p\, dv.$$

The *weight of the fluid displaced* is

$$\int_v \mathfrak{F}\, \delta\, dv.$$

But by the basic equation of hydrostatics,

$$\mathfrak{F}\, \delta = \nabla p.$$

Hence the weight of the displaced fluid is

$$\int_v \nabla p\, dv.$$

Thus *buoyant force and weight of displaced fluid are equal and opposite.*

EXERCISES

1. A cylinder of length l and specific gravity σ oscillates vertically in water about its equilibrium position. (*a*) Is the oscillation in simple harmonic motion? (*b*) What is the period? (*c*) What fraction of the length is above water at the equilibrium position?

2. Consider an enclosed liquid in equilibrium having a pressure function $p(\mathbf{R})$. Now let the pressure at a part of the boundary be increased by a distinct small amount q_0 (as by driving in the plunger in Fig. 15.9). The pressure function throughout the fluid changes. Show that when equilibrium is restored the new pressure function $p'(\mathbf{R})$ is given by

$$p'(\mathbf{R}) = p(\mathbf{R}) + q_0.$$

This means that the impressed pressure has been transmitted equally throughout the volume (*Pascal's law*).

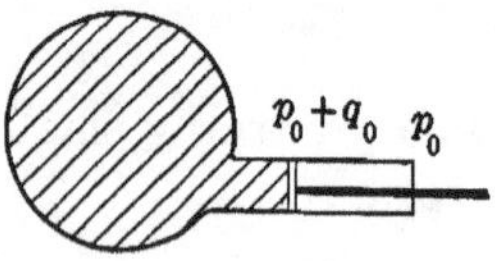

FIG. 15.9.

15.4. Velocity Fields. When a fluid is in motion, a velocity vector may be associated with each point in the region. This vector may be constant (this is known as *steady flow*), but often it will vary. In this sense, velocity is a vector function of position *and* time:

$$\mathbf{V} = \mathbf{V}(\mathbf{R},t).$$

At any given moment, velocity constitutes a specific *vector field*. It is often convenient to express $\mathbf{V}$ in terms of components in fixed directions.

$$\mathbf{V} = v_x\mathbf{I} + v_y\mathbf{J} + v_z\mathbf{K}.$$

For each choice of axes, v_x, v_y, and v_z are scalar functions of position and determine *three scalar fields.*

With t still held constant, we can consider the *directional derivative* of the vector **V**. This concept was presented in Sec. 14.1 which should be reviewed at this time. Using the symbolism of Sec. 14.1 the directional derivative of **V** in the direction of the unit vector **T** is given by

$$\frac{d\mathbf{V}}{ds} = (\mathbf{T} \cdot \nabla)\mathbf{V}. \tag{15.13}$$

When we were discussing force fields, we were concerned especially with the conservative case for which the *work around a closed path* vanished:

$$\text{Work} = \oint \mathbf{F} \cdot d\mathbf{R} = 0.$$

The analogous concept with a velocity field is the *circulation around a closed path.*

$$\text{Circulation} = \oint \mathbf{V} \cdot d\mathbf{R}. \tag{15.14}$$

If for *every* closed path in the fluid the circulation is zero, the motion is *irrotational.* The value of the circulation generally depends on the path taken. In Fig. 15.10, for instance, several vectors are drawn to illustrate the field

$$\mathbf{V} = |y|\mathbf{I}.$$

The circulation is zero for circuit a but not zero for circuit b. This can be seen mathematically and it also may be visualized intuitively. Suppose that the circles a and b represented inflated rafts floating on water whose current pattern is indicated by the arrows. It is clear that raft a would not tend to rotate but that raft b would rotate in a clockwise fashion.

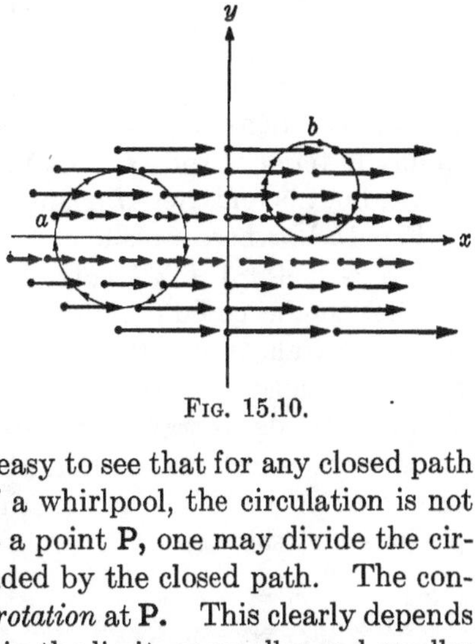

FIG. 15.10.

In the case of *motion in a plane* it is easy to see that for any closed path in the plane and around the center of a whirlpool, the circulation is not zero. As a measure of the *vorticity* at a point **P**, one may divide the circulation by the area of a surface bounded by the closed path. The concept so defined is sometimes called the *rotation* at **P**. This clearly depends on the choice of path and surface, but in the limit, as smaller and smaller curves are used, the limit will be unique if the function **V** and its derivatives are continuous. For example, if the motion is like a rigid body in rotation at angular speed ω and if we take a circle with the center of rotation as its center, we get

$$c = \text{circulation} = \omega r(2\pi r)$$

and for our measure of the vorticity at the center

$$\text{(15.15)} \qquad \text{rot.} = \text{rotation} = \lim_{r\to 0}\left(\frac{2\pi\omega r^2}{\pi r^2}\right) = 2\omega.$$

This shows how in this special case the result is independent of the radius of the circle even before the limit is taken. A better measure of vorticity might be defined as one-half the rotation; so that for our special case it would be equal to ω. If a small raft were floated on the liquid, its angular velocity would tend to equal one-half the rotation at the point it occupied.

If the motion is not necessarily plane, another complication arises. Through a point **P** we may draw various planes for which the rotation might be computed. These planes are designated by the unit normal vector **N** directed so that **N** is parallel to the corresponding angular velocity vector. Referring to Fig. 15.11, we may define the **N** rotation thus:

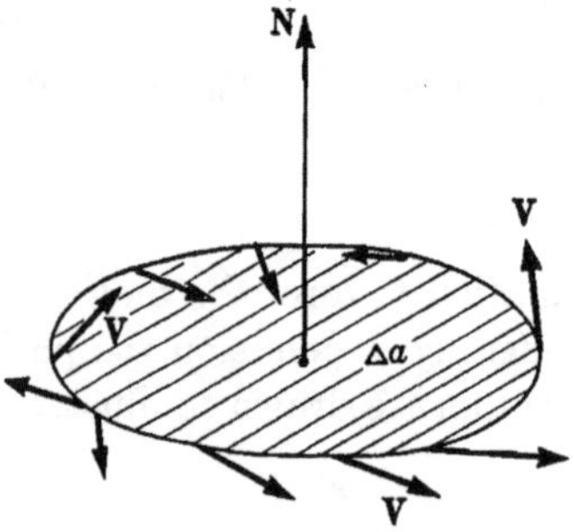

FIG. 15.11.

$$\text{(15.16)} \qquad \text{rot.}_N\, \mathbf{V} = \lim_{\Delta a\to 0}\frac{c_N}{\Delta a},$$

where c_N is the circulation about the curve bounding Δa.

It is a remarkable fact, reminiscent of similar situations met in other contexts, that $\text{rot.}_N\,\mathbf{V}$ can be expressed simply in terms of $\text{rot.}_I\,\mathbf{V}$, $\text{rot.}_J\,\mathbf{V}$, $\text{rot.}_K\,\mathbf{V}$. Consider the possible circulations about boundaries of triangles in Fig. 15.12 where a plane of normal $\mathbf{N} = l\mathbf{I} + m\mathbf{J} + n\mathbf{K}$ cuts axes parallel to the coordinate axes to form a tetrahedron. If each triangle is circulated in the direction shown, each edge is traversed twice, in opposite directions, so that the sum is zero. Let us use at once the obvious fact that

$$\text{(15.17)} \qquad \begin{aligned} c_I &= -c_{(-I)},\\ c_J &= -c_{(-J)},\\ c_K &= -c_{(-K)}, \end{aligned}$$

so that

$$\text{(15.18)} \qquad c_N = c_I + c_J + c_K.$$

If we denote the areas of the triangles by Δa, Δa_x, etc., we have

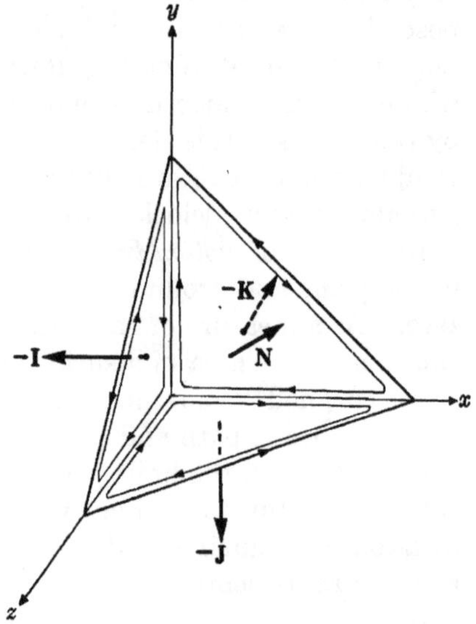

FIG. 15.12.

$$\Delta a_x = l\,\Delta a,$$
$$\Delta a_y = m\,\Delta a,$$
$$\Delta a_z = n\,\Delta a,$$

so that

$$\frac{1}{\Delta a} = \frac{l}{\Delta a_x} = \frac{m}{\Delta a_y} = \frac{n}{\Delta a_z}. \tag{15.19}$$

Multiplying successive entries in (15.18) by the equal quantities of (15.19), we get

$$\frac{c_N}{\Delta a} = l\,\frac{c_I}{\Delta a_x} + m\,\frac{c_J}{\Delta a_y} + n\,\frac{c_K}{\Delta a_z}. \tag{15.20}$$

Now let us take limits as Δa approaches zero. We clearly get

$$\text{rot.}_N\,\mathbf{V} = l\,\text{rot.}_I\,\mathbf{V} + m\,\text{rot.}_J\,\mathbf{V} + n\,\text{rot.}_K\,\mathbf{V}. \tag{15.21}$$

This expression bears a distinct resemblance to (14.55) and (13.3).

EXERCISES

1. A cylinder of fluid is in uniform rotation about the y axis; so

$$\mathbf{V} = \omega\mathbf{J} \times \mathbf{R}.$$

Show that $(\mathbf{V} \cdot \nabla)\mathbf{V} = -\omega^2(x\mathbf{I} + z\mathbf{K})$.

2. A velocity field parallel to the xy plane is given by

$$\mathbf{V} = 2x\mathbf{J}.$$

Compute the circulation for a clockwise trip around the square whose corners have coordinates (0,0), (0,1), (1,1), (1,0).

3. Suppose that a fluid travels in a horizontal circular ring-shaped conduit in such a way that the linear speed is a constant, that is, the fluid traveling along a circle of large radius moves no faster than fluid traversing a smaller circle. Find how the circulation about these circles varies with the radius. For what kind of circular velocity pattern would these circulations be equal?

4. If the flow described in the first part of Exercise 3 were imagined to continue right up to the center of the circle, what would be the rotation at that point?

5. For rotation in a plane like a rigid body about a fixed axis, consider the circulation around the closed path bounded by concentric circles and radii whose corners are given in polar coordinates (origin on axis in plane) as (r,θ), $(r + \Delta r,\theta)$, $(r + \Delta r,\theta + \Delta\theta)$, $(r,\theta + \Delta\theta)$. From this find the rotation at (r,θ).

15.5. The Notion of Curl. As in our treatment of (13.3) we note how convenient it would be to regard (15.21) as the scalar product of **N** with a new vector usually called the *curl* of **V** and here defined by

$$\textbf{curl}\ \mathbf{V} = (\text{rot.}_I\,\mathbf{V})\mathbf{I} + (\text{rot.}_J\,\mathbf{V})\mathbf{J} + (\text{rot.}_K\,\mathbf{V})\mathbf{K}. \tag{15.22}$$

In terms of this we can rewrite (15.21) as

$$\text{rot.}_N\,\mathbf{V} = \mathbf{N} \cdot \textbf{curl}\ \mathbf{V}. \tag{15.23}$$

This is analogous to Eq. (13.5). We note that when **N** is chosen parallel to the vector **curl V**, we get a maximum rotation and that the magnitude of the vector is equal to this maximum rotation. Thus curl plays the same role for rotation and vorticity that gradient does for directional derivative. Paraphrasing (13.7), we have

(15.24) **Curl V** *has the direction for which the rotation of* **V** *is maximum. It has the magnitude of this maximum rotation.*

Next let us seek analytical expressions for the components of **curl V**. Consider a rectangle of normal **K** and edges Δx and Δy about a point **P** as center as shown in Fig. 15.13. Average velocity components parallel to the respective edges are approximately

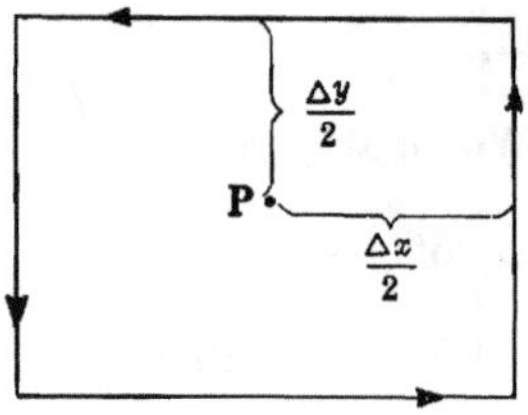

FIG. 15.13.

$$v_x - \frac{\partial v_x}{\partial y}\frac{\Delta y}{2}, \qquad v_y + \frac{\partial v_y}{\partial x}\frac{\Delta x}{2},$$
$$-\left(v_x + \frac{\partial v_x}{\partial y}\frac{\Delta y}{2}\right), \qquad -\left(v_y - \frac{\partial v_y}{\partial x}\frac{\Delta x}{2}\right).$$

The circulation is then, since several terms of opposite sign cancel each other,

$$c_K = -\frac{\partial v_x}{\partial y}\Delta y\,\Delta x + \frac{\partial v_y}{\partial x}\Delta x\,\Delta y$$

and we get

$$\text{rot.}_K\,\mathbf{V} = \lim_{\substack{\Delta x\to 0\\ \Delta y\to 0}} \frac{c_K}{\Delta x\,\Delta y} = \frac{\partial v_y}{\partial x} - \frac{\partial v_x}{\partial y}.$$

Similar evaluations may be carried out for $\text{rot.}_I\,\mathbf{V}$ and $\text{rot.}_J\,\mathbf{V}$, yielding the formula

$$\text{(15.25)} \quad \mathbf{curl\ V} = \left(\frac{\partial v_z}{\partial y} - \frac{\partial v_y}{\partial z}\right)\mathbf{I} + \left(\frac{\partial v_x}{\partial z} - \frac{\partial v_z}{\partial x}\right)\mathbf{J} + \left(\frac{\partial v_y}{\partial x} - \frac{\partial v_x}{\partial y}\right)\mathbf{K}.$$

We used the symbol ∇ in dealing with gradients. If we regard it as a symbolic vectorial operator, it will have further use for us. The use of operator equations has been met earlier, for example,

$$\frac{d}{dt} = \mathbf{\Omega}\times\ , \qquad \frac{d}{dt} = \frac{d'}{d't} + \mathbf{\Omega}\times\ .$$

Here we write

$$\text{(15.26)} \qquad \nabla = \mathbf{I}\frac{\partial}{\partial x} + \mathbf{J}\frac{\partial}{\partial y} + \mathbf{K}\frac{\partial}{\partial z}.$$

When this "operates" on a scalar, we merely use symbolic multiplication by a scalar φ to get a formula for an actual operation; thus

$$\nabla\varphi = \mathbf{I}\frac{\partial\varphi}{\partial x} + \mathbf{J}\frac{\partial\varphi}{\partial y} + \mathbf{K}\frac{\partial\varphi}{\partial z} = \mathbf{grad}\ \varphi.$$

In this sense we may write

(15.27) $$\text{curl } \mathbf{V} = \nabla \times \mathbf{V},$$

for, symbolically,

(15.28)
$$\text{curl } \mathbf{V} = \begin{vmatrix} \frac{\partial}{\partial x} & \frac{\partial}{\partial y} & \frac{\partial}{\partial z} \\ v_x & v_y & v_z \\ \mathbf{I} & \mathbf{J} & \mathbf{K} \end{vmatrix}$$
$$= \mathbf{I} \begin{vmatrix} \frac{\partial}{\partial y} & \frac{\partial}{\partial z} \\ v_y & v_z \end{vmatrix} + \mathbf{J} \begin{vmatrix} \frac{\partial}{\partial z} & \frac{\partial}{\partial x} \\ v_z & v_x \end{vmatrix} + \mathbf{K} \begin{vmatrix} \frac{\partial}{\partial x} & \frac{\partial}{\partial y} \\ v_x & v_y \end{vmatrix}.$$

This last expression expands to give (15.25). Since the symmetric determinant (15.28) is easily written down from (15.27), the symbolic approach is a real crutch for flagging memories when computations of curls are desired.

Example 1

$$\mathbf{V} = x\mathbf{I} + xy\mathbf{K}.$$

Find curl **V**.

SOLUTION

$$\text{curl } \mathbf{V} = \begin{vmatrix} \frac{\partial}{\partial x} & \frac{\partial}{\partial y} & \frac{\partial}{\partial z} \\ x & 0 & xy \\ \mathbf{I} & \mathbf{J} & \mathbf{K} \end{vmatrix} = \mathbf{I}(x - 0) + \mathbf{J}(0 - y) + \mathbf{K}(0 - 0)$$
$$= x\mathbf{I} - y\mathbf{J}.$$

Example 2. Let us consider the field of Fig. 15.10 for points above the x axis. Then $\mathbf{V} = y\mathbf{I}$. It follows easily that

$$\text{curl } \mathbf{V} = -\mathbf{K}.$$

EXERCISES

1. Show that for rigid-body motion the following equation holds for any point of the body:

$$\text{curl } \mathbf{V} = 2\mathbf{\Omega}.$$

2. Evaluate **curl** V for

(*a*) $\mathbf{V} = x^2y\mathbf{I} + (x - y)\mathbf{K}$. (*b*) $\mathbf{V} = \dfrac{\mathbf{R}}{\mathbf{R} \cdot \mathbf{R}}$.

3. Rephrase (13.16) in terms of the ideas of this section.

4. Referring to (14.31) and (14.32), show that **curl H** = **O** is a condition for a pure strain.

5. Evaluate **curl V** for **V** = **L** (**L** being the unit radial vector, as usual).

6. Investigate the curl of $\nabla\varphi$ for a suitable scalar function of position φ.

7. Get a formula for **curl** **V** for a fluid rotating in circles in the xy plane about the z axis at an angular speed $\omega = k/r^2$, where k is a constant.

15.6. Stokes' Theorem. For a very small element of area Δa and of normal **N** one may write approximately, according to (15.23) and (15.16),

$$\Delta c_N = \mathbf{N} \cdot (\mathbf{curl\ V})\Delta a. \tag{15.29}$$

When two such small elements are adjacent, as in Fig. 15.14, it is apparent that the sum of the two circulations c_1 and c_2 is equal to the circulation c about the periphery of the combined area, since a cancellation occurs on the common boundary: $c = c_1 + c_2$. For any larger area, as in Fig. 15.15, the circulation around the boundary is equal to the sum of the circulations around all the elements, however small, into which the area may be divided,

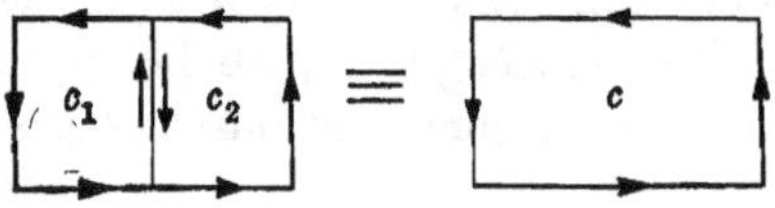

FIG. 15.14.

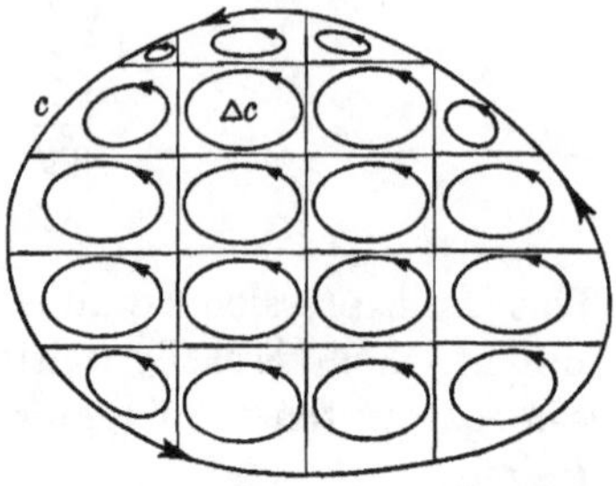

FIG. 15.15.

$$c = \Sigma \Delta c.$$

Let any simply connected (*i.e.*, no holes) surface bounded by the simple curve in Fig. 15.16 be divided into very small elements Δa. Thus (15.29) applies for each such element. Adding these equations, we get

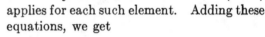

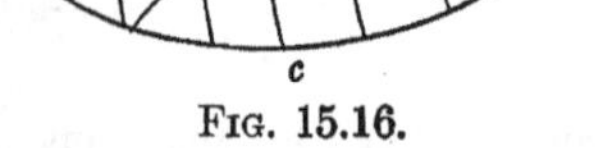

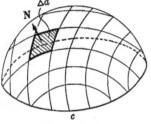

FIG. 15.16.

$$c = \Sigma \mathbf{N} \cdot (\mathbf{curl\ V})\Delta a. \tag{15.30}$$

Taking the limit as Δa gets smaller and smaller, the left member remains constant, but the right member normally approaches a limit. Writing c in the form of (15.14), we have

$$\oint \mathbf{V} \cdot d\mathbf{R} = \int_a \mathbf{N} \cdot \nabla \times \mathbf{V}\, da. \tag{15.31}$$

In words:

(15.32) *The circulation around a simple curve is equal to the area integral over any simply connected surface bounded by the curve of the normal component of the curl of the velocity.* This is a form of Stokes' theorem.

Example. Let us use Stokes' theorem to determine how a fluid in a circular conveyor must travel to have a zero curl. Assume that the velocity is always transverse (normal to radius) and constant for a given radius. Suppose that the speed is v_1 for $r = r_1$ and v_2 for $r = r_2$. Then the circulation around the closed path shown in Fig. 15.17 is

$$c = -v_1r_1\theta + 0 + v_2r_2\theta + 0 = (v_2r_2 - v_1r_1)\theta.$$

If **curl V** is zero throughout, the condition on the speeds is

$$v_2r_2 = v_1r_1 \qquad \text{or} \qquad v_2 = v_1\left(\frac{r_1}{r_2}\right),$$

that is, the speed varies inversely as the radius. This conclusion may be compared with the result of Exercise 7 of the preceding section.

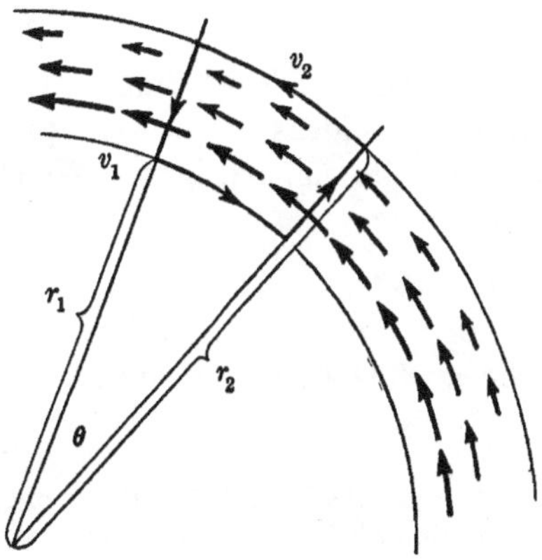

FIG. 15.17.

This important theorem assists us in arriving at a very useful conclusion. We have seen that a force field $\mathbf{F}(\mathbf{R})$ is conservative if and only if it is possible to express $\mathbf{F}$ as equal to the gradient of a scalar function φ. Similarly, a velocity field $\mathbf{V}(\mathbf{R})$ is irrotational if a corresponding function may be found. But can one tell by looking at an analytic expression of $\mathbf{F}(\mathbf{R})$ or $\mathbf{V}(\mathbf{R})$ whether there is such a φ? Clearly, a more direct test is desirable. We shall demonstrate that (for a simply connected region and suitably smooth functions),

(15.33) *A vector function of position* $\mathbf{F}(\mathbf{R})$ *can be expressed as the gradient of a scalar function* $\varphi(\mathbf{R})$ *if and only if* **curl F** = **O** *at every point.*

First suppose that $\mathbf{F}(\mathbf{R})$ can be written as $\nabla\varphi$. Then

$$\textbf{curl F} = \begin{vmatrix} \dfrac{\partial}{\partial x} & \dfrac{\partial}{\partial y} & \dfrac{\partial}{\partial z} \\ \dfrac{\partial\varphi}{\partial x} & \dfrac{\partial\varphi}{\partial y} & \dfrac{\partial\varphi}{\partial z} \\ \mathbf{I} & \mathbf{J} & \mathbf{K} \end{vmatrix}$$

$$= \mathbf{I}\left(\frac{\partial^2\varphi}{\partial y\,\partial z} - \frac{\partial^2\varphi}{\partial z\,\partial y}\right) + \mathbf{J}\left(\frac{\partial^2\varphi}{\partial z\,\partial x} - \frac{\partial^2\varphi}{\partial x\,\partial z}\right) + \mathbf{K}\left(\frac{\partial^2\varphi}{\partial x\,\partial y} - \frac{\partial^2\varphi}{\partial y\,\partial x}\right).$$

If these second-order partial derivatives are continuous, as we assume, each expression in parentheses vanishes; thus

$$\textbf{curl F} = \mathbf{O}.$$

Suppose on the other hand that **curl F** = **O** everywhere. Then let us take a closed path and evaluate the circulation of **F** around this path. By Stokes' theorem

$$\oint \mathbf{F}\cdot d\mathbf{R} = \int_a \mathbf{N}\cdot \textbf{curl F}\, da,$$

for some surface bounded by the closed path. But if **curl F** is zero everywhere, we get

$$\oint \mathbf{F} \cdot d\mathbf{R} = 0.$$

We have considered simple curves only. For a simply connected region, the same ideas are easily applied to less simple curves, although the details are omitted here. We shall conclude then that **F** is conservative and hence

$$\mathbf{F} = \nabla \varphi.$$

In the remaining sections we shall be concerned only with irrotational flow. Thus vortices will not be considered.

EXERCISES

1. Show that **curl V** $= \mathbf{O}$ if and only if **V** is irrotational.

2. Show briefly that any irrotational velocity field can be expressed as the gradient of a scalar "velocity potential."

3. Determine which of the following velocity fields are irrotational:

(*a*) $\mathbf{V} = (2 - 2y - z)\mathbf{I} + (2 + 2x - z)\mathbf{J} + (x + y)\mathbf{K}$.

(*b*) $\mathbf{V} = (x^2 - 4)\mathbf{I} + 4y\mathbf{J} - (z^2 + z)\mathbf{K}$.

(*c*) $\mathbf{V} = (yz^2 + 2yzx + zy^2)\mathbf{I} + (zx^2 + 2zxy + xz^2)\mathbf{J} + (xy^2 + 2xyz + yx^2)\mathbf{K}$.

15.7. The Notion of Divergence. For a velocity field, the volume of fluid crossing a boundary area per second is called the *flux*. For an element of area Δa of normal **N**, the flux is (see Fig. 15.18)

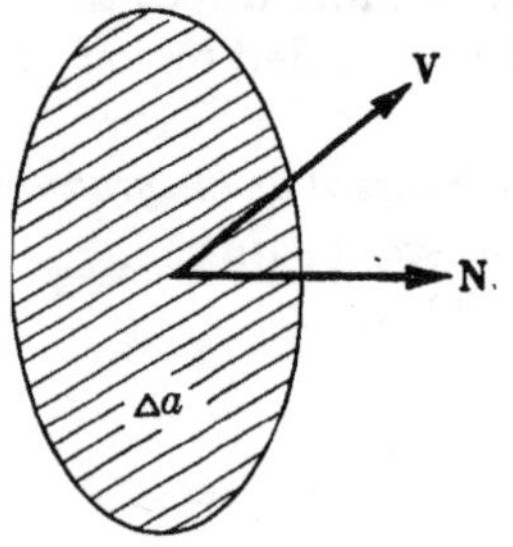

FIG. 15.18.

(15.34) $$\Delta(\text{flux}) = \mathbf{N} \cdot \mathbf{V}\, \Delta a,$$

and for an extended area it is given by

(15.35) $$\text{Flux} = \int_a \mathbf{N} \cdot \mathbf{V}\, da.$$

In the special case of a plane boundary of normal **I**, the flux is

(15.36) $$\text{Flux} = (\mathbf{I} \cdot \bar{\mathbf{V}})a = \bar{v}_x a,$$

where $\bar{\mathbf{V}}$ and $\bar{v}_x$ indicate average values for the surface. If the velocity is uniform across this surface, no averaging is necessary.

Now consider a small boxlike element of volume $\Delta x\, \Delta y\, \Delta z$. Let **V** be the velocity at the center of the box. As usual, we estimate the average velocity across the various faces by using formula (13.1). The net outward flux across faces perpendicular to **I** is then

$$\left(v_x + \frac{\partial v_x}{\partial x}\frac{\Delta x}{2}\right) \Delta y\, \Delta z - \left(v_x - \frac{\partial v_x}{\partial x}\frac{\Delta x}{2}\right) \Delta y\, \Delta z,$$

or

$$\frac{\partial v_x}{\partial x}\, \Delta x\, \Delta y\, \Delta z.$$

Similar terms describe the net efflux in the y and z directions. Adding these three, dividing by the volume of the box, and taking the limit as the size of the box shrinks, we get an expression for the *net outward flux per volume* which is given the name *divergence of the velocity*. It is written div **V**.

$$\text{div } \mathbf{V} = \frac{\partial v_x}{\partial x} + \frac{\partial v_y}{\partial y} + \frac{\partial v_z}{\partial z}. \tag{15.37}$$

It is interesting that this formula can be given a symbolic representation in terms of the operator ∇:

$$\nabla \cdot \mathbf{V} = \left(\mathbf{I}\frac{\partial}{\partial x} + \mathbf{J}\frac{\partial}{\partial y} + \mathbf{K}\frac{\partial}{\partial z}\right) \cdot (v_x\mathbf{I} + v_y\mathbf{J} + v_z\mathbf{K})$$

or

$$\nabla \cdot \mathbf{V} = \text{div } \mathbf{V}. \tag{15.38}$$

For an incompressible fluid, a point of positive divergence is a *source* (such as the end of a nozzle). Correspondingly (see Fig. 15.19), a point of negative divergence is a *sink* or negative source. For steady flow, similar conclusions can be drawn about any reasonable fluid.

Example. Find div $\dfrac{\mathbf{R}}{\mathbf{R} \cdot \mathbf{R}}$.

FIG. 15.19.

SOLUTION

$$\frac{\mathbf{R}}{\mathbf{R} \cdot \mathbf{R}} = \frac{x}{r^2}\mathbf{I} + \frac{y}{r^2}\mathbf{J} + \frac{z}{r^2}\mathbf{K},$$

where

$$r^2 = x^2 + y^2 + z^2$$

$$\text{div } \frac{\mathbf{R}}{\mathbf{R} \cdot \mathbf{R}} = \frac{x^2 + y^2 + z^2 - 2x^2}{r^4} + \frac{x^2 + y^2 + z^2 - 2y^2}{r^4} + \frac{x^2 + y^2 + z^2 - 2z^2}{r^4} = \frac{1}{r^2}.$$

The Equation of Continuity. The rate at which *mass* streams across an element of area da in a moving fluid is

$$\delta \mathbf{N} \cdot \mathbf{V}\, da.$$

The vector **V** in the definition of flux has been replaced by $\delta\mathbf{V}$. Hence the net outward flow of mass per volume at a point is

$$\nabla \cdot \delta \mathbf{V}.$$

But this is precisely the rate at which the density is decreasing (*if there are no sources or sinks)*; so

$$\nabla \cdot \delta \mathbf{V} = -\frac{\partial \delta}{\partial t},$$

or

$$\frac{\partial \delta}{\partial t} + \nabla \cdot \delta \mathbf{V} = 0. \tag{15.39}$$

This is one of the fundamental results of hydrodynamics. It is known as the *equation of continuity*. For an incompressible fluid (δ constant) this gives

$$\nabla \cdot \mathbf{V} = 0. \tag{15.40}$$

That is, for any fluid where there are no sources or sinks mass is conserved; while for an incompressible fluid, volume also is conserved. To get a mental picture of the two equations of continuity, visualize a football being inflated (*a*) with air and (*b*) with water. In the first case (see Fig. 15.20), the air slows up as it passes through a tube to the ball: more enters the tube than leaves it since the pressure and hence the density increase. Here the divergence of the velocity pattern is positive. In the second case, the density cannot change appreciably: as much water leaves the tube as enters it. Here the divergence is zero.

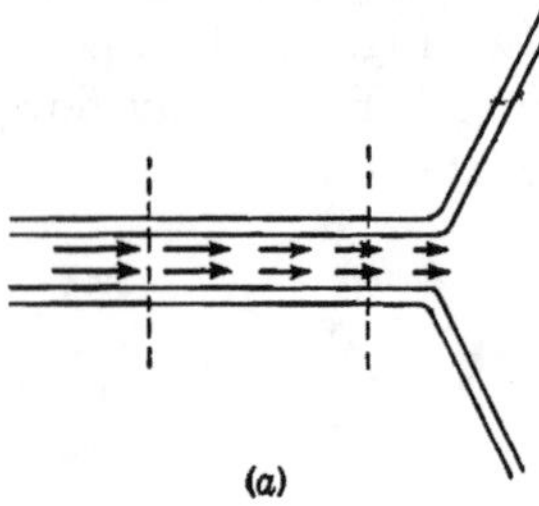
(a)

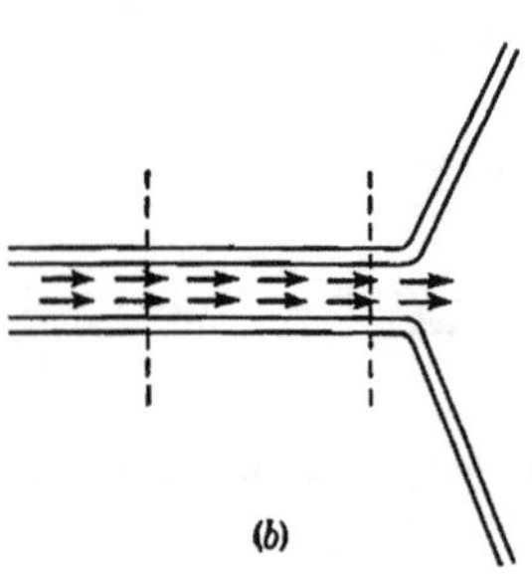
(b)

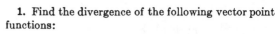

FIG. 15.20.

EXERCISES

1. Find the divergence of the following vector point functions:

(*a*) $x\mathbf{I}$. (*b*) $\mathbf{R}$.
(*c*) $\mathbf{L}$. (*d*) **grad** xy^2z^3.
(*e*) **grad** $1/r$.

2. $\mathbf{V}(x,y,z)$ is a vector point function. $f(x,y,z)$ is a scalar point function. Show that

$$\nabla \cdot (f\mathbf{V}) = f\nabla \cdot \mathbf{V} + \mathbf{V} \cdot \nabla f.$$

3. Show that the velocity potential ψ of an irrotational velocity field $\mathbf{V}$ where $\nabla \cdot \mathbf{V}$ is zero satisfies the equation

$$\frac{\partial^2 \psi}{\partial x^2} + \frac{\partial^2 \psi}{\partial y^2} + \frac{\partial^2 \psi}{\partial z^2} = 0.$$

(This is *Laplace's equation.*)

4. Show that div **curl** $\mathbf{V} = 0$ for any $\mathbf{V}$.

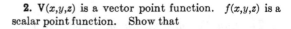

5. Evaluate (*a*) $\nabla \cdot r^n\mathbf{R}$, where $r = |\mathbf{R}|$; (*b*) $\nabla \cdot \mathbf{A} \times \mathbf{R}$ for a constant $\mathbf{A}$.

15.8. The Divergence Theorem. Consider within a fluid a surface (see Fig. 15.21) enclosing a volume having inside it sinks and sources. If we note that

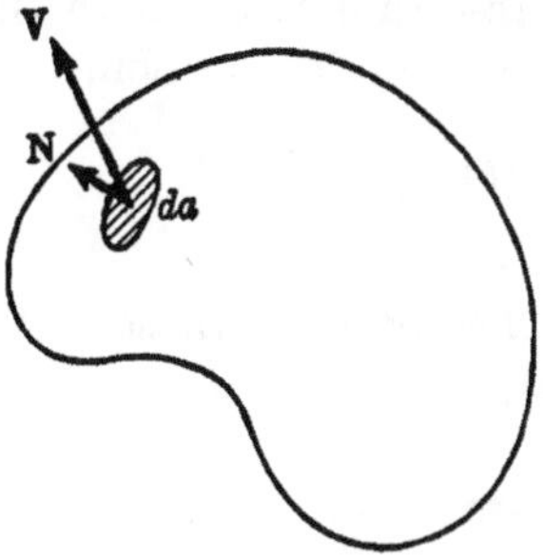

FIG. 15.21.

$$(15.41)\quad \nabla \cdot \mathbf{V} = \mathbf{I} \cdot \nabla v_x + \mathbf{J} \cdot \nabla v_y + \mathbf{K} \cdot \nabla v_z,$$

we may apply the gradient theorem as follows (b denotes volume to avoid confusion with the use of v for speed):

$$\begin{aligned}\int_b \nabla \cdot \mathbf{V}\, db &= \mathbf{I} \cdot \int_b \nabla v_x\, db + \mathbf{J} \cdot \int_b \nabla v_y\, db + \mathbf{K} \cdot \int_b \nabla v_z\, db \\ &= \mathbf{I} \cdot \int_a \mathbf{N} v_x\, da + \mathbf{J} \cdot \int_a \mathbf{N} v_y\, da + \mathbf{K} \cdot \int_a \mathbf{N} v_z\, da\end{aligned}$$

or, finally,

$$(15.42)\quad \int_b \nabla \cdot \mathbf{V}\, db = \int_a \mathbf{N} \cdot \mathbf{V}\, da.$$

This is the *divergence theorem.* This, like the gradient theorem, enables us to go from local information to surface information, and vice versa.

EXERCISES

1. Derive (15.41).

2. Consider an incompressible nonviscous fluid flowing steadily in a pipe of variable cross section as in Fig. 15.22. There are no sinks or sources. For two normal cross sections of areas a_1 and a_2, prove that

FIG. 15.22.

$$\frac{v_1}{v_2} = \frac{a_2}{a_1},$$

using the equation of continuity and the divergence theorem. This result is often called the *equation of continuity* in elementary courses. State any additional assumptions which you make.

3. A region has surface a and unit outward normal $\mathbf{N}$ (see Fig. 15.23). Prove that its volume is

$$\tfrac{1}{3} \int_a \mathbf{R} \cdot \mathbf{N}\, da.$$

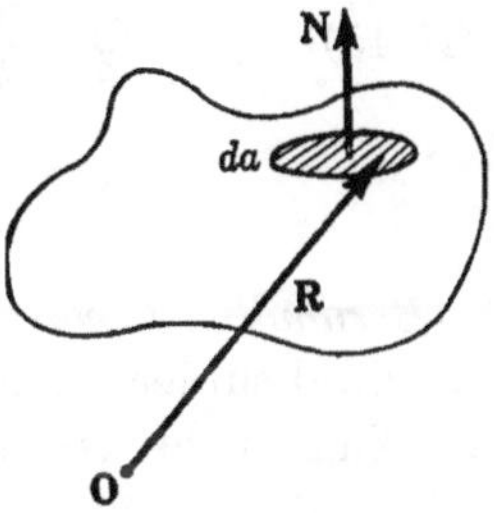

FIG. 15.23.

4. Write an expression for $\nabla \times \mathbf{V}$ analogous to (15.41). Use this to construct a proof of the *curl theorem:*

$$\int_b \nabla \times \mathbf{V}\, db = \int_a \mathbf{N} \times \mathbf{V}\, da.$$

15.9. The Equations of Euler. In our discussion of hydrostatics, we had the resultant of forces per mass set equal to zero as a condition for equilibrium. In the more general case, this resultant is equal to the acceleration experienced by a particle at the position in question.

$$\mathfrak{F} - \frac{1}{\delta}\nabla p = \mathbf{A}. \tag{15.43}$$

The particle whose motion is examined traces out a path

$$\mathbf{R} = \mathbf{R}(t).$$

Its velocity is

$$\mathbf{V} = \mathbf{V}(\mathbf{R},t),$$

where $\mathbf{R}$ satisfies the preceding equation. The acceleration is

$$\mathbf{A} = \frac{d\mathbf{V}}{dt} = \frac{\partial \mathbf{V}}{\partial s}\frac{ds}{dt} + \frac{\partial \mathbf{V}}{\partial t} = v\frac{\partial \mathbf{V}}{\partial s} + \frac{\partial \mathbf{V}}{\partial t}.$$

Note that two types of velocity change are involved:

1. The change due to variations in the field at each fixed point $\partial\mathbf{V}/\partial t$.
2. The change due to variations in the field along the path, *i.e.*, the directional derivative:

$$\frac{\partial \mathbf{V}}{\partial s} = (\mathbf{T}\cdot\nabla)\mathbf{V}.$$

Since $v\mathbf{T} = \mathbf{V}$, we have finally

$$\mathfrak{F} - \frac{1}{\delta}\nabla p = \mathbf{A} = \frac{\partial \mathbf{V}}{\partial t} + (\mathbf{V}\cdot\nabla)\mathbf{V}. \tag{15.44}$$

This is *Euler's equation of motion.* This is equivalent to the following three scalar equations:

$$\begin{aligned} f_x - \frac{1}{\delta}\frac{\partial p}{\partial x} &= \frac{\partial v_x}{\partial t} + v_x\frac{\partial v_x}{\partial x} + v_y\frac{\partial v_x}{\partial y} + v_z\frac{\partial v_x}{\partial z}, \\ f_y - \frac{1}{\delta}\frac{\partial p}{\partial y} &= \frac{\partial v_y}{\partial t} + v_x\frac{\partial v_y}{\partial x} + v_y\frac{\partial v_y}{\partial y} + v_z\frac{\partial v_y}{\partial z}, \\ f_z - \frac{1}{\delta}\frac{\partial p}{\partial z} &= \frac{\partial v_z}{\partial t} + v_x\frac{\partial v_z}{\partial x} + v_y\frac{\partial v_z}{\partial y} + v_z\frac{\partial v_z}{\partial z}. \end{aligned} \tag{15.45}$$

Bernoulli's Theorem. We shall consider steady flow of an incompressible fluid subject to gravity. Several of these limitations have a precise bearing on the use of Euler's equation.

Steady:

$$\frac{\partial \mathbf{V}}{\partial t} = 0.$$

Incompressible:

$$\delta \text{ is a constant so that } \frac{1}{\delta}\nabla p = \nabla \frac{p}{\delta}.$$

Gravity:

$$\mathfrak{F} = -g\mathbf{J} = -\nabla gy.$$

Euler's equation now may be written

$$(\mathbf{V}\cdot\nabla)\mathbf{V} + \nabla gy + \nabla\frac{p}{\delta} = \mathbf{O}.$$

Recall now that

$$(\mathbf{V}\cdot\nabla)\mathbf{V} = v\frac{d\mathbf{V}}{ds},$$

where ds is in the direction of $\mathbf{V}$; consequently,

$$\mathbf{T}\cdot(\mathbf{V}\cdot\nabla)\mathbf{V} = \mathbf{T}\cdot\left(v\frac{d\mathbf{V}}{ds}\right) = \mathbf{V}\cdot\frac{d\mathbf{V}}{ds} = \frac{1}{2}\frac{d}{ds}(\mathbf{V}\cdot\mathbf{V}).$$

Recall also that for a scalar point function φ (such as gy or p/δ),

$$\mathbf{T}\cdot\nabla\varphi = \frac{d\varphi}{ds}$$

(that is, the directional derivative of φ).

Let us now multiply our modified form of Euler's equation by $\mathbf{T}$. The result

$$\mathbf{T}\cdot(\mathbf{V}\cdot\nabla)\mathbf{V} + \mathbf{T}\cdot\nabla gy + \mathbf{T}\cdot\nabla\frac{p}{\delta} = 0$$

means

(15.46) $$\frac{d}{ds}\left(\frac{1}{2}v^2 + gy + \frac{p}{\delta}\right) = 0.$$

Therefore

$$\frac{1}{2}v^2 + gy + \frac{p}{\delta}$$

is a constant along the curve determined by $\mathbf{T}$, that is, *along a streamline.* For irrotational fields, this constant is independent of the particular streamline.

EXERCISES

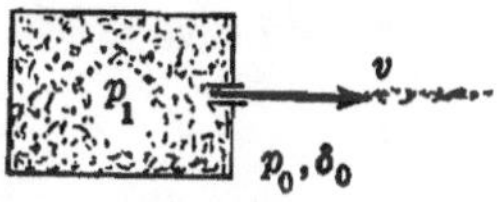

FIG. 15.24.

1. Gas under pressure (p_1) escapes from a container (see Fig. 15.24) through a small aperture in a steady stream of speed v. At atmospheric pressure (p_0) the density of the gas is δ_0. Assume that temperature is constant throughout, that the weight of the gas is negligible, and that the motion of flow is essentially all in one direction. Find v.

2. What is the velocity of efflux (see Fig. 15.25) of an incompressible ideal fluid from a small opening at the bottom of a very large tank of depth h (*Torricelli's theorem*)?

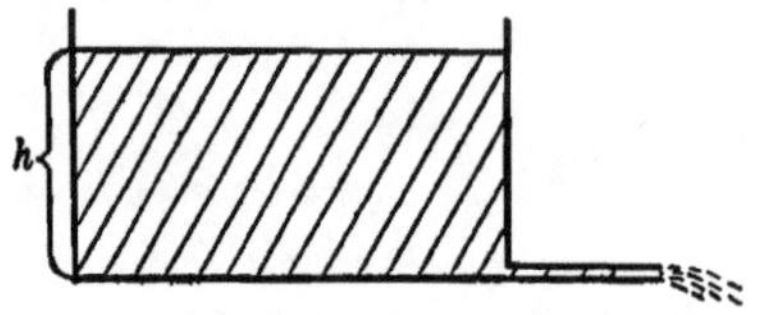

FIG. 15.25.

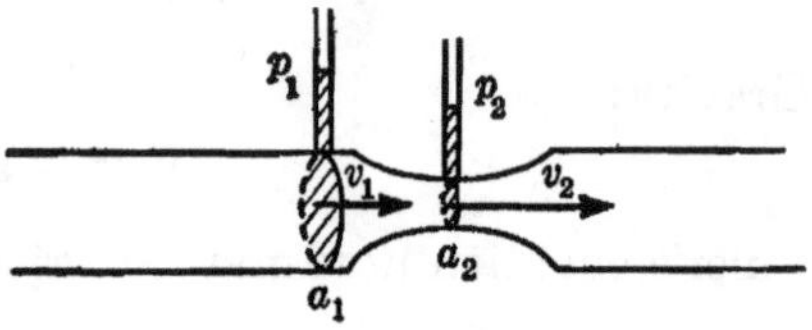

FIG. 15.26.

3. In the *Venturi flowmeter* (see Fig. 15.26) the pressure variation in a constricted pipe is used to measure flux of a liquid. Show that the flux is given by

$$\text{Flux} = a_1 \sqrt{\frac{2(p_1 - p_2)}{\left[\left(\frac{a_1}{a_2}\right)^2 - 1\right]\delta}}.$$

4. Consider, as in Fig. 15.6, a cylindrical volume of liquid rotating in steady state about a vertical axis.

(*a*) Use Euler's equation (see Exercise 1, Sec. 15.4) to show that

$$\nabla p = \delta\omega^2 x\mathbf{I} - \delta g\mathbf{J} + \delta\omega^2 z\mathbf{K}.$$

(*b*) Compute $\nabla p \cdot d\mathbf{R} = dp$, and integrate, evaluating the constant of integration for the center point on the free surface of the fluid.

(*c*) What is an equation for the free surface?

CHAPTER 16

WAVE MOTION IN ONE DIMENSION

The preceding chapter gave an introduction to one important branch of the dynamics of deformable bodies. The emphasis was on actual flow of material from one position to another. In this chapter another important branch will be introduced. The motions investigated will involve the flow of energy from one place to another. The energy will be transmitted mechanically, but no material will move from the source to the destination. These two phases of deformation dynamics have an analogy in the field of electricity. When there is electric current in a wire, we say that electric charge actually flows along it. But when a radio signal is picked up with an antenna, we do not pretend that a charge carried the signal from the transmitter. The analogy must not be carried too far, for in the electrical case no mechanism for energy transmission is apparent: a vacuum will do. In our present study the elastic mechanism is to be very much in evidence; therefore a medium is necessary.

16.1. The Nature of Wave Motion. The transmission of energy without an actual transfer of material is accomplished in a way that is easily visualized. Imagine a hundred people lined up in single file with Mr. A at one end and Mr. B at the other. If Mr. A has a note for Mr. B, he may get out of line and carry it to him. That epitomizes the subject matter of the last chapter. Or the note may be passed from person to person down the line until B receives it. The note has been delivered, but the carriers are still in their original positions. This epitomizes the sort of transmission to be studied in the present chapter. Suppose, for example, that one part of an elastic body is subjected to a deforming force and is then released. The deforming force creates strains with their corresponding stresses. Upon removal of this applied force, the stresses institute a motion. Each moving portion acquires momentum and in being halted imparts a shove to its neighbor, setting it in motion. In this way motion is transmitted elastically throughout the body. This is an example of *wave motion*. Mechanical wave motion may be characterized as a traveling disturbance in a medium without any net displacement of the medium. The word "disturbance" is used in a very broad sense: it might for example be a displacement, a change in pressure, a change in tension, a change in angular orientation.

We have seen in our discussions of springs and pendulums that when restoring forces are proportional to displacements they tend to cause simple harmonic oscillations. It is not surprising then that in studying elastic transmission of energy subject to Hooke's law we shall give particular attention to periodic or repetitive disturbances. When a note is sounded on a whistle, a periodic compressional pattern travels out in all directions. This is a periodic sound wave. If the end of a steel rail is struck by a hammer, a longitudinal elastic wave travels along it. This too is a sound wave although not periodic. If a long, taut string is struck normally near the middle, transverse kinks may be seen traveling in both directions. This too is wave motion. Classical physics abounds in such examples, and in modern physics wavelike aspects of observable phenomena motivate the use of a mathematical model closely akin to the mathematics of wave motion as we shall study it in this chapter.

16.2. Simple Harmonic Waves. Among mechanical periodic waves the most important are the ones for which the disturbance at any one point is a simple harmonic oscillation. Such a wave is a *simple harmonic wave.* There are other instances. In fact, any disturbance which can be described as sinusoidal and which is propagated as a wave may be regarded as a simple harmonic wave. By means of Fourier analysis any periodic wave may be regarded as an aggregate of simple harmonic waves superimposed. These ideas may even be extended to a harmonic analysis of nonperiodic waves.

In this section we shall review some of the properties of periodic waves by looking closely at equations for simple harmonic waves. Suppose that the disturbance at the source is measured by y_0. y_0 might be a transverse or a longitudinal displacement, an increment in pressure or tension, or any other such disturbance. We assume that y_0 is simple harmonic and can be represented thus:

$$y_0 = y_m \sin \omega t. \tag{16.1}$$

Let us assume that this disturbance travels parallel to the x axis at speed c. Then, if the source is at the origin, the disturbance y at a point with coordinate x is at a given moment exactly the same as the disturbance at the origin x/c sec earlier.

$$y = y_m \sin \omega \left(t - \frac{x}{c}\right). \tag{16.2}$$

Equation (16.1) is then the special case of (16.2) for $x = 0$.

For a random position x and time t, y is determined by (16.2). y is thus a function of the two variables x and t. Suppose we select a particular instant, say $t = 7.8$ sec. Then the equation is

$$y = y_m \sin \omega \left(7.8 - \frac{x}{c}\right), \tag{16.3}$$

which is merely a sine curve showing the *wave profile* in the position corresponding to that particular moment. Figure 16.1 is a graph of this

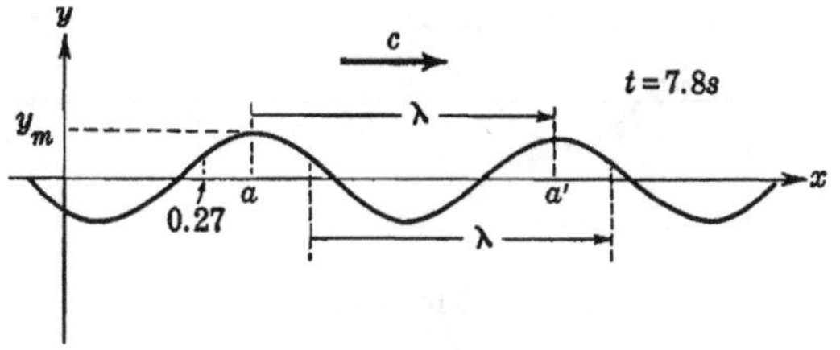

FIG. 16.1.

wave profile. There are regularly spaced points such as a and a' on the x axis for which the disturbance is maximum. Their separation λ is called the *wavelength* of the wave. Actually *any* two points separated by a distance λ have at any one moment equal disturbances. As we have seen in setting up Eq. (16.2), the wave profile moves in the positive x direction at speed c. Since c is the rate at which a peak or a zero or any other particular phase of the oscillation appears to move, it is called the *phase velocity*. By analyzing (16.3) it is easy to show that

$$\frac{\lambda}{c} = \frac{2\pi}{\omega} = \tau. \tag{16.4}$$

As in Sec. 5.9, τ is called the *period* of the oscillation given by (16.1). The reciprocal of τ is the *frequency* ν; thus we may write

$$\lambda\nu = c. \tag{16.5}$$

This is one of the most important equations of wave physics. The reciprocal of λ is the *wave number* k; so

$$\nu = ck. \tag{16.6}$$

Now let us select a point, say $x = 0.27$ m, on the x axis. The wave equation becomes

$$y = y_m \sin \omega \left(t - \frac{0.27}{c}\right). \tag{16.7}$$

This is merely the equation of an oscillation like that of the source having period $2\pi/\omega$. It is out of phase with the source unless $0.27/c$ happens to be an integral number of periods. A graph of the oscillation at $x = 0.27$ would be like Fig. 16.2.

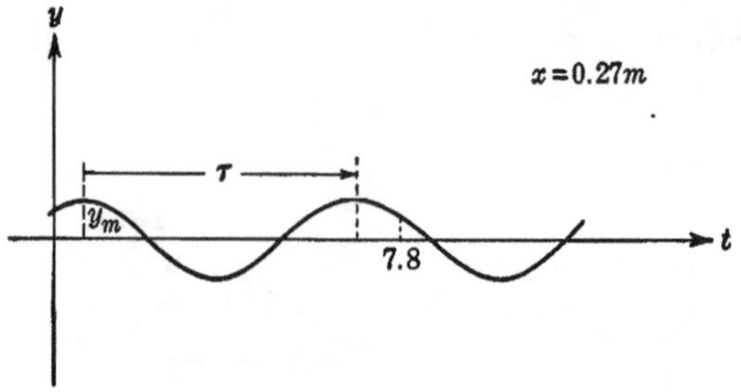

FIG. 16.2.

We have seen then that a uniform simple harmonic wave has a dual aspect. *At each point* the disturbance is simple harmonic, the period being the same for all points. Neighboring points have oscillations out of phase. Points a wavelength apart have oscillations in phase. *At each moment* the sinusoidal pattern of disturbance or wave profile may be observed. This pattern moves at a certain phase velocity, but the net displacement of the oscillating substance is zero.

Two more symmetric forms of (16.2) are often used. The first is obtained by substituting $2\pi/\tau$ for ω.

$$y = y_m \sin 2\pi \left(\frac{t}{\tau} - \frac{x}{\lambda}\right), \tag{16.8}$$

$$y = y_m \sin 2\pi(\nu t - kx). \tag{16.9}$$

EXERCISES

1. Derive (16.4) from (16.3).
2. Derive (16.9) from (16.2).
3. Rewrite (16.2) in terms of ν and c.
4. Plot $y = 10 \sin 2\pi(4{,}000t - 4x)$ as a function of x for $t = 12.5, 25.0, 37.5, 50.0, 62.5$ μsec. Use a single set of axes so that the progressive nature of the wave will be evident. (The prefix *micro-* is equivalent to a factor of 10^{-6}.)
5. Plot $y = 10 \sin 2\pi(4{,}000t - 4x)$ as a function of t for $x = 0.00, 0.05, 0.10$ ft.

16.3. Doppler Effect. One interesting property of mechanical periodic waves may be studied as an application of Eq. (16.5) and of the kinematics of relative motion. It is well known that the observed pitch of a whistle varies with the relative velocity of the source and the observer. Here we shall consider motion along the x axis. Let us assume that the x axis is fixed in the medium and that the source and observer have velocities along the x axis denoted by v_s and v_o. These may be either positive or negative or zero. The frequency of the signal emitted by the source is ν, and the observer experiences a frequency ν'.

There are two quite distinct aspects of this problem. The source causes waves of length λ to be set up in the medium. If v_s is positive, the wave leaves the source at a slower relative speed and the wavelength, according to (16.5), is shorter. When v_s is negative, the relative speed is greater, and the wave is stretched out. In either case

$$\lambda\nu = c - v_s,$$

or

$$\lambda = \frac{c - v_s}{\nu}. \tag{16.10}$$

This part of the deduction concerns only the source. Nothing has been said about the observer.

Now let us consider the frequency ν' experienced by the observer. ν' is merely the rate at which peaks in the waves already set up are encountered by the observer. If v_o is positive, the waves overtake the observer with a smaller relative speed. If v_o is negative, he is rushing to meet the oncoming waves. In either case (16.5) applies:

$$\nu' = \frac{c - v_o}{\lambda}. \tag{16.11}$$

This part of the argument has nothing to do with the source: given the wave train of wavelength λ moving at speed c in the medium, then the observed frequency ν' depends only on the speed of the observer relative to the medium.

Equations (16.10) and (16.11) may be combined to get a formula relating ν' and ν:

$$\nu' = \nu\left(\frac{c - v_o}{c - v_s}\right). \tag{16.12}$$

EXERCISES

1. A train going north at 60 mph whistles at a southbound train approaching at 90 mph. If the true frequency of the whistle is 350 per sec, what is the observed frequency on the second train? (Take c as 1,100 ft/sec.)

2. If c is much larger than both v_o and v_s and if the medium is stationary, show that the Doppler formula may be written

$$\nu' = \nu\left(1 - \frac{v'}{c}\right),$$

where v' is the velocity of the observer relative to the source.

3. A steamship heads south at 10 mph. The wind, from the south, is 30 mph. A motorboat sails north toward the steamer at 20 mph. The steamer blows a whistle of frequency 150 cycles/sec. What frequency is observed at the motorboat? (Take c as 1,100 ft/sec.)

16.4. Vibration of a Tense String. Suppose that a long, light, flexible string is held taut with a tension f. If a portion of the string is suddenly deflected slightly and released, a wave travels along the string. This phenomenon is very familiar, although of course a string used in an experiment would not be ideally light or perfectly flexible. Let us isolate a portion of the string at a given moment and see what dynamical conclusions may be reached. Let q denote the linear density, m/l, of the string. Refer now to Fig. 16.3. The angle between the deflected string and its equilibrium direction is θ. This is assumed to be small. We shall isolate the portion of the string between x and $x + \Delta x$. Since the string is flexible, no torque is transmitted to the isolated portion. Since the string is light, the tensions f of the two ends are the only forces. We shall apply the dynamics equation for y components:

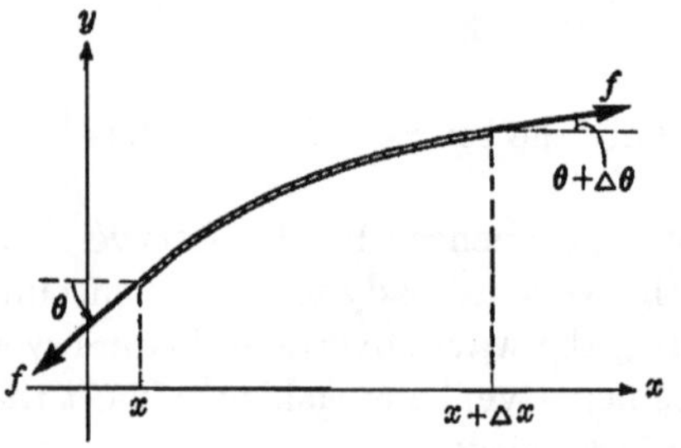

FIG. 16.3.

$$\sum f_y = m \frac{d^2y}{dt^2}.$$

The derivative will be a partial derivative here, since y varies with x as well as t. We shall call the mass $q\,\Delta x$, but it should be realized that some small approximation is involved: once the string is deflected, the distribution of mass along the x axis is no longer uniform. We get

$$-f \sin \theta + f \sin (\theta + \Delta\theta) = (q\,\Delta x) \frac{\partial^2 y}{\partial t^2}$$

or

$$\frac{f\,\Delta(\sin \theta)}{\Delta x} = q \frac{\partial^2 y}{\partial t^2}.$$

Since θ is small, we shall make the approximation

$$\sin \theta = \theta = \tan \theta = \frac{\partial y}{\partial x}.$$

Then taking the limit as Δx approaches zero, we get this condition for wave motion along such a string

$$f \frac{\partial^2 y}{\partial x^2} = q \frac{\partial^2 y}{\partial t^2}. \tag{16.13}$$

Equation (16.13) is an example of an extremely important differential equation. It can be satisfied only by equations of wave profiles traveling in either direction along the x axis. From what we know of kinks on taut strings, this assertion is hardly surprising. In courses on differential equations a demonstration is usually given. Most students using this book will not have had such a course; therefore we shall give a brief statement of results here. The general solution of the *differential equation of wave motion parallel to the x axis*

$$\frac{\partial^2 y}{\partial x^2} = \frac{1}{c^2} \frac{\partial^2 y}{\partial t^2} \tag{16.14}$$

has the form

$$y = y_1(x - ct) + y_2(x + ct), \tag{16.15}$$

where y_1 is any wave profile traveling in the positive x direction and y_2 is any wave profile traveling in the negative x direction, the speed of propagation being c. Our simple harmonic wave of Sec. 16.2 can be written in this form:

$$y = -y_m \sin \frac{\omega}{c} (x - ct).$$

A comparison of the general equation (16.14) with the special result for a string (16.13) gives us an important formula for the speed of a transverse wave along a string:

$$c = \sqrt{\frac{f}{q}}. \tag{16.16}$$

In the introductory paragraphs on waves the concept of energy played a conspicuous role. Now that we have the theory of one type of wave to scrutinize, let us evaluate the energy. First, let us see what potential energy is involved in taking the string, under tension, from the equilibrium position to a displaced position. The only forces which can do work are tensions (assumed uniform) along the string. The potential energy then is equal to this tension times the increase in length of the string. In computing, we shall avoid the complication of lateral displacements during stretching (that is, the problem of nonuniform x density already mentioned) by isolating either a long piece of the string or, to include a fair sample of all aspects of the phenomenon, for simple harmonic waves an integral number of quarter-wavelengths. Let x range from 0 to l for the portion isolated. Then

$$\text{p.e.} = f \int_0^l (ds - dx),$$

where ds is the arc length corresponding to dx. Now

$$ds = \sqrt{1 + \left(\frac{dy}{dx}\right)^2}\, dx.$$

But for sufficiently small smooth displacements, the square of the derivative is very small; therefore we shall substitute an *approximate* value based on the binomial theorem.

$$\sqrt{1 + \left(\frac{dy}{dx}\right)^2} = 1 + \frac{1}{2}\left(\frac{dy}{dx}\right)^2.$$

Our conclusion is, using partial derivatives since here y is a function of both t and x,

$$\text{p.e.} = \frac{1}{2} f \int_0^l \left(\frac{\partial y}{\partial x}\right)^2 dx. \tag{16.17}$$

A similar sample of the string has kinetic energy which can readily be expressed. For an element corresponding to dx, the mass is approximately $q\,dx$ and the kinetic energy $\frac{1}{2} q\,dx \left(\frac{\partial y}{\partial t}\right)^2$. This ignores the slight energy of lateral displacement. Integrating

$$\text{k.e.} = \frac{1}{2} q \int_0^l \left(\frac{\partial y}{\partial t}\right)^2 dx. \tag{16.18}$$

It is left as an exercise to use (16.16) in proving that for a wave going in one direction on a string these two expressions for energies are equal.

EXERCISES

1. Show by direct substitution that Eq. (16.9) satisfies the wave equation (16.14).

2. How long will it take a transverse wave to travel the length of a string 3 m long, of radius 2 mm, weighing 300 g, and subjected to a tension of 10 newtons?

3. If $y_1 = y_1(x,t)$ and $y_2 = y_2(x,t)$ are solutions of (16.14) and if a_1 and a_2 are constants, show that the following also is a solution:

$$y = a_1 y_1 + a_2 y_2.$$

4. Check Eq. (16.16) dimensionally.

5. Verify that for a wave on a string given by $y = y(x - ct)$ the kinetic energy and potential energy are equal.

6. Use Eq. (16.9) to verify that for a simple harmonic wave on a string the potential energy and kinetic energy are equal.

7. Show that the total energy (k.e. + p.e.) of a simple harmonic transverse wave on a string is proportional to the square of the amplitude.

16.5. Superposition Theorem. Beats. The differential equation of wave motion is linear; therefore any linear combination

$$y = a_1 y_1 + a_2 y_2$$

of solutions y_1 and y_2 (a_1 and a_2 are constants) is also a solution. This is called a *superposition theorem.* The proof is omitted in this section since it was the content of Exercise 3, Sec. 16.4. As a first application, consider what happens when two waves of slightly different frequency but the same amplitude travel in the same medium in the same direction. Let their equations be

$$y_1 = y_m \sin 2\pi\nu_1 \left(t - \frac{x}{c}\right),$$

$$y_2 = y_m \sin 2\pi\nu_2 \left(t - \frac{x}{c}\right).$$

We shall use the trigonometric identity

$$\sin \alpha + \sin \beta = 2 \sin \frac{\alpha + \beta}{2} \cos \frac{\alpha - \beta}{2}.$$

We get

$$\begin{aligned} y &= y_1 + y_2 \\ &= 2y_m \sin 2\pi \left(\frac{\nu_1 + \nu_2}{2}\right)\left(t - \frac{x}{c}\right) \cos 2\pi \left(\frac{\nu_1 - \nu_2}{2}\right)\left(t - \frac{x}{c}\right). \end{aligned}$$

This is the product of a wave of average frequency $(\nu_1 + \nu_2)/2$ times a wave of low frequency $(\nu_1 - \nu_2)/2$. The general effect is shown in Fig. 16.4. At any point along the x axis an oscillation of the average fre-

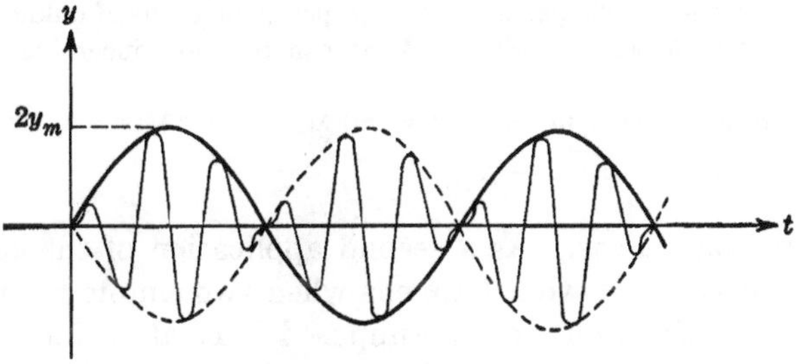

FIG. 16.4.

quency takes place but its amplitude varies between 0 and $2y_m$, achieving two moments of maximum amplitude (approximately) in each period of the slower oscillation. These pulses of maximum amplitude are called *beats*. They occur at a frequency twice that of the slow oscillation:

$$\nu_{\text{beat}} = \nu_1 - \nu_2 = \Delta\nu, \tag{16.19}$$

where ν_1 is the faster of the two initial frequencies.

Whenever the phase velocity of waves depends on the frequency, the preceding deduction is incomplete, for we used c as the velocity in each case. Let us repeat, using the symmetric form (16.9) and writing $\nu_1 - \nu_2$ as $\Delta\nu$. The development is as follows:

$$\begin{aligned} y_1 &= y_m \sin 2\pi[(\nu + \Delta\nu)t - (k + \Delta k)x] \\ y_2 &= y_m \sin 2\pi(\nu t - kx) \\ y &= y_1 + y_2 \\ &= 2y_m \sin 2\pi \left[\left(\nu + \frac{\Delta\nu}{2}\right)t - \left(k + \frac{\Delta k}{2}\right)x\right] \cos 2\pi \left(\frac{\Delta\nu}{2}t - \frac{\Delta k}{2}x\right). \end{aligned}$$

The result as before is the product of a wave of average frequency by a wave of frequency $\frac{1}{2}\Delta\nu$. But this time it is easy to express the rate at which the grouping of waves into pulses progresses. The velocity with which such beat formations move is called the *group velocity u*. Just as $c = \nu/k$ as in (16.6), so here

$$u = \frac{\Delta\nu}{\Delta k}. \tag{16.20}$$

Since the frequencies are assumed to be close (and since in some cases a whole continuous range of frequencies might be involved), we write

$$u = \frac{d\nu}{dk}. \tag{16.21}$$

The concept of group velocity is especially important in electromagnetic theory.

EXERCISES

1. A tone of frequency 300 per sec is superimposed on a tone of unknown frequency. Beats of frequency 5 per sec result. What can be said concerning the unknown frequency?

2. Express group velocity in terms of ν and λ.

3. Verify the equation $u = c - \lambda \frac{dc}{d\lambda}$.

16.6. Standing Waves. As a second application of the superposition theorem let us consider what happens when two simple harmonic waves differing only in direction are superimposed. To allow for various phase relationships, epoch angles ϵ_1 and ϵ_2 are added. The equations of the waves are written thus

$$y_1 = y_m \sin [2\pi(\nu t + kx) + \epsilon_1],$$
$$y_2 = y_m \sin [2\pi(\nu t - kx) + \epsilon_2].$$

Then the net disturbance is given by

$$y = y_1 + y_2.$$

$$y = 2y_m \sin\left(2\pi\nu t + \frac{\epsilon_1 + \epsilon_2}{2}\right) \cos\left(2\pi kx + \frac{\epsilon_1 - \epsilon_2}{2}\right). \tag{16.22}$$

This pattern of disturbance is quite different from the ones looked at so far. It is not going anywhere. The first factor, depending only on t, shows that there is a simple harmonic oscillation of frequency ν at each point. The amplitude of this oscillation varies from point to point. The second factor, depending only on x, allows us to evaluate this amplitude. This second factor describes the limits between which the oscillation can take place. In Fig. 16.5 the black curve is merely a graph of

$$y = 2y_m \cos\left(2\pi kx + \frac{\epsilon_1 - \epsilon_2}{2}\right).$$

The dotted lines show how the disturbance pattern oscillates when the remaining factor, $\sin [2\pi\nu t + (\epsilon_1 + \epsilon_2)/2]$, assumes values other than

+1. It is clear that there are some points where the amplitude is always zero. These are called *nodes* and are indicated by N_1, N_2, N_3 in the figure. They are points where the two waves always cancel each other. The points of maximum amplitude halfway between the nodes are *antinodes* or *loops*. Since both nodes and antinodes are fixed in position and

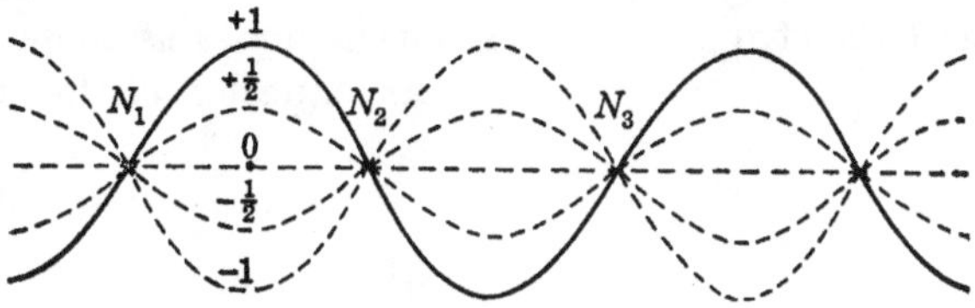

FIG. 16.5.

since each point partakes of an oscillation of constant amplitude, the phenomenon is called a *standing wave* or *stationary wave.*

The location of certain nodes and antinodes is usually fixed by the conditions of a specific problem. For instance, a string with both ends fixed must have nodes at these ends if stationary waves are set up. Other nodes may occur between but the fixed ends are nodes anyway. A free end of a one-dimensional oscillating medium is normally a loop. Equation (16.22) may be adapted to such situations, with convenient coordinates, by taking suitable values for ϵ_1 and ϵ_2. First, let us take $\epsilon_1 = \epsilon_2 = 0$. We have

$$y = 2y_m \sin 2\pi\nu t \cos 2\pi kx. \tag{16.23}$$

This form will be convenient when a loop is at the origin. Now take $-\epsilon_1 = +\epsilon_2 = \pi/2$. We then have

$$y = 2y_m \sin 2\pi\nu t \sin 2\pi kx. \tag{16.24}$$

This indicates a node at the origin.

Let us see how stationary waves might be set up in a string of length l. Nodes must occur at $x = 0$ and $x = l$; therefore we shall use Eq. (16.24) and insist that

$$\sin 2\pi kl = 0.$$

This is satisfied if $2\pi kl = n\pi$ for any integer $n = 0, 1, 2, 3, \ldots$, but the case $n = 0$ is not interesting here. An equivalent statement is

$$\lambda = \frac{2}{n}\,l = \frac{1}{k}, \qquad n = 1, 2, 3, \ldots .$$

Let us see what frequencies are possible, assuming that the phase velocity c is fixed:

$$\nu = ck = \frac{nc}{2l}, \qquad n = 1, 2, 3, \ldots .$$

These frequencies correspond to the various *normal modes of oscillation* given by the successive integers. The lowest frequency, for $n = 1$, is called *fundamental.*

These basic facts about stationary waves on a string enable us to check formula (16.16) for c. Suppose that transverse sinusoidal stationary waves are set up in a string of linear density q and tension f. Isolate the portion of the string between adjacent nodes as shown in Fig. 16.6.

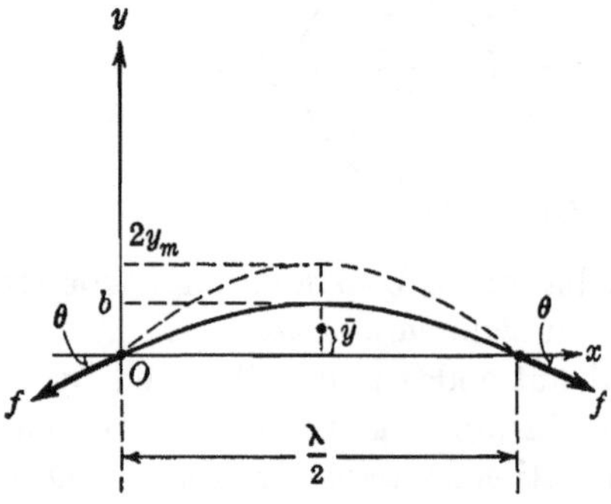

FIG. 16.6.

An equation of the curve at time t is

$$y = b \sin 2\pi kx,$$

where b is, by (16.24), given by

$$b = 2y_m \sin 2\pi\nu t.$$

The center of mass of the isolated segment is in simple harmonic motion; so

$$\bar{a} = -\omega^2\bar{y}.$$

As usual

$$\Sigma f_y = m\bar{a}. \tag{16.25}$$

First, let us compute the forces:

$$\Sigma f_y = -2f \sin \theta.$$

But for small displacements we have at the origin

$$\sin \theta = \frac{dy}{dx} = 2\pi kb \cos 2\pi kx = 2\pi kb.$$

Thus

$$\Sigma f_y = -4\pi kbf.$$

Next $\bar{y}$ is computed as

$$\begin{aligned}\bar{y} &= \frac{1}{m}\int_0^{\lambda/2} y\,dm = \frac{2}{\lambda q}\int_0^{\lambda/2} qb \sin 2\pi kx\,dx \\ &= \frac{b}{\pi}\Big[-\cos 2\pi kx\Big]_0^{\lambda/2} = \frac{2b}{\pi}.\end{aligned}$$

Substituting in (16.25),

$$-4\pi kbf = \frac{\lambda}{2}q\left(-\omega^2\frac{2b}{\pi}\right).$$

Regrouping, and substituting $k = 1/\lambda$,

$$\frac{f}{q} = \frac{\lambda^2\omega^2}{4\pi^2}.$$

By (16.4) we recognize the right member of this equation as c^2; so

$$c^2 = \frac{f}{q}. \tag{16.26}$$

EXERCISES

1. A string 3 m long and weighing 50 g is subjected to a tension of 200 newtons. Both ends are fixed. Find the frequency and the location of the nodes for the first and third normal modes of oscillation.

2. Derive a formula for normal frequencies for a string of length l, mass m, and tension f.

3. Show that the total energy (p.e. + k.e.) of a string with its ends fixed and experiencing stationary waves in the nth normal mode is given by

$$\text{t.e.} = 4\pi^2 q l \nu^2 y_m^2,$$

where the symbols have the same meaning as in the preceding section.

16.7. Longitudinal Vibrations in a Narrow Uniform Bar. As a second concrete illustration of wave motion, let us consider a straight narrow uniform bar of cross section a, density δ, and Young's modulus ψ. We shall suppose that a state of longitudinal strain is caused to exist in part of the rod and that this disturbance is allowed to be transmitted along the rod. Because of the narrowness of the bar, we shall neglect all transverse effects such as contractions given by Poisson's ratio. We shall assume that each plane normal to the rod acts as a unit. In other words all points in a given plane section always have the same displacements. We shall find a basic equation, analogous to (16.13), which must be satisfied. We isolate the portion of the undisturbed rod determined by coordinates x and $x + \Delta x$ as shown in Fig. 16.7. When the rod is dis-

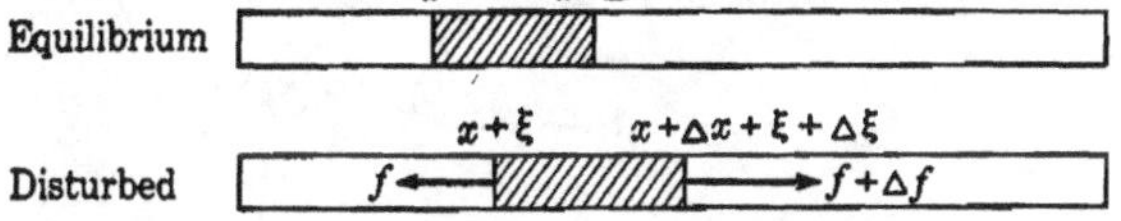

FIG. 16.7.

turbed, to each point x is associated a displacement ξ. The isolated portion is then bounded by planes at $x + \xi$ and $x + \Delta x + \xi + \Delta\xi$. Let the corresponding tensions be f and $f + \Delta f$. By Hooke's law (see 14.70), we have at any point

$$\frac{f}{a} = \psi \frac{\partial \xi}{\partial x}. \tag{16.27}$$

Therefore Δf can be expressed

$$\Delta f = a\psi \, \Delta \left(\frac{\partial \xi}{\partial x}\right). \tag{16.28}$$

But the equation of motion, $f = ma$, for the isolated portion is

$$\Delta f = a \, \delta \, \Delta x \, \frac{\partial^2 \xi}{\partial t^2}. \tag{16.29}$$

Equate the two expressions for Δf, divide by Δx, and take the limit as Δx is allowed to approach zero. We get

$$\psi \frac{\partial^2 \xi}{\partial x^2} = \delta \frac{\partial^2 \xi}{\partial t^2}. \tag{16.30}$$

Comparison with (16.14) shows this to be the condition for waves traveling at speed

$$c = \sqrt{\frac{\psi}{\delta}}. \tag{16.31}$$

Since each normal section acts as a unit, the resulting motion is an example of a *plane wave*.

Problems involving standing waves follow a pattern similar to those for transverse waves on a string. A fixed end of a bar is automatically a node. For it, $\xi = 0$. A free end on the other hand is characterized by $f = 0$ or, according to (16.27), by $\partial\xi/\partial x = 0$. Specific cases are left as exercises.

Let us now look at the energies carried by such a wave. When an arbitrarily small segment of length dx is stretched by an amount $d\xi$, the work done is $\frac{1}{2}f\,d\xi$; so, in the limit, the potential energy per length is $\frac{1}{2}f(\partial\xi/\partial x)$. Using (16.27), we get

$$\text{p.e. per volume} = \frac{1}{2}\psi\left(\frac{\partial\xi}{\partial x}\right)^2. \tag{16.32}$$

The kinetic energy per volume is at once seen to be

$$\text{k.e. per volume} = \frac{1}{2}\delta\left(\frac{\partial\xi}{\partial t}\right)^2. \tag{16.33}$$

In the case of a traveling wave given by

$$\xi = \xi(z) = \xi(x - ct)$$

the derivatives are

$$\frac{\partial\xi}{\partial x} = \frac{d\xi}{dz}\frac{\partial z}{\partial x} = \frac{d\xi}{dz}(1),$$
$$\frac{\partial\xi}{\partial t} = \frac{d\xi}{dz}\frac{\partial z}{\partial t} = \frac{d\xi}{dz}(-c),$$

so that

$$\frac{\partial\xi}{\partial t} = -c\frac{\partial\xi}{\partial x}. \tag{16.34}$$

Substituting in (16.33), we get

$$\text{k.e. per volume} = \frac{1}{2}c^2\delta\left(\frac{\partial\xi}{\partial x}\right)^2,$$

which, by (16.31), is equal to the expression in (16.32); thus for a progressive longitudinal wave along a bar at a given instant and at a given position

(16.35) k.e. per volume = p.e. per volume.

The preceding conclusion may seem startling. In simple oscillators such as pendulums the kinetic energy and potential energy are out of phase. For waves, we have just seen that they can rise and fall together. Perhaps, too, there may seem to be complications involving conservation of energy. But we are discussing merely the energy *at a point:* the energy flows in pulses in the direction of the wave. Some of these points may be cleared up by Fig. 16.8. A section of the bar is shown in unstrained

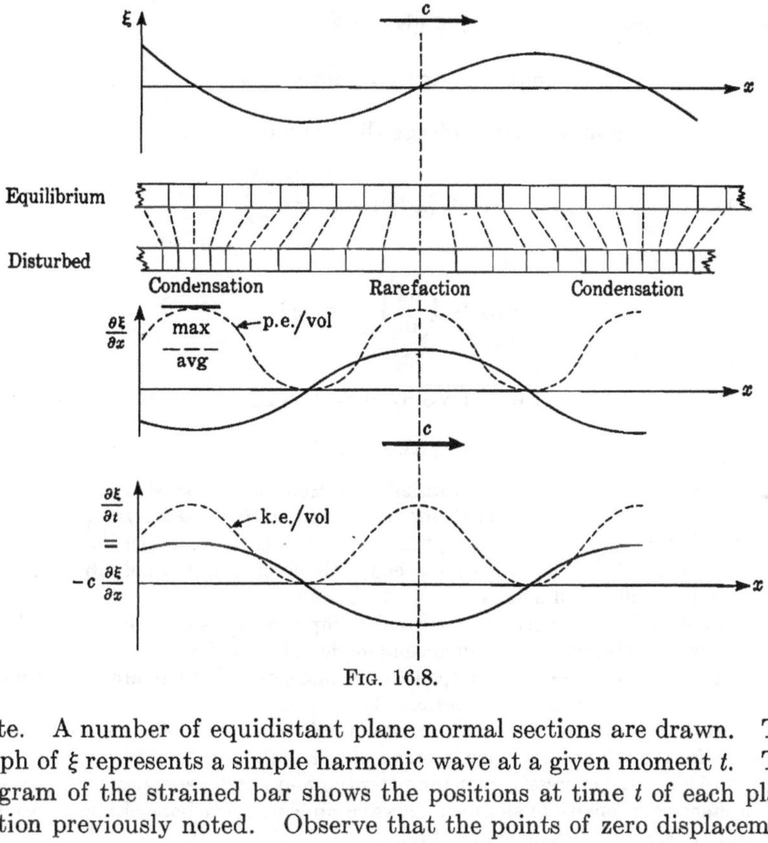

FIG. 16.8.

state. A number of equidistant plane normal sections are drawn. The graph of ξ represents a simple harmonic wave at a given moment t. The diagram of the strained bar shows the positions at time t of each plane section previously noted. Observe that the points of zero displacement are points of *rarefaction* and *condensation.* The graph of $\partial\xi/\partial x$ (showing the slope of the other graph) has peaks at the rarefactions and valleys at the condensations. The graph of $\partial\xi/\partial t$, based on (16.34), shows that points in the section at the middle of the condensation are moving to the right at maximum speed while those at the rarefactions are moving to the left with maximum speed. This clearly has the effect of moving the condensations and rarefactions to the right—and of course all the patterns shown must move to the right at speed c. The two dotted graphs, of the energies per volume, based on the squares of the other curves in accordance with (16.32) and (16.33), have peaks at the points of condensation (maximum compression) and points of rarefaction (maximum stretch). For the simple harmonic case, it is clear that the average total energy per volume is equal to the peak value of either the kinetic or the potential energy per volume. The following outlines the argument, using overlines for averages, on a per volume basis,

$$\overline{\text{t.e.}} = \overline{\text{p.e.} + \text{k.e.}} = 2\,\overline{\text{k.e.}} = (\text{k.e.})_{\text{max}}.$$

Assuming constant density this gives us

$$\text{max k.e. per volume} = \tfrac{1}{2}\delta v_{\text{max}}^2.$$

Now let us take an equation of the disturbance to be

$$\xi = \xi_m \sin \omega\left(t - \frac{x}{c}\right). \tag{16.36}$$

Then we get

$$v_{\text{max}} = \left(\frac{\partial \xi}{\partial t}\right)_{\text{max}} = \omega \xi_m$$

and so

$$\overline{\text{t.e. per volume}} = \tfrac{1}{2}\,\delta(\omega\xi_m)^2. \tag{16.37}$$

EXERCISES

1. What is the speed of a longitudinal vibration along a steel wire for which the density is 7,900 kg/m^3 and Young's modulus is 20×10^{10} newtons/m^2?

2. A uniform bar is stretched with a force f. Its length, area, density, and Young's modulus are l, a, δ, and ψ. Find the speed with which longitudinal vibrations travel along the bar. Show all details of your deduction.

3. A uniform bar of length l has one end clamped and the other end free. Write a standing-wave equation for the nth normal mode in terms of n, c, l.

4. A steel bar 1 m long is clamped at its mid-point. What are its normal frequencies? Use the constants of Exercise 1.

5. A free uniform bar of length l carries standing waves. Write a standing-wave equation for the nth normal mode in terms of n, c, l.

6. Find algebraic expressions for the potential and kinetic energies per volume for a simple harmonic longitudinal traveling wave on a uniform bar. Express results in terms of ξ_m, ν, c, and δ as functions of t and x.

7. Show that the total energy in a long bar of length l and cross section a carrying a wave given by (16.36) is equal to $2\pi^2 k^2 \psi a l \xi_m^2$.

8. Show that the average rate at which energy is propagated by a longitudinal wave given by (16.36) along a narrow bar of cross section a is equal to $2\pi^2\nu^2\delta a c \xi_m^2$.

16.8. Plane Sound Waves in a Column of Fluid. The analysis of the preceding section can easily be adapted to cover plane longitudinal waves in a fluid. We may apply the Euler equation from the chapter on hydromechanics:

$$\mathfrak{F} - \frac{1}{\delta} \nabla p = \mathbf{A}. \tag{16.38}$$

For this application we are concerned only with the wave motion; thus we ignore the $\mathfrak{F}$. Since we shall consider only motion in the x direction where each plane normal to the x direction moves as a unit, the equation for us is

$$\frac{\partial p}{\partial x} = -\delta \frac{\partial^2 \xi}{\partial t^2}. \tag{16.39}$$

(The partial derivative is still used for p, since p varies with t as well as with x.) Denoting the equilibrium pressure by p_0 and the instantaneous pressure by p, we may write

$$p = p_0 + p'$$

and

$$\frac{\partial p}{\partial x} = \frac{\partial p'}{\partial x}. \tag{16.40}$$

The excess pressure p' (positive, zero, or negative) will interest us more than the absolute pressure p.

At any point in the fluid the excess pressure p' goes hand in hand with a strain $\Delta v/v$. This strain, assuming the column of fluid to be of uniform cross section, is given by

$$\frac{\Delta v}{v} = \frac{\partial \xi}{\partial x}.$$

For, as in Fig. 16.9, if $v = a\,\Delta x$ and $\Delta v = a\,\Delta\xi$, then in the limit the

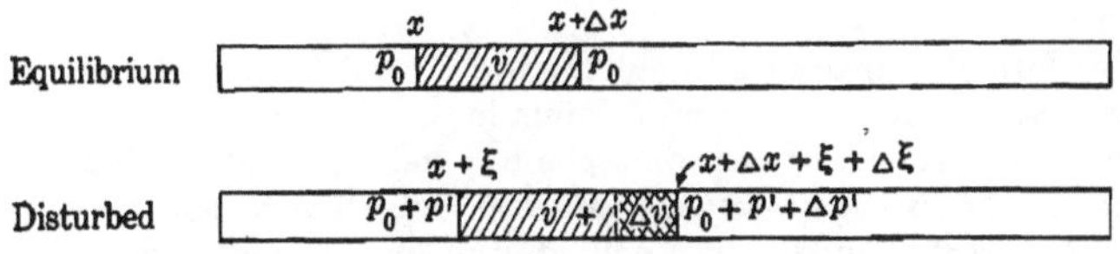

FIG. 16.9.

preceding evaluation of $\Delta v/v$ must hold. Hence, using the bulk modulus equation (14.74),

$$p' = -\beta \frac{\partial \xi}{\partial x}.$$

(The student should convince himself that it is valid to use this equation with only the excess pressure p' taken account of.) Differentiating the last equation with respect to x,

$$\frac{\partial p'}{\partial x} = -\beta \frac{\partial^2 \xi}{\partial x^2}. \tag{16.41}$$

We may now eliminate p and p' from (16.39), (16.40), and (16.41) to get

$$\beta \frac{\partial^2 \xi}{\partial x^2} = \delta \frac{\partial^2 \xi}{\partial t^2}. \tag{16.42}$$

This is satisfied by waves of velocity

$$c = \sqrt{\frac{\beta}{\delta}}. \tag{16.43}$$

For gases, the bulk modulus β depends conspicuously on the way in which compressions take place. If the processes are *isothermal*, an ideal gas satisfies

$$\beta = p,$$

as will be shown in the chapter on the kinetic theory of gases. If the process is *adiabatic*,

$$\beta = \gamma p,$$

where γ is the ratio of two important specific heats of a gas. These matters also will be taken up in the last chapter. For air, this ratio has the value 1.4. Since the longitudinal motion in a sound wave is too rapid to allow temperature to remain constant, the hypothesis of adiabatic processes gives results more nearly in accord with experiment.

EXERCISES

1. Compute the speed of sound in air under standard conditions assuming (*a*) isothermal compressions and (*b*) adiabatic compressions. Take the density of air as 1.2 kg/m^3.

2. What is the speed of sound in water? Take bulk modulus as 2.1×10^9 newtons/m^2.

3. Derive formulas analogous to (16.32) and (16.33) for energies per volume for a plane sound wave. (Recall the work formula for ideal fluids: $\int p\, dv$.)

4. Show that when simple harmonic plane sound waves are set up in a tube, the excess pressure always has its extreme values at displacement nodes.

5. The *intensity* of a sound wave is equal to the average power transmitted per area. Show that for a plane simple harmonic sound wave in a tube of fluid of uniform cross section the intensity is proportional to the square of the amplitude of the oscillation.

CHAPTER 17

KINETIC THEORY

In the fitting of mathematical descriptions to physical phenomena, some conscious approximations are always made. Max Planck remarks "Nature does not allow herself to be exhaustively expressed in human thought." No theory is the last word, but rather a partial description. A theory is good as long as it is useful. The model of a gas which we are about to study is based on admittedly inadmissible assumptions. It is not a modern theory; it was in its prime many years ago, and some of its ideas were advanced two thousand years ago. One justification for studying this doctrine is that it is still a useful one, for many verifiable conclusions can be easily deduced from the simple mechanical model postulated.

17.1. Clausius' Postulates for the Kinetic Theory of Gases. The supposition that *temperature* is closely related to the *kinetic energy of molecules* in motion had antecedents in the meditations of Democritus (400 B.C.) and Lucretius (A.D. 55), in the deductions of Gassendi (1620) and Hooke (1650), and in the theorizing of Daniel Bernoulli (1730). In the middle of the last century the relationship between heat and mechanical energy was investigated experimentally by Joule and Rowland. Soon after this the kinetic theory was established as a sound mathematical theory by the efforts of Clausius and Maxwell. As a starting point, we shall accept Clausius' postulates for gases:

(17.1) *For a monatomic gas, molecules are identical solid spheres traveling in straight lines except for collisions.*

(17.2) *Collisions are instantaneous and perfectly elastic. No other forces are exerted between molecules.*

(17.3) *The size of molecules is negligible in comparison with the space in which they move.*

From these postulates one may deduce many of the classical properties of ideal gases. These results may then be modified when necessary in order that the behavior of real gases be understood.

17.2. An Elementary Approach to Molecular Velocities. As a first exercise in treating molecules as perfectly elastic spheres, let us consider a single sphere rattling around in an otherwise empty spherical room. This molecule will be subject only to forces of collisions when it strikes the wall. These forces are normal, since the wall is smooth, and radial, since it is spherical. This implies that the motion is plane, for each impulse is a vector in the plane determined by the path before collision and by the center of the sphere. In other terms one might note that the forces are central; so plane motion results. The great circle shown in Fig. 17.1 is in this plane of motion. **R** and **R′** are successive points of collision. Since the coefficient of restitution is 1, it follows that

$$v' \cos \theta' = v \cos \theta.$$

Taking the tangential component of the impulse-momentum equation, we have

$$-mv \sin \theta + mv' \sin \theta' = 0.$$

Hence

$$v' \sin \theta' = v \sin \theta,$$

and dividing by the previous equation,

$$\tan \theta' = \tan \theta;$$

thus

$$\theta' = \theta, \qquad v = v'.$$

The impulse at such a collision has magnitude (see Fig. 17.1*b*)

$$\left|\int \mathbf{F}\, dt\right| = 2mv \sin (90° - \theta) = 2mv \cos \theta.$$

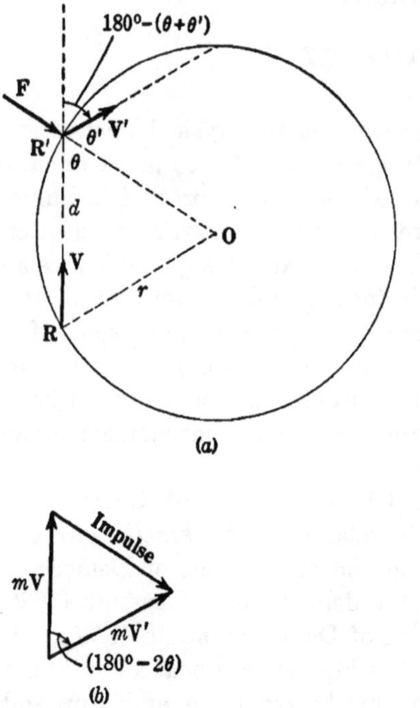

FIG. 17.1.

The distance traveled between collisions is

$$d = 2r \cos \theta;$$

hence the time between collisions is

$$t = \frac{d}{v} = \frac{2r \cos \theta}{v}.$$

Now the force in the preceding discussion is intermittent. Its average magnitude, however, has some interest

$$(17.4) \qquad \bar{f} = \frac{1}{t}\left|\int \mathbf{F}\, dt\right| = \frac{2mv \cos \theta}{\dfrac{2r \cos \theta}{v}} = m\frac{v^2}{r}.$$

Note that this value is independent of θ: it is the same for $\theta = 0°$ and $\theta = 90°$. The extreme case of $\theta = 90°$ we must interpret as uniform circular motion; therefore it is reassuring to observe that the value $\bar{f}$ is correct for the corresponding centripetal force.

Let us now consider what changes there would be if there were a large number, n, of molecules in the room. Collisions between molecules are perfectly elastic; therefore we shall assume that on the average the total force exerted by the room will be the same as if the molecules did not interfere with each other. If there are enough spheres as with a gas, the force magnitude may be described in terms of the pressure:

$$p = \frac{n\bar{f}}{4\pi r^2} = \frac{nm\bar{v}^2}{4\pi r^3}, \tag{17.5}$$

where $\bar{v}^2$ is the result of averaging v^2 for the different molecules. Now the density of the gas in the room is evaluated as the mass of the gas divided by the volume of the room:

$$\delta = \frac{nm}{\frac{4}{3}\pi r^3}. \tag{17.6}$$

We have then

$$p = \frac{\delta \bar{v}^2}{3}, \tag{17.7}$$

or

$$\bar{v} = \sqrt{\frac{3p}{\delta}}. \tag{17.8}$$

Since $\bar{v}$ was defined as the square root of the average of the squares of velocities, it is called the *root-mean-square speed* or *rms speed.*

For oxygen at standard temperature and pressure, this formula gives the value

$$\bar{v} = 460 \text{ m/sec.}$$

EXERCISES

1. Find the rms molecular speed of hydrogen under standard conditions (density is 9.0×10^{-2} kg/m^3).

2. Two molecules collide; the first having mass m has velocities **U** and **V** before and after impact. The second has mass m' and corresponding velocities **U**$'$ and **V**$'$. Take their line of centers at impact as the x axis. Show that the energy gained by the first molecule is

$$\frac{2mm'}{(m+m')^2}[(m'u_x'^2 - mu_x^2) + (m - m')u_x u_x'].$$

Compare this result with that of Exercise 4, Sec. 13.14.

3. A rectangular box contains perfectly elastic spherical molecules. Assume that the molecules all travel at speed $\bar{v}$, one-third of them parallel to each edge. Show that Eq. (17.8) is satisfied.

17.3. The Virial Theorem of Clausius. The derivation of the preceding section gave us a formula which actually is valid for containers of other shapes. In this section a more general derivation is given. The method used makes it possible to deduce further results in later sections.

Consider a finite set of particles of masses m_i and position vectors $\mathbf{R}_i$ moving in a *confined space* with finite speeds. Let $\mathbf{F}_i$ be the resultant of all forces acting on the ith particle. For each particle we consider the quantity $-0.5\mathbf{R}_i \cdot \mathbf{F}_i$. The time average of the sum of these quantities is called the *virial* of the system of particles:

$$\text{Virial} = -0.5 \overline{\sum_{i=1}^{n} \mathbf{R}_i \cdot \mathbf{F}_i} = -0.5 \overline{\sum_{i=1}^{n} m_i \mathbf{R}_i \cdot \mathbf{A}_i}. \tag{17.9}$$

We shall compare the virial with the average translational kinetic energy of the system.

$$\overline{\text{k.e.}} - \text{virial} = 0.5 \overline{\sum_{i=1}^{n} m_i(\mathbf{V}_i \cdot \mathbf{V}_i + \mathbf{R}_i \cdot \mathbf{A}_i)}$$

$$= 0.5 \overline{\sum_{i=1}^{n} m_i \frac{d}{dt} (\mathbf{R}_i \cdot \mathbf{V}_i)}$$

$$= 0.25 \overline{\sum_{i=1}^{n} m_i \frac{d^2}{dt^2} (\mathbf{R}_i \cdot \mathbf{R}_i)}.$$

In random chaotic motion of gas molecules within a confined space the distribution of particles tends to become statistically steady even though the motion of any individual may be far from regular. For this reason, the sum of the quantities $\mathbf{R}_i \cdot \mathbf{R}_i$ is practically constant, and its derivatives are practically zero.

The average value of its second derivative is certainly indistinguishable from zero if the average is taken over a sufficiently long time (say a thousandth of a second, during which time a typical molecule would have experienced a million collisions). With the right member of the last equation equal to zero, we have the conclusion

$$\overline{\text{k.e.}} = \text{virial}. \tag{17.10}$$

This is the *virial theorem of Clausius.* This theorem will be employed in computing the average kinetic energy of gas molecules under given conditions of pressure and density.

Consider now gas molecules in a closed container. By our postulates only forces of collision are exerted on the molecules. Since the forces of impact between particles occur in equal and opposite pairs, the only forces which contribute to the virial are the contact forces at the boundary. These contact forces are best described in terms of the average pressure. For an element of boundary having area da and outward normal $\mathbf{N}$ (see Fig. 17.2), the total average force on the gas is

$$d\mathbf{F} = -p\mathbf{N}\,da. \tag{17.11}$$

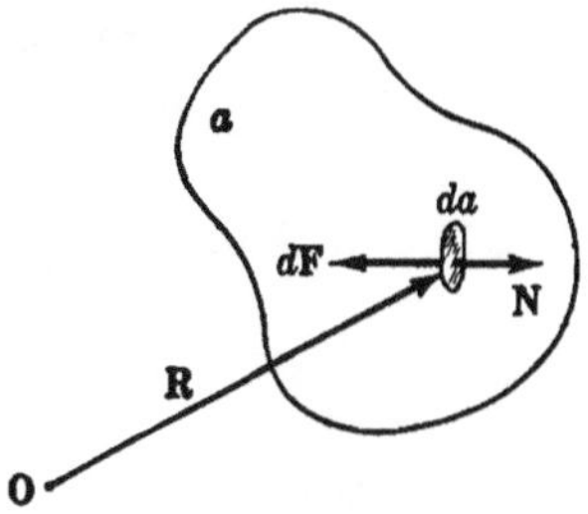

FIG. 17.2.

The virial is then given by

$$\text{Virial} = -\tfrac{1}{2}\int_a \mathbf{R}\cdot(-p\mathbf{N})da. \tag{17.12}$$

By the divergence theorem this may be rewritten as

$$\text{Virial} = \frac{1}{2}p\int_b \nabla\cdot\mathbf{R}\,db = \frac{3pb}{2}, \tag{17.13}$$

where b denotes volume. By the virial theorem then

$$\overline{\text{k.e.}} = \frac{1}{2}\overline{\sum_{i=1}^{n} m_i v_i^2} = \frac{3pb}{2}. \tag{17.14}$$

This result has been derived for gases whose molecules are particles, *i.e.*, for monatomic molecules. It may be used for other gases if it is understood that the virial theorem concerns only translational kinetic energy.

We shall denote by $\bar{v}$ the rms molecular speed defined for this more general situation by

$$\bar{v}^2 = \frac{\overline{\Sigma m_i v_i^2}}{\Sigma m_i}. \tag{17.15}$$

The rms speed is then given by

$$\bar{v}^2 = \frac{3pb}{\Sigma m_i}.$$

Since the average density δ of the gas is precisely mass divided by volume, we conclude as before:

$$\bar{v} = \sqrt{\frac{3p}{\delta}}. \tag{17.16}$$

In Chap. 15 gas velocities were discussed, but in that treatment our gas model was quite different. We then treated gas as a continuous homogeneous fluid. The chaotic motion of individual molecules was ignored and only motion of the fluid as a whole was investigated. It should be emphasized that the results just derived concern the individual motion of a fairly typical molecule. In this course we shall not follow up the statistical question about to what extent individuals may have speeds differing from the rms value. The distribution of velocities is suggested qualitatively in Fig. 17.3.

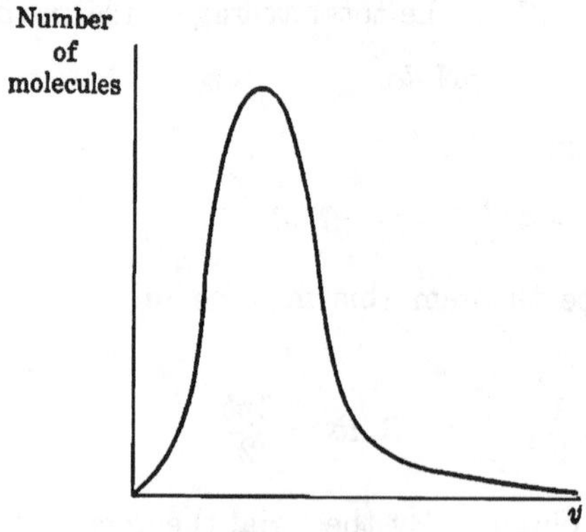

FIG. 17.3.

EXERCISES

1. A perfectly elastic spherical molecule of mass 4.0×10^{-26} kg travels in a repetitive path around a cubical box 5.0 cm wide as shown in Fig. 17.4. Its speed is 500 m/sec. (*a*) Taking the center **O** as origin, compute the contributions to the virial at **A**, **B**, **C**, and **D**. (*b*) Taking the corner **O′** as origin, compute the contributions to the virial at **A**, **B**, **C**, and **D**. (*c*) What is the kinetic energy?

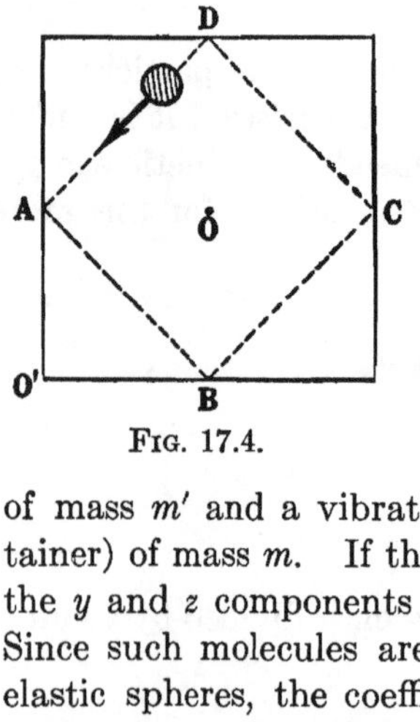

FIG. 17.4.

2. Use the virial theorem directly to compute the rms molecular velocity of a gas in a spherical vessel without appealing to the divergence theorem. (HINT: Use center of sphere as origin.)

17.4. Equipartition of Energy. Consider a collision as in Fig. 17.5 between a gas molecule of mass m' and a vibrating wall molecule (in the boundary of the container) of mass m. If the line of centers at impact is taken as the x axis, the y and z components of velocity will be unchanged by the collision. Since such molecules are considered as perfectly elastic spheres, the coefficient of restitution is 1. A direct calculation (see Exercise 2, Sec. 17.2) shows that the energy gained at impact by the wall molecule is

$$\frac{2mm'}{(m+m')^2}\left[(m'u_x'^2 - mu_x^2) + (m - m')u_x u_x'\right].$$

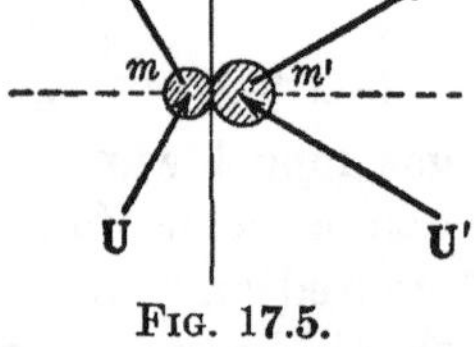

FIG. 17.5.

Assuming that the wall molecule is in harmonic oscillation, the average value of u_x is zero; thus *on the average* the gas molecules gain kinetic energy from such collisions only if their energy before collision is less than that of wall molecules. This average molecular kinetic energy may be taken as a measure of temperature. The temperatures of gas and container thus tend to become equal.

If two gases are in the same container, their temperatures approach that of the container, and when equal temperatures exist, the average molecular kinetic energies are equal:

$$\tfrac{1}{2}m_1\bar{v}_1^2 = \tfrac{1}{2}m_2\bar{v}_2^2. \tag{17.17}$$

At a given temperature, then, big molecules move more slowly on the average than small ones.

These examples show how energy tends to become uniformly distributed among molecules of gases. Thus far we have considered only monatomic molecules (spherical) having three degrees of freedom (three of translation; rotation is ignored because of the trivial moment of inertia). A diatomic molecule (dumbbell-shaped) has five degrees of freedom (two of rotation in addition to three of translation). At a given temperature such a molecule will have on the average 60 per cent more total kinetic energy than a monatomic molecule. Thus the principle of equipartition of energy extends to degrees of freedom: energy tends to become uniformly distributed among degrees of freedom of molecular motion.

17.5. The Laws of Dalton, Boyle, and Avogadro. In Sec. 17.3 we concluded that

$$\overline{\text{k.e.}} = \text{virial} = \tfrac{3}{2}pb$$

for gas in a container. Let us now consider what happens when two distinct families of molecules are mixed together in the same container. As before

$$(\overline{\text{k.e.}}) = (\overline{\text{k.e.}})_1 + (\overline{\text{k.e.}})_2 = \text{virial} = \tfrac{3}{2}pb.$$

Also, considering each of the gases by itself,

$$(\overline{\text{k.e.}})_1 = (\text{virial})_1, \qquad (\overline{\text{k.e.}})_2 = (\text{virial})_2.$$

Now, $(\text{virial})_1$ has two parts: that due to the boundary and that due to the other gas.

$$(\text{virial})_1 = (\text{virial})_{1b} + (\text{virial})_{1g}.$$

Similarly,

$$(\text{virial})_2 = (\text{virial})_{2b} + (\text{virial})_{2g}.$$

The contributions of the walls are already known:

$$(\text{virial})_{1b} = \tfrac{3}{2}p_1 b,$$
$$(\text{virial})_{2b} = \tfrac{3}{2}p_2 b,$$

where p_1 is the pressure that would be caused by the first gas if it alone occupied the container and p_2 likewise is the pressure which would exist if only the second gas were present. The other terms will, of course, be equal and opposite:

$$(\text{virial})_{1g} = -(\text{virial})_{2g}$$

because whenever there are collisions between the two families of molecules, the forces are equal and opposite. Combining the equations, we have

$$\tfrac{3}{2}pb = \tfrac{3}{2}p_1b + \tfrac{3}{2}p_2b$$

or

$$p = p_1 + p_2. \tag{17.18}$$

This is *Dalton's law of partial pressures.* The pressure of a mixture of gases is the sum of the pressures which would be caused by the constituent gases taken singly.

For constant temperature, the average molecular kinetic energy is, we shall assume, constant. Under this interpretation of constancy of temperature, the equation

$$pb = \tfrac{2}{3}(\overline{\text{k.e.}}) \tag{17.19}$$

is merely a restatement of *Boyle's law* concerning isothermal behavior of an ideal gas. In the next section we shall discuss this equation for the general case where $\overline{\text{k.e.}}$ is not constant.

If we have two samples of gases occupying equal volumes at equal pressures and equal temperatures, the number of molecules is the same for both samples. This is *Avogadro's hypothesis.* It is easily deduced from the principles already examined. By Boyle's law,

$$pb = (\tfrac{2}{3}n_1)(\tfrac{1}{2}m_1\bar{v}_1^2) = (\tfrac{2}{3}n_2)(\tfrac{1}{2}m_2\bar{v}_2^2),$$

where n_1 and n_2 are the numbers of molecules and m_1 and m_2 are the masses of single molecules. Equality of temperature implies equality of average molecular kinetic energy; thus

$$\tfrac{1}{2}m_1\bar{v}_1^2 = \tfrac{1}{2}m_2\bar{v}_2^2.$$

Consequently,

$$n_1 = n_2. \tag{17.20}$$

Under standard conditions (0°C, barometer 76 cm), one molecular weight (mole, gram molecule) of an ideal gas occupies 22.4 liters. The number of molecules is called Avogadro's number: 6.02×10^{23}.

EXERCISES

1. Oxygen has rms molecular speed of 460 m/sec under standard conditions. Oxygen has molecular weight 32. Helium has molecular weight 4.0. What is its rms speed under standard conditions?

2. The bulk modulus of a gas is defined as

$$\beta = -b\frac{dp}{db}.$$

Evaluate it in terms of pressure for *isothermal* compressions.

3. What in joules is the total kinetic energy of a roomful of air under standard conditions, taking the volume as 30 m^3? (Treat as monatomic and then correct to allow for rotation of diatomic molecules.)

4. Explain qualitatively in terms of the virial why *real* gases do not obey Boyle's law at (*a*) low temperatures and (*b*) high pressures.

17.6. Temperature and Molecular Energy. For a gas consisting of n molecules, Boyle's law (17.19) may be written

$$pb = \tfrac{2}{3}n(\tfrac{1}{2}m\bar{v}^2). \tag{17.21}$$

This may be compared with the general ideal-gas law of elementary physics

$$pb = nm\bar{g}\theta, \tag{17.22}$$

where m is the mass of a single molecule and hence nm is the total mass, $\bar{g}$ is a gas constant depending on the particular gas considered, and θ is the absolute temperature. From this comparison we get a precise statement as to how temperature and average molecular energy are related:

$$\tfrac{1}{2}m\bar{v}^2 = \tfrac{3}{2}(m\bar{g})\theta.$$

Now the product $m\bar{g}$ turns out to be independent of the gas used. It is equal to the famous *Boltzmann gas constant per molecule, k.* Its value is 1.38×10^{-23} joule/°C.

$$m\bar{g} = k. \tag{17.23}$$

We have then

$$\tfrac{1}{2}m\bar{v}^2 = \tfrac{3}{2}k\theta, \tag{17.24}$$

and for the *general ideal-gas law,*

$$pb = nk\theta. \tag{17.25}$$

Now the mean molecular energy used in (17.24) is that of translation only; thus only three degrees of freedom are involved. By the principle of equipartition, the energy associated with each degree of freedom is one-third of this amount. In general, if f is the number of degrees of freedom of a molecule, the total kinetic energy of the gas is given by

$$\text{k.e.} = \tfrac{1}{2}fnk\theta. \tag{17.26}$$

17.7. The Specific Heats of a Gas. When a gas is heated, the heat or added energy e is equal to the gain in kinetic energy plus the work done by the gas in expansion:

$$\Delta e = \Delta(\text{k.e.}) + \int p\, db. \tag{17.27}$$

This is a statement of the *first law of thermodynamics* for this situation. In differential form,

$$de = d(\text{k.e.}) + p\, db. \tag{17.28}$$

A *specific heat* c of a gas is defined as heat per temperature change per mass:

$$c = \frac{1}{nm}\frac{de}{d\theta}. \tag{17.29}$$

The specific heat *at constant pressure*, c_p, will first be evaluated. From (17.25), we get

$$p\,db = nk\,d\theta$$

and from (17.26)

$$d(\text{k.e.}) = \tfrac{1}{2}fnk\,d\theta.$$

Using (17.28), we have

$$c_p = \frac{1}{nm}\left(\frac{1}{2}fnk + nk\right)$$

or

$$c_p = \frac{(f+2)k}{2m}. \tag{17.30}$$

The specific heat *at constant volume* c_v is more easily computed since we assume that no work is done.

$$c_v = \frac{fk}{2m}. \tag{17.31}$$

The ratio γ of these two principal specific heats occurs often in physics.

$$\gamma = \frac{c_p}{c_v} = \frac{f+2}{f}. \tag{17.32}$$

It is interesting to compare the last result with experimental values for real gases. A few selected ones are tabulated below.

Gas	Temperature, °C	γ
Argon	15	1.67
Helium	18	1.63
Mercury vapor	360	1.67
Carbon monoxide	15	1.40
Hydrogen	15	1.41
Nitrogen	15	1.40
Oxygen	15	1.40
Ammonia	15	1.31
Carbon dioxide	15	1.30
Water vapor	100	1.32

Less convincing examples are easy to find. For example, at −181° hydrogen has the value 1.60.

EXERCISES

1. What value of γ would be predicted by elementary kinetic theory for the 10 gases listed previously?

2. Show that

$$c_p - c_v = \bar{g} = \frac{k}{m}.$$

3. *Molecular heat* is defined as the product of molecular weight by specific heat at constant volume. Show that

$$\text{Molecular heat} = 0.99f \qquad \text{cal/°C.}$$

This is essentially the *law of Dulong and Petit* (1819). This result may be compared with the following laboratory results for selected temperatures:

Argon:	3.0	Helium:	3.0	Mercury vapor:	3.0
Oxygen:	5.0	Hydrogen:	4.8	Nitrogen:	5.0

This law may be extended to solids by recognizing that in addition to the kinetic energy of three degrees of vibratory freedom there is an equal potential energy; so that here $f = 6$.

Compare with laboratory results:

Aluminum:	5.8	Iron:	6.0	Copper:	5.9
Zinc:	6.0	Silver:	6.0	Tin:	6.4
Gold:	6.2				

4. Find the rms molecular velocity of hydrogen (compare Exercise 1, Sec. 17.2) at a pressure of 0.2 atm and a temperature of 100°C.

17.8. Adiabatic Processes. We have noted that when heat is added to a gas, it may result in an expansion as well as in a change in the energy of the gas. It is possible for a gas to expand or contract without the addition or removal of heat. In a very quick expansion, for instance, there may not be time for the gradual transfer of energy from walls of a cylinder; therefore the decrease in the virial caused by the withdrawal of a piston must be matched by a decrease in the kinetic energy of the gas. A process involving no transfer of heat is called *adiabatic*. It is characterized by the equation

$$de = 0, \tag{17.33}$$

or, using (17.28),

$$d(\text{k.e.}) = -p\,db. \tag{17.34}$$

We shall now derive an equation relating the pressure and volume of a gas. Using (17.26) to express the general ideal-gas law (17.25) in terms of kinetic energy rather than temperature, we have

$$pb = \frac{2}{f}(\text{k.e.}). \tag{17.35}$$

Differentiating and substituting (17.34),

$$p\,db + b\,dp = \frac{2}{f}\,d(\text{k.e.}) = -\frac{2}{f}\,p\,db.$$

Rearranging terms,

$$b\,dp = -\left(1 + \frac{2}{f}\right)p\,db.$$

Using (17.32) and dividing by bp,

(17.36) $$\frac{dp}{p} = -\gamma\,\frac{db}{b}.$$

This may be integrated to give

(17.37) $$pb^{\gamma} = \text{const},$$

which is a standard equation for adiabatic behavior of an ideal gas.

EXERCISES

1. Derive a formula in terms of pressure for the bulk modulus of a gas for *adiabatic* compressions. Compare with Exercise 2, Sec. 17.5.

2. Show that for an adiabatic process $\theta b^{\gamma-1}$ is a constant.

3. The volume of a sample of air is suddenly doubled. The original temperature was 27°C. What is the final temperature?

4. A flask of gas is allowed to expand adiabatically. The original temperature is θ_1, the final temperature is θ_2. Show that the work done by the gas in expanding is

$$mc_v(\theta_1 - \theta_2),$$

where m is the total mass of the gas.

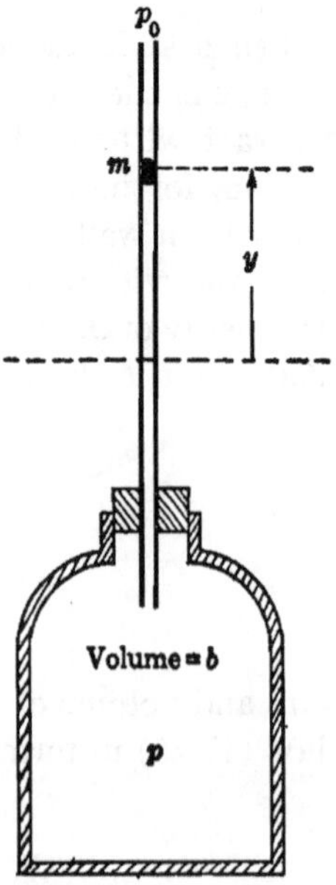

FIG. 17.6.

17.9. An Adiabatic Oscillator. In this section we shall look briefly at a dynamic method of determining the ratio of specific heats, γ, of a gas. A flask of volume b is fitted with a precision-bore glass tube as shown in Fig. 17.6. A pellet of mass m and radius r (very slightly less than that of the tube) is dropped down the tube. If b is of a suitable size and if the fit is sufficiently snug, there will be an equilibrium position (shown by the dotted axis in the figure) for which the weight of the pellet and the net force due to pressure of the air outside and gas inside will just balance:

(17.38) $$mg = \pi r^2(p - p_0).$$

When the pellet is at some other position, the net force is a restoring force. For a displacement y, let the pressure increase be Δp; then the equation of motion is

$$\pi r^2(p + \Delta p - p_0) - mg = m\frac{d^2y}{dt^2},$$

or, using the equilibrium equation,

$$\pi r^2 \, \Delta p = m\frac{d^2y}{dt^2}.$$

To find how Δp and y are related, we assume that the process is adiabatic, and hence we use (17.36)

$$\Delta p = -\gamma p\frac{\Delta b}{b}.$$

For a displacement y, the volume change is

$$\Delta b = \pi r^2 y;$$

thus we may substitute

$$\Delta p = -\gamma p\frac{\pi r^2}{b}y$$

and find for an equation of motion

$$-\gamma p\frac{\pi^2 r^4}{bm}y = \frac{d^2y}{dt^2}. \tag{17.39}$$

This represents a simple harmonic oscillation of period

$$\tau = \frac{2}{r^2}\sqrt{\frac{mb}{\gamma p}}. \tag{17.40}$$

In this equation b is the volume up to the equilibrium position of the pellet and p is given by (17.38). If m, b, τ, r, and p are measured, γ may be computed. This method is due to Rüchhardt.

EXERCISES

1. An experiment of the type described in this section was carried out with a 5-liter jar and a tube of inner diameter $\frac{5}{8}$ in. The pellet had mass 33.2 g. Its equilibrium position was 44 cm above the top of the jar. The barometer reading was 76 cm. The period of oscillation was measured as 1.14 sec. On the basis of these data compute γ.

17.10. Mean Free Path. The speed with which a typical gas molecule travels has been considered: in air at normal temperature it is roughly the speed of sound. In the section on the virial theorem it was mentioned that collisions occur with very great frequency. We shall now investigate this matter by seeking a rough answer to the question: On the average how far is any given molecule likely to go before it has a collision? This distance is called the *mean free path.*

In the first place, we must now recognize that molecules have size. The effective or kinetic diameter of a molecule will be written as d. The problem of computing the mean free path is complex. In order to get an estimate without too much labor, we shall make some assumptions and guesses. First, let us temporarily assume that the mean free path of a given molecule will be unchanged if all the other molecules are made to stand still in typical positions. It will be convenient to replace our moving molecule by a sphere of radius d and the stationary ones by points as shown in Fig. 17.7. The occurrence of collisions will not be changed by this substitution. The moving molecule sweeps out each second a cylinder of volume

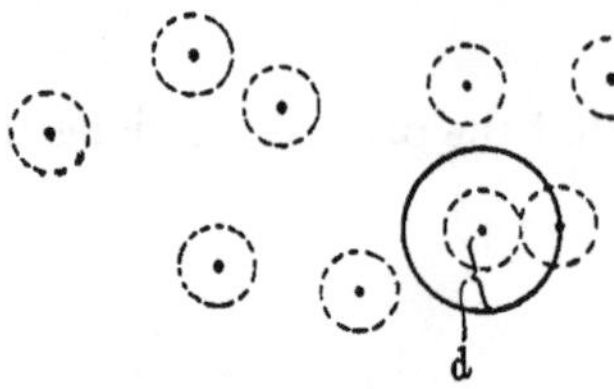

FIG. 17.7.

$$\pi\, d^2 v,$$

v being the average molecular velocity. If n_0 is the number of molecules per cubic centimeter, there will be $\pi\, d^2 n_0\, v$ collisions each second. The mean free path λ is then

$$\lambda = \frac{v}{\pi n_0\, d^2 v} = \frac{1}{\pi n_0\, d^2}. \tag{17.41}$$

This result, based on untenable assumptions, turns out to be wrong only by a factor of about 1.4.

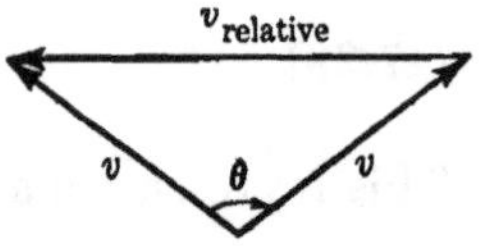

FIG. 17.8.

Now let us admit that all molecules are in motion but assume at least that each one is moving at the average speed v. We now use the average value of the *relative speed* of two molecules, *i.e.*, the average value of the magnitude of the vector difference of two velocities. For the case where all actual speeds are v, the relative speed is (see Fig. 17.8)

$$v' = 2v \sin\frac{\theta}{2},$$

where θ is the angle between the velocity vector of the molecule we are studying and the velocity vector of a second molecule. Since all directions for this second vector are equally likely, we compute the space average of the relative speed; that is, we multiply each element of area on a unit sphere about our molecule by the relative speed for a second molecule moving in that direction, integrate, and then divide by the area of the sphere. The computation of the average relative speed, $\bar{v}'$, follows. The coordinates are shown in Fig. 17.9.

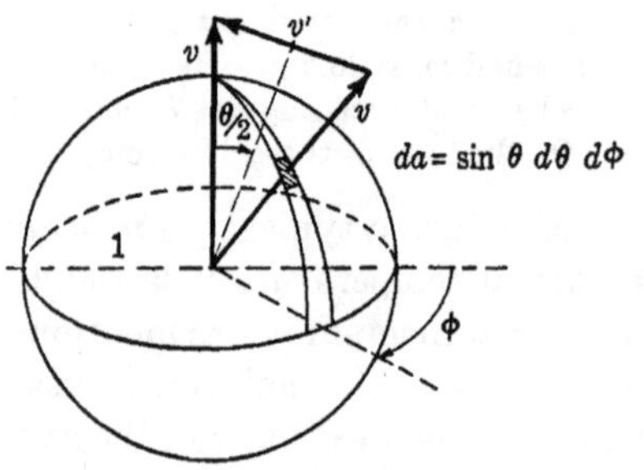

FIG. 17.9.

$$\bar{v}' = \frac{1}{\text{area}} \int v'\, da = \frac{1}{4\pi} \int_0^{2\pi} \int_0^{\pi} 2v \sin\frac{\theta}{2} \sin\theta\, d\theta\, d\phi = \frac{4}{3}\, v.$$

The number of collisions per second is now

$$\tfrac{4}{3}\pi n_0 \, d^2 v,$$

and the mean free path is

$$\lambda = \frac{3}{4\pi n_0 \, d^2}. \tag{17.42}$$

This formula is due to Clausius.

If allowance is made for the fact that velocities are not uniform but follow a distribution curve such as indicated in Fig. 17.3, a slightly different value is indicated. Since the statistical question of velocity distribution is omitted in this course, we shall use the result just derived. It should, however, be pointed out that rms and average speeds will differ slightly. The ratio according to Maxwell, the pioneer in these distribution researches, is

$$\frac{\text{Rms}}{\text{Average}} = \sqrt{\frac{3\pi}{8}}.$$

EXERCISES

1. Under standard conditions what would be the mean free path of a gas molecule having kinetic diameter 2.97×10^{-8} cm? What would the mean free path be at normal pressure but a temperature of 27,027°C? What would the mean free path be at 0°C at a pressure of 0.1 mm of mercury?

17.11. Transport Phenomena. Let an imaginary plane divide a gas into two portions as shown in Fig. 17.10. The division is soon violated, for the molecules in their chaotic motion cross the "boundary" repeatedly. In crossing, they transport physical characteristics. For instance, if the lower region has a tendency to drift parallel to the plane, the tendency will soon appear above the plane also. This phenomenon is one of *viscosity*. Molecules acquiring momentum below the boundary *transport the momentum* to the upper region. Again if the lower region is hotter than the upper, the molecules emigrating carry with them excessive kinetic energy. This is a case of *thermal conduction*, the *transport of energy*. As such interpenetrations take place, it is obvious that *mass* is transported across the boundary. This is called *diffusion*.

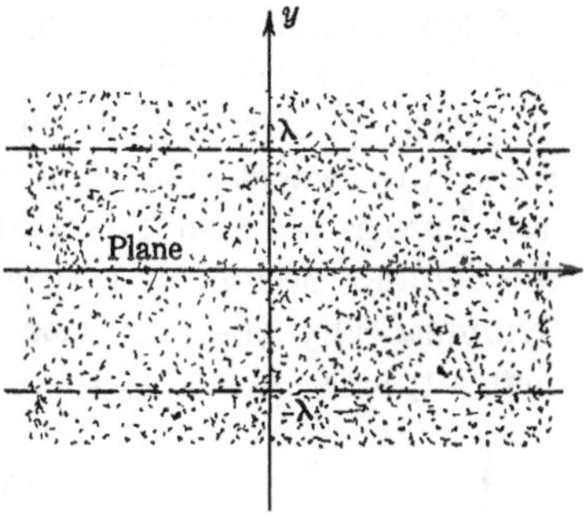

FIG. 17.10.

These three transport phenomena can be investigated quantitatively in terms of the kinetic theory. We shall formulate the viscosity problem. To make the task simpler, we shall assume that the viscosity would be unchanged if all molecules had the same speed (*i.e.*, we assign the average speed to each molecule). We shall assume, moreover, that the laminar (plane) drift of the gas as a whole can be thought of as a regular motion superimposed on the chaotic thermal agitation already discussed.

The drift of the gas will be parallel to the xz plane, as indicated in Fig. 17.11. The speed u of the drift is

$$u = u_0 + y\frac{du}{dy}.$$

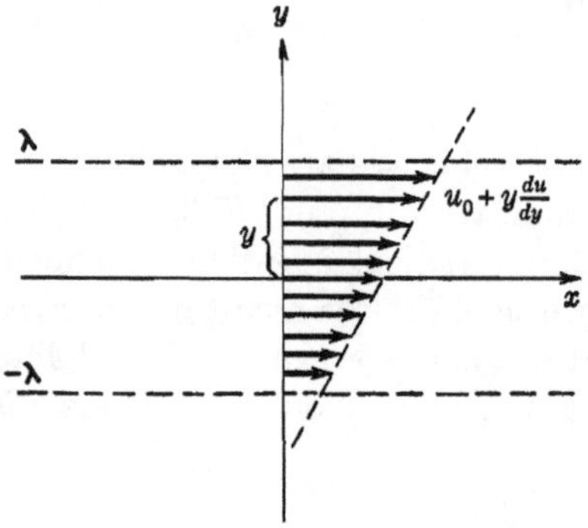

FIG. 17.11.

Within the limits

$$-2\lambda \leqq y \leqq 2\lambda;$$

at least, we shall treat du/dy as a constant.

Let dn_θ be the number of molecules per unit volume traveling toward the xz plane at an angle of between θ and $\theta + d\theta$ with the y axis. The average number of these crossing a unit area of the xz plane per second is then (see Fig. 17.12)

$$2dn_\theta\, v \cos\theta,$$

where v is the average molecular speed (quite aside from the superimposed drift).

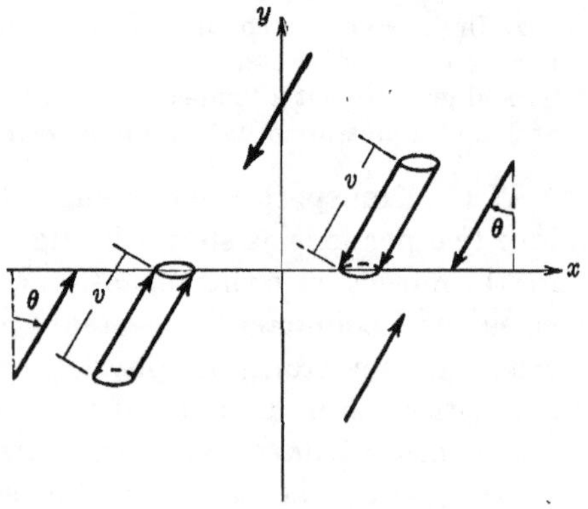

FIG. 17.12.

A typical molecule crossing the xz plane upward will travel one mean free path *after* crossing the plane (its expectation of unmolested progress does not depend on the distance previously traveled). Symmetrically one may also say that a typical molecule crossing the plane upward will have traveled one mean free path since its last collision. A similar statement may be made for molecules traveling downward. Since as many molecules travel down as up, we may merely evaluate the transfer of momentum associated with the interchange of particles separated by a distance 2λ as in Fig. 17.13. For each pair this amounts to

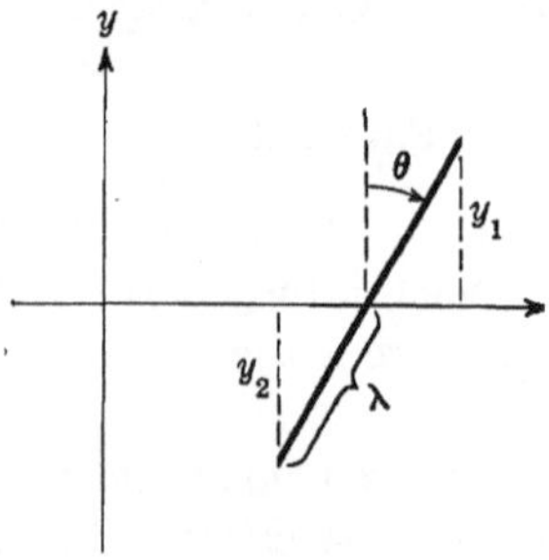

FIG. 17.13.

$$m\left(u_0 + y_2\frac{du}{dy}\right) - m\left(u_0 + y_1\frac{du}{dy}\right)$$

or, ignoring the minus sign,

$$m(y_2 - y_1)\frac{du}{dy} = 2m\lambda\frac{du}{dy}\cos\theta.$$

There are $dn_\theta/2$ such pairs per unit volume; thus the exchange per second of momentum for tracks with angles between θ and $\theta + d\theta$ is, per unit area,

$$2dn_\theta\, m\lambda v\cos^2\theta\frac{du}{dy}.$$

All directions of travel from the original location of a molecule are equally likely. The fraction of the molecules taking courses in the $d\theta$ range toward the xz plane is proportional to the area which they would pierce on a sphere of unit radius about their origin. If n_0 is the total number per unit volume, this fraction is, referring to the shaded strip of width $d\theta$ in Fig. 17.14,

$$\frac{dn_\theta}{n_0} = \frac{\text{area of strip}}{\text{area of sphere}} = \frac{2\pi\sin\theta\, d\theta}{4\pi} = 0.5\sin\theta\, d\theta.$$

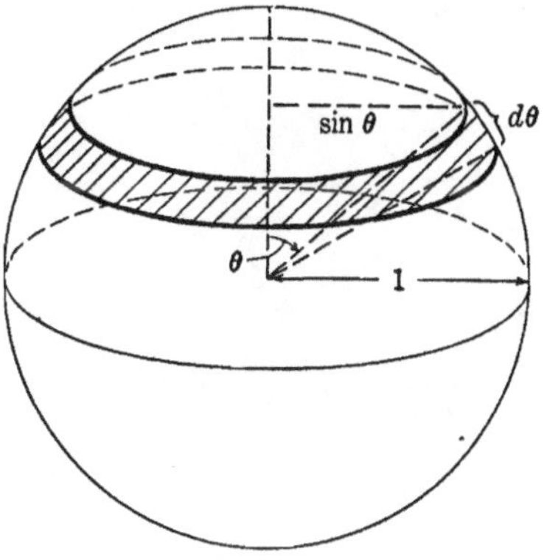

FIG. 17.14.

The total change of momentum per second per area (or in other words the force per area) on one side of the plane is then

$$\frac{f}{a} = n_0 m\lambda v\frac{du}{dy}\int_0^{\pi/2}\cos^2\theta\sin\theta\, d\theta = \frac{1}{3}n_0 m\lambda v\frac{du}{dy}.$$

As usual (see almost any elementary physics book) the *coefficient of viscosity* η is defined as the ratio of force per area to the speed-of-drift gradient; thus

(17.43) $$\eta = \frac{f/a}{du/dy};$$

so

$$\eta = \tfrac{1}{3}n_0 m\lambda v,$$

or

(17.44) $$\eta = \tfrac{1}{3}\delta\lambda\, v.$$

EXERCISES

1. Show that the coefficient of viscosity of a gas is given by

$$\eta = \frac{mv}{4\pi d^2}$$

and hence that it is independent of density and pressure.

2. The viscosity coefficient of helium under standard conditions is 1.891×10^{-5} mks units, while the density is 0.1785 kg/m^3. The molecular weight is 4.0. (*a*) Compute the mean free path. (*b*) From part (*a*), compute the kinetic diameter of the helium atom.

3. Using arguments similar to those of the preceding section, show that the thermal conductivity of a monatomic gas is equal to

$$\tfrac{1}{3} n_0 c_v m \lambda v = \eta c_v.$$

HINT: Show that the energy of each molecule is

$$e = \frac{3}{2} k\theta = c_v m \left(\theta_0 + y \frac{d\theta}{dy} \right).$$

4. Show that the thermal conductivity of a monatomic gas is equal to

$$\frac{c_v m v}{4\pi d^2}$$

and hence is independent of pressure.

SUGGESTED REFERENCES

GENERAL REFERENCES AT INTERMEDIATE LEVEL

BRAND, L., *Vectorial Mechanics*, Wiley.
An excellent textbook emphasizing the postulational approach to mechanics. Considerable detail is given on engineering structures and mechanisms, cables, and belts.

CAMPBELL, J. W., *An Introduction to Mechanics*, Pitman.
An intermediate text giving unusual attention to chains and cables.

CREW, H., and K. K. SMITH, *Mechanics for Students of Physics and Engineering*, Macmillan.
An intermediate text with numerous historical references. Special topics such as friction, elasticity, hydrodynamics, and waves are developed.

KARELITZ, G. B., J. ORMONDROYD, and J. M. GARRELTS, *Problems in Mechanics*, Macmillan.
A good collection of problems, mostly of an applied nature, with answers.

LINDSAY, R. B., *Physical Mechanics*, Van Nostrand.
An excellent treatment of the mechanical aspects of physics, including kinetic theory of gases, acoustic resonators, surface phenomena and viscosity, and an introduction to advanced mechanics.

OSGOOD, W. F., *Mechanics*, Macmillan.
A critical approach with good examples.

RAMSAY, A. S., *Dynamics* (2 vols), Cambridge.
A rich source of problems. Supplementary work on orbits may be found here. Methods of advanced as well as intermediate mechanics are developed.

SCOTT, M., *Mechanics: Statics and Dynamics*, McGraw-Hill.
A good source of supplementary information on gravitational fields and applied elasticity.

SEELY, F. B., and N E. ENSIGN, *Analytical Mechanics for Engineers*, Wiley.
A good all-round book on practical mechanics.

SLOAN, A., *Fundamentals of Engineering Mechanics*, Prentice-Hall.
An additional reference for engineering mechanisms and structures, and especially for problems involving distributed forces.

SYNGE, J. L., and B. A. GRIFFITH, *Principles of Mechanics*, McGraw-Hill.
An admirable book developing plane mechanics and three-dimensional mechanics separately. This is a good reference for supplemental reading on the foundations of mechanics, and on advanced methods, the motion of a charged particle, and the special theory of relativity.

TIMOSHENKO, S., and D. H. YOUNG, *Engineering Mechanics*, McGraw-Hill.
A fine text. The separate volumes on "Statics" and "Dynamics" contain many detailed solutions of practical problems.

ADVANCED OR SPECIALIZED REFERENCES

APPELL, P., *Traité de mécanique rationnelle*, Gauthier-Villars.
A singularly lucid treatise of which the first volume especially is a suitable reference for intermediate students.

BINDER, R. C., *Fluid Mechanics* and *Advanced Fluid Mechanics and Fluid Machinery*, Prentice-Hall.

Interesting and practical treatments well suited for supplementary reading.

BIRKHOFF, G., *Hydromechanics*, Princeton University.

Contains an account of dimensional analysis applied to modeling.

BRIDGMAN, P. W., *Dimensional Analysis*, Yale University.

The standard monograph on this subject.

CHAMPION, F. C., and N. DAVY, *Properties of Matter*, Blackie.

A good source for supplementary reading. It contains both theory and descriptions of experimental procedures. Among the topics covered are dimensional analysis, measurement of *g*, elasticity, seismic waves, surface phenomena, and viscosity.

COE, C. J., *Theoretical Mechanics*, Macmillan.

A splendid treatise on vectorial mechanics emphasizing mathematical niceties.

COFFIN, J. G., *Vectorial Analysis*, Wiley.

An older book, very good on the use of vectors.

COULSON, C. A., *Waves*, Oliver & Boyd.

A concise treatment of mechanical, acoustical, and electrical waves.

DEN HARTOG, J. P., *Strength of Materials*, McGraw-Hill.

For further information, pleasingly presented, concerning elastic properties of engineering structures.

GEIRINGER, H., *Geometrical Foundations of Mechanics*, mimeographed notes, Brown University.

An advanced treatment, unusual in its perspective as well as in its methods.

GOLDSTEIN, H., *Classical Mechanics*, Addison-Wesley.

A modern treatment of advanced dynamics. Contains an excellent bibliography.

JEANS, SIR JAMES, *An Introduction to the Kinetic Theory of Gases*, Macmillan.

For further reading concerning the statistical use of mechanics in the theory of heat.

JOHNSON, W. C., *Mathematical and Physical Principles of Engineering Analysis*, McGraw-Hill.

A systematic approach to the setting up of practical problems. Use is made of electrical analogues of mechanical systems.

JOOS, G., *Theoretical Physics*, Hafner.

A considerable range of topics including relativistic mechanics.

KINSLEY, L. E., and A. R. FREY, *Fundamentals of Acoustics*, Wiley.

For a more extensive treatment of waves in elastic media.

LASS, H., *Vector and Tensor Analysis*, McGraw-Hill.

A source for further information on the theory and use of vectors.

MACELWANE, J. B., *Geodynamics*, Wiley.

The early part of this book is a good reference on elasticity.

MACMILLAN, W. D., *Statics and the Dynamics of a Particle*, McGraw-Hill.

For more mathematical detail on orbits and on elastic behavior.

———, *Theoretical Mechanics (Theory of the Potential)*, McGraw-Hill.

For additional material concerning gravitational fields.

MILNE-THOMSON, L. M., *Theoretical Hydrodynamics*, Macmillan.

An outstanding text using vector methods.

MORSE, P. M., *Vibration and Sound*, McGraw-Hill.

A standard source for material on mechanical oscillations and waves.

NEWMAN, F. H., and V. H. L. SEARLE, *The General Properties of Matter*, Benn.

An alternate reference having a table of contents similar to that of the book by Champion and Davy.

OLSON, H. F., *Dynamical Analogies*, Van Nostrand.
A very suggestive book emphasizing performance of mechanical, acoustical, and electrical systems.

OXTOBY, J. C., "What Are Physical Dimensions?" American Physics Teacher, 2, 85–90 (1934).

RUARK, A. E., and H. C. UREY, *Atoms, Molecules, and Quanta*, McGraw-Hill.
A source of further material on atomic mechanics.

SLATER, J. C., and N. H. FRANK, *Mechanics*, McGraw-Hill.
A good reference for advanced mechanics including oscillating systems.

SOKOLNIKOFF, I. S., *Mathematical Theory of Elasticity*, McGraw-Hill.

———, and E. S. SOKOLNIKOFF, *Higher Mathematics for Engineers and Physicists*, McGraw-Hill.
Suggested here mainly for its brief survey of vector analysis.

STEWART, G. W., and R. B. LINDSAY, *Acoustics*, Van Nostrand.
An interesting text on sound using the notion of acoustic impedance.

THOMSON, W. T., *Mechanical Vibrations*, Prentice-Hall.
Contains many exercises (with answers) for oscillating systems.

TIMOSHENKO, S., and D. H. YOUNG, *Advanced Dynamics*, McGraw-Hill.
For a more detailed account of small vibrations and of gyrostatic phenomena.

WEBSTER, A. G., *The Dynamics of Particles and of Rigid, Elastic, and Fluid Bodies*, Teubner.
A masterly treatise recommended here primarily for its sections on elasticity and hydromechanics.

WILSON, W., *Theoretical Physics*, Vol. I, Methuen.
A good source for further study concerning gases, fluids, and elastic media.

PARTIAL LIST OF ANSWERS TO EXERCISES

(Generally to slide-rule accuracy)

CHAPTER 1

Sec. 1.4. **1.** 911 ft. **3.** 0.663, 0.500, 0.557. **5.** 60° or 120°.
Sec. 1.7. **3.** (*a*) $5.00\underline{/53^\circ}$; (*c*) $5.00\underline{/120^\circ}$.
Sec. 1.9. **1.** (*a*) $1.00\underline{/45^\circ}$; (*c*) $1.00\underline{/105^\circ}$. **3.** (*a*) 8.66, 5.00; (*c*) −10, 0.
Sec. 1.10. **1.** (*a*) −5.00; (*c*) −8.66; (*e*) 0.00.
Sec. 1.11. **1.** (*a*) $0.707\mathbf{I} + 0.707\mathbf{J}$; (*c*) $0.800\mathbf{I} - 0.600\mathbf{J}$; (*e*) $0.667\mathbf{I} - 0.333\mathbf{J} - 0.667\mathbf{K}$; (*g*) $-0.333\mathbf{I} + 0.667\mathbf{J} - 0.667\mathbf{K}$. **3.** (*a*) 65, −0.508, 0.000, 0.862; (*c*) 30, 0.000, 0.000, −1.000. **5.** (*a*) 0.333, 0.333; (*c*) 0, 0.
Sec. 1.12. **1.** (*a*) 0.707, 0.000, 0.707; (*c*) −0.570, 0.684, −0.456. **3.** $3.50\mathbf{I} - 2.54\mathbf{J} + 3.50\mathbf{K}$, $-1.50\mathbf{I} + 4.54\mathbf{J} - 1.50\mathbf{K}$. **7.** $\mathbf{P} = \frac{1}{2}(\mathbf{P}' + \mathbf{P}'')$.

CHAPTER 2

Sec. 2.1. **1.** (*a*) −85.5; (*c*) 0.500; (*e*) 6.34; (*g*) −5.00. **3.** −1.00. **5.** $|\mathbf{A}| = |\mathbf{B}|$ **7.** (*a*) $-6\mathbf{J}$; (*b*) $5.52\mathbf{I} - 7.36\mathbf{K}$. **9.** −5.0, 7.0. **11.** The angle between **E** and **F** is 60°.
Sec. 2.2. **3.** 3.61. **5.** $x - 2y - 3z = 0$. **7.** 2.2. **9.** 2.01.
Sec. 2.3. **1.** (*a*) $-19.8\mathbf{K}$; (*c*) $-17.1\mathbf{K}$; (*e*) $\mathbf{I} - \mathbf{J} + \mathbf{K}$. **3.** $\mathbf{R} = x\mathbf{I} + \mathbf{J}$ (*i.e.*, the locus is the line $y = 1$).
Sec. 2.4. **1.** (*a*) $2\mathbf{I} - 2\mathbf{K}$; (*c*) **O**. **3.** $n_x = f_z y - f_z y' - f_y z + f_y z'$, etc.
Sec. 2.5. **1.** $\pm(0.667\mathbf{I} - 0.667\mathbf{J} - 0.333\mathbf{K})$. **3.** 0.8, 0.0, −0.6 or −0.8, 0.0, 0.6. **5.** 2, 2. **7.** 0.707. **9.** $x - 1 = \dfrac{y-2}{-2} = \dfrac{z-3}{4}$.
Sec. 2.6. **1.** 4. **3.** 7. **7.** −0.393.

CHAPTER 3

Sec. 3.4. **1.** (*d*) $9.3\underline{/38^\circ}$. **3.** 10.6 lb; 0.48, 0.62, 0.61.
Sec. 3.7. **1.** $16.0\underline{/213.4^\circ}$ lb. **3.** 190.4 lb, 123.7 lb. **7.** 1.7 lb, 2.0 lb. **9.** 981 newtons, 1,690 newtons; or 490 newtons, 849 newtons.
Sec. 3.8. **1.** 33.8 lb. **3.** 44.1 lb, 21.8° above plane.
5. $p_{\max} = w(\sin\theta + \mu\cos\theta)/(\cos\theta - \mu\sin\theta)$,
$p_{\min} = w(\sin\theta - \mu\cos\theta)/(\cos\theta + \mu\sin\theta)$.
6. 0.36. **7.** $|\mathbf{T}'| = 3.59$ newtons, $|\mathbf{T}| = 12.3$ newtons. **9.** The answers in pounds are shown in the accompanying figure. Compressions are indicated by a minus.

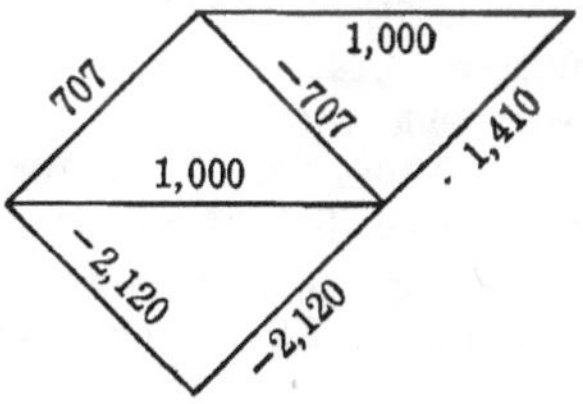

CHAPTER 4

Sec. 4.2. **1.** 2.60 ft.
Sec. 4.3. **1.** 20.8 ft-lb; −0.481, 0.144, 0.865.
Sec. 4.4. **3.** (*a*) −5**K** ft-lb; (*b*) −20**K** ft-lb. **5.** 728 ft-lb.
Sec. 4.5. **3.** (−)580 ft-lb. **5.** 3.33 ft-lb. **7.** −14 ft.
Sec. 4.6. **1.** Couple: 2.45d (where d is length of cube); 0.408, −0.817, 0.408. Force: 5.39; 0.371, 0.557, 0.743. **3.** $\bar{\Gamma} = -6\mathbf{I} + 40\mathbf{J} - 72\mathbf{K}$ ft-lb, $\bar{\mathbf{F}} = 10\mathbf{I} + 2\mathbf{J}$ lb.
Sec. 4.7. **3.** A force 16**I** lb acting at (0,9.5,0) ft. **5.** A force 8**J** lb acting at (−23.75,0,−3.75) ft.
Sec. 4.8. **1.** 2.1 ft from side and 2.5 ft from end or 1.5 ft from end and 1.5 ft from side. **3.** $(\gamma - \gamma')/d$, γ'/d, γ/d.
Sec. 4.9. **1.** 66.7 lb, 66.7 lb. **3.** $w/2$. **5.** 5,190 lb. **7.** 3.36 lb. **9.** (*a*) 393 lb; (*b*) 314 lb, 364 lb. **11.** 44.7 lb. **13.** 25 lb. **15.** The answers in pounds are shown

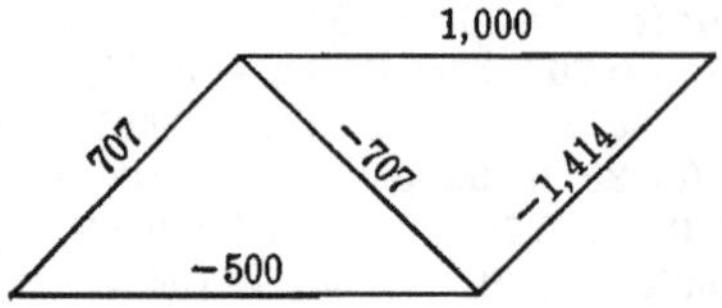

in the accompanying figure. Compressions are indicated by a minus sign. **17.** 13.3 lb, 13.3 lb. **19.** 292 lb, 527 lb, 667 lb.
Sec. 4.10. **3.** 4.24 lb, 3.61 lb, 3.00 lb, 4.24 lb, 33.7°. −45°.

CHAPTER 5

Sec. 5.2. **3.** −0.898**J** ft/sec. **5.** $(2t + \Delta t)\mathbf{I} + (1 - 4t - 2\Delta t)\mathbf{J}$.
Sec. 5.3. **3.** (*a*) $4t^3$; (*c*) $8t^3\mathbf{I} - 5t^4\mathbf{J} - 6t^2\mathbf{K}$. **5.** 1.414, −0.612, 0.353, 0.707. **7.** 3,980/29.6°, 3,920/28.0°, 3,720/21.4° ft/sec.
Sec. 5.4. **1.** 175.6 mph. **3.** 2 mph. **5.** 50 mph at an angle 36.9° with rear of train. **7.** 36.9° north or south of west. **9.** 7.45 miles, 41.8° ahead of line of sight. **11.** 10.4 mph from southeast.
Sec. 5.5. **1.** For example, $t = \pi/3$ sec, 30 ft/sec. **3.** 2. **5.** (*a*) 104 ft/sec; (*b*) 0.385**I** + 0.923**K**, 0.385**I** − 0.923**K**; (*c*) 144 ft; (*d*) 101 ft/sec.
Sec. 5.6. **3.** 50 ft/sec, 12 ft/sec^2. **5.** 50 ft/sec^2, 8 ft/sec^2. **7.** 3.35 cm/sec^2.
Sec. 5.7. **1.** 45.0 ft/sec^2, 30.0 ft/sec^2, 54.1 ft/sec^2. **3.** 5.29 ft/sec.
Sec. 5.8. **3.** 205 ft, 115 ft/sec, 56.7 ft/sec. **5.** 6 ft/sec^2, 1.15 sec. **7.** 6 m/sec. **9.** 0.347 sec. **11.** 2.
Sec. 5.10. **1.** 20, 0.22. **3.** 9.43 ft/sec, 29.6 ft/sec^2. **5.** (*a*) 642 ft/sec; (*b*) 1,284 ft/sec. **11.** $(1/3)(\bar{\mathbf{R}}_1 + \bar{\mathbf{R}}_2 + \bar{\mathbf{R}}_3)$. **13.** 1.5 ft and 1.0 ft from the perpendicular sides of the triangle.

CHAPTER 6

Sec. 6.1. **3.** 3**J**. **5.** 0.5 rad/sec, 3.14 sec. **7.** 1 sec, 2 rad/sec^2. **9.** 3.33 rad. **11.** 0.667 rad. **13.** 50 ft/sec^2, 36.9° with radius. **15.** 138.2 rad/sec.
Sec. 6.2. **1.** 693; 0.408, −0.816, 0.408. **3.** 5.14×10^{-5} rad/sec.
Sec. 6.3. **1.** 40**I** + 20**J** ft/sec, −400**I** + 800**J** ft/sec^2.
Sec. 6.4. **3.** 533 ft/sec. **5.** $\mathbf{A} = \mathbf{A}_{O'} + \boldsymbol{\alpha} \times \mathbf{R}' + \boldsymbol{\Omega} \times (\boldsymbol{\Omega} \times \mathbf{R}')$.
Sec. 6.5. **1.** 0.733 ft below center. **5.** 2.24 ft below center.

Sec. 6.6. **1.** 100**J** − 1,050**K** mph, −1,150**K** mph, −100**J** − 1,050**K** mph, −950**K** mph.

Sec. 6.7. **3.** $(v'^2 + \omega^2 r^2)^{\frac{1}{2}}$, $(4\omega^2 v'^2 + \omega^4 r^2)^{\frac{1}{2}}$. **5.** 0, 78.6 mph². **9.** 30 ft/sec, 26 ft/sec, 51.9 ft/sec², 120 ft/sec², 180 ft/sec², 93.2 ft/sec², 31.1 ft/sec.

CHAPTER 7

Sec. 7.1. **1.** 9.81 newtons. **3.** 8.05 ft/sec². **5.** 32.2 ft/sec². **7.** 4.45×10^5. **9.** 10^5.

Sec. 7.2. **1.** 1.99 sec. **3.** 8.05 ft/sec². **5.** 2.34 tons. **7.** 9.54 sec. **9.** 2.28 ft. **11.** Greater than 0.171. **13.** 10.4 m/sec. **15.** 40 sec. **17.** 0.433, 34.6 ft.

Sec. 7.3. **1.** 8.02 ft/sec. **3.** 17.9 ft/sec.

Sec. 7.4. **1.** 4.30 ft/sec², 2.15 ft/sec², 2.34 lb. **3.** −19.3 ft/sec², 6.44 ft/sec², 6.44 ft/sec², 8 lb. **5.** 8.59 ft/sec², 17.2 ft/sec², 4.67 lb, 2.33 lb.

Sec. 7.5. **3.** (*a*) $\ddot{\mathbf{R}} = 0.2\mathbf{I} + 0.6\mathbf{J}$ m; (*b*) $\mathbf{A} = 0.2\mathbf{I} + 0.6\mathbf{J}$ m/sec².

Sec. 7.6. **1.** 1.57 sec. **3.** (*a*) 1.28 sec; (*c*) 1.32 sec. **5.** 4.01 rad/sec. **7.** $2m\omega v'$, $m\omega^2 r$.

Sec. 7.7. **1.** 2,220 lb, north. **3.** 0. **7.** 45°, 0.00174 rad. **11.** 192 ft, west. **13.** 271°/day.

CHAPTER 8

Sec. 8.1. **1.** 0.533 m from end. **3.** 1.5 ft and 5.0 ft from the perpendicular rods. **5.** 0.5 in. and 1.5 in. from inside edges. **7.** $0.636r$ from center. **9.** 0.70 ft from bottom of square. **11.** $0.417b$ from base.

Sec. 8.2. **1.** 5.47 lb, 4.53 lb. **3.** $|\mathbf{F}| = al + \frac{1}{3}bl^3$, $\bar{x} = l(6a + 3bl^2)/(12a + 4bl^2)$.

Sec. 8.3. **1.** 143.4 lb (vertical), 12.8° with vertical. **3.** r/h. **5.** $ar'/g(r - r')$. **7.** 80.2 ft. **9.** $\tan\theta = a/g$.

Sec. 8.4. **1.** 310 sec. **3.** 150.5 rev, 60.2 sec. **5.** 0.593 kg-m². **7.** $i = i_1(r_2^2 - r_0^2)/(r_1^2 - r_0^2)$.

Sec. 8.5. **1.** $(\frac{7}{5})mr^2$. **3.** 0.90 kg-m², 2.70 kg-m². **5.** $0.5r$. **7.** (*a*) 2.95 sec; (*b*) 2.09 sec; (*c*) 3.61 sec.

Sec. 8.6. **1.** $0.548r$. **3.** $1.118a$.

Sec. 8.7. **3.** $(2/3)^{\frac{1}{2}}ab(a^2 + b^2)^{-\frac{1}{2}}$.

Sec. 8.8. **1.** (*a*) 2.01 sec; (*b*) 1.74 sec. **3.** 1.54 ft. **5.** 9.795 m/sec². **7.** 0.41 m. **9.** 0.74/sec. **11.** 256 ft-lb-sec². **15.** $7.38(r/g)^{\frac{1}{2}}$.

Sec. 8.9. **1.** 1.33, 13.3 ft. **3.** 2.60 sec. **5.** 3.99 in. **7.** 0.194. **9.** 1.40 ft/sec², 3.66 lb. **11.** 0.917 sec.

Sec. 8.10. **1.** 4.72 rad/sec. **3.** 572 lb, 381 lb.

Sec. 8.12. **1.** (*a*) $[lft^2]$; (*b*) $[lf]$; (*c*) $[ft\mathbf{E}]$; (*d*) $[lft\mathbf{E}]$; (*e*) $[l^{-1}f\mathbf{E}]$. **5.** 7.37. **7.** const $g^{\frac{1}{2}}\lambda^{\frac{1}{2}}$. **9.** const $\gamma^{\frac{1}{2}}m^{\frac{1}{2}}\lambda^{-\frac{1}{2}}$.

CHAPTER 9

Sec. 9.1. **1.** (*a*) −290 ft-lb; (*b*) 0; (*c*) 790 ft-lb; (*d*) −500 ft-lb. **3.** (*a*) 0; (*b*) 25 joules. **5.** (*a*) 25 ft-lb; (*b*) 5.9 ft-lb. **7.** 12 ft-lb. **9.** 0.0114 ft-lb. **11.** $wd(1 - s)^2/2s$.

Sec. 9.2. **1.** 0.6 joule. **3.** 66.7 ft-lb.

Sec. 9.3. **3.** 1,040 m. **5.** 0.74. **7.** 1.96 in. **9.** 68.2°. **11.** 400 ft. **15.** 41.8°.

Sec. 9.4. **1.** 1.34 m/sec. **3.** 1.40 m/sec. **7.** 7.77 ft/sec.

Sec. 9.5. **1.** 0.174 ft-lb. **3.** 1,550 ft-lb. **5.** 4,000 ft-lb.

Sec. 9.6. **1.** 2.48 ft/sec. **3.** 7.22 ft/sec. **5.** 18.4 rad/sec. **7.** 17.9 lb, 11.1 lb. **9.** 9.27 rad/sec, 13.7 lb at an angle of 12.7° with the horizontal. **11.** 0.205. **13.** (*a*) 41.8° with horizontal; (*b*) 19.5°. **15.** 0.32 rad/sec.

CHAPTER 10

Sec. 10.1. **1.** -21 ft-lb.
Sec. 10.2. **1.** 727 rad/sec. **3.** 42.8 rad/sec. **5.** $(\frac{2}{3})m^{\frac{1}{2}}g^{\frac{1}{2}}k^{-\frac{1}{2}}$.
Sec. 10.3. **1.** $\pi[(8/g)(r' - r)]^{\frac{1}{2}}$. **3.** $\pi[(2r/g)(9\pi - 16)(r' - r)]^{\frac{1}{2}}[(3\pi - 4)r + 4r']^{-\frac{1}{2}}$. **5.** 1.18 sec. **7.** (*a*) $2\pi(d/6g)^{\frac{1}{2}}$; (*b*) $2\pi(2d/3g)^{\frac{1}{2}}$.
Sec. 10.4. **1.** 110 lb. **3.** 346 lb. **5.** 24.5 lb. **7.** 25.7°. **11.** $(18 \sec \theta)f_m$. **13.** $[a + (\theta/2\pi)b]w$.
Sec. 10.5. **1.** 25.7°, unstable. **3.** $h < 2r$. **5.** 26.6°, unstable. **7.** $\sin^3 \theta = \cos \theta$, $\theta = 55.7°$.

CHAPTER 11

Sec. 11.1. **1.** 28.8 lb-sec. **3.** 0.8 lb-sec.
Sec. 11.2. **1.** 2.58**I** + 5**J** − 4.51**K** ft/sec. **3.** 0.355. **5.** $0.99\underline{/105°}$ lb-sec. **7.** 30.4 ft. **9.** 2π. **11.** $2mv \cos \theta$.
Sec. 11.3. **1.** 174.5 lb. **3.** 172 newtons. **5.** 69 lb.
Sec. 11.4. **1.** 1.33 ft/sec. **3.** 51.3°.
Sec. 11.5. **1.** (*a*) $fr\theta/\omega$; (*b*) $(fr/\omega) \sin \theta$. **5.** (*a*) −3**I** + 6**J** − 4**K** kg-m/sec; (*b*) −0.3**I** + 0.6**J** − 0.4**K** m/sec; (*c*) 2.5**I** − 2**J** m; (*d*) 20**I** + 25**J** + 35**K** kg-m²/sec; (*e*) 12**I** + 15**J** + 26**K** kg-m²/sec.
Sec. 11.6. **1.** 115 ft-lb. **3.** $(iv/wr^2) + (v/g)$. **7.** 0.289 m. **9.** 21.9 in. **11.** 0.894 ft.
Sec. 11.7. **1.** (*a*) $(1/e) \tan \theta_1$; (*b*) $(1/e)(\tan \theta_1 - \mu - \mu e)$. **7.** 0.25. **9.** 2.89 rad/sec, 9.64 ft/sec.

CHAPTER 12

Sec. 12.1. **1.** $[l^{-1}ft^{-1}]$, $[lf^{-1}]$. **3.** $c'c''/(2c'' + c')$. **5.** $\frac{1}{2}c'c''/(c' + c'')$.
Sec. 12.3. **1.** (*a*) 3.33 ft-lb; (*b*) 0.452 sec; (*c*) 2.32 ft/sec. **3.** 0.43 slug, 0.052 ft/lb. **5.** (*a*) 0.625 ft-lb; (*b*) 0.625 ft-lb; (*c*) 0.261 sec.
Sec. 12.4. **5.** (*a*) 23.7 ft; (*b*) 5.7 ft. **7.** (*a*) 4.99 mph; (*b*) 89.5 ft.
Sec. 12.5. **1.** 10.8 lb-sec/ft. **3.** (*a*) 0.0167 m/sec; (*b*) 10.4 sec; (*c*) 10.4 sec. **5.** 1.39 sec.
Sec. 12.6. **5.** 20.0, −19.3, 18.6. **9.** (*a*) 0.0063 m/newton; (*b*) 0.2 newton-sec/m.
Sec. 12.7. **3.** (*a*) 0.0309 m/newton; (*b*) 6.00 newton-sec/m; (*c*) 11.4 newton-sec/m. **5.** (*a*) 0.079 sec, 0.13 ft; (*b*) 0.050 sec, 0.056 ft.
Sec. 12.9. **1.** $[l^{-1}ft]$. **3.** (*a*) 91.3 rad/sec; (*b*) 5.0 newton-sec/m; (*c*) 1.42 cm. **5.** $\pi/2\lambda$. **7.** 7.2×10^{-4} ft/lb.

CHAPTER 13

Sec. 13.2. **1.** $0.577(1 - x + y + yz - xz - xy)$. **5.** 3.03.
Sec. 13.3. **3.** (*a*) $-\dfrac{\gamma m'm}{r^2}\mathbf{L}$; (*b*) **L**; (*c*) **L**. **5.** 8.
Sec. 13.4. **5.** $r_2 = r_1[1 - (m/k)v_0^2r_1^2]^{-\frac{1}{2}}$.
Sec. 13.5. **1.** 9.81. **3.** (*a*) $-3x + 7z$; (*b*) 10.02 ft/sec. **5.** 9,810 joules/kg.
Sec. 13.6. **1.** $\dfrac{2\gamma m}{a^2}\left[1 - \dfrac{x}{\sqrt{x^2 + a^2}}\right]$. **3.** 5.30 ft/sec². **5.** 4.55 m.
Sec. 13.7. **1.** 1,640 miles. **3.** 6.95 mps. **5.** (*a*) 82 miles; (*b*) 84 miles. **7.** 3,960 miles. **9.** 1.38 mps.
Sec. 13.9. **1.** 1.034. **3.** 1.94.
Sec. 13.10. **1.** Hyperbolic.
Sec. 13.11. **3.** $[l^2t^{-1}]$, $[l^3t^{-2}]$.

Sec. 13.12. **5.** (*a*) 6500 A; (*b*) 1200 A. **7.** $f/\nu = (2/n)(n-1)^2(2n-1)^{-1}$, lim $=1$.
Sec. 13.13. **3.** 1.414.
Sec. 13.14. **1.** 258 days.

CHAPTER 14

Sec. 14.1. **1.** $\mathrm{I} - (\frac{4}{3})\mathrm{J} + 36\mathrm{K}$.
Sec. 14.2. **1.** $2\sigma e_l$. **3.** 0.004 rad.
Sec. 14.3. **1.** (*a*) $\dfrac{\partial\xi}{\partial y} = -\theta$, $\dfrac{\partial\eta}{\partial x} = \theta$, others are zero; (*b*) 0.
Sec. 14.4. **1.** $e_{xx} = a_{11} - 1$, $e_{yy} = a_{22} - 1$, $e_{xy} = 0.5(a_{12} + a_{21})$, others are zero. **5.** $(e/2)(1-\sigma)$.
Sec. 14.8. **3.** 45°. **5.** 0.0033, −0.00193.
Sec. 14.9. **1.** $(f\cos\theta - g\sin\theta)/rh$, $(f\sin\theta + g\cos\theta)/rh$.
Sec. 14.10. **1.** $\cos^2\theta\, x_x + \sin 2\theta\, x_y + \sin^2\theta\, y_y$, $\sin\theta\cos\theta(y_y - x_x) + x_y\cos 2\theta$.
Sec. 14.11. **1.** −1,000 lb/in.², 3,000 lb/in.² **3.** 3,640 lb/in.²
Sec. 14.13. **1.** 0.0212%, 0.0085%. **5.** 0.286, 1.40×10^{11} newtons/m². **7.** 333 newtons on each lateral face. **9.** 1.04×10^{-2} ft.
Sec. 14.14. **1.** $(\pi\mu/2l)(a^4 - a'^4)$. **3.** $4\pi m r^2 l/\tau^2 a^4$.
Sec. 14.15. **1.** $wl^3/4\psi bd^3$. **3.** $y = (w/24i'\psi l)(6x^2l^2 - 4lx^3 + x^4)$.

CHAPTER 15

Sec. 15.2. **3.** 6.75×10^6 lb (net). **5.** $h/2$.
Sec. 15.3. **1.** (*b*) $2\pi l^{\frac{1}{2}}\sigma^{\frac{1}{2}}g^{-\frac{1}{2}}$; (*c*) $1-\sigma$.
Sec. 15.5. **5.** 0. **7.** 0.
Sec. 15.7. **1.** (*a*) 1; (*c*) $2/r$; (*e*) 0. **5.** (*a*) $(n+3)r^n$; (*b*) 0.
Sec. 15.9. **1.** $[(2p_0/\delta_0)\ln(p_1/p_0)]^{\frac{1}{2}}$.

CHAPTER 16

Sec. 16.3. **1.** 426 per sec. **3.** 156.3 per sec.
Sec. 16.6. **1.** 18.3 per sec, 54.8 m/sec.
Sec. 16.7. **1.** 5,030 m/sec. **3.** $\xi = 2\xi_m \sin[(2n-1)\pi ct/2l]\sin[(2n-1)\pi x/2l]$. **5.** $\xi = 2\xi_m\sin(\pi cnt/l)\cos(\pi nx/l)$.
Sec. 16.8. **1.** (*a*) 291 m/sec; (*b*) 344 m/sec. **3.** $\frac{1}{2}\beta(\partial\xi/\partial x)^2$, $\frac{1}{2}\delta(\partial\xi/\partial t)^2$.

CHAPTER 17

Sec. 17.2. **1.** 1,840 m/sec.
Sec. 17.3. **1.** (*a*) 5×10^{-21} joules at each point; (*b*) 0, 0, 10×10^{-21}, 10×10^{-21} joule; (*c*) 5×10^{-21} joule.
Sec. 17.5. **1.** 1,300 m/sec. **3.** 7.6×10^6 joule.
Sec. 17.8. **1.** γp. **3.** −46° C.
Sec. 17.10. **1.** 1.0×10^{-7} m, 1.0×10^{-5} m, 7.7×10^{-4} m.

INDEX

F

M

N

S

T

U

V

CPSIA information can be obtained
at www.ICGtesting.com
Printed in the USA
BVHW041442140219
540301BV00006B/32/P

9 781258 246143